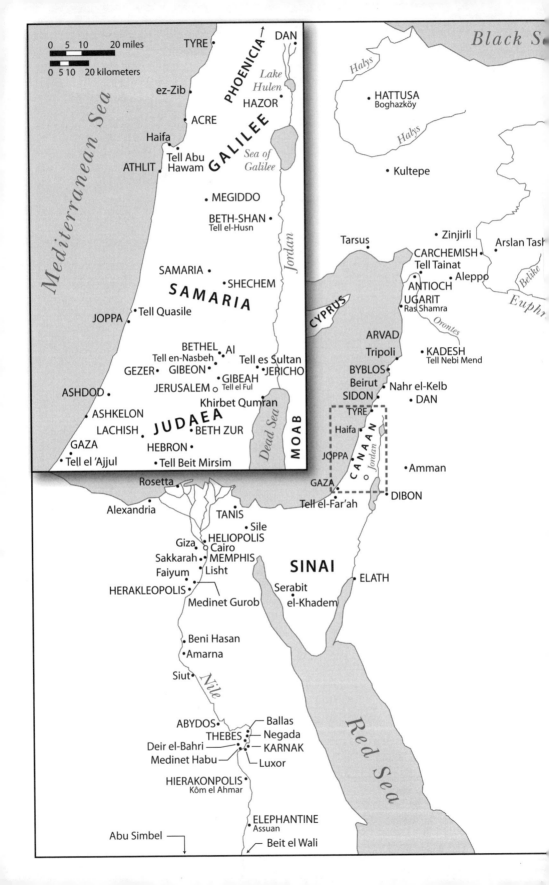

The Ancient Near East

Caspian Sea

Lake Van

ozan

Tell Billa
Khorsabad •
• NINEVEH
Mosul • — Balawat
ASHUR • NIMRUD
NUZI
• Yorghan Tepe

Khabur

RI •
ri

Tigris

Diyala

• BEHISTUN

ESHNUNNA
• Tell Asmar
Baghdad •
• Khafaje
SIPPAR •
Abu Habbah

BABYLON • •
KISH
Tell el Obeimir
SHURUPPAK •
WARKA •
• LARSA
Tell el-'Obeid • • UR
ERIDU
Basra

• NIPPUR

• SUSA

LAGASH
Tello

PASARGADAE •
Naqsh-i-Rustam •
PERSEPOLIS

Abadan

Persian Gulf

0   50   100   200   300 miles

0   50 100   200   400 kilometers

The Ancient Near East

Translators and Annotators

W. F. Albright, Johns Hopkins University

Robert D. Biggs, Oriental Institute, University of Chicago

J. J. Finkelstein, Yale University

H. L. Ginsberg, Jewish Theological Seminary

Albrecht Goetze, Yale University

A. K. Grayson, University of Toronto

A. Jamme, W. F., The Catholic University

S. N. Kramer, University of Pennsylvania Museum of Archaeology
     and Anthropology, Philadelphia

Theophile J. Meek, University of Toronto

William L. Moran, Harvard University

A. Leo Oppenheim, Oriental Institute, University of Chicago

Robert H. Pfeiffer, Harvard University

Erica Reiner, University of Chicago

Franz Rosenthal, Yale University

E. A. Speiser, University of Pennsylvania

Ferris J. Stephens, Yale University

John A. Wilson, Oriental Institute, University of Chicago

The Ancient Near East

An Anthology of Texts and Pictures

Edited by JAMES B. PRITCHARD

Foreword by DANIEL E. FLEMING

PRINCETON UNIVERSITY PRESS | PRINCETON AND OXFORD

This anthology includes material originally published in *Ancient Near Eastern Texts Relating to the Old Testament* (Copyright © 1950, 1955, 1969 by Princeton University Press) and *The Ancient Near East in Pictures Relating to the Old Testament* (Copyright © 1954, 1969 by Princeton University Press); *The Ancient Near East, Volume 1: An Anthology of Text and Pictures* (Copyright © 1958 by Princeton University Press) and *The Ancient Near East, Volume 2: A New Anthology of Texts and Pictures* (copyright © 1975 by Princeton University Press)

Library of Congress Cataloging-in-Publication Data

The ancient Near East : an anthology of texts and pictures / edited by James B. Pritchard ; foreword by Daniel E. Fleming.
   p. cm.
  Includes index.
   ISBN 978-0-691-14725-3 (hardback : alk. paper) —
ISBN 978-0-691-14726-0 (pbk. : alk. paper)   1. Bible. O.T.—History of contemporary events.   2. Middle Eastern literature—Translations into English.   3. Bible. O.T.—Antiquities.   I. Pritchard, James B. (James Bennett), 1909–1997.   II. Fleming, Daniel E.
  BS1180.P83   2011
   221.9′5—dc22   2010009121

British Library Cataloging-in-Publication Data is available

Contents

Egyptian Myths and Tales · JOHN A. WILSON   I

Myths and Epics from Mesopotamia   II

Assyrian and Babylonian Historical Texts   VIII

A. LEO OPPENHEIM

Palestinian Inscriptions · W. F. ALBRIGHT   IX

Illustrations

A consolidated map will be found on the endpaper. References in the following list to *The Ancient Near East in Pictures Relating to the Old Testament* are abbreviated *ANEP* (1st edition, 1954) and *ANEP²* (2nd edition, 1969).

1. Statuettes of Sumerians from Khafajah (*ANEP*, 18–19); University of Pennsylvania Museum of Archaeology and Anthropology.
2. Asiatics bringing eye paint to Egypt (3) wall painting in tomb of Khnum-hotep III at Beni Hasan.
3. A Mede carved on the stairway at Persepolis (26).
4. Syrian captive on staff of Tut-ankh-Amon (43); Cairo Museum.
5. Syrian tribute bearers from tomb painting at Thebes (47); British Museum.
6. Hittite prisoner on wall of temple at Abu Simbel (32).
7. Prisoners of Ramses III from Amor (7), Medinet Habu.
8. Kneeling Syrians and Negroes (4), wall painting of tomb 226 at Thebes.
9. Bronze mirror from 'Athlit (71); Palestine Archaeological Museum.
10. Ivory comb from Megiddo (67); Oriental Institute, University of Chicago.
11. Gold and electrum jewelry from Tell el-'Ajjul (74); Palestine Archaeological Museum.
12. An Egyptian barber, wall painting in hall of tomb of User-het (80), Thebes.
13. Egyptian razor blade of bronze from Ballas or Negada (82); University of Pennsylvania Museum of Archaeology and Anthropology.
14. Woman holding mirror and painting her lips (78); Turin Museum.

Foreword

Some time ago, an editor from Princeton University Press approached me with the question, "Is there still a place for James Pritchard's old volume of translations?" The first edition of *Ancient Near Eastern Texts Relating to the Old Testament* (ANET) appeared in 1950, with significant new material added for the third edition in 1969 (ANET³), already forty years ago. Naturally, the various fields represented by these translated texts have advanced enormously, with both new texts and better knowledge of their contents.

Nevertheless, I responded that Pritchard surely still has a place. Especially in the two paperback volumes that have continued in print—now integrated into one volume—the collection remains a convenient, well-conceived, reliable companion to study of the Bible and introduction to writing from the ancient Near East. The work still stands on its merits, after all this time. I can still send students to its translations as a solid starting point for work with these ancient materials, and even scholars still cite them. This new edition undertakes to preserve the qualities that made this a great collection while simplifying its structure for easier use.

Beyond their intrinsic value, the translations in Pritchard's ANET bear witness to a great period in the history of ancient Near Eastern studies. Unlike earlier collections of ancient Near Eastern evidence, this one became a basic reference for a generation of students and scholars, based on its range of materials and the authority of its translations. The figures who contributed their work include scholars of such influence that their names have become icons to generations of students up to the present: W. F. Albright and H. L. Ginsberg for their work on ancient Israel; A. Leo Oppenheim for his irreplaceable *Ancient Mesopotamia*; Erica Reiner as long-standing editor of the *Chicago Assyrian Dictionary*; William Moran for the Amarna letters.

Their translations reflect a degree of conceptual and technical mastery that we do not easily match today. Collectively, study of the ancient Near East has progressed, but individually, few scholars today match the systematic knowledge and accompanying perspective that many of these past figures possessed. So far as a translation may be more than the sum of its parts, it is still worth reading the work of these masters.

The craft of the ANET translators finds expression in various forms, and a few examples may offer a taste. E. A. Speiser's *Gilgamesh* includes a wonderful try at an impossibly difficult line in the Old Babylonian Pennsylvania Tablet, where Enkidu is first to be socialized for human companionship: "Food they placed before him; He gagged, he gaped and stared. Nothing does Enkidu know of eating food" (page 46). This is reading with a sense of humor. In contrast, H. L. Ginsberg translates as if handling material from King Arthur's court, complete with "thou" and "thine." When Baal's palace is forged of gold and silver, Ginsberg lets the literal "eating" of fire add to his alliteration: "Fire is set to the house, flame to the palace. Lo, a day and a second, fire feeds on the house, flame upon the palace" (page 120). Ginsberg's style invokes the feel of tales from time gone by, as at the start of the Aqhat legend: "Unhappy is Daniel the Rapha-man, a-sighing is Ghazir the Harnamiyy-man; who hath no son like his brethren, nor scion hath like his kindred" (page 135).

In general, these translations are straightforward, clear, true to the indigenous wording without taking refuge in woodenness. Erica Reiner offers a fluid version of a classic curse sequence in the Vassal Treaties of Esarhaddon: "If you try to reverse the curse, to avert the consequences of the oath, think up and carry out stratagems in order to reverse the curse" (page 220). In his translation of a letter between kings known from the Mari letters, William Moran preserves palpably one ruler's attempt to provoke guilt in the other ("The God of My Father," page 446): "Right now, just to relieve my feelings, I must speak about this matter which should not be spoken about. You are a great king; you made a request to me for two horses, and I had them conducted to you. But you sent me twenty minas of tin! Without any formal agreement with me you have not gone wanting (what you requested), (and yet) you sent me this bit of tin! Had you simply not sent me (anything), by the name of the god of my father my feelings would not have been hurt." Sometimes, the simple choice of an English word is striking. J. J. Finkelstein offers "taverness" for the term usually rendered as "ale-wife" (The Edict of Ammusaduqa, page 183); and A. Leo Oppenheim calls Bunene "the great plenipotentiary of Shamash" rather than simply his "vizier" ("The Dedication of the Shamash Temple by Yahdun-Lim," page 246).

With this new printing of Pritchard's *The Ancient Near East*, we have streamlined the table of contents to combine like with like, but as far as possible, most of the section headings have been left as they were. The goal of this reprinting is not to update the perspective represented in every aspect of the original publication. After all, even the choice of categories and organization of texts reflects the priorities and points of view of Pritchard and his contributors. Nevertheless, one feature of the original offers a potential obstacle to today's readers. The original two paperback volumes were divided by the two main episodes of Pritchard's compilation. Volume 1 (1958) incorporated only the work of the initial project, published as ANET in 1950, with W. F. Albright, H. L. Ginsberg, Albrecht Goetze, S. N. Kramer, Theophile J. Meek, A. Leo Oppenheim, Robert H. Pfeiffer, Franz Rosenthal, E. A. Speiser, Ferris J. Stephens, and John A. Wilson. Volume 2 (1975) then presented separately the new work from the 1969 third edition (ANET³), even where some of the categories and contributors overlap, with W. F. Albright, Robert D. Biggs, J. J. Finkelstein, H. L. Ginsberg, Albrecht Goetze, A. K. Grayson, A. Jamme, S. N. Kramer, William L. Moran, A. Leo Oppenheim, Erica Reiner, Franz Rosenthal, and John A. Wilson. In this new printing, we have combined the contents into a single sequence, so that the myths, the laws, the "historical texts," the "Palestinian inscriptions," and so on are found side by side. Adjustments of section headings were required only in order to allow the combination of material that is most naturally read together, and in these cases, we have adapted Pritchard's categories rather than attempting to create new ones. These slight changes occur at the end of the collection, in the "Didactic and Wisdom Literature" (XV), "Oracles and Prophecies" (XVI), and "Love Poetry" (XVII). The "Other Literary Texts" (XVIII) combine the pieces that did not suit any of the previous three.

Beyond these changes, the basic character of the original volumes remains in this new edition. The text itself dominates. Pritchard had the translators provide only very brief introductions, and bibliographic information was omitted, with reference only to the appropriate pages in ANET, where more was provided. For contemporary readers, there are now more up-to-date sources for text editions in any case, and the value of the translations lies in the renditions themselves. This new edition nevertheless keeps the marginal citations for ANET (1950) and ANET³ (1969), to guarantee exact identification of each translated text. In the earlier two-volume set, only volume 1 included marginal citations of biblical texts for comparison, and these were relatively sparse.

Recognizing the priority of the texts themselves, which have an enduring standing based on the mastery of their translators, it is still possible to use the classic volumes of Pritchard's *Ancient Near East* with profit. These remain some of the most important writings from the ancient world, especially as useful for students of the Hebrew Bible, and the very antiquity of the presentation—now more than forty years after the finished collection—allows a simplicity of vision. So much has been discovered and published since that time, and it is difficult to decide what to include. Pritchard has made some good choices already, with the wisdom of his age, and it is good to see the result still in play.

Daniel E. Fleming

Preface to the 1975 Edition

In this volume we have sought to make readily available to the serious student some of the most important recently discovered source materials for the history of the ancient Near East. In aim and format it is a sequel to a volume which we edited seventeen years ago, *The Ancient Near East: An Anthology of Texts and Pictures* (Princeton, 1958). Since that volume appeared, however, archaeology has provided a wealth of new material for understanding the peoples of the ancient Near East and their cultures. Not only have new literary texts come to light but previously known ones have been more precisely interpreted, and scientifically controlled excavations have succeeded in supplying new documentation for the art, architecture, religion, and daily life in the ancient world. It is the increment of the more recent discoveries that we have sought to present in this volume.

The anthology published in 1958 was an abridgment of two larger volumes intended for the professional student of the ancient Near East: *Ancient Near Eastern Texts Relating to the Old Testament* (abbreviated ANET), 1950, 2nd ed. 1955; and *The Ancient Near East in Pictures Relating to the Old Testament* (ANEP), 1954. Both of these volumes have been published in new editions that incorporate the newly discovered materials, ANET (3rd edition, 1969) and ANEP (2nd edition, 1969). (The supplementary material was published simultaneously in a volume, *The Ancient Near East: Supplementary Texts and Pictures Relating to the Old Testament*, 1969.) The present volume is an abridgment intended for the more general public of the supplementary materials in the latest editions of ANET and ANEP.

The reference in the margin at the beginning of each text is to the third edition of ANET, where the interested reader can find more detailed bibliographic information and footnotes that give philological discussions by the translator. Similarly, references in the List of

Illustrations to the publication in the second edition of ANEP will direct the reader to the detailed descriptions and bibliography for each of the pictures.

It is obvious that the text section of this book is the work of the translators and annotators of the individual texts. Each has taken time from a busy schedule of scholarly research to make available an entirely new translation of each of the ancient texts and to write introductions and footnotes. It is appropriate that the editor express his and the reader's appreciation to each of these scholars for his labor: the late W. F. Albright, Robert D. Biggs, the late J. J. Finkelstein, H. L. Ginsberg, the late Albrecht Goetze, A. K. Grayson, A. Jamme, S. N. Kramer, William L. Moran, the late A. Leo Oppenheim, Erica Reiner, Franz Rosenthal, and John A. Wilson.

Within the translations certain conventions have been followed in the signs and notations. Italics have been used to designate doubtful translations of a known text and for transliterations of the original text. Square brackets are employed for restorations in the text made by the translator; round brackets (parentheses) have been put around interpolations made for a better understanding of the translation; obvious scribal omissions have been placed between triangular brackets. A lacuna has been indicated by three dots; in case the lacuna comes before a final sentence dot, four dots appear.[1] References to the tablets, columns, and lines of the text have been given usually in parentheses either within the translation, as in prose, or in the right-hand margin when the form is poetry. Capital Roman numerals indicate the number of the tablet or some other well-recognized division; lower-case Roman numerals have been used for columns; Arabic numerals indicate the line or lines.

It is fitting that acknowledgment be made and thanks expressed to the many excavators, museum directors, and scholarly friends who have kindly supplied photographs and given permission for their inclusion in the second edition of ANEP, from which this selection is taken. It is appropriate, too, that the editor express his deep appreciation to the Princeton University Press for its support of this project of publishing various editions of texts and pictures from the ancient Near East for now more than two decades. Its former director, Datus C. Smith, first published ANET; Herbert S. Bailey, Jr., the present director of the Press, has been an unfailing source of help and encouragement.

---

[1] *Editor's note to the 2010 edition:* In addition to the signs and notations outlined above, the Egyptian hieratic texts often used rubrics for emphasis or punctuation: passages in red ink, where the general context was in black ink. The translations of these texts use small capital letters to indicate such rubrics.

Preface to the 1958 Edition

The aim of this volume is to make available in convenient form those ancient Near Eastern documents which are important for an understanding of biblical peoples and their writings. For many centuries the Old Testament and a few Greek sources provided the sole witness to life in the ancient Near East. In comparatively recent years, however, the sources for the history of the peoples of the biblical world have been greatly augmented by archaeological discovery. Writings of Egyptians, Syrians, Hittites, Assyrians, Babylonians, and other contemporary peoples have been recovered, deciphered, and reliably understood. In addition to the words of the ancient Near Eastern people, there has been amassed a significant additional documentation in art, architecture, and artifacts of daily life.

The selection offered here has been made from the point of view of relevance to the Old Testament, the most widely studied and the most significant legacy from the ancient Near East. Some suggested points of contact with specific biblical passages have been entered beside the texts; the wide margins provide space for others which may occur to the user of the volume.

Most of the translations are taken from *Ancient Near Eastern Texts Relating to the Old Testament*, edited by James B. Pritchard, 2nd edition, Princeton University Press, 1955 (abbreviated ANET). In the side margins the reader may find references to the pages of ANET, where these translations are accompanied by full bibliographical references and footnotes.

The more pertinent information about the photographs has been given in the captions. A full documentation for most of them may be had by referring to the *Catalogue of the Ancient Near East in Pictures Relating to the Old Testament*, by James B. Pritchard, Princeton University Press, 1954 (abbreviated ANEP), where details of size, provenience, publication, and present location of the object can be found. An account of the discovery and of the significance of some of the most important extra-biblical materials from the ancient Near East is given in the editor's *Archaeology and the Old Testament*, Princeton University Press, 1958.

Italics have been used in the translations to designate a doubtful translation of a known text or for transliterations. Square brackets have been employed for restorations in the text; round brackets (parentheses) have been put around interpolations made for a better understanding of the translation; obvious scribal omissions have been placed between triangular brackets. In the translations from Ugaritic, half square brackets have been used to designate a text which has been partly restored. A lacuna has been indicated by three dots; in case the lacuna comes before a final sentence dot, four dots appear. References to the tablets, columns, and lines of the text have been given usually in parentheses either within the translation, as in prose, or in the right-hand margin, when the form is poetry. Capital Roman numerals indicate the number of the tablet or some other well-recognized division; lowercase Roman numerals have been used for columns; Arabic numerals indicate the line or lines.

In the difficult task of making a choice of the most relevant texts and pictures the editor has benefited from earlier collections, such works as those of Barton, Rogers, Gressmann, and Galling. Twenty-five teachers of graduate courses in the fields of Near Eastern and Old Testament history have given helpful opinions as to the most essential material to be included. The editor's thanks are due to those predecessors and colleagues who have helped in a measure to check his own judgment in the choice of the most relevant material.

With pleasure the editor of this volume acknowledges his great debt to Herbert S. Bailey, Jr., director of the Princeton University Press, who first suggested the making of this anthology from the larger and more expensive collections of texts and pictures. Helen Van Zandt's skill in solving many of the technical problems connected with the making of this book has constituted no small part of the undertaking. In addition to the translators listed opposite the title page, Dr. Edmund I. Gordon, of the University Museum, University of Pennsylvania, participated by supplying translations of important Sumerian proverbs.

J. B. P.
Berkeley, California, February, 1958

The Ancient Near East

Egyptian Myths and Tales

TRANSLATOR: JOHN A. WILSON

The Memphite Theology of Creation   ANET, 4–5

When the First Dynasty established its capital at Memphis, it was necessary to justify the sudden emergence of this town to central importance. The Memphite god Ptah was therefore proclaimed to have been the First Principle, taking precedence over other recognized creator-gods. Mythological arguments were presented that the city of Memphis was the "place where the Two Lands are united" and that the Temple of Ptah was the "balance in which Upper and Lower Egypt have been weighed."

The extracts presented here are particularly interesting, because creation is treated in an intellectual sense, whereas other creation stories (like *ANET*, pp. 3–4) are given in purely physical terms. Here the god Ptah conceives the elements of the universe with his mind ("heart") and brings them into being by his commanding speech ("tongue"). Thus, at the beginning of Egyptian history, there was an approach to the Logos Doctrine.

The extant form of this document dates only to 700 B.C., but linguistic, philological, and geopolitical evidence is conclusive in support of its derivation from an original text more than two thousand years older.

(53) There came into being as the heart and there came into being as the tongue (something) in the form of Atum. The mighty Great One is Ptah, who transmitted [*life* to all gods], as well as (to) their *ka*'s, through this heart, by which Horus became Ptah, and through this tongue, by which Thoth became Ptah.[1]

---

[1] Ptah thought of and created by speech the creator-god Atum ("Totality"), thus transmitting the divine power of Ptah to all other gods. The gods Horus and Thoth, a commonly associated pair, are equated with the organs of thought and speech.

(Thus) it happened that the heart and tongue gained control over [every] (other) member of the body, by teaching that he[2] is in every body and in every mouth of all gods, all men, [all] cattle, all creeping things, and (everything) that lives, by thinking and commanding everything that he wishes.

(55) His Ennead is before him in (the form of) teeth and lips. That is (the equivalent of) the semen and hands of Atum. Whereas the Ennead of Atum came into being by his semen and his fingers, the Ennead (of Ptah), however, is the teeth and lips in this mouth, which pronounced the name of everything, from which Shu and Tefnut came forth, and which was the fashioner of the Ennead.

Fig. 158

The sight of the eyes, the hearing of the ears, and the smelling the air by the nose, they report to the heart. It is this which causes every completed (concept) to come forth, and it is the tongue which announces what the heart thinks.

Thus all the gods were formed and his Ennead was completed. Indeed, all the divine order really came into being through what the heart thought and the tongue commanded. Thus the *ka*-spirits were made and the *hemsut*-spirits were appointed, they who make all provisions and all nourishment, by this speech. (*Thus justice was given to*) him who does what is liked, (*and injustice to*) him who does what is disliked. Thus life was given to him who has peace and death was given to him who has sin. Thus were made all work and all crafts, the action of the arms, the movement of the legs, and the activity of every member, in conformance with (this) command which the heart thought, which came forth through the tongue, and which gives value to everything.

(Thus) it happened that it was said of Ptah: "He who made all and brought the gods into being." He is indeed Ta-tenen, who brought forth the gods, for everything came forth from him, nourishment and provisions, the offerings of the gods, and every good thing. Thus it was discovered and understood that his strength is greater than

Gen. 2:2

(that of the other) gods. And so Ptah was satisfied,[3] after he had made everything, as well as all the divine order. He had formed the gods, he had made cities, he had founded nomes, he had put the gods in their shrines, (60) he had established their offerings, he had founded their shrines, he had made their bodies like that (with which) their hearts were satisfied. So the gods entered into their bodies of every (kind of) wood, of every (kind of) stone, of every (kind of) clay, or anything which might grow upon him,[4] in which they had taken form.

---

[2] Ptah, as heart and tongue.

[3] Or, "so Ptah rested."

[4] Upon Ptah, in his form of the "rising land." Note that divine images were not the gods themselves, but only places.

So all the gods, as well as their *ka*'s gathered themselves to him, content and associated with the Lord of the Two Lands.

Deliverance of Mankind from Destruction

The themes of this myth are the sin of mankind, the destructive disappointment of their creator, and the deliverance of mankind from annihilation. However, the setting of the present text shows that its purpose was magical protection rather than moral teaching. On the walls of three royal tombs of the Empire, it accompanies certain charms to protect the body of the dead ruler. This implies that the former deliverance of mankind from destruction will be valid also in this individual case.

ANET, 10–11

It happened that ... Re, the god who came into being by himself, when he was king of men and gods all together. Then mankind plotted something in the (very) presence of Re. Now then, his majesty— life, prosperity, health!—was old. His bones were of silver, his flesh of gold, and his hair of genuine lapis lazuli.

Gen. 6:5–7

Then his majesty perceived the things which were being plotted against him by mankind. Then his majesty—life, prosperity, health!— said to those who were in his retinue: "Pray, summon to me my Eye,[5] Shu, Tefnut, Geb, and Nut, as well as the fathers and mothers who were with me when I was in Nun,[6] as well as my god Nun also. He is to bring his court (5) with him. Thou shalt bring them *secretly*: let not mankind see; let not their hearts escape.[7] Thou shalt come with them to the Great House, that they may tell their plans, since *the* [*times*] *when* I came from Nun to the place in which I came into being."

Fig. 158

Then these gods were brought in, and these gods [*came*] beside him, putting their heads to the ground in the presence of his majesty, so that he might make his statement in the presence of the father of the eldest, he who made mankind, the king of people. Then they said in the presence of his majesty: "Speak to us, so that we may hear it."

Then Re said to Nun: "O eldest god, in whom I came into being, O ancestor gods, behold mankind, which came into being from my Eye[8]—they have plotted things against me. Tell me what ye would do about it. Behold, I am seeking; I would not slay them until I had heard what (10) ye might say about it." Then the majesty of Nun said: "My son Re, the god greater than he who made him and mightier than they who created him, sitting upon thy throne, the fear of thee

---

[5] The eye of the sun-god was an independent part of himself, with a complicated mythological history.

[6] The abysmal waters, in which creation took place.

[7] Was Re unwilling that mankind repent its rebellious purposes?

[8] Mankind originated as the tears of the creator-god.

is great when thy Eye is (directed) against them who scheme against thee!" Then the majesty of Re said: "Behold, they have fled into the desert, their hearts being afraid because I *might* speak to them." Then they said in the presence of his majesty: "May thy Eye be sent, that it may *catch* for thee them who scheme with evil things. (But) the Eye is not (*sufficiently*) prominent therein to smite them for thee. It should go down as Hat-Hor."

Fig. 162

So then this goddess came and slew mankind in the desert. Then the majesty of this god said: "Welcome, Hat-Hor, who hast done for me *the deed for which I came!*" Then this goddess said: "As thou livest for me, I have prevailed over mankind, and it is pleasant in my heart!" Then the majesty of Re said: "I shall prevail over them *as a king* (15) by diminishing them!"[9] That is how Sekhmet came into being, the (beer)-mash of the night, to wade in their blood from Herakleopolis.[10]

Then Re said: "Pray, summon to me swift and speedy messengers, so that they may run like the shadow of a body." Then these messengers were brought immediately. Then the majesty of this god said: "Go ye to Elephantine and bring me red ochre very abundantly." Then this red ochre was brought to him. Then the majesty of this great god caused . . . , [and He-With]-the-Side-Lock who is in Heliopolis[11] ground up this red ochre. When further maidservants crushed barley to (make) beer, then this red ochre was added to this mash. Then (it) was like human blood. Then seven thousand jars of the beer were made. So then the majesty of the King of Upper and Lower Egypt: Re came, together with these gods, to see this beer.

Now when day broke for (20) the slaying of mankind by the goddess at their season of going upstream, then the majesty of Re said: "How good it is! I shall protect mankind with it!" Then Re said: "Pray, carry it to the place in which she expected to slay mankind." Then the majesty of the King of Upper and Lower Egypt: Re went to work early in the depth of the night to have this sleep-maker poured out. Then the fields were filled with liquid *for* three palms, through the power of the majesty of this god.

Then this goddess went at dawn, and she found this (place) flooded. Then her face (looked) beautiful therein. Then she drank, and it was good in her heart. She came (back) drunken, without having perceived mankind.

(The remainder of this story has to do with the origin of certain names and customs, such as the use of strong drink at the Feast of Hat-Hor.)

---

[9] It soon becomes clear that Re wishes the destruction to cease, whereas Hat-Hor is unwilling to halt her lustful annihilation.

[10] The formula by which the origin of a name was explained.

[11] An epithet of the High Priest of Re.

The Story of Si-nuhe

ANET, 18–22

A strong love of country was a dominant characteristic of the ancient Egyptian. Though he might feel the responsibilities of empire-building, he wished the assurance that he would close his days on the banks of the Nile. That sentiment made the following story one of the most popular classics of Egyptian literature. An Egyptian official of the Middle Kingdom went into voluntary exile in Asia. He was prosperous and well established there, but he continued to long for the land of his birth. Finally he received a royal invitation to return and join the court. This was his real success in life, and this was the popular point of the story. Much of the tale is pompous and over-styled in wording and phrasing, but the central narrative is a credible account, which fits the period as we know it. If this was fiction, it was based on realities and deserves a respected place in Egyptian literature.

The story opens with the death of Amen-em-het I (about 1960 B.C.) and continues in the reign of his successor, Sen-Usert I (about 1971–1928 B.C.). Manuscripts are plentiful and run from the late Twelfth Dynasty (about 1800 B.C.) to the Twenty-first Dynasty (about 1000 B.C.). There are five papyri and at least seventeen ostraca. The most important papyri are in Berlin.

(R1) THE HEREDITARY PRINCE AND COUNT, Judge and District Overseer of the domains of the Sovereign in the lands of the Asiatics, real acquaintance of the king, his beloved, the Attendant Si-nuhe. He says:

I was an attendant who followed his lord, a servant of the royal harem (and of) the Hereditary Princess, the great of favor, the wife of King Sen-Usert in (the pyramid town) Khenem-sut, the daughter of King Amen-em-het (R5) in (the pyramid town) Qa-nefru, Nefru, the lady of reverence.

Fig. 105

YEAR 30, THIRD MONTH OF THE FIRST SEASON, DAY 7.[12] The god ascended to his horizon; the King of Upper and Lower Egypt: Sehetep-ib-Re was taken up to heaven and united with the sun disc. The body of the god merged with him who made him.[13] The Residence City was in silence, hearts were in mourning, the Great Double Doors were sealed shut. (R10) The courtiers (sat) head on lap, and the people were in grief.

Now his majesty had sent an army to the land of the Temeh-Libyans, with his eldest son as the commander thereof, the good god Sen-Usert, (R15) and even now he was returning and had carried off living captives of the Tehenu-Libyans and all (kinds of) cattle without number.

---

[12] Around 1960 Amen-em-het I's death would have fallen early in March.

[13] The pharaoh was the "Son of Re," the sun-god. At death he was taken back into the body of his creator and father.

The courtiers of the palace sent to the western border to let the King's Son know the events which had taken place at the court. The messengers met him on the road, (R20) and they reached him in the evening time. He did not delay a moment; the falcon[14] flew away with his attendants, without letting his army know it. Now the royal children who had been following him in this army had been sent for, (B1) and one of them was summoned. While I was standing (near by) I heard his voice as he was speaking and I was a little way off. My heart was distraught, my arms spread out (in dismay), trembling fell upon all my limbs.[15] I removed myself *by leaps and bounds* to seek a hiding place for myself. I placed (5) myself between two bushes, in order to *cut (myself) off from* the road and its *travel.*

I set out southward, (but) I did not plan to reach this Residence City, (for) I thought that there would be civil disorder, and I did not expect to live after him. I crossed Lake Ma'aty near Sycamore, and I came to Snefru Island. I spent the day there on the *edge* of (10) the fields, I *came into the open* light, while it was *(still)* day, and I met a man standing near by. He stood in awe of me, for he was afraid. When the time of the evening meal came, I drew near to Ox-town. I crossed over in a barge without a rudder, by aid of the west wind. I passed by the east of the quarry (15) above Mistress-of-the-Red-Mountain.[16] I gave (free) road to my feet going northward, and I came up to the Wall-of-the-Ruler, made to oppose the Asiatics and to crush the Sand-Crossers. I took a crouching position in a bush, for fear lest the watchmen upon the wall where their day's (duty) was might see me.

I set out (20) at evening time, and when day broke I reached Peten. I halted at the Island of Kem-wer. An attack of thirst overtook me. I was parched, and my throat was dusty. I said: "This is the taste of death!" (But then) I lifted up my heart and collected myself, for I had heard the sound of the lowing of cattle, (25) and I spied Asiatics. The sheikh among them, who had been in Egypt, recognized me. Then he gave me water while he boiled milk for me. I went with him to his tribe. What they did (for me) was good.

One foreign country gave me to another. I set off for Byblos and approached Qedem, and spent (30) a year and a half there. Ammi-enshi—he was a ruler of Upper Retenu—took me and said to me:

[14] The new king Sen-Usert I.

[15] We are never directly told the reason for Si-nuhe's sudden fright and voluntary exile. Later both he and the king protest his innocence. He may have been legally guiltless, but the transition between kings was a dangerous time for one who was not fully identified with the new king. Assume that Si-nuhe had adequate reason for his sudden and furtive departure and his long stay in Asia.

[16] Gebel el-Ahmar, east of Cairo.

"Thou wilt do well with me, and thou wilt hear the speech of Egypt."
He said this, for he knew my character, he had heard of my wisdom,
and the people of Egypt who were there with him[17] had borne witness for me. . . .

He set me at the head of his children. He married me to his eldest
daughter. He let me choose for myself of his country, (80) of the
choicest of that which was with him on his frontier with another
country. It was a good land, named Yaa. Figs were in it, and grapes.   Num. 13:23, 27
It had more wine than water. Plentiful was its honey, abundant its olives. Every (kind of) fruit was on its trees. Barley was there, and
emmer. There was no limit to any (kind of) cattle. (85) Moreover,
great was that which accrued to me as a result of the love of me. He
made me ruler of a tribe of the choicest of his country. Bread was
made for me as daily fare, wine as daily provision, cooked meat and
roast fowl, beside the wild beasts of the desert, for they hunted (90)
for me and laid before me, beside the catch of my (own) hounds.
Many . . . were made for me, and milk in every (kind of) cooking.

I spent many years, and my children grew up to be strong men,
each man as the restrainer of his (own) tribe. The messenger who
went north or who went south to the Residence City (95) stopped
over with me, (for) I used to make everybody stop over. I gave water
to the thirsty. I put him who had strayed (back) on the road. I rescued him who had been robbed. When the Asiatics became so bold
as to oppose the rulers of foreign countries, I counseled their movements. This ruler of (100) (Re)tenu had me spend many years as
commander of his army. Every foreign country against which I went
forth, when I had made my attack on it, was driven away from its
pasturage and its wells. I plundered its cattle, carried off its inhabitants, took away their food, and slew people in it (105) by my strong
arm, by my bow, by my movements, and by my successful plans. I
found favor in his heart, he loved me, he recognized my valor, and he
placed me at the head of his children, when he saw how my arms
flourished.

A mighty man of Retenu came, that he might challenge me (110)
in my (own) camp. He was a hero without his peer, and he had re-
pelled all of it.[18] He said that he would fight me, he intended to despoil me, and he planned to plunder my cattle, on the advice of his
tribe. That prince discussed (it) with me, and I said: "I do not know
him. Certainly I am no confederate of his, (115) so that I might move
freely in his encampment. Is it the case that I have (ever) opened his
door or overthrown his fences? (Rather), it is hostility because he
sees me carrying out thy commissions. I am really like a stray bull

[17] Other exiles like Si-nuhe? He is in a land of refuge from Egypt.
[18] He had beaten every one of the land of Retenu.

in the midst of another herd, and a bull of (these) cattle attacks him. . . . "[19]

During the night I strung my bow and shot my arrows,[20] I gave free play to my dagger, and polished my weapons. When day broke, (Re)tenu was come. (130) It had *whipped up* its tribes and collected the countries of a (good) half of it. It had thought (only) of this fight. Then he came to me as I was waiting, (for) I had placed myself near him. Every heart burned for me; women and men groaned. Every heart was sick for me. They said: "Is there another strong man who could fight against him?" Then (*he took*) his shield, his battle-axe, (135) and his *armful of javelins. Now* after I had let his weapons issue forth, I made his arrows pass by me uselessly, one close to another. He charged me, and I shot him, my arrow sticking in his neck. He cried out and fell on his nose. (140) I felled him with his (own) bat-tle-axe and raised my cry of victory over his back, while every Asiatic roared. I gave praise to Montu,[21] while his adherents were mourning for him. This ruler Ammi-enshi took me into his embrace. Then I carried off his goods and plundered his cattle. What he had planned to do (145) to me I did to him. I took what was in his tent and stripped his encampment. I became great thereby, I became exten-sive in my wealth, I became abundant in my cattle.

I Sam. 17:51

Thus did god to show mercy to him upon whom he had *laid blame*, whom he had led astray to another country. (But) today his heart is assuaged.[22] . . .

Now when the majesty of the King of Upper and Lower Egypt: Kheper-ka-Re, the justified,[23] was told about this situation in which I was, then his majesty kept sending (175) to me with presentations from the royal presence, that he might gladden the heart of this ser-vant like the ruler of any foreign country. The royal children in his palace let me hear their commissions.[24] . . .

Then they came for this servant. . . . I was permitted to spend a day in Yaa handing over my property to my children, my eldest son being responsible for my tribe. (240) My tribe and all my property were in his charge: my serfs, all my cattle, my fruit, and every pleas-ant tree of mine.

---

[19] Si-nuhe goes on to state that he accepts the challenge, which has come to him because he is an outsider.

[20] In practice.

[21] The Egyptian god of war.

[22] It is not clear how Si-nuhe expiated his sins, except by being a successful Egyp-tian in another country.

[23] Sen-Usert I.

[24] They also wrote to Si-nuhe.

Then this servant came southward. I halted at the "Ways of Horus."[25] The commander there who was responsible for the patrol sent a message to the Residence to make (it) known. Then his majesty sent a capable overseer of peasants of the palace, with loaded ships in his train, (245) carrying presentations from the royal presence FOR THE ASIATICS WHO HAD FOLLOWED ME, ESCORTING ME TO THE "WAYS OF HORUS." I called each of them by his name.[26] Every butler was (busy) at his duties. When I started and set sail, the kneading and straining (of beer) was carried on beside me, until I had reached the town of Lisht.

Gen. 45:21–23

When day had broken, very early, they came and summoned me, ten men coming and ten men going to usher me to the palace. I put my brow to the ground between the sphinxes, (250) while the royal children were waiting in a *recess* to meet me. The courtiers who usher into the audience hall set me on the way to the private chambers. I found his majesty upon the Great Throne in a *recess* of fine gold. When I was stretched out upon my belly, I knew not myself in his presence, (although) this god greeted me pleasantly. I was like a man caught in the dark: (255) my soul departed, my body was powerless, my heart was not in my body, that I might know life from death.

THEN HIS MAJESTY SAID TO ONE OF THESE COURTIERS: "Lift him up. Let him speak to me." Then his majesty said: "Behold, thou art come. Thou hast trodden the foreign countries *and made a flight.* (But now) elderliness has attacked thee; thou hast reached old age. It is no small matter that thy corpse be (properly) buried; thou shouldst not be interred by bowmen. Do not, do not act thus any longer: (for) thou dost not speak (260) when thy name is pronounced!" Yet (I) was afraid to respond, and I answered it with the answer of one afraid: "What is it that my lord says to me? I should answer it, (but) there is nothing that I can do: it is really the hand of a god. It is a terror that is in my belly like that which produced the fated flight. BEHOLD, I AM BEFORE THEE. THINE IS LIFE. MAY THY MAJESTY DO AS HE PLEASES."

THEREUPON the royal children WERE ushered in. Then his majesty said to the Queen: "Here is Si-nuhe, (265) come as a Bedu, (in) *the guise of* the Asiatics." She gave a very great cry, and the royal children clamored all together. Then they said to his majesty: "It is not really he, O Sovereign, my lord!" Then his majesty said: "It is really he!" Now when they had brought with them their bead-necklaces, their rattles, and their sistra, then they presented them to his majesty. ". . . Loose the horn of thy bow and relax thy arrow! (275) Give breath

Exod. 15:20–21

---

[25] The Egyptian frontier station facing Sinai, probably near modern Kantarah.

[26] He introduced the Asiatics to the Egyptians.

to him that was stifled! Give us our goodly gift in this sheikh Si-Mehit, a bowman born in Egypt. He made a flight through fear of thee; he left the land through terror of thee. (But) the face of him who beholds thy face shall not *blench*; the eye which looks at thee shall not be afraid!"

Then his majesty said: "He shall not fear. (280) He has no *title* to be in dread. He shall be a courtier among the nobles. He shall be put in the ranks of the courtiers. Proceed ye to the inner chambers of the *morning* (*toilet*), in order to make his position."[27]

Gen. 41:42

So I went forth from the midst of the inner chambers, with the royal children giving me their hands. (285) Thereafter we went to the Great Double Door. I was put into the house of a royal son, in which were splendid things. A cool room was in it, and images of the horizon.[28] Costly things of the Treasury were in it. Clothing of royal linen, myrrh, and prime oil of the king and of the nobles whom he loves were in every room. (290) Every butler was (busy) at his duties. Years were made to pass away from my body. I was *plucked*, and my hair was combed. A load (of dirt) was given to the desert, and my clothes (to) the Sand-Crossers. I was clad in fine linen and anointed with prime oil. I slept on a bed. I gave up the sand to them who are in it, (295) and wood oil to him who is anointed with it. I was given a house *which had a garden*, which had been in the possession of a courtier. Many *craftsmen* built it, and all its wood(work) was newly restored. Meals were brought to me from the palace three or four times a day, apart from that which the royal children gave, without ceasing a moment.

Gen. 41:14

Fig. 192

(300) There was constructed for me a pyramid-tomb of stone in the midst of the pyramid-tombs. The stone-masons who hew a pyramid-tomb took over its ground-area. The outline-draftsmen designed in it; the chief sculptors carved in it; and the overseers of works who are in the necropolis made it their concern. (305) Its necessary materials were made from all the outfittings which are placed at a tomb-shaft. Mortuary priests were given to me. There was made for me a necropolis garden, with fields in it *formerly* (*extending*) as far as the town, like that which is done for a chief courtier. My statue was overlaid with gold, and its skirt was of fine gold. It was his majesty who had it made. There is no poor man for whom the like has been done.

(So) I was under (310) the favor of the king's presence until the day of mooring had come.[29]

---

[27] Si-nuhe's new rank is to be established by a change of dress in a properly designated place.

[28] Painted decorations. "Cool room" may have been either a bathroom or a cellar for preserving foods.

[29] Until the day of death.

The Story of Two Brothers

ANET, 23–25

This folk tale tells how a conscientious young man was falsely accused of a proposal of adultery by the wife of his elder brother, after he had actually rejected her advances. This part of the story has general similarity to the story of Joseph and Potiphar's wife. The two chief characters are brothers named Anubis and Bata. These were the names of Egyptian gods, and the tale probably does have a mythological setting. However, it served for entertainment, rather than ecclesiastical or moral purpose. The story is colloquial and is so translated.

Gen. 39:1–20

Papyrus D'Orbiney is now British Museum 10183. Facsimiled in *Select Papyri in the Hieratic Character from the Collections of the British Museum*, 11 (London, 1860), Pls. ix–xix, and in G. Möller, *Hieratische Lesestücke*, 11 (Leipzig, 1927), 1–20. The manuscript can be closely dated to about 1225 B.C. in the Nineteenth Dynasty. Transcription into hieroglyphic in A. H. Gardiner, *Late-Egyptian Stories* (*Bibliotheca Aegyptiaca*, 1, Brussels, 1932), 9–29, Translation in Erman, *LAE*, 150–61.

NOW THEY SAY THAT (ONCE) THERE WERE two brothers of one mother and one father. Anubis was the name of the elder, and Bata was the name of the younger. Now, as for Anubis, he [had] a house and had a wife, [and] his younger brother (lived) with him as a sort of minor. He was the one who made clothes for him and went to the fields driving his cattle. He was the one who did the plowing and who harvested for him. He was the one who did all (kinds of) work for him which are in the fields. Really, his younger [brother] was a good (grown) man. There was no one like him in the entire land. Why, the strength of a god was in him.

[NOW] AFTER MANY DAYS AFTER THIS,[30] his younger brother (5) [was tending] his cattle in his custom of every [day], and he [left off] (to go) to his house every evening, loaded [with] all (kinds of) plants of the field, [with] milk, with wood, and [with] every [good thing of] the fields, and he laid them in front of his [elder brother], who was sitting with his wife. And he drank and he ate, and [he *went out to sleep* in] his stable among his cattle [*by himself*].

NOW WHEN IT WAS DAWN AND A SECOND DAY HAD COME, [he *prepared food*], which was cooked, and laid it before his elder brother. [And he] gave him bread for the fields. And he drove his cattle out to let them feed in the fields. He went along after his cattle, [and] they would say to him: "The grass [of] such-and-such a place is good," and he would understand whatever they said and would take them to the place (ii 1) of good grass which they wanted. So the cattle which were before him became very, very fine. They doubled their calving very, very much.

[30] The unthinking formula of a storyteller making a transition.

Fig. 16

NOW AT THE TIME OF plowing his [elder] brother said to him: "Get a yoke [*of oxen*] ready for us for plowing, for the fields have come out, and it is fine for plowing. Also come to the fields with seed, for we shall be busy (with) plowing [in] the morning." So he spoke to him. THEN [his] (5) younger brother did all the things which his elder brother had told him to [do].

NOW WHEN IT WAS DAWN [AND A SECOND] DAY HAD COME, they went to the fields with their [seed], and they were busy [with] plowing, and [their hearts] were very, very pleased with their activity at the beginning of [their] work.

NOW [AFTER] MANY [DAYS] AFTER THIS, they were in the fields and ran short of seed. THEN HE sent his younger brother, saying: "Go and fetch us seed from the village." And his younger brother found the wife of his elder brother sitting and doing her hair. THEN HE said to her: "Get up and give me (some) seed, (iii 1) for my younger[31] brother is waiting for me. Don't delay!" THEN SHE said to him: "Go and open the bin and take what you want! Don't make me leave my combing unfinished!" THEN the lad went into his stable, and he took a big jar, for he wanted to carry off a lot of seed. So he loaded himself with barley and emmer and came out carrying them.

Fig. 10

THEN SHE said to him: "How much (is it) that is on your shoulder?" [And he] said to her: (5) "THREE sacks of emmer, two sacks of barley, FIVE IN ALL, is what is on your shoulder."[32] So he spoke to her. THEN SHE [talked with] him, saying "There is [great] strength in you! Now I see your energies every day!" And she wanted to know him as one knows a man.

THEN SHE stood up and took hold of him and said to him: "Come, let's spend an [hour] sleeping (together)! This will do you good, because I shall make fine clothes for you!" THEN the lad [became] like a leopard with [great] rage at the wicked suggestion which she had made to him, and she was very, very much frightened. THEN HE argued with her, saying: "See here—you are like a mother to me, and your husband is like a father to me! Because—being older than I—he was the one who brought me up. What (iv 1) is this great crime which you have said to me? Don't say it to me again! And I won't tell it to a single person, nor will I let it out of my mouth to any man!" And he lifted up his load, and he went to the fields. THEN HE reached his elder brother, and they were busy with activity (at) their work.

NOW AT THE [TIME] OF EVENING, THEN his elder brother left off (to go) to his house. And his younger brother tended his cattle, and [he] loaded himself with everything of the fields, and he took his

---

[31] Read "elder."

[32] Read "my shoulder." He was carrying more than 11 bushels.

cattle (5) in front of him, to let them sleep (in) their stable which was in the village.

But the wife of his elder brother was afraid (because of) the suggestion which she had made. THEN SHE took fat and grease,[33] and she became like one who has been criminally beaten, wanting to tell her husband: "It was your younger brother who did the beating!" And her husband left off in the evening, after his custom of every day, and he reached his house, and he found his wife lying down, terribly sick. She did not put water on his hands, after his custom, nor had she lit a light before him, and his house was in darkness, and she lay (there) vomiting. So her husband said to her: "Who has been talking with you?" Then she said to him: "Not one person has been talking with me except your (v 1) younger brother. But when he came [to] take the seed to you he found me sitting alone, and he said to me: 'Come, let's spend an hour sleeping (together)! Put on your curls!'[34] So he spoke to me. But I wouldn't listen to him: 'Aren't I your mother?—for your elder brother is like a father to you!' So I spoke to him. But he was afraid, and he beat (me), so as not to let me tell you. Now, if you let him live, I'll kill myself! Look, when he comes, *don't* [*let him speak*], for, if I accuse (him of) this wicked suggestion, he will be ready to do it *tomorrow* (*again*)!"

THEN his elder brother became (5) like a leopard, and he made his lance sharp, and he put it in his hand. THEN his elder (brother) stood behind the door (of) his stable to kill his younger brother when he came back in the evening to put his cattle in the stable.

Now when the sun was setting, he loaded himself (with) all plants of the fields, according to his custom of every day, and he came back. When the first cow came into the stable, she said to her herdsman: "Here's your elder brother waiting before you, carrying his lance to kill you! Run away from him!" THEN HE understood what his first cow had said. And (vi 1) another went in, and she said the same. So he looked under the door of his stable, and he saw the feet of [his] elder brother, as he was waiting behind the door, with his lance in his hand. So he laid his load on the ground, and he started to run away and escape. And his elder brother went after him, carrying his lance.

THEN his younger brother prayed to the Re-Har-akhti, (5) saying: "O my good lord, thou art he who judges the wicked from the just!" Thereupon the Re heard all his pleas, and the Re made a great (body of) water appear between him and his elder (brother), and it was full of crocodiles. So one of them came to be on one side and the other on the other. And his elder brother struck his hand twice because of his not killing him. THEN his younger brother called to him from the

---

[33] Apparently to make her vomit.

[34] The wig of her festive attire.

(other) side, saying: "Wait here until dawn. When the sun disc rises, I shall (vii 1) be judged with you in his presence, and he will turn the wicked over to the just, for I won't be with you ever [*again*]; I won't be in a place where you are—I shall go to the Valley of the Cedar!"

NOW WHEN IT WAS DAWN AND A SECOND DAY HAD COME, the Re-Har-akhti arose, and one of them saw the other. THEN the lad argued with his elder brother, saying: "What do you (mean by) coming after me to kill (me) falsely, when you wouldn't listen to what I had to say? Now I am still your younger brother, and (5) you are like a father to me, and your wife is like a mother to me! Isn't it so? When I was sent to fetch us (some) seed, your wife said to me: 'Come, let's spend an hour sleeping (together)!' But, look, it is twisted for you into something else!" THEN HE let him know all that had happened to him and his wife. THEN HE swore to the Re-Har-akhti, saying "As for your killing (me) falsely, you carried your lance on the word of a filthy whore!" And he took a reed-knife, and he cut off his phallus, and he threw it into the water. And the shad swallowed (it).[35] And he (viii 1) was faint and became weak. And his elder brother's heart was very, very sad, and he stood weeping aloud for him. He could not cross over to where his younger brother was because of the crocodiles. . . .

THEN (the younger brother) went (7) off to the Valley of the Cedar, and his elder brother went off to his house, with his hand laid upon his head, and he was smeared with dust.[36] So he reached his house, and he killed his wife, and he threw her out (to) the dogs. And he sat in mourning for his younger brother. . . .

Josh. 7:6;
II Kings 9:33, 36

(The story continues with a number of episodes).

ANET, 25–29 ## The Journey of Wen-Amon to Phoenicia

When the Egyptian Empire disintegrated, it left a vacuum in its place for a generation or two. Egyptians, Asiatics, and Africans continued to think in terms of an authority which was no longer real. In the following tale Egypt had already become a "bruised reed" but was continuing to assert traditional Isa. 36:6 expressions of dominance. The Asiatics were beginning to express their scepticism and their independence of their great neighbor to the south.

The story is almost picaresque in its atmosphere and must be classed as a narrative. Nevertheless, it deals at close range with actual individuals and

---

[35] The mutilation was a self-imposed ordeal to support his oath to the sun-god. There was a familiar element in the swallowing of the phallus by the fish. In the Plutarch account of the Osiris myths, it is related that Seth dismembered Osiris and scattered the pieces. Then Isis went about and buried each piece as she found it. However, she could not find the phallus, which had been thrown into the river and eaten by certain fishes, which thereby became forbidden food.

[36] Thus showing his grief.

situations and must have had a basis of fact, here exaggerated by the conscious and unconscious humor of the narrator. It does represent the situation in Hither Asia about 1100 B.C. more tellingly than a document of the historical-propagandistic category could do.

Wen-Amon, an official of the Temple of Amon at Karnak, tells how he was sent to Byblos on the Phoenician coast to procure lumber for the ceremonial barge of the god. Egypt had already split into small states and did not support his mission with adequate purchasing value, credentials, or armed force.

The papyrus, now in the Moscow Museum, comes from el-Hibeh in Middle Egypt and dates to the early Twenty-first Dynasty (11th century B.C.), shortly after the events it relates.

YEAR 5, 4TH MONTH OF THE 3RD SEASON, DAY 16: the day on which Wen-Amon, the Senior of the Forecourt of the House of Amon, [Lord of the Thrones] of the Two Lands, set out to fetch the woodwork for the great and august barque of Amon-Re, King of the Gods, *Fig. 99* which is on [the River and which is named:] "User-het-Amon." On the day when I reached Tanis, the place [where Ne-su-Ba-neb]-Ded and Ta-net-Amon were,[37] I gave them the letters of Amon-Re, King of the Gods, and they (5) had them read in their presence. And they said: "Yes, I will do as Amon-Re, King of the Gods, our [lord], has said!" I SPENT UP TO THE 4TH MONTH OF THE 3RD SEASON in Tanis. And Ne-su-Ba-neb-Ded and Ta-net-Amon sent me off with the ship captain Mengebet, and I embarked on the great Syrian sea IN THE 1ST MONTH OF THE 3RD SEASON, DAY 1.

I reached Dor, a town of the Tjeker, and Beder, its prince, had *Judg. 1:27* 50 loaves of bread, one jug of wine, (10) and one leg of beef brought to me. And a man of my ship ran away and stole one [*vessel*] of gold, [amounting] to 5 *deben*, four jars of silver, amounting to 20 *deben,* and a sack of 11 *deben* of silver. [Total of what] he [stole]: 5 *deben* of gold and 31 *deben* of silver.[38]

I got up in the morning, and I went to the place where the Prince was, and I said to him: "I have been robbed in your harbor. Now you are the prince of this land, and you are its investigator who should look for my silver. Now about this silver—it belongs to Amon-Re, (15) King of the Gods, the lord of the lands; it belongs to

[37] Ne-su-Ba-neb-Ded was the *de facto* ruler of the Delta, with Tanis as its capital. Ta-net-Amon was apparently his wife. At Thebes in Upper Egypt, the High Priest of Amon, Heri-Hor, was the *de facto* ruler. Ne-su-Ba-neb-Ded and Heri-Hor were in working relations with each other, and were shortly to become contemporary pharaohs.

[38] This value—about 450 grams (1.2 1b. troy) of gold and about 2.8 kilograms (7.5 1b. troy) of silver—was to pay for the lumber.

Ne-su-Ba-neb-Ded; it belongs to Heri-Hor, my lord, and the other great men of Egypt! It belongs to you; it belongs to Weret; it belongs to Mekmer; it belongs to Zakar-Baal, the Prince of Byblos!"[39]

And he said to me: "Whether you are important or whether you are eminent—look here, I do not recognize this accusation which you have made to me! Suppose it had been a thief who belonged to my land who went on your boat and stole your silver, I should have repaid it to you from my treasury, until they had (20) found this thief of yours—whoever he may be. Now about the thief who robbed you—he belongs to you! He belongs to your ship! Spend a few days here visiting me, so that I may look for him."

I spent nine days moored (in) his harbor, and I went (to) call on him, and I said to him: "Look, you have not found my silver. [*Just let*] me [*go*] with the ship captains and with those who go (to) sea!" But

Fig. 98 he said to me: "Be quiet!". . . I went out of Tyre at the break of dawn. . . . Zakar-Baal, the Prince of Byblos, . . . (30) ship. I found 30 *deben* of silver in it, and I seized upon it.[40] [And I said to *the Tjeker: "I have seized upon*] your silver, and it will stay with me [until] you find [my silver or the thief] who stole it! Even though *you have not stolen,* I shall take it. But as for you . . ." So they went away, and I enjoyed my triumph [in] a tent (on) the shore of the [sea], (in) the harbor of Byblos. And [*I hid*] Amon-of-the-Road, and I put his property inside *him.*[41]

And the [Prince] of Byblos sent to me, saying: "Get [out of (35) my] harbor!" And I sent to him, saying: "Where *should* [*I go to*]? . . . If [*you have a ship*] to carry me, have me taken to Egypt again!" So I spent twenty-nine days in his [harbor, while] he [spent] the time sending to me every day to say: "Get out (of) my harbor!"

NOW WHILE HE WAS MAKING OFFERING to his gods, the god seized

I Sam. 19:24 one of his youths and made him possessed.[42] And he said to him: "Bring up [*the*] god! Bring the messenger who is carrying him! (40) Amon is the one who sent him out! He is the one who made him come!" And while the possessed (youth) was having his frenzy on this night, I had (already) found a ship headed for Egypt and had loaded everything that I had into it. While I was watching for the darkness, thinking that when it descended I would load the god

---

[39] On the one hand, the gold and silver belong to the Egyptians who sent Wen-Amon. On the other hand, they belong to the Asiatics who would receive it. Beder thus has double responsibilities to recover them.

[40] Nearly the same amount as the silver which had been stolen from him, without account of the gold.

[41] The divine image would have its daily cult and therefore its cultic apparatus would be stored within the hollow image.

[42] Perhaps a court page was seized with a prophetic frenzy.

(also), so that no other eye might see him, the harbor master came to me, saying: "Wait until morning—so says the Prince." So I said to him: "Aren't you the one who spend the time coming to me every day to say: 'Get out (of) my harbor'? Aren't you saying 'Wait' tonight (45) in order to let the ship which I have found get away—and (then) you will come again (to) say: 'Go away!'?" So he went and told it to the Prince. And the Prince sent to the captain of the ship to say: "Wait until morning—so says the Prince!"

When MORNING CAME, he sent and brought me up, but the god stayed in the tent where he was, (on) the shore of the sea. And I found him sitting (in) his upper room, with his back turned to a window, so that the waves of the great Syrian sea broke against the back (50) of his head.[43]

So I said to him: "*May* Amon *favor you!*" But he said to me "How long, up to today, since you came from the place where Amon is?" So I said to him: "Five months and one day up to now." And he said to me: "Well, you're truthful! Where is the letter of Amon which (should be) in your hand? Where is the dispatch of the High Priest of Amon which (should be) in your hand?" And I told him: "I gave them to Ne-su-Ba-neb-Ded and Ta-net-Amon." And he was very, very angry, and he said to me: "Now see—neither letters nor dispatches are in your hand! Where is the cedar ship which Ne-su-Ba-neb-Ded gave to you? Where is (55) its Syrian crew? Didn't he turn you over to this foreign ship captain to have him kill you and throw you into the sea? (Then) with whom would they have looked for the god? And you too—with whom would they have looked for you too?" So he spoke to me.

BUT I SAID TO HIM: "Wasn't it an Egyptian ship? Now it is Egyptian crews which sail under Ne-su-Ba-neb-Ded! He has no Syrian crews." And he said to me: "Aren't there twenty ships here in my harbor which are in commercial relations with Ne-su-Ba-neb-Ded? As to this Sidon, (ii 1) the other (place) which you have passed, aren't there fifty more ships there which are in commercial relations with Werket-El, and which are drawn up to his house?" And I was silent in this great time.

Ezek. 27:8–9

And he answered and said to me: "On what business have you come?" So I told him: "I have come after the woodwork for the great and august barque of Amon-Re, King of the Gods. Your father did (it), (5) your grandfather did (it), and you will do it too!" So I spoke to him. But he said to me: "To be sure, they did it! And if you give me (something) for doing it, I will do it! Why, when my people carried out this commission, Pharaoh—life, prosperity, health!—sent six

---

[43] Pictorially, not literally. Wen-Amon gives his vivid first view of Zakar-Baal, framed in an upper window overlooking the surf of the Mediterranean.

ships loaded with Egyptian goods, and they unloaded them into their storehouses! You—what is it that you're bringing me—me also?" And he had the journal rolls of his fathers brought, and he had them read out in my presence, and they found a thousand *deben* of silver and all kinds of things in his scrolls.

(10) So he said to me: "If the ruler of Egypt were the lord of mine, and I were his servant also, he would not have to send silver and gold, saying: 'Carry out the commission of Amon!' There would be no carrying of a royal-gift, such as they used to do for my father. As for me—me also—I am not your servant! I am not the servant of him who sent you either! If I cry out to the Lebanon, the heavens open up, and the logs are here lying (on) the shore of the sea! Give (15) me the sails which you have brought to carry your ships which would hold the logs for (Egypt)! Give me the ropes [which] you have brought [*to lash the cedar*] logs which I am to cut down to make you . . . which I shall make for you (as) the sails of your boats, and the *spars* will be (too) heavy and will break, and you will die in the middle of the sea! See, Amon made thunder in the sky when he put Seth near him.[44] Now when Amon (20) founded all lands, in founding them he founded first the land of Egypt, from which you come; for craftsmanship came out of it, to reach the place where I am, and learning came out of it, to reach the place where I am. What are these silly trips which they have had you make?"

And I said to him: "(That's) not true! What I am on are no 'silly trips' at all! There is no ship upon the River which does not belong to Amon! The sea is his, and the Lebanon is his, of which you say; 'It is mine!' It forms (25) the *nursery* for User-het-Amon, the lord of [every] ship! Why, he spoke—Amon-Re, King of the Gods—and said to Heri-Hor, my master: 'Send me forth!' So he had me come, carrying this great god. But see, you have made this great god spend these twenty-nine days moored (in) your harbor, although you did not know (it). Isn't he here? Isn't he the (same) as he was? You are stationed (here) to carry on the commerce of the Lebanon with Amon, its lord. As for your saying that the former kings sent silver and gold—suppose that they had life and health; (then) they would not have had such things sent! (30) (But) they had such things sent to your fathers in place of life and health![45] Now as for Amon-Re, King of the Gods—he is the lord of this life and health, and he was the lord of your fathers. They spent their lifetimes making offering to

----

[44] As god of thunder. Thus Amon and Seth were gods of all lands, not of Egypt alone.

[45] In contrast with the past, Wen-Amon has brought an actual god in "Amon-of-the-Road," so that there may be spiritual rather than material advantages for Zakar-Baal.

Amon. And you also—you are the servant of Amon! If you say to Amon: 'Yes, I will do (it)!' and you carry out his commission, you will live, you will be prosperous, you will be healthy, and you will be good to your entire land and your people! (But) don't wish for your-self anything belonging to Amon-Re, (King of) the Gods. Why, a lion wants his own property! Have your secretary brought to me, so that (35) I may send him to Ne-su-Ba-neb-Ded and Ta-net-Amon, the *officers* whom Amon put in the north of his land, and they will have all kinds of things sent. I shall send him to them to say: 'Let it be brought until I shall go (back again) to the south, and I shall (then) have every bit of the debt still (due to you) brought to you.'" So I spoke to him.

So he entrusted my letter to his messenger, and he loaded in the *keel*, the bow-post, the stern-post, along with four other hewn tim-bers—seven in all—and he had them taken to Egypt. And in the first month of the second season his messenger who had gone to Egypt came back to me in Syria. And Ne-su-Ba-neb-Ded and Ta-net-Amon sent: (40) 4 jars and 1 *kak-men* of gold; 5 jars of silver; 10 pieces of clothing in royal linen; 10 *kherd* of good Upper Egyptian linen; 500 (rolls of) finished papyrus; 500 cowhides; 500 ropes; 20 sacks of lentils; and 30 baskets of fish. And she sent to me (personally): 5 pieces of clothing in good Upper Egyptian linen; 5 *kherd* of good Upper Egyptian linen; 1 sack of lentils; and 5 baskets of fish.

And the Prince was glad, and he detailed three hundred men and three hundred cattle, and he put supervisors at their head, to have them cut down the timber. So they cut them down, and they spent the second season lying there.[46]

Fig. 89

In the third month of the third season they dragged them (to) the shore of the sea, and the Prince came out and stood by them. And he sent to me, (45) saying: "Come!" Now when I presented myself near him, the shadow of his lotus-blossom fell upon me. And Pen-Amon, a butler who belonged to him, cut me off, saying: "The shadow of Pharaoh—life, prosperity, health!—your lord, has fallen on you!" But he was angry at him, saying: "Let him alone!"[47]

So I presented myself near him, and he answered and said to me: "See, the commission which my fathers carried out formerly, I have carried it out (also), even though you have not done for me what your fathers would have done for me, and you too (should have done)! See, the last of your woodwork has arrived and is lying (here). Do as I wish, and come to load it in—for aren't they going to give it

---

[46] Seasoning in the mountains.

[47] Perhaps we have to do with the blight of majesty. The butler's jest has point if the shadow of pharaoh was too intimate and holy to fall upon a commoner.

to you? (50) Don't come to look at the terror of the sea! If you look at the terror of the sea, you will see my own (too)![48] Why, I have not done to you what was done to the messengers of Kha-em-Waset, when they spent seventeen years in this land—they died (where) they were!" And he said to his butler: "Take him and show him their *tomb* in which they are lying."

But I said to him: "Don't show it to me! As for Kha-em-Waset— they were men whom he sent to you as messengers, and he was a man himself. You do not have one of his messengers (here in me), when you say: 'Go and see your companions!' Now, shouldn't you rejoice (55) and have a stela [made] for yourself and say on it: 'Amon-Re, King of the Gods, sent to me Amon-of-the-Road, his messenger—[life], prosperity, health!—and Wen-Amon, his human messenger, after the woodwork for the great and august barque of Amon-Re, King of the Gods. I cut it down. I loaded it in. I provided it (with) my ships and my crews. I caused them to reach Egypt, in order to ask fifty years of life from Amon for myself, over and above my fate.' And it shall come to pass that, after another time, a messenger may come from the land of Egypt who knows writing, and he may read your name on the stela. And you will receive water (in) the West, like the gods who are (60) here!"[49]

And he said to me: "This which you have said to me is a great testimony of words!"[50] So I said to him: "As for the many things which you have said to me, if I reach the place where the High Priest of Amon is and he sees how you have (carried out this) commission, it is your (carrying out of this) commission (which) will *draw out* something for you."

And I went (to) the shore of the sea, to the place where the timber was lying, and I spied eleven ships belonging to the Tjeker coming in from the sea, in order to say: "Arrest him! Don't let a ship of his (go) to the land of Egypt!" Then I sat down and wept. And the letter scribe of the Prince came out to me, (65) and he said to me: "What's the matter with you?" And I said to him: "Haven't you seen the birds go down to Egypt a second time?[51] Look at them—how they travel to the cool pools! (But) how long shall I be left here! Now don't you see those who are coming again to arrest me?"

So he went and told it to the Prince. And the Prince began to weep because of the words which were said to him, for they were

---

[48] If you use wind or weather as excuses for delay, you will find me just as dangerous.

[49] A libation to help maintain the dead.

[50] We cannot be sure whether the irony was conscious or unconscious.

[51] Wen-Amon had been away from Egypt for more than a year, seeing two flights of birds southward.

painful. And he sent out to me his letter scribe, and he brought to me two jugs of wine and one ram. And he sent to me Ta-net-Not, an Egyptian singer who was with him,[52] saying: "Sing to him! Don't let his heart take on cares!" And he sent to me, (70) to say: "Eat and drink! Don't let your heart take on cares, for tomorrow you shall hear whatever I have to say."

When morning came, he had his assembly summoned, and he stood in their midst, and he said to the Tjeker: "What have you come (for)?" And they said to him: "We have come after the *blasted* ships which you are sending to Egypt with our opponents!" But he said to them: "I cannot arrest the messenger of Amon inside my land. Let me send him away, and you go after him to arrest him."

So he loaded me in, and he sent me away from there at the harbor of the sea. And the wind cast me on the land of (75) Alashiya. And they of the town came out against me to kill me, but I *forced my way* through them to the place where Heteb, the princess of the town, was. I met her as she was going out of one house of hers and going into another of hers.

So I greeted her, and I said to the people who were standing near her: "Isn't there one of you who understands Egyptian?" And one of them said: "I understand (it)." So I said to him: "Tell my lady that I have heard, as far away as Thebes, the place where Amon is, that injustice is done in every town but justice is done in the land of Alashiya. Yet injustice is done here every day!" And she said: "Why, what do you (mean) (80) by saying it?" So I told her: "If the sea is stormy and the wind casts me on the land where you are, you should not let them take me *in charge* to kill me. For I am a messenger of Amon. Look here—as for me, they will search for me all the time! As to this crew of the Prince of Byblos which they are bent on killing, won't its lord find ten crews of yours, and he also kill them?"

So she had the people summoned, and they stood (there). And she said to me: "Spend the night. . . ."

(At this point the papyrus breaks off. Since the tale is told in the first person, it is fair to assume that Wen-Amon returned to Egypt to tell his story, in some measure of safety or success.)

The Tradition of Seven Lean Years in Egypt   ANET, 31–32

The prosperity of Egypt depends upon the satisfactory flow of the Nile, particularly upon its annual inundation, and that river is antic and unpredictable. Ancient Egyptian texts have frequent references to hunger, "years of

---

[52] Egyptian women who entertained or participated in cult ceremonies in Asia are known in the inscriptions on the Megiddo ivories.

misery," "a year of low Nile," and so on.[53] The text which follows tells of seven years of low Niles and famine. In its present form the text derives from the Ptolemaic period (perhaps around the end of the 2nd century B.C.). However, its stated setting is the reign of Djoser of the Third Dynasty (about 28th century B.C.). It states the reasons why a stretch of Nile land south of Elephantine had been devoted to Khnum, god of Elephantine. It is a question whether it is a priestly forgery of some late period, justifying their claim to territorial privileges, or whether it correctly recounts an actual grant of land more than 2,500 years earlier. This question cannot be answered in final terms. We can only affirm that Egypt had a tradition of seven lean years, which, by a contractual arrangement between pharaoh and a god, were to be followed by years of plenty.

Fig. 162

Year 18 of the Horus: Netjer-er-khet; the King of Upper and Lower Egypt: Netjer-er-khet; the Two Goddesses: Netjer-er-khet; the Horus of Gold: Djoser, *and under* the Count, Mayor, *Royal Acquaintance,* and Overseer of Nubians in Elephantine, Madir. There was brought to him[54] this royal decree:

To let thee know. I was in distress on the Great Throne, and those who are in the palace were in heart's affliction from a very great evil, since the Nile had not come in my time for a space of seven years. Grain was scant, fruits were dried up, and everything which they eat was short. Every man *robbed* his companion. They moved without going (*ahead*). The infant was wailing; the youth was *waiting*; the heart of the old men was in sorrow, their legs were bent, crouching on the ground, their arms were *folded.* The courtiers were in need. The temples were shut up; the sanctuaries held [*nothing but*] air. Every[*thing*] was found empty.

Gen. 41:27

I extended my heart back to the beginnings, and I asked him who was the *Chamberlain,* the Ibis, the Chief Lector Priest Ii-em-(ho)tep,[55] the son of Ptah, South-of-His-Wall: "What is the birthplace of the Nile? *Who is* . . . the god there? Who is the god?"

Then he answered (5) me: "I need the guidance of Him Who Presides over the House of the Fowling Net,[56] . . . *for the heart's confidence*

[53] Vandier gives a previously unpublished text from the First Intermediate Period (23rd–21st century B.C.), from a tomb some distance south of Thebes. "When the entire Upper Egypt was dying because of hunger, with every man eating his (own) children, I never allowed death to occur from hunger in this nome. I gave a loan of grain to Upper Egypt. . . . Moreover, I kept alive the domain of Elephantine and kept alive Iat-negen in these years, after the towns of Hefat and Hor-mer had been satisfied." He took care of his home districts first.

[54] To Madir, the Governor at Elephantine.

[55] The famed minister of Djoser, whose reputation for wisdom later brought him deification.

[56] Thoth of Hermopolis, the god of wisdom and of priestly lore.

of all men about what they should do. I shall enter into the House of Life and spread out the Souls of Re,[57] (to see) if some guidance be in them."

So he went, and he returned to me immediately, that he might *instruct* me on the inundation of the Nile, . . . and everything about which they had written. He uncovered for me the hidden spells thereof, to which the ancestors had taken (their) way, without their equal among kings since the limits *of time. He said* to me:

"There is a city in the midst of the waters [*from which*] the Nile *rises*, named Elephantine. It is the Beginning of the Beginning, the Beginning Nome, (*facing*) *toward* Wawat. It is the *joining* of the land, the primeval hillock *of earth, the throne* of Re, when he *reckons to cast* life beside everybody. 'Pleasant of Life' is the name of its dwelling. 'The Two Caverns' is the name of the water; they are the two breasts which pour forth all good things. It is the couch of the Nile, in which he becomes young (again). . . . He fecundates (the land) by mounting as the male, the bull, to the female; he renews (his) virility, assuaging his desire. He rushes twenty-eight cubits (high at Elephantine); he hastens at Diospolis seven cubits (high). Khnum is there as a god. . . . " . . .

(18) . . . As I slept in life and satisfaction, I discovered the god standing over against me. I propitiated him with praise; I prayed to him in his presence. He *revealed* himself to me, *his face* being fresh. His words were:

I Kings 3:5

"I am Khnum, thy fashioner. . . . I know the Nile. When he is introduced into the fields, his introduction gives life to every nostril, like the introduction (of life) to the fields . . . The Nile will pour forth for thee, without a year of cessation or laxness for any land. Plants will grow, bowing down under the *fruit*. Renenut[58] will be at the head of everything. . . . Dependents *will fulfill* the purposes in their hearts, (22) as well as the master. The starvation year will have gone, and (people's) *borrowing* from their granaries will have departed. Egypt will come into the fields, the banks will sparkle, . . . and contentment will be in their hearts more than that which was formerly."

Gen. 41:56

Then I awoke *quickly*, my heart cutting off weariness. I made this decree beside my father Khnum:[59]

"An offering which the King gives to Khnum, the Lord of the Cataract Region, Who Presides over Nubia, in recompense for these things which thou wilt do for me:

---

[57] The scriptorium in which the sacred and magic books "The Souls of Re," were kept.

[58] The goddess of the harvest.

[59] That is, in the temple of Khnum.

"I offer to thee thy west in Manu and thy east (in) Bakhu,[60] from Elephantine as far as [Takompso], for twelve *iters*[61] on the east and west, whether arable land or desert or river in every part of these *iters*. . . ."

(The remainder of the text continues Djoser's promise to Khnum, the essence of which is that the land presented to the god shall be tithed for his temple. It is finally provided that the decree shall be inscribed on a stela in the temple of Khnum.)

[60] Manu was the western and Bakhu the eastern mountain range bordering the Nile.

[61] The *Dodekaschoinos* known from the Greek writers.

Myths and Epics from Mesopotamia

A Sumerian Myth

TRANSLATOR: S. N. KRAMER

The Deluge

ANET, 42–44

This Sumerian myth concerning the flood, with its Sumerian counterpart of the antediluvian Noah, offers the closest and most striking parallel to biblical material as yet uncovered in Sumerian literature. Moreover, its introductory passages are of considerable significance for Mesopotamian cosmogony; they include a number of important statements concerning the creation of man, the origin of kingship, and the existence of at least five antediluvian cities.

(approximately first 37 lines destroyed)
"My mankind, *in* its destruction I will . . . ,[1]
To Nintu[2] I will *return the . . . of* my creatures,
I will *return* the people *to* their *settlements,*   (40)
Of the cities, verily they will build their *places of (divine) ordinances,*
    I will make peaceful their shade,
Of *our*[3] houses, verily they will lay their bricks in pure places,
The places of our decisions verily they will found in pure places."
He directed the . . . *of the temenos,*

[1] There is some possibility that it is more than one deity who is speaking. Our interpretation of the text assumes that the speaking deity (or deities) plans to save mankind from destruction, but this is uncertain.

[2] Nintu is the Sumerian mother goddess known also under the names Ninhursag and Ninmah.

[3] Perhaps "of the houses of the (divine) ordinances."

Perfected the rites (and) the exalted (divine) ordinances,
On the earth he . . . d, placed the . . . there.
After Anu, Enlil, Enki, and Ninhursag
Had fashioned the black-headed (people),[4]
Vegetation luxuriated from the earth,
Animals, four-legged (creatures) of the plain, were brought
      artfully into existence.   (50)
              (approximately 37 lines destroyed)
After the . . . of kingship had been lowered from heaven,
After the exalted [*tiara*] (and) the throne of kingship had been
      lowered from heaven,
He[5] [pe]rfected the [rites (and) the ex]alted [(divine)
      ordinances] . . . ,   (90)
Founded the [*five*] *ci*[*ties*] in . . . p[ure places],
Cal[led] their names, [appor]tioned them *as*[*cu*]*lt-centers.*
The *first* of these cities, Eridu, he gave to Nudimmud,[6] the leader,
The second, Badtibira, he gave to . . . ,
The third, Larak, he gave to Endurbilhursag,
The fourth, Sippar, he gave to the hero Utu,[7]
The fifth, Shuruppak, he gave to Sud.[8]
When he had called the names of these cities, apportioned them as
      cult-centers,
He *brought* . . . ,[9]
Established the *cleaning* of the small *rivers as* . . .   (100)
            (approximately 37 lines destroyed)
Gen. 6   The flood . . .
     . . .
Thu[s w]as treated . . .
Then did Nin[tu *weep*] like a . . . ,
The pure Inanna [set up] a lament for *its*[10] people,
Enki took coun[sel] with himself,
Anu, Enlil, Enki, (and) Ninhursag . . . ,
The gods of heaven and earth [uttered] the name of[11] Anu (and)
      Enlil.

---

[4] The word "black-headed" usually refers to inhabitants of Sumer and Babylon; in
the present context, it seems to refer to mankind as a whole.

[5] Identity of deity or deities uncertain; perhaps it is Anu Enlil.

[6] Nudimmud is a name for the water-god Enki.

[7] The sun-god, known as the tutelary deity of both Sippar and Larsa.

[8] The tutelary goddess of Shuruppak identified by the later Babylonian theologians
with the goddess Ninlil, the wife of Enlil.

[9] It may deal with rain and water supply.

[10] That is "the earth's" or "the land's."

[11] "Conjured by Anu (and) Enlil."

Then did Ziusudra, the king, the *pašišu* [of] . . . ,
Build giant . . . ;
Humbly obedient, reverently [he] . . . ,
Attending daily, constantly [he] . . . ,
Bringing forth all kinds of dreams, [he] . . . ,
Uttering the name of heaven (and) earth,
    [he] . . .   (150)
  . . . the gods a *wall* . . . ,
Ziusudra, standing at *its* side, list[ened].
"Stand *by the wall* at my left side . . . ,[12]
By *the wall* I will say a word to thee, [take my word],
[Give] ear to my instruction:
By *our* . . . a flood [*will sweep*] over the cult-centers;
To destroy the seed of mankind . . . ,
Is the decision, the word of the assembly [of the gods].
By the word commanded by Anu (and) Enlil . . . ,
Its kingship, its rule [*will be put to an end*]."   (160)
           (approximately 40 lines destroyed)
All the windstorms, exceedingly powerful, attacked as one,   (201)
At the same time, the flood sweeps *over the cult-centers.*
After, for seven days (and) seven nights,
The flood had *swept over* the land,
(And) the huge boat had been tossed about by the windstorms on
    the great waters,
Utu came forth, who sheds light on heaven (and) earth.
Ziusudra opened *a window of* the huge boat,
The hero Utu *brought his rays into* the giant boat.
Ziusudra, the king,
Prostrated himself before Utu,   (210)
The king kills an ox, *slaughters* a sheep.
          (approximately 39 lines destroyed)
"Ye will utter 'breath of heaven,' 'breath of earth,' verily it will
    stretch itself by *your*. . ."   (251)
Anu (and) Enlil *uttered* "breath of heaven," "breath of earth," *by*
    their . . . , it stretched itself.
Vegetation, coming up out of the earth, rises up.
Ziusudra, the king,
Prostrated himself before Anu (and) Enlil.
Anu (and) Enlil cherished Ziusudra,
Life like (that of) a god they give him,
Breath eternal like (that of) a god they *bring down* for him. Then,
    Ziusudra the king,

---

[12] The name of the speaking deity is not given; no doubt, Enki.

The *preserver of the name of vegetation (and) of the seed of*
   mankind.   (260)
In the land[13] *of crossing,*[14] the land of Dilmun, the place where the
   sun rises, they[15] caused to dwell.
(Remainder of the tablet, about 39 lines of text, destroyed.)

ANET, 60,
66–69, 514

Akkadian Myths and Epics
The Creation Epic (Enuma elish)

TRANSLATOR: E. A. SPEISER

The struggle between cosmic order and chaos was to the ancient Mesopota-
mians a fateful drama that was renewed at the turn of each new year. The
epic which deals with these events was therefore the most significant expression of the religious literature of Mesopotamia. The work, consisting of
seven tablets, was known in Akkadian as *Enūma eliš* "When on high," after
its opening words. It was recited with due solemnity on the fourth day of the
New Year's festival.

There is as yet no general agreement as regards the date of composition.
None of the extant texts antedates the first millennium B.C. On the internal
evidence, however, of the context and the linguistic criteria, the majority of
the scholars would assign the epic to the Old Babylonian period, i.e., the
early part of the second millennium B.C. There does not appear to be any
convincing reason against this earlier dating.

(Tablets I–III recount the birth of the gods, who spring from the pri-
mordial Apsu and Tiamat, and the choice of Marduk as the champion of the younger gods in the battle against Tiamat.)

Tablet IV

They erected for him a princely throne.
Facing his fathers, he sat down, presiding.
"Thou art the most honored of the great gods,
Thy decree is unrivaled, thy command is Anu.[16]

Fig. 141 Thou, Marduk, art the most honored of the great gods,
Thy decree is unrivaled, thy word is Anu.
From this day unchangeable shall be thy pronouncement.

I Sam. 2:7 To raise or bring low—these shall be (in) thy hand.

---

[13] The Sumerian word twice rendered by "land" in this line may also be translated
as "mountain" or "mountain-land."

[14] Perhaps the crossing of the sun immediately upon his rising in the east; the Sumerian word used may also mean "of rule."

[15] That is, probably Anu and Enlil.

[16] I.e., it has the authority of the sky-god Anu.

Thy utterance shall be true, thy command shall be unimpeachable.

No one among the gods shall transgress thy bounds! (10)

Adornment being wanted for the seats of the gods,

Let the place of their shrines ever be in thy place.

O Marduk, thou art indeed our avenger.

We have granted thee kingship over the universe entire.

When in Assembly thou sittest, thy word shall be supreme.

Thy weapons shall not fail; they shall smash thy foes!

O lord, spare the life of him who trusts thee,

But pour out the life of the god who seized evil." Judg. 6:36–40

Having placed in their midst a piece of cloth,

They addressed themselves to Marduk, their first-born: (20)

"Lord, truly thy decree is first among gods.

Say but to wreck or create; it shall be.

Open thy mouth: the cloth will vanish!

Speak again, and the cloth shall be whole!"

At the word of his mouth the cloth vanished.

He spoke again, and the cloth was restored.

When the gods, his fathers, saw the fruit of his word,

Joyfully they did homage: "Marduk is king!"

They conferred on him scepter, throne, and *vestment*;

They gave him matchless weapons that ward off the foes: (30)

"Go and cut off the life of Tiamat.

May the winds bear her blood to places undisclosed."

Bel's destiny thus fixed, the gods, his fathers,

Caused him to go the way of success and attainment.

He constructed a bow, marked it as his weapon,

Attached thereto the arrow, fixed its bow-cord.

He raised the mace, made his right hand grasp it;

Bow and quiver he hung at his side.

In front of him he set the lightning,

With a blazing flame he filled his body. (40)

He then made a net to enfold Tiamat therein.

The four winds he stationed that nothing of her might escape,

The South Wind, the North Wind, the East Wind, the West Wind.

Close to his side he held the net, the gift of his father, Anu.

He brought forth Imhullu "the Evil Wind," the Whirlwind, the
  Hurricane,

The Fourfold Wind, the Sevenfold Wind, the Cyclone, the
  Matchless Wind;

Then he sent forth the winds he had brought forth, the seven of
  them.

To stir up the inside of Tiamat they rose up behind him.

Then the lord raised up the flood-storm, his mighty weapon.

He mounted the storm-chariot irresistible [and] terrifying. (50)

He harnessed (and) yoked to it a team-of-four,
The Killer, the Relentless, the Trampler, the Swift.
Sharp were their teeth, bearing poison.
They were versed in ravage, in destruction skilled.
On his right he posted the *Smiter*, fearsome in battle,
On the left the Combat, which repels all the zealous.
For a cloak he was wrapped in an armor of terror;
With his fearsome halo his head was turbaned.
The lord went forth and followed his course,
Towards the raging Tiamat he set his face.   (60)
In his lips he held a spell;
A plant to put out poison was grasped in his hand.
Then they milled about him, the gods milled about him,
The gods, his fathers, milled about him, the gods milled about him.
The lord approached to scan the inside of Tiamat,
(And) of Kingu, her consort, the scheme to perceive.
As he looks on, his course becomes upset,
His will is distracted and his doings are confused.
And when the gods, his helpers, who marched at his side,
Saw the valiant hero, blurred became their vision.   (70)
Tiamat emitted [a cry], without turning her neck,
Framing savage[17] defiance in her lips:[18]

Judg. 12:6 "Too [imp]ortant art thou [for] the lord of the gods to rise up
    against thee!
Is it in their place that they have gathered, (or) in thy place?"
Thereupon the lord, having [raised] the flood-storm, his mighty
    weapon,
[To] enraged [Tiamat] he sent word as follows:
"*Why* art thou risen, art haughtily exalted,
Thou hast charged thine own heart to stir up conflict, . . . sons reject
    their own fathers,
Whilst thou, who hast born them, hast foresworn love!   (80)
Thou hast appointed Kingu as thy consort,
Conferring upon him the rank of Anu, not rightfully his.
Against Anshar, king of the gods, thou seekest evil;
[Against] the gods, my fathers, thou hast confirmed thy
    wickedness.
[Though] drawn up be thy forces, girded on thy weapons,
Stand thou up, that I and thou meet in single combat!"
When Tiamat heard this,
She was like one possessed; she took leave of her senses.
In fury Tiamat cried out aloud.

---

[17] "Her incantation" is not impossible.
[18] Tiamat's taunt, as recorded in the next two lines, is not clear.

To the roots her legs shook both together.   (90)
She recites a charm, keeps casting her spell,
While the gods of battle sharpen their weapons.
Then joined issue Tamat and Marduk, wisest of gods.
They strove in single combat, locked in battle.
The lord spread out his net to enfold her,
The Evil Wind, which followed behind, he let loose in her face.
When Tiamat opened her mouth to consume him,
He drove in the Evil Wind that she close not her lips.
As the fierce winds charged her belly,
Her body was distended and her mouth was wide open.   (100)
He released the arrow, it tore her belly,
It cut through her insides, splitting the heart.
Having thus subdued her, he extinguished her life.
He cast down her carcass to stand upon it.
After he had slain Tamat, the leader,
Her band was shattered, her troupe broken up;
And the gods, her helpers who marched at her side,
Trembling with terror, turned their backs about,
In order to save and preserve their lives.
Tightly encircled, they could not escape.   (110)
He made them captives and he smashed their weapons.
Thrown into the net, they found themselves ensnared;
Placed in cells, they were filled with wailing;
Bearing his wrath, they were held imprisoned.
And the eleven creatures which she had charged with awe,
The band of demons that marched . [. .] before her,
He cast into fetters, their hands [. . .].
For all their resistance, he trampled (them) underfoot.
And Kingu, who had been made chief among them,
He bound and accounted him to Uggae.[19]   (120)
He took from him the Tablets of Fate, not rightfully his,
Sealed (them) with a seal[20] and fastened (them) on his breast.
When he had vanquished and subdued his adversaries,
Had . . . the vainglorious foe,
Had wholly established Anshar's triumph over the foe,
Nudimmud's desire had achieved, valiant Marduk
Strengthened his hold on the vanquished gods,
And turned back to Tiamat whom he had bound.
The lord trod on the legs of Tiamat,
With his unsparing mace he crushed her skull.   (130)
When the arteries of her blood he had severed,

---

[19] God of death.

[20] This was an essential act of attestation in Mesopotamian society.

The North Wind bore (it) to places undisclosed.
On seeing this, his fathers were joyful and jubilant,
They brought gifts of homage, they to him.
Then the lord paused to view her dead body,
That he might divide the monster and do artful works.
He split her like a shellfish into two parts:
Half of her he set up and ceiled it as sky,
Pulled down the bar and posted guards.
He bade them to allow not her waters to escape.   (140)
He crossed the heavens and surveyed the regions.
He squared Apsu's quarter, the abode of Nudimmud,
As the lord measured the dimensions of Apsu.
The Great Abode, its likeness, he fixed as Esharra,
The Great Abode, Esharra, which he made as the firmament.

Figs. 167, 168 Anu, Enlil, and Ea he made occupy their places.

Tablet V

He constructed stations for the great gods,
Fixing their astral likenesses as constellations.
He determined the year by designating the zones:
He set up three constellations for each of the twelve months.
After defining the days of the year [by means] of (heavenly)
      figures,
He founded the station of Nebiru[21] to determine their (heavenly)
      bands,
That none might transgress or fall short.
Alongside it he set up the stations of Enlil and Ea.
Having opened up the gates on both sides,
He strengthened the locks to the left and the right.   (10)
In her[22] belly he established the zenith.
The Moon he caused to shine, the night (to him) entrusting.
He appointed him a creature of the night to signify the days:
"Monthly, without cease, form designs with a crown.
At the month's very start, rising over the land,
Thou shalt have luminous horns to signify six days,
On the seventh day reaching a [half]-crown.
At full moon[23] stand in opposition[24] in mid-month.

---

[21] I.e., the planet Jupiter. This station was taken to lie between the band of the north, which belonged to Enlil, and the band of the south, which belonged to Ea.

[22] Tiamat's.

[23] Akkadian *šapattu*, the prototype of the "Sabbath" in so far as the injunctions against all types of activity are concerned.

[24] I.e., with regard to the sun. This verb was a technical term in Babylonian astronomy.

When the sun [overtakes] thee at the base of heaven,
Diminish [thy crown] and retrogress in light. (20)
[At the time of disappearance] approach thou the course of the sun,
And [on the twenty-ninth] thou shalt again stand in opposition to
    the sun."
  (The remainder of this tablet is broken away or too fragmentary
           for translation.)

Tablet VI

When Marduk hears the words of the gods,
His heart prompts (him) to fashion artful works.
Opening his mouth, he addresses Ea
To impart the plan he had conceived in his heart:
"Blood I will mass and cause bones to be.   Gen. 1:26
I will establish a savage, 'man' shall be his name.
Verily, savage-man I will create.
He shall be charged with the service of the gods
    That they might be at ease!
The ways of the gods I will artfully alter.
Though alike revered, into two (groups) they shall be
    divided." (10)
Ea answered him, speaking a word to him,
Giving him another plan for the relief of the gods:
"Let but one of their brothers be handed over;
He alone shall perish that mankind may be fashioned.[25]
Let the great gods be here in Assembly,
Let the guilty be handed over that they may endure."
Marduk summoned the great gods to Assembly;
Presiding graciously, he issues instructions.
To his utterance the gods pay heed.
The king addresses a word to the Anunnaki: (20)
"If your former statement was true,
Do (now) the truth on oath by me declare!
Who was it that contrived the uprising,
And made Tiamat rebel, and joined battle?
Let him be handed over who contrived the uprising.
His guilt I will make him bear. You shall dwell in peace!"
The Igigi, the great gods, replied to him,
To Lugaldimmerankia,[26] counselor of the gods, their lord:
"It was Kingu who contrived the uprising,
And made Tiamat rebel, and joined battle." (30)
They bound him, holding him before Ea.

[25] Out of his blood.
[26] "The king of the gods of heaven and earth."

They imposed on him his guilt and severed his blood (vessels).
Out of his blood they fashioned mankind.
He[27] imposed the service and let free the gods.
After Ea, the wise, had created mankind,
Had imposed upon it the service of the gods—
That work was beyond comprehension;
As artfully planned by Marduk, did Nudimmud create it—
Marduk, the king of the gods divided
All the Anunnaki above and below.[28]   (40)
He assigned (them) to Anu to guard his instructions.
Three hundred in the heavens he stationed as a guard.
In like manner the ways of the earth he defined.
In heaven and on earth six hundred (thus) he settled.
After he had ordered all the instructions,
To the Anunnaki of heaven and earth had allotted their portions,
The Anunnaki opened their mouths
And said to Marduk, their lord:
"Now,[29] O lord, thou who hast caused our deliverance,
What shall be our homage to thee?   (50)
Let us build a shrine whose name shall be called
'Lo, a chamber for our nightly rest'; let us repose in it!
Let us build a throne, a recess for his abode!
On the day that we arrive[30] we shall repose in it."
When Marduk heard this,
Brightly glowed his features, like the day:
"Like that of *lofty* Babylon, whose building you have requested,
Let its brickwork be fashioned. You shall name it 'The Sanctuary.' "
The Anunnaki applied the implement;
For one whole year they molded bricks.   (60)
When the second year arrived,

Fig. 189 They raised high the head of Esagila equaling Apsu.[31]
Having built a stage-tower *as high as* Apsu,
They set up *in it* an abode for Marduk, Enlil, (and) Ea
In their presence he *adorned* (it) in grandeur.
To the base of Esharra its horns look down.
After they had achieved the building of Esagila,
The Anunnaki *themselves* erected their shrines.

---

[27] Ea.

[28] Here and elsewhere in this epic the Anunnaki are understood to be the celestial gods (normally Igigi) as well as those of the lower regions.

[29] Not "O Nannar," as translated by some.

[30] For the New Year's festival.

[31] Meaning apparently that the height of Esagila corresponded to the depth of Apsu's waters.

[. . .] all of them gathered,
[. . .] they had built as his dwelling. (70)
The gods, his fathers, at his banquet he seated:
"This is Babylon, the place that is your home!
Make merry in its precincts, occupy its broad [places]."
The great gods took their seats,
They set up festive drink, sat down to a banquet.
After they had made merry within it,
In Esagila, the *splendid,* had performed their rites,
The norms had been fixed (and) *all* [their] portents,
All the gods apportioned the stations of heaven and earth.
The fifty great gods took their seats. (80)
The seven gods of destiny set up the three hundred [in heaven].
Enlil raised the bo[w, his wea]pon, and laid (it) before them.
The gods, his fathers, saw the net he had made.
When they beheld the bow, how skillful its shape,
His fathers praised the work he had wrought.
Raising (it), Anu spoke up in the Assembly of the gods,
As he kissed the bow: "This is my daughter!"
He named the names of the bow as follows:
"Longwood is the first, the second is [. . .];
Its third name is Bow-Star, in heaven I have made it shine." (90)
He fixed a place which the gods, its[32] brothers, [. . .].
After Anu had decreed the fate of the Bow,
And had placed the *exalted* royal throne before the gods,
Anu seated it in the Assembly of the gods.
When the great gods had assembled, (95)
And had [. . .] the fate which Marduk had exalted,
They pronounced among themselves a curse,
Swearing by water and oil to place life in jeopardy.
When they had granted him the exercise of kingship of the gods,
They confirmed him in dominion over the gods of heaven and
    earth. (100)
Anshar pronounced supreme his name Asar(u)luhi:
"Let us make humble obeisance at the mention of his name;
When he speaks, the gods shall pay heed to him.
Let his utterance be supreme above and below!"
"Most exalted be the Son, our avenger;
Let his sovereignty be surpassing, having no rival.
May he shepherd the black-headed ones,[33] his creatures.
To the end of days, without forgetting, let them acclaim his ways.
May he establish for his fathers the great food-offerings; (110)

---

[32] Referring to the Bow.

[33] A common Akkadian metaphor for "the human race."

Their support they shall furnish, shall tend their sanctuaries.
May he cause incense to be smelled, . . . their spells,
A likeness on earth of what he has wrought in heaven.
May he order the black-headed to re[*vere him*],
May the subjects ever bear in mind their god,
And may they at his word pay heed to the goddess.
May food-offerings be borne for their gods and goddesses.
Without fail let them support their gods!
Their lands let them improve, build their shrines,
Let the black-headed wait on their gods.   (120)
As for us, by however many names we pronounce, he is our god!
Let us then proclaim his fifty names. . . ."

ANET³, 501–3   ## Additions to Tablet V

TRANSLATOR: A. K. GRAYSON

Research and new discoveries have filled some gaps in this composition and corrected some erroneous ideas. It is now widely held that the date of composition of the Creation Epic is later than the Old Babylonian period. Beyond this there is little agreement for while some would place its origin in the Kassite period, others would date it even later.

Among recent publications of overall significance must be included the composite cuneiform text of the epic edited by W. G. Lambert and Simon B. Parker, *Enuma Eliš* (Oxford, 1966). Also worthy of note is an article by W. G. Lambert, "A New Look at the Babylonian Background of Genesis" in *The Journal of Theological Studies,* XVI (1965), 287–300. New texts that have appeared come mainly from Ashur and Sultantepe.

"I [have appointed] a sign, follow its path,   (23)
. . . [. . . a]pproach and give judgement."

(Lines 25–44 are too broken for translation. It is clear from the traces, however, that after completing his creation of the moon Marduk turned his attention to establishing the sun.)

After he [had appointed] the days [to Shamash],   (45)
[And had established] the precincts of night and d[ay],
[*Taking*] the spittle of Tia[mat]
Marduk created [. . .] . . .
He formed the c[louds] and filled (them) with [water].
The raising of winds, the bringing of rain (and) cold,   (50)
Making the mist smoke, piling up her poison:
. (These) he appointed to himself, took into his own charge.
Putting her head into position he formed the[reon the mountai]ns,
Opening the deep (which) was in flood,
He caused to flow from her eyes the Euphr[ates (and) T]igris,

Stopping her nostrils he left . . . ,
He formed at her udder the lofty m[ountain]s,
(Therein) he drilled springs for the wells to carry off (the water).
Twisting her tail he bound it to Durmah,
[. . .] . . . Apsu at his foot,   (60)
[. . .] her crotch, she was fastened to the heavens,
(Thus) he covered [the heavens] (and) established the earth.
[. . .] . . . in the midst of Tiamat he made flow,
[. . .] his net he completely let out,
(So) he *created* heaven and earth . . . ,
[. . .] their bounds . . . established.
When he had designed his rules (and) fashioned [his] ordinances,
He founded [the shr]ines (and) handed them over to Ea.
[The Tablet of] Destinies which he had taken from Kingu he
    carried,
He brought (it) as the first gift of greeting, he gave (it) to Anu. (70)
[The go]ds who had *done battle* (and) been scattered,
He led [bou]nd into the presence of his fathers.
Now the eleven creatures which Tiamat had made . . . ,
Whose weapons he had shattered, which he had tied to his foot:
[Of these] he made statues and set (them) up [at the Gate of] Apsu
    (saying):
"Let it be a token that this may never be forgotten!"
When [the gods] saw (this) they were exceedingly glad,
[La]hmu, Lahamu, and all of his fathers
[Crossed] over to him, and Anshar, the king, made manifest his
    greeting,
[An]u, Enlil, and Ea presented to him gifts.   (80)
[With a gi]ft Damkina, his mother, made him joyous,
She sent offerings, his face brightened.
[T]o Usmi who brought her gift to a secret place
[He entru]sted the chancellorship of Apsu (and) the stewardship of
    the shrines.
Being [assem]bled, all the Igigi bowed down,
While everyone of the Anunnaki kissed his feet,
[. . .] their assembly to do obeisance,
They stood [before h]im, bowed (and said): "He is the king!"
[After] the gods, his fathers, were satiated with his charms.   (89)

(Lines 90–106 are too mutilated for translation. In this passage the
seating of Marduk on the throne with his weapons was described.)

Ea and Damkina [. . .],   (107)
They opened their mouths to [speak to the great gods], the Igigi:
"Formerly [Mard]uk was (merely) our beloved son,
Now he is your king, proclaim his title!"   (110)

A second (speech) they made, they all spoke:
"His name shall be Lugaldimmerankia,[34] trust in him!"
When they had given the sovereignty to Marduk,
They declared for him a *formula* of good fortune and success:
"Henceforth thou wilt be the patron of our sanctuaries,
Whatever thou dost command we will do."
Marduk opened his mouth to speak,
To say a word to the gods, his fathers:
"Above the Apsu where you have resided,
The counterpart of Esharra which I have built over you,   (120)
Below I have hardened the ground for a building site,
I will build a house, it will be my luxurious abode.
I will found therein its temple,
I will appoint cellas, I will establish my sovereignty.
When you come up from the Apsu for assembly,
You will spend the night therein, (it is there) to receive all of you.
When you des[cend] from heaven [for assem]bly,
You will spend the night there[in] (it is there) to receive all of you.
I will call [its] name ['Babylon'] (which means) 'the houses of the
          great gods,'
I shall build it [with] the skill of craftsmen."   (130)
[When the gods], his fathers, h[eard] this [speech] of his,
[They put] the following question [to Marduk, their firstborn]:
"Over all that your hands have created,
Who will have thy [*authority*]?
Over the ground which your hands have created,
Who will have thy [*power*]?
Babylon, which thou didst give a fine name,
Ther[ein] establish our [abod]e forever!
[. . .], let them bring our daily ration,
[. . .] our [. . .],   (140)
Let no one [*usurp*] our tasks which we [*previously performed*],
Therein [. . .] its labor [. . .]."
Marduk rejoiced [*when he heard this and*]
He [answered] those gods [who had ques]tioned him,
He that sle[w Tiamat sho]wed them light,
He opened [his mouth], his [speec]h was noble:
" . . . [. . .] them [. . .],
[. . .] will be entrusted to thee."
The gods bowed down before him, they spoke [to him],
They said to Lugaldimmeran[ki]a: (150)
"Formerly the lord [was (merely) our beloved] son,
Now he is our king, [proclaim his title]!

---

[34] "King of the gods of heaven and underworld." Cf. Tablet VI, 140.

He whose pure incantation gave us life,
[*He is the lord* of sple]ndor, mace, and sceptre.
[Ea who knows the ski]ll of all crafts,
Let him prepare the plans, we [*will be the workers*]."

The Epic of Gilgamesh

TRANSLATOR: E. A. SPEISER

The theme of this epic is essentially a secular one. The poem deals with such earthy things as man and nature, love and adventure, friendship and combat—all masterfully blended into a background for the stark reality of death. The climactic struggle of the protagonist to change his eventual fate, by learning the secret of immortality from the hero of the Great Flood of long ago, ends in failure; but with the failure comes a sense of quiet resignation. For the first time in the history of the world a profound experience on such a heroic scale has found expression in a noble style. The scope and sweep of the epic, and its sheer poetic power, give it a timeless appeal. All but a few of the Akkadian texts come from the library of Ashurbanipal at Nineveh. Unlike the Creation Epic, however, the Gilgamesh Epic is known also from versions which antedate the first millennium B.C. From the middle of the second millennium have come down fragments of an Akkadian recension current in the Hittite Empire, and the same Boğazköy archives have yielded also important fragments of a Hittite translation, as well as a fragment of a Hurrian rendering of the epic. From the first half of the second millennium we possess representative portions of the Old Babylonian version of the epic, which pertain to Tablets I–III, and X. That this version was itself a copy of an earlier text is suggested by the internal evidence of the material. The original date of composition of the Akkadian work has to be placed at the turn of the second millennium, if not slightly earlier.

ANET, 72–79, 83–90, 92–97, 514–15

Fig. 69

Tablet I

(i)
He who saw everything [to the end]s of the land,
[Who all thing]s experienced, [conside]red all!
[. . .] together [. . .],
[. . .] of wisdom, who all things .[. .].
The [hi]dden he saw, [laid bare] the undisclosed.
He brought report of before the Flood,
Achieved a long journey, weary and [w]orn.
All his toil he engraved on a stone stela.
Of ramparted Uruk the wall he built,
Of hallowed Eanna,[35] the pure sanctuary. (10)

---

[35] The temple of Anu and Ishtar in Uruk.

Behold its outer wall, whose cornice is like copper,
Peer at the inner wall, which none can equal!
Seize upon the threshold, which is from of old!
Draw near to Eanna, the dwelling of Ishtar,
Which no future king, no man, can equal.
Go up and walk on the walls of Uruk,
Inspect the base terrace, examine the brickwork:
Is not its brickwork of burnt brick?
Did not the Seven [Sages][36] lay its foundations?

(Remainder of the column broken away. A Hittite fragment [cf., J. Friedrich, *ZA*, xxxix (1929), 2–5] corresponds in part with the damaged initial portion of our column ii, and hence appears to contain some of the material from the end of the first column. We gather from this fragment that several gods had a hand in fashioning Gilgamesh, whom they endowed with superhuman size. At length, Gilgamesh arrives in Uruk.)

    (ii)
Two-thirds of him is god, [one-third of him is human].
The form of his body [. . .]
                    (mutilated or missing)   (3–7)
[. . .] like a wild ox lofty [. . .];   (8)
The onslaught of his weapons verily has no equal.
By the *drum*[37] are aroused [his] companions.   (10)
The nobles of Uruk *are gloo[my]* in [their chamb]ers:
"Gilgamesh leaves not the son to [his] father;
[Day] and [night] is unbridled his arro[gance].
[Is this Gilga]mesh, [the shepherd of ramparted] Uruk?
Is this [our] shepherd, [bold, stately, wise]?
[Gilgamesh] leaves not [the maid to her mother],
The warrior's daughter, [the noble's spouse]!"
The [gods hearkened] to their plaint,
The gods of heaven Uruk's lord [they . . .]:
"Did not [*Aruru*][38] bring forth this strong wild ox?   (20)
[The onslaught of his weapons] verily has no equal.
By the *drum* are aroused his [companions].
Gilgamesh leaves not the son to his father;
        Day and night [is unbridled his arrogance].
Is this the shepherd of [ramparted] Uruk?
Is this their [. . .] shepherd,

---

[36] The seven sages, who brought civilization to seven of the oldest cities.

[37] Here perhaps the reference is to the abuse for personal purposes of an intrument intended for civic or religious use.

[38] A goddess.

Bold, stately, (and) wise? . . .
Gilgamesh leaves not the maid to [her mother],
The warrior's daughter, the noble' spouse!"
When [Anu] had heard out their plaint,
The great Aruru they called: (30)
    "Thou, Aruru, didst create [the man];
Create now his double;
    His stormy heart let him match.
Let them contend, that Uruk may have peace!"
When Aruru heard this,
    A double of Anu she conceived within her.
Aruru washed her hands,
    Pinched off clay and cast it on the steppe.
[On the step]pe she created valiant Enkidu,
    Offspring of . . . , essence of Ninurta.
[Sha]ggy with hair is his whole body,
    He is endowed with head hair like a woman.
The locks of his hair sprout like Nisaba.[39]
He knows neither people nor land;
    Garbed is he like Sumuqan.[40]
With the gazelles he feeds on grass,
With the wild beasts he jostles at the watering-place,   (40)
With the teeming creatures his heart delights in water.
(Now) a hunter, a trapping-man,
Faced him at the watering-place.
[One] day, a second, and a third
    He faced him at the watering-place.
When the hunter saw him, his face became motionless.
He and his beasts went into his house,
[Sore a]fraid, still, without a sound,
(While) his heart [was disturbed], overclouded his face.
For woe had [entered] his belly;
His face was like that [of a wayfarer] from afar.   (50)
    (iii)
The hunter opened [his mouth] to speak,
    Saying to [his father]:
"My father, there is [a] fellow who [has come from the hills],
He is the might[iest in the land]; strength he has.
[Like the essence] of Anu, so mighty his strength!
[Ever] he ranges over the hills,
[Ever] with the beasts [he feeds on grass].
[Ever sets he] his feet at the watering-place.

[39] Goddess of grain.
[40] God of cattle.

[I am so frightened that] I dare not approach him!
[He filled in] the pits that I had dug,
[He tore up] my *traps* which I had [set], (10)
The beasts and creatures of the steppe
    [He has made slip through my hands].[41]
[He does not allow] me to engage in fieldcraft!

[His father opened his mouth to speak],
    Saying to the hunter:
"[My son], in Uruk [there lives] Gilgamesh.
[No one is there more mighty] than he.
[Like the essence of Anu, so mi]ghty is his strength!
[Go, then, toward Uruk set] thy face,
[Speak to him of] the power of the man.
[Let him give thee a harlot-lass]. Take (her) [with thee];
[Let her prevail against him] by dint of [greater] might. (20)
[When he waters the beasts at] the watering-place,
[She shall pull off] her cloth[ing, laying bare] her ripeness.
[As soon as he sees] her, he will draw near to her.
Reject him[42] will his beasts [that grew up on] his steppe!"
[Giving heed to] the advice of his father,
The hunter went forth [to Gilgamesh].
He took the road, in Uruk he set [his foot]:
"[. . .] Gilga[mesh . . .],
There is a fellow [who has come from the hills],
He is the might[iest in the land; strength he has]. (30)
Like the essence of Anu, so mighty [his strength]!
[Ever] he ranges over the hills,
Ever with the beasts [he feeds on grass],
Ever [sets] he his feet at the watering-place.
I am so frightened that I dare not approach [him]!
He filled in the pits that [I] had dug,
He tore up my *traps* [which I had set],
The beasts and creatures [of the steppe]
    He has made slip through my hands.
He does not allow me to engage in fieldcraft!"
Gilgamesh says to him, [to] the hunter: (40)
"Go, my hunter, take with thee a harlot-lass.
When he waters the beasts at the watering-place,
She shall pull off her clothing, laying bare her ripeness.
As soon as he sees her, he will draw near to her.
Reject him will his beasts that grew up on his steppe!"
Forth went the hunter, taking with him a harlot-lass.

[41] Perhaps "he has made me forfeit."
[42] Lit., "regard as stranger, deny."

They took the road, going straight on the(ir) way.
On the third day at the appointed spot they arrived.
The hunter and the harlot sat down in their places.
One day, a second day, they sat by the watering-place.   (50)
The wild beasts came to the watering-place to drink.
    (iv)
The creeping creatures came, their heart delighting in water.
But as for him, Enkidu, born in the hills—
With the gazelles he feeds on grass,
With the wild beasts he drinks at the watering-place,
With the creeping creatures his heart delights in water—
The lass beheld him, the savage-man,
The barbarous fellow from the depths of the steppe:
"There he is, O lass! Free thy breasts,
Bare thy bosom that he may possess thy ripeness!
Be not bashful! Welcome his ardor!   (10)
As soon as he sees thee, he will draw near to thee.
Lay aside thy cloth that he may rest upon thee.
Treat him, the savage, to a woman's task!
Reject him will his wild beasts that grew up on his steppe,
As his love is drawn unto thee."
The lass freed her breasts, bared her bosom,
    And he possessed her ripeness.
She was not bashful as she welcomed his ardor.
She laid aside her cloth and he rested upon her.
She treated him, the savage, to a woman's task,
As his love was drawn unto her.   (20)
For six days and seven nights Enkidu comes forth,
    Mating with the lass.
After he had had (his) fill of her charms,
He set his face toward his wild beasts.
On seeing him, Enkidu, the gazelles ran off,
The wild beasts of the steppe drew away from his body.
Startled was Enkidu, as his body became taut,
His knees were motionless—for his wild beasts had gone.
Enkidu had to slacken his pace—it was not as before;
But he now had [wi]sdom, [br]oader understanding.
Returning, he sits at the feet of the harlot.   (30)
He looks up at the face of the harlot,
His ears attentive, as the harlot speaks;
[The harlot] says to him, to Enkidu:
"Thou art [wi]se, Enkidu, art become like a god!
Why with the wild creatures dost thou roam over the steppe?
Come, let me lead thee [to] ramparted Uruk,
To the holy temple, abode of Anu and Ishtar,

Where lives Gilgamesh, accomplished in strength,
And like a wild ox lords it over the folk."
As she speaks to him, her words find favor, (40)
His heart enlightened, he yearns for a friend.
Enkidu says to her, to the harlot:
"Up, lass, escort thou me,
To the pure sacred temple, abode of Anu and Ishtar,
Where lives Gilgamesh, accomplished in strength,
And like a wild ox lords it over the folk.
I will challenge him [and will bo]ldly address him,
(v)
[I will] shout in Uruk: 'I am he who is mighty!
[I am the] one who can alter destinies,
[(He) who] was born on the steppe is mighty; strength he has.'"
"[Up then, let us go, that he may see] thy face.
[I will show thee Gilgamesh; where] he is I know well.
Come then, O Enkidu, to ramparted [Uruk],
Where people are re[splend]ent in festal attire,
(Where) each day is made a holiday,
Where [. . .] lads . . . ,
And la[ss]es [. .] . of figure. (10)
Their ripeness [. . .] full of perfume.
They drive the great ones from their couches!
To thee, O Enkidu, who rejoicest in living,
I will show Gilgamesh, the joyful man!
Look thou at him, regard his face;
He is radiant with manhood, vigor he has.
With ripeness gorgeous is the whole of his body,
Mightier strength has he than thou,
Never resting by day or by night.
O Enkidu, renounce thy presumption! (20)

Fig. 144   Gilgamesh—of him Shamash is fond;
Anu, Enlil, and Ea have broadened his wisdom.
Before thou comest down from the hills,
Gilgamesh will see thee in (his) dreams in Uruk: . . ."

(Remaining lines of the Assyrian Version of Tablet I are here omitted since the Old Babylonian Version of Tablet II takes up at this point.)

Tablet II

Old Babylonian Version
(ii)
Gilgamesh arose to reveal the dream,
Saying to his mother:

"My mother, in the time of night
I felt joyful and I walked about
In the midst of the nobles.
The stars appeared in the heavens.
The essence of Anu descended towards me.
I sought to lift it; it was too heavy for me!
I sought to move it; move it I could not!   (10)
Uruk-land was gathered about it,
While the nobles kissed its feet.
As I set my forehead,[43]
They gave me support.
I raised it and brought it to thee."
The mother of Gilgamesh, who knows all,
Says to Gilgamesh:
"Forsooth, Gilgamesh, one like thee
Was born on the steppe,
And the hills have reared him.
When thou seest him, [*as (over) a woman*] thou wilt rejoice.   (20)
The nobles will kiss his feet;
Thou wilt embrace him and [..] . him;
Thou wilt lead him to me."
He lay down and saw another
[Dream]: he says to his mother:
[My mother], I saw another
[. . .] in *the confusion*. In the street
[Of] broad-marted Uruk
There lay an axe, and
They were gathered round it.   (30)
That axe, strange was its shape.
As soon as I saw it, I rejoiced.
I loved it, and as though to a woman,
I was drawn to it.
I took it and place it
At my side."
The mother of Gilgamesh, who knows all,
[Says to Gilgamesh]:   (small break)
        (ii)
"Because I made it vie with thee."
While Gilgamesh reveals his dream,
Enkidu sits before the harlot.
[. . .] *the two of them.*
[Enki]du forgot where he was born.

---

[43] To press the carrying strap against it; this method, which is witnessed on the Ur   *Fig. 97*
Standard, is still practiced in modern Iraq.

For six days and seven nights Enkidu came forth
Mating with the l[ass].
Then the harlot opened her mouth,   (10)
Saying to Enkidu:
"As I look at thee, Enkidu, thou art become like a god;
Wherefore with the wild creatures
Dost thou range over the steppe?
Up, I will lead thee
To broad-marted Uruk,
To the holy temple, the abode of Anu,
Enkidu, arise, I will lead thee
To Eanna, the abode of Anu,
Where lives [Gilgamesh, accomplished] in deeds,
And thou, li[ke . . .],   (20)
Wilt love [him like] thyself.
Up, arise from the ground,
The shepherd's bed!"
He hearkened to her words, approved her speech;
The woman's counsel
Fell upon his heart.
She pulled off (her) clothing;
With one (piece) she clothed him,
With the other garment
She clothed herself.   (30)
Holding on to his hand,
She leads him like a mother
To the board of shepherds,
The place of the sheepfold.
Round him the shepherds gathered.
                              (several lines missing)
          (iii)
The milk of wild creatures
He was wont to suck.
Food they placed before him;
He gagged, he gaped
And he stared.
Nothing does Enkidu know
Of eating food;
To drink strong drink
He has not been taught.
The harlot opened her mouth,   (10)
Saying to Enkidu:
"Eat the food, Enkidu,
As is life's due;

Drink the strong drink, as is the custom of the land."
Enkidu ate the food,
Until he was sated;
Of strong drink he drank
Seven goblets.
Carefree became his mood (and) cheerful,
His heart exulted   (20)
And his face glowed.
He rubbed [the *shaggy growth*],
The hair of his body,
Anointed himself with oil,
Became human.
He put on clothing,
He is like a groom!
He took his weapon
To chase the lions,
That shepherds might rest at night.   (30)
He caught wolves,
He captured lions,
The chief cattlemen could lie down;
Enkidu is their watchman,
The bold man,
The unique hero!
To [. . .] he said:

(several lines missing)

    (iv)

(some eight lines missing)

He made merry.
When he lifted his eyes,   (10)
He beheld a man.
He says to the harlot:
"Lass, fetch the man!
Why has he come hither?
His name let me hear."
The harlot called the man,
Going up to him and saying to him:
"Sir, whither hastenest thou?
What is this thy toilsome course?"
The man opened his mouth,   (20)
Saying to En[kidu]:
"Into the meeting-house he has [*intruded*],
Which is set aside for the people,
. . . for *wedlock*.
On the city he has heaped *defilement*,

Imposing strange things on the *hapless* city.
For the king of broad-marted Uruk
The *drum*[44] of the people is free for nuptial choice.   (30)
For Gilgamesh, king of broad-marted Uruk,
The *drum* of the people is free
For nuptial choice,
That with lawful wives he might mate!
He is the first,
The *husband* comes after.
By the counsel of the gods it has (so) been ordained.
With the cutting of his umbilical cord
It was decreed for him!"
At the words of the man
His face grew pale.

                    (some three lines missing)
         (v)
                    (some six lines missing)
[Enkidu] walks [in front]
And the lass behind him.
When he entered broad-marted Uruk,
The populace gathered about him.   (10)
As he stopped in the street
Of broad-marted Uruk,
The people were gathered,
Saying about him:
"He is like Gilgamesh *to a hair*!
Though shorter in stature,
He is stronger of bone.
[. . .] . . .
[He is the strongest in the land]; strength he has.
The milk of wild creatures   (20)
He was wont to suck.
In Uruk (there will be) a constant (*clatter of*) *arms*."
The nobles rejoiced:
"A hero has appeared
For the man of proper mien!
For Gilgamesh, the godlike,
His equal has come forth."
For Ishhara[45] the bed
Is laid out.
Gilgamesh. [. .],
At night . . [.],

---

[44] Instrument to summon the listeners.
[45] A form of Ishtar, as goddess of love.

As he approaches,
[Enkidu] stands in the street
To bar the way
To Gilgamesh
[...] in his might.

(some three lines missing)

    (vi)

(some five lines missing)

Gilgamesh [...]
On the steppe [...]
Sprouts [...].
He rose up and [...]
Before him.   (10)
They met in the Market-of-the-Land.
Enkidu barred the gate
With his foot,
Not allowing Gilgamesh to enter.
They grappled each other,
Holding fast like bulls.
They shattered the doorpost,
As the wall shook.
Gilgamesh and Enkidu
Grappled each other,   (20)
Holding fast like bulls;
They shattered the doorpost,
As the wall shook.
As Gilgamesh bent the knee—
His foot on the ground—
His fury abated
And he turned away.
When he had turned away,
Enkidu to him
Speaks up, to Gilgamesh:
"As one alone thy mother
Bore thee,
The wild cow of the steer-folds,
Ninsunna!
Raised up above men is thy head.
Kingship over the people
Enlil has granted thee!"

Tablet III

Old Babylonian Version

(From fragments of text it is clear that Gilgamesh has decided on an expedition against monstrous Ḫuwawa [Assyrian Ḫumbaba], who lives in the Cedar Forest. Enkidu tries to dissuade him, but Gilgamesh's determination is apparent from the following lines of the Old Babylonian Version:)

| Gilgamesh opened his mouth, | (3) |

Gilgamesh opened his mouth,   (3)
Saying to [Enkidu]:
"Who, my friend can scale he[aven]?
Only the gods [live] forever under the sun.

Eccles. 1:2–4   As for mankind, numbered are their days;
Whatever they achieve is but the wind!
Even here thou art afraid of death.
What of thy heroic might?   (10)
Let me go then before thee,
Let thy mouth call to me, 'Advance, fear not!'
Should I fall, I shall have made me a name:
'Gilgamesh'—they will say—against fierce Huwawa
Has fallen!'(Long) after
My offspring has been born in my house,"

(From the fragmentary text of Tablets IV and V it is clear that the hazardous expedition of the two heroes against Ḫuwawa is successful.)

Tablet VI

He[46] washed his grimy hair, polished his weapons,
The braid of his hair he shook out against his back.
He cast off his soiled (things), put on his clean ones,
Wrapped a fringed cloak about and fastened a sash.
When Gilgamesh had put on his tiara,
Glorious Ishtar raised an eye at the beauty of Gilgamesh:
"Come, Gilgamesh, be thou (my) lover!
Do but grant me of thy fruit.
Thou shalt be my husband and I will be thy wife.
I will harness for thee a chariot of lapis and gold,   (10)
Whose wheels are gold and whose horns are brass.
Thou shalt have storm-demons to hitch on for mighty mules.
In the fragrance of cedars thou shalt enter our house.
When our house thou enterest,
Threshold (and) dais shall kiss thy feet!
Humbled before thee shall be kings, lords, and princes!
The *yield* of hills and plain they shall bring thee as tribute.
Thy goats shall cast triplets, thy sheep twins,
Thy he-ass in lading shall surpass thy mule.
Thy chariot horses shall be famed for racing,   (20)
[Thine ox] under yoke shall not have a rival!"

---

[46] Gilgamesh.

[Gilgamesh] opened his mouth to speak,
[Saying] to glorious Ishtar:
["What am I to give] thee, that I may take thee in marriage?
[Should I give oil] for the body, and clothing?
[Should I give] bread and victuals?
[. . .] food fit for divinity,
[. . .] drink fit for royalty.

(mutilated) (29–31)

[. . . if I] take thee in marriage?
[Thou art but a brazier which goes out] in the cold;
A back door [which does not] keep out blast and wind-storm;
A palace which crushes the valiant [. . .];
A *turban* whose cover [. . .];
Pitch which [soils] its bearers;
A waterskin which [soaks through] its bearer;
Limestone which [*springs*] the stone rampart;
Jasper [which . . .] enemy land; (40)
A shoe which [pinches the foot] of its owner!
Which lover didst thou love forever?
Which of thy shepherds pleased [thee for all time]?Come, and I will
   na[*me* for thee] thy lovers:

Of . . . [. . .] . . .
For Tammuz, the lover of thy youth,
Thou hast ordained wailing year after year.
Having loved the dappled shepherd-bird,
Thou smotest him, breaking his wing.
In the groves he sits, crying 'My wing!'[47] (50)
Then thou lovedst a lion, perfect in strength;
Seven pits and seven thou didst dig for him.
Then a stallion thou lovedst, famed in battle;
The whip, the spur, and the lash thou ordainedst forhim.
Thou decreedst for him to gallop seven leagues,
Thou decreedst for him the muddied to drink;
For his mother, Silili, thou ordainedst wailing!
Then thou lovedst the keeper of the herd,
Who ash-cakes ever did heap up for thee,
Daily slaughtered kids for thee; (60)
Yet thou smotest him, turning him into a wolf,
So that his own herd boys drive him off,
And his dogs bite his thighs.
Then thou lovedst Ishullanu, thy father's gardener,
Who baskets of dates ever did bring to thee,

---

[47] Akk., *kappi*, plainly a word play on the cry of the bird.

And daily did brighten thy table.
Thine eyes raised at him, thou didst go to him:
'O my Ishullanu, let us taste of thy vigor!
Put forth thy "hand" and touch our "modesty!" '
Ishullanu said to thee: (70)
'What dost thou want with me?
Has my mother not baked, have I not eaten,
That I should taste the food of stench and foulness?
Does reed-work afford cover against the cold?[48]
As thou didst hear this [his talk],
Thou smotest him and turn[edst] him into a *mole*.
Thou placedst him in the midst of .. [.];
He cannot go up . . . nor can he come down . . .
If thou shouldst love me, thou wouldst [treat me] like them."

When Ishtar heard this,
Ishtar was enraged and [mounted] to heaven.   (80)
Forth went Ishtar before Anu, her father,
To Antum, her mother, she went and [said]:
"My father, Gilgamesh has heaped insults upon me!
Gilgamesh has recounted my stinking deeds,
My stench and my foulness."
Anu opened his mouth to speak,
Saying to glorious Ishtar:
"But surely, thou didst invite .[..],
And so Gilgamesh has recounted thy stinking deeds,
Thy stench and [thy] foulness."   (91)

Ishtar opened her mouth to speak,
Saying to [Anu, her father]:
"My father, make me the Bull of Heaven [that he smite Gilgamesh],
[And] fill Gil[gamesh . . .]!
If thou [dost not make] me [the Bull of Heaven],
I will smash [the doors of the nether world],
I will [. . .],
I will [raise up the dead eating (and) alive],
So that the dead shall outnumber the living!"   (100)

Anu [opened his mouth to speak],
Saying [to glorious Ishtar]:
"[If I do what] thou askest [of me],
[There will be] seven years of (barren) husks.
Hast thou gathered [grain for the people]?
Hast thou grown grass [for the beasts]?"

---

[48] This appears to be a proverbial expression.

[Ishtar opened her mouth] to speak,
[Saying to A]nu, her father:
"[Grain for the people] I have stored,
[Grass for the beasts] I have provided.   (110)
[If there should be seven] years of husks,
[I have ga]thered [grain for the people],
[I have grown] grass [for the beasts]."

(Lines 114–28 are too fragmentary for translation. It is plain, however, that Anu did Ishtar's bidding, for the Bull comes down and kills hundreds of men with his first two snorts.)

With [his] third snort [*he sprang*] at Enkidu.
Enkidu *parried* his onslaught.   (130)
Up leaped Enkidu, seizing the Bull of Heaven by the horns.
The Bull of Heaven hurled [his] foam in [his] face,
Brushed him with the thick of his tail.

Enkidu opened his mouth to speak,
Saying [to Gilgamesh]:
"My friend, we have gloried [. . .]."

(Lines 137–51 mutilated, but the course of the battle is made plain by the following:)

Between neck and horns [he thrust] his sword.   (152)
When they had slain the Bull, they tore out his heart,
Placing it before Shamash.
They drew back and did homage before Shamash.
The two brothers sat down.

Then Ishtar mounted the wall of ramparted Uruk,
Sprang on the battlements, uttering a curse:
"Woe unto Gilgamesh because he insulted me
        By slaying the Bull of Heaven!"
When Enkidu heard this speech of Ishtar,   (160)
He *tore loose* the right thigh of the Bull of Heaven
        And tossed it in her face:
"Could I but get thee, like unto him
I would do unto thee.
His entrails I would hang at thy side!"
(Thereupon) Ishtar assembled the votaries,
The (pleasure-)lasses and the (temple-)harlots.
Over the right thigh of the Bull of Heaven she set up a wail.
But Gilgamesh called the craftsmen, the armorers,
All (of them).
The artisans admire the thickness of his horns: (170)
Each is cast from thirty minas of lapis;

The coating on each is two fingers (thick);
Six measures of oil, the capacity of the two,
He offered as ointment to his god, Lugalbanda.
He brought (them) and hung them in his princely bedchamber.

In the Euphrates they washed their hands,
They embraced each other as they went on,
Riding through the market-street of Uruk.
The people of Uruk are gathered to gaze [upon them].

I Sam. 18:7   Gilgamesh to the *lyre maids*[49] [of Uruk]   (180)
Says (these) words:
"Who is most splendid among the heroes?
Who is most glorious among men?"
"Gilgamesh is most splendid among the heroes,
[Gilgamesh is most glori]ous among men."
                    (mutilated)   (186–88)

Gilgamesh in his palace holds a celebration.
Down lie the heroes on their beds of night.   (190)
Also Enkidu lies down, a dream beholding.
Up rose Enkidu to relate his dream,
Saying to his friend:
"My friend, why are the great gods in council?"

Tablet VII

The first two columns of this tablet, Enkidu's dream, are missing in the Assyrian Version.

"[. . .] . . . Then daylight came."
[And] Enkidu answered Gilgamesh:
"[*He*]*ar* the dream which I had last night:
Anu, Enlil, Ea, and heavenly Shamash
        [Were in council].
And Anu said to Enlil:
'Because the Bull of Heaven they have slain, and Huwawa
They have slain, therefore'—said Anu—'the one of them
Who stripped the mountains of the cedar [Must die!]'
But Enlil said: 'Enkidu must die;
Gilgamesh, however, shall not die!'   (10)

Then heavenly Shamash answered valiant Enlil:
'Was it not at my command
That they slew the Bull of Heaven and Huwawa?
        Should now innocent
Enkidu die?' But Enlil turned

---

[49] The context calls clearly for musicians or singers, not servant girls.

In anger to heavenly Shamash: 'Because, *much like*
One of their comrades, thou didst daily go down to them.' "
Enkidu lay down (ill) before Gilgamesh.
And as his[50] tears were streaming down, (he said):
"O my brother, my dear brother! Me they would
Clear at the expense of my brother!"
  Furthermore: (20)
"Must I by the spirit (of the dead)
Sit down, at the spirit's door,
Never again [to behold] my dear brother with (mine) eyes?"

 (The remainder is lost. In a deathbed review of his life, Enkidu
seems to bemoan the events that had led up to this sorry state, cursing the successive steps in his fated life. One of his courses, preserved
in an Assyrian fragment, is directed against the gate that lamed
his hand.)

Enkidu [. . .] lifted up [his eyes],   (36)
Speaking with the door as though [it were human]:
"Thou door of the woods, uncom[prehending],
Not endowed with understanding!
At twenty leagues away I found choice thy wood,   (40)
(Long) before I beheld the lofty cedar.
There is no counterpart of thy wood [*in the land*].
Six dozen cubits is thy height, two dozen thy breadth [. . .].
Thy pole, thy pole-ferrule, and thy pole-knob [. . .].
A *master-craftsman* in Nippur built thee [. . .].   *Fig. 61*
Had I known, O door, that this [*would come to pass*]
And that this [thy] beauty [. . .],
I would have lifted the axe, would have [. . .],
I would have *set* a reed frame *upon* [*thee*]!"

 (A long gap follows. When the text sets in again, Enkidu—
continuing his bitter survey—invokes the curse of Shamash upon
the hunter.)

  (iii)
"[. . .] destroy his wealth, diminish his power!
May his [way be *repugnant*] before thee.
May [*the beasts he would trap*] escape from before him.
[Let not] the hunter at[tain] the fullness of his heart!"
[Then his heart] prompted (him) to curse [the harlo]t-lass:
"Come, lass, I will decree (thy) [fa]te,
[A fa]te that shall not end for all eternity!
[I will] curse thee with a great curse,

---

[50] Referring to Gilgamesh.

[*An oath*], whose curses shall soon overtake thee.
[. . .] surfeit of thy charms.   (10)
                    (mutilated)   (11–17)
[. . .] shall cast into thy house.
[. . .] the road shall be thy dwelling place,
[The shadow of the wall] shall be thy station,   (20)
[. . .] thy feet,
[The besotted and the thirsty shall smite] thy cheek!
                    (mutilated)   (23–30)
Because me [thou hast . . .]
And because [. . .] upon me."
When Shamash heard [these words] of his mouth,
Forthwith he called down to him [from] heaven:
"Why, O Enkidu, cursest thou the harlot-lass,
Who made thee eat food fit for divinity,
And gave thee to drink wine fit for royalty,
Who clothed thee with noble garments,
And made thee have fair Gilgamesh for a comrade?
And has (not) now Gilgamesh, thy bosom friend,   (40)
Made thee lie on a noble couch?
He has made thee lie on a couch of honor,
Has placed thee on the seat of ease, the seat at the left,
That [the prin]ces of the earth may kiss thy feet!
He will make Uruk's people weep over thee (and) lament,
Will fill [joyful] people with woe over thee.
And, when thou art gone,
      He will his body with uncut hair invest,
Will don a lion skin and roam over the steppe."

[When] Enkidu [heard] the words of valiant Shamash,
[. . .] his vexed heart grew quiet.

     (Short break. Relenting, Enkidu changes his curse into a blessing.
He addresses himself once again to the girl:)
                    (iv)
"May [. . .] return to thy pl[ace . .].
[Kings, prin]ces, and nobles shall love [thee].
[None shall on account of thee] smite his thigh.[51]
[Over thee shall the old man]shake his beard.
[. . . *the young*] shall unloose his girdle.
[. . .] *carnelian*, lapis, and gold.
[May he be paid] back who defiled thee,
[*May his home be emptied*], his heaped-up storehouse.
[To the presence of] the gods [the priest] shall let thee enter,

---

[51] In derision or embarrassment.

[On thy account] shall be forsaken the wife,
    (though) a mother of seven."   (10)
[. . . Enki]du, whose mood is bitter,
[. . .] lies down all alone.
That night [he pours out] his feelings to his friend:
"[My friend], I saw a dream last night:
The heavens [moaned], the earth responded;[52]
[. . .] I stood [alo]ne.
[. . .] his face was darkened.
Like unto [. . .] was his face.
[. . . like] the talons of an eagle were his claws.
[. . .] he *overpowered* me.   (20)
[. . .] he leaps.
[. . .] he submerged me.
           (mutilated or missing)   (23–30)
[. . .] . . . he transformed me,
So that my arms were [. . .] like those of a bird.
Looking at me, he leads me to the House of Darkness,
    The abode of Irkalla,
To the house which none leave who have entered it,
On the road from which there is no way back,
To the house wherein the dwellers are bereft of light,
Where dust is their fare and clay their food.
They are clothed like birds, with wings for garments,
And see no light, residing in darkness.
In the House of Dust, which I entered,   (40)
I looked at [rulers], their crowns put away;
I [saw princes], those (born to) the crown,
    Who had ruled the land from the days of yore.
[These *doubl*]es of Anu and Enlil were serving meat roasts;
They were serving bake[meats] and pouring
    Cool water from the waterskins.
In the House of Dust, which I entered,
Reside High Priest and acolyte,
Reside incantatory and ecstatic,
Reside the lover-anointers of the great gods,
Resides Etana,[53] resides Sumuqan.[54]
Ereshkigal [lives there], Queen of the nether world,   (50)
[And Belit-]Seri, recorder of the nether world, kneels
    before her.
[She holds a tablet] and reads out to her.

[52] A portent of death.

[53] King of Kish who was carried to heaven by an eagle.

[54] God of cattle.

[Lifting] up her head, she beheld me:
[Saying: 'Who] has brought this one hither?' "

(The remainder of the tablet in the Assyrian Version is missing.
The following fragment may be relevant.)

"Remember all my travels [with him]!   (4)
My friend saw a dream whose [*portents*] were un[favorable]:
The day on which he saw the dream was ended.
Stricken is Enkidu, one day, [a second day].
Enkidu's [suffering], on his bed, [increases].
A third day, a fourth day [. . .].
A fifth day, a sixth, and a seventh;   (10)
        An eighth, a ninth, [and a tenth day],
Enkidu's suffering, on his bed, [increases].
        An eleventh and a twelfth day [. . .].
[Stricken] is Enkidu on his bed [*of pain*]!
At length he called Gilgamesh [and said to him]:
'My friend, [. . .] has cursed me!
[Not] like one [fallen] in battle [shall I die],
For I feared the battle [. . .].
My friend, he who [is slain] in battle [is blessed].
But as for me, [. . .]' "

Tablet VIII

        (obverse, i)
With the first glow of dawn Gilgamesh said to his friend:
"Enkidu, thy [moth]er a gazelle, a wild ass thy father, [produce]d
        thee.
They whose *mark* is their tails reared thee, and the cattle
Of the steppe and of all the pastures.
        May the tracks of Enkidu in the Cedar Forest
Weep for thee, may they not *hush* night and day.
May the elders of wide, ramparted Uruk weep for thee.
        [May weep for thee]
The finger that is extended behind us in blessing.
        May weep for thee
And echo the countryside as though it were thy mother.
        May weep for thee [. . .]
In whose midst we . . . May weep for thee
        bear, hyena, [panther],
Tiger, hart, *leopard,* lion; oxen, deer, [ibex],   (10)
And the wild creatures of the steppe.
        May weep for thee the river Ula [. . .]
By whose banks we used to walk.
        May weep for thee the pure Euphrates, [*where we drew*]

Water for the skin. May weep for thee
    The warriors of wide, [ramparted] Uruk
[. . .] we slew the Bull . . . May weep for thee [. . .]
[Who] in Eridu extolled thy name. May weep for thee . . .]
[Who . . .] extolled thy name. May weep for thee [. . .]
[Who] provided . . . grain for thy mouth. May weep for thee [. . .]
[Who] put salve on thy back. May weep for thee [. . .]
[Who] put ale in thy mouth. May weep for thee the [*harlot*]
[Who] anointed thee with fragrant oil.
    May we[ep for thee . . .]   (20)
[Of the *h*]arem who [*brought to thee*]
    The wife and the ring *of* thy choice.[55]
May brothers weep for thee like sisters [. . .
    and may they let grow long]
Their head-hair over thee [. . .]!"
    (ii)
"Hear me, O elders [and give ear] unto me!
It is for Enkidu, my [friend], that I weep,
Moaning bitterly like a wailing woman.
The axe at my side, my hand's trust,
The dirk in my belt, [the shield] in front of me,
My festal robe, my richest trimming—
An evil [*demon*] rose up and robbed me!
[O my younger friend], thou chasedst
    The wild ass of the hills, the panther of the steppe!
Enkidu, my younger friend, thou who chasedst
    The wild ass of the hills, the panther of the steppe!
We who [have conquered] all things, scaled [the mountains],   (10)
Who seized the Bull [and slew him],
Brought affliction on Hubaba,[56] who [dwelled in the Cedar Forest]!
What, now, is this sleep that has laid hold [on thee]?
Thou art benighted and canst not hear [me]!"
But he lifts not up [his eyes];
He touched his heart, but it does not beat.
Then he veiled (his) friend like a bride [. . .],
Storming over him like a lion,
Like a lioness deprived of [her] whelps.
He paces back and forth before [*the couch*],   (20)
Pulling out (his hair) and strewing [it . . .],   Jer. 16:6; 48:37
Tearing off and flinging down (his) finery,
    [As though] unc[lean]!
With the first glow [of dawn], Gil[gamesh . . .].

[55] Or perhaps, "a wife, a ring, thy counsel."
[56] Variant of Ḫumbaba, Ḫuwawa.

Then Gilgamesh issued a call to the land: "O smith, [...],
Coppersmith, goldsmith, lapidary! Make my friend [...]!"
[Then] he fashioned a statue for his friend,
> The friend whose stature [...]:
"[...], of lapis is thy breast, of gold thy body, [...]."
> (iii)
"On a couch [of honor I made thee lie],
I placed thee [on the seat of ease, the seat at the left],
That the princes of the earth [might kiss thy feet]!
Over thee I will make [Uruk's] people weep (and) [lament],
Joyful people [I will fill with woe over thee].
And, when thou art gone,
> [I shall invest my body with uncut hair],
And, clad in a [lion] skin, [I shall roam over the steppe]!"

With the first glow of dawn, [Gilgamesh]
Loosened his band [...].

(The remainder of the tablet is missing or too fragmentary for
translation, with the exception of the following lines:)
> (v)
With the first glow of dawn, Gilgamesh fashioned [...],   (45)
Brought out a large table of *elammaqu* wood,
Filled with honey a bowl of *carnelian*,
Filled with curds a bowl of lapis,
[...] he decorated and exposed to the sun.

Tablet IX

> (i)
For Enkidu, his friend, Gilgamesh
Weeps bitterly, as he ranges over the steppe:
"When I die, shall I not be like Enkidu?
Woe has entered my belly.
Fearing death, I roam over the steppe.
To Utnapishtim,[57] Ubar-Tutu's son,
I have taken the road to proceed in all haste.
When arriving by night at mountain passes,
I saw lions and grew afraid,
I lifted my head to Sin[58] to pray.   (10)
To [...] of the gods went out my orisons.
[...] preserve thou me!"
[As at night] he lay, he awoke from a dream.
[There were ...], rejoicing in life.

[57] Mesopotamian hero of the Flood—Sumerian Ziusudra and Greek Xisouthros.
[58] The moon-god.

He raised his axe in his hand,
He drew [the dirk] from his belt.
Like an ar[row] he descended among them.
He smote [them] and hacked away at them.

(The remainder of Tablet IX gives the adventures of Gilgamesh as
he passes successfully the darkness of the mountain range of Mashu
guarded by scorpionmen.)

Tablet X

This tablet, which traces further the successive stages in Gilgamesh's quest of
immortality, happens to be represented by as many as four separate versions.
Two of these, however, the Hittie and Hurrian, are extant only in fragments
that are too slight for connected translation. Substantial portions are available, on the other hand, in the Old Babylonian and Assyrian recensions.

 Old Babylonian Version
 (i)
     (top broken away)
"[. . .] . . .
With their skins [he clothes himself], as he eats flesh.
[.] . . , O Gilgamesh, which has not happened
As long as my wind drives the waters."
Shamash was distraught, as he betook himself to him;
He says to Gilgamesh:
"Gilgamesh, whither rovest thou?
The life thou pursuest thou shalt not find."
Gilgamesh says to him, to valiant Shainash:
"After marching (and) roving over the steppe,   (10)
Must I lay my head in the heart of the earth
That I may sleep through all the years?
Let mine eyes behold the sun
  That I may have my fill of the light!
Darkness withdraws when there is enough light.
May one who indeed is dead behold yet the radiance of the sun!"
  (ii)
  (Beginning lost. Gilgamesh is addressing Siduri, the ale-wife:)
"He who with me underwent all hard[ships]—
Enkidu, whom I loved dearly,
Who with me underwent all hardships—
Has now gone to the fate of mankind!
Day and night I have wept over him.
I would not give him up for burial—
In case my friend should rise at my plaint—
Seven days and seven nights,

Until a worm fell out of his nose.
Since his passing I have not found life, (10)
I have roamed like a hunter in the midst of the steppe.
O ale-wife, now that I have seen thy face,
Let me not see the death which I ever dread."
The ale-wife said to him, to Gilgamesh:
　　　(iii)
"Gilgamesh, whither rovest thou?

Ps. 115:17　The life thou pursuest thou shalt not find.
When the gods created mankind,
Death for mankind they set aside,
Life in their own hands retaining.
Thou, Gilgamesh, let full be thy belly,

Eccles. 5:18　Make thou merry by day and by night.
Of each day make thou a feast of rejoicing,

Eccles. 8:15　Day and night dance thou and play!

Eccles. 9:8–9　Let thy garments be sparkling fresh, (10)
Thy head be washed; bathe thou in water.
Pay heed to the little one that holds on to thy hand,
Let thy spouse delight in thy bosom!
For this is the task of [mankind]!"
　　　　　　(remainder of the column broken away)
　　　(iv)
In his wrath he shatters them.[59]
When he returned, he goes up to him.[60]
Sursunabu[61] his eyes behold.
Sursunabu says to him, to Gilgamesh:
"Tell me, thou, what is thy name?
I am Sursunabu, (he) of Utanapishtim[62] the Faraway."
Gilgamesh said to him, to Sursunabu:
"As for me, Gilgamesh is my name,
Who have come from Uruk-Eanna,
Who have traversed the mountains, (10)
A distant journey, as the sun *rises*.
O Surusunabu, now that I have seen thy face,
Show me Utanapishtim the Faraway."
Sursnabu [says] to him, to Gilgamesh.
　　　　　　(remainder broken away)

(The Assyrian Version of Tablet X gives the episodes of the meet-
ings with Siduri and with Sursunabu [Urshanabi in the Assyrian

[59] Apparently the mysterious "Stone Things."
[60] To the boatman.
[61] The Urshanabi of the Assyrian Version.
[62] Assyrian Utnapishtim.

Version] and an account of the crossing of the Waters of Death to the abode of Utnapishtim. The concluding part of Tablet X follows:)

> (v)

Gilgamesh also said to him, to Utnapishtim: (23)
"That now I might come and behold Utnapishtim,
> Whom they call the Faraway,

I ranged and wandered over all the lands,
I traversed difficult mountains,
I crossed all the seas!
My face was not sated with sweet sleep,
I fretted myself with wakefulness;
> I filled my joints with misery.

I had not reached the ale-wife's house,
> When my clothing was used up.   (30)

[I sl]ew bear, hyena, lion, panther,
> Tiger, stag, (and) ibex—

The wild beasts and creeping things of the steppe.
Their [flesh] I ate and their skins I *wr[apped about me]*."

(The remainder of this column is too mutilated for translation. The beginning of the last column is broken away, except for the conclusion of the sage observations of Utnapishtim:)

> (vi)

"Do we build a house for ever?   (26)
> Do we seal (contracts) for ever?

Do brothers divide shares for ever?
Does hatred persist for ever in [the land]?   Eccles. 9:6
Does the river for ever raise up (and) bring on floods?
The dragon-fly [leaves] (its) shell   (30)
That is face might (but) glance at the face of the sun.
Since the days of yore there has been no [permanence];   Eccles. 1:11; 1:4;
The *resting* and the dead, how alike [they are]   2:16; 9:5; 3:19
Do they not compose a picture of death,
The commoner and the noble,
> Once they are near to [their fate]?

The Anunnaki, the great gods, foregather;
Mammetum, maker of fate, with them the fact decrees:
Death and life they determine.   Deut. 30:19
(But) of death, its days are not revealed."

Tablet XI

Gilgamesh said to him, to Utnapishtim the Faraway:
"As I look upon thee, Utnapishtim,
Thy features are not strange; even as I art thou.
Thou art not strange at all; even as I art thou.

My heart had regarded thee as resolved to do battle,
[Yet] thou liest indolent upon thy back!
[Tell me,] how joinedst thou the Assembly of the gods,
        In thy quest of life?"

Utnapishtim said to him, to Gilgamesh:
"I will reveal to thee, Gilgamesh, a hidden matter
And a secret of the gods will I tell thee: (10)
Shurippak—a city which thou knowest,
[(And) which] on Euphrates' [banks] is situate—
That city was ancient, (as were) the gods within it,
When their heart led the great gods to produce the flood.
[*There*] *were* Anu, their father,
Valiant Enlil, their counselor,
Ninurta, their assistant,
Ennuge, their irrigator.[63]
Ninigiku-Ea was also present with them;
Their words he repeats to the reed-hut:[64]   (20)
'Reed-hut, reed-hut! Wall, wall!
Reed-hut, hearken! Wall, reflect!
Man of Shuruppak, son of Ubar-Tutu,

Gen. 6:14   Tear down (this) house, build a ship!
Give up possessions, seek thou life.
Forswear (worldly) goods and keep the soul alive!

Gen. 6:19–20   Aboard the ship take thou the seed of all living things.
The ship that thou shalt build,
Her dimensions shall be to measure.

Gen. 6:15   Equal shall be her width and her length.   (30)
Like the Apsu thou Shalt ceil her.'
I understood, and I said to Ea, my lord:
'[Behold], my lord, what thou hast thus ordered,
I will be honored to carry out.
[But what] shall I answer the city, the people and elders?'
Ea opened his mouth to speak,
Saying to me, his servant:
'Thou shalt then thus speak unto them:
"I have learned that Enlil is hostile to me,
So that I cannot reside in your city,   (40)
Nor set my f[oo]t in Enlil's territory.
To the Deep I will therefore go down,
        To dwell with my lord Ea.
[But upon] you he will shower down abundance,

---

[63] More specifically, "inspector of canals."

[64] Presumably, the dwelling place of Unapishtim. Ea addresses him through the barrier of the wall.

[The *choicest*] birds, the *rarest* fishes.
[*The land shall have its fill*] of harvest riches.
[He who at dusk orders] the husk-greens,
Will shower down upon you a rain of wheat." '65

With the first glow of dawn,
The land was gathered [about me].
    (too fragmentary for translation)   (50–53)
The little ones [carr]ied bitumen,
While the grown ones brought [all else] that was needful.
On the fifth day I laid her framework.
One (whole) acre was her floor space,
    Ten dozen cubits the height of each of her walls,   Gen. 6:15
Ten dozen cubits each edge of the square deck.66
I laid out the contours (and) joined her together.
I provided her with six decks,   (60)   Gen. 6:16
Dividing her (thus) into seven parts.
Her floor plan I divided into nine parts.
I hammered water-plugs into her.
I saw to the punting-poles and laid in supplies.
Six 'sar'67 (measures) of bitumen I poured into the furnace,   Gen. 6:14
Three sar of asphalt [I also] poured inside.
Three sar of oil the basket-bearers carried,
Aside from the one sar of oil which the *calking* consumed,
And the two sar of oil [which] the boatman stowed away.
Bullocks I slaughtered for the [people],   (70)   Gen. 6:21
And I killed sheep every day.
Must, red wine, oil, and white wine
[I gave the] workmen [to drink], as though river water,
That they might feast as on New Year's Day.
I op[ened . . .] ointment, applying (it) to my hand.
[On the sev]enth [day] the ship was completed.
[*The launching*] was very difficult,
So that they had to shift the floor planks above and below,
[*Until*] two-thirds of [*the structure*] [*had g*]one [*into the water*].
[Whatever I had] I laded upon her: (80)
Whatever I had of silver I laded upon her;
Whatever I [had] of gold I laded upon her;

---

65 As has long been recognized, these lines feature word plays in that both *kukku* and *kibāti* may designate either food or misfortune; Wily Ea plays on this ambiguity: To the populace, the statement would be a promise of prosperity; to Utnapishtim it would signalize the impending deluge.

66 The ship was thus an exact cube.

67 The number 3,600. If the measure understood with it was the *sutu* (seah), each *sar* designated about 8,000 gallons.

Gen. 7:7–8   Whatever I had of all the living beings I [laded] upon her.
            All my family and kin I made go aboard the ship.
Gen. 7:13–16   The beasts of the field, the wild creatures of the field,
                 All the craftsmen I made go aboard.
            Shamash had set for me a stated time:
            'When he who orders unease at night,
                 Will shower down a rain of blight,
            Board thou the ship and batten up the entrance!'
            That stated time had arrived:
            'He who orders unease at night, showers down a rain of
                 blight.'   (90)
            I watched the appearance of the weather.
            The weather was awesome to behold.
            I boarded the ship and battened up the entrance.
            To batten down the (whole) ship, to Puzur-Amurri, the boatman,
            I handed over the structure together with its contents.

            With the first glow of dawn,
Gen. 7:11   A black cloud rose up from the horizon.
            Inside it Adad thunders,
            While Shullat and Hanish[68] go in front,
            Moving as heralds over hill and plain.   (100)
            Erragal[69] tears out the posts;[70]
            Forth comes Ninurta and causes the dikes to follow.
            The Anunnaki lift up the torches,
            Setting the land ablaze with their glare.
            Consternation over Adad reaches to the heavens,
            Who turned to blackness all that had been light.
            [The wide] land was shattered like [a pot]!
            For one day the south-storm [blew],
Gen. 7:20–22   Gathering speed as it blew, [submerging the mountains],
            Overtaking the [people] like a battle.   (110)
            No one can see his fellow,
            Nor can the people be recognized from heaven.
            The gods were frightened by the deluge,
            And, shrinking back, they ascended to the heaven of Anu.[71]
            The gods cowered like dogs
                 Crouched against the outer wall.
            Ishtar cried out like a woman in travail,
            The sweet-voiced mistress of the [gods] moans aloud:
Gen. 7:23   'The olden days are alas turned to clay,

---

[68] Two heralds.

[69] Nergal, god of the nether world.

[70] Of the world dam.

[71] The highest heaven in the Mesopotamian conception of the cosmos.

Because I bespoke evil in the Assembly of the gods.
How could I bespeak evil in the Assembly of the gods,   (120)
Ordering battle for the destruction of my people,   Gen. 8:21
When it is I myself who give birth to my people!
Like the spawn of the fishes they fill the sea!'
The Anunnaki gods weep with her,
The gods, all humbled, sit and weep,
Their lips *drawn tight*, [. . .] one and all.
Six days and [six] nights
Blows the flood wind, as the south-storm sweeps the land.
When the seventh day arrived,
     The flood (-carrying) south-storm subsided in the battle,
Which it had fought like an army.   (130)
The sea grew quiet, the tempest was still, the flood ceased.   Gen. 8:1–2
I looked at the weather: stillness had set in,
And all of mankind had returned to clay.
The landscape was as level as a flat roof.
I opened a hatch, and light fell upon my face.   Gen. 8:6
Bowing low, I sat and wept,
Tears running down on my face.
I looked about for coast lines in the expanse of the sea:
In each of fourteen (regions)
     There emerged a region(-mountain).
On Mount Nisir the ship came to a halt.   (140)   Gen. 8:4
Mount Nisir held the ship fast,
     Allowing no motion.
One day, a second day, Mount Nisir held the ship fast,
     Allowing no motion.
A third day, a fourth day, Mount Nisir held the ship fast,
     Allowing no motion.
A fifth, and a sixth (day), Mount Nisir held the ship fast,
     Allowing no motion.
When the seventh day arrived,
I sent forth and set free a dove.
The dove went forth, but came back;   Gen. 8:8–10
Since no resting-place for it was visible, she turned round.
Then I sent forth and set free a swallow.
The swallow went forth, but came back;   (150)
Since no resting-place for it was visible, she turned round.
Then I sent forth and set free a raven.   Gen. 8:7
The raven went forth and, seeing that the waters had diminished,
He eats, circles, caws, and turns not round.
Then I let out (all) to the four winds
     And offered a sacrifice.
I poured out a libation on the top of the mountain.   Gen. 8:19–20

Seven and seven cult-vessels I set up,
Upon their pot-stands I heaped cane, cedarwood, and myrtle.
Gen. 8:21   The gods smelled the savor,
The gods smelled the sweet savor,   (160)
The gods crowded like flies about the sacrificer.
When at length as the great goddess [72] arrived,
She lifted up the great jewels which Anu had fashioned to her
        liking:
'Ye gods here, as surely as this lapis
        Upon my neck I shall not forget,
I shall be mindful of these days, forgetting (them) never.
Let the gods come to the offering;
(But) let not Enlil come to the offering,
For he, unreasoning, brought on the deluge
And my people consigned to destruction.'
When at length as Enlil arrived,   (170)
And saw the ship, Enlil was wroth,
He was filled with wrath over the Igigi gods:[73]
'Has some living soul escaped?
        No man was to survive the destruction!'
Ninurta opened his mouth to speak,
        Saying to valiant Enlil:
'Who, other than Ea, can devise plans?[74]
It is Ea alone who knows every matter.'
Ea opened his mouth to speak,
        Saying to valiant Enlil:
'Thou wisest of gods, thou hero,
How couldst thou, unreasoning, bring on the deluge?
On the sinner impose his sin,   (180)
        On the transgressor impose his transgression!
(Yet) be lenient, lest he be cut off,
Be patient, lest he be dis[lodged]!
Ezek. 14:13–21   Instead of thy bringing on the deluge,
        Would that a lion had risen up to diminish mankind!
Instead of thy bringing on the deluge,
        Would that a wolf had risen up to diminish mankind!
Instead of thy bringing on the deluge,
        Would that a famine had risen up to l[ay low] mankind!
Instead of thy bringing on the deluge,
        Would that pestilence had risen up to smi[te down] mankind!

[72] Ishtar.
[73] The heavenly gods.
[74] An allusion to one of the common epithets of Ea.

It was not I who disclosed the secret of the great gods.
I let Atrahasis[75] see a dream,
    And he perceived the secret of the gods.
Now then take counsel in regard to him!'
Thereupon Enlil went aboard the ship.
Holding me by the hand, he took me aboard.   (190)
He took my wife aboard and made (her) kneel by my side.
Standing between us, he touched our foreheads to bless us:
'Hitherto Utnapishtim has been but human.
Henceforth Utnapishtim and his wife shall be like unto us gods.
Utnapishtim shall reside far away, at the mouth of the rivers!'
Thus they took me and made me reside far away,
    At the mouth of the rivers.
But now, who will for thy sake call the gods to Assembly
That the life which thou seekest thou mayest find?
Up, lie not down to sleep
    For six days and seven nights."
As he sits there on his haunches,   (200)
Sleep fans him like the whirlwind.
Utnapishtim says to her, to his spouse:
"Behold this hero who seeks life!
Sleep fans him like a mist."
His spouse says to him, to Utnapishtim the Faraway:
"Touch him that the man may awake,
That he may return safe on the way whence he came,
That through the gate by which he left he may return to his land."
Utnapishtim says to her, to his spouse:
"Since to deceive is human, he will seek to deceive thee.   (210)   Gen. 8:21
Up, bake for him wafers, put (them) at his head,
And mark on the wall the days he sleeps."
She baked for him wafers, put (them) at his head,
And marked on the wall the days he slept.
His first wafer is dried out
The second is gone bad, the third is soggy;
    The crust of the fourth has turned white;
The fifth has a moldy cast,
    The sixth (still) is fresh-colored;
The seventh—just as he touched him the man awoke.[76]
Gilgamesh says to him, to Utnapishtim the Faraway:
"Scarcely had sleep surged over me,   (220)
When straightway thou dost touch and rouse me!"

---

[75] "Exceeding Wise," an epithet of Utnapishtim.

[76] By asserting that he had not slept at all.

Utnapishtim [says to him], to Gilgamesh:
"[Go], Gilgamesh, count thy wafers,
[That the days thou hast slept] may become known to thee:
Thy [first] wafer is dried out,
[The second is gone] bad, the third is soggy;
 The crust of the fourth has turned white;
[The fifth] has a moldy cast,
 The sixth (still) is fresh-colored.
[The seventh]—at this instant thou hast awakened."
Gilgamesh says to him, to Utnapishtim the Faraway:
"[What then] shall I do, Utnapishtim,   (230)
 Whither shall I go,
[Now] that the Bereaver has laid hold on my [members]?
In my bedchamber lurks death,
And wherever I se[t my foot], there is death!"

Utnapishtim [says to him], to Urshanabi, the boatman:
"Urshanabi, may the landing-pl[ace not rejoice in thee],
 May the place of crossing renounce thee!
To him who wanders on its shore, deny thou its shore!
The man thou hast led (hither), whose body is covered with
 grime,
The grace of whose members skins have distorted,
Take him, Urshanabi, and bring him to the washing-place.
Let him wash off his grime in water
 clean as snow,   (240)
Let him cast off his skins, let the sea carry (them) away,
 That the fairness of his body may be seen.
Let him renew the band round his head,
Let him put on a cloak to clothe his nakedness,
That he may arrive in his city,
That he may achieve his journey.
Let not (his) cloak have a moldy cast,
 Let it be wholly new."
Urshanabi took him and brought him to the washing-place.
He washed off his grime in water clean as snow.
He cast off his skins, the sea carried (them) away,
That the fairness of his body might be seen.   (250)
He renewed [the band] round his head,
He put on a cloak to clothe his nakedness,
That he might ar[rive in his city],
That he might achieve his journey.
[The cloak had not a moldy cast, but] was [wholly] new.
Gilgamesh and Urshanabi boarded the boat,
[They launch]ed the boat on the waves (and) they sailed away.

His spouse says to him, to Utnapishtim the Faraway:
"Gilgamesh has come hither, toiling and straining.
What wilt thou give (him) that he may return to his land?"   (260)
At that he, Gilgamesh, raised up (his) pole,
To bring the boat nigh to the shore.
Utnapishtim [says] to him, [to] Gilgamesh:
"Gilgamesh, thou hast come hither, toiling and straining.
What shall I give thee that thou mayest return to thy land?
I will disclose, O Gilgamesh, a hidden thing,
And [a secret of the gods I will] tell thee:
This plant, like the buckthorn is [its . . .].
Its thorns will pr[ick thy hands] just as does the *rose*.
If thy hands obtain the plant, [thou wilt find new life]."   (270)
No sooner had Gilgamesh heard this,
        Than he opened the wa[ter-pipe],
He tied heavy stones [to his feet].
They pulled him down into the deep [and he saw the plant].
He took the plant, though it pr[icked his hands].
He cut the heavy stones [from his feet].
The [s]ea cast him up upon its shore.

Gilgamesh says to him, to Urshanabi, the boatman:
"Urshanabi, this plant is a plant *apart*,
Whereby a man may regain his *life's breath*.
I will take it to ramparted Uruk,   (280)
        Will cause [. . .] to eat the plant . . . !
Its name shall be 'Man Becomes Young in Old Age.'[77]
I myself shall eat (it)
        And thus return to the state of my youth."
After twenty leagues they broke off a morsel,
After thirty (further) leagues they prepared for the night.
Gilgamesh saw a well whose water was cool.
He went down into it to bathe in the water.
A serpent snuffed the fragrance of the plant;
It came up [from the water] and carried off the plant.
Going back it shed [its] slough.

Thereupon Gilgamesh sits down and weeps,   (290)
His tears running down over his face.
[He took the hand] of Urshanabi, the boatman:
"[For] whom, Urshanabi, have my hands toiled?
For whom is being spent the blood of my heart?
I have not obtained a boon for myself.

---

[77] Note that the process is one of rejuvenation, not immortality.

For the earth-lion[78] have I effected a boon!
And now the tide will bear (it) twenty leagues away!
When I opened the *water-pipe* and [. . .] the year,[79]
I found that which has been placed as a sign for me:
    I shall withdraw,
And leave the boat on the shore!"   (300)
    After twenty leagues they broke off a morsel,
After thirty (further) leagues they prepared for the night.
    When they arrived in ramparted Uruk,
Gilgamesh says to him, to Urshanabi, the boatman:
"Go up, Urshanabi, walk on the ramparts of Uruk.
Inspect the base terrace, examine its brickwork,
    If its brickwork is not of burnt brick,
And if the Seven Wise Ones laid not its foundation!
One 'sar' is city, one sar orchards,
    One sar margin land; (further) the *precinct* of the Temple of
    Ishtar.
Three sar and the *precinct* comprise Uruk."

(Tablet XII has been omitted from this abridgment, since it is an
inorganic appendage to the epic proper.)

A Cosmological Incantation: The Worm and the Toothache

ANET, 100–101

TRANSLATOR: E. A. SPEISER

Among the incantations which contain cosmological material, one of the
best-known attributes toothache to a worm that had obtained the permission of the gods to dwell among the teeth and gums. The present text, which
is designated ideographically as an "Incantation against Toothache," dates
from Neo-Babylonian times and was published by R. Campbell Thompson
in *CT*, XVII (1903), Pl. 50. But the colophon indicates that the copy had been
made from an ancient text. And indeed, the Mari documents of the Old
Babylonian period include a tablet with the Akkadian label *ši-pa-at tu-ul-
tim* "Toothache Incantation." The text itself, however, is in Hurrian. But although it cites various deities of the Hurrian pantheon—and is thus clearly
religious in nature—the context does not correspond to the Neo-Babylonian
legend, to judge from the intelligible portions.

---

[78] An allusion to the serpent?

[79] The opening of the *rāṭu* (normally "pipe, tube") apparently took place in connection with Gilgamesh's dive (cf., also 1. 271). But the details remain obscure. In the
Eridu Creation Story, II, the same term is used, perhaps for a pipe connecting with a
source of sweet waters which would nourish the miraculous plant.

After Anu [had created heaven],
Heaven had created [the earth],
The earth had created the rivers,
The rivers had created the canals,
The canals had created the marsh,
(And) the marsh had created the worm—
The worm went, weeping, before Shamash,
His tears flowing before Ea:
"What wilt thou give for my food?
What wilt thou give me for my sucking?"   (10)
"I shall give thee the ripe fig,
(And) the apricot"
"Of what use are they to me, the ripe fig
And the apricot?
Lift me up and among the teeth
And the gums cause me to dwell!
The blood of the tooth I will suck,
And of the gum I will gnaw
Its *roots*!"
    Fix the pin and seize its foot.[80]   (20)
Because thou hast said this, O worm,
May Ea smite thee with the might
Of his hand!

Adapa

ANET, 101–3

TRANSLATOR: E. A. SPEISER

The story of Adapa shares with the Epic of Gilgamesh the *motif* of man's squandered opportunity for gaining immortality. It is extant in four fragmentary accounts. The oldest and longest of these (B) comes from the El-Amarna archives (fourteenth century B.C.), whereas the other three (A, C, and D) derive from the library of Ashurbanipal. The order of presentation is contextual, except that C is roughly parallel to parts of B.

    A
[Wis]dom . . . [. . .].
His command was indeed . . . [. . .] like the command of [Ea].
Wide understanding he had perfected for him to disclose the
    designs of the land.
To him he had given wisdom; eternal life he had not given him.
In those days, in those years, the sage from Eridu,
Ea, created him as the *model* of men.
The sage—his command no one can vitiate—

---

[80] This is the instruction to the dentist.

The capable, the most wise among the Anunnaki is he;
The blameless, the clean of hands, the ointment priest,

Ps. 24:4   the observer of rites.
With the bakers he does the baking   (10)
With the bakers of Eridu he does the baking;
Bread and water for Eridu daily he provides,
With his clean hand(s) he arranges the (offering) table,
Without him the table cannot be cleared.
He steers the ship, he does the prescribed fishing for Eridu.
In those days Adapa, the one of Eridu,
While [. . .] Ea . . . upon the couch,
Daily did attend to the sanctuary of Eridu.
At the holy quay, the Quay of the New Moon, he boarded the
          sailboat;
Then a wind blew thither and his boat drifted;   (20)
[With the o]ar he steers his boat
[. . .] upon the wide sea.
                              (remainder destroyed)
                    B
. . . [. . .]
The south wind b[lew and submerged him],
[causing him to go down] to the home [of the *fish*]:
"South wind, [. .]. me all thy *venom* . . . [. . .].
I will break thy wi[ng]!" Just as he had said (this) with his mouth,
The wing of the sou[th wi]nd was broken. For seven days
The [south win]d blew not upon the land. Anu
Calls [to] Ilabrat, his vizier:
"Why has the south wind not blown over the land these seven
          days?"
His vizier, Ilabrat, answered him: "My lord,   (10)
Adapa, the son of Ea,[81] the wing of the south wind
Has broken." When Anu heard this speech,
He cried, "Mercy!" Rising from his throne: "[Let] them fetch him
          hither!"
At that, Ea, he who knows what pertains to heaven, took hold of
          him,
[Adapa], caused him to wear (his) [hai]r unkempt, a mourning
          garb
[He made him put on], and gave him (this) [ad]vice:
"[Adapa], thou art going [before Anu], the king;

---

[81] It should be added that Adapa's purpose was plainly to catch fish for Ea's temple,
hence that god's primary interest in Adapa. For the importance of fishing to the temple economy, cf., the so-called Weidner Chronicle, which employs this *motif* as a reason for the rise and fall of dynasties (and, incidentally, mentions Adapa).

[The road to heaven thou wilt take. When to] heaven
[Thou hast] go[ne up and] hast [approached the gate of Anu],
[Tammuz and Gizzida] at the gate of Anu   (20)
Will be standing. When they see thee, they will [as]k thee: 'Man,
For whom dost thou look thus? Adapa, for whom
Art thou clad with mourning garb?'
        'From our land two gods have disappeared,
Hence I am thus.' 'Who are the two gods who from the land
Have disappeared?' 'Tammuz and Gizzida.' They will glance at each
        other
And will smile. A good word they
Will speak to Anu, (and) Anu's benign face
They will cause to be shown thee. As thou standest before Anu,
When they offer thee bread of death,
Thou shalt not eat (it). When they offer thee water of death,   (30)
Thou shalt not drink (it). When they offer thee a garment,
Put (it) on. When they offer thee oil, anoint thyself (therewith).
(This) advice that I have given thee, neglect not; the words
That I have spoken to thee, hold fast!" The messenger
Of Anu arrived there (saying as follows): "Adapa the south wind's
Wing has broken, bring him before me!"

He made him take the road to heaven, and to heaven he went up.
When he had ascended to heaven and approached the gate
        of Anu,
Tammuz and Gizzida were standing at the gate of Anu.
When they saw Adapa, they cried, "Mercy!   (40)
Man, for whom dost thou look thus? Adapa,
For whom art thou clad with mourning garb?"
"Two gods have disappeared from the land, therefore with
        mourning garb
I am clad." "Who are the two gods who from the land have
        disappeared?"
"Tammuz and Gizzida." They glanced at each other
And smiled.[82] As Adapa before Anu, the king,
Drew near and Anu saw him, he called:
"Come now, Adapa, wherefore the south wind's wing
Didst thou break?" Adapa replied to Anu: "My lord,
For the household of my master, in the midst of the sea   (50)
I was catching fish. The sea was like a mirror.
But the south wind came blowing and submerged me,
Causing (me) to go down to the home of the *fish*. In the wrath of
        my heart

---

[82] Apparently pleased because Adapa mourned their loss.

I cursed the [south wind]." Speaking up at [his] side, Tammuz
[And] Gizzida to Anu [a g]ood word
Addressed. His heart quieted as he was . . .
"Why did Ea to a *worthless* human of the heaven
And of the earth the plan disclose,
Rendering him *distinguished* and making a name for him?
As for us, what shall we do about him? Bread of life   (60)
Fetch for him and he shall eat (it)." When the bread of life
They brought him, he did not eat; when the water of life
They brought him, he did not drink. When a garment
They brought him, he put (it) on; when oil
They brought him, he anointed himseif (therewith).
As Anu looked at him, he laughed at him:
"Come now, Adapa! Why didst thou neither eat nor drink?
Thou shalt not have (eternal) life! Ah, *per[ver]se* mankind!"
          "Ea, my master,
Commanded me: 'Thou shalt not eat, thou shalt not drink' "
"Take him away and return him to his earth."
                    (remainder destroyed)
          C
When [Anu] heard th[is],
[. . . in the wr]ath of his heart
[. . .] he dispatches a messenger,
[. . . , who] knows the heart of the great gods,
That he [. . .] . . .
To reach [. . . of Ea], the king.
[. . .] he discussed the matter.
[. . .] to Ea, the king.
[. . .] . . .   (10)
[. . .], the wise, who knows the heart of the great gods
[. . .] heaven . . .
[. . .] unkempt hair he caused him to wear,
[. . .] . . . and clad him with a mourning garb,
[He gave him advice], saying to him (these) [wor]ds:
["Adapa,] thou art going [before Anu], the king;
[Neglect not my advice], my words hold fast!
[When thou hast gone up to heaven and] hast approached the gate
          of Anu,
[Tammuz and Gizzida] will be standing [at the gate of Anu]."
                    (remainder missing)
          D
[. . .] he [. . .]
[Oil] he commanded for him, and he an[ointed himself].
[A ga]rment he commanded for him, and he was clothed.
Anu laughed aloud at the doing of Ea, [saying]:

"Of the gods of heaven and earth, as many as there be,
    Who [ever] gave such a command,
So as to make his own command exceed the command of Anu?"
As Adapa from the horizon of heaven to the zenith of heaven
Cast a glance, he saw its awesomeness.
[Th]en Anu imposed on Adapa [. . .];
For [the city] of Ea he decreed release,   (10)
His [pri]esthood to glorify in the future he [*decreed*] as destiny.
[. . .] . . . as for Adapa, the human offspring,
[Who . . .], lord-like, broke the south wind's wing,
Went up to heaven—and so forth—
[. . .] what ill he has brought upon mankind,
[And] the disease that he brought upon the bodies of men,
These Ninkarrak[83] will allay.
[Let] malady be lifted, let disease turn aside.
[Upon] this [. . .] let horror fall,
Let him [*in*] sweet sleep not lie down,
[. . .] . . . joy of human heart(s).
                (remainder broken off)

Descent of Ishtar to the Nether World   ANET, 106–9

TRANSLATOR: E. A. SPEISER

This myth has as its central theme the detention of the goddess of fertility—
Sumerian Inanna, Akkadian Ishtar—in the realm of the dead and her eventual return to the land of the living. The cuneiform material is extant in Sumerian and Akkadian formulations. The Sumerian version is obviously
primary. But although the Semitic version has various points of contact with
the older source, it is by no means a mere translation from the Sumerian.

    (obverse)
To the Land of no Return, the realm of [*Ereshkigal*],
Ishtar, the daughter of Sin, [set] her mind.
Yea, the daughter of Sin set [her] mind
To the dark house, the abode of Irkal[la],[84]
To the house which none leave who have entered it,
To the road from which there is no way back,
To the house wherein the entrants are bereft of li[ght],
Where dust is their fare and clay their food,
(Where) they see no light, residing in darkness,
(Where) they are clothed like birds, with wings for garments,   (10)
(And where) over door and bolt is spread dust.

---

[83] Goddess of healing.
[84] Ereshkigal, Queen of the Nether World.

When Ishtar reached the gate of the Land of no Return,
She said (these) words to the gatekeeper:
"O gatekeeper, open thy gate,
Open thy gate that I may enter!
If thou openest not the gate so that I cannot enter,
I will smash the door, I will shatter the bolt,
I will smash the doorpost, I will move the doors,
I will raise up the dead, eating the living,
So that the dead will outnumber the living." (20)
The gatekeeper opened his mouth to speak,
Saying to exalted Ishtar:
"Stop, my lady, do not throw it[85] down!
I will go to announce thy name to Queen E[reshk]igal."
The gatekeeper entered, saying [to] Eresh[kigal]:
"Behold, thy sister Ishtar is waiting at [the gate],
She who upholds the great festivals,
    Who stirs up the deep before Ea, the k[ing]."
When Ereshkigal heard this,
Her face turned pale like a cut-down tamarisk,
While her lips turned dark like a bruised *kunīnu*-reed.[86] (30)
"What drove her heart to me? What impelled her spirit hither?
Lo, should I drink water with the Anunnaki?
Should I eat clay for bread, drink muddied water for beer?
Should I bemoan the men who left their wives behind?
Should I bemoan the maidens who were wrenched from the laps of
    their lovers?
(Or) should I bemoan the tender little one who was sent off before
    his time?[87]
Go, gatekeeper, open the gate for her,
Treat her in accordance with the ancient rules."
Forth went the gatekeeper (to) open the door for her:
"Enter, my lady, that Cutha[88] may rejoice over thee, (40)
That the palace of the Land of no Return may be glad at thy
    presence."
When the first door he had made her enter,
    He stripped and took away the great crown on her head.
"Why, O gatekeeper, didst thou take the great crown on my head?"
"Enter, my lady, thus are the rules of the Mistress of the Nether
    World."

---

[85] The door.

[86] Word play *Jabat* "bruised": *Japat-š[a]* "her lips."

[87] I.e., Ereshkigal would have cause for weeping if all these occupants of the nether
world should be liberated by Ishtar.

[88] A name of the nether world, the Akkadian city-name *Kutu*.

When the second gate he had made her enter,
    He stripped and took away the pendants on her ears.
"Why, O gatekeeper, didst thou take the pendants on my ears?"
"Enter, my lady, thus are the rules of the Mistress of the Nether
    World."
When the third gate he had made her enter,
    He stripped and took away the chains round her neck.
"Why, O gatekeeper, didst thou take the chains round my neck?"
"Enter, my lady, thus are the rules of the Mistress of the Nether
    World."   (50)
When the fourth gate he had made her enter,
    He stripped and took away the ornaments on her breast.
"Why, O gatekeeper, didst thou take the ornaments on my breast?"
"Enter, my lady, thus are the rules of the Mistress of the Nether
    World."
When the fifth gate he had made her enter,
    He stripped and took away the girdle of birthstones on her
    hips.
"Why, O gatekeeper, didst thou take the girdle of birthstones on my
    hips?"
"Enter, my lady, thus are the rules of the Mistress of the Nether
    World."
When the sixth gate he had made her enter,
    He stripped and took away the clasps round her hands and
    feet.
"Why, O gatekeeper, didst thou take the clasps round my hands and
    feet?"
"Enter, my lady, thus are the rules of the Mistress of the Nether
    World."
When the seventh gate he had made her enter,   (60)
    He stripped and took away the breechcloth round her body.
"Why, O gatekeeper, didst thou take the breechcloth on my body?"
"Enter, my lady, thus are the rules of the Mistress of the Nether
    World."
As soon as Ishtar had descended to the Land of no Return,
Ereshkigal saw her and burst out at her presence.
Ishtar, unreflecting, flew at her.
Ereshkigal opened her mouth to speak,
Saying (these) words to Namtar, her vizier:
"Go, Namtar, lock [her] up [in] my [palace]!
Release against her, [against] Ishtar, the sixty mis[eries]:
Misery of the eyes [against] her [eyes],   (70)
Misery of the sides ag[ainst] her [sides],
Misery of the heart ag[ainst her heart],
Misery of the feet ag[ainst] her [feet],

Misery of the head ag[ainst her head]—
Against every part of her, against [her whole body]!"
After Lady Ishtar [had descended to the nether world],
The bull springs not upon the cow, [the ass impregnates not the
    jenny],
In the street [the man impregnates not] the maiden.
The man lies [in his (own) chamber, the maiden lies on her side],
[. . . l]ies [. . .].   (80)
    (reverse)
The countenance of Papsukkal, the vizier of the great gods,
    Was fallen, his face was [clouded].
He was clad in mourning, long hair he wore.
Forth went Papsukkal before Sin his father, weeping,
[His] tears flowing before Ea, the king:
"Ishtar has gone down to the nether world, she has not come up.
Since Ishtar has gone down to the Land of no Return,
The bull springs not upon the cow, the ass impregnates not the
    jenny,
In the street the man impregnates not the maiden.
The man lies down in his (own) chamber,
The maiden lies down on her side."   (10)
Ea in his wise heart conceived an image,
And created Asushunamir, a eunuch:
"Up, Asushunamir, set thy face to the gate of the Land of no Return;
The seven gates of the Land of no Return shall be opened for thee.
Ereshkigal shall see thee and rejoice at thy presence.
When her heart has calmed, her mood is happy,
Let her utter the oath of the great gods.
(Then) lift up thy head, paying mind to the life-water bag:
"Pray, Lady, let them give me the life-water bag
    That water therefrom I may drink."[89]
As soon as Ereshkigal heard this,
She smote her thigh,[90] bit her finger:
"Thou didst request of me a thing that should not be requested.
Come, Asushunamir, I will curse thee with a mighty curse![91]
The food of the city's *gutters* shall be thy food,
The *sewers* of the city shall be thy drink.
The shadow of the wall shall be thy station,

---

[89] The scheme evidently succeeds as Ereshkigal, distracted by the beauty of
Aṣūšunamir, "His Appearance is Brilliant," does not recover until too late.

[90] A gesture of annoyance, or derision.

[91] Or read "I will decree for thee a fate not to be forgotten,
    A fate will I decree for thee,
    Not to be forgotten throughout eternity."

The threshold shall be thy habitation,
The besotted and the thirsty shall smite thy cheek!"
Ereshkigal opened her mouth to speak,
Saying (these) words to Namtar, her vizier: (30)
"Up, Namtar, knock at Egalgina,[92]
Adorn the thresholds with *coral*-stone,
Bring forth the Anunnaki and seat (them) on thrones of gold,
Sprinkle Ishtar with the water of life and take her from my
    presence!"
Forth went Namtar, knocked at Egalgina,
Adorned the thresholds with *coral*-stone,
Brought forth the Anunnaki, seated (them) on thrones of gold,
Sprinkled Ishtar with the water of life and took her from her
    presence.
When through the first gate he had made her go out,
    He returned to her the breechcloth for her body.
When through the second gate he had made her go out,   (40)
    He returned to her the clasps for her hands and feet.
When through the third gate he had made her go out,
    He returned to her the birthstone girdle for her hips.
When through the fourth gate he had made her go out,
    He returned to her the ornaments for her breasts.
When through the fifth gate he had made her go out,
    He returned to her the chains for her neck.
When through the sixth gate he had made her go out,
    He returned to her the pendants for her ears.
When through the seventh gate he had made her go out,
    He returned to her the great crown for her head.
"If she does not give thee her ransom price, bring her back.[93]
As for Tammuz, the lover of her youth,
Wash him with pure water, anoint him with sweet oil;
Clothe him with a red garment, let him *play* on a flute of lapis.
Let courtesans *turn* [*his*] mood."
[When] Belili was string[ing] her jewelry,
[And her] lap was filled with "eye-stones,"
On hearing the sound of her brother, Belili struck the jewelry on
    [...]

---

[92] "Palace of Justice."

[93] This continuation of Ereshkigal's instructions appears to be out of place here, as regards the Ninevah version. The older Ashur vesrion speaks of the ransom before Ishtar is led away. The mention of Tammuz is likewise startling in this context. There is no indication in the Sumerian version—contrary to earlier assumptions—that Tammuz had gone down to the nether world. The concluding part of the myth, therefore, will remain obscure in its allusions so long as additional material is not available.

So that the "eye-stones" filled the [. . .]. . . .
"My only brother, bring no harm to me!
On the day when Tammuz comes up to me,
    When with him the lapis flute (and) the carnelian ring come
      up to me,
When with him the wailing men and the wailing women come up
Ezek. 8:14   to me,
May the dead rise and smell the incense."

ANET, 119 # The Legend of Sargon
TRANSLATOR: E. A. SPEISER

Sargon, the mighty king, king of Agade, am I.
My mother was a *changeling*,[94] my father I knew not.
The brother(s) of my father *loved* the hills.
My city is Azupiranu, which is situated on the banks of the
    Euphrates.
Exod. 2:3 My *changeling* mother conceived me, in secret she bore me.
She set me in a basket of rushes, with bitumen she sealed my lid.
She cast me into the river which rose not (over) me.
The river bore me up and carried me to Akki, the drawer of water.
Akki, the drawer of water lifted me out as he dipped his e[w]er.
Akki, the drawer of water, [took me] as his son (and)
      reared me.   (10)
Akki, the drawer of water, appointed me as his gardener.
While I was a gardener, Ishtar granted me (her) love,
And for four and [. . .] years I exercised kingship.
The black-headed [people] I ruled, I gov[erned];
Mighty [moun]tains with chip-axes of bronze I conquered,
The upper ranges I scaled,
The lower ranges I [trav]ersed,
The sea [lan]ds three times I circled.
Dilmun my [hand] cap[tured],
[To] the great Der I [went up], I [. . .],   (20)
[. . .] I altered and [. . .].
Whatever king may come up after me,
[. . .],
Let him r[ule, let him govern] the black-headed [peo]ple;
[Let him conquer] mighty [mountains] with chip-axe[s of bronze],
[Let] him scale the upper ranges,
[Let him traverse the lower ranges],
Let him circle the sea [lan]ds three times!

[94] There is no indication as to whether the term refers to a change in the social, religious, or national status.

[Dilmun let his hand capture],
Let him go up [to] the great Der and [...]! (30)
[...] from my city, Aga[de ...]
[...] ... [...].
(Remainder broken away.)

Nergal and Ereshkigal

ANET³, 507–2

TRANSLATOR: A. K. GRAYSON

In recent years a Neo-Assyrian version of this myth was discovered at Sultantepe and this find was announced by O. R. Gurney, *Proceedings of the British Academy*, XLI (1955), 27–33. The Sultantepe tablet provides us with a much fuller version of the story but there are lacunae in it, some of which may be filled in from the Amarna tablet.

The beginning of the myth is very fragmentary and it is not absolutely certain that this small piece belongs to the tablet. It appears to be a hymn in praise of a deity, presumably Ereshkigal.

(i)
I will praise [... queen of mankind],
[...] continually.
I will praise [*Ereshkigal, queen of mankind*],
[...] c[ontinua]lly.
[...] ...
[...] favor.
[...] among all the goddesses.
[...] *thou art merciful.* (8′)

(There is a lacuna of about thirteen lines in which the preparations for a banquet of the gods were probably described.)

[Anu opened his mouth to say something to Kaka:] (6′)
[*"I will send thee, Kaka, to the Land of no Return,*]
[*To Ereshkigal ... thou shalt say*:]
['Thou art not able to come up,]
[In thy year thou canst not ascend to our presence,] (10′)
[And we cannot go down,]
[In our month we cannot descend to thy presence.]
[(Therefore) let thy messenger come,]
[Let him remove (the dish) from the table, let him take thy share.]
[Whatever I give to him he will hand over all of it ...] to thee.' "
[Kaka descended the long staircase of] the heavens.
[When] he reac[hed the gate of Ereshkigal (he said)]:
["Porter], o[pen for m]e the gate!"
["*Enter*, Kaka,] and may the gate ble[ss thee!"]

He led [the god K]aka through [the first gat]e, (20′)
He led [the god] Kaka through [the second] gate,
He led [the god] Kaka through [the third] gate,
He led the god Kaka through the fourth gate,
He led the god Kaka through the fifth gate,
He led the god Kaka [through] the sixth gate,
He led the god Kaka [through] the seventh gate.
He entered her wide courtyard,
He bowed down, he [kissed] the ground in front of her.
He straightened up and standing there said to her:
"Anu, [thy] father, has sent me (30′)
With these words: 'Thou art not able to come up,
In thy year thou canst not ascend to our presence,
And we cannot go down,
In our month we cannot descend to thy presence.
(Therefore) let thy messenger come,
Let him remove (the dish) from the table, let him take thy share.
Whatever I give to him he will hand over all of it . . . to thee.' "

Ereshkigal opened her mouth to say something to K[aka]:
"O messenger of Anu, our father, who has come to us,
Is it well with Anu, Enlil, and Ea, the great gods? (40′)
Is it well with Nammu and Nash, the pure god?
Is it well with the spouse of the mistress of the heavens?
Is it well with Nin[urta, mightiest] in the land?"

Kaka opened [his mouth] to say something to Ereshkigal:
"It is well with Anu, Enlil, and Ea, the great gods,
It is well with [Namm]u and Nash, the pure (god),
It is well [with the spouse of the m]istress of the heavens,
It is we[ll with] Ni[nurta, migh]tiest in the land."
[K]aka (again) opened his mouth to say some[thing] to
        Ereshkigal:
"[. . .] may it be well with thee!" (50′)

[Ereshkiga]l opened her mouth to say something to Namtar, her
        vizier:
"O Nam[tar], my [vizier], I will send thee [to] the heaven of Anu,
        our father.
Ascend, Namtar, the long [staircase of the heavens],
Remove (the dish) from the table, [take my share],
Whatever Anu give[s to thee, bring it all to me]."

(There is a large lacuna of about twenty-six lines in which Namtar's ascent to heaven and entrance into the presence of the upper
deities was narrated. After the lacuna there is a section, part of which
is translated below, in which it is narrated that all the gods except

Nergal bowed to Namtar. Because of the insult Nergal must descend to the nether world to apologize to Ereshkigal. Ea gives him advice on how to conduct himself on his journey.)

(ii)

[*Ea* opened his mouth to say something to Nergal]:

["...] (1')

[*When* he] arrived a[t...]

[...] the path...[...]

[*The gods*] altogether were b[owing *before*] him,

[*The great god*]s, the lords of destinies.

[*He*] was holding the authority, he was holding the authority [of the gods],

[The gods] who dwell in Ir[kalla].[95]

Why dost thou not b[ow i]n his presence?

[...] I keep squinting at thee,

Thou hast turned into an ignoramus. (10')

[...] thine e[yes] stare at the ground."

(Lines 12'–16' are missing.)

[*Nergal* opened his mouth to say something to Ea]:

[...I w]ill get up,

[...] thou hast spoken.

[...]...he/I will twine it double." (20')

When Ea heard this he said to himself:

"[*I will*] do...send/rule."

Ea opened his mouth to say something to Nergal:

"O traveller, dost thou wish to go on thy errand with *a sword* in thy hand?

Descend to the forest of *mesu*-trees,

Cut down a *mesu*-tree, a *hash*[*urru*-tree, and] a *supalu*-tree,

Break off a...[...and] a staff."

[He descended to the forest] of *mesu*-trees,

[He cut down a *mesu*-tree, a *hashurru*-tree, and a s]*upalu*-tree,

He bro[ke off a...and] a staff, (30')

He will make complete [...] *and Ningishzida.*

Like lapis [lazuli] he painted his [...],

Like go[ld] he painted [his...],

Like lapis lazuli he painted [his staff],

The works...th[rone...]...

He (Ea) called to him to give him instructions:

"O traveller, dost [thou] wish...?

Whatever instructions [...]...[...]

[95] Nether world.

As soon as they bring thee a throne,
Thou must not go and sit on it;   (40')
When a baker brings [thee] bread, [thou must not g]o and *eat* his
  bread;
When a butcher brings [thee] meat, [thou must not g]o and *eat* his
  meat;
When a brewer brings thee beer, thou must not go and [*dr*]*ink* the
  beer;
When water for (thy) feet is brought to thee, thou must not go and
  wash thy [feet];
(When) she (Ereshkigal) has gone in to bathe,
To put on her . . . -garment,
She will reveal to thee *her body.*
Thou must not . . . [what is normal for m]an and woman."
Nergal [. . .]   (49')

(About twelve lines are missing. The end of the second column
can be restored from the parallel in the Descent of Ishtar 1–10.)

[Nergal turned his face toward the Land of no Return,]
[To the dark house, the abode of Irkalla,]
[To the house which none leave who have entered it,]
        (iii)
[To the road from which] there is no way back,
[To the house wherein the entrants] are bereft of light,
[Where dust is their fare and] clay [thei]r food,
[(Where) they are clothed like bir]ds, with wings for garments,
[(Where) they see no light,] residing [in] darkness,
[. . .] *moaning*
[. . . they *moan*] like [d]oves.
[. . .] . . .
[The porter opened his mouth to s]ay something to Nergal:
"I will take back a report [*about a traveller standing*] at
  the gate."   (10)
[The porter *went in* to Ereshkiga]l to s[ay] something:
["*O mistress, a certain traveller*] has com[e to us],
[. . .], wh[o *will identify*] him?"   (13)

(A few lines are missing. When the text is again legible, Ereshkigal is giving instructions to Namtar, her vizier.)

[". . .] seize him!"   (16')
[". . . *I will*] identify him.[96]
[. . . *I will look at* h]im in the outer gate,

---

[96] There is a change of speaker in lines 17' or 18'. It is not certain who will do the
identifying but clearly Namtar is speaking in line 18'.

I will bring back [*a report*] to my *mistress*."
Namtar went to look at Erra[97] [*at the s*]*ide* of the door. (20′)
Namtar's face turned pale like a cut-down tamarisk,
His lips turned dark like a bruised *kunīnu*-reed.
Namtar went to say something to his mis[tress]:
"O mistress, wh[en] thou didst send me [to] thy father,
[When] I entered the courtyard of [Anu],
[*The gods altogether*] were bowed down humbly,
[*The gods of the land* . . .] were bowed down."
(Five lines are missing.)
[*Ereshkigal opened her mouth to speak*],
[*To say something*] to [*Namtar, her vizier*]:
["*Namtar,* . . .]
(Two lines are missing.)
And I [. . .]
[Let him eat] the bread of the An[unnaki,
    Let him drink the water of the Anunnaki].
Go, [*bring*] this god [*into my presence*]!" (40′)
[He led Nergal through the fir]st gate, that of N[edu],
[He led Nergal through the second gat]e, that of K[ishar],
[He led Nergal through the third gate, that of Endashurimma],
[He led Nergal through the fourth gate, that of] En[urulla],
[He led Nergal through the fifth gate], that of Endu[kuga],
[He led Nergal through the sixth] gate, that of Endu[shuba],
[He led Nergal through the seven]th gate, that of Ennug[igi].
He entered [her] wide [courtyard],
He bowed down, he kissed the groun[d before her], (saying):
"Anu, thy father, *sent* me [. . .]" (50′)
(Ereshkigal replied): "Sit down on a throne [. . .]
Determine the verdicts . . . [. . . of the great gods],
The great gods which dw[ell in Irkalla]."
As soon as [they brought him a throne],
He did *not* go and [sit on it];
When a baker brought him bread, [*he* did not go] and eat the
    bread;
When [a but]cher brou[ght him] meat, *he* did [not] go and eat his
    meat;
[When a brewer brought him beer], *he* did not go and [dr]ink his
    beer;
[When water for his feet was broug]ht to him, *he* did not go and
    [wash his feet];
[(When) she (Ereshkigal)] w[ent in to ba]the, (60′)
To put on her [. . . -garment],

---

[97] Another name for Nergal.

[. . .] *she revealed* [*her body*].

[He, what is normal for man and wo]man [. . .] his heart.

         (About ten lines are missing.)

      (iv)

    (The first three lines are too fragmentary for translation.)

[When] Nergal [heard] thi[s . . .]   (4′)

She [went in]to the b[ath]room,

[To put on her . . .]-garment,

 . . . [*she revealed her body*].

He, what is normal for m[an and woman . . .].

They [both] embraced [one another],

Pas[sionately they got into] bed.   (10′)

The first day, the second day, they lay, [*queen Ereshkigal and Erra*];

[The third] day, the fourth day, [they lay, *queen Ereshkigal and Erra*];

[The fifth day], the sixth day, [they lay, *queen Ereshkigal and Erra*];

[When the seventh] day [came],

Since Nergal *was not there* [. . .]

After him carried off . . . [. . .]

"Release me, [my] sister, [. . .]

[*Do not*] raise the alarm [. . .]

I will go and [come back] to the Land of no Return."

With regard to her, [. . .] turned dark.   (20′)

[*Nergal*] w[ent str]aight [*to* . . .],

[To . . .] the porte[r *to say something*]:

"[Ereshkigal], thy mistress, [*sent me*]

With these words:

[*'I will send thee to the heaven*] of An[u, *our father*].'

Let me go [*that I might deliver*] the message!"

Nergal ascended [the long staircase of the heavens].

[When he reached] the gate of Anu, En[lil, and Ea],

Anu, Enlil, and [Ea looked at him and (said)]:

"*The son of* Ishtar [*has come up to us*].

[. . .] *will seek* [*him*] and [. . .]   (30′)

[*Let*] Ea, his *father*, [*sprinkle him with*] s[pring] water, [so that he is bald],

Twitching, la[me . . . *let him sit in the assembly of all the gods*]."

Ereshkigal [. . .]

[*She went in*]to the bathroom

 . . . [. . .]

Her body [. . .]

 . . . [. . .]

She called [. . .]:

A thro[ne . . .]

"[*Sprinkle the house with*] water of [. . .]
S[prinkle] the house with water of [. . .]   (40′)
Sprin[kle] the house with wa[ter of . . .]
[. . .] two daughters, [. . .] and Enmeshar,
S[prin]kle them [*with water of*] . . .
[*The messenger*] of Anu, our father, who came to us,
[Let] him ea[t our bread,] let him drink our [water]!"

[*Namtar*] opened [his mouth] to speak,
To say something [to Ereshkigal], his mistress:
"[*The messenger* of Anu], our father, who came to us,
[. . .] to lie."   (49′)
                    (A few lines are missing.)
Tears were running down her cheeks.   (52′)
"O Erra, my voluptuous mate!
I was not sated with his charms (and) he has left me.
O Erra, my voluptuous mate!
I was not sated with his charms (and) he has left me."
Namtar opened his mouth to say something to Ereshkigal:
"[. . .] . . . [. . .] I will seize that god,
[. . . that he might k]iss thee."
        (v)
[Ereshkigal opened her mouth to speak],
[To say something to Namtar, her vizier]:
["Go, Namtar, . . .]
Set your face [toward the gate of] Anu, Enlil, and Ea,   (1′)
[Say]: 'Since I, thy daughter, was young,
I have not known the play of maidens,
 I have not kn[own] the frolic of young girls.
[That god whom] thou didst send and who had intercourse with me,
        Let him lie with me,
Send [that god] to me that he might be my husband,
        That he might lodge with me.
I am sexually defiled, I *am* not *pure,*
        I cannot determine the verdicts of the great gods,
The great gods who dwell in Irkalla.
If [thou dost not] send t[hat] god,
According [to the *ordinances of Irkall*]a and the great
        underworld,   (10′)
I shall send up the dead that they might devour the living,
I shall make the dead more numerous than the living.' "
Namtar ascended the long staircase of the heave[ns].
When he reached the gate of Anu, Enlil, and Ea,
[An]u, Enlil, and Ea looked at him and (said):
"[Wh]y dost thou come, Namtar?"

"Your [daughte]r has sent me,
With these words: 'Since I, thy daughter, was young,
I have not known the play of maidens,
I have not known the frolic of young girls. (20′)
That god whom thou didst send and who had intercourse
    [with me],
    [Let] him lie [with me],
Send that god to me that he might be [my] husband,
    That [he might lodge with me].
I am sexually defiled, I *am* not [*pure*],
    I cannot determine the verdict[s of the great gods],
The great gods who d[well] in Irkal[la].
If thou dost [not] send that god,
I shall send up [the dead that they might devour] the living,
[I shall make] the dead more numerous than the living.' "

Ea opened his mouth [to speak], to say something [to Namtar]:
"Na[mtar, come in]to the cour[tyard of Anu]."
[. . .] (30′)
When he entered [the courtyard of An]u,
All of [the gods were humbly] bowed down [. . .],
[The god]s of the land were b[owed down . . .].
[He went straight up to] one, [but did not] recognize that god,
He went straight up to [a second (and) thi]rd, but did not recognize
    that god.
N[amt]ar went to say something to his mistress:
"My mistress, [in the heaven of] Anu, thy father, to which thou
    didst send me,
My mistress [*there was a certain god*] who was bald,
    Twitching, lame . . . , sitting in the assembly of all the gods,"
"Go, seize that god, b[ri]ng (him) to [me]!
Ea, his *father, has* sprin[*kled him with*] spring water, (40′)
So that he is bald, twitching, lame . . . ,
    [As he sits] in the assembly of all the g[ods]."
Namtar ascended the long staircase of the heave[ns]. When he
reached the gate of Anu, Enlil, and Ea, Anu, Enlil, and Ea looked at
him [and (said)]:
"Why dost thou come, Namtar?"
    "Your daughter has sent m[e]
With these words:
    'Seize that god and bring (him) to me!' "
"Namtar, come into the courtyard of Anu,
Seek (redress) from him for (his) *offences* against thee.
    T[ake him]!"
He went straight up to one, but did not recognize [that god],

He went straight up to [a second (and) thi]rd, but [did not
   recognize that god], (50′)
He went straight up to [a fourth (and) fifth], but [did not recognize
   that god].
[. . .] opened his mouth to speak, [to say something] to Ea:
"[. . . Na]mtar, the messenger who came [to us],
[*Let him*] *drink* [*water*], let him bathe,
   Let him ano[int *his body*]."

(About six lines are missing in which it was narrated that Namtar
found Nergal/Erra. In the following broken section, which is trans-
lated below, Namtar instructs Nergal that he must give up a piece of
clothing or some other object at each of the seven gates to the nether
world. Cf., the Descent of Ishtar.)
    (vi)
"May he not remove [. . .]"[98]
"Erra, I shall make thee go [. . .] upon him [. . .],
I shall *kill* thee,[99] I shall [. . .]"
"Namtar, thy task to [. . .]"
"Erra, . . . [. . .]
All the ordinances of the great underworld I *will reveal to thee.*
When [thou] hast departed from this place,
I *shall provide* a throne for [thee to carry],[100]
[*I shall provide* . . .] for [thee to carry],
[*I shall provide* . . .] for [thee to carry], (10)
[*I shall provide* . . .] for thee [to carry],
[*I shall provide* . . .] for thee to [ca]rry,
[*I shall provide* . . .] for thee to [c]arry.
[. . .] *dwellings.*
[. . .] . . . thy breast."
[*Erra*] *took* to heart [*the speech of Namtar*],
[. . .] he . . . his . . . and *drew* his bow.
[*Ne*]rgal [*descended*] *the long stairc*[*ase of the hea*]*vens.*
When he re[ached] the gate of Eresh[kigal (he said)]:
"Open [for me], O porter, *the gate!*" (20)
The porter of the gate hung up [*his throne at*] the gate,
He did not let him take [it] away.
The second (porter) of the g[ate] did the same to his [. . .].
The third (porter) [of the gate] did the same to his [. . .].
The fourth (porter) [of the gate] did the same [to his . . .].

---

[98] Nergal/Erra must be speaking.

[99] To become a permanent resident of the nether world.

[100] Nergal is being provided with seven objects to give to each of the seven porters
of the nether world so that he will not have to remove his clothing.

The fifth (porter) [of the gate] did the same to his [. . .].
[The sixth (porter) of the gate] did the same to his [. . .].
[The seventh (porter) of the gate] did the same to his [. . .].
He entered her wide courtyard,
He *went up* to her and laughed.   (30)
He seized her by her coiffure,
He [*dragged*] *her* from [the *throne*].
He seized her [*by*] *her locks,*
. . . *love* of his heart.
They both embraced one another,
Passionately they got into bed.
The first day, the second day, they lay, *queen Eresh*[*kigal and E*]*rra;*
The third day they lay, *queen Ereshkigal and Erra;*
The fourth day they lay, *queen Ereshkigal and Erra;*
The fifth day they lay, *queen Ereshkigal and Erra;*   (40)
[The sixth day] they lay, *queen Ereshkigal and Erra;*
[When the seventh day] came,
[*Anu* opened his mouth] to speak,
To say something [*to Kaka, his vizier*]:
"I will send thee, [*Kaka, to the Land of no Return*],
[*To the house* of Ereshkiga]l, who dwells in Irkalla.
[*With these words: 'That god*] whom I sent to thee,
[*He shall dwell with thee* for] ever.
[. . .] those above,   (50)
[. . .] those below.'"
                    (The remainder of the text is missing.)

ANET³, 514   # The Myth of Zu (Anzu)

Assyrian Version

TRANSLATOR: A. K. GRAYSON

Tablet I

The son of the king of inhabited places,
        The illustrious, beloved of Mami,
The strong one, the god, child of [Enli]l, I will ever praise.
Ninurta, the illustrious, beloved of Mami,
[The strong] one, the god, child of Enlil, I will ever glorify,
[(He is): The offsp]ring of Ekur, foremost among the Annunaki,
        Strength of Eninnu,
[*He who made*] the animal-stalls (and) founded houses, streets
        and cities;
The hero, [experienc]ed in battle, *the active fighter,*
[Whose] tireless attack the savage [*demons*] fear;
[. . .] the strong one, praise of his might,

[Who] bound his [enemi]es (and) tied up the Stone Things;   (10)
[*Who vanquished* the f]ugitive Zu with his weapon,
[Who *subdued* the K]usarikku in the midst of the sea;
[. . .] . . . goes, moves with his weapon,
[. . .] directs strife (and) battle.
[. . .] the shrines were made,
[. . .] Igigi.
                (The remainder of the column is missing.)
        (ii)   ANET³, 112–13
And all the decrees of the gods he directed.
To *convey them* he dispatched Zu,
Enlil entrusted to him the . . . of the entrance to his shrine.
The [. . .]ing of pure water before him.
The exercise of his Enlilship his eyes view.
The crown of his sovereignty, the robe of his godhead,
His divine Tablet of Destinies Zu views constantly.
As he views constantly the father of the gods, the god of Duranki,
The removal of Enlilship he conceives in his heart.
As Zu views constantly the father of the gods, the god of
        Duranki,
The removal of Enlilship he conceives in his heart.
"I will take the divine Tablet of Destinies, I,
And the decrees of all the gods I will rule!
I will make firm my throne and be the master of the norms,
I will direct the totality of all the Igigi."
His heart having thus plotted aggression,
At the entrance of the sanctuary, which he had been viewing,
        He awaits the start of day.
As Enlil was washing with pure water,
His crown having been removed and deposited on the throne,
He seized the Tablet of Destinies in his hands,   (20)
Taking away the Enlilship; suspended were [the norms].
When Zu had flown away and repaired to his mountain,
Father Enlil, their counselor, was speechless.
Stillness spread abroad, si[lence] prevailed.
The sanctuary took off its brilliance.
[The gods of the l]and rallied at the ne[ws].
Anu op[ened] his mouth to speak,
Saying to the gods, his sons:
"[Wh]o will slay Zu,
And make his name the greatest [in] the settlements?"   (30)

They called the [Irriga]tor, the son of Anu;
[He who gi]ves the orders addressed him,
They called Adad, the Irrigator, the son of Anu;

[He who gi]ves the orders addressed him:
"[Tho]u potent one, all-conquering Adad—immovable thy onslaught—
[Bring] lightning on Zu with thy weapons!
Thy [name] shall be the greatest in the Assembly of the great gods,
[Among the god]s, thy brothers, thou shalt have no equal!
[Let] built shrines [app]ear,
[In the] four [qu]arters establish thy cult sites,   (40)
Let thy [cult si]tes re-enter Ekur!
[Glori]fied before the gods and potent shall be thy name!"
[Ada]d replied to the command,
Saying (these) words [to A]nu, his father:
"[My father, to the] trackless [mountain] who will hasten?
[Who is li]ke Zu among the gods, thy sons?
[The Tablet of Destinies] he has seized in his hands,
[The Enlilship] he has taken away; suspended are the norms.
[Zu] has flown away repairing to his mountain.
His [utteran]ce has become like that of the god of Duranki.   (50)
[He who opposes] him will become [like clay],
[At] his [. . . the gods waste away]."
[Anu bade him to forego the] journey.
        (iii)
    (The first twenty-three lines of this column [54–76 in consecutive
line count] are almost totally destroyed, except for portions of the
last five lines. These correspond to lines 49–53 above. Apparently
another deity had been called in, but declined to go against Zu. It
should be noted that in the Susa Version the first-born of Ishtar is the
second god to be called [the third in the Assyrian Version]. Moreover, he appears to have accepted the challenge, unlike his counterpart in the present instance.)

[They] called [Shara], the first-born of Ishtar.   (77)
[He who gives the or]ders addressed him:
"[Thou pot]ent one, all-conquering Shara—
        immovable thy onslaught—   (80)
[Bring lightning upon] Zu with thy weapons!
[Thy name] shall be the greatest in the Assembly of the great gods,
[Am]ong the gods, thy brothers, thou shalt have no equal!
Let built shrine appear,
In the four quarters establish thy cult sites,
Let thy cult sites re-enter Ekur!
Glorified before the gods and potent shall be thy name!"
Shara replied to the command,
Saying (these) words to Anu, his father:
"My father, to the trackless mountain who will hasten?
Who is like Zu among the gods, thy sons?   (90)

The Tablet of Destinies he has seized in his hands,
The Enlilship he has taken away; suspended are the norms.
Zu has flown away repairing to his mountain.
[His] utter[ance] has [be]come [like that of the god of Duranki].
[He who opposes him will become like clay],
[At his . . . the gods waste away]."
[Anu bade Shara to forego the journey].
                    (gap of seven lines)
[. . .] . . . Anu says: (105)   ANET³, 514–17
"[. . .] I will find a god [. . .]
And will appoint (him) in the Assembly as the vanquisher of Zu.

Yea, I will find a god
And appoint (him) in the Assembly as the vanquisher of Zu."
When the Igigi heard this speech of his,
The Igigi trembled and kissed his feet.
Ninigiku opened his mouth to speak,
To say something to Anu and Dagan.
   (Column iii ends at this point and column iv is entirely missing.)

Tablet II

When the narration begins, Mami is speaking.

" . . . to appoint a time;
  . . . send forth brilliance.
Launch thy full offensive,
Let thy seven ill winds go against him.
Vanquish the fugitive Zu,
And (thus) bring peace to the *earth* [which] I created,
    While bringing chaos to his abode.
Heap up things to frighten him,
Let thy terrifying offensive rage against him;
Cause the entire whirlwind *to attack* him,
Draw the bow (and) let the arrows carry poison.   (10)
Let thy countenance become like a demon's,
Send out a fog so he cannot recognize thy face.
Let thy radiance go against him,
[In . . . and] steppe thou wilt have brilliance.
May the sun not shine over him,
May the bright [day] turn to gloom on him.
Slit his throat, vanquish Zu,
Let the winds carry his wings to a secret place,
Toward Ekur, to thy father Enlil.
Take flood (and) confusion in to the midst of the [mountain]s, (20)
Cut the throat of evil Zu.

Let the sovereignty (again) enter Ekur,
Let the norms return [t]o the fa[ther who] begot thee.
Let built shrines [appear],
Establish thy cult sites [in the] four [quarters].
[Let] thy [cult sites] enter (again) into Ekur,
(And) may thy mighty name be splendid before the gods!"
When the hero heard the speech of his mother,
He was wroth, he raged (and) departed for his (Zu's) mountain.
My lord hitched the Seven-of-the-Battle, (30)
The hero hitched the seven ill winds,
The seven whirlwinds which stir up the dust,
He launched a terrifying war, a fierce conflict.
While the gale at his side shrieked for strife,
Zu and Ninurta met on the mountainside.
When Zu saw him he raged at him,
He ground (his teeth) like a demon, his brilliance covered the
     mountain,
He roared like a lion seized with anger,
In his rage he called [to the h]ero:
"I have carried off everyone of the norms, (40)
And (therefore) the decrees of all the gods I direct;
Who art thou to come to fight with me?
     Explain thyself!"
He advanced aggressively toward him and the word of his mouth
     went forth to him,
[The hero] Ninurta [answered] Zu:
"*I* [*am* . . .] and the god of Duranki,
[*I*] received wide [*understanding*] (*from*) Ea, king of the Destinies.
I have come [*to thee*] to fight with thee . . . "
When Zu heard the word of his mouth,
In the midst of the mountain range he let loose a piercing shriek.
There was darkness, the face of the mountain was covered, (50)
Ninurta, the light of the gods, entered the gloom.
Adad . . . roared, his thunder pursued Zu,
In the midst of the conflict, (in the midst of) the war,
     He launched fourteen storm floods,
Dressed in armor he bathed in blood,
Clouds of death sent rain, the lightning flashes were arrows.
He *stood* in their midst while the battle roared,
The strong, the illustrious, the child of Mami,
The hope of Anu and Dagan, the beloved of Ninigiku,
He loaded [the . . .] of the bow with an arrow,
From the breast of the bow he loosed the arrow at him, (60)
But the arrow could not approach Zu, it turned back,
(For) Zu called to it:

"O arrow that [has] come, return to thy canebrake,
Stave [of the bow] (return) to thy wood,
(Return, bow)-gut, to the sheep's rump, return wings to the birds!"
While he bore the [Tablet of De]stinies of the gods in his hand,
... [... the arrows] could not approach his body.
The ba[tt]le [was st]illed, the conflict ceased,
The weapons were stopped, in the midst of the mountain
    They vanquished not Zu.
He (Ninurta) called to Adad and gave him instructions: (70)
"Repeat to him, to Ea Ninigiku, the deeds which thou hast
    observed:
'O lord, Ninurta was encircling Zu,
Ninurta *was girding up* the dust of destruction;
He loaded [the ...] of the bow with an arrow,
He *drew* the bow and loosed the arrow at him,
But the arrow could not approach Zu, it turned back,
(For) Zu called to it:
"O arrow that has come, return to thy canebrake,
Stave of the bow (return) to thy wood,
(Return, bow)-gut, to the sheep's rump, return wings
    to the birds!"   (80)
While he bore the Tablet of Destinies of the gods in his hand,
... the arrows could not approach his body.
The battle was stilled, the conflict ceased,
The weapons were stopped, in the midst of the mountain they
    vanquished not Zu.' "
Adad, the prince, took the report,
The news of the fight he bore to Ea Ninigiku.
Whatever the lord had spoken to him he repeated to Ea:
"O lord, Ni[nurta] was encircling Zu,
Ninurta *was gir[ding up]* the dust of destruction;
[He loaded the ... of the bow with an arrow],   (90)
He *drew* the bow and loosed the arrow at him,
But the arrow could not approach [Z]u, it turned back,
(For) Zu called to it:
'O arrow that has come, return to [thy] canebrake,
Stave of the bow (return) to thy wood,
[(Return, bow-)gu]t, to the sheep's [rump], [return] wings to the
    birds!'
[While he bore the Tablet of Destinies] of the gods [in his] h[and],
[... the arrows could not approach his body].
[The battle was] s[tilled, the conflict ceased],
[The weapons were] s[topped, in the midst of the mountain they
    vanquished not Zu]."   (100)
When [Ea Ninigi]ku heard the word of his son,

He called to [Adad and] gave him instructions:
"Repeat [to him], to thy lord, my instructions,
Wha[te]ver I say outline to him:
'In battle do not tire, prove thy strength,
Subdue him, by the onslaught of the south wind let his pinions be
    overcome.
Take the . . . weapon to the back of thy darts,
Cut off his pinions, *scatter* (them) to the right and left.
When he sees his wings (the sight) will rob him of speech:
"Wing to wing!" he will cry, fear him no (longer). (110)
Draw thy bow (and) from its breast let fly the arrows like lightning,
Let pinions (and) wings dance like bloody things.
Slit his throat, vanquish Zu,
Let the winds carry his wings to a secret place,
Toward Ekur, to thy father Enlil.
Take flood (and) confusion into the midst of the mountains,
Cut the throat of evil Zu.
Let the sovereignty (again) enter Ekur,
Let the norms return [to] the fat[her] who begot thee.
Let built shrines appear, (120)
Establish thy cult sites in the four quarters.
Let thy cult sites enter (again) into Ekur,
(And) may thy mighty name be splendid bef[ore the g]ods!' "
[Adad], the prince, took the directions,
Instructions for the fight [he b]ore to Ninurta, his lord,
Wha[tev]er Ea said he repeated to him:
"In battle do not tire, prove thy strength,
Subdue him, [by the onslaught] of the south wind let his pinions be
    overcome.
Take the . . . -weapon to the back of thy darts,
[Cut of]f [his] pinions, *scatter* (them) [to the right and left]. (130)
When he sees his wings (the sight) will rob him of speech:
'Wing to wing!' he will cry, [fear] him no (longer).
Draw thy bow (and) from its breast let fly the arrows [like lightning],
Let pinions (and) wings dance like bloody things.
Slit his throat, vanquish Zu,
Let the winds c[arry] his wings to a secret place,
Toward Ekur, to thy father Enlil.
Take flood (and) [confusion] into the midst of the mountains,
Cut [the throat] of evil Zu.
Let thy sovereignty (again) enter [Ekur], (140)
[Let] the norms [return] to the father who begot thee.
Let built [shri]nes appear,
[Establish] thy cult sites [in the four quarters].
[Let thy cult sites enter (again) in]to Ekur,

(And) may thy mighty name [be splendid before the gods]!"
When the lord [heard the words of] Ea Ninigiku,
[He was w]roth, he raged (and) departed for his (Zu's) mountain.
[My] lord hitched the Seven-of-the-Battle,
The hero hitched the seven ill winds,
The seven whirlwinds which stir up the dust.   (150)

Fragmentary descriptions of the subsequent battle which took place between Ninurta and Zu have been recently published. Presumably these pieces come from Tablet III of the epic. Mention is made of the south, north, east, and west winds and this is followed by a description of Zu becoming frightened and the general confusion that prevailed. Note particularly line 27:

He routed Zu and cut his throat.

Ninurta is mentioned in line 13 and he may be the god responsible for vanquishing Zu. Finally, it should be noted that the beginning of the battle is described in the last four lines of the third tablet of the Old Babylonian Susa version:

[. . .] He (Ningirsu) sent forth the four winds [to d]o battle.
[. . .] the earth shook, filled [. . .]
[. . .] its [. . .] became dark, the heavens [became] black,
[. . .] at the onset of the south wind the pinions of Zu [were
     overcome].

A Babylonian Theogony   ANET³, 517–18
TRANSLATOR: A. K. GRAYSON

The present text apparently contains the tradition of only one city. The gods are paired, male and female, the first two being Hain, an otherwise unknown male deity, and Earth. These two brought into existence the next pair of deities, Amakandu and Sea, as well as the city, Dunnu. In the subsequent lines of the text is found the stereotyped account of how, by means of incest and murder, one divine pair succeeded another. Only the names of one more pair, Lahar and River, are completely preserved. The names of the male consorts of Ga'um and Ningeshtinna are missing. The dates upon which each new god took control are given and these were obviously related to important festivals of the city, Dunnu.

[. . .] in the beginn[ing . . .]
[. . .] and [. . .]
They [. . .] . . . their plough.
[With the c]ut of their plough they created Sea.

[Second]ly, by themselves they gave birth to Amaka[ndu].
[Thi]rdly, they built the two Pillars of Dunnu.
[Ha]in bestowed the lordship in Dunnu on himself.
[Earth] turned her attention to Amakandu, her son,
She said to him, "Come, I will make love to you!"
Ama[kandu] married Earth, his mother;   (10)
He killed Hain, his [father, and]
Laid [him] to rest in Dunnu, the city which he loved.
Then Amakandu [too]k the lordship of his father [and]
[Ma]rried Sea, his sister, . . .
Lahar, son of Amakandu, went [and]
Killed Amakandu and in Dunnu,
In the . . . of [hi]s father, he laid [him] to rest.
He married [Se]a, [hi]s mother.
Then Sea *laid to rest* Earth, her mother.
On the sixteenth day of the month Kislim he took the lordship
    and sovereignty.   (20)

[. . .] son of Lahar married River, his own sister.
He killed [Lahar], his father, and Sea, his mother.
[. . .] laid them to rest . . .
On the first day [of the month . . . he took] the sovereignty and
    lordship for himself.
[. . . , son of] . . . , ma[rr]ied Ga'um, his sister.
He . . . [. . .] earth
He . . . [. . .] . . .
[. . .] fathers and [. . .]
He [. . .] for the . . . of the gods.
[. . .] killed River, his mother.   (30)
He settled the[m . . .]
[On the . . . day of the month . . .] he to[ok] the lordship and
    sovereignty for himself.
[. . . , son of . . .], marr[ied] Ningeshtinna, his sister.
He ki[lled . . . , his father, and] Ga'um, [hi]s mother.
He settled th[em . . .].
On the sixteenth (variant: twenty-ninth) day [of the month . . . he
    took] the sovereignty (and) lordship.

[. . .] the child/servant of Haharnu [. . .]
Marr[ied . . .], his own [si]ster.
[. . .] took the lordship of his father and [. . .]
. . .   (40)
[. . .] to the city Shupat-[. . .]

    (Illegible traces of one more line are preserved before the text is
completely broken. The reverse is too mutilated to translate.)

Hittite Myths

TRANSLATOR: ALBRECHT GOETZE

The Telepinus Myth

ANET, 126–28

a. The God's Anger, His Disappearance, and Its Consequences

(The upper third of the tablet, about 20 lines, is broken off. It probably told the reasons for the god's anger.)

(i) Telepinus [flew into a rage and shouted:] "There must be no inter[ference!" In his agitation] he tried to put [his right shoe] on his left foot and his left [shoe on his right foot]. . . . [. . .].

(5) *Mist* seized the windows, *vapor* seized the house. In the fireplace the logs were stifled, at the altars the gods were stifled, in the fold the sheep were stifled, in the stable the cattle were stifled. The sheep neglected its lamb, the cow neglected its calf.

(10) Telepinus walked away and took grain, (fertile) breeze, . . . , . . . and satiation to the country, the meadow, the *steppes.* Telepinus went and lost himself in the *steppe; fatigue* overcame him. So grain (and) spelt thrive no longer. So cattle, sheep and man no longer (15) breed. And even those with young cannot bring them forth.

The *vegetation* dried up; the trees dried up and would bring forth no fresh shoots. The pastures dried up, the springs dried up. In the land famine arose so that man and gods perished from hunger. The great Sun-god arranged for a feast and invited the thousand gods. They ate, (20) but they did not satisfy their hunger; they drank, but they did not quench their thirst.

b. The Search for the Vanished God

The Storm-god became anxious about Telepinus, his son: "Telepinus, my son, (he said) is not here. He has flown into a rage and taken (with him) every good thing." The great gods and the lesser gods began to search for Telepinus. The Sun-god sent out the swift Eagle (saying): "Go! Search every high (25) mountain!"

"Search the deep valleys! Search the watery depth!" The Eagle went, but he could not find him. Back to the Sun-god he brought his message: "I could not find him, him, Telepinus, the noble god." The Storm-god said to Hannahannas:[1] "What shall we do? (30) We shall die of hunger." Hannahannas said to the Storm-god: "Do something, O Storm-god! Go! Search for Telepinus thyself!"

The Storm-god began to search for Telepinus. In his city he [knock]s at the gate, but he is not there and opens not. He broke open his bolt and his lock, [but he has no luck], the Storm-god. So he gave up and sat down to rest. Hannahannas (35) sent [out the Bee]: "Go! Search thou for Telepinus!"

[The Storm-god s]aid [to Hannahannas]: "The great gods (and) the lesser gods have searched for him, but [did not find] him. Shall then this [Bee] go out [and find him]? Its wings are small, it is small itself. Shall they admit that it is greater than they?"

Hannahannas said to the Storm-god: "Enough! It will go (and) find him." Hannahannas sent out the little Bee: "Go! Search thou for Telepinus! When thou findest him, sting him on his hands (and) his feet! Bring him to his feet! Take wax and wipe his eyes and his feet, purify him and bring him before me!"

The Bee went away and searched ... the streaming rivers, and searched the murmuring springs. The honey within it gave out, [the wax within it] gave out. Then [it found] him in a meadow in the grove at Lihzina. It stung him on his hands and his feet. It brought him to his feet, it took wax and wiped his eyes (and) his feet, [it purified him] and [...].

[Telepinus . . .] declares: "For my part I had flown into a rage [and walked away. How dare] ye a[rouse me] from my sleep? How dare ye force me to talk when enraged?" He grew [still more infu]riated. [He stopped] the murmuring springs, he diverted the flowing rivers and made them flow over their banks. He [*blocked off*] the clay pits, he shattered [the windo]ws, he shattered the houses.

He had men perish, he had sheep and cattle perish. [It came to] pass that the gods [*despaire*]d (asking): "Wh[y has Te]lepinus become [so infur]iated? [Wh]at shall we do? [What shall we do?"

[The great Sun-god (??) decl]ares: "[Fetch ye] man! Let him [t]ake the spring Hattara on mount Ammuna [as . . .]! Let him (man) make him move! With the eagle's wing let him make him move! Let man make him move! With the eagle's wing [let man make him move]!"[2]

---

[1] The name is ideographically written NIN.TU or MAH; mother of the gods.
[2] A certain ritual.

(A gap follows in which Kamrusepas, the goddess of magic and healing, is commissioned to pacify Telepinus and to bring him back.)

c. The Ritual

Entreaty

(The beginning is mutilated.)

(ii) "O Telepinus! [Here lies] sweet and soothing [cedar essence. Just as it is . . .], [even so let] the stifled [be set right] again!

"Here [I have] *upthrusting sap* [with which to purify thee]. (10) Let it [invigorate] thy heart and thy soul, O Telepinus! Toward the king [turn] in favor!

"Here lies *chaff.* [Let his heart (and) soul] be *segregated* [like it]! Here lies an ear [of grain]. Let it attract his heart [(and) his soul]!

"(15) Here lies sesame. [Let his heart (and) his soul] be *comforted* by it. Here [lie] figs. Just as [figs] are sweet, even so let Te[lepinus' heart (and) soul] become sweet!

"Just as the olive [holds] oil within it, [as the grape] (20) holds wine within it, so hold thou, Telepinus, in (thy) heart (and thy) soul good feelings [toward the king]!

"Here lies *ointment.* Let it anoint Telepin[us' heart (and) soul]! Just as malt (and) malt-loaves are harmoniously fused, even so let thy soul be in harmony with the affairs of mankind! [Just as spelt] (25) is clean, even so let Telepinus' soul become clean! J[ust as] honey is sweet, as cream is smooth, even so let Telepinus' soul become sweet and even so let him become smooth!

"See, O Telepinus! I have now sprinkled thy ways with fine oil. So walk thou, Telepinus, over these ways that are sprinkled with fine oil! (30) Let *šaḫiš* wood and *ḫappuriašaš* wood be at hand! Let us set thee right, O Telepinus, into whatever state of mind is the right one!"

Telepinus came in his fury. Lightning flashed, it thundered while the dark earth was in turmoil. (35) Kamrusepas saw him. The eagle's wing made him move out there. It took off him (iii) the rage, it took off him the anger, it took off him [the ire], it took off him the fury.

Kamrusepas' Ritual of Purification

Kamrusepas tells the gods: "Come ye, O gods! See! Hapantallis is shepherding the Sun-god's sheep. (5) Select ye twelve rams! I want to fix long days for Telepinus. I have taken death, one thousand eyes. I have strewn about the selected sheep of Kamrusepas.

"Over Telepinus I have swung them this way and that. (10) From Telepinus' body I have taken the evil, I have taken the malice. I have taken the rage, I have taken the anger, I have taken the ire, I have taken the fury.

"When Telepinus was angry, his heart (and) his soul were stifled (like) firebrands. (15) Just as they burned these brands, even so let Telepinus' rage, anger, malice (and) fury burn themselves out! Just as [malt] is barren, (as) people do not bring it to the field to use it for seed, (as) people do not make it into bread (or) put it in the storehouse, even so let Telepinus' rage, [anger], (20) malice (and) fury become barren!

"When Telepinus was angry, [his heart (and) his soul] were a burning fire. Just as this fire [is quenched], even so let (his) rage, anger (and) fury [be quenched] too!

"O Telepinus, give up thy rage, [give up] thine anger, (25) give up thy fury! Just as (water in) a pipe flows not upward, even so let Telepinus' [rage, anger (and)] fury not [come] back!

"The gods [were gathered] in assembly under the *ḫatalkešnaš* tree. For the *ḫatalkešnaš* tree I have fixed long [years]. (30) All gods are now present, (including) the [*Is*]*tustayas,* the Good-women (and) the Mother-goddesses, the Grain-god, Miyatanzipas, Telepinus, the Patron-god. Hapantaliyas (and) the Patron of the field. For these gods I have fixed long years; I have purified him, [O Telepinus]!

(35) "[. . .] I have taken the evil [from] Telepinus' body, I have taken away his [rage], [I have taken away] his an[ger], I have taken away his [ire], [I have taken away] his fury, I have taken away his malice, [I have taken away his] ev[il]." (small gap)

Man's Ritual

(The beginning is lost, but Telepinus is addressed:)

". . . (When) thou [departedst] from the *ḫatalkešnaš* tree on a summer day, the crop got *smutted*. (When) the ox departed [with thee], (iv) thou *wastedst* its *shape*. (When) the sheep departed with thee, thou *wastedst* its form. O Telepinus, stop rage, anger, malice (and) fury!

"(When) the Storm-god comes in his wrath, the Storm-god's priest (5) stops him. (When) a pot of food boils over, the (stirring) *spoon* stops it. Even so let the word of me, the mortal, stop Telepinus' rage, anger, and fury!

"Let Telepinus' rage, anger, malice, (and) fury depart! Let the house let them go, let the interior . . . let them go, (10) let the window let them go! In the . . . let the interior courtyard let them go, let the gate let them go, let the gateway let them go, let the road of the king let them go! Let it not go to the thriving field, garden (or) grove! Let it go the way of the Sun-god of the nether world!

"The doorkeeper has opened the seven doors, has unlocked the seven bolts. (15) Down in the dark earth there stand bronze cauldrons, their lids are of *abaru*-metal, their *handles* of iron. Whatever goes in there comes not out again; it perishes therein. Let them also receive Telepinus' rage, anger, malice (and) fury! Let them not come back!"

d. The God's Home-Coming

(20) Telepinus came home to his house and cared (again) for his land. The *mist* let go of the windows, the *vapor* let go of the house. The altars were set right for the gods, the hearth let go of the log. He let the sheep go to the fold, he let the cattle go to the pen. The mother tended her child, the ewe tended her lamb, (25) the cow tended her calf. Also Telepinus tended the king and the queen and provided them with enduring life and vigor.

Telepinus cared for the king. A pole was erected before Telepinus and from this pole the fleece of a sheep was suspended. It signifies fat of the sheep, it signifies grains of corn (and) (30) wine, it signifies cattle (and) sheep, it signifies long years and progeny.

It signifies the lamb's favorable message.[3] It signifies . . . . . . It signifies *fruitful* breeze. It signifies . . . satiation. . . .

(end of the text lost)

El, Ashertu, and the Storm-god (Elkunirsha and Ashertu)

ANET³, 519

This "Canaanite Myth" is only a fragment from a larger context. One may hope that more of it will turn up in the future.

(i) [". . . . Give thyself to me, then] I shall give myself to thee; I shall *harass* thee with my word, [with my sp]indle I shall prick thee. [. . .] I shall *stir* thee up." The Storm-god heard the words. (5) He went on his way and betook himself to the well-spring of the Mala-River. [He] came to El-kunirsha, the husband of Ashertu, and entered El-kunirsha's tent.

El-kunirsha beheld the Storm-god and asked him: "[Why] didst thou come?" Thus said the Storm-god: "When I entered thy house, (10) Ashertu sent out (her) maidens to me (saying). 'Come, sleep with me!' [When] I refused, she became *aggressive* and said to me as follows: 'Give thyself to me, [then] I shall give myself to thee; I shall *harass* thee with my word, (15) with my spindle I shall prick thee.' This is why I have come, my father. For, [with a message] I did not come, I have come to thee on my own. Ashertu is impugning thy virility. Although she is thy wife she keeps on sending to me: 'Come, sleep with me.'" El-kunirsha began to reply to the Storm-god: (20) "Go, sleep with her! Lie with my wife and humble her!"

---

³ Favorable omens when intestines of the sacrificial lamb are inspected.

The Storm-god hearkened to the word of El-kunirsha. With Ashertu he slept. The Storm-god said to Ashertu: "Of thy sons I slew 77, I slew 88." Ashertu (25) heard this humiliating word of the Storm-god and her mind got incensed against him. She appointed wailing-women and began to wail for 7 years. They keep eating (and) drinking. . . .

(gap)

(ii?) [". . . I shall listen . . . [. . . and] I shall sleep with thee." [When El-kunirsha] heard these words, he said to his wife: "[. . .] the Storm-god, I shall turn him over to thee. (5) As thou pleasest, thus d[eal] with him!"

ISHTAR heard those words. In El-kunirsha's hand she became a *cup*; she became a *ḫapupiš* bird and roosted on his wall. Whatever words husband and wife speak, those ISHTAR (10) overhears. El-kunirsha and his wife went upon her bed and slept with each other. But ISHTAR flew like a bird across the . . . and found the Storm-god in the. . . . (The column breaks off. Apparently ISHTAR tells the Storm-god of El and Ashertu's plot.)

(Of the other columns too little is preserved to yield a comprehensible context.)

Ugaritic Myths and Epics

TRANSLATOR: H. L. GINSBERG

Poems about Baal and Anath (The Baal Cycle)

ANET, 129–35, 138–42

Both large and small fragments of tablets containing poetic mythological texts in which the leading role is played by the rain- and fertility-god Baal and the next in importance by the warrior-goddess Anath came to light in the French excavations of Ras Shamra-Ugarit in the years 1930, 1931, and 1933, and at least one small fragment (which may be a duplicate of one of the others) in 1929. Because so many letters, words, lines, columns, and probably some whole tablets are missing, not all of the tablets can be declared, with certainty, to be parts of the great epic of Baal and arranged in their proper order within it. However, in the following translations, even small fragments whose pertinence to the larger epic is probable have, for the most part, been included (if only, in a few desperate cases, in the form of sketchy summaries) and assigned tentative positions within it. Tablets whose pertinence to the larger poem is doubtful have been added at the end by way of an appendix.

a. VI AB

Editions: Ch. Virolleaud, *La déesse 'Anat* (Paris, 1938), pp. 91–102 and the last photograph; C. H. Gordon, *Ugaritic Handbook*, II, pp. 189–90, 'nt, pls. ix–x (transliteration only). Studies: A. Herdner, *Syria*, XXIII (1942–43), 283–85. Owing to the very poor state of preservation, connected translation is possible only for groups of lines which, because they are stereotyped, can be completed with the help of parallels; while just the crucial passages are very doubtful. It seems, however, that El, the head of the pantheon, (1) instructs the craftsman-god Kothar wa-Khasis to build a palace on his (El's) grounds, the name of the latter being Khurshan-zur-kas (col. iii), (2) announces that his (eldest? favorite?) son is to be known as El's Beloved Yamm (= Sea) and as Master (cf. iv 15, 20 with II AB ii 34–35, and iv 17 with III AB B 17, 33–34), and (3) perhaps authorizes Yamm to banish Baal from his throne (iii 22–25).

b. III AB C

Editions: Ch. Virolleaud, *Syria*, xxiv (1944–45), 1–12; C. H. Gordon, *Ugaritic Handbook*, ii, Text 129. This fragment comprises 24 very mutilated lines from the right-hand column on one of the sides of a tablet with two very broad columns on each side. Such a tablet is the one of whose col. i, III AB B is the lower part, and of whose col. iv, III AB A is the upper part; Virolleaud therefore surmises that III AB C is part of (the lower half of) col. iii of the same tablet. For its content, however, a position between III AB B and III AB A seems strange; so, perhaps, it belongs to a tablet which preceded, and in outward disposition resembled, the tablet of which III AB B-A is a remnant.

In it, El instructs Kothar to build a palace for Yamm. Ashtar complains of not being accorded the like favor.

[. . . There] he is off on his way (3)
>To El of the Sources [of the Floods,
>In the midst of the headwaters of the Two Oceans.

Fig. 138 He penetrates] E[l]'s *field* and *enter*
>The [pa]vilion of King [Father Shunem.[1]
At El's feet he bows] and falls down,
>Prostrates himself, doing [him] *homage*.
(. . .". . . O) Kothar wa-Kha[sis!
Quic]*kly* bu(ild the h)ouse of Yamm,
>[Ere]ct the palace of Judge Nahar.

. . .

> . . .

Build the house of Prince Yamm,
>[Ere]ct the pala[ce *of Judge*] Nahar,
>In the midst of [. . .
Quickly] his [hou]se shalt thou build, (10)
>Quickly erec[t his palace].
. . ."

(All that can be made out is that Ashtar is displeased.)
Quoth the God's Torch Shapsh,[2]
>Raising her voice and [crying:
"Heark]en, I pray thee!
Thy father Bull El *favors*
>Prince Yamm . . . [. . .] . . .
[Sh]ould thy father Bull [E]l hear thee,
>He will pull out [the *pillars* of thy dwelling!
Yea, overt]urn [the throne of thy] kingship!
>Yea, break the sce[pter] of thy dominion!"

---

[1] One of El's epithets; vocalization uncertain. Some render "Father of Years."
[2] The sun-goddess.

Quoth [Ashtar] of the [. . .] . . . :
"*Oh,* my father Bull El!
I have no house [like] the gods,
    [Nor] court like [*the holy on*]es.   (20)
. . ."

(the rest obscure)

c. III AB B-A

Editions: (1) Of III AB B: *Ugaritic Handbook,* ii, Text 137. (2) Of III AB A:
Ch. Virolleaud, *Syria,* xvi (1935), 29–45, with Pl. xi; H. L. Ginsberg, *JPOS,*
xv (1935), 327–31; *Kitbe Ugarit,* 73–76; H. Bauer, *AKTRSch.,* Ca. Studies:
W. F. Albright, *JPOS,* xvi (1936), 17–20; T. H. Gaster, *Iraq,* 4 (1937), 21–23;
J. Obermann, *JAOS,* lxvii (1947), 195–208. See the paragraph preceding the
translation of III AB C.

(1) III AB B

. . . [. . . Quoth] Puissant Baal: (3)   *Fig. 136*
"[May'st thou be driven from the throne of thy kingship,
    From the seat of thy do]minion!
. . . [. . .]
Ayamur[3] upon thy head, [O Yamm;
    Upon thy back Yagrush,[4][5] Judge Nahar.
May [Horon] break, [O Yamm,
    May Horon break] thy head,
    Ashtoreth [Name of Baal thy pate.
. . .] down may'st thou fall in . . . [. . .]   (10)
    . . . [. . .]."
[Me]ssengers Yamm doth send.
(Two lines defective and unintelligible.)
"Depart ye, lad[s, don't tarry.
    There now, be off] on your way
Towards the Assembled Body[6]
    In the m[idst of the Mount of Lala.
At the feet of El] fall not down,
    Prostrate you not to the Assembled [Body.
Proudly standing] say ye your speech.
And say unto Bull [my] father [El,
    Declare unto the Assembled] Body:
'Message of Yamm your lord,
    Of your master Ju[dge Nahar].

---

[3] Name of a bludgeon, meaning something like "Driver"; see episode (2).

[4] Name of a bludgeon, meaning "Chaser"; see episode (2).

[5] Evidently Kothar has already promised Baal the two cudgels which he wields so
effectively in episode (2).

[6] The assembly of the gods.

Surrender the god *with a following,*
> *Him whom the multitudes worship:*
Give Baal [to me to lord over],
> Dagon's son whose spoil I'll possess.'"—
The lads depart, they delay not.
[There, they are off] on their way   (20)
> To the midst of the Mount of Lala,
> Towards the Assembled Body.
Now, the gods were sitting to e[at],
> The holy ones for to dine,
> Baal attending upon El.
As soon as the gods espy them,
> Espy the messengers of Yamm,
> The envoys of Judge Nahar,
The gods do drop their heads
> Down upon their knees
> And on the thrones of their princeship.
Them doth Baal rebuke:
"Why, O gods, have ye dropt
> Your head[s] down upon your knees
> And on your thrones of princeship?
I see the gods are cowed
> With terror of the messengers of Yamm,
> Of the envoys of Judge Naha[r].
Lift up, O gods, your heads
> From upon your knees,
> From upon the thrones of your princeship,
And I'll answer[7] the messengers of Yamm,
> The envoys of Judge Nahar."
The gods lift up their heads
> From upon their knees,
> From upon [their] thrones of prin[ceship].
Then come the messengers of Yamm,   (30)
> The envoys of Judge Nahar.
At El's feet they do [not] fall down,
> Prostrate them not to the Assembled Body.
Prou[dly] standing, [they] say their speech.
> Fire, burning fire, *doth flash;*
> A whetted sword [are their e]*yes.*
They say to Bull his father El:
"Message of Yamm your lord,
> Of your master Judge Nahar.
Surrender the god *with* a following,
> etc." (see 18–19)

---

[7] Or, perhaps, humble.

[Quoth] Bull, his father, El: (36)
"Thy slave is Baal, O Yamm,
    Thy slave is Baal [for eve]r,
Dagon's Son is thy captive;
    He shall be brought as thy tribute.
For the gods bring [thy gift],
    The holy ones are thy tributaries."—
Now, Prince Baa[l] *was wroth.*
[Sei]zing [*a cudgel*] in his hand,
    A *bludgeon* in his right hand,
    He r[*eached*] to strike the lads.
[His right hand Ashtore]th seizes,   (40)
    Ashtoreth seizes his left hand.
"How [canst thou strike the messengers of Yamm,
    The en]voys of Judge Nahar?
A messenger . . . [. . .
    . . .] a messenger [bears];
Upon his shoulders the words of his lord,
    And . . . [. . .]."
But Prince Baal was wroth.
The *cudgel* in ha[nd he . . .
    He con]*fronts* the messengers of Yamm,
    The [en]voys of Judge Naha[r.
. . .] . . . "I say unto Yamm your lord,
    [Your] ma[ster Judge Nahar]:
. . ."

        (lines 46–47 too defective for understanding)

    (2) III AB A
          (1–4 defective and obscure)
". . . [ho]uses.
To the earth shall fall the strong,
    To the dust the mighty."—
Scarce had the word lef[t] her mouth,
    Her speech left her lips,
As she uttered her . . . voice
    Under the throne of Prince Yamm,
    Quoth Kothar wa-Khasis:
"I tell thee, O Prince Baal,
    I declare, O Rider of the Clouds.
Now thine enemy, O Baal,   Ps. 92:9
    Now thine enemy wilt thou smite,
    Now wilt thou cut off thine adversary.
Thou'lt take thine eternal kingdom,   (10)   Ps. 145:13
    Thine everlasting dominion."

Kothar brings down two clubs
>And gives them names.
"Thou, thy name is Yagrush ('Chaser').
>Yagrush, chase Yamm!
Chase Yamm from his throne,
>[Na]har from his seat of dominion.
Do thou swoop in the hand of Baal,
>Like an eagle between his fingers;
Strike the back of Prince Yamm,
>Between the arms[8] of [J]udge Nahar."
The club swoops in the hand of Baal,

II Kings 9:24

>Like an eagle between his [fi]ngers;
It strikes the back of Prince Yamm,
>Between the arms of Judge Nahar.
Yamm is firm, he is not bowed;
>His joints bend not,
>>Nor breaks his frame.—
Kothar brings down two clubs
>And gives them names.
"Thou, thy name is Ayamur ('Driver'?).
>Ayamur, drive Yamm!
Drive Yamm from his throne,   (20)
>Nahar from his seat of dominion.
Do thou swoop in the hand of Baal,
>Like an eagle between his fingers;
Strike the pate of Prince Yamm,

Exod. 13:9, 16;
Deut. 6:8; 11:18;
Dan. 8:5

>Between the eyes[9] of Judge Nahar.
Yamm shall collapse
>And fall to the ground."
The club swoops in the hand of Baal,
>[Like] an eagle between his fingers;
It strikes the pate of Prince [Yamm],
>Between the eyes of Judge Nahar.
Yamm collapses,
>He falls to the ground;
His joints bend,
>His frame breaks.
Baal would rend, would smash Yamm,
>Would annihilate Judge Nahar.
By name Ashtoreth rebukes [him].
"For shame, O Puissant [Baal];
>For shame, O Rider of the Clouds!

[8] I.e., on the back.
[9] On the front of the head.

For our captive is Prin[ce Yamm],
    Our captive is Judge Nahar."   (30)
As [the word] left [her mouth],
    Puissant Baal was ashamed . . .

(The rest is too defective for any meaning to be extracted, except that Yamm seems to say twice "I am dying, Baal will reign." But apparently Yamm does not die, but is only confined to his proper sphere, the seas. Hence there is still talk of him, e.g., at the end of col. ii of episode e.)

d. Fragment b

". . . Homage to Lady Asherah of [the Sea],
    Obeisance to the Progenitress of the Gods,
(So) [she] will give a house to Baal like the [g]ods',
    And a court like [A]sherah's sons'."—
Loudly to his lads Baal cries:
"Look ye, Gapn and Ugar sons of Ghulumat,[10]
    'Amamis twain, *sons* of Zulumat (*Ẓlmt*)[10]
    The stately, win[g]-spreading, . . . ;
Winged ones twain, flock of clouds,   (10)
    'Neath [. . .];
Birdlike ones twain, *fl*[*ock* of . . . snow].
    . . ."
        (obscure beginnings of 5 more lines)

e. II AB

At the beginning, Baal's messengers explain to Anath why a démarche before Asherah is indicated.

   . . .   (some 20 lines missing, 3 obliterated)

But alas!
He cri]es unto Bull El [his father,   (5)
    To E]l the King [his begetter;
He cries] unto Ashe[rah and her children],
    To [E]lath [and the band of] her [kindred:
Look, no house has Baal like the gods,   (10)
    Nor court like the children of Ashe]r[ah].
The abode of El is the shelter of his son.
    The abode of Lady Asherah of the Sea
    Is the abode of the perfect brides:
'Tis the dwelling of Padriya daughter of Ar,
    The shelter of Talliya(*ṭly*) the daughter of Rabb,

---

[10] Means "darkness," Ghulumat is also known as the name of a goddess.

(And) the abode of Arsiya (*arṣy*) the daughter of
   Ya'abdar.[11]
And here's something more I would tell thee: (20)
Just try doing homage to Lady Asherah of the Sea,
   Obeisance to the Progenitress of the Gods.
Hayyin[12] would go up to the bellows,
   In Khasis' hands would be the tongs,
To melt silver,
   To beat out gold.
He'd melt silver by the thousands (of shekels),
   Gold he'd melt by the myriads.
He'd melt . . . and . . . :   (30)
A gorgeous dais weighing twice ten thousand (shekels),
   A gorgeous dais cast in silver,
   Coated with a film of gold;
A gorgeous throne resting above
   A gorgeous footstool o'erspread with a mat;
A gorgeous couch having a . . . ,
   He pours it over with gold;
A gorgeous table which is filled
   With all manner of game[13] from the foundations of
   the earth;   (40)
Gorgeous bowls shaped like small beasts like those of Amurru,
   Stelae shaped like the wild beasts of Yam'an,
   Wherein are wild oxen by the myriads.

Fig. 126

(The first lines of the following scene perhaps show Asherah,
"Lady Asherah of the Sea," presenting an offering of fish to El.)
   (ii)
(Some 16 lines entirely missing, then 4 defective and obscure.)
   Its[14] *skin*, the covering of its flesh.
She[15] *flings* its vestment into the sea,
   Both its *skins* into the deeps.
She puts fire on the brazier,
   A pot upon the coals,
(And) *propitiates* Bull El Benign,   (10)
   Does obeisance to the Creator of Creatures.—
Lifting up her eyes she beholds.

---

[11] The three names mean "Flashie (or, Lightningette) daughter of Light, Dewie
daughter of Distillation, Earthie daughter of . . . " They are Baal's wives or daughters,
and Baal is the god of rain and dew and "the Prince, Lord of the Earth."

[12] "Deft," another name of the craftsman-god.

[13] If the translation is correct: rhytons, or vessels having the shape of animals.

[14] Of some beast of fish.

[15] Apparently, Lady Asherah or the Sea.

The advance of Baal Asherah doth espy,
>   The advance of the Maiden Anath,
>   The onrush of Yabamat [Liimmim].
Thereat her feet [do stumble];
>   Her loins [do crack be]hind her,
>   Her [face breaks out in s]weat [above her].
Bent are the [joints of her loins],
>   *Weakened* those of [her] back.[16]   (20)
She lifts up her voice and cries:
"*Why* is Puissant [Ba]al come?
>   And why the Ma[id]en Anath?
Have my children slain [each other],
>   O[r the b]and of my kinsmen [destroyed one another]?"
[The *work*] of silver Asherah doth espy,
>   The *work* of silver and [. . .] of gold.
Lady A[sherah] of the Sea rejoices;
>   Loudly unto her lad [she] doth [cry]:
"Look thou, Deft One, yea [give heed],   (30)
>   O fisherman of Lady Asher[ah of the Sea].
Take a net in thy hand,
>   A large [*seine*] *on thy two hands.*
[*Cast it*] into El's Beloved [Yamm][17]
>   Into the Sea of El Be[nign,
>   Into the De]ep of El . . . [. . .] . . . ."

(Only the beginnings of 37–47 preserved, and no connected sense
recoverable.)
>   (iii)
>   (about 12 lines missing, 9 lines defective)
C[ome]s Puissant Baal,   (10)
>   *Advances* the Rider of the Clouds.
Lo, he takes his stand and *cries defiance*,
>   He stands erect and spits
>   In the midst of the *as*[*sem*]*bly* of the divine beings:
"Ab[omination] has been placed upon my table,
>   Filth in the cup I drink.
For two [kinds of] banquets Baal hates,
>   Three the Rider of the Clouds:
A banquet of shamefulness,
>   A banquet {banquet} of baseness,   (20)
>   And a banquet of handmaids' *lewdness.*

---

[16] Because she fears the unexpected visitors bring bad news (cf. Ezek. 21:11–12).
This is the standard reaction of a female character to an unexpected visit.

[17] Yamm (= Sea) is apparently still El's Beloved, despite what he went through
above, in episode III AB A.

Yet herein is flagrant shamefulness,
> And herein is handmaids' *lewdness*."—

After this goes Puissant Baal,
> Also goes the Maiden Anath.

As they do homage to Lady Asherah of the Sea,
> Obeisance to the Progenitress of the Gods,
> Quoth Lady Asherah of the Sea:

"Why do ye homage to Lady Asherah of the Sea,
> Obeisance to the Progenitress of the Gods?   (30)

Have ye done homage to Bull El Benign,
> Or obeisance to the Creator of Creatures?"

Quoth the Maiden Anath:

"We do homage to [*th*]*ee*, Lady Asherah of the Sea,
> [Obei]sance to the Progenitress of the Gods. . . ."

(Rest of column badly damaged. It is clear that Asherah makes a feast for her visitors, and it may be inferred that they urge her to intercede for Baal with El, as she does in the next column.)

(iv–v)

(Some 10 lines missing; lines 1–2a too fragmentary to be restored.)

[Loudly unto her lad] Ashe[rah doth cry:

"Look thou, Qadesh wa-Amrur,
> Fisherman of Lady] Asherah of the Sea!

[Saddle a donkey],
> Harness a jackass.

[Attach trappings of] silver,   (10)
> [A housing] of gol[d],
> Put on the trappings of [thy] she-asses."

Qad[esh] wa-Amrur obeys.

He saddles a donkey,
> Harnesses a jackass.

He attaches trappings of silver,   (10)
> A *housing* of gold,
> Puts on the trappings of his she-asses.

Qadesh wa-Amrur embraces
> And places Asherah on the donkey's back,
> On the beautiful back of the jackass.

Qadesh proceeds to lead,
> Amrur is like a star in front;

The Maiden Anath follows,
> While Baal leaves for Zaphon's summit.—

There, she[18] is off on her way   (20)
> Towards El of the Sources of the Two Floods
> In the midst of the headwaters of the Two Oceans.

---

[18] Asherah.

She penetrates El's field and enters
    The pavilion of King Father Shunem.
At El's feet she bows and falls down,
    Prostrates her and does him reverence.
As soon as El espies her,
    He *parts his jaws* and laughs.
His feet upon the footstool he puts
    And doth twiddle his fingers.   (30)
He lifts up his voice and [cri]es:
"Why is come Lady Asher[ah of the S]ea?
    Why hither the Progenitress of the G[ods]?
Art thou become hungry and *fa*[*int*],
    Or art become thirsty and *pa*[*rched*]?
Eat, pray, yea drink.
Ea[t] thou from the tables bread;
    Drink from the flagons wine,
    From the golden gob⟨lets⟩ blood of vines.
See, El the King's love stirs thee,
    Bull's affection arouses thee."
Quoth Lady Asherah of the Sea: (40)
"Thy decree, O El, is wise:
    Wisdom with ever-life thy portion.
Thy decree is: our king's Puissant Baal,
    Our sovereign second to none;
All of us must bear his gi[ft],
    All of us [must b]ear his purse.[19]
[But alas!]
He cries unto Bull El his father,
    To [El] the King his begetter;
He cries unto *Asherah* and her children,
    Elath and the band of her kin[dred]:
Look, no house has Baal like the gods,   (50)
    Nor court like the children of Asherah.
The abode of El is the shelter of his son.
The abode of Lady Asherah of the Sea
    Is the abode of the perfect brides:
The abode of Padriya daughter of Ar,
    The shelter of Talliya daughter of Rabb,
    (And) the abode of Arsiya daughter of Ya'abdar."
Quoth the Kindly One El Ben[ign]:
"Am I a slave, an attendant of Asherah?
    Am I a slave, to handle . . . ?   (60)
Or is Asherah a handmaid, to make bricks?

---

[19] Must be tributary to him. But the translation is uncertain.

(v)

Let a house be built for Baal like the gods',
    And a court like the children of Asherah's!"
Quoth Lady Asherah of the Sea:
"Art great indeed, O El, and wise,
    Thy beard's gray hair instructs thee,
    ..., [...] to thy breast.
Now, too, the *seasons* of his rains will Baal *observe*,
    The *seasons* of ... with *snow*;
And ⟨he will⟩ peal his thunder in the clouds,   (70)
    Flashing his lightnings to the earth.
The house of cedar—*let him burn it*;
    Yea, the house of brick—*remove it.*
Be it told to Puissant Baal:
Summon *weeds* into thy house,
    Herbs into the midst of thy palace.[20]
The mountains shall bring thee much silver,
    The hills a treasure of gold;
    They'll bring thee *god's grandeur aplenty.*
So build thou a silver and gold house,   (80)
    A house of most pure lapis lazuli."
The Maiden Anath rejoices,
    Stamps with her foot so the earth *quakes.*
There, she is off on her way
    Unto Baal upon Zaphon's summit,
    O'er a thousand fields, ten thousand acres.
Laughing, the Maiden Anath
    Lifts up her voice and cries:
"Receive, Baal, the glad tidings I bring thee.
They will build thee a house like thy brethren's   (90)
    And a court like unto thy kindred's.
Summon *weeds* into thy house,
    Herbs into the midst of thy palace.
The mountains shall bring thee much silver,
    The hills a treasure of gold;
    They 'll bring thee *god's grandeur aplenty.*
So build thou a silver and gold house,
    A house of most pure lapis lazuli."
Puissant Baal rejoiced.
He summoned *weeds* into his house,
    Herbs into the midst of his palace.

---

[20] This seems—if the sense is correctly guessed—to imply that Baal had some sort of habitation before, but that it was not one worthy of a "ranking" god, such as Baal had become by vanquishing Yamm.

The mountains did bring him much silver,   (100)
    The hills a treasure of gold;
They brought him *god's grandeur aplenty.*
    Then he ⟨se⟩nt unto Kothar wa-Khasis.
(Direction to the reciter):
    Now turn to the account of the sending of the lads.[21]

After this comes Kothar wa-Khasis.
Before him an ox is set,
    A fatted one at his disposal.
A throne is placed and he's seated
    To the right of Puissant Baal.   (110)
So ate [the gods] and drank.
Then answered *Puiss[ant Baal,*
    Responded the Ri]d[er of the Clouds]:
"Quickly, a house, O K[othar],
    Quickly raise up a pal[ace].
Quickly the house shalt thou build,
    Quickly shalt raise up the pa[lace]
    In the midst of the fastness of Zaphon.
A thousand fields the house shall cover,
    A myriad of acres the palace."
Quoth Kothar wa-Khasis: (120)
"Hearken, O Puissant Baal:
    Give heed, O rider of the Clouds.
A window I'll make in the house,
    A casement within the palace."
But Puissant Baal replied:
"Make not a window in [the house],
    [A casement] within the pal[ace]."
                (2 or 3 lines missing?)
     (vi)
Quoth Ko[thar wa-Khas]is:
    "Thou'lt heed [my words], O Baal."
Again spake Ko[thar wa]-Khasis:
    "Hark, pray, Pu[is]sant Baal!
A wi[nd]ow I'll make in the house,
    A casement withi[n the pa]lace."
But Puissa[nt] Baal replied:
"Make not a w[ind]ow in the house,
    A casement with[in the pa]lace.

---

[21] No doubt refers to an earlier passage, lost to us, in which Baal dispatched Gapn and Ugar to Kothar. The reciter is directed simply to repeat that passage verbatim here.

Let not [Padriya] daughter of Ar [*be seen*]   (10)
    Or T[alliya] daughter of Rabb *be espied*
    By [. . .] El's Beloved Yamm!"
[. . .] *cried defiance*
    And spat [. . .].
Quoth Kothar [wa-Khasis]:
    "Thou'lt heed my words, O Baal."
[*As for Baal*] his house is built,
    [*As for Hadd*][22] his palace is raised.
They [. . .] from Lebanon and its trees,
    From [Siri]on its precious cedars.
. . . [. . . Le]banon and its trees,   (20)
    Si[r]ion its precious cedars.
Fire is set to the house,
    Flame to the palace.
Lo, a [d]ay and a second,
    Fire feeds on the house,
    Flame upon the palace:
A third, a fourth day,
    [Fi]re feeds on the house,
    Flam[e] upon the palace.
A fifth, a s[ix]th day,
    Fire feeds [on] the house,
    Flame u[pon] the palace.   (30)
There, on the seventh d[ay],
    The fire *dies down* in the house,
    The f[la]me in the palace.
The silver turns into blocks,
    The gold is turned into bricks.
Puissant Baal exults:
"My h⟨ouse⟩ have I builded of silver;
    My palace, indeed, of gold."
For (his) house preparations [Baa]l makes,
    [Prepa]rations makes Hadd for his palace.   (40)
He slaughters both neat [and] small cattle,
    Fells bulls [*together with*] fatlings;
    Rams (and) one-year-ol[d] calves;
    Lambs . . . k[i]ds.
He summons his brethren to his house,
    His ki[nd]red within his palace:
    Summons Asherah's seventy children.
He sates the he-lamb gods with w[ine],
    He sates the ewe-lamb goddesses [. . . ?]

---

[22] Another name of Baal.

He sates the bull-gods with w[ine],
　　He sates the cow-goddesses [. . . ?]
He sates the throne-gods with wi[ne],
　　He sates the chair-goddesses [. . . ?]
He sates the gods with jars of wine,
　　He sates the goddesses with pitchers.
So eat the gods and drink.
They sate them with fatness abundant,
　　With tender [fat]ling by bounteous knife;[23]   Isa. 60:16; 66:11
While drinking the [wine] from flag[ons,
　　From gold cups the blood of vines].
　　　　　　　　(some 9–10 lines missing)
　　(vii)
(The first 8 lines are very defective. El's Beloved Yamm—see above
vi 12—figures in lines 3–4. Since Baal's misgivings about a window
are thereupon dispelled—15ff.—perhaps Yamm is here given his
quietus.)

Sixty-six towns he took,
　　Seventy-seven hamlets;   (10)
Eighty (took) Baal of [Zaphon's] s[ummit],
　　Ninety Baal of the sum[mit.
Baal] dwells in his house,
　　Baal in the midst of the house.
Quoth Puissant Baal:
"I will make (one), Kothar, this day;
　　Kothar, this very hour.
A casement shall be opened in the house,
　　A window within the palace.
Yea, I'll open rifts in the clouds
　　At thy word, O Kothar wa-Khasis!"   (20)
Kothar wa-Khasis laughs,
　　He lifts up his voice and cries:
"Said I not to thee, Puissant Baal,
　　'Thou'lt heed my words, O Baal'?"—
He opens a casement in the house,
　　A window within the pa[lace].
　　Baal op[ens] rifts in [the cloud]s.
Ba[al gives] forth his holy voice,
　　Baal discharges the ut[terance of his li]ps.   (30)
His h[oly] voice [convulses] the earth, . . . the mountains quake,
　　A-tremble are . . .

---

[23] Literally: They were sated with sucking of breast; by milch knife, with fatling's
teat.

East and west, earth's high places reel.
Baal's enemies take to the woods,
      Hadd's foes to the sides of the mountain.
Quoth Puissant Baal:
"Baal's enemies, why do you quake?
      Why do you quake . . . ?"
Baal's eye seeks out for his hand   (40)
      When the yew-club swings in his right hand.
So Baal dwells in his house.
      "Nor king nor commoner
      The earth my dominion shall . . .
Tribute I'll send not to Divine Mot,[24]
      Not dispatch to El's Darling Ghazir.
Mot calls out in his soul,
      The Beloved thinks in his heart,
'I alone will have sway o'er the gods   (50)
      So that gods and men may feed,
      Who satisfies the multitudes of the earth.' "
Aloud unto [his l]ads Baal doth cry:
"Look ye, [Gapn and] Ugar so⟨ns⟩ of Ghulumat,
      ['*Amami*]s twain, sons of Zulumat
      [The stately, wing]-spreading, . . . ;
Winged ones twain, flock of clouds,
      ['Neath . . . ;
Birdlike ones twain, *flock* of . . . snow].
                        (some 5 lines missing)
      (viii)
There now, be off on your way
      Unto the Mount of Targhuzizza,
Unto the Mount of Tharumegi,
      Unto the Ridge of the Loam of the Earth.
Lift the mount on your hands,
      The elevation upon your palms,
And descend to the depth of the earth,
      Be of those who descend into earth.
There now, be off on your way   (10)
      Into his city *Pit*,
Low the throne that he sits on,
      Filth the land of his inheritance.
Yet beware, divine messengers.
      Approach not Divine Mot,
Lest he make you like a lamb in his mouth,
      Ye be crushed like a kid in his *gullet*.   (20)

---

[24] God of the rainless season and, apparently, of the nether world.

Even the Gods' Torch Shapsh,
> *Who wings over heaven's expanse,*
> Is in Mot El's Beloved's hand![25]
From a thousand fields, ten thousand acres,[26]
> To Mot's feet bow and fall down,
> Prostrate you and show him honor.
And say unto Divine Mot,   (30)
> Declare unto El's Darling Ghazir:
Message of Puissant Baal,
> Work of the Mighty Wa[rrior]:
'My house I have builded [of silver,
> My palace, indeed, of gold.]
. . .'"

(Ten lines of which only the ends are preserved, and approximately another 15 lines missing altogether.)
(Broken colophon in margin:)
[Written by Elimelech(?) Do]nated by Niqmadd, King of Ugarit.

f. V AB

(For the provisional assignment of V AB to this position in the epic and for a translation of the preserved portions of the text, see *ANET*, 135–38.)

g. I*AB

(i)

"
. . .
If thou smite Lotan, the serpent slant,   Ps. 74:14; Isa. 27:1
> Destroy the serpent tortuous,
> Shalyat (*šlyṭ*) of the seven heads,
. . ."

(two couplets very obscure)
From the *tomb* of the Godly Mot,
> *From* the pit of El's Belov'd Ghazir,
> The gods twain[27] depart, tarry not.
There, they are off on their way   (10)
> To Baal of the Summit of Zaphon.
Then Gapn and Ugar declare:
"Message of Godly Mot,
> Word of the God-Belov'd Ghazir:
> (even the gist of 14–27 still eludes savants)

[25] After Yamm, this is the next favorite-and-bully of El that Baal has to vanquish. That is logical: first the earth—Baal's domain—must be made safe from the encroachments of the sea, then from the blight of sterility.

[26] From a safe distance.

[27] Gapn and Ugar.

If thou smite Lotan, the serpent slant,
>Destroy the serpent tortuous,
>Shalyat of the seven heads,
>>. . ."

(Traces of the two obscure couplets mentioned above. Some
30 lines missing.)

(ii)

(12 lines missing at the top)
One lip to earth and one to heaven,[28]
>[He stretches his to]ngue to the stars.
Baal enters his mouth,
>Descends into him like an olive-cake,[29]
>Like the yield of the earth and trees' fruit.
Sore afraid is Puissant Baal,
>Filled with dread is the Rider of Clouds:
"Begone![30] Say unto Godly Mot,
>Repeat unto El's Belov'd Ghazir:
'Message of Puissant Baal,   (10)
>Word of the Powerful Hero:
Be gracious, O Godly Mot;
>Thy slave I, thy bondman for ever.'"—
The gods depart, tarry not.
There, they are off on their way
>Unto Godly Mot,
Into his city Hamriya,
>Down to the throne that [he] sits on
>His [filthy] land of inher'tance.
They lift up their voice and cry:
"Message of Puissant Son Baal,
>Word of the Powerful Hero:
Be gracious, O Godly Mot;
>Thy slave I, thy bondman for ever."—
The Godly Mot rejoices   (20)
>[And lifting] his [vo]ice he cries:
"How *humbled is* [. . .]."

(Several ends of lines, then about 20–25 lines missing. Cols. iii–iv
too damaged for connected sense.)

---

[28] Also occurs elsewhere in describing some ravenous creature opening its
mouth.

[29] Apparently a flat loaf of bread with olives, a common meal in ancient and modern times.

[30] Said by Baal to Gapn and Ugar. A quotation without an introduction.

(v)

(About 25 lines missing at the top. Then 1–5 defective.)

" . . .[31]

But thou, take thy cloud, thy wind,
 Thy . . . , thy rains;
With thee thy seven lads,
 Thine eight *boars*.
With thee Padriya, daughter of Ar;   (10)
 With thee Tatalliya (*Ṭṭly*), daughter of Rabb.
There now, be off on thy way
 Unto the Mount of Kankaniya.
Lift the mount upon thy hands,
 The elevation upon thy palms,
And descend to the depth of the earth,
 Be of those who descend into earth,
 And . . ."—
Puissant Baal complies.
He desires a cow-calf in Dubr,
 A heifer in Shihlmemat-field (*šd šḥlmmt*);
Lies with her times seventy-seven,   (20)
 [. . .] . . . times eighty-eight.
 She [conc]eives and gives birth to Math.
  (fragments of 3 more lines; another 11 missing)
 (vi)
   (about 30 lines missing at the top)
[They[32] penetrate El's Field and enter
 The pavilion of King El Father] Shunem.
[And lifting their voice they cr]y:
"We went [. . .],
 . . .
We [ca]me to the pleasance of Dabr-land,
 To the beauty of Shihlmemat-field.
We came upon Baal
 Fallen on the ground:
Puissant Baal is dead,
 The Prince, Lord of Earth, is perished."   (10)
Straightway Kindly El Benign
 Descends from the throne,
 Sits on the footstool,
From the footstool;
 And sits on the ground;

---

[31] Addressed (by Mot?) to Baal.
[32] Probably Gapn and Ugar.

Pours dust of mourning on his head,
>Earth of mortification on his pate;
>And puts on *sackcloth and loincloth*.
He *cuts a gash* with a stone,
>*Incisions* with . . .
He *gashes* his cheeks and his chin,
>He *harrows* the *roll* of his *arm*.   (20)
He plows his chest like a garden,
>*Harrows* his back like a plain.
He lifts up his voice and cries:
"Baal's dead!—What becomes of the people?
>Dagon's Son!—What of the masses?
>After Baal I'll descend into earth."
Anath also goes and wanders
>Every mount to the heart of the earth,
>Every hill to the earth's very bo[we]ls.
She comes to the pleasance of Dabr-[land],
>To the beauty of Shihlmemat-field.   (30)
She [comes] upon Baal
>Fal[len] on the ground:
>She puts on [*sackcloth*] *and loincloth*.

h. I AB

(Pertaining to "Baal.")
She *cuts a gash* with a stone,
>*Incisions* with . . . etc.

(See g, col. vi.)

Then weeps she her fill of weeping;

Ps. 42:3

>Deep she drinks tears, like wine.   (10)

Ps. 80:5   Loudly she calls
>Unto the Gods' Torch Shapsh.
"Lift Puissant Baal, I pray,
>Onto me."
Hearkening, Gods' Torch Shapsh
>Picks up Puissant Baal,
>Sets him on Anath's shoulder.
Up to Zaphon's *Fastness* she brings him,
>Bewails him and buries him too,
>Lays him in the hollows of the earth-ghosts.
She slaughters seventy buffaloes
>As tribute to Puissant Baal;
She slaughters seventy neat   (20)
>[As tr]ibute to Puissant Baal;
[She slaugh]ters seventy small cattle
>[As tribu]te to Puissant Baal;

[She slaugh]ters seventy deer
    [As tribute to] Puissant Baal;
[She slaughters] seventy mountain-goats
    [As tribute to Pu]issant Baal;
[She slaughters seventy ro]ebucks
    [As tribu]te to Puissant Baal.
. . .] . . . A[nath],   (30)
    [. . .] Yabama[t] Liimmim.—
[The]re, she is off on her way
    To [E]l of the Sources of the Floods,
    In the midst of [the Hea]dwaters of the Two Deeps.
She penetrates El's Field and enters
    The pavilion of King Father Shunem.
At El's feet she bows and falls down,
    Prostrates her and does him honor.
She lifts up her voice and cries:
"Now let Asherah rejoice and her sons,   (40)
    Elath and the band of her kinsmen;
For dead is Puissant Baal,
    Perished the Prince, Lord of Earth."[33]
Loudly El doth cry
    To Lady Asherah of the Sea:
"Hark, Lady A[sherah of the S]ea,
    Give one of thy s[ons] I'll make king."
Quoth Lady Asherah of the Sea:
    "Why, let's make Yadi' Yalhan (*yd' ylḥn*) king."
Answered Kindly One El Benign:
"Too weakly. He can't race with Baal,   (50)
    Throw jav'lin with Dagon's Son *Glory-Crown!*"
Replied Lady Asherah of the Sea:
    "Well, let's make it Ashtar the Tyrant;
    Let Ashtar the Tyrant be king."—
Straightway Ashtar the Tyrant
    Goes up to the *Fastness* of Zaphon
    (And) sits on Baal Puissant's throne.
(But) his feet reach not down to the footstool,
    Nor his head reaches up to the top.   (60)
So Ashtar the Tyrant declares:
    "I'll not reign in Zaphon's *Fastness!*"
Down goes Ashtar the Tyrant,
    Down from the throne of Baal Puissant,
    And reigns in El's Earth, all of it.   [. . .] . . .

---

[33] Now a son of Asherah can rule the earth. In col. v Asherah's sons are Baal's enemies. His epithet "Dagon's Son" may echo a stage of tradition in which he was not a
son of El, either.

(ii)

(some 30 lines missing on top)

[. . .]. A day, days go by,   (4)
    [And Anath the Lass] draws nigh him.
Like the heart of a c[ow] for her calf,
    Like the heart of a ew[e] for her lamb,
    So's the heart of Ana[th] for Baal.
She grabs Mot by the fold of his garment,
    Seizes [him] by the hem of his robe.   (10)
She lifts up her voice and [cries]:
    "Now, Mot! Deliver my brother."
Responds the Godly Mot:
    "What wouldst thou, O Maiden Anath?
I indeed have gone and have wander'd
    Every mount to the heart of the earth,
    Every hill to the earth's very bowels.
Lifebreath was wanting 'mong men,
    Lifebreath among earth's masses.
I came to the pleasance of Dabr-land,
    The beauty of Shihlmemat-field.   (20)
I did *masticate* Puissant Baal.
I made him like a lamb in my mouth;
    Like a kid in my gullet he's crushed.
Even the Gods' Torch Shapsh,
    Who wings over heaven's expanse,
    Is in Mot the Godly's hand."
A day, even days pass by,
    From days unto months.
    Then Anath the Lass draws nigh him.
Like the heart of a cow for her calf,
    Like the heart of a ewe for her lamb,
    So's the heart of Anath for Baal.   (30)
She seizes the Godly Mot—
    With sword she doth cleave him.
With fan she doth winnow him—
    With fire she doth burn him.[34]
With hand-mill she grinds him—
    In the field she doth sow him.
Birds eat his *remnants,*
    Consuming his *portions,*
    Flitting from remnant to remnant.[35]

[34] That is to say, the parts of him corresponding to chaff and straw.
[35] But somehow Mot comes to life entire in col. vi, and Baal even earlier.

(iii–iv)

"...[36]

(some 40 lines missing on top of col. iii)
[That Puissant Baal had died],
    That the Prince [Lord of Earth] had perished.
And behold, alive is [Puissant Baal]!
    And behold, existent the Prince, Lo[rd of Earth]!
In a dream, O Kindly El Benign,
    In a vision, Creator of Creatures,
The heavens fat did rain,
    The wadies flow with honey.
So I knew
That alive was Puissant Baal!
    Existent the Prince, Lord of Earth!
In a dream, Kindly El Benign,   (10)
    In a vision, Creator of Creatures,
The heavens fat did rain,
    The wadies flow with honey!"—
The Kindly One El Benign's glad.
    His feet on the footstool he sets,
    And parts his *jaws* and laughs.
He lifts up his voice and cries:
    "Now will I sit and rest
    And my soul be at ease in my breast.
For alive is Puissant Baal,   (20)
    Existent the Prince, Lord of Earth!"   (edge)
Loudly El doth cry
    Unto the Maiden Anath.
"Hearken, O Maiden Anath!
    Say to the Gods' Torch Shapsh:
    (iv)
'Parch'd is the furrow of Soil, O Shapsh;
    Parched is El's Soil's furrow:
    Baal neglects the furrow of his tillage.
Where is Puissant Baal?
    Where is the Prince, Lord of Earth?'"—
The Maiden Anath departs.   (30)
There, she is off on her way
    Unto the Gods' Torch Shapsh.
She lifts up her voice and cries:
"Message of Bull El thy father,
    Word of the Kindly, thy begetter:

---

[36] Who the speaker is is not known.

Parch'd is the furrow of Soil, O [Shapsh];
> Parched is El's Soil's furrow:
> Baal ne[glects] the furrow of his tillage.

Where is Puissant Baal?
> Where is the Prince, Lord of Earth?"—   (40)

Answer'd the Gods' Torch Sha[psh]:
". . . in the . . . [of thy brother],
> In the . . . of thy sibling,
> And I'll look for Puissant Baal."—

Quoth the Maiden Anath:
". . . . . . , O Shapsh;

> . . .

May . . . [. . .] guard thee,
> . . . [. . .]." (?)   (some 35 lines missing)
> (v)

Baal seizes the sons of Asherah.
> Rabbim[37] he strikes in the back.

Dokyamm he strikes with a bludgeon,
> . . . he fells to the earth.

Baal [mounts] his throne of kingship,
> [Dagon's Son] his seat of dominion.

[From] days to months, from months to years.
> Lo, after seven years,

The Godly Mot [. . .]
> Unto Puissant Baal.   (10)

He lifts up his voice and says:
"Upon thee . . . may I see,
> *Downfall* upon thee may I see.

Winnowing ⟨with fan
> Upon thee may I see.

Cleaving⟩ with sword
> Upon thee may I see.

Burning with fire
> Upon thee [may I see.

Gri]nding with hand-mill
> Up[on thee] may I s[ee

Siftin]g with *sieve*
> Upon thee [may I] see.

[. . .] . [. . .] in the soil
> Upon thee may I see.

Sowing on the sea
> [. . .] . . [. . .]."

---

[37] According to tablet f (V AB, between lines 30 and 40), Anath has already destroyed Rabbim once.

(Lines 20–28 defective and obscure. Some further 35 lines missing.)
    (vi)
Returning to Baal of Zaphon's *Fastness,*   (12)
    He lifts *up* his voice and cries:
"My brothers hast thou given, Baal, my . . . [s?];
    My mother's sons, my . . ."
They . . . like *camels:*
    Mot's firm, Baal's firm.
They gore like buffaloes:
    Mot's firm. Baal's firm.
They bite like snakes:
    Mot's firm. Baal's firm.   (20)
They *kick* like *chargers:*
    Mot falls. Baal falls.
Above Shapsh cries to Mot:
"Hearken, now, Godly Mot!
    Why striv'st thou with Puissant Baal? Why?
Should Bull El thy father hear thee,
    He'll pull out thy dwelling's *pillars.*
Overturn thy throne of kingship,
    Break thy staff of dominion!"
Sore afraid was Godly Mot,   (30)
    Filled with dread El's Belovèd Ghazir.
Mot . . .
    . . [. . . .]
Baal seats him [on] his kingdom's [throne],
    Upon his dominion's [seat].
        (36–42 missing, defective, or unintelligible)
          " . . .[38]
Thou'lt[39] eat the bread of honor,   (46)
    Thou'lt drink the wine of favor.
Shapsh *shall govern* the *gathered ones,*[40]
    Shapsh *shall govern* the divine ones.
. . . gods . . . mortals,
    . . . Kothar thy fellow,
    Even Khasis thine intimate."
On the sea of *monster* and dragon,   (50)
    Proceedeth Kothar wa-Khasis,
    Kothar wa-Khasis doth journey.[41]

---

[38] Apparently Baal is handing out rewards to his allies.
[39] Or, "she'll."
[40] The *rephaim,* or shades?
[41] Perhaps the quotation should be closed here.

(colophon)
Written by Elimelech the Shabnite.
Dictated by Attani-puruleni, Chief of Priests, Chief of
(Temple)-herdsmen.
Donated by Niqmadd, King of Ugarit, Master of Yargub, Lord of
Tharumeni.

Appendix. *IV AB + RŠ 319*

There exist a large (IV AB) and a very small piece (RŠ 319) of a tablet with three columns of writing on only one side. That they both belong to the same tablet is not certain but very probable. That only one side of the tablet is written on is probably due to the fact that it contained the whole of the composition in question, which was quite short. It has no colophon. It is distinct from the Baal epic which we have been following in the preceding pieces. RŠ 319, which is apparently the missing top right-hand corner of IV AB, contains a graphic account of sexual intercourse between Baal and Anath; and IV AB itself is suggestive of something more than platonic relations between the two. This is entirely at variance with the epic, as everyone will realize who has read the former.

(col. i too fragmentary for use)

(ii)

(some 20 lines missing on top?)

". . . Baal in his house,
    The God Hadd in the midst of his palace?"[42]
The lads of Baal make answer:
"Baal *is not* in his house,
    [The God] Hadd in the midst of his palace.
His bow he has ta'en in his hand,
    Also his *darts* in his right hand.
There he is off on his way
    To Shimak Canebrake,[43] the [buf]falo-*filled*."—
The Maiden Ana[th] lifts her wing,   (10)
    Lifts her wing and speeds in flight,
    To Shimak Canebrake, the [buf]falo-*filled.*—
Puissant Baal lifts up his eyes,
    Lifts up his eyes and beholds,
Beholds the Maiden Anath,
    Fairest *among* Baal's sisters.
Before her he rises, he stands,
    At her feet he kneels and falls down.
And he lifts up his voice and cries:
"Hail, sister, and . . . !   (20)

[42] The inquirer is evidently Anath.
[43] Semachonitis, the modern Lake Ḥûleh in Galilee?

The horns of thy . . . , O Maiden Anath,
 The horns of thy . . . Baal will anoint,
 Baal will *anoint* them in flight.
We'll thrust my foes into the earth,
 To the ground them that rise 'gainst thy brother!"—
The Maiden Anath lifts up her eyes,
 Lifts up her eyes and beholds,
Beholds a cow and proceeds a-walking,
 Proceeds a-walking and proceeds *a-dancing,*
 In the pleasant spots, in the lovely places.   (30)

(RŠ 319)

   (8 or 9 badly damaged lines at the bottom)
He seizes and holds [her] womb;
 [She] seizes and holds [his] stones.
Baal . . . *to an ox.*
[. . . the Mai]den Anath
 [. . .] to conceive and bear.
    (another 14 lines very fragmentary)

(IV AB iii)

[Calve]s the cows dr[op]:
 An ox for Maiden Anath
 And a heifer for Yahamat Liimmim.
Quoth Puissant [Baal]:
". . . that our progenitor is eternal,
 To all generations our begetter."
Baal scoops [his hands] full,
 ⌐The God⌐ Hadd [his] fin[gers] full.
. . . the mouth of Maiden An[ath],   (10)
 E'en the mouth of [his] fairest sister.
Baal goes up in the mou[ntain],
 Dagon's Son in the s[ky].
Baal sits upon [his th]rone,
 Dagon's Son upon [his se]at.

 (In lines 16–29, which are poorly preserved, there is again talk of a buffalo being born to Baal, it being still not absolutely clear that his bovine mother was Anath herself.)

And so she goes up to Arar,   (30)
 Up to Arar and Zaphon.
In the pleasance, the Mount of Possession,
 She cries aloud to Baal:
"Receive, Baal, godly tidings,
 Yea receive, O Son of Dagon:

A wild-ox is [born] to Baal,
>A buffalo to Rider of Clouds."
Puissant Baal rejoices.

ANET, 149–55

The Tale of Aqhat

The rich epigraphic harvests of the French excavations of 1930 and 1931 at the site of ancient Ugarit included large portions of three tablets, and a possible fragment of a fourth, belonging to an epic about a youth whose name is spelled *a-q-h-t* and conventionally vocalized *Aqhat.* The text was at first *Fig. 68* called the Epic of Daniel, or Danel, for Aqhat's father; but on the one tablet of which the first line, containing the title of the composition to which the tablet belongs, is preserved, it reads "Pertaining to ʿAqhat,'" and closer study reveals that the text really tells about Daniel only what concerns Aqhat.

AQHT A

(i)

(about 10 lines missing at top)

II Sam. 21:16, 18, 20, 22; Gen. 14:5; Deut. 2:11, 20; 3:11, 13

[. . . Straightway Daniel[44] the Raph]a[45]-man, (1)
>Forthwith [Ghazir[46] the Harnamiyy[47]-man],
Gives oblation to the gods to eat,
>Gives oblation to drink to the holy ones.
A couch of sackcloth he mounts and lies,
>*A couch of* [loincloth] and ⌜passes the night⌝.
Behold a day and a second,
>Oblation to the gods gives Daniel,
Oblation to the gods to eat,
>Oblation to drink to the holy ones.
A third, a fourth day,
>Oblation to the gods gives Daniel, (10)
Oblation to the gods to eat,
>Oblation to drink to the holy ones.
A fifth, a sixth, a seventh day,
>Oblation to the gods gives Daniel,
Oblation to the gods to eat,
>Oblation to drink to the holy ones.
A *sackcloth couch* doth Daniel,

[44] The name means "God judges." Judging the cause of the widow and the fatherless is Daniel's special concern; see v 4–8 etc. His wife's name, Danatiya (v 16, 22), is from the same root.

[45] This Rapha is perhaps identical with the aboriginal giant race of Canaan.

[46] As a common noun, *gzr* means "boy."

[47] Perhaps connected with *Hrnm,* a Syrian locality named in an early Egyptian source (Harnaim).

A *sackcloth couch* mount and lie,
    A couch of loincloth and pass the night.
But lo, on the seventh day,
    Baal approaches with his plea:
"Unhappy is Daniel the Rapha-man,
    A-sighing is Ghazir the Harnamiyy-man;
Who hath no son like his brethren,   (20)
    Nor scion hath like his kindred.
Surely there's a son for him ⌐like⌐ his brethren's,
    And a scion like unto his kindred's!
He gives oblation to the gods to eat,
    Oblation to drink to the holy ones.
Wilt thou not bless him, O Bull El, my father,
    Beatify him, O Creator of Creatures?
So shall there be a son in his house,
    A scion in the midst of his palace:
Who sets up the stelae of his ancestral spirits,
    In the holy place the protectors of his clan;
Who frees his spirit from the earth,
    From the dust guards his footsteps;
Who smothers the life-force of his detractor,   (30)
    Drives off who attacks his abode;
Who takes him by the hand when he's drunk,
    Carries him when he's sated with wine;   Isa. 51:17–18
Consumes his funerary offering in Baal's house,
    (Even) his *portion in* El's house;
Who plasters his roof when it leaks,
    Washes his clothes when they're soiled."—
[*By the hand*] El takes his servant,
    Blessing Daniel the Rapha-man,
    Beatifying Ghazir the Harnamiyy-man:
"With life-breath shall be quickened Daniel the Rapha-man,
    With spirit Ghazir the Harnamiyy-man.
[*With life-breath*] he is *invigorated*.[48]
    Let him mount his bed [. . .].   (40)
In the kissing of his wife [she'll conceive],
    In her embracing become pregnant.
[By conception] (and) pregnancy she'll bear
    [A man-child to Daniel the Ra]pha-[man].
So shall there be a son [in his house,
    A scion] in the midst of his palace:
[Who sets up the stelae of his ances]tral spirits,
    In the holy place [the protectors of his clan];

---

[48] This does not imply that Daniel's vigor was previously below average.

Who frees [his spirit from the e]arth,
> [From the dust gu]ards his footsteps;
[Who smothers the life-force of his detractor],
> Drives off who attacks [his abode;
Etc.]"

(After line 48 some 10 lines are missing, but the first 4 of these were obviously identical with lines 31–34 above. After that it was related that somebody was instructed to tell the good news to Daniel.)

(ii)

(Another 10 lines, approximately, missing here. The messenger obeyed instructions and addressed Daniel as follows:

". . . A son shall be borne thee like thy brethren's,
> A scion like unto thy kindred's:
Who sets up the stelae of thine ancestral spirits,
> In the holy place)
> > the pro[tectors of thy clan;
Who frees thy spirit from the earth],   (1)
> From the dust etc., etc."   (2–8c)
> > (see above, i 25ff.)

Daniel's face lights up,   (8d)
> While above his forehead shines.
He *parts his jaws* and laughs,   (10)
> Places his foot on the footstool,
> And lifts up his voice and cries:
Now will I sit and rest
> And my soul be at ease in my breast.
For a son's born to me like my brethren's
> A scion like unto my kindred's
Etc., etc.
Daniel goes to his house,
> To his palace Daniel betakes him.   (25)
Into his house come skillful ones,[49]
> Daughters of joyful noise, *swallows*.
Straightway Daniel the Rapha-man,
> Forthwith Ghazir the Harnamiyy-man,
Prepares an ox for the skillful ones,   (30)
> Gives food to the [ski]llful ones and gives drink
> To the daughters of joy[ful noise], the *swallows*.
Behold a day and a second,
> He give[s f]ood to the skillful ones and dr[in]k
> To the daughters of joyful noise, the *swallows*;

---

[49] "Artistes."

A third, a fo[urth] day,
>He gives food to the skillful ones and drink
>To the daughters of joyful noise, the *swallows;*

A fifth, a sixth day,
>He gives food to the skill[ful] ones and d[rink
>To the d]aughters of joyful noise, the *swallows.*

Lo, on the seventh day,
>Away from his house go the skillful ones,   (40)
>The daughters of joyful noise, the *swallows.*—

[. . .] the fairness of the bed [*of conception*],
>The beauty of the bed of *childbirth.*

Daniel sits [and cou]nts her months.
A month follows a month;
>A third, a fou[rth (a fifth?) month.

But in the fifth (sixth?)] month,
>He goes [*to the shrine of* . . .].

>(ten lines of col. ii and all of cols. iii–iv missing)

>(v)

(Some 13 lines missing at the top. The preserved portion begins in the middle of a speech of the craftsman-god addressed to Daniel:)

". . . (abraded except for traces)   (1)

I myself will bring the bow,
>*Even I* will convey the *darts.*"

And behold, on the seventh day—
Straightway Daniel the Rapha-man,
>Forthwith Ghazir the Harnam[iyy]-man,

Is upright, sitting before the gate,
>Beneath *a mighty tree* on the threshing floor,

Judging the cause of the widow,
>Adjudicating the case of the fatherless.

Lifting up his eyes, he beholds:
>From a thousand fields, ten thousand acres,[50]   (10)

The march of Kothar[51] he espies,
>He espies the onrush of Khasis,[52]

See, he bringeth a bow;
>Lo, he conveyeth *darts.*

Straightway Daniel the Rapha-man,
>Forthwith Daniel the Harnamiyy-man,

Loudly unto his wife doth call:
"Hearken, Lady Danatiya,
>Prepare a lamb from the flock

---

[50] I.e., in the distance.
[51] "Skillful," a common name of the craftsman-god.
[52] "Clever," another of his names.

For the desire of Ko[th]ar wa-Khasis,[53]
    For the appetite of Hayyin[54] of the Handicrafts.
Give food, give drink to the godhead;   (20)
    Serve, honor him,
    The Lord of Hikpat-El,[55] all of it."
Lady Danatiya obeys,
    She prepares a lamb from the flock
For the desire of Kothar wa-Khasis,
    For the appetite of Hayyin of the Handicrafts.
Afterwards, Kothar wa-Khasis comes.
The bow he delivers into Daniel's hand;
    The *darts* he places upon his knees.
Straightway Lady Danatiya
    Gives food, gives drink to the godhead;
She serves, honors him,   (30)
    The Lord of Hikpat-El, all of it.
Kothar departs for[56] his tent,
    Hayyin departs for[56] his tabernacle.
Straightway Daniel the Rapha-man,
    Forthwith Ghazir the Harnamiyy-man,
The bow doth [...] ... , upon Aqhat he doth ...
    [...]:
"*The choicest* of thy game, O my son,
    The choicest of thy game ... [...],
    The game of thy ... [...]."[57]
                (some 12 lines missing)
    (vi)

(Some 19 lines missing. Then come 15 broken lines which tell about a feast and about the warrior-goddess Anath coveting Aqhat's bow: Aqhat will have been entertaining her tête-à-tête.)

[She lifts up her voice and] cries: (16)
    "Hearken, I pray thee, [Aqhat the Youth!
A]sk for silver, and I'll give it thee;
    [For gold, and I'll be]stow't on thee;
But give thou thy bow [to me;
    Let] Yabamat-Liimmim[58] *take* thy *darts*."
But Aqhat the Youth answers: (20)

---

[53] "Skillful and Clever."

[54] "Deft."

[55] *Hkpt il,* the name of the craftsman-god's "estate."

[56] Or "from," if Daniel's tent is meant rather than Kothar's.

[57] Perhaps Daniel here impresses upon his son the duty of offering some of his game to the gods.

[58] Alternative designation of the Maiden Anath.

"*I vow yew trees* of Lebanon,
    I vow sinews from wild oxen;
I vow horns from mountain goats,
    Tendons from the hocks of a bull;
I vow from a *cane-forest* reeds:
    Give (these) to Kothar wa-Khasis.
He'll make a bow for thee,
    Darts for Yabamat-Liimmim."[59]
Then quoth the Maiden Anath:
"Ask for life, O Aqhat the Youth.
Ask for life and I'll give it thee,
    For deathlessness, and I'll bestow't on thee.
I'll make thee count years with Baal,
    With the sons of El shalt thou count months.[60]
And Baal when he gives life gives a feast,   (30)
    Gives a feast to the life-given and bids him drink;
Sings and chants over him,
    Sweetly serenad[es] him:
So give I life to Aqhat the Youth."
But Aqhat the Youth answers:
"Fib not to me, O Maiden;
    For to a Youth thy fibbing is *loathsome.*
Further life—how can mortal attain it?
    How can mortal attain life enduring?
Glaze will be poured [on] my head,
    Plaster upon my pate;[61]
And I'll die as everyone dies,
    I too shall assuredly die.
Moreover, this will I say:
My bow is [*a weapon for*] warriors.   (40)
    Shall now females [*with it*] to the chase?"
—[Loud]ly Anath doth laugh,
    While forging [a plot] in her heart:
"Give heed *to* me, Aqhat the Youth,
    Give heed to me for thine own good.
[. . .] I'll meet thee in the path of arrogance,
    [Encounter thee] in the path of presumption,
Hurl thee down at [my feet *and trample*] thee,
    My darling great big he-man!"—
[She *stamps* with her fe]et and *traverses* the earth.

---

[59] Yew-wood, horn, sinew, and tendon go into the making of a composite bow; reed into that of arrows.

[60] I.e., shalt be immortal like them.

[61] My hair will turn white.

There, [she is off on her w]ay
>Towards El of the Source of the Floods
>[In the midst of the headwaters] of the Two Oceans.
She penetrates El's field [and enters
>The pavili]on of King Father Shunem.[62]
[At El's feet she] bows and falls down,   (50)
>Prostr[ates herself, doing him rever]ence.
She denounces Aqhat the Youth,
>[Damns the child of Dani]el the Rapha-man.
Quoth [the Maiden Anath,
>Lifting up] her [voice] and crying:

(In 54–55 only the word "Aqhat" can be made out. A further 10 lines or so are missing. In them Anath may well have told a cock-and-bull story about the unaccommodating youth. In any case, El declared he could, or would, do nothing against Aqhat.)

(colophon on edge of tablet)

[Dictated by Attani]-puruleni.[63]

AQHT B

(The preserved fragment of this four-column tablet bears the top of col. i on the obverse and the bottom of col. iv on the reverse, the surface of the obverse being largely abraded.)

(i)

[. . . But the Maiden Anath] [replied]:
"[. . .], O El!
>[. . . rejoice not.
Re]joice not [. . . ,
>Exult] not [. . . .   (10)
With] the *might* [of my] *lon*[*g hand,*
>I'll verily smash] thy [pa]te,
Make [thy gray hair] flow [with blood,
>The gray hair of] thy [beard] with gore.
And [call] Aqhat and let him save thee,
>The son [of Daniel] and let him deliver thee,
>From the hand of the Maiden [Anath]!"—
Answered the Kindly One El Be[nign]:
"I ween'd, daughter mine, thou wast *gentle,*
>And goddesses fr[ee from] *contumely.*
On, then, *perverse* daughter;
>[Thou'lt ta]ke whatsoever thou wilt.

---

[62] One of El's names.

[63] Known from the colophon at the end of the Baal epic to have been chief of priests in the reign of Niqmadd, king of Ugarit, second quarter of the 14th century B.C.

Thou'lt compass [whatever thou] list:
>   Who hinders thee will be crushed."—
[The Maid]en Anath [rejoices].   (20)
There, she is off [on her way
>   Towards A]qhat the Youth,
>   O'er thousand fi[elds, ten thousand a]cres.
Now laughs the Maiden [Anath,
>   And lifts up] her voice and cries:
"Oh, hearken bu[t, Aqhat the Youth],
>   Thou'rt my brother, and I [*thy sister*]. . . ."

(Lines 25–35 too damaged to yield anything but the probable general sense that Anath offers to show Aqhat a particularly good place to hunt in, namely, the environs of the home-town of Yatpan [*yṭpn*], on whom see further on. Probably in the additional 20 lines of this column and in the whole of cols. ii–iii, which are missing altogether, the twain betook them thither; Aqhat had good luck, and Anath left him for a while.)

>   (iv)
>   (some 20 lines missing, 4 lines fragmentary)
The Maiden Anath [depar]ts.   (5)
[There, she is off on her way]
>   Towards Yatpan [*the Drunken*] *Soldier*.
[She lifts up her voice] and cries:

(The sense of her imperfectly preserved utterance has not yet been determined, except that it shows that Yatpan dwelt in "the city of Abelim, Abelim the city of Prince Yarikh [= Moon].")

Quoth Yatpan [*the Drunken Soldier*]:   (11)
>   "Hearken, O Maiden Anath.
Wouldst thou slay him[64] fo[r his bow],
>   Slay him for his *darts*,
>   Him ma[ke live again]?
The darling Youth has set meat and [*drink*].
>   He is left in the fields and . . . [. . .]."
Quoth the Maiden Anath:
>   "Give heed, Yatp,[65] and [I'll tell] thee.
I'll make thee like a vulture in my girdle,
>   Like a swift flier in my pouch.
[As] Aqhat [sits] to eat,
>   The son of Daniel to [dine],
[Over him] vultures will soar,   (20)
>   [A flock of sw]ift fliers will *coast*.

[64] Aqhat.
[65] Hypocoristicon of, or mistake for, Yatpan.

'Mong the vultures will I be soaring;
    Above Aqhat will I pose thee.
Strike him twice on the crown,
    Thrice above the ear;
Pour out his blood like *sap*,
    Like *juice* to his knees.
Let his breath escape like wind,
    His soul like vapor,
    Like smoke from his nostrils {from nostrils}.
⌜His vigor⌝ I will revive."
—She takes Yatpan *the Drunken Soldier*,
    Makes him like a vulture in her girdle,
    Like a swift flier in her pouch.
As Aqhat sits to e[at],
    The son of Daniel to dine, (30)
Over him vulture[s] soar,
    A flock of swift flier[s] coasts.
[Among] the vultures soars Anath;
    Above [Aqhat] she poses him.
He smites him twice [on the crown],
    Thrice above the ear;
Pou[rs out] his blood [like] *sap*,
    Like *ju[ice* to his knees.
His] breath escapes like wind,
    His soul [like vapor],
    Like smoke [from his nostrils].
Anath, [seeing] his vigor extinguished—
    [The vigor of] Aqhat—doth weep.
"*Woe!* [Would] I could heal [thy corse]! (40)
'Twas but for [thy bow I slew thee,
    'Twas but for] thy *darts*.
    But thou, would thou didst l[ive.
. . .] and perished . . . [. . .]."

AQHT C

(i)

(In the first 13 lines, defective in various degrees, it is only clear that Anath figures there. She is apparently speaking; it is not known to whom.)
    " . . .
I smote him *but* for his bow,
    I smote him for his *darts*.
    So his bow has been given to me.
But *through his death* . . . ,
    The [*fr*]uits of summer *are withered*,
    The ear [in] its husk."—

Straightway Daniel the Rapha-man, (20)
    Forthwith Gha*zir* [the Harna]miyy-[man],
*Is up*right, [sitting before the g]at[e,
    Un]der [a mighty tree on the threshing floor,
Judging] the cause [of the widow,
    Adjudicating] the case [of the fatherless.
   ...]   (lines 25–28 almost entirely missing)
[Lift]ing her eyes she[66] beholds:
[...] on the threshing floors *dries up*; (30)
    [...] *droops*;
    Blasted are the buds [...].
O'er her father's house vultures are soaring
    A flock of swift fliers is coasting.
Paghat weeps in her heart,
    Cries in her inward parts.
She rends the garment of Daniel the Rapha-man,
    The vest⟨ment⟩ of Ghazir the Harnamiyy-man.[67]
Straightway Daniel the Rapha-man,
... s a cloud in the heat of the *season*; (40)
    ... s a cloud raining upon the figs,
    Dew distilling upon the grapes.[68]
"Seven years shall Baal fail,
    Eight the Rider of the Clouds.
No dew,   II Sam. 1:21
    No rain;
No welling-up of the deep,[69]   Gen. 7:11
    No sweetness of Baal's voice.[70]
For rent
Is the garment of Daniel the Rapha-man,
    The vestment of Ghazir [the Harnamiyy-man]."—
Loudly to h[is] daughter he doth cry:
    (ii)
"Hearken, Paghat who observes the wat[er], (50)
    Who studies the dew from the drip,
    Who knows the course of the stars.[71]
Saddle a donkey, harness a jackass.
    Attach my trappings of silver,
    My golden housing."—

[66] Daniel's daughter Paghat.

[67] Because she realizes the blight upon the land must be due to the murder of some innocent person. She has the gift of divination; see below.

[68] In Syria rain sometimes falls in September.

[69] Through springs; what Daniel here either predicts or wishes, David wishes for Gilboa, the scene of Saul and Jonathan's death in battle.

[70] Baal is the god of rain and thunder.

[71] Apparently forms of weather-wisdom bordering on divination.

She obeys, Paghat who observes the water,
>Who studies the ⌜dew [from the drip]⌝,
>Who knows the course of the stars. ⌜ . . . ⌝
See, she saddles a donkey;
>See, she harnesses a ja⌜ck⌝ass.
See, she lifts up her father,
>Places him on the donkey's back,
>On the comely back of the jackass.— (60)
Yadinel[72] turns to the *vegetable-patch*;
>He sees a *stalk* in the *vegetable-patch*;
Seeing a *stalk* in the *seedbeds*,
>H[e embraces] the *stalk* and kisses it:
"Ah, if it may be, *stalk*,
>Let the *stalk* grow in the *vegetable-patch*;
>Let it grow in the *beds* of the *plants*.
May the hand of Aqhat the Youth gather thee,
>Deposit thee in the granary."—
Yadin⌜e⌝ ⟨l⟩ turns to the *grainfields*;
>In the *grainfi[el]ds* he sees a corn-ear;
Seeing an ear in the unwatered land, (70)
>He em[braces] the ear and kisses it:
"Ah, if it may be, co[rn-ear],
>Let the corn-ear grow in the unwatered land;
>Let it grow in the [*beds*] of the *plants*.
May the hand of Aqhat the You[th] gather thee,
>Deposit thee in the granary."—
Scarce hath the word left his mouth,
>His speech left his lips,
When he lifts up his eyes and they behold:[73]

(Lines 77–89 rather mutilated and obscure. The gist of them is that somebody finds out what has happened to Aqhat; either because Paghat sees two supernatural beings act it out in dumb show, or because two attendants of Daniel hear the tale from the dying boy.)

[. . .] they come.
They lift up [their] voice, [and cry]:
"Hearken, O Daniel the [Rapha]-man! (90)
>Aqhat the Youth is dead.
The Maiden Anath [has caused
>His breath to escape] like [wind],
>His soul like vapor."

---

[72] Apparently variant of "Daniel."

[73] Or "as she (Paghat) lifts up her eyes, she beholds."

[Daniel's legs] tremble.
>Abo[ve, his face sweats;
>Behind, he is broken] in the loins.
[The joints of his loins are bent],
>*Weakened* [those of his back.[74]
He lifts up his voice] and cri[es:
"*Cursed be*] the slayer [of my son].
>>(lines 100–104 missing)
Lift[ing up his eyes he beholds:
>... vultures ....
>(iii)
He lifts up his voice] and cries: (107)
"The vultures' wings may Baal bre⟨ak⟩,
>May Ba[a]l br[eak the pinions of them].
Let them fall down at my feet.
>I'll spl[it their bellies and] gaze. (110)
An there be fat,
>An the[re be] bone,
I'll w⌜ee⌝p and inter it,
>Lay't in the hollows of the ear⌜th⌝-ghosts."
Scarce hath the word left his mouth,
>[His] speech left his lips,
The vultures' wings Baal doth break,
>Baal doth break the pinions of them.
They do fall down at his feet,
>He splits their bellies a[nd gazes]:
No fat is there,
>No bone.
He lifts up his voice and cr*ies*:
"The vultures' wings may Baa*l* mend,
>May ⟨Baal⟩ mend the pinions of them.
>Vultures, flutter and fly." (120)
Lifting his eyes, he s[ees];
>Beholds Hargab, the *vul*tures' father.
He lifts up his voice and cries:
>"The *wi*ngs of Har[ga]b may Baal bre⟨ak⟩,
>May Baal b[re]ak the pinions of [him].
And let him fall down at my feet.
>I'll split [his] b[elly] and gaze.
An there be fat,
>An there be [bone],
I'll weep and inter it,
>Lay't in the *ho*[llo]*ws* of [the earth-ghosts]."

[74] He is overcome with dismay.

[Scarce hath the word left his mouth],
> *His speech* [left] his [li]ps,
Hargab's wings Baal doth [br]eak,
> Baal doth break the pinions of him.
He doth fall down at his feet.   (130)
> So he splits his belly and gazes:
No fat is there,
> No bone.
He lifts up [his] voice *and* cries:
"The wings of Hargab may Baal [mend,
> May Ba]al mend the pinions of him.
> Hargab, may'st flutter and fly."—
Lifting his eyes he sees,
> Beholds Samal (*ṣml*), the vultures' mother.
He lifts up his voice and cries:
"The wings of Samal may Baal break,
> May Baal break the [pi]nions of her.
Let her fall down at my feet.
> I'll split her belly and gaze.
An there be fat,
> An there be bone,   (140)
I'll weep and inter it,
> Lay't in the hollows of the earth-ghosts."
Scarce hath the word [left] his mouth,
> His speech left his lips,
Samal's wings [Ba]a[l doth break],
> Baal doth break the pinions of her.
She doth fa[ll down at] his feet.
> So he splits her belly and gazes.
There is fat,
> There is bone.
Taking them for Aqhat he ⟨*we*⟩*eps,*
> Weeps and inters him.
He inters him in . . . , in . . . ,
> Then lifts up his voice and cries:
"The wings of the vultures may Baal break,
> May Baal break the pinions of them,   (150)
An they fly over the grave of my son,
> Rousing him from his sleep."—
Qiru-mayim[75] the king doth *curse:*
> "Woe to thee, O Qiru-mayim,
O[n] which rests the blood-guilt of Aqhat the Youth!
> . . . the dwellers of the house of El;

---

[75] Perhaps "Water-Sources." In any case a locality near the scene of the murder.

Now, *tomorrow*, and for evermore,
    From now unto all generations!"
Again he waves the staff of his hand,
    And comes to Marurat-taghullal-banir.[76]
He lifts up his voice and cries:
"Woe to thee, Marurat-taghullal-banir,
    On which rests the blood-guilt of Aqhat the Youth!
Thy root grow not in the earth;
    In uprooter's hand droop thy head—   (160)
Now, *tomorrow,* and for evermore,
    From now unto all generations!"
Again he waves the staff of his hand,
    (iv)
    And comes to the city of Abelim,
    Abelim the city of Prince Yarikh.[77]
He lifts up his voice and cries:
"Woe to thee, city of Abelim,
    On which rests the blood-guilt of Aqhat the Youth!
May Baal make thee blind
    From now for evermore,
    From now unto all generations!"
Again he waves the staff of his hand.
    Daniel goes to his house,   (170)
    To his palace Daniel betakes him.
Into his palace come weeping-women,
    Wailing-women into his court *Pzǵm ǵr*.[78]
He weeps for Aqhat the Youth,
    Cries for the child, does Daniel the Rapha-man.
From days to months, from months to years,
    Until seven years,
He weeps for Aqhat the Youth,
    Cr[ie]s for the child, does Daniel the [Rapha]-man.
But after seven years,   (180)
    [Daniel] the Rapha-[man] speaks up,
    Ghazir [the Harnamiyy-m]an makes answer.
[He] lifts up his voice and cries:
"De[part], weeping-women, from my pala[ce];
    Wailing-women, from my court *Pzǵm ǵr*."—
He ta[kes] a sacrifice for the gods,
    Offers up a *clan-offering* to heaven,
    The *clan-offering* of Harnamiyy to the stars.
          (three and one-half lines mutilated)

---

[76] Perhaps "Blessed One Harnessed with a Yoke,"

[77] The actual home of the murderer; see B i end and B iv.

[78] It has been suggested that this is the proper name of Daniel's court.

Quoth Paghat who observes the *flowing* water: (190)
"Father has sacrificed to the gods,
    Has offered up a *clan-offering* to heaven,
    The *clan-offering* of Harnamiyy to the stars.
Do thou bless me, so I'll go blessed;
    Beatify me, so I'll go beatified.
I'll slay the slayer of my brother,
    [Destroy] the [de]stroyer of my [si]bling."—
[Dani]e[l] the Ra[p]ha-man makes answer:
"With life-breath shall be quickened [Paghat],
    She who observes the water,
Who studies the dew from the drip,   (200)
    Who knows the courses of the stars.
With life-breath she is *invigorated.*
She'll slay the slayer [of her brother],
    Destroy the destroyer of [her] sibling."
. . . in the sea she bat[hes],
    And stains herself red with murex,
She emerges, dons a youth's raiment,
    Puts a k[*nife*] in her sheath,
A sword she puts in her scabbard,
    And o'er all dons woman's garb.
At the rising of Gods' Torch Shapsh,[79]
    Paghat . . .   (210)
At the set[ting] of Gods' Torch Shapsh,
    Paghat arriv[es] at the tents.
Word [is b]rought to Yat[pan]:
"*Our hired woman* has entered thy fields,
    [. . .] has entered the t⟨e⟩nts."
And Yatpan *the Drunken Soldier* makes answer:
    "Take her and let her give me wine to drink.
[Let her place] the cup in my hand,
    The goblet in my right hand."
Paghat [t]akes and gives him drink:
    Pl[aces the cup] in his hand,
    The goblet in his right hand.
Then spake Yat[pa]n *the Drunken [Sold]ier*:
    (one and one-half lines partly defective and obscure)
"The hand that slew [Aqha]t the Youth   (220b)
    Can slay thousands of foes."

(Two and one-half lines obscure, except that Paghat's "heart is like
a serpent's," i.e., filled with fury.)

[79] The sun-goddess.

A second time she gives the mixture to him to drink,

    Gives the [mi]xt[ure] to drink   (224)

(Direction to the reciter, along the edge to the left of 172–86:) Here one proceeds to tell about the daughter.

(The story, continuing on one or more missing tablets, no doubt went on to relate that [a] Paghat killed Yatpan while he lay unconscious in the arms of Bacchus, and [b] between El's pity and Anath's remorse some modus was found for restoring Aqhat to his father, perhaps only for half—the fertile half—of the year. The familiar Adonis-Tammuz theme.)

V

Legal Texts

Collections of Laws from Mesopotamia

ANET, 161–63 The Laws of Eshnunna

TRANSLATOR: ALBRECHT GOETZE

Texts: Iraq Museum 51059 and 52614 excavated at Tell Abu Harmal[1] near Baghdad by the Iraq Directorate of Antiquities in Pre-Hammurabi layers.

1: 1 kor of barley is (priced) at 1 shekel of silver; 3 *qa* of "best oil" are (priced) at 1 shekel of silver; 1 seah (and) 2 *qa* of sesame oil are (priced) at 1 shekel of silver; 1 seah (and) 5 *qa* of lard are (priced) at 1 shekel of silver; 4 seah of "river oil" are (priced) at 1 shekel of silver; 6 minas of wool are (priced) at 1 shekel of silver; 2 kor of salt are (priced) at 1 shekel of silver; 1 kor . . . is (priced) at 1 shekel of silver; 3 minas of copper are (priced) at 1 shekel of silver; 2 minas of refined copper are (priced) at 1 shekel of silver.

2: 1 *qa* of sesame oil *ša nišḫātim*—its (value in) barley is 3 seah; 1 *qa* of lard *ša nišḫātim*—its (value in) barley is 2 seah and 5 *qa*; 1 *qa* of "river oil" *ša nišḫātim*—its (value in) barley is 8 *qa*.

3: The hire for a wagon together with its oxen and its driver is 1 pan (and) 4 seah of barley. If it is (paid in) silver, the hire is one third of a shekel. He shall drive it the whole day.

---

[1] Abu Harmal formed part of the kingdom of Eshnunna—the Diyala region east of Baghdad—which flourished between the downfall of the Third Dynasty of Ur (about 2000 B.C.) and the creation of Hammurabi's empire. Eshnunna was one of the numerous Amurrite-controlled states of the period. The city of Eshnunna itself is located at Tell Asmar, which was excavated by the Oriental Institute of the University of Chicago.

4: The hire for a boat is 2 *qa* per kor (of capacity), 1 seah 1 *qa* is the hire for the boatman. He shall drive it the whole day.

5: If the boatman is negligent and causes the sinking of the boat, he shall pay in full for everything the sinking of which he caused.

6: If a man . . .[2] takes possession of a boat (which is) not his, he shall pay 10 shekels of silver.

7: The wages of a harvester are 2 seah of barley; if they are (paid in) silver, his wages are 12 grain.

8: The wages of winnowers are 1 seah of barley.

9: Should a man pay 1 shekel of silver to a hired man for harvesting—if he (the hired man) does not place himself at his disposal and does not complete for him the harvest work everywhere, he [shall p]ay 10 shekels of silver. Should he have received 1 seah (and) 5 *qa* (of barley) as wages and leave the rations of [barley], oil (and) cloth shall also be refunded.

10: The hire for a donkey is 1 seah of barley, and the wages for its driver are 1 seah of barley. He shall drive it the whole day.

11: The wages of a hired man are 1 shekel of silver; his provender is 1 pan of barley. He shall work for one month.

12: A man who is caught in the field of a *muškēnum*[3] in the *crop* during daytime, shall pay 10 shekels of silver. He who is caught in the *crop* [at ni]ght, shall die, he shall not get away alive.

13: A man who is caught in the house of a *muškēnum*, in the house, during daytime, shall pay 10 shekels of silver. He who is caught in the house at night, shall die, he shall not get away alive.

14: The fee of a . . .[4]—should he bring 5 shekels of silver the fee is 1 shekel of silver; should he bring 10 shekels of silver the fee is 2 shekels of silver.

15: The *tamkarrum*[5] and the *sabītum*[6] shall not receive silver, barley, wool (or) sesame oil from a slave or a slave-girl *as an investment*.

16: To a coparcener or a slave a mortgage cannot be furnished.

17: Should the son of a man bring bride-money to the house of (his) father-in-law—, if one of the two deceases, the money shall revert to its owner.

18: If he takes her (the girl) and she enters his house, but *afterward* the young woman should decease, he (the husband) can not

---

[2] Possibly "(who finds himself) in *great peril.*"

[3] The *muškēnum* is a member of a social class which at Eshnunna seems to be closely connected with the palace or the temple.

[4] The word must denote some kind of "money-lender" or "merchant."

[5] The official "finance officer" who has a state monopoly on certain commercial transactions.

[6] The woman to whom trade in liquor is entrusted.

obtain refunded that which he brought (to his father-in-law), but will retain the excess (in) his (hand).

18A: Per 1 shekel (of silver) there will accrue ⅙ shekel and 6 grain as interest; per 1 kor (of barley) there will accrue 1 pan and 4 seah as interest.

19: The man who gives (a loan) in terms of his retake shall make (the debtor) pay on the threshing floor.

20: If a man gives a loan ... expressing the value of the silver in barley, he shall at harvest time receive the barley and its interest, 1 pan (and) 4(?) seah per kor.

21: If a man gives silver (as a loan) *at face value,* he shall receive the silver and its interest, one sixth (of a shekel) and [6 grain] per shekel.

22: If a man has no claim against a(nother) man, but (nevertheless) distrains the (other) man's slave-girl, the owner of the slave-girl shall [decla]re under oath: "Thou hast no claim against me" and he shall pay (him) silver in full compensation for the slave-girl.

23: If a man has no claim against a(nother) man, but (nevertheless) distrains the (other) man's slave-girl, detains the distrainee in his house and causes (her) death, he shall give two slave-girls to the owner of the slave-girl as a replacement.

24: If he has no claim against him, but (nevertheless) distrains the wife of a *muškēnum* (or) the child of a *muškēnum* and causes (their) death, it is a capital offence. The distrainer who distrained shall die.

25: If a man calls at the house of (his) father-in-law, and his father-in-law *accepts* him *in servitude,* but (nevertheless) gives his daughter to [another man], the father of the girl shall refund the bride-money which he received twofold.

26: If a man gives bride-money for a(nother) man's daughter, but another man seizes her forcibly without asking the permission of her father and her mother and deprives her of her virginity, it is a capital offence and he shall die.

27: If a man takes a(nother) man's daughter without asking the permission of her father and her mother and concludes no formal marriage contract with her father and her mother, even though she may live in his house for a year, she is not a housewife.

28: *On the other hand,* if he concludes a formal contract with her father and her mother and cohabits with her, she is a housewife. When she is caught with a(nother) man, she shall die, she shall not get away alive.

29: If a man has been made prisoner during a raid or an invasion or (if) he has been carried off forcibly and [stayed in] a foreign [count]ry for a [long] time, (and if) another man has taken his wife and she has born him a son—when he returns, he shall [get] his wife back.

30: If a man hates his town and his lord and becomes a fugitive, (and if) another man takes his wife—when he returns, he shall have no right to claim his wife.

31: If a man deprives another man's slave-girl of her virginity, he shall pay one-third of a mina of silver; the slave-girl remains the property of her owner.

32: If a man gives his son (away) for having (him) nursed and brought up, but does not give (the nurse) rations of barley, oil (and) wool for three years, he shall pay (her) 10 minas (of silver) for bringing up his son and shall take back his son.

33: If a slave-girl by subterfuge gives her child to a(nother) man's daughter, (if) its lord sees it when it has become older, he may seize it and take it back.

34: If a slave-girl of the palace gives her son or her daughter to a *muškēnum* for bringing (him/her) up, the palace may take back the son or the daughter whom she gave.

35: Also the adoptant of the child of a slave-girl of the palace shall recompense the palace with its equivalent.

36: If a man gives property of his as a deposit to ... and if the property he gives disappears without that the house was burglarized, the *sippu*[7] broken down (or) the window forced, he (the depositary) will replace his (the depositor's) property.

37: If the man's (the depositary's) house either collapses or is burglarized and together with the (property of the) deposit(or) which he gave him loss on the part of the owner of the house is incurred, the owner of the house shall swear him an oath in the gate of Tishpak[8] (saying): "Together with your property my property was lost; I have done nothing *improper* or fraudulent." If he swears him (such an oath), he shall have no claim against him.

38: If one of several brothers wants to sell his share (in a property common to them) and his brother wants to buy it, he shall pay. . . .[9]

39: If a man is hard up and sells his house, the owner of the house shall (be entitled to) redeem (it) whenever the purchaser (re)sells it.

40: If a man buys a slave, a slave-girl, an ox or any other valuable good but cannot (legally) establish the seller, he is a thief.

41: If an *ubarum*, a *naptarum* or a *mudūm*[10] wants to sell his beer, the *sabītum* shall sell the beer for him at the current price.

42: If a man bites the nose of a(nother) man and severs it, he shall pay 1 mina of silver. (For) an eye (he shall pay) 1 mina of silver; (for)

---

[7] Part of the house at or near the door.

[8] The main god of Eshnunna.

[9] This expression seems to imply a preferential treatment.

[10] Social classes who seem to be entitled to a ration of beer.

a tooth ½ mina; (for) an ear ½ mina; (for) a slap in the face 10 shekels of silver.

43: If a man severs a(nother) man's finger, he shall pay two-thirds of a mina of silver.

44: If a man throws a(nother) man to the floor in an *altercation* and breaks his *hand*, he shall pay ½ mina of silver.

45: If he breaks his foot, he shall pay ½ mina of silver.

46: If a man assaults a(nother) man and breaks his . . . , he shall pay two-thirds of a mina of silver.

47: If a man *hits* a(nother) man *accidentally*, he shall pay 10 shekels of silver.

48: And in *addition*, (in cases involving penalties) from two-thirds of a mina to 1 mina, they shall formally try the man. A capital offence comes before the king.

49: If a man is caught with a stolen slave (or) a stolen slave-girl, he shall surrender slave by slave (and) slave-girl by slave-girl.

50: If the governor, the river commissioner (or) an(other) official whoever it may be seizes a lost slave, a lost slave-girl, a lost ox, a lost donkey belonging to the palace or a *muškēnum* and does not surrender it to Eshnunna but keeps it in his house, even though he may let pass only seven days, the palace shall prosecute him for theft.

51: A slave or a slave-girl of Eshnunna which is marked with a *kannum*, a *maškanum* or an *abbuttum*[11] shall not leave the gate of Eshnunna without its owner's permission.

52: A slave or a slave-girl which has entered the gate of Eshnunna in the custody of a (foreign) envoy shall be marked with a *kannum*, a *maškanum* or an *abbuttum* but remains in the custody of its master.

53: If an ox gores an(other) ox and causes (its) death, both ox owners shall divide (among themselves) the price of the live ox and also the equivalent of the dead ox.

54: If an ox is known to gore habitually and the authorities have brought the fact to the knowledge of its owner, but he does not have his ox *dehorned*, it gores a man and causes (his) death, then the owner of the ox shall pay two-thirds of a mina of silver.

55: If it gores a slave and causes (his) death, he shall pay 15 shekels of silver.

56: If a dog is vicious and the authorities have brought the fact to the knowledge of its owner, (if nevertheless) he does not keep it in, it bites a man and causes (his) death, then the owner of the dog shall pay two-thirds of a mina of silver.

57: If it bites a slave and causes (its) death, he shall pay 15 shekels of silver.

[11] Markings that can easily be removed.

58: If a wall is threatening to fall and the authorities have brought the fact to the knowledge of its owner, (if nevertheless) he does not strengthen his wall, the wall collapses and causes a free man's death, then it is a capital offence; jurisdiction of the king.

59: If a man divorces his wife after having made her bear children and takes [ano]ther wife, he shall be driven from his house and from whatever he owns and may go after him who will accept him.

(60 and 61 badly mutilated and therefore incomprehensible)

The Code of Hammurabi

TRANSLATOR: THEOPHILE J. MEEK

ANET, 163–64, 166–77

Hammurabi (also spelled Hammurapi) was the sixth of eleven kings in the Old Babylonian (Amorite) Dynasty. He ruled for 43 years, from 1728 to 1686 according to the most recent calculations. The date-formula for his second year, "The year he enacted the law of the land," indicates that he promulgated his famous lawcode at the very beginning of his reign, but the copy which we have could not have been written so early because the Prologue refers to events much later than this. Our copy was written on a diorite stela, topped by a bas-relief showing Hammurabi in the act of receiving the commission to write the lawbook from the god of justice, the sun-god Shamash. The stela was carried off to the old Elamite capital, Susa (the Shushan of Esther and Daniel), by some Elamite raider (apparently Shutruk-Nahhunte, about 1207–1171 B.C.) as a trophy of war. It was discovered there by French archaeologists in the winter of 1901–1902 and was carried off by them to the Louvre in Paris as a trophy of archaeology. All the laws from col. xvi 77 to the end of the obverse (from the end of §65 to the beginning of §100) were chiseled off by the Elamites, but these have been preserved in large part on other copies of the Code.

Fig. 59

The Laws

1: If a seignior[12] accused a(nother) seignior and brought a charge of murder against him, but has not proved it, his accuser shall be put to death.

Deut. 5:20; 19:16–21; Exod. 23:1–3

2: If a seignior brought a charge of sorcery against a(nother) seignior, but has not proved it, the one against whom the charge of sorcery was brought, upon going to the river,[13] shall throw himself into the river, and if the river has then overpowered him, his accuser shall

---

[12] Awēlum seems to be used in at least three senses: (1) sometimes to indicate a man of the higher class, a noble; (2) sometimes a free man of any class, high or low; and (3) occasionally a man of any class, from king to slave. I follow the ambiguity of the original and use the rather general term "seignior," as employed in Italian and Spanish, to indicate any free man of standing.

[13] The river (the Euphrates) as judge in the case was regarded as god.

take over his estate; if the river has shown that seignior to be innocent and he has accordingly come forth safe, the one who brought
the charge of sorcery against him shall be put to death, while the one
who threw himself into the river shall take over the estate of his
accuser.

3: If a seignior came forward with false testimony in a case, and
has not proved the word which he spoke, if that case was a case involving life, that seignior shall be put to death.

4: If he came forward with (false) testimony concerning grain or
money, he shall bear the penalty of that case.

Fig. 57   5: If a judge gave a judgment, rendered a decision, deposited a
sealed document, but later has altered his judgment, they shall prove
that that judge altered the judgment which he gave and he shall pay
twelvefold the claim which holds in that case; furthermore, they shall
expel him in the assembly from his seat of judgment and he shall
never again sit with the judges in a case.

6: If a seignior stole the property of church or state, that seignior
shall be put to death; also the one who received the stolen goods
from his hand shall be put to death.

7: If a seignior has purchased or he received for safekeeping either
silver or gold or a male slave or a female slave or an ox or a sheep or
an ass or any sort of thing from the hand of a seignior's son or a seignior's slave without witnesses and contracts, since that seignior is a
thief, he shall be put to death.

8: If a seignior stole either an ox or a sheep or an ass or a pig or a
Exod. 20:15; Deut.   boat, if it belonged to the church (or) if it belonged to the state, he
5:19; 22:1–4; Lev.   shall make thirtyfold restitution; if it belonged to a private citizen,[14]
19:11, 13   he shall make good tenfold. If the thief does not have sufficient to
make restitution, he shall be put to death.

9: When a seignior, (some of) whose property was lost, has found
his lost property in the possession of a(nother) seignior, if the seignior in whose possession the lost (property) was found has declared, "A seller sold (it) to me; I made the purchase in the presence
of witnesses," and the owner of the lost (property) in turn has declared, "I will produce witnesses attesting to my lost (property)"; the
purchaser having then produced the seller who made the sale to him
and the witnesses in whose presence he made the purchase, and the
owner of the lost (property) having also produced the witnesses attesting to his lost (property), the judges shall consider their evidence,
and the witnesses in whose presence the purchase was made, along
with the witnesses attesting to the lost (property), shall declare what
they know in the presence of god, and since the seller was the thief,

[14] Ordinarily indicates a man of the middle class, a commoner, but here it mani-
festly refers to a private citizen as distinct from the church and state.

he shall be put to death, while the owner of the lost (property) shall take his lost (property), with the purchaser obtaining from the estate of the seller the money that he paid out.[15]

10: If the (professed) purchaser has not produced the seller who made the sale to him and the witnesses in whose presence he made the purchase, but the owner of the lost property has produced witnesses attesting to his lost property, since the (professed) purchaser was the thief, he shall be put to death, while the owner of the lost property shall take his lost property.

11: If the (professed) owner of the lost property has not produced witnesses attesting to his lost property, since he was a cheat and started a false report, he shall be put to death.

12: If the seller has gone to (his) fate, the purchaser shall take from the estate of the seller fivefold the claim for that case.

13: If the witnesses of that seignior were not at hand, the judges shall set a time-limit of six months for him, and if he did not produce his witnesses within six months, since that seignior was a cheat, he shall bear the penalty of that case.

14: If a seignior has stolen the young son of a(nother) seignior, he shall be put to death.   Exod. 21:16; Deut. 24:7

15: If a seignior has helped either a male slave of the state or a female slave of the state or a male slave of a private citizen or a female slave of a private citizen to escape through the city-gate, he shall be put to death.

16: If a seignior has harbored in his house either a fugitive male or female slave belonging to the state or to a private citizen and has not brought him forth at the summons of the police, that householder shall be put to death.

17: If a seignior caught a fugitive male or female slave in the open and has taken him to his owner, the owner of the slave shall pay him two shekels[16] of silver.

18: If that slave has not named his owner, he shall take him to the palace in order that his record may be investigated, and they shall return him to his owner.

19: If he has kept that slave in his house (and) later the slave has been found in his possession, that seignior shall be put to death.

20: If the slave has escaped from the hand of his captor, that seignior shall (so) affirm by god to the owner of the slave and he shall then go free.

21: If a seignior made a breach in a house, they shall put him to death in front of that breach and wall him in.   Exod. 22:2–3

---

[15] In the time of Hammurabi coinage had of course not yet been invented and the money (usually silver, as here) was weighed out in bars.

[16] A weight of about 8 gr.

22: If a seignior committed robbery and has been caught, that seignior shall be put to death.

23: If the robber has not been caught, the robbed seignior shall set forth the particulars regarding his lost property in the presence of god, and the city and governor, in whose territory and district the robbery was committed, shall make good to him his lost property.

Deut. 21:1ff.

24: If it was a life (that was lost), the city and governor shall pay one mina[17] of silver to his people.

25: If fire broke out in a seignior's house and a seignior, who went to extinguish (it), cast his eye on the goods of the owner of the house and has appropriated the goods of the owner of the house, that seignior shall be thrown into that fire.

26: If either a private soldier or a commissary,[18] whose despatch on a campaign of the king was ordered, did not go or he hired a substitute and has sent (him) in his place, that soldier or commissary shall be put to death, while the one who was hired by him shall take over his estate.

27: In the case of either a private soldier or a commissary who was carried off while in the armed service of the king, if after his (disappearance) they gave his field and orchard to another and he has looked after his feudal obligations—if he has returned and reached his city, they shall restore his field and orchard to him and he shall himself look after his feudal obligations.

28: In the case of either a private soldier or a commissary, who was carried off while in the armed service of the king, if his son is able to look after the feudal obligations, the field and orchard shall be given to him and he shall look after the feudal obligations of his father.

29: If his son is so young that he is not able to look after the feudal obligations of his father, one-third of the field and orchard shall be given to his mother in order that his mother may rear him.

30: If either a private soldier or a commissary gave up his field, orchard, and house on account of the feudal obligations and has then absented himself, (and) after his (departure) another took over his field, orchard, and house and has looked after the feudal obligations for three years—if he has returned and demands his field, orchard, and house, they shall not be given to him; the one who has taken over and looked after his feudal obligations shall himself become the feudatory.

---

[17] About 500 gr., divided into 60 shekels.

[18] The exact meaning of the two military terms used here, *redum* and *ba'irum*, is uncertain. The former means literally "follower" and is regularly used for the ordinary foot-soldier; the latter means literally "fisher, hunter," hence "commissary" here.

31: If he has absented himself for only one year and has returned, his field, orchard, and house shall be given back to him and he shall look after his feudal obligations himself.

32: If a merchant has ransomed either a private soldier or a commissary, who was carried off in a campaign of the king, and has enabled him to reach his city, if there is sufficient to ransom (him) in his house, he himself shall ransom himself; if there is not sufficient to ransom him in his house, he shall be ransomed from the estate of his city-god; if there is not sufficient to ransom him in the estate of his city-god, the state shall ransom him, since his own field, orchard, and house may not be ceded for his ransom.

33: If either a sergeant or a captain has obtained a soldier by conscription or he accepted and has sent a hired substitute for a campaign of the king, that sergeant or captain shall be put to death.

34: If either a sergeant or a captain has appropriated the household goods of a soldier, has wronged a soldier, has let a soldier for hire, has abandoned a soldier to a superior in a lawsuit, has appropriated the grant which the king gave to a soldier, that sergeant or captain shall be put to death.

35: If a seignior has bought from the hand of a soldier the cattle or sheep which the king gave to the soldier, he shall forfeit his money.

36: In no case is the field, orchard, or house belonging to a soldier, a commissary, or a feudatory[19] salable.

37: If a seignior has purchased the field, orchard, or house belonging to a soldier, a commissary, or a feudatory, his contract-tablet shall be broken and he shall also forfeit his money, with the field, orchard, or house reverting to its owner.

38: In no case may a soldier, a commissary, or a feudatory deed any of his field, orchard, or house belonging to his fief to his wife or daughter, and in no case may he assign (them) for an obligation of his.

39: He may deed to his wife or daughter any of the field, orchard, or house which he purchases and accordingly owns,[20] and he may assign (them) for an obligation of his.

40: A hierodule,[21] a merchant, and a feudatory extraordinary may sell his field, orchard, and house, with the purchaser assuming the feudal obligations of the field, orchard, and house which he purchases.

41: If a seignior acquired by barter the field, orchard, or house belonging to a soldier, a commissary, or a feudatory, and also made an

---

[19] Or, officers of some sort.

[20] I.e., in fee simple and not as a fief.

[21] The exact meaning of the term used here, *naditum*, is unknown, but it indicates some kind of religious functionary.

additional payment, the soldier, commissary, or feudatory shall re-possess his field, orchard, or house, and he shall also keep the additional payment that was made to him.

42: If a seignior rented a field for cultivation, but has not produced grain in the field, they shall prove that he did no work on the field and he shall give grain to the owner of the field on the basis of those adjoining it.

43: If he did not cultivate the field, but has neglected (it), he shall give grain to the owner of the field on the basis of those adjoining it; furthermore, the field which he neglected he shall break up with mattocks, harrow, and return to the owner of the field.

44: If a seignior rented a fallow field for three years for development, but became so lazy that he has not developed the field, in the fourth year he shall break up the field with mattocks, plow and harrow (it), and he shall return (it) to the owner of the field; furthermore, he shall measure out ten *kur*[22] of grain per eighteen *iku*.[23]

45: If a seignior let his field to a tenant and has already received the rent of his field, (and) later Adad has inundated the field or a flood has ravaged (it), the loss shall be the tenant's.

46: If he has not received the rent of the field, whether he let the field for one-half or one-third (the crop), the tenant and the owner of the field shall divide proportionately the grain which is produced in the field.

47: If the tenant has asked (another) to cultivate the field because he did not get back his investment in the previous year, the owner of the field shall not object; his (new) tenant shall cultivate his field and at harvest-time he shall take grain in accordance with his contracts.

48: If a debt is outstanding against a seignior and Adad has inundated his field or a flood has ravaged (it) or through lack of water grain has not been produced in the field, he shall not make any return of grain to his creditor in that year; he shall cancel[24] his contract-tablet and he shall pay no interest for that year.

49: When a seignior borrowed money from a merchant and pledged to the merchant a field prepared for grain or sesame, if he said to him, "Cultivate the field, then harvest (and) take the grain or sesame that is produced," if the tenant has produced grain or sesame in the field, the owner of the field at harvest-time shall himself take the grain or sesame that was produced in the field and he shall give to the merchant grain for his money, which he borrowed from the merchant, together with its interest, and also for the cost of cultivation.

---

[22] A measure equal to a little more than 7 bushels, divided into 300 *qu*.

[23] A land measure equal to about ⅞ of an acre.

[24] Lit., "he shall wash off."

50: If he pledged a field planted with ⟨grain⟩ or a field planted with sesame, the owner of the field shall himself take the grain or sesame that was produced in the field and he shall pay back the money with its interest to the merchant.

51: If he does not have the money to pay back, ⟨grain or⟩ sesame at their market value in accordance with the ratio fixed by the king[25] he shall give to the merchant for his money, which he borrowed from the merchant, together with its interest.

52: If the tenant has not produced grain or sesame in the field, he may not change his contract.

53: If a seignior was too lazy to make [the dike of] his field strong and did not make his dike strong and a break has opened up in his dike and he has accordingly let the water ravage the farmland, the seignior in whose dike the break was opened shall make good the grain that he let get destroyed.

54: If he is not able to make good the grain, they shall sell him and his goods, and the farmers whose grain the water carried off shall divide (the proceeds).

55: If a seignior, upon opening his canal for irrigation, became so lazy that he has let the water ravage a field adjoining his, he shall measure out grain on the basis of those adjoining his.

56: If a seignior opened up the water and then has let the water carry off the work done on a field adjoining his, he shall measure out ten *kur* of grain per eighteen *iku*.

57: If a shepherd has not come to an agreement with the owner of a field to pasture sheep on the grass, but has pastured sheep on the field without the consent of the owner of the field, when the owner of the field harvests his field, the shepherd who pastured the sheep on the field without the consent of the owner of the field shall give in addition twenty *kur* of grain per eighteen *iku* to the owner of the field.

58: If after the sheep have gone up from the meadow, when the whole flock has been shut up within the city-gate,[26] the shepherd drove the sheep into a field and has then pastured the sheep on the field, the shepherd shall look after the field on which he pastured and at harvest-time he shall measure out sixty *kur* of grain per eighteen *iku* to the owner of the field.

59: If a seignior cut down a tree in a(nother) seignior's orchard without the consent of the owner of the orchard, he shall pay one-half mina of silver.

---

[25] In ancient Mesopotamia the ratio between silver (the money of the time) and various commodities was fixed by the state.

[26] The reference to the city-gate evidently reflects the Near Eastern custom in both ancient and modern times of bringing the sheep into the shelter of the town or village at night.

Lev. 19:23–25

60: If, when a seignior gave a field to a gardener to set out an orchard, the gardener set out the orchard, he shall develop the orchard for four years; in the fifth year the owner of the orchard and the gardener shall divide equally, with the owner of the orchard receiving his preferential share.

61: If the gardener did not set out the whole field, but left a portion bare, they shall assign the bare portion to him as his share.

62: If he did not set out the field that was given to him as an orchard, if it was a cultivated field, the gardener shall pay[27] to the owner of the field rent for the field for the years that it was neglected on the basis of those adjoining it; also he shall do the (necessary) work on the field and return (it) to the owner of the field.

63: If it was fallow land, he shall do the (necessary) work on the field and return (it) to the owner of the field; also he shall measure out ten *kur* of grain per eighteen *iku* for each year.

64: If a seignior gave his orchard to a gardener to pollinate,[28] the gardener shall give to the owner of the orchard two-thirds of the produce of the orchard as rent of the orchard as long as the orchard is held, with himself taking one-third.

65: If the gardener did not pollinate the orchard and so has let the yield decline, the gardener [shall measure out] rent for the orchard on the basis of those adjoining it.

66: When a seignior borrowed money from a merchant and his merchant foreclosed on him and he has nothing to pay (it) back, if he gave his orchard after pollination to the merchant and said to him, "Take for your money as many dates as there are produced in the orchard," that merchant shall not be allowed; the owner of the orchard shall himself take the dates that were produced in the orchard and repay the merchant for the money and its interest in accordance with the wording of his tablet and the owner of the orchard shall in turn take the remaining dates that were produced in the orchard.

67: If a seignior built a house, his neighbor . . .

68: f.: (not preserved)

70: . . . he shall give to him.

71: If he is giving grain, money, or goods for a fief estate belonging to an estate adjoining his, which he wishes to purchase, he shall forfeit whatever he paid, while the estate shall revert to its [owner]. If that estate does not carry feudal obligations, he may purchase (it), since he may give grain, money, or goods for such an estate.

72–77: (Only a few words preserved, having to do with house building.)

---

[27] Lit., "measure out," indicating that the rent was to be paid in grain.

[28] The orchard was a date orchard (see §66) and hence had to be artificially fertilized.

78: [If a seignior let a house to a(nother) seignior and] the seignior (who was) the tenant paid his rental money in full for the year
to the owner of [the house] and the owner of the house has then said
to the [tenant] while his term was (still) incomplete, "Move out," the
owner of the house [shall forfeit] the money which the tenant paid to
him [because] he made the tenant [move out] of his house while his
term was (still) incomplete.

79–87: (not preserved)

88: If a merchant [lent] grain at interest, he shall receive sixty *qu*
of grain per *kur* as interest.[29] If he lent money at interest, he shall receive one-sixth (shekel) six *še* (i.e., one-fifth shekel) per shekel of silver as interest.[30]

89: If a seignior, who [incurred] a debt, does not have the money
to pay (it) back, but has the grain, [the merchant] shall take grain for
his money [with its interest] in accordance with the ratio fixed by
the king.

90: If the merchant increased the interest beyond [sixty *qu*] per
kur [of grain] (or) one-sixth (shekel) six *še* [per shekel of money] and
has collected (it), he shall forfeit whatever he lent.

91: If a merchant [lent] grain at interest and has collected money
[for the full interest] on the grain, the grain along with the money
may not [*be charged to the account*].

92: (not preserved)

93: [If the merchant] ... or he has not had the full amount of
grain [which he received] deducted and did not write a new contract, or he has added the interest to the principal, that merchant
shall pay back double the full amount of grain that he received.

94: If a merchant lent grain or money at interest and when he lent
(it) at interest he paid out the money by the small weight and the
grain by the small measure, but when he got (it) back he got the
money by the [large] weight (and) the grain by the large measure,
[that merchant shall forfeit] whatever he lent.

95: If a [merchant lent grain or money] at interest and gave ... ,
he shall forfeit whatever he lent.

96: If a seignior borrowed grain or money from a merchant and
does not have the grain or money to pay (it) back, but has (other)
goods, he shall give to his merchant whatever there is in his possession, (affirming) before witnesses that he will bring (it), while the
merchant shall accept (it) without making any objections.

97: ... , he shall he put to death.

98: If a seignior gave money to a(nother) seignior for a partner-
ship, they shall divide equally in the presence of god the profit or loss
which was incurred.

---

[29] Since there were 300 *qu* in a *kur*, the interest rate was 20%.

[30] Since there were 180 *še* in a shekel, the interest rate was again 20%.

99: If a merchant lent money at interest to a trader[31] for the purpose of trading [and making purchases] and sent him out on the road, the trader shall ... on the road [the money which was entrusted] to him.

100: If he has realized a profit where he went, he shall write down the interest on the full amount of money that he borrowed and they shall count up the days against him and he shall repay his merchant.

101: If he has not realized a profit where he went, the trader shall repay to the merchant double the money that he borrowed.

102: If a merchant has lent money to a trader as a favor[32] and he has experienced a loss where he went, he shall pay back the principal of the money to the merchant.

103: If, when he went on the road, an enemy has made him give up whatever he was carrying, the trader shall (so) affirm by god and then he shall go free.

104: If a merchant lent grain, wool, oil, or any goods at all to a trader to retail, the trader shall write down the value and pay (it) back to the merchant, with the trader obtaining a sealed receipt for the money which he pays to the merchant.

105: If the trader has been careless and so has not obtained a sealed receipt for the money which he paid to the merchant, the money with no sealed receipt may not be credited to the account.

106: If a trader borrowed money from a merchant and has then disputed (the fact) with his merchant, that merchant in the presence of god and witnesses shall prove that the trader borrowed the money and the trader shall pay to the merchant threefold the full amount of money that he borrowed.

107: When a merchant entrusted (something) to a trader and the trader has returned to his merchant whatever the merchant gave him, if the merchant has then disputed with him whatever the trader gave him, that trader shall prove it against the merchant in the presence of god and witnesses and the merchant shall pay to the trader sixfold whatever he received because he had a dispute with his trader.

108: If a woman wine seller, instead of receiving grain for the price of a drink, has received money by the large weight and so has made the value of the drink less than the value of the grain, they shall prove it against that wine seller and throw her into the water.

109: If outlaws have congregated in the establishment of a woman wine seller and she has not arrested those outlaws and did not take them to the palace, that wine seller shall be put to death.

[31] I.e., a traveling salesman peddling his wares.
[32] I.e., without interest.

110: If a hierodule, a nun,[33] who is not living in a convent, has opened (the door of) a wineshop or has entered a wineshop for a drink, they shall burn that woman.

111: If a woman wine seller gave one (flask) of *pīhum*-drink on credit, she shall receive fifty *qu*[34] of grain at harvest-time.

112: When a seignior was engaged in a (trading) journey and gave silver, gold, (precious) stones, or (other) goods in his possession to a(nother) seignior and consigned (them) to him for transport, if that seignior did not deliver whatever was to be transported where it was to be transported, but has appropriated (it), the owner of the goods to be transported shall prove the charge against that seignior in the matter of whatever was to be transported, but which he did not deliver, and that seignior shall pay to the owner of the goods to be transported fivefold whatever was given to him.

113: If a seignior held (a debt of) grain or money against a(nother) seignior and he has then taken grain from the granary or threshing floor without the consent of the owner of the grain, they shall prove that that seignior took grain from the granary or threshing floor without the consent of the owner of the grain and he shall return the full amount of grain that he took and he shall also forfeit everything else that he lent.

114: If a seignior did not hold (a debt of) grain or money against a(nother) seignior, but has distrained (someone as) his pledge, he shall pay one-third mina of silver for each distraint.

115: If a seignior held (a debt of) grain or money against a(nother) seignior and distrained (someone as) his pledge and the pledge has then died a natural death in the house of his distrainer, that case is not subject to claim.

116: If the pledge has died from beating or abuse in the house of his distrainer, the owner of the pledge shall prove it against his merchant, and if it was the seignior's son, they shall put his son to death; if it was the seignior's slave, he shall pay one-third mina of silver and also forfeit everything else that he lent.

117: If an obligation came due against a seignior and he sold (the services of) his wife, his son, or his daughter, or he has been bound over to service, they shall work (in) the house of their purchaser or obligee for three years, with their freedom reestablished in the fourth year.

Exod. 21:2–11; Deut. 15:12–18

118: When a male slave or a female slave has been bound over to service, if the merchant foreclosed, he may sell (him), with no possibility of his being reclaimed.

---

[33] The ideogram means literally "lady of a god."

[34] A measure equal to a little more than ¾ of a quart, dry measure.

119: If an obligation came due against a seignior and he has accordingly sold (the services of) his female slave who bore him children, the owner of the female slave may repay the money which the merchant paid out and thus redeem his female slave.

120: If a seignior deposited his grain in a(nother) seignior's house for storage and a loss has then occurred at the granary or the owner of the house opened the storage-room and took grain or he has denied completely (the receipt of) the grain which was stored in his house, the owner of the grain shall set forth the particulars regarding his grain in the presence of god and the owner of the house shall give
Exod. 22:7–9
to the owner of the grain double the grain that he took.

121: If a seignior stored grain in a(nother) seignior's house, he shall pay five *qu* of grain per *kur* of grain[35] as the storage-charge per year.

122: If a seignior wishes to give silver, gold, or any sort of thing to a(nother) seignior for safekeeping, he shall show to witnesses the full amount that he wishes to give, arrange the contracts, and then commit (it) to safekeeping.

123: If he gave (it) for safekeeping without witnesses and contracts and they have denied (its receipt) to him at the place where he made the deposit, that case is not subject to claim.

124: If a seignior gave silver, gold, or any sort of thing for safekeeping to a(nother) seignior in the presence of witnesses and he has denied (the fact) to him, they shall prove it against that seignior and he shall pay double whatever he denied.

125: If a seignior deposited property of his for safekeeping and at the place where he made the deposit his property has disappeared along with the property of the owner of the house, either through breaking in or through scaling (the wall), the owner of the house, who was so careless that he let whatever was given to him for safekeeping get lost, shall make (it) good and make restitution to the owner of the goods, while the owner of the house shall make a thorough search for his lost property and take (it) from its thief.

126: If the seignior's property was not lost, but he has declared,
Ruth 3:11; 4:10
"My property is lost," thus deceiving his city council, his city council shall set forth the facts regarding him in the presence of god, that his property was not lost, and he shall give to his city council double whatever he laid claim to.

127: If a seignior pointed the finger at a nun or the wife of a(nother) seignior, but has proved nothing, they shall drag that seignior into the presence of the judges and also cut off half his (hair).

128: If a seignior acquired a wife, but did not draw up the contracts for her, that woman is no wife.

---

[35] 1 2/3% since there were 300 *qu* in a *kur*.

129: If the wife of a seignior has been caught while lying with another man, they shall bind them and throw them into the water. If the husband of the woman wishes to spare his wife, then the king in turn may spare his subject.

Deut. 22:22

130: If a seignior bound the (betrothed) wife of a(nother) seignior, who had had no intercourse with a male and was still living in her father's house, and he has lain in her bosom and they have caught him, that seignior shall be put to death, while that woman shall go free.

Deut. 22:23–27

131: If a seignior's wife was accused by her husband, but she was not caught while lying with another man, she shall make affirmation by god and return to her house.

132: If the finger was pointed at the wife of a seignior because of another man, but she has not been caught while lying with the other man, she shall throw herself into the river[36] for the sake of her husband.

Num. 5:11–31

133: If a seignior was taken captive, but there was sufficient to live on in his house, his wife [shall not leave her house, but she shall take care of her person by not] entering [the house of another].[37]

133a: If that woman did not take care of her person, but has entered the house of another, they shall prove it against that woman and throw her into the water.[38]

134: If the seignior was taken captive and there was not sufficient to live on in his house, his wife may enter the house of another, with that woman incurring no blame at all.

135: If, when a seignior was taken captive and there was not sufficient to live on in his house, his wife has then entered the house of another before his (return) and has borne children, (and) later her husband has returned and has reached his city, that woman shall return to her first husband, while the children shall go with their father.

136: If, when a seignior deserted his city and then ran away, his wife has entered the house of another after his (departure), if that seignior has returned and wishes to take back his wife, the wife of the fugitive shall not return to her husband because he scorned his city and ran away.

137: If a seignior has made up his mind to divorce a lay priestess,[39] who bore him children, or a hierodule who provided him with children, they shall return her dowry to that woman and also give

---

[36] I.e., submit to the water ordeal, with the river as divine judge.

[37] I.e., in order to live there as another man's wife.

[38] I.e., to be drowned.

[39] The exact meaning of the word used here, šu.ge₄-tum, is unknown, but it indicates some kind of priestess.

her half of the field, orchard and goods in order that she may rear her children; after she has brought up her children, from whatever was given to her children they shall give her a portion corresponding to (that of) an individual heir in order that the man of her choice may marry her.

138: If a seignior wishes to divorce his wife who did not bear him children, he shall give her money to the full amount of her marriage-price and he shall also make good to her the dowry which she brought from her father's house and then he may divorce her.

139: If there was no marriage-price, he shall give her one mina of silver as the divorce-settlement.

140: If he is a peasant, he shall give her one-third mina of silver.

141: If a seignior's wife, who was living in the house of the seignior, has made up her mind to leave in order that she may engage in business, thus neglecting her house (and) humiliating her husband, they shall prove it against her; and if her husband has then decided on her divorce, he may divorce her, with nothing to be given her as her divorce-settlement upon her departure. If her husband has not decided on her divorce, her husband may marry another woman, with the former woman living in the house of her husband like a maidservant.

142: If a woman so hated her husband that she has declared, "You may not have me," her record shall be investigated at her city council, and if she was careful and was not at fault, even though her husband has been going out and disparaging her greatly, that woman, without incurring any blame at all, may take her dowry and go off to her father's house.

143: If she was not careful, but was a gadabout, thus neglecting her house (and) humiliating her husband, they shall throw that woman into the water.

144: When a seignior married a hierodule and that hierodule gave a female slave to her husband and she has then produced children, if that seignior has made up his mind to marry a lay priestess, they may not allow that seignior, since he may not marry the lay priestess.

145: If a seignior married a hierodule and she did not provide him with children and he has made up his mind to marry a lay priestess, that seignior may marry the lay priestess, thus bringing her into his house, (but) with that lay priestess ranking in no way with the hierodule.

146: When a seignior married a hierodule and she gave a female slave to her husband and she has then borne children, if later that female slave has claimed equality with her mistress because she bore children, her mistress may not sell her; she may mark her with the slave-mark and count her among the slaves.

147: If she did not bear children, her mistress may sell her.

148: When a seignior married a woman and a fever has then seized her, if he has made up his mind to marry another, he may marry (her), without divorcing his wife whom the fever seized; she shall live in the house which he built and he shall continue to support her as long as she lives.

149: If that woman has refused to live in her husband's house, he shall make good her dowry to her which she brought from her father's house and then she may leave.

150: If a seignior, upon presenting a field, orchard, house, or goods to his wife, left a sealed document with her, her children may not enter a claim against her after (the death of) her husband, since the mother may give her inheritance to that son of hers whom she likes, (but) she may not give (it) to an outsider.

151: If a woman, who was living in a seignior's house, having made a contract with her husband that a creditor of her husband may not distrain her, has then had (him) deliver a written statement;[40] if there was a debt against that seignior before he married that woman, his creditors may not distrain his wife; also, if there was a debt against that woman before she entered the seignior's house, her creditors may not distrain her husband.

152: If a debt has developed against them after that woman entered the seignior's house, both of them shall be answerable to the merchant.[41]

153: If a seignior's wife has brought about the death of her husband because of another man, they shall impale that woman on stakes.

154: If a seignior has had intercourse with his daughter, they shall make that seignior leave the city.

155: If a seignior chose a bride for his son and his son had intercourse with her, but later he himself has lain in her bosom and they have caught him, they shall bind that seignior and throw him into the water.

156: If a seignior chose a bride for his son and his son did not have intercourse with her, but he himself has lain in her bosom, he shall pay to her one-half mina of silver and he shall also make good to her whatever she brought from her father's house in order that the man of her choice may marry her.

157: If a seignior has lain in the bosom of his mother after (the death of) his father, they shall burn both of them.

158: If a seignior after (the death of) his father has been caught in the bosom of his foster mother who was the bearer of children, that seignior shall be cut off from the parental home.

Lev. 18:6–18; 20:10–21; Deut. 27:20, 22–23

---

[40] Lit., "a tablet."
[41] I.e., the money-lender who made the loan.

159: If a seignior, who had the betrothal-gift brought to the house of his (prospective) father-in-law (and) paid the marriage-price, has then fallen in love with another woman and has said to his (prospective) father-in-law, "I will not marry your daughter," the father of the daughter shall keep whatever was brought to him.

160: If a seignior had the betrothal-gift brought to the house of the (prospective) father-in-law (and) paid the marriage-price, and the father of the daughter has then said, "I will not give my daughter to you," he shall pay back double the full amount that was brought to him.

161: If a seignior had the betrothal-gift brought to the house of his (prospective) father-in-law (and) paid the marriage-price, and then a friend of his has so maligned him that his (prospective) father-in-law has said to the (prospective) husband, "You may not marry my daughter," he shall pay back double the full amount that was brought to him, but his friend may not marry his (intended) wife.

162: If, when a seignior acquired a wife, she bore him children and that woman has then gone to (her) fate, her father may not lay claim to her dowry, since her dowry belongs to her children.

163: If a seignior acquired a wife and that woman has gone to (her) fate without providing him with children, if his father-in-law has then returned to him the marriage-price which that seignior brought to the house of his father-in-law, her husband may not lay claim to the dowry of that woman, since her dowry belongs to her father's house.

164: If his father-in-law has not returned the marriage-price to him, he shall deduct the full amount of her marriage-price from her dowry and return (the rest of) her dowry to her father's house.

165: If a seignior, upon presenting a field, orchard, or house to his first-born, who is the favorite in his eye, wrote a sealed document for him, when the brothers divide after the father has gone to (his) fate, he shall keep the present which the father gave him, but otherwise they shall share equally in the goods of the paternal estate.

166: If a seignior, upon acquiring wives for the sons that he got, did not acquire a wife for his youngest son, when the brothers divide after the father has gone to (his) fate, to their youngest brother who did not acquire a wife, to him in addition to his share they shall assign money (enough) for the marriage-price from the goods of the paternal estate and thus enable him to acquire a wife.

167: If, when a seignior acquired a wife and she bore him children, that woman has gone to (her) fate (and) after her (death) he has then married another woman and she has borne children, when later the father has gone to (his) fate, the children shall not divide according to mothers; they shall take the dowries of their (respective) mothers and then divide equally the goods of the paternal estate.

168: If a seignior, having made up his mind to disinherit his son, has said to the judges, "I wish to disinherit my son," the judges shall investigate his record, and if the son did not incur wrong grave (enough) to be disinherited, the father may not disinherit his son.

169: If he has incurred wrong against his father grave (enough) to be disinherited, they shall let him off the first time; if he has incurred grave wrong a second time, the father may disinherit his son.

170: When a seignior's first wife bore him children and his female slave also bore him children, if the father during his lifetime has ever said "My children!" to the children whom the slave bore him, thus having counted them with the children of the first wife, after the father has gone to (his) fate, the children of the first wife and the children of the slave shall share equally in the goods of the paternal estate, with the first-born, the son of the first wife, receiving a preferential share.

171: However, if the father during his lifetime has never said "My children!" to the children whom the slave bore him, after the father has gone to (his) fate, the children of the slave may not share in the goods of the paternal estate along with the children of the first wife; freedom for the slave and her children shall be effected, with the children of the first wife having no claim at all against the children of the slave for service; the first wife shall take her dowry and the marriage-gift which her husband, upon giving (it) to her, wrote down on a tablet for her, and living in the home of her husband, she shall have the usufruct (of it) as long as she lives, without ever selling (it), since her heritage belongs to her children.

172: If her husband did not give her a marriage-gift, they shall make good her dowry to her and she shall obtain from the goods of her husband's estate a portion corresponding to (that of) an individual heir; if her children keep plaguing her in order to make her leave the house, the judges shall investigate her record and place the blame on the children, so that woman need never leave her husband's house; if that woman has made up her mind to leave, she shall leave to her children the marriage-gift which her husband gave her (but) take the dowry from her father's house in order that the man of her choice may marry her.

173: If that woman has borne children to her later husband in the place that she entered, and afterwards that woman has died, the earlier with the later children shall divide the dowry.

174: If she has not borne children to her later husband, only the children of her first husband shall receive her dowry.

175: If either a palace slave or a private citizen's slave married the daughter of a seignior and she has borne children, the owner of the slave may not lay claim to the children of the seignior's daughter for service.

176: Furthermore, if a palace slave or a private citizen's slave married the daughter of a seignior and when he married her she entered the house of the palace slave or the private citizen's slave with the dowry from her father's house and after they were joined together they set up a household and so acquired goods, but later either the palace slave or the private citizen's slave has gone to (his) fate, the seignior's daughter shall take her dowry, but they shall divide into two parts whatever her husband and she acquired after they were joined together and the owner of the slave shall take one-half, with the seignior's daughter taking one-half for her children.

176a: If the seignior's daughter has no dowry, they shall divide into two parts whatever her husband and she acquired after they were joined together and the owner of the slave shall take one-half, with the seignior's daughter taking one-half for her children.

177: If a widow, whose children are minors, has made up her mind to enter the house of another, she may not enter without the consent of the judges; when she wishes to enter the house of another, the judges shall investigate the condition of her former husband's estate and they shall entrust her former husband's estate to her later husband and that woman and they shall have them deposit a tablet (to the effect that) they will look after the estate and also rear the young (children), without ever selling the household goods, since the purchaser who purchases the household goods of a widow's children shall forfeit his money, with the goods reverting to their owner.

178: In the case of a nun, a hierodule, or a votary, whose father, upon presenting a dowry to her, wrote a tablet for her, if he did not write for her on the tablet which he wrote for her (permission) to give her heritage to whom she pleased and did not grant her full discretion, after the father has gone to (his) fate, her brothers shall take her field and orchard and they shall give her food, oil and clothing proportionate to the value of her share and thus make her comfortable; if her brothers have not given her food, oil and clothing proportionate to the value of her share and so have not made her comfortable, she may give her field and orchard to any tenant that she pleases and her tenant shall support her, since she shall have the usufruct of the field, orchard or whatever her father gave her as long as she lives, without selling (it or) willing (it) to another, since her patrimony belongs to her brothers.

179: In the case of a nun, a hierodule, or a votary, whose father, upon presenting a dowry to her, wrote a sealed document for her, if he wrote for her on the tablet which he wrote for her (permission) to give her heritage to whomever she pleased and has granted her full discretion, after her father has gone to (his) fate, she may give her heritage to whomever she pleases, with her brothers having no claim against her.

180: If a father did not present a dowry to his daughter, a hierodule in a convent or a votary, after the father has gone to (his) fate, she shall receive as her share in the goods of the paternal estate a portion like (that of) an individual heir, but she shall have only the usufruct of (it) as long as she lives, since her heritage belongs to her brothers.

181: If a father dedicated (his daughter) to deity as a hierodule, a sacred prostitute, or a devotee and did not present a dowry to her, after the father has gone to (his) fate, she shall receive as her share in the goods of the paternal estate her one-third patrimony, but she shall have only the usufruct of (it) as long as she lives, since her heritage belongs to her brothers.

182: If a father, since he did not present a dowry to his daughter, a hierodule of Marduk of Babylon, did not write a sealed document for her, after the father has gone to (his) fate, she shall share along with her brothers in the goods of the paternal estate to the extent of her one-third patrimony, but she shall not assume any feudal obligations, since a hierodule of Marduk may give her heritage to whomever she pleases.

183: If a father, upon presenting a dowry to his daughter, a lay priestess, when he gave her to a husband, wrote a sealed document for her, after the father has gone to (his) fate, she may not share in the goods of the paternal estate.

184 : If a seignior did not present a dowry to his daughter, a lay priestess, since he did not give her to a husband, after the father has gone to (his) fate, her brothers shall present her with a dowry proportionate to the value of the father's estate and they shall give her to a husband.

185: If a seignior adopted a boy in his own name and has reared him, that foster child may never be reclaimed.

186: If a seignior, upon adopting a boy, seeks out his father and mother when he had taken him, that foster child may return to his father's house.

187: The (adopted) son of a chamberlain, a palace servant, or the (adopted) son of a votary, may never be reclaimed.

188: If a member of the artisan class[42] took a son as a foster child and has taught him his handicraft, he may never be reclaimed.

189: If he has not taught him his handicraft, that foster child may return to his father's house.

190: If a seignior has not counted among his sons the boy that he adopted and reared, that foster child may return to his father's house.

---

[42] Lit., "the son of an artisan," where "son" is used in the technical sense of "belonging to the class of, species of," so common in the Semitic languages.

191: If a seignior, who adopted a boy and reared him, set up a family of his own, has later acquired children and so has made up (his) mind to cut off the foster child, that son shall not go off empty-handed; his foster father shall give him from his goods his one-third patrimony and then he shall go off, since he may not give him any of the field, orchard, or house.

192: If the (adopted) son of a chamberlain or the (adopted) son of a votary has said to his foster father or his foster mother, "You are not my father," "You are not my mother," they shall cut out his tongue.

193: If the (adopted) son of a chamberlain or the (adopted) son of a votary found out his parentage and came to hate his foster father and his foster mother and so has gone off to his paternal home, they shall pluck out his eye.

194: When a seignior gave his son to a nurse and that son has died in the care of the nurse, if the nurse has then made a contract for another son without the knowledge of his father and mother, they shall prove it against her and they shall cut off her breast because she made a contract for another son without the knowledge of his father and mother.

Exod. 21:15

195: If a son has struck his father, they shall cut off his hand.

196: If a seignior has destroyed the eye of a member of the aristocracy,[43] they shall destroy his eye.

Exod. 21:23–25;
Lev. 24:19–20;
Deut. 19:21

197: If he has broken a(nother) seignior's bone, they shall break his bone.

198: If he has destroyed the eye of a commoner or broken the bone of a commoner, he shall pay one mina of silver.

199: If he has destroyed the eye of a seignior's slave or broken the bone of a seignior's slave, he shall pay one-half his value.

200: If a seignior has knocked out a tooth of a seignior of his own rank, they shall knock out his tooth.

201: If he has knocked out a commoner's tooth, he shall pay one-third mina of silver.

202: If a seignior has struck the cheek of a seignior who is superior to him, he shall be beaten sixty (times) with an oxtail whip in the assembly.

203: If a member of the aristocracy has struck the cheek of a(nother) member of the aristocracy who is of the same rank as himself, he shall pay one mina of silver.

204: If a commoner has struck the cheek of a(nother) commoner, he shall pay ten shekels of silver.

205: If a seignior's slave has struck the cheek of a member of the aristocracy, they shall cut off his ear.

---

[43] Lit., "the son of a man," with "son" used in the technical sense already explained above and "man" clearly in the sense of "noble, aristocrat"; or it is possible that "son" here is to be taken in its regular sense to indicate a person younger than the assailant.

206: If a seignior has struck a(nother) seignior in a brawl and has inflicted an injury on him, that seignior shall swear, "I did not strike him deliberately";[44] and he shall also pay for the physician.

207: If he has died because of his blow, he shall swear (as before), and if it was a member of the aristocracy, he shall pay one-half mina of silver.

208: If it was a member of the commonalty, he shall pay one-third mina of silver.

209: If a seignior struck a(nother) seignior's daughter and has caused her to have a miscarriage,[45] he shall pay ten shekels of silver for her fetus.

Exod. 21: 22–25

210: If that woman has died, they shall put his daughter to death.

211: If by a blow he has caused a commoner's daughter to have a miscarriage, he shall pay five shekels of silver.

212: If that woman has died, he shall pay one-half mina of silver.

213: If he struck a seignior's female slave and has caused her to a have a miscarriage, he shall pay two shekels of silver.

214: If that female slave has died, he shall pay one-third mina of silver.

215: If a physician performed a major operation on a seignior with a bronze lancet and has saved the seignior's life, or he opened up the eye-socket of a seignior with a bronze lancet and has saved the seignior's eye, he shall receive ten shekels of silver.

216: If it was a member of the commonalty, he shall receive five shekels.

217: If it was a seignior's slave, the owner of the slave shall give two shekels of silver to the physician.

218: If a physician performed a major operation on a seignior with a bronze lancet and has caused the seignior's death, or he opened up the eye-socket of a seignior and has destroyed the seignior's eye, they shall cut off his hand.

219: If a physican performed a major operation on a commoner's slave with a bronze lancet and has caused (his) death, he shall make good slave for slave.

220: If he opened up his eye-socket with a bronze lancet and has destroyed his eye, he shall pay one-half his value in silver.

221: If a physician has set a seignior's broken bone, or has healed a sprained tendon, the patient[46] shall give five shekels of silver to the physician.

222: If it was a member of the commonalty, he shall give three shekels of silver.

---

[44] Lit., "while I was aware of (it)."

[45] Lit., "caused her to drop that of her womb (her fetus)."

[46] "Owner of the injury."

223: If it was a seignior's slave, the owner of the slave shall give two shekels of silver to the physician.

224: If a veterinary surgeon performed a major operation on either an ox or an ass and has saved (its) life, the owner of the ox or ass shall give to the surgeon one-sixth (shekel) of silver as his fee.

225: If he performed a major operation on an ox or an ass and has caused (its) death, he shall give to the owner of the ox or ass one-fourth its value.

226: If a brander cut off the slave-mark of a slave not his own without the consent of the owner of the slave, they shall cut off the hand of that brander.

227: If a seignior deceived a brander so that he has cut off the slave-mark of a slave not his own, they shall put that seignior to death and immure him at his gate; the brander shall swear, "I did not cut (it) off knowingly," and then he shall go free.

228: If a builder constructed a house for a seignior and finished (it) for him, he shall give him two shekels of silver per *sar*[47] of house as his remuneration.

229: If a builder constructed a house for a seignior, but did not make his work strong, with the result that the house which he built collapsed and so has caused the death of the owner of the house, that builder shall be put to death.

230: If it has caused the death of a son of the owner of the house, they shall put the son of that builder to death.

231: If it has caused the death of a slave of the owner of the house, he shall give slave for slave to the owner of the house.

232: If it has destroyed goods, he shall make good whatever it destroyed; also, because he did not make the house strong which he built and it collapsed, he shall reconstruct the house which collapsed at his own expense.

233: If a builder constructed a house for a seignior and has not done his work properly so that a wall has become unsafe, that builder shall strengthen that wall at his own expense.

234: If a boatman calked a boat of sixty *kur* for a seignior, he shall give him two shekels of silver as his remuneration.

235: If a boatman calked a boat for a seignior and did not do his work well with the result that that boat has sprung a leak in that very year, since it has developed a defect, the boatman shall dismantle that boat and strengthen (it) at his own expense and give the strengthened boat back to the owner of the boat.

236: If a seignior let his boat for hire to a boatman and the boatman was so careless that he has sunk or wrecked the boat, the boatman shall make good the boat to the owner of the boat.

---

[47] A measure equal to about 42 1/5 square yds.

237: When a seignior hired a boatman and a boat and loaded it with grain, wool, oil, dates, or any kind of freight, if that boatman was so careless that he has sunk the boat and lost what was in it as well, the boatman shall make good the boat which he sank and whatever he lost that was in it.

238: If a boatman sank the boat of a seignior and has then refloated it, he shall give one-half its value in silver.

239: If a seignior hired a boatman, he shall give him six *kur* of grain per year.

240: If a rowboat ramined a sailboat and has sunk (it), the owner of the boat whose boat was sunk shall in the presence of god set forth the particulars regarding whatever was lost in his boat and the one in charge of the rowboat which sank the sailboat shall make good to him his boat and his lost property.

241: If a seignior has distrained an ox as a pledge, he shall pay one-third mina of silver.

242, 243: If a seignior hired (it) for one year, he shall give to its owner four *kur* of grain as the hire of an ox in tandem, three *kur* of grain as that of a young lead-ox.

244: If a seignior hired an ox or an ass and a lion has killed it in the open, (the loss) shall be its owner's.

245: If a seignior hired an ox and has caused its death through carelessness or through beating, he shall make good ox for ox to the owner of the ox.

246: If a seignior hired an ox and has broken its foot or has cut its neck tendon, he shall make good ox for ox to the owner of the ox.

247: If a seignior hired an ox and has destroyed its eye, he shall give one-half its value in silver to the owner of the ox.

248: If a seignior hired an ox and has broken its horn, cut off its tail, or injured the flesh of its back, he shall give one-quarter its value in silver.

249: If a seignior hired an ox and god struck it and it has died, the seignior who hired the ox shall (so) affirm by god and then he shall go free.

250: If an ox, when it was walking along the street, gored a seignior to death, that case is not subject to claim.

Exod. 21:28–36

251: If a seignior's ox was a gorer and his city council made it known to him that it was a gorer, but he did not pad its horns (or) tie up his ox, and that ox gored to death a member of the aristocracy, he shall give one-half mina of silver.

252: If it was a seignior's slave, he shall give one-third mina of silver.

253: If a seignior hired a(nother) seignior to oversee his field, and lending him *feed-grain,* entrusting him with oxen, contracted with him to cultivate the field, if that seignior stole the seed or fodder and it has been found in his possession, they shall cut off his hand.

254: If he appropriated the *feed-grain* and thus has starved the oxen, he shall make good twofold the grain which he received.

255 : If he has let the seignior's oxen out on hire or he stole the seed-grain and so has raised nothing in the field, they shall prove it against that seignior and at harvest-time he shall measure out sixty *kur* of grain per eighteen *iku*.

256: If he was not able to meet his obligation, they shall drag him through that field with the oxen.

257: If a seignior hired a *cultivator*, he shall give him eight *kur* of grain per year.

258: If a seignior hired a cattle-herder, he shall pay him six *kur* of grain per year.

259: If a seignior stole a plow from a field, he shall give five shekels of silver to the owner of the plow.

260: If he has stolen a *seeder* or a harrow, he shall give three shekels of silver.

261: If a seignior hired a shepherd to pasture cattle or sheep, he shall give him eight *kur* of grain per year.

262 : If a seignior . . . and ox or a sheep to . . .

263: If he has lost [the ox] or sheep which was committed to him, he shall make good ox for [ox], sheep for [sheep] to their owner.

264: If [a shepherd], to whom cattle or sheep were given to pasture, being in receipt of his wages in full, to his satisfaction, has then let the cattle decrease, has let the sheep decrease, thus lessening the birth rate, he shall give increase and profit in accordance with the terms of his contract.

265: If a shepherd, to whom cattle or sheep were given to pasture, became unfaithful and hence has altered the cattlemark or has sold (them), they shall prove it against him and he shall make good in cattle and sheep to their owner tenfold what he stole.

266: If a visitation of god has occurred in a sheepfold or a lion has made a kill, the shepherd shall prove himself innocent in the presence of god, but the owner of the sheepfold shall receive from him the animal stricken in the fold.

Exod. 22:10ff.

267: If the shepherd was careless and has let lameness develop in the fold, the shepherd shall make good in cattle and sheep the loss through the lameness which he let develop in the fold and give (them) to their owner.

268: If a seignior hired an ox to thresh, twenty *qu* of grain shall be its hire.

269: If he hired an ass to thresh, ten *qu* of grain shall be its hire.

270: If he hired a goat to thresh, one *qu* of grain shall be its hire.

271: If a seignior hired oxen, a wagon and a driver for it, he shall give 180 *qu* of grain per day.

272: If a seignior hired simply a wagon by itself, he shall give forty *qu* of grain per day.

273: If a seignior hired a laborer, he shall give six *še* of silver per day from the beginning of the year till the fifth month; from the sixth month till the end of the year he shall give five *še* of silver per day.

274: If a seignior wishes to hire an artisan, he shall pay per day as the wage of a . . . five [*še*] of silver; as the wage of a *brickmaker* five *še* of silver; [as the wage of] a *linen-weaver* . . . [*še*] of silver; [as the wage] of a *seal-cutter* . . . [*še*] of silver; [as the wage of] a *jeweller* . . . [*še* of] silver; [as the wage of] a *smith* . . . [*še* of] silver; [as the wage of] a carpenter four *še* of silver; as the wage of a leatherworker . . . *še* of silver; as the wage of a basketmaker . . . *še* of silver; [as the wage of] a builder . . . *še* of silver.

275: [If] a seignior hired a *long-boat,* its hire shall be three *še* of silver per day.

276: If a seignior hired a rowboat, he shall give two and one-half *še* of silver per day as its hire.

277: If a seignior hired a boat of sixty *kur*, he shall give one-sixth (shekel) of silver per day as its hire.

278: If a seignior purchased a male (or) female slave and when his month was not yet complete, epilepsy attacked him, he shall return (him) to his seller and the purchaser shall get back the money which he paid out.

279: If a seignior purchased a male (or) female slave and he has then received a claim (against him), his seller shall be responsible for the claim.

280: If a seignior has purchased in a foreign land the male (or) female slave of a(nother) seignior and when he has arrived home the owner of the male or female slave has identified either his male or his female slave, if that male and female slave are natives of the land, their freedom shall be effected without any money (payment).

281: If they are natives of another land, the purchaser shall state in the presence of god what money he paid out and the owner of the male or female slave shall give to the merchant the money he paid out and thus redeem his male or female slave.

282: If a male slave has said to his master, "You are not my master," his master shall prove him to be his slave and cut off his ear.

The Laws of Ur-Nammu

ANET³, 523–25

TRANSLATOR: J. J. FINKELSTEIN

Ur-Nammu (2112–2095 B.C.) was the founding ruler of the Third Dynasty of Ur, the builder of the best preserved ziggurat in ancient Mesopotamia, whose reign inaugurated the last great period of Sumerian literary creativity. Although some contemporary examples of this creative effort have begun to come to light in recent excavations at Nippur, most of the literary and scholarly production of this period is known only from copies produced in the scribal schools in Nippur and Ur some two to three hundred years later, i.e., between 1800 and 1700 B.C.

(lines 1–23 destroyed or fragmentary) (24–30) . . . (of) the land . . . , . . . monthly, he established for him 90 *kōr* of barley, 30 sheep, and 50 quarts of butter, as a regular offering.

(31–35) After An and Enlil had turned over the Kingship of Ur to Nanna, (36–40) at that time did Ur-Nammu, son born of (the goddess) Ninsun, for his beloved mother who bore him, (41–42) in accordance with his (i.e., of the god Nanna) principles of equity and truth, . . . (lines 43–72 destroyed or fragmentary).

(col. ii 73–74) He set up the seven . . . (75–78) Nammahni, the *ensi* of Lagash he slew. (79–84) By the might of Nanna, lord of the city (of Ur), he returned the Magan-boat of Nanna to the *boundary* (-*canal*), (85–86) (and) made it famous in Ur.

(87–96) At that time, the field(s) had been subject to the *nisqum*-official, the maritime trade was subject to the seafarers' overseer, (col. iii) the herdsman was subject to the "oxen-taker," the "sheep-taker," and the "donkey-taker."

(lines 97–103 destroyed) (104–13) Then did Ur-Nammu, the mighty warrior, king of Ur, king of Sumer and Akkad, by the might of Nanna, lord of the city (of Ur), and in accordance with the true word of Utu, establish equity in the land (114–16) (and) he banished malediction, violence and strife. (117–22) *By granting immunity in Akkad to* the maritime trade from the seafarers' overseer, to the herdsman from the "oxen-taker," the "sheep-taker," and the "donkey-taker," he (123–24) set Sumer and Akkad *free.*

(125–29) At that time, the . . . . *of* Mar[ad] (and) Kazal[lu] *he* . . . . (130–34) [By] the might [of Nanna] (his) lord . . . . , he . . . . (135–42) The copper . . . , the (wooden) . . . (three lines missing), the copper . . . , the wooden . . . , [these] seven . . . , he standardized. (143–44) He fashioned the bronze *silá*-measure, (145–49) he standardized the one *mina* weight, (and) standardized the stone-weight of a shekel of silver *in relation to* one mina.

(150–52) At that time, the bank of the Tigris, the bank of the Euphrates . . . (153–60 destroyed) . . . (161) the king (or "owner") provided a head gardener.

(162–68) The orphan was not delivered up to the rich man; the widow was not delivered up to the mighty man; the man of one shekel was not delivered up to the man of one mina.

(From line 169 to line 205, the A text is almost completely destroyed. It is likely that the series of law-cases began towards the lower end of col. iv on the obverse of the tablet, or at the very beginning of col. v on the reverse, since traces strongly suggest the beginning of a law-case with line 196, which will be considered here as § 1.)

2: (206–15) . . . . . . he shall plant for him, his . . . the planted . . . apple trees and cedars . . . [he . . .] without the owner's knowledge, . . . he shall bring in.

3: (216–21, destroyed)

4: (222–31 = B § 1). If the wife of a man, *by employing her charms,* followed after another man and he slept with her, they (i.e., the authorities) shall slay that woman, but that male (i.e., the other man) shall be set free.

5: (232–39 = B § 2). If a man proceeded by force, and deflowered the virgin (lit.: "undeflowered") slave-woman of another man, that man must pay five shekels of silver.

6: (app. 240–44 = B § 3). If a man divorces his primary wife, he must pay (her) one mina of silver.

7: (app. 245–49 = B § 4). If it is a (former) widow (whom) he divorces, he must pay (her) one-half mina of silver.

8: (250–55 = B § 5). If (however) the man had slept with the widow without there having been any marriage contract, he need not pay (her) any silver.

9: (= 256–69 mostly destroyed)

10: (270–80). If a man had accused a(nother) man of . . . and he (i.e., the accuser) had him (i.e., the accused) brought to the river-ordeal, and the river-ordeal proved him innocent, then the man who had brought him (i.e., the accuser) must pay him three shekels of silver.

11: (281–90 = B § 10). If a man accused the wife of a man of fornication, and the river(-ordeal) proved her innocent, then the man who had accused her must pay one-third of a mina of silver.

12: (291–301 = B § 11). If a (prospective) son-in-law entered the house of his (prospective) father-in-law, but his father-in-law later gave [his daughter (i.e., the prospective bride) to] another man, he (the father-in-law) shall return to him (i.e., the rejected son-in-law) *two*-fold the amount of bridal presents he had brought.

13: (302–12 = B § 12). (Only traces remain.)

14: (313–23, omitted in B). If [. . .] a slavewoman [*or a male slave fled from the master's house*] and crossed beyond the territory of the city, and (another) man brought her/him back, the owner of the slave shall pay to the one who brought him back *two* shekels of silver.

15: (324–30 = B § 13 + § 21). If a [man . . .] cut off the foot (var.: limb) of [another man *with his* . . .], he shall pay ten shekels of silver.

16: (331–38, omitted in B). If a man, in the course of a scuffle, smashed the limb of another man with a club, he shall pay one mina of silver.

17: (339–44 = B § 22). If someone severed the nose of another man with a *copper knife,* he must pay two-thirds of a mina of silver.

18: (A 345–? = B § 23). If a man cut off the [. . .] of [another man] with a [. . .] he shall pay [x shekels(?) of silv]er.

19: (B § 24 + § 16). If he [*knocked out*] his to[*oth*] with [a . . .] he shall pay two shekels of silver.

20: (missing). (There is a gap of close to 30 lines, which contained not more than three sections, including § 20, § 21, and the beginning of § 21'.)

21': (B § 28). . . . he shall surely bring. If he has no slave-woman, he must surely pay ten shekels of silver. If he has no silver, *he shall pay him (with) whatever possessions he (owns).*

22': (B § 29). If a man's slave-woman, comparing herself to her mistress, speaks insolently to her (or: him), her mouth shall be scoured with 1 quart of salt.

23': (B § 30). If a man's slave-woman, comparing herself to her mistress, struck her . . . (rest missing).

24': (almost completely missing, possibly more than one section in the gap)

25': (B § 34). If a man appeared as a witness (in a lawsuit), and was shown to be a perjurer, he must pay fifteen shekels of silver.

26': (B § 35). If a man appeared as a witness (in a lawsuit), but declined to testify on oath, he must make good as much as is involved in that lawsuit.

27': (B § 36). If a man proceeded by force, and plowed the arable field of a(nother) man, and he (i.e., the latter) brought a lawsuit (against him), but he (i.e., the squatter) reacts in contempt, that man will forfeit his expenses.

28': (B § 37). If a man flooded the field of a(nother) man with water, he shall measure out (for him) three *kōr* of barley per *ikū* of field.

29': (B § 38). If a man had leased an arable field to a(nother) man for cultivation, but he (the lessee) did not plow it, so that it turned into wasteland, he shall measure out (to the lessor) three *kōr* of barley per *ikū* of field.

(remainder of text largely destroyed)

Sumerian Laws

TRANSLATOR: J. J. FINKELSTEIN

Yale Babylonian Collection, YBC 2177

ANET³, 525–26

Since the first publication of this text in 1912, it was thought to represent a part of the "lawcode" of some unknown ruler of the pre-Hammurabi period. In actual fact, however, the text is a student exercise executed in one of the scribal schools of Southern Mesopotamia (i.e., Sumer) some time during the

Old Babylonian period, probably *ca.* 1800 B.C. The obverse of the tablet has never been published due to its very poor state of preservation, but from those lines of it which are still legible it can be ascertained that it consisted in considerable part of disconnected legal phrases and sentences revolving about a limited number of topics, such as pledges for loans, and loss of animals, and that it contained a number of repetitions.

(rev. col. iv) 1: If (a man accidentally) buffeted a woman of the free-citizen class and caused her to have a miscarriage, he must pay 10 shekels of silver.

2: If (a man deliberately) struck a woman of the free-citizen class and caused her to have a miscarriage, he must pay one-third mina of silver.

3: If (*a boat captain*) violated the itinerary to which he was committed, and (thereby) brought about the loss of the boat, he shall measure out to *its* owner as much as the boat . . . , (*and*) its hire of . . .

4: If (a son) has said to his father and to his mother: "You are not my father; you are not my mother," he forfeits (his heir's rights to) house, field, orchard, slaves, and (any other) property, and they may sell him (into slavery) for money at full value.

5: (If) his father and his mother (say): "You are not our son," they will forfeit the estate.

6: (If) his father and his mother (say): "You are not our son," (col. v) [. . .] . . . [. . .] shall forfeit.

7: If (a man) deflowered the daughter of a free citizen in the street, her father and her mother not having known (that she was in the street), and she (then) says to her father and her mother: "*I was raped,*" her father and her mother may give her to him (forcibly) as a wife.

8: If (a man) deflowered the daughter of a free citizen in the street, her father and her mother having known (that she was in the street) but the man who deflowered her denied that he knew (her to be of the free-citizen class), and, standing at the temple gate, swore an oath (to this effect, he shall be freed).

9: If a lion has devoured a *straying* ox, he (i.e., the herdsman or the person who hired it) must *deliver* the . . . *in full,* to its owner.

10: If an ox caused the loss of a *straying* ox, ox for ox . . . . (remainder lost)

The Edict of Ammisaduqa

ANET³, 526–28

TRANSLATOR: J. J. FINKELSTEIN

It was the custom in Mesopotamia during the Old Babylonian period, but going back possibly to late Early Dynastic times, for the kings to proclaim an act of "justice" or "equity" (Sumerian n í g . s i . s á = Akkadian *mīšarum*) at the beginning of their reigns and at intervals of seven or more years thereafter. Such acts, concerned mainly with the remission of debts and other obligations, as well as the reversion of land holdings to their original owners, were known heretofore from allusions to them in royal year-names, and references to them in certain private legal documents. The Edict of Ammisaduqa, the 10th ruler of the Hammurabi Dynasty in Babylon (1646–1626 B.C.), represents the only extant substantial text proper of such an edict, the only other one known being a fragment of a similar edict issued by Samsuiluna (1749–1712 B.C.), the great-grandfather of Ammisaduqa. There is good reason to believe, however, that the early law-"codes," such as those of Ur-Nammu, Lipit-Ishtar, the kingdom of Eshnunna, and the great "code" of Hammurabi incorporate within their texts at least some of the provisions of the *misharum*-acts proclaimed by them during the course of their reigns, and it is likely that the well-known "reform" inscription of Urukagina, the last king of Lagash of the Early Dynastic period (*ca.* 2350 B.C.), is a text of a closely related type.

1: (Text C). The tablet [of the decree which the land was ordered] to hear at the time that the king invoked a *misharum* for the land.

2: (5) The arrears of the farming agents, the shepherds, the *šusikku*-(agents) of the provinces, and (other) crown tributaries—the . . . of their *firm agreements* and the *promissory notes* . . . of their payments are herewith remitted. (10) The collecting officer may not sue the crown tributary for payment.

3: The "market" of Babylon, the "markets" of the country(side), the *ra'ibānum*-officer, which in the . . . tablet, are . . . *to* the collecting officer—(15) their arrears dating from the "Year in which King Ammiditana remitted the debts which the land had contracted (= year 21 of Ammiditana)" until the month of Nisan of the "Year: Ammisaduqa the king, Enlil having (20) magnified his noble lordship, like Shamash (Text A) he rose forth in steadfastness over his country, and instituted justice for the whole of his people (= year 1 of Ammisaduqa)"—because the king has invoked the *misharum* for the land, (25) the collecting officer may not sue the [. . .] for payment.

4: Whoever has given barley or silver to an Akkadian or an Amorite as an interest-bearing loan, or on the *melqētum* basis (30) [*or* . . .], and had a document executed—because the king has invoked the *misharum* for the land, his document is voided; (35) (Text C) he may not collect the barley or silver on the basis of his document.

5: But if, commencing with the month of Addar II of the "Year in which King Ammiditana destroyed the wall of Udinim constructed by Damqiilishu" (= Year 37 of Ammiditana), (40) he collected by constraint, he shall refund whatever he had received through collection. He who does not (thus) make a refund (45) in accordance with the royal decree, shall die.

6: Whoever has given barley or silver to an Akkadian or an Amorite as an interest-bearing loan or on the *melqētum* basis, and in the document which he executed (50) perpetrated a deception by having it drawn up as a sale or a bailment and then persisted in taking interest, he (i.e., the debtor) shall produce his witnesses, and they shall indict him (i.e., the creditor) for taking interest; because he had distorted his document, his document shall be voided.

(55) A creditor may not sue against the house of an Akkadian or an Amorite for whatever he had loaned him; should he sue for payment, he shall die.

7: (Text A) If anyone had given barley or silver as an interest-bearing loan and had a document executed, (ii 30) retaining the document in his own possession, and then stated: "I have certainly not given it to you as an interest-bearing loan or on the *melqētum* basis; the barley or silver which I have given you, I have given (as an advance) for purchases, or for the production of profit, or for some other objective," the person who had received the barley or silver from the creditor shall produce his witnesses to the wording of the document which the lender had denied, and they shall speak (their testimony) before god. (ii 40) Because he (i.e., the creditor) had distorted his document and denied the (truth of the) matter, he must pay (to the borrower) six-fold (the amount he had lent him). If he (the creditor) cannot make good his liability, he must die.

8: (iii) An Akkadian or an Amorite who has received barley, silver, or (other) goods either as merchandise for a commercial journey, or as a joint enterprise for the production of profit, (5) his document is not voided (by the *misharum* act); he must repay in accordance with the stipulations of his agreements.

9: Whoever has given barley, silver, or (other) goods to an Akkadian or an Amorite either (as an advance) for purchases, for a commercial journey, or as a joint enterprise for the production of profit, (10) and had a document executed, (but) in the document he had executed, the creditor stipulated in writing that at the expiration of the term (of the contract) the money would accrue interest (15) or if he made any (other) additional stipulations, he (i.e., the obligee) shall not repay on the terms of the (added) stipulations, but shall repay (only) the barley or silver [on the terms of the (basic) document]. The (obligations of the supplementary) stipulations upon the Akkadian (20) or the Amorite are remitted.

10: [. . .] . . . *to* Babylon, [the market of . . .], the market of Borsippa, [the market of . . .], the market of Isin, [the market of . . .], the market of Larsa, (25) [the market of . . .]aṣ, the market of Malgium, [the market of Manki]sum, the market of Shitullum, [. . .] half (their) investment capital was given [*them*] (in the form of) merchandise out of the palace—the (other) half to be made up by them (i.e., the market associations of the named cities)—(30) *any* such merchandise shall be disbursed to them from the palace at the going price of the respective city.

11: If a (state) trading merchant, who customarily disposes of merchandise of the palace, made out a document in favor of the palace against the (collectable) arrears of crown tributaries as if he actually received (such) merchandise from the palace, and received (in turn) the (payable) document of the palace-tributary—thus no merchandise was actually given him from the palace in accordance with his document, nor did he receive (any funds) from the palace tributary—(40) because the king has remitted the arrears of the palace-tributary, (iv) that merchant shall declare on divine oath: "(I swear that) I have not received anything in payment from the palace-tributaries as stated in this document." After having (thus) declared, (5) he shall produce the document of the palace-tributary, they (i.e., the authorities and the principals) shall settle the accounts jointly, and out of the merchandise stipulated in the document made out by the merchant in favor of the palace they shall remit in behalf of the merchant as much as was stipulated by the document made out by the palace-tributary (10) in favor of the merchant.

12: The *šusikku*-agent of the land who (15) customarily receives [*the carcasses*] from the palace cattle-herdsmen, shepherds, and goatherds under divine oath, (and) who (21) customarily renders to the palace: For every cow carcass: one (quantity) of sin[ews] together with the skin; for every ewe-carcass: one-sixth . . . *barley,* together with the skin, plus 1¾ minas of wool; for every goat-carcass: one-sixth of [*a shekel*] of *silver* plus ⅔ of a mina of goat-wool,—because the king has instituted the *misharum* for the land, their arrears will not be collected. The . . . (*of*) the *šusikku*-agent of the land (25) (*the quotas*) . . . will not be filled.

13: The arrears of the porter(s) which had been assigned to the collecting-agent for collection are remitted; they will not be collected.

14: (30) The arrears of the Suhu country consisting of *šibšum*-rents and/(*or*) half-share rents—because the king has instituted the *misharum* for the land, it is remitted; it will not be collected. (35) He (i.e., the collecting-agent) shall not sue for collection against the houses of Suhu (var.: the Suhian population).

15: The crop impost officer who customarily receives the impost proportions of fields (planted to) [barley,] sesame, or minor crops belonging to the palace-tributaries, the . . . , the crown dependents, the infantrymen, the sergeants, or other special feudatories—(v) because the king has instituted the *misharum* for the land, it is remitted; it will not be proportioned (i.e., the impost shares of each crop will not be collected). (However,) the barley destined for sale or profit will be proportioned according to the customary ratio(s).

16: (5) The taverness(es) of the provinces who customarily pay silver (and/or) barley to the palace—because the king has instituted the *misharum* in the land, the collecting agent (10) will not sue for payment of their arrears.

17: A taverness who has given beer or barley as a loan may not collect any of what she had given as a loan.

18: A taverness or a merchant who [...] (15) dishonest *weight* shall die.

19: The infantryman or the sergeant who has leased [a ... field] for three years does not perform the [...] service. (20) In the present [*year*], because the king has instituted the *misharum* in the land, the infantryman or the sergeant pays according to the (prevailing) ratio of his city ... , a third or half (of the crop).

20: (25) If an obligation has resulted in foreclosure against a citizen of Numhia, a citizen of Emutbalum, a citizen of Idamaras, a citizen of Uruk, a citizen of Isin, a citizen of Kisurra, or a citizen of Malgium, (in consequence of which) he [placed] his own person, his wife (30) or his [children] in debt servitude for silver, or as a pledge—because the king has instituted the *misharum* in the land, he is released; his freedom (35) is in effect.

21: If a house-born slavewoman or male slave of a citizen of Numhia, a citizen of Emutbalum, a citizen of Idamaras, a citizen of Uruk, a citizen of Isin, a citizen of Kisurra, (vi) or a citizen of Malgium ... whose price ... , has been sold for money, or was (5) given over for debt servitude, or was left as a pledge, his freedom will not be effected.

22: (10) The *ra'ibānum* or regional governor who gives barley, silver, or wool to the "house" of an infantryman or a sergeant for harvest labor, or for the performance of (other) labor, (15) as the result of force, shall die. (That) infantryman or sergeant may (at the same time) keep (lit.: "carry off") whatever had been given him.

Documents from the Practice of Law
Mesopotamian Legal Documents

ANET, 219–20

Translator: Theophile J. Meek

Nuzi Akkadian

(1) Sale-Adoption[48]

The tablet of adoption belonging to Kuzu, the son of Karmishe: he adopted Tehip-tilla, the son of Puhishenni. As his share[49] (of the estate) Kuzu gave Techiptilla 40 imers[50] of land in the district of Iphushshi. If the land should have a claimant, Kuzu shall clear (it) and give (it) back to Tehip-tilla. Tehip-tilla in turn gave 1 mina of silver to Kuzu as his honorarium. Who ever defaults shall pay 2 minas of silver (and) 2 minas of gold.

[48] Sale-adoption was a legal device used in Nuzi whereby a landowner could circumvent the law prohibiting the sale of land outside the family by going through the form of adopting the purchaser. The Nuzi tablets come from the middle of the 2nd millennium B.C.

[49] The word used here, *zittu*, means the double share of the first-born son.

[50] An imer was approximately 4½ acres.

(The names of fourteen persons and the scribe as witnesses, each preceded by the witness-sign.)

(The names of two of the witnesses, one other person, and the scribe, each preceded by "The seal of.")

(2) Sale-Adoption

The tablet of adoption belonging to Nashwi, the son of Ar-shenni: he adopted Wullu, the son of Puhi-shenni. As long as Nashwi is alive, Wullu shall provide food and clothing; when Nashwi dies, Wullu shall become the heir. If Nashwi has a son of his own, he shall divide (the estate) equally with Wullu, but the son of Nashwi shall take the gods of Nashwi. However, if Nashwi does not have a son of his own, then Wullu shall take the gods of Nashwi.[51] Furthermore, he gave his daughter Nuhuya in marriage to Wullu, and if Wullu takes another wife he shall forfeit the lands and buildings of Nashwi. Whoever defaults shall make compensation with 1 mina of silver and 1 mina of gold.

Gen. 31:26ff.

(The names of five persons and the scribe as witnesses, each preceded by the witness-sign.)

(The names of four of the witnesses and the scribe, each preceded by "The seal of.")

(3) Real Adoption

The tablet of adoption belonging to [Zike], the son of Akkuya: he gave his son Shennima in adoption to Shuriha-ilu, and Shuriha-ilu, with reference to Shennima, (from) all the lands . . . (and) his earnings of every sort gave to Shennima one (portion) of his property. If Shuriha-ilu should have a son of his own, as the principal (son) he shall take a double share; Shennima shall then be next in order (and) take his proper share. As long as Shuriha-ilu is alive, Shennima shall revere him. When Shuriha-ilu [dies], Shennima shall become the heir. Furthermore, Kelim-ninu has been given in marriage to Shennima. If Kelim-ninu bears (children), Shennima shall not take another wife; but if Kelim-ninu does not bear, Kelim-ninu shall acquire a woman of the land of Lullu as wife for Shennima, and Kelim-ninu may not send the offspring away. Any sons that may be born to Shennima from the womb of Kelim-ninu, to (these) sons shall be given [all] the lands (and) buildings of every sort. [However], if she does not bear a son, [then] the daughter of Kelim-ninu from the lands (and) buildings shall take one (portion) of the property. Furthermore, Shuriha-ilu shall not adopt another son in addition to Shennima.

[51] Possession of the household gods marked a person as the legitimate heir, which explains Laban's anxiety to recover his household gods from Jacob. It is to be noted too that Laban binds Jacob in verse 50 to marry no other wives besides his daughters, just as Wullu is bound in our text.

Whoever among them defaults shall compensate with 1 mina of silver (and) 1 mina of gold.

Furthermore, Yalampa is given as a handmaid to Kelim-ninu and Shatim-ninu has been made co-parent. As long as she is alive, she (i.e., Yalampa) shall revere her Shatim-ninu shall not annul the [*agreement*].

If Kelim-ninu bears (children) and Shennima takes another wife, she may *take* her dowry and leave.

(The names of nine persons and the scribe as witnesses, each preceded by the witness-sign.)

The remaining sons of Zike may not lay claim to the lands (and) buildings belonging to the (above) one (portion) of the property.

The tablet was written after the proclamation.

(Sealed by eight persons, seven of whom were already named as witnesses.)

(4) Lawsuit

Tarmiya, the son of Huya, appeared with Shukriya and Kula-hupi, with (these) two brothers of his, the sons of Huya, in a lawsuit before the judges of Nuzi with reference to the female slave [Sululi-Ishtar], whereupon Tarmiya spoke thus before the judges, "My father, Huya, was sick and lay on a couch; then my father seized my hand and spoke thus to me, 'My other sons, being older, have acquired wives, but you have not acquired a wife; so I give you herewith Sululi-Ishtar as your wife.'" Then the judges demanded the witnesses to Tarmiya [and Tarmiya] had his witnesses appear [before the judges]: . . . , the son of Hurshaya, . . . , the son of Ikkiya, . . . , the son of Itrusha, (and) . . . , the son of Hamanna. [These] witnesses of [Tarmiya] were examined before the judges, whereupon the judges spoke to Shukriya and Kula-hupi, "Go and take the oath of the gods against the witnesses of Tarmiya." Shukriya and Kula-hupi shrank from the gods[52] so that Tarmiya prevailed in the lawsuit and the judges assigned the female slave, Sululi-Ishtar, to Tarmiya.

(The names of three persons, each preceded by "The seal of.")

The signature of Iliya.

(5) Hebrew Slave Document

Mar-Idiglat, a Hebrew from the land of Assyria, on his own initiative has entered (the house of) Tehip-tilla, the son of Puhi-shenni, as a slave.

(The names of eleven persons and the scribe as witnesses, each preceded by the witness-sign.)

(The names of two of the witnesses and the scribe, each preceded by "The seal of.")

---

[52] I.e., they refused to take the oath in fear of its consequences and thus showed themselves in the wrong.

(6) Hebrew Slave Document

Sin-balti, a Hebrew woman, on her own initiative has entered the house of Tehip-tilla as a slave. Now if Sin-balti defaults and goes into the house of another, Tehip-tilla shall pluck out the eyes of Sin-balti and sell her.

(The names of nine persons and the scribe as witnesses, each preceded by the witness-sign.)

(The names of two of the witnesses and the scribe, each preceded by "The seal of.")

TRANSLATOR: J. J. FINKELSTEIN

ANET³, 542–47

(1) A Trial for Murder

Nanna-sig son of Lu-Suen, Ku-Enlilla son of Ku-Nanna the barber, and Enlil-ennam son of Adda-kalla, the orchard-keeper, murdered Lu-Inanna son of Lugaluru, the *nishakku*-priest.

(6) After Lu-Inanna son of Lugal-uru was dead, they (i.e., the murderers) told Nin-dada daughter of Lu-Ninurta, wife of Lu-Inanna, that her (husband) Lu-Inanna had been murdered. (13) Nin-dada daughter of Lu-Ninurta did not open her mouth; she kept it secret. Their case was brought to Isin before the king. Ur-Ninurta the king[53] ordered that the case be tried by the Assembly of Nippur.

(20) Ur-gula son of Lugal-ibila, Dudu the bird-catcher, Ali-ellati the *muškēnu*,[54] Puzu son of Lu-Suen, Eluti son of Tizqar-Ea, Shesh-kalla the potter, Lugal-kam the orchard keeper, Lugal-azida son of Suen-andul, Sheshkalla son of Shara-ḤAR (var.: ḤAR-*abi*) addressed (the Assembly): (30) "As men who have killed a man, they are not (fit to be) alive; those three males and that woman should be killed in front of the (official) chair of Lu-Inanna son of Lugal-uru the *nishakku*-priest," they said. (35) Shuqalilum the ERIN-GAL-GAL of the infantry of Ninurta (and) Ubar-Suen the orchard-keeper then addressed (the Assembly): "Nin-data daughter of Lu-Ninurta—granted that she killed her husband—(40) what can a woman do that she should be killed?,"[55] they said. In the Assembly of Nippur they[56] [respond and] addressed it thus: "A woman who does not treasure her husband—(45) she may surely have had intercourse with a stranger, (and) he would then murder her husband. Should he then let her know that her husband had been killed—why should she then not keep silent

---

[53] King of Isin, 1923–1896 B.C.

[54] The social class consisting of crown dependents.

[55] I.e., she was an accessory to, but not a direct participant in the act.

[56] Presumably, the nine persons who first proposed the verdict, who were most likely the "elders" of the Assembly.

about him?[57] (50) It is certainly she, who murdered her husband; her guilt exceeds that of the ones who (actually) killed a man," they said.

The Assembly of Nippur having (thus) resolved the issue, Nanna-sig son of Lu-Suen, Ku-Enlilla son of Ku-Nanna, the barber, Enlil-ennam son of Adda-kalla, the orchard-keeper, and Nin-dada daughter of Lu-Ninurta, the wife of Lu-Innanna, were condemned to execution.

(Subscription:) A case before the Assembly of Nippur.

(2) Dissolution of Partnership

Old Assyrian, Cappadocia, 19th century B.C.

Ashurpilah, trustee for the estate of Amur-Ishtar, Su'in-re'um, Ilibani, Ashurnishu, and Shulaban—the sons of (5) Amur-Ishtar (appearing) in their own right—and representing Abshalim, daughter of Amur-Ishtar and Iddin-Adad their brother, (vs.) Ashurmuttabbil, Buzazu, and Ikupasha, sons of (10) Pushuken (appearing) in their own right, and representing Ahaha their sister, the abbess, and their brother Shue'a, empaneled us (as judges) respecting their mutual obligations. (15) They swore the oath by the "City" (i.e., Ashur) and we terminated their litigations, (namely): (Regardless) whether (in the past) Amur-Ishtar had acted as (lawful) agent for Pushuken, or whether Pushuken acted as agent (20) for Amur-Ishtar; whether either one had sent the other (goods for) deposit; whether either one had (25) received money of the other on outstanding deliveries; whatever (business involved in) an encased tablet bearing the seal of (either of) them; whatever was in transit, whatever either had stored in the other's warehouse—whether it was in the (30) "City" (i.e., Ashur), or in the "Country" (i.e., central Anatolia)—the sons of Amur-Ishtar, the daughter of Amur-Ishtar, the abbess, and the sons of Pushuken, the daughter of Pushuken, (35) the abbess,—none will return (in litigation) against the other for any cause whatever. Usanum son of Amur-Ashur, Kuluma'a son of Ashur-imitti, (40) Huni'a son of Ashur-imitti, Tabsil-Ashur son of Ashur-idi, Puzurenna son of Enna-Ashur, Ashurtaklaku son of Alahum, Belanum son of Shu-Ashur, Idi-Ashur son of Dan-Ashur—these persons were those who terminated the litigation.

(3) Acknowledgment of Liability for a Parental Obligation

Old Assyrian, 19th century B.C.

Ashurtab empaneled us (as judges) against Ashurlamassi, and thus (spoke) Ashurtab to Ashurlamassi: (5) "This tablet—(does it bear) the seal of your father, or (does it) not (bear) the seal of your father?"

---

[57] Probably referring to her murdered husband, as in line 14, rather than the murderers, who were three men.

Thus (spoke) Ashurlamassi: "(It does bear) the seal of my father; I shall bring you evidence of satisfaction (of the obligation) (10) within six months. If I do not produce for you (this evidence within six months), I assume the debt. Month of Sha-sarate, (15) eponymate of a subordinate of Enna-Su'in. Witness (i.e., the judges): Abuziya son of Shu-Su'in, [. . .] son of Ashur-Shamshi, Anina son of Shu-Erra.

(4) Marriage Contract

Old Assyrian, 19th century B.C.

Laqipum has married Hatala, daughter of Enishru. In the country (i.e., Central Anatolia) Laqipum (5) may not marry another (woman)—(but) in the City (i.e., Ashur) he may marry a hierodule. If within two years she (i.e., Hatala) does not provide him with offspring, (10) she herself will purchase a slavewoman, and later on, after she will have produced a child by him, (15) he may then dispose of her by sale wheresoever he pleases. Should Laqipum choose to divorce her (text: "him"), he must pay (her) five minas of silver; (20) and should Hatala choose to divorce him, she must pay (him) five minas of silver. Witnesses: Masa, Ashurishtikal, (25) Talia, Shupianika.

(5) Inheritance of Priestly Office

Old Babylonian period, Nippur.

Sinabushu son of Nanna-lu-ti having (formerly) conveyed the sealed titles of (his) office of incantatory-priest and his inheritance into the possession of Nannatum the *nishakku* priest—(7) two years having passed since the death of Sinabushu—Aba-Enlil-dim took possession of (these) sealed titles from the hand of Nannatum.

In the future, any claims with reference to (these) sealed titles will be answerable by Aba-Enlil-dim.

Names of Witnesses: Month of Addar, 13th year of Samsuiluna.

(6) Sale of Temple Prerogatives

Old Babylonian period, Larsa.

The term office(s) of anointer, brewer, and "chef" of the temple of Damu[58]—fourteen days a year during the month of Marcheshwan— (5) the prebend of Damiqilishu son of Ana-Damu-taklaku, Puzur-Gula son of Ibku-Nisaba has (10) purchased from Damiqilishu. He has paid out its full sale price of 15 shekels of silver. That in the future (15) Damiqilishu and his heirs—as many as they may be—will not institute any claim with reference to (these) prebends, (20) he swore the oath by the king.

---

[58] A healing god, whose temple was located in Isin.

List of witnesses. Date: 45th year of Rim-Sin.

(7) Litigation over Inheritance
Old Babylonian period.

Text A
Concerning a house-plot of ⅓-sar in area[59] within the cloister,[60] adjoining the house of Lamassi the *hierodule, the full share of a jointly held prior estate*[61] which Amat-Shamash daughter of Supapum (5) had bequeathed to her (adopted) daughter, the (natural) daughter of Sin-eribam, Nidnusha and Shamash-apili, sons of Iddinunim (10) brought suit against the daughter of Sineribam, stating thus: "Amat-Shamash did not bequeath to you any house whatever, and executed no document in your favor; upon her death, you yourself drew up (such a document)," (15) that is what they stated. They (i.e., the litigants) pleaded before Sumu-Akshak.[62] For (the purpose of hearing the testimony of) her (i.e., the defendant's) male and female witnesses, the Standard of Shamash, the Saw of Shamash, and (20) the Serpent of Ishhara[63] entered the cloister. Her male and female witnesses having (25) testified that she[64] had, while still alive, bequeathed (to the defendant) the house and drawn up the document, the judges proceeded with the case; the judge(s) pronounced the penalty to be imposed upon them (i.e., the plaintiffs); the judge(s) cast . . . upon them (30) Nidnusha, Shamash-apili, and the brothers of Amat-Shamash—as many as there may be *who held joint shares in the earlier (estate)*—may not re-institute suit against the daughter of Sin-eribam. If any among the brothers of Amat-Shamash—as many as may be so counted—should (again) (35) institute suit, since their case has been terminated, it is they (i.e., the plaintiffs) who will be held responsible.

A legal case before Shamash. Names of three or four judges.

Text B
(Beginning lost) . . . (After) [Nidnusha and Shamashapil]i, his brother, [the sons of] Iddinunim had instituted suit, (and) the judges tried the

[59] About 133 square feet.

[60] The compound for the votaries of the gods Shamash and his consort Aya in the city of Sippar.

[61] The reading of the third line of the text is in some doubt, but the context, and parallel phraseology from later periods leave no doubt about the general sense; see the list of four defendants in text B.

[62] The burgomaster of Sippar (see text B), and the chief judicial authority in the city.

[63] Three emblems which were brought to the cloister from their temples or chapels to solemnize the witness' testimony.

[64] Amat-Shamash.

case in the temple of Shamash, (and) (5) drew up a non-contestable document in favor of Lamassi, Beltani, Iltani, and the daughter of Sin-eribam, Nidnusha son of Iddinunim once again filed suit. Sumu-Akshak the burgomaster of Sippar (10′) and the judges of Sippar implemented judicial process: Because he had again filed suit in face of a duly executed non-contestable document, they (i.e., the authorities) shaved half his head hair, (15′) pierced his nose, extended his arm(s) (and) marched him around the city. His contest and suit are terminated. Never again shall (20′) Nidnusha son of Iddinunim bring suit against Lamassi, the votary of Shamash, daughter of Puzur-Akshak, Beltani, the votary of Shamash, daughter of Manium, Iltani, the votary of Shamash, daughter of Irra-gamil, and the daughter of Sin-eribam, with respect to anything which Amat-Shamash, the votary of Shamash, daughter of Supapum had (25′) bequeathed to them, from chaff to gold. He may not plead: "I have forgotten this." Nor shall the brothers of Amat-Shamash, as many as there may be, bring suit against them. Because Nidnusha (30′) has terminated *their case*, Nidnusha will be held responsible for their (future) contest and suit.

They swore the oath by Shamash, Marduk, Sinmuballit, and the city of Sippar.

Names of witnesses (mostly destroyed).

(8) Marriage Contract

Old Babylonian period.

Sabitum daughter of Ibbatum—Ibbatum, her father, delivered her into the house of Ilushu-ibni, her father-in-law, (5) as wife to Warad-kubi, his son. 2 beds, 2 chairs, 1 table, 2 baskets, 1 millstone, 1 *mortar*, 1 *sūtu*-measure, (10) 1 grinding-bowl—all these items which Ibbatum has given to Sabitum, his daughter, she brought into the house of Ilushu-ibni, her father-in-law. (15) Her bride-price of ten shekels of silver, (which) Ibbatum has received, having kissed her, he bound (the money) up in the *sissiktu*[65] of his daughter, Sabitum; it was (thus) (20) returned to Warad-kubi.

Should Sabitum ever say to her husband Warad-kubi: "(You) are not my husband," they shall bind her and cast her into the water. (25) And should Warad-kubi ever say to his wife Sabitum: "(You) are not my wife," he shall weigh out her divorce money of one-third mina of silver. Emuq-Adad, her brother(!), (30) shall be responsible for her word.

---

[65] The hem of her garment, having legal and symbolic significance in the event of divorce. The bride-price money was in this instance transferred by the bride's father to the bride, for her husband's use but the principal remaining ultimately the property of the wife.

Five witnesses, including the scribe. Date: 15 Tishre, unknown
year of Ammiditana.

(9) Judicial Disherison

Old Babylon period.

(Beginning lost) . . . (2′) spoke thus, declaring: (3′) "Shamash-nasir is
not my brother; Awil-Nabium, my father, did not (4′) adopt him,"
thus he declared. (5′) Shamash-nasir thus responded to him, saying:
(7′) "Awil-Nabium, my father, while I was a small child, (8′) took me
in adoption and reared me, (9′) I can produce my witness (to that effect)," thus he spoke. (10′) In the presence of the judges they (thus)
charged and replied to each other. (11′) The judges examined their
case and (12′) requested of him his witness. Witness (13′) was
ushered into the presence of the judges, who then (14′) listened carefully to their testimony and (15′–16′) dispatched them to the temple
of Shamash in order to declare their testimony (under oath). (rev.)
(1–2) In the temple of Shamash, the witnesses took the stand (before)
the Golden Standard,[66] his heralds, and (3) thus declared their testimony, saying: (4–5) "Awil-Nabium took Shamash-nasir in adoption
as a small child, (6) and reared him; we certify his being reared," thus
they stated. (7) [Word] having been brought back to the judges,
(8) [the judges] thereupon reinstated Shamash-nasir as the son of
Awil-Nabium, and (9) his brother . . . -nasir, they disinherited (10)
[. . .] *waived* the imposition of (any additional) penalty against him.
  (Names of witnesses follow; date lost.)

(10) Litigation over a House in Susa

Old Babylonian period.

Concerning the house which Abi-ili sold at full price to Kuk-adar in
(the time of the viceroy) Temti-raptash and Kuduzulush the burgomaster, (5) Puzur-Teppuna, son of Abi-ili, and his heirs, rose up in
litigation against Iqishuni (son of Kuk-Adar), (declaring) thus: "Our
father's house was not sold to your father; (10) your tablet is forged."
Many men were present and, acting as a court, imposed upon Iqishuni the oath by the god. In the temple of Innanna Iqishuni (15)
pronounced the oath, saying: "Thou, O Innanna, knowest that I did
not fabricate a forged document and that my father bequeathed this
tablet to me." Iqishuni having thus sworn, (20) they cleared for him
(his title to) the house. (21–47) Names of witnesses. (48ff.) In the
presence of these *34* witnesses Iqishuni took the oath in the temple of

---

[66] The emblem of Shamash in his temple Ebabbar in Sippar, before which the oath
procedure is performed.

Innanna; Puzur-Teppuna [and his heirs] caused him to take the oath [. . .] (and) they (the judges) cleared (for him title to) the house.

(11) Trial for Assault

Old Babylonian period, Diyala region.

Bir-ilishu the Amorite infantryman struck the cheek of Apil-ilishu son of Ahushina, then denied it, saying: "I did not strike (him)." (6) The viceroy and the judges then remanded him to the Gate of Ishtar (where he was) to stand and swear (his denial). (11) (But) he turned away. As he would not pay (voluntary compensation), did not take the stand, and did not swear, he must pay 3⅓ shekels of silver.

4 witnesses.

(12) A Trial for Theft

Old Babylonian period.

Ilushunasir and Belshunu—because Taribum had (5) trespassed . . . in the house of Ilushunasir—arrested him. Taribum son of . . . , before the elders of the city confessed: "I am a thief." (10) Since he [confessed] : "I have committed theft," the stolen good having been found in his possession, the city elders, in the (presence of) the Axe of Sin and the Mace of Isharkidissu, delivered him up to Ilushunasir for penal servitude.

17 witnesses, including the viceroy (šakanakku).

(13) Adoption

Old Babylonian period. Mari.

Yahatti-el is the son of Hillalum and Alitum. He shall rejoice in their joys (5) and commiserate in their miseries. Should Hillalum, his father, and Alitum, his mother (ever) say to their son Yahatti-el: "You are not our son," (10) they shall forfeit house and belongings. Should Yahatti-el say to Hillalum, his father, and to Alitum, his mother (15): "You are not my father; you are not my mother," they shall have him shaved, and shall sell him for money. (As for) Hillalum and (20) Alitum—regardless of how many sons they shall have acquired— Yahatti-el is primary heir, and he shall take a double share of the estate of Hillalum, his father. (25) His younger brothers shall divide (the remainder) in equal shares. Whichever (among the brothers) shall contest (this) against him, will (be deemed to) have eaten the taboo of Shamash, Itur-Mer, Shamshi-Adad, and Yasmah-Adad, (30) and shall pay three and one-third minas of silver, the penalty in a capital case.

Eighteen witnesses. Month of Hibirtum, 28th day; eponymy of Asqudum.

MESOPOTAMIAN LEGAL DOCUMENTS • 197

(14) Litigation concerning Inheritance

Alalakh, Old Babylonian period.

Concerning the estate of the wife of Ammurapi, Abba'ēl brought legal suit against his sister Bittatti, declaring thus: "The entire house belongs to me only; you, Bittatti, are not reckoned (as an heir) in (this) house." Thus (replied) Bittatti: "[...] in the city of Suharuwa, [...] I am (indeed) reckoned (as an heir) in [the estate of] my mother; *why* have *you* then taken the extra share (of the estate)? You and I must (rather) divide our father's house equally."

They entered upon legal proceedings before King Niqmepa. Abi-adu declared in testimony before King Niqmepa the king that Bittatti held (rights to) a share in the estate. The king thereupon declared: "Let Abba'ēl take as his preferential share that (portion of) the house which he pleases; Bittatti shall then take that (portion of the) house which he declines." That is what the king declared.

Gimil-Addu and Niwariadu, [officials] of the Throne were detailed to arrange the division of the house. Abba'ēl took as his preferred share the upper house with loft; the lower house he left (text: gave) for his sister, Bittatti. From this day henceforward Abba'ēl may not re-institute proceedings against Bittatti—nor Bittatti against Abba'ēl—with respect to the house which is the portion of Bittatti. Whichever (of them) does open such proceedings will pay into the palace five hundred shekels of gold and will forfeit his portion of the estate.

Nine witnesses. Date: 13th day of the month of Izalli, year in which King Niqmepa took the city of Arazik.

(15) Abrogation of a Marriage Agreement

Alalakh, fifteenth century B.C.

Seal of Niqmepa (seal impression of Idrimi).[67]
Shatuwa son of Zuwa, citizen of Luba, asked Apra for (the hand of) his daughter to be his daughter-in-law, (5) and, in accordance with the rules of Aleppo, brought him the marriage gift. Apra (sub-sequently) committed treason, was executed for his crime, (10) and his estate was confiscated by the palace. Shatuwa came, in the light of his (rights to his) possessions—six *ingots* of copper and two bronze daggers—and took them (back). (15) And as of this day, Niqmepa (is considered to have) satisfied Shatuwa. For (all) future time, Shatuwa [will have no further] legal claim with reference to his pos[sessions]. Seven witnesses, including the scribe.

---

[67] Niqmepa was the son of Idrimi, kings of Alalakh in the first half of the 15th century B.C.

(16) Manumission and Marriage

Ugarit.

As of this day, before witnesses, Gilben, chamberlain of the queen's palace, set free (5) Eliyawe his maid-servant, from among the women of the harem, and by pouring oil on her head, made her free, (saying:) (10) "Just as I am quit towards her, so is she quit towards me, forever."

Further, Buriyanu, the *namū*, has taken her as his wife, (15), and Buriyanu, her husband has rendered 20 (shekels) of silver into the hands of Gilben. Four witnesses.

(Inscribed on seal:) Should Buriyanu, tomorrow or the following day, refuse to consummate (his marriage) with Eliyawe—

(17) Will and Testament

Ugarit.

As of this day, before witnesses, Yarimanu spoke as follows: "Now therefore, (5) whatever I possess (and) that which Bidawe acquired together with me (to wit): my large cattle, my small cattle, my asses, my male slaves, my female slaves, my bronze bowls, bronze kettles, (10) bronze jugs, baskets, the field of Bin-Harasina (bordering) upon the Ra'abani stream—I have bequeathed to Bidawe, my wife.

And now therefore, my two sons (15)—Yatlinu, the elder, and Yanhamu, the younger—whichever of them shall bring a lawsuit against Bidawe, or shall abuse Bidawe, (20) their mother, shall pay 500 shekels of silver to the king; he shall set his cloak upon the door-bolt, and shall depart into the street. But whichever of them (25) shall have paid respect to Bidawe, his mother—to that one will she bequeath (the possessions).

Five witnesses and the name of the scribe.

(18) Trial for Homicide

Ugarit, thirteenth century B.C.

Before Ini-Teshup, king of Carkemish, Arishimiga, a merchant in the service of the king of Tarhudashshi, and the citizens of Ugarit met in trial. Arishimiga deposed thus: (5) "The citizens of Ugarit killed a merchant of the king of Tarhudashsha." And Arishimiga had not re-trieved any of the goods belonging to the merchant who was slain in Ugarit. The king then (10) decided their case thus: "Let Arishimiga take the oath (in support of his testimony) and the citizens of Ugarit shall then pay the full compensation for that merchant." (15) Arishi-miga then took the oath, and the citizens of Ugarit paid the full com-pensation of 180 shekels of silver to Arishimiga, servant of the king of Tarhudashshi. In future time, Arishimiga (20) shall enter no (fur-ther) claim against the citizens of Ugarit in respect of the merchant who was slain, and the citizens of Ugarit shall enter no claim against Arishimiga in respect to the 180 shekels of silver of their compensation payment. Whichever (of them) does so enter a claim—(25) this document will prevail against him.

(19) Adoption of the Son of a Prostitute

Neo-Babylonian.

Innin-shum-ibni son of Nabu-ahhe-shullim came to Balta daughter of Nabu-ahhe-shullim, his sister, stating as follows: (5) "Give me your seventeen-day-old son Dannu-ahhe-ibni, that I will rear him, and he will be my son." Balta acceded to him, and gave him her seventeen-day-old son Dannu-ahhe-ibni for adoption. He then inscribed him as next-(heir-)in-line to his own son Labashi. For as long as Balta continues (10) to practice prostitution, Dannu-ahhe-ibni will grow up in her care. As soon as Balta goes to the house of a respectable citizen, he (i.e., Innin-shum-ibni) will pay Balta one-third shekel of silver for the feeding and rearing of Dannu-ahhe-shullim (and with) bread, beer, salt, cress, and *muṣibtum*-clothes.

(16) Innin-shum-ibni swore by Anu and Ishtar: "Verily, in good faith and as (your) brother, I will never give away Dannu-ahhe-ibni to Nabu-zer-lishir my brother, or to Eshirtu my sister. Dannu-ahhe-ibni and Labashi together will serve the king and the "Mistress-of-Uruk."

Witnesses: six names including that of the scribe.

Date: Ninth to Tammuz, 32nd year of Nebuchadnezzar (= 573/2 B.C.). (30) May Anu and Ishtar and the solemn oath of Nebuchadnezzar, king of Babylon, decree the destruction of whomsoever alters this agreement.

(20) Sale of Temple Benefice

Seleucid era.

Nana-iddin son of Parak-Anu son of Anu-ahhe-iddin, descendant of Kuzu, by his own will, has sold to Parak-Anu son of Nur son of Anu-ah-ushabshi, descendant of Ekur-zakir, the twelfth-part of the day for each day from the first day (of the month) to the thirtieth day, his prebend of the post of brewer before the gods Anu, Antum, Ishtar, Nana, Belit-sha-bit-resh, Sharriyahitum, and all the deities of their chapels, monthly throughout the year, the *guqqanu*-offerings on the days of the monthly festivals and all else that accrues to those prebends (which the seller owns) together with his brothers and all other shareholders, in perpetuity and at the full price of $\frac{5}{6}$ mina of pure silver by the true stater-weights of Antochus. Nana-iddin has received from the hands of Parak-Anu, the money of $\frac{5}{6}$th mina, the price of the total of those prebends; it is paid. Should any (future) claim arise with respect to those prebends, Nana-iddin son of Parak-Anu, vendor of those prebends, will clear it by paying twelve-fold to Parak-Anu son of Nur. (reverse 15) Joint responsibility for clearing those prebends (of other claims) in favor of Parak-Anu son of Nur, rests in perpetuity upon Nana-iddin, vendor of those prebends, and (upon) Parak-Anu, his son. The twelfth-part of the day, which is the prebend of the brewership, is the possession of Parak-Anu son of Nur son of Anu-ah-ush-abshi descendant of Ekur-zakir, forever. (19–27) List of witnesses.[68]

(28) Uruk, 12th day of the month of Tammuz, year 144—Antiochus (IV), king—July 21, 168 B.C.

On side of tablet: seal legend of five witnesses, followed by:
Seal of Nana-iddin, vendor of those prebends;
Seal of Parak-Anu, his son, guarantor.

ANET, 222–23

Aramaic Papyri from Elephantine

TRANSLATOR: H. L. GINSBERG

Mibtahiah's First Marriage

Deed of 459 B.C., relating to reversion of property. Text: Sayce-Cowley, C; Cowley, 9.

On the 21st of Chisleu, that is the 1st of Mesore,[69] year 6 of King Artaxerxes, Mahseiah b. Yedoniah, a Jew of Elephantine, of the detachment of Haumadata, said to Jezaniah b. Uriah of the said detachment as follows: There is the site of 1 house belonging to me, west of the house belonging to you, which I have given to your wife, my daughter Mibtahiah (*Mbṭhyh*), and in respect of which I have written her a deed. The measurements of the house in question are 8 cubits and a handbreadth (5) by 11, *by the measuring-rod.* Now do I, Mahseiah, say to you, Build and equip that site . . . and dwell thereon with your wife. But you may not sell that house or give it as a present to others; only your children by my daughter Mibtahiah shall have power over it after you two. If tomorrow or some other day you build upon this land, and then my daughter divorces you and leaves you, she shall have no power to take it or give it to others; only your children by (10) Mibtahiah shall have power over it, in return for the work which you shall have done. If, on the other hand, she recovers from you,[70] she [may] take half of the house, and [the] othe[r] half shall be at your disposal in return for the building which you will have done on that house. And again as to that half, your children by Mibtahiah

---

[68] It should be noted that all the witnesses and the principals in the transaction are priests and descendants of priestly families.

[69] Egyptian month-name.

[70] This must mean, "In the event of your divorcing her, in which case she does not forfeit all rights as when she divorces you." Perhaps there is a lacuna in the text.

shall have power over it after you. If tomorrow or another day I should institute suit or process against you and say I did not give you this land to build on and did not draw up this deed for you, I (15) shall give you a sum of 10 *karshin* by royal weight, at the rate of 2 R^{71} to the ten, and no suit or process shall lie. This deed was written by 'Atharshuri b. Nabuzeribni in the fortress of Syene at the dictation of Mahseiah. Witnesses hereto (signatures).

In Liquidation of Mibtahiah's Second Marriage

See the Aramaic letter, "Settlement of Claim by Oath," Chap. XIX.

Contract of Mibtahiah's Third Marriage

Text: Sayce-Cowley, G; Cowley, 15. Date: about 440 B.C.

On the 2[5]th of Tishri, that is the 6th day of the month Epiphi, [year . . . of] Kin[g Artaxerx]es, said Ashor b. [Seho],[72] builder to the king, to Mah[seiah, A]ramean of Syene, of the detachment of Varizata, as follows: I have [co]me to your house that you might give me your daughter Mipht⟨ah⟩iah in marriage. She is my wife and I am her husband from this day for ever. I have given you as the bride-price (5) of your daughter Miphtahiah (a sum of) 5 shekels, royal weight. It has been received by you and your heart is content there-with.[73] (Lines 6–16, Miphtahiah's dowry.) (17) Should Ashor die tomorrow or an[othe]r day having no child, male or female, by his wife Mi[phtah]iah, Miphtahiah shall be entitled to the house, chattels and all worldly goods of Ashor. (20) Should Miphtahiah die tomorrow or ⟨another⟩ day having no child, male or female, by her husband Ashor, Ashor shall inherit her property and chattels. Should [Miph]tahiah, tomorrow [or] another [d]ay stand up in a congregation and say, I divorce my husband Ashor, the price of divorce shall be upon her head: she shall sit by the balance and weigh out to [As]hor a sum of 7 shekels 2 R.[74] But all that which she has brought in (25) with her she shall take out, shred and thread, and go whither she will, without suit or process. Should Ashor tomorrow or another day stand up in a congregation and say, I divorce my [wif]e Miphtahiah, [he shall] forfeit her bride-price, and all that she has brought in with her she

---

[71] Probably stands for *rub'in*, "quarters" (of a shekel). Does 2/4 × 10 (= 1/5) indicate the proportion of alloy?

[72] The name of Ashor's father (*ṣḥ'*) is preserved in another document. Both it and his own are Egyptian, but he eventually adopted the Hebrew one of Nathan.

[73] The bride-price was regularly added to the bride's dowry. In the following lines the value of each item of the dowry is given, and so is the total value; but the latter exceeds the value of the items by exactly the amount of the bride-price.

[74] This sum is exactly 1½ times the bride-price Ashor paid for her (line 5).

shall take out, shred and thread, on one day at one stroke, and shall go whither she will, without suit or process. And [whoever] arises against Miphtahiah (30) to drive her away from the house, possessions, and chattels of Ashor shall give her the sum of 20 *karash*,[75] and the law of this deed shall [. . .] for her. And I shall have no right to say I have another wife besides Mipht⟨ah⟩iah or other children besides any Miphtahiah may bear to me. If I say I have chi[ldren] and wife other than Miphtahiah and her children, I shall give to Miphtahiah a su[m] of 20 *karash*, royal weight. (35) Neither shall I have the right to [wre]st my property and chattels from Miph[tah]iah. If I take *them* away from her (erasure), I shall give to Miphtahiah [a sum of] 20 *karash*, royal weight. [This deed] was written by Nathan b. *Ananiah* [at the dictation of Ashor]. Witnesses: (signatures).

Manumission of a Female Slave and Her Daughter, June 12, 427 B.C.

ANET³, 548–49

(1) On the 20th of Siwan,[76] that is the 7th day of Phamenoth,[77] the year 38 of King Artaxerxes[78]—at that time, (2) Meshullam son of Zakkur, a Jew of the fortress Elephantine, of the detachment of Arpakhu said to the woman Tapmut (as she is called), (3) his slave,[79] who has on her right hand the marking "Of Meshullam," as follows: I have taken kindly thought of you (4) in my lifetime. I hereby declare you released at my death and likewise declare released the daughter Yehoyishma̔ (as she is called) whom (5) you have borne to me. No son or daughter, close or distant relative, kinsman, or clansman of mine (6) has any right to you or to the daughter Yehoyishma̔ whom you have borne to me; none has any right (7) to mark you or to *deliver you as a payment of money*. Whoever attempts such action against you or the daughter Yehoyishma̔ (8) whom you have borne to me must pay you a fine of 50 karsh of silver by the king's weights. You (9) are released, with your daughter Yehoyishma̔, from the shade for the sun, and no other man is master (10) of you or your daughter Yehoyishma̔. You are released for God.

(11) And Tapmut and her daughter Yehoyishma̔ declared: We shall serve you [a]s a son or daughter supports his or her father (12)

---

[75] A *karash* is 10 heavy shekels or 20 light ones.

[76] By the Babylonian calendar, adopted by the Persians.

[77] By the Egyptian calendar.

[78] Artaxerxes II (464–424).

[79] Though she was acquired in marriage 22 years earlier by a contract (Brooklyn, 2) between her master and her husband, and though her daughter has issued from that marriage, she has remained in law the slave of her master, and her daughter has been born into that status.

as long as you live; and when you die, we shall support your son Zak-kur like a son who supports his father, just as we shall have been doing (13) for you while you were alive. (. . . .) If we ever say, "We will not support you as a son supports (14) his father, and your son Zak-kur after your death," we shall be liable to you and your son Zakkur for a fine (15) in the amount of 50 karsh of refined silver by the king's weights without suit or process.

Written by Haggai (16) the scribe, at Elephantine, at the dictation of Meshullam son of Zakkur, the witnesses herein being: Atarparan son of Nisai (17) the Mede; witness Micaiah son of Ahio; witness Berechiah son of Miptah; witness Dalah son of Gaddul.

(Endorsement) Quit-claim written by Meshullam son of Zakkur to Tapmut and Yehoyishma[ʿ].

Marriage Contract of a Former Slave Girl Who Is Subject to Paramonē, 420 B.C.

(1) On (the first day of) the month of Tishri,[80] that is Epiphi,[81] the year 4 of King Darius,[82] in the fortress Elephantine, said Ananiah son of Haggai, (2) an Aramean of the fortress Elephantine, [of] the de-tachment of [Iddin]-Nabu, to Zakkur son of Me[shullam, *an Arame*]*an* of Syene, of the same detachment, as follows: (3) I have come to your [hous]e and asked you for your sister the woman Yehoyishmaʿ (as she is called) in marriage, and you have given her (4) to me. She is my wife and I am [her] husband from this day to eternity. I have paid to you as the bride price of your sister Yehoyishmaʿ (5) 1 karsh of silver; you have received it [and have been satisfied therewi]th. Your sister Yehoyishmaʿ has brought into my house a cash sum (6a) of two karsh, (two) 2 shekels, and 5 hallurs of silver, . . . (Lines 6b–13a defective, a list of probably 12 articles of wool and linen with their respective values; 13b–15a, 5 articles of copper with their respective values; 15b missing.) (15c) [Garments and articles of co]pper with the cash and the bride price: seven (that is, 7) karsh, eight (that is, 8) shekels, and 5 hallurs of silver by the king's (17a) weights, silver of 2 R to the ten. (17b–21aa, containers of palm leaves, reeds, wood, and stone and quantities of various sorts of oil—no values specified.)

(21 cont.) If at some future date Ananiah should arise in an/the assembly and declare, "I divorce my wife Yehoyishmaʿ; (22) she shall not be a wife to me," he shall become liable for divorce money. ⟨He shall forfeit her bride price:⟩ he must surrender to her all that she brought into his house. Her dowry of cash (23) and clothing, worth karsh seven, sh[ekels eight, and hallurs 5] of silver, and the rest of

---

[80] Of the Babylonian calendar, adopted by the Persians.
[81] Of the Egyptian calendar.
[82] Darius II (423–405).

the goods listed (above) (24a–b) he must hand over to her on one day and in a single act, and she may [leave him for where]ver [she will]. . . .

(24c) If, on the other hand, Yehoyishmaʿ should divorce her husband (25) Ananiah and say to him, "I divorce you, I will not be wife to you," she shall become liable for divorce money. []. (26) She shall sit by the scales and weigh out to her husband Ananiah 7 shekels and 2 R and shall leave him with the balance of her (27) cash, goods, and pos[sessions, worth karsh 7, shekels 5+] 3, and hallurs 5; and the rest of her goods, (28) which are listed (above), he shall hand over to her on one day and in a single act, and she shall depart for her father's house.

If Ananiah should die having no male or (29) female child from his wife [Yehoyi]shmaʿ, Yehoyishmaʿ shall be [mistress] of his [pr]operty: of his house, his goods, (30) his possession, [and all that he owns. Anyone who] attempts to banish Yehoyishmaʿ from his house, [goods, possessions], and all that [he] owns, [shall p]ay to [her a fi]ne of silver, (32) twenty karsh by [the king's] weights, silver of 2 R to the 10, and shall accord [her] her due under this deed without lawsuit. (33) However, Yeh[oyishmaʿ] is not permitted [to] *acquire* a husband other [than] Anani. Should she do so, (34) that shall constitute a divorce, and [*the provisions for divorcement*] shall be applied to [her]. (So, too,) if [Yehoyishmaʿ] should die having no (35) [male] or female child by [her] hus[band] Anani, [Anani] shall inherit from her her [cash], goods, possessions, and all (36) that she own[s]. And [Anani] likewise [may] no[t ta]ke any woman [other than his wife Yehoyishmaʿ] (37) in marriage. Should he do [so, that shall constitute a divorce, and the provisions for di]vorcement [shall be applied to him].

Further, Ananiah (38) may not omit to accord to his wife Yehoyishmaʿ the right of any of the wives of his fellows.[83] Should (39) he fail to do so, that shall constitute a divorce, and he shall implement for her the provisions for divorcement. Neither may Yehoyishmaʿ (40) omit to accord to her husband Ananiah the right of any (husband).[83] Should she fail to accord it to him, that shall constitute a divorce.

Further, (41) Zakkur may not say with reference to [his] sis[ter], "I gave those [goo]ds to Yehoyishmaʿ gratis; now I wish (42) to take them back." If he speaks [thus], no attention shall be paid to him; he is in the wrong.

This deed was written by Maʿuziah son of Nathan (43) at the dictation of Ananiah son of Haggai [and] Zakkur son of Meshullam, and the witnesses thereto are: (There followed the names of six witnesses and those of their fathers, making twelve names in all, of which nine are preserved, all of them Jewish, and all of them *in the handwriting of the scribe*.)

---

[83] I.e., conjugal rights.

Treaties

Hittite Treaty

TRANSLATOR: ALBRECHT GOETZE

Treaty of Suppiluliumas and Aziras of Amurru   ANET³, 529–30

Preamble

These are the words of the Sun Suppiluliumas, the great king, the king of the Hatti land, the valiant, the favorite of the Storm-god.

(gap)

Historical Introduction

I, the Sun, [made you my vassal.] And if you, [Aziras, "protect" the king of the Hatti land, your master,] the king of the Hatti land, your ma[ster, will "protect" you in the same way.] (5) The way [you "protect"] your own [soul, your own person, your own body] and your own land, ["protect" the soul of the king, the person of the king,] the body of the king and the [Hatti] land [in the same way!] In the days to come "protect" [you, Aziras, the king of the Hatti land] and the Hatti land, [my sons and my grandsons.] 300 she[kels of refined gold,] (10) first class (and) pure, shall be the tribute to the king of the Hatti land per year. Let them weigh [it out with the weighing stones of the merchants o]f the Hatti land. [And, you, Az]iras, should come to the Hatti land to the Sun once a year.

Formerly, *in fact*, the king of the land of Egypt, (15) the king of the Hurri land, the king [of . . . , the king of the country Kinza, the ki]ng of the country Nuhassa, the king of the country Niya, the king of the country [. . . , the king of the country Mukis], the king of the country Halba, the king of the country Kargamis—all these kings were hostile [to the Sun]. But Aziras, the king of [Amurru] land, parted from the gate of Egypt and became subservient to the Sun, the k[ing of H]atti land. (20) And the Sun, the great king, was ve[ry happy] about. . . . that Aziras fell down at the feet of the Sun. Aziras parted from the gate of Egypt and (25) fell d[own at the feet of the Sun.] I, the Sun, the great king, [accepted] Aziras [in vassalage] and added him to his brethren.

[Th]en Azi[ras . . . .] To [the Sun, the great king], his lord, he spoke as follows: [". . .] together with my house [. . .] (30) I have surrendered and . . . [. . .].

(gap)

Military Clauses

(ii). . . . He who [lives in peace] with the Sun (10) shall live in peace also with you. But he who is an enemy of the Sun, shall also be an enemy [with you]. When the king of [the Hatti] land (is on a campaign) in the [Hurri] land, or in the land of Egypt, or [in the land Ka]raduniy[as,] o[r in the country Astata,] or in the country Alsi—(15) countries bordering on your territory [but] enemies [of the Su]n, countries that are at peace (with you), [but] bordering [on your territory]—[(when) the country Kinza and the country] Nuhassa turn about [and go to wa]r [with the Hatti land,] (20) [when the king of the Hatti land gives battle] against such a country—if (then) you, Aziras, on your own decision [do not] march out with troops (and) charioteers and on your own [decision] will not give battle—

(25) [or i]f I, the Sun, send out to you, Aziras, either a prince or a notable [with] his troops (and) charioteers as aid, or (if) I send (them) out to another country to make an attack, [and if] (then) Aziras on his own decision (30) does not march out [with] troops (and) charioteers and you do not attack [such] an enemy—if you commit some [treachery and speak as follows]: "True, I am under a treaty [properly sworn to], but whether he is to vanquish his enemy or his enemy is to vanquish him, (35) this [I cannot] know in any way" [and if] you write to [such] an enemy: "[See! Troops (and) charioteer]s of the Hatti land [are coming to attack (you)]; so be on your guard!" [thereby] you will transgress the oath.

(40) [Out of] the troops (and) charioteers of the Hatti land [. . . .] Hatti land they must not seize a single man. [If you] on your own decision [will not let him go] and to the king of the Hatti land (45) [will not hand him over, thereby] you will transgress the oath.

[If] against the king of the Hatti land [. . .] another enemy rises and [ravages the Hatti] land, [if against the king of the] Hatti [land somebody revolts] (50) [and you,] Aziras, hear about [it, if then] you on your own decision [with troops (and) charioteers] do not rush to the aid—[if] for you, Aziras, it is impossible to come yourself, send [either a son of yours] or a brother of yours with troops (55) [(and) charioteers to the aid of the ki]ng of the Hatti land. [. . . .]

(iii) [And if somebody presses Aziras hard . . . or (if) somebody starts a revolt, (if) you (then) wr]ite to the king of the Hatti land: "send troops (and) charioteers to my aid!" (5) I shall h[it] that enemy for [you].

[. . .] because Aziras . . . [. . .] and *returned* [to] the Sun in vassalage, I, the Sun, dispatched notables of the Hatti land, troops (and) charioteers of mine [*from* the] Hatti land down to Amurru land. (10) [If] they march up to towns of yours, treat them well and furnish them with the necessities of life. Before [the people of Amurru land] let them walk like brethren! Treat [the Hi]ttites well! But if any Hittite (15) [*misbehaves* an]d shows evil intentions towards Aziras and tries to get hold of either a town of his or a (piece of) land of his, thereby he will transgress the oath.

Dealings with Foreigners, Etc.

The deportees of these countries whom (20) the Sun moved—deportees of the Hurri lands, deportees of the country Kinza, deportees of the country Niya and deportees of the country Nuhassi—[if] from Hattusa somebody, man or woman, escapes and comes to your country, (25) you will not say as follows: "True! [I] am under a treaty properly sworn to, but I can [not] know in any way where amidst my country these (people) [*hide.*]" You, Aziras, will seize [them] (30) and hand [them] over to the king of the Hatti land.

[If . . .] before you, Aziras, somebody speaks [evil words concerning] the Sun, be it a [notable] or be it an (ordinary) subject of yours, (if) you, [Azir]as, will not seize [him] (35) and will not hand him over to the king of the Hatti land, thereby you will transgress the oath.

Also people of Amurru land who reside in the Hatti land, be it a notable or be it an (ordinary) subject of the country of Aziras, (40) or be it (that) you consider him a [subject] of the king of the Hatti land—if the king of the Hatti land re[turns] him to you, keep him. But if the king of the Hatti land does not return it, he escapes [and he] comes to you, (45) [if . . .] you, Azi[ras, do not] seize [him and do not hand him over to the king of the Hatti land, thereby you will transgress the oath].

(small gap)

(iv) And if a Hittite [. . .] as a fugitive comes [into your country . . .] comes back [to . . . , you will seize him and will hand] him over to the king of the [Hatti land. . .].

(gap)

(The rest of col. iv is too mutilated for translation. It is however recognizable that it closes with a list of gods called to serve as witnesses at the conclusion of the treaty.)

Akkadian Treaties from Syria and Assyria
TRANSLATOR: ERICA REINER

Before the discovery of the treaty of Esarhaddon with the vassal princes only a few treaties imposed by Mesopotamian sovereigns were known, and those were in a fragmentary state of preservation. The newly found Esarhaddon treaty not only increases the actually available textual material but also serves to restore and to increase the understanding of the previously known treaty fragments. Understandably, the parallelism with biblical material has given rise to a vast literature.

Treaty between Niqmepa of Alalakh and Ir-ᵈIM of Tunip

ANET³, 531–32

Heading
Seal of Ir-ᵈIM, king of Tunip.

Preamble
Text (of the agreement) sanctioned by an oath to the gods, between Niqmepa, king of Mukishhe [and Alalakh], and Ir-ᵈIM, king of Tunip; Niqmepa and Ir-ᵈIM have now established [this agreement] between them as follows:

1. [If *anyone*], whether [*mer*]*chants*, whether Suteans, . . . [wants to *sell*], be it barley, (be it) emmer, (be it) oil, [. . .] . . . [he must not] sell [it without *authorization*].

2. [If in your land] there is [a plot against me, and] they plot [to . . . , and you hear of it], you will search for them, [*if*] they say, [". . .] we [are *citizens* of] Mukishhe," you must not kill those men [but you have to extradite them].

3. If someone from my land [*plots against me*], if you hear of it, you must [. . .] and you must not conceal it from me, and if he lives in your land, you must extradite him.

4. If any booty coming from my land is sold in your land, you must seize it, together with the one who sells it, and hand it over to me.

5. If a fugitive slave, male or female, of my land flees to your land, you must seize and return him to me, (or), if someone else seizes him and takes him to you, [you must keep him] in your prison, and whenever his owner comes forward, you must hand him over to [him]. If (the slave) is not to be found, you must give him (the owner) an escort, and he may seize him in whatever town he (the slave) is found; (in any town where) he is not found, the mayor and five elders will declare under oath: "Your slave does not live among us and we do not conceal him"—if they are unwilling to take the oath, but (eventually) return his slave, [they go free], but if they take the oath

and later he discovers his slave [among them], they are considered thieves and their hands are cut off, (moreover) they will pay 6,000 (shekels of) copper to the palace.

6. If a man, woman, ox, donkey, or horse [is *found*] in the house of somebody (and the *owner*) *identifies* it, but (the man in whose possession it was found) declares: "I have bought it," if he can produce the merchant, he goes free, but if he cannot produce the merchant, he who has *identified* it, . . . he will declare under oath: ["It is my . . ."], but if he is unwilling to take the oath, [he is considered a thief and his hands are cut off].

7. If you hold a man in custody, he *may* do (forced) labor with/for a [. . .]-man, (but) if he (the latter) [*takes off*] his fetters, shaves off his slavemark, [. . .] and they catch him, he is considered a thief. If he declares: ["The man is mine"] he will declare under oath as follows: ["(I swear) that the man is mine"]; if he is unwilling to take the oath, [he is a th]ief [. . .]. If the *criminal*, man, woman, or boy, does (forced) labor in his house, and (the owner?) seizes him, he is considered a thief, and his (*the criminal's*) master will have him declare under oath: "I have captured him in the open country *personally*" [. . .].

8. If a brigand from your land commits a robbery or breaks into a house or town in my land, and they seize him and [put him] in prison, whenever his (the robber's) owner [*claims him*], the owner of the house (broken into) will declare under oath: "I(!) have caught him as he was breaking and entering (lit.: at the breach or the . . . of the moat)," and he has to bring witnesses, and they can convict him and . . . him. But a slave cannot be made to take the oath, and he (the accused robber) goes free.

9. [If *families* from my land] enter your land to find subsistence, you must take them into custody in your land, and *feed* them, (but) whenever they want to [return to my land, you must gather them and return them to [my land], and you must not detain one single family in your land.

10. If a man from your land enters my land to find subsistence, and says: "In my city [there is nothing] to [eat,]" [. . .] if he is a criminal, [. . .].

11. If there is a city or a [. . .], they live with the people [in] my city, [. . .] . . . you must seize them, . . . you must [not] seize them.

12. [If] (any) Hurrian (*subject of*) our lord becomes an enemy of the king of the Hurrians, I will not break the oath made with the king of the Hurrians, my lord, (*unless*) he releases me from these stipulations of the oath.

76. Seal of Niqmepa, king of Alalakh.

77. Whosoever transgresses these agreements, Adad, [. . .] and Shamash, the lord of judgment, Sin, and the great gods will make him perish, [will make disappear] his name and (his) descendants

from the lands, [...], they will make him forsake his throne and *scepter* [...].

ANET³, 532

Treaty between Idrimi and Pilliya

1. Tablet of agreement.

2. When Pilliya and Idrimi took an oath by the gods and made this binding agreement between themselves: they will always return their respective fugitives, (i.e.) if Idrimi seizes a fugitive of Pilliya, he will return him to Pilliya, and if Pilliya seizes a fugitive of Idrimi, he will return him to Idrimi. Anyone who seizes a fugitive, and returns him to his master, (the owner) will pay as prize of capture 500 (shekels of) copper if it is a man, one thousand as prize of capture if it is a woman. However, if a fugitive from Pilliya enters the land of Idrimi and nobody seizes him, but his own master seizes him, he need not pay a prize of capture to anyone. In whatever city (it is suspected that) they conceal a fugitive, the mayor and five elders will make a declaration under oath. From the very day on which Barattarna has sworn (this) oath by the gods together with Idrimi, from that day on it is decreed that fugitives have to be returned.

Whoever transgresses this agreement, ᵈIM, Shamash and Ishhara, and all the (other) gods will destroy him.

ANET³, 532–33

Treaty between Ashurnirari V of Assyria and Mati'ilu of Arpad

(i)

(break)

(may) Mati'ilu [...] his sons and daughters, his officials, [...] altogether [turn into ...], his land altogether into wasteland, may his soil be [as narrow] as a brick of one cubit, not enough for his sons, [his daughters, his officials, the people of his land] to stand upon. May Mati'ilu [together with his sons,] daughters, officials, the people of his land [be ...] like ..., and he himself, together with the people of his land, be crushed like gypsum.

(10) This spring lamb has been brought from its fold not for sacrifice, not for a banquet, not for a purchase, not for (divination concerning) a sick man, not to be slaughtered for [...]: it has been brought to sanction the treaty between Ashurnirari and Mati'ilu. If Mati'ilu sins against (this) treaty made under oath by the gods, then, just as this spring lamb, brought from its fold, will not return to its fold, will not behold its fold again, alas, Mati'ilu, together with his sons, daughters, officials, and the people of his land [will be ousted] from his country, will not return to his country, and not behold his

country again. This head is not the head of a lamb, it is the head of Mati'ilu, it is the head of his sons, his officials, and the people of his land. If Mati'ilu sins against this treaty, so may, just as the head of this spring lamb is torn off, and its knuckle placed in its mouth, [. . .], the head of Mati'ilu be torn off, and his sons [. . .]. This shoulder is not the shoulder of a spring lamb, it is the shoulder of Mati'ilu, it is the shoulder of his sons, his officials, and the people of his land. If Mati'ilu sins against this treaty, so may, just as the shoulder of this spring lamb is torn out, and [. . .], the shoulder of Mati'ilu, of his sons, his officials, and the people of his land be torn out and [. . .] in [. . .].

(iii)

(1'9' fragmentary) [. . .] if you conceal (or) protect (him/it), if you send it to another country, if you are not loyal to Ashurnirari, if your heart is not devoted to Ashurnirari, king of Assyria, then you, your sons, the people of your land [. . .]. (break)

(iv)

(If the Assyria army) goes to war at the orders of Ashurnirari, king of Assyria, and Mati'ilu, together with his officials, his army, his chariotry, does not leave (on the campaign) in full loyalty, may the great lord Sin who dwells in Harran, clothe Mati'ilu, his sons, his officials, and the people of his land in leprosy as in a cloak so that they have to roam the open country, and may he have no mercy on them. Let there be no milk to suck for the oxen, asses, sheep, and horses in his land. May Adad, the canal inspector of heaven and earth, put an end to Mati'ilu, his land and the people of his land through hunger, want, and famine, so that they eat the flesh of their sons and daughters and it taste as good to them as the flesh of spring lambs. May they be deprived of Adad's thunder so that rain be denied them. Let dust be their food, pitch their ointment, donkey's urine their drink, rushes their clothing, let their sleeping place be in the corners (of *walls*). If Mati'ilu, his sons, or his nobles, who sin against this treaty—let the farmers of his land not sing the harvest song in the fields, no vegetation should spring forth in the open country and see the sunlight, [the . . .] not draw water from the springs, may [. . .] be their food, [. . .] their drink, [. . .]. (break)

(v)

If our death is not your death, if our life is not your life, if you do not seek the life of Ashurnirari, his sons and his officials as your own life, and the life of your sons and officials, then may Ashur, father of the gods, who grants kingship, turn your land into *wasteland,* your people into . . . , your cities into ruin mounds, your house into ruins.

(8) If Mati'ilu sins against this treaty with Ashurnirari, king of Assyria, may Mati'ilu become a prostitute, his soldiers women, may they receive [*a gift*] in the square of their cities (i.e., publicly) like any

prostitute, may one country ... them to the next; may Mati'ilu's (seed) be that of a mule, his wives *barren,* may Ishtar, the goddess of men, the lady of women, take away their "bow," cause their [steri]lity, ... may they say, "Woe, we have sinned against the treaty with Ashurnirari, king of Assyria." (break)

(vi)

May [*locusts*] appear and devour his land, may [...] blind their eyes; let one thousand houses decrease to one house, let one thousand tents decrease to one tent, let only one man be spared in the city to tell about my feats.

(6) Be adjured by Ashur, king of heaven and earth; be adjured by Anu and Antu; be adjured by Enlil and Ninlil; be adjured by Ea and Damkina; be adjured by Sin and Ningal; be adjured by Shamash and Aja; be adjured by Adad and Shala; be adjured by Marduk and Zar-panitu; be adjured by Nabu and Tashmetu; be adjured by Ninurta and Gula; be adjured by Urash and Ninegal; be adjured by Zababa and Bau; be adjured by Nergal and Laz; be adjured by Madanu and Ningirsu; be adjured by Humhummu and Ishum; be adjured by Girra and Nusku; be adjured by Ishtar, Lady of Nineveh; be adjured by Ishtar, Lady of Arbela; be adjured by Adad of Kurba-il; be adjured by Adad of Alep; be adjured by Palil, who marches in front; be ad-jured by the Seven warrior gods; ...

(break)

ANET³, 533–34   ## Treaty of Esarhaddon with Baal of Tyre

(i)

[Treat]y of [*Esarhaddon*], king of Assyria, eldest son of [...], with Baal, king of Tyre, ... (break)

(ii broken)

(iii)

... Esarhaddon ... Esarhaddon, king of Assyria, ... these cities which ...

(6) [The royal deputy whom] I have appointed over you, ... the elders of your country, ... the royal deputy [...] with them ... the ships ... do not listen to him, [do not ...] without the royal *deputy*; nor must you open a letter which I send you without (the presence) of the royal deputy. If the royal deputy is absent, wait for him and then open it, [do] not ....

(15) If a ship of Baal or of the people of Tyre is ship-wrecked off (the coast of) the land of the Philistines or anywhere on the borders of Assyrian territory, everything that is on the ship belongs to Esar-haddon, king of Assyria, but one must not do any harm to any per-son on board ship, they should li[st] their names [and inform the king of Assyria].

(18) These are the ports of trade and the trade roads which Esar-haddon, king of Assyria, [granted] to his servant Baal: (to wit): to-ward Akko, Dor, in the entire district of the Philistines, and in all the cities within Assyrian territory, on the seacoast, and *in* Byblos, (across) the Lebanon, all the cities in the mountains, all the cities of Esarhaddon, king of Assyria, which Esarhaddon, king of Assyria, gave [*to*] Baal [. . .], [to] the people of Tyre, . . . [. . .], in their ships or all those who cross over, in the towns of [*Baal*], his towns, his manors, his wharves, which [. . .], to [. . .], as many as lie in the outlying regions, as in the past [. . .] they . . . , nobody should harm their ships. Inland, in his district, in his manors . . . . (break)

(iv)

[May Ninlil, who resides in Nineveh, "tie to you" a swift dagger]. [May] Ishtar, [who resides in Arbela, not grant] you [mercy and for-giveness]. May Gula, the great physician, [put illness and weariness in] your [hearts], an unhealing sore in your body, bathe [in your own blood as if in water]. May the Seven gods, the warrior gods, cause your [downfall] with their [fierce] weapons. May Bethel and Anath-Bethel deliver you to a man-eating lion. May the great gods of heaven and earth, the gods of Assyria, the gods of Akkad, and the gods of Eber-nari curse you with an indissoluble curse. May Baal-sameme, Baal-malage, and Baal-saphon raise an evil wind against your ships, to undo their moorings, tear out their mooring pole, may a strong wave sink them in the sea, a violent tide [. . .] against you. May Melqart and Eshmun deliver your land to destruction, your people to be deported; from your land [. . .]. May they make disappear food for your mouth, clothes for your body, oil for your ointment. May Astarte break your bow in the thick of battle, and have you crouch at the feet of your enemy, may a foreign enemy divide your belongings.

Tablet of the treaty established with Baal of Tyre.

The Vassal-Treaties of Esarhaddon

ANET[3], 534–41

Heading

Seal of the god Ashur, king of the gods, lord of all lands, which is
not to be altered;
seal of the great ruler, the father of the gods, which is not to be
contested.

1. (1) (This is) the treaty of Esarhaddon, king of the world, king of Assyria, son of Sennacherib, likewise king of the world, king of As-syria, with Ramataya, city-ruler of Urakazabanu,
with his sons, grandsons, with all the people of Urakazabanu,
(all the men under his command) young and old, from sunrise (east) to sunset (west),

all those over whom Esarhaddon, king of Assyria, acts as king and lord; with you, your sons, your grandsons, all those who will live in the future after this treaty;

(—the treaty that he has made with you on behalf of the crown prince designate Ashurbanipal,

the son of Esarhaddon, king of Assyria—)

2. (13) (the treaty) which he has made binding with you before Jupiter, Venus,

Saturn, Mercury,

Mars, and Sirius;

before Ashur, Anu, Enlil, and Ea,

Sin, Shamash, Adad, and Marduk,

Nabu, Nusku, Urash, and Nergal,

(the goddesses) Ninlil, Sherua, and Belet-ili,

Ishtar of Nineveh and Ishtar of Arbela;

all the gods dwelling in heaven and earth,

the gods of Assyria, the gods of Sumer and Akkad,

the gods of every (foreign) country.

3. (25) You are adjured by Ashur, the father of the gods, lord of all lands;

you are adjured by Anu, Enlil, and Ea,

you are adjured by Sin, Shamash, Adad, and Marduk,

you are adjured by Nabu, Nusku, Urash, and Nergal,

you are adjured by Ninlil, Sherua, and Belet-ili,

you are adjured by Ishtar of Nineveh and Ishtar of Arbela,

you are adjured by all the gods of the city Assur,

you are adjured by all the gods of Nineveh,

you are adjured by all the gods of Calah,

you are adjured by all the gods of Arbela,

you are adjured by all the gods of Kalzi,

you are adjured by all the gods of Harran,

you are adjured by all the gods of Assyria,

you are adjured by all the gods of Babylon, Borsippa, and Nippur,

you are adjured by all the gods of Sumer and Akkad,

you are adjured by all the gods of every land, you are adjured by the gods of heaven and earth.

4. (41) (This is) the treaty which Esarhaddon, king of Assyria, has established with you before the great gods of heaven and earth, on behalf of the crown prince designate Ashurbanipal, the son of your lord Esarhaddon, king of Assyria, who has designated and appointed him for succession. When Esarhaddon, king of Assyria, departs from the living, you will seat the crown prince designate Ashurbanipal upon the royal throne, he will exercise the kingship and overlordship of Assyria over you. (If) you do not serve him in the open country

and in the city, do not fight and even die on his behalf, do not always speak the full truth to him, do not always advise him well in full loyalty, do not smooth his way in every respect; if you remove him, and seat in his stead one of his brothers, younger or older, on the throne of Assyria, if you change or let anyone change the decree of Esarhaddon, king of Assyria, if you will not be subject to this crown prince designate Ashurbanipal, son of Esarhaddon, king of Assyria, your lord, so that he cannot exercise kingship and lordship over you—

5. (62) If you do not serve the crown prince designate Ashurbanipal, whom Esarhaddon, king of Assyria, has presented to you and ordered you (to serve), on behalf of whom he has made this binding treaty with you, if you sin against him, lift your hands with evil intent against him, set afoot a rebellion, or wrong or evil plans against him, if you remove him from the kingship of Assyria, and help one of his brothers, younger or older, to take the throne of Assyria in his stead, and install another king, another lord over yourselves and swear the oath of loyalty to another king or lord—

6. (73) If you hear any wrong, unseemly, improper plans, which are improper or detrimental to the exercise of kingship by the crown prince designate Ashurbanipal, whether they be spoken by his brothers, his father's brothers, his cousins, or any other member of his father's lineage, or by officials or governors, or by the court personnel, eunuchs or not, or by the army, or any human being whatsoever, and conceal it and do not come and report it to the crown prince designate Ashurbanipal—

7. (83) If Esarhaddon departs from the living while his sons are minors, you will help Ashurbanipal, the crown prince designate, take the throne of Assyria, and seat Shamashshumukin, his dear brother, the crown prince designate of Babylonia, upon the royal throne of Babylonia, and entrust to him the rule over all of Sumer, Akkad, and Karduniash, and you will not hold back any gift that his father Esarhaddon, king of Assyria, gave him, but let him take it with him.

8. (92) If you do not always offer complete truth to the crown prince designate Ashurbanipal whom Esarhaddon, king of Assyria, has presented to you, as well as to the brothers by the mother of the crown prince designate Ashurbanipal, concerning whom Esarhaddon, king of Assyria, has established this treaty with you; if you do not treat them with proper loyalty, speak to them with a true heart, and serve them in the open country and in the city—

9. (101) If you sin against the crown prince designate Ashurbanipal whom Esarhaddon, king of Assyria, has ordered you (to serve), against the brothers by the mother of the crown prince designate Ashurbanipal, concerning whom he has established this treaty with you, if you lift your hands with evil intent against them, set afoot rebellion, or evil plans against them—

10. (108) If any (of you) hears some wrong, evil, unseemly plan which is improper or detrimental to the crown prince designate Ashurbanipal, son of your lord Esarhaddon, king of Assyria, whether they be spoken by his enemy or his ally, by his brothers, by his sons, by his daughters, by his brothers, his father's brothers, his cousins, or any other member of his father's lineage, or by your own brothers, sons, or daughters, or by a prophet, an ecstatic, a dream-interpreter, or by any human being whatsoever, and conceals it, does not come and report it to the crown prince designate Ashurbanipal, son of Esarhaddon, king of Assyria—

11. (123) If you do something wrong and evil against the crown prince designate Ashurbanipal, whom Esarhaddon, king of Assyria, has ordered you (to serve), if you seize him and kill him or hand him over to his enemy, if you remove him from the kingship of Assyria, and swear the oath of loyalty to another king or lord—

12. (130) If anyone instigates you to a revolt or rebellion against the crown prince designate Ashurbanipal, son of your lord Esarbaddon, king of Assyria, concerning whom he has established (this) treaty with you, in order to kill, harm and destroy him, and you, upon hearing such a thing from anybody, do not seize the instigators of the revolt, do not bring them before the crown prince designate Ashurbanipal, (and) if you, being able to seize and kill them, do not seize and kill them, do not eradicate their name and descendants from the country, or, being unable to seize and kill them, you do not inform the crown prince designate Ashurbanipal, do not stand by him and seize and kill the instigators of the revolt—

13. (147) If you side with the instigators of a revolt, be they few or many, and hear something, whether good or detrimental, and do not report it, do not come to the crown prince designate Ashurbanipal, son of Esarhaddon, king of Assyria, and do not give him your full loyalty, (if) you establish this treaty before the gods who are placed (as witnesses), and swear by the laden table, by drinking from the cup, by the glow of fire, by water and oil, by touching one another's breast, and (still) do not come and report to the crown prince designate Ashurbanipal, son of your lord Esarhaddon, king of Assyria, do not seize and kill the instigators of the revolt and the criminal persons, do not eradicate their name and descendants from the country—

14. (162) If either an Assyrian, subject of Assyria, a member of the court personnel, eunuch or not, or a citizen of Assyria, or a citizen of another country, or any living human being, holds prisoner the crown prince designate Ashurbanipal in the open country or inside the city and sets afoot revolt and rebellion, and you do not side with the crown prince designate Ashurbanipal, and do not serve him, do not kill the persons who set afoot revolt in full loyalty, do not save

the crown prince designate Ashurbanipal and his brothers by the same mother—

15. (173) If someone rebels against the crown prince designate Ashurbanipal, son of your lord Esarhaddon, king of Assyria, concerning whom he has established this treaty with you, and you side with him, if, should they seize you by force, you do not escape and come to the crown prince designate Ashurbanipal—

16. (180) If you reside in (this) country as *ḫurādu-soldiers*, or as . . . , or enter it in a *pirru*-troupe and nurture evil thoughts in your hearts against the crown prince designate Ashurbanipal, rebel against him, or set afoot against him rebellion and evil plans—

17. (188) If the crown prince designate Ashurbanipal, son of your lord Esarhaddon, king of Assyria, is not your king and lord on the day when your lord Esarhaddon, king of Assyria, departs from the living, if he cannot abase the mighty, lift up the lowly, kill him who is fit to be put to death, keep alive him who deserves to be kept alive, and you do not listen to whatever he orders, do not act according to his command, seek to place another king, another lord over him—

18. (198) If someone in the palace starts a revolt, whether by day or by night, whether on the road or in the hinterland, against Esarhaddon, king of Assyria, you must not listen to him; (or), whether by day or by night, at an improper time, a messenger from the palace comes to the crown prince and says, "Your father has elevated you (to the throne), let Your Majesty come," you must not let him go, he must not leave, you will keep him under severe guard until one of you who is devoted to his lord, and who is concerned about the house of his lord can go and find out (himself) about the king your lord in the palace, only after that may you follow the crown prince your lord to the palace.

19. (212) If you convene an assembly and take an oath with each other to give the kingship to one among you—

20. (214) If you help onto the throne one of his brothers, his uncles, his cousins, or any other member of his father's lineage, whether they live in Assyria or have fled to another country, or someone from nearby palace . . . , or from outlying palace . . . , or from large or small . . .-s, or (anyone) young or old, from the wellborn citizens or from the clients (of noblemen), or from the court officials, eunuchs or not, from the slaves, from the bought servants, from among the Assyrians or among citizens of another country, or anyone from among living human beings, and give him the kingship and lordship over Assyria, if you do not help unto the throne of Assyria the crown prince designate Ashurbanipal, so that he cannot exercise over you the kingship and lordship over Assyria—

21. (229) If you do not fight for the crown prince Ashurbanipal, son of your lord Esarhaddon, king of Assyria, if you do not die for

him, if you do not seek to do what is good for him, if you act wrongly toward him, do not give him sound advice, lead him on an unsafe course, do not treat him with proper loyalty—

22. (237) If Esarhaddon departs from the living while his sons are minor, and one of the palace personnel, eunuch or not, kills the crown prince designate Ashur-banipal, and usurps the kingship over Assyria, if you side with him, agree to be subject to him, do not rebel, do not start hostilities and do not make all other countries hostile to him, do not foment revolt against him, do not seize and kill him, and do not place the son of the crown prince designate Ashurbanipal upon the throne of Assyria—

23. (249) Or, if the child is yet unborn, if you do not subject yourselves to the widow of Esarhaddon, king of Assyria, or the wife of the crown prince designate Ashurbanipal, do not raise (the child) when he is born, do not place him upon the throne of Assyria, do not seize and kill the instigators of the revolt, do not eradicate their name and descendants from the country, do not shed blood for blood, do not avenge the crown prince designate Ashurbanipal; if you give the crown prince designate Ashurbanipal, son of your lord Esarhaddon, king of Assyria, a deadly herb to eat, to drink, or to anoint himself, if you practice witchcraft against him, and bring the anger of his personal god and goddess upon him—

24. (266) If you do not love the crown prince designate Ashurbanipal, son of your lord Esarhaddon, king of Assyria, as you do your own lives, if you slander his brothers by the same mother in front of the crown prince designate Ashurbanipal, speak evil things about them, lift your hands against their households, commit a sin against them, take away something from the gifts that their father, Esarhaddon, king of Assyria, has given them or the property they have acquired, if the gifts in fields, houses, orchards, persons, equipment, horses, mules, donkeys, cattle, sheep, which Esarhaddon, king of Assyria, has given to his sons do not remain theirs, if you do not speak in their favor before the crown prince designate Ashurbanipal, so that they cannot live at his court and associate with you—

25. (283) This treaty which Esarhaddon, king of Assyria, has established with you in a binding fashion, under oath, on behalf of the crown prince designate Ashurbanipal and his brothers, sons by the mother of the crown prince designate Ashurbanipal,

—(if) you do not say and do not give orders to your sons, grandsons, to your offspring, to your descendants, who will live in the future after this treaty, saying: "Keep this treaty, do not sin against this treaty with you, lest you lose your lives, deliver your land to destruction, and your people to be deported. Let this order, which is acceptable to god and man, be acceptable to you too, let it be pleasing to you. Let Ashurbanipal, the crown prince designate, be preserved to be lord over the land and the people, and later be called to kingship. Do not set over yourselves another king, another lord."—

26. (302) If anyone sets afoot a revolt or rebellion against Esarhaddon, king of Assyria, and seats himself upon the royal throne, if you rejoice at his (having taken over the) kingship, and do not seize and kill him, if, not being able to seize and kill him, you accept his kingship, swear an oath of vassalage to him, do not rebel against him, do not fight against him with full loyalty, do not make all other countries hostile to him, do not make razzias against him, do not defeat him, do not eradicate his name and descendants from the country, do not help the crown prince designate Ashurbanipal onto the throne of his father—

27. (318) If one of his brothers, his father's brothers, his cousins, his kin, or any member of his father's lineage, or a descendant of former kings, or any prince, governor, Assyrian or foreigner, involves you in a plot and tells you, "Denounce the crown prince designate Ashurbanipal to his father, speak wrong and evil things about him," (if) you (thus) cause strife between him and his father, and incite them to hate each other—

28. (328) A . . . who gives you orders (or) *instigates* you, saying, "I am able (to . . .) his brothers or the retinue who *agitate* before his father, and denounce him to his father,"—*what* Ashur, (Shamash, and . . .) have spoken was established, without Ashur and Shamash . . . your father, honor your brother and (thus) save your lives.

29. (336) If one of his brothers, his father's brothers, his cousins, his kin, or any member of his father's lineage, of the court personnel, eunuchs or not, whether an Assyrian or a foreigner, or any living human being, involves you in a plot and tells you, "Denounce his brothers by the same mother to him, create strife between them, alienate his brothers by the same mother from him," (and) you listen to him and speak evil of his brothers to him, alienate him from his brothers, if you let go free the person who has spoken such things to you, if you do not go and tell it to the crown prince designate Ashurbanipal, saying, "Your father has established a treaty under oath with us about (such things)"—

30. (353) If you are *subjects* . . . the crown prince designate Ashurbanipal, his brothers . . . the throne . . . and you, of [*your*] *own accord* do not turn hostile to them, do not [. . .] among them, saying, "Your father has established a treaty under oath about (this)"—

31. (360) If you, after your lord Esarhaddon, king of Assyria, has departed from the living, and the crown prince designate Ashurbanipal has seated himself upon the royal throne, speak evil of his brothers or his [dear] brother to their brother, and *instigate* him, saying, "Lift your hand against them," if you estrange them from the crown prince designate Ashurbanipal, speak evil rumors of them

before Ashurbanipal, say to the crown prince designate Ashurbanipal that the rank that Esarhaddon, king of Assyria, has assigned them [is *unfit* so that] he removes them [from *it*]—

32. (373) If you smear your face, your hands, or your throats with red paste which (*is like*) *šapuḫru* in the eyes of the gods, or tie it to the hem of your garments in order to avert the consequences of the oath—

33. (377) If you try to reverse the curse, to avert the consequences of the oath, think up and carry out *stratagems* in order to reverse the *curse,* to avert the consequences of the oath, you and your sons who will live in the future will be *adjured* by this oath on behalf of the crown prince designate Ashurbanipal, son of your lord Esarhaddon, which will stay (in vigor) from today until after this treaty.

34. (385) If you, as you stand on the soil where this oath (is sworn), swear the oath with words and lips (only), do not swear with your entire heart, do not transmit it to your sons who will live after this treaty, if you take this *curse* upon yourselves but do not plan to keep the treaty of Esarhaddon, king of Assyria, on behalf of the crown prince designate Ashurbanipal, may your sons and grandsons because of this fear in the future, forever, your god Ashur and your lord, the crown prince designate Ashurbanipal.

35. (397) He who changes, neglects, transgresses, erases the words of this tablet, falsifies [...], the ... oath [...], [...] of this treaty tablet [...]. (If) you do not respect as your own god Ashur, king of the gods, and the great gods, my lords, [...] or the image of Esarhaddon, king of Assyria, or the image of Ashurbanipal, crown prince designate, or the image of ...-s, the seal [...] the crown prince designate [Ashurbanipal]—[...] [the tablet] sealed with the seal of Ashur, king of the gods, and placed before you—

36. (410) If you remove it, consign it to fire, throw it into water, bury it in dust, or by some trick destroy, annihilate, or turn it face down—

37. (414) May Ashur, king of the gods, who determines the fates, decree for you an evil, unpropitious fate, and not grant you fatherhood, old age, ... ripe old age.

38. (417) May Ninlil, his beloved wife, induce him to pronounce evil for you and may she not intercede for you.

38A. (418 ff.) May Anu, king of the gods, rain upon all your houses disease, exhaustion, *di'u*-disease, sleeplessness, worries, ill health.

39. (419) May Sin, the luminary of heaven and earth, clothe you in leprosy and (thus) not permit you to enter the presence of god and king; roam the open country as a wild ass or gazelle!

40. (422) May Shamash, the light of heaven and earth, not give you a fair and equitable judgment, may he take away your eyesight; walk about in darkness!

41. (425) May Ninurta, leader of the gods, fell you with his fierce arrow, and fill the plain with your corpses, give your flesh to eagles and vultures to feed upon.

42. (428) May Venus, the brightest among the stars, let your wives lie in the embrace of your enemy before your very eyes, may your sons not have authority over your house, may a foreign enemy divide your possessions.

43. (431) May Jupiter, the exalted lord of the gods, not let you see the entrance of Bel into Esagila, may he put an end to your lives.

44. (433) May Marduk, the eldest son, determine a grievous sin and an indissoluble curse as your fate.

45. (435) May Zarpanitu, who grants offspring and descendants, eradicate your offspring and descendants from the land.

46. (437) May Belet-ili, the Lady of all creatures, put an end to birth giving in your land, so that the nurses among you shall miss the cry of babies in the streets.

47. (440) May Adad, the canal inspector of heaven and earth, put an end [to vegetation] in your land, may he *avoid* your meadows and hit your land with a severe destructive downpour, may locusts, which diminish the (produce) of the land, [devour] your crops, let there be no sound of the grinding stone or the oven in your houses, let barley rations to be ground disappear for you, so that they grind your bones, (the bones of) your sons and daughters instead of barley rations, and not even the (first) joint of your finger should be able to dip into the dough, may the [. . .] eat the dough from your troughs. Mother shall [bar the door to] her daughter, may you eat in your hunger the flesh of your children, may, through want and famine, one man eat the other's flesh, clothe himself in the other's skin; let dogs and pigs eat your flesh, and may your spirit have no one to take care of and pour libations to him.

48. (453) May Ishtar, lady of battle, break your bow in a heavy battle, tie your arms, and have you crouch at the feet of your enemy.

49. (455) May Nergal, the warrior among the gods, extinguish your life with his merciless dagger, may he plant carnage and pestilence among you.

50. (457) May Ninlil, who resides in Nineveh, . . . (lit.: may *they* tie with you) a swift dagger.

51. (459) May Ishtar, who resides in Arbela, not grant you mercy and forgiveness.

52. (461) May Gula, the great physician, put illness and weariness [into your *hearts*], an unhealing sore in your body, so that you bathe in [your own blood] as if in water.

53. (464) May the Seven gods, the warrior gods, cause your downfall with their fierce weapons.

54. (466) May [. . .] hand you over to a man-eating lion.

55. (469) May Ishtar [of . . .], Ishtar [. . . of] Carchemish put a severe . . . into your heart, so that your blood dribbles down to the ground like rain.

56. (472) May the great gods of heaven and earth, who inhabit the world, all those that are named in this tablet, strike you down, look with disfavor upon you, curse you angrily with a baleful curse, on earth, may they uproot you from the living, below, may they deprive your spirit of water (libations), may they chase you away from both shade and sunlight so that you cannot take refuge in a hidden corner, may food and drink *forsake* you, and hunger, want, famine, and pestilence never leave you, may dogs and pigs drag around in the squares of Ashur the . . . of your young women, the . . . of your young men before your very eyes, may the earth not receive your body for burial, may the bellies of dogs and pigs be your burial place, your days should be somber, your years dark, may they decree for you an unrelieved darkness, your lives should end in sighs and sleeplessness, may a flood, an irresistible deluge, rise from the bowels of the earth and devastate you, may all that is good be abhorrent to you, all that is evil be bestowed upon you, let tar and pitch be your food, donkey urine your drink, naphtha your ointment, river rushes your covers, and evil spirits, demons, and lurkers select your houses (as their abode).

57. (494) "May these gods look on if we rebel or revolt against Esarhaddon, king of Assyria, or the crown prince designate Ashurbanipal, or his brothers by the mother of the crown prince designate Ashurbanipal, or against the rest of the sons begotten by our lord Esarhaddon, king of Assyria, if we plot with his enemies, if we hear agitators, plotters, whispers of evil, wrong, unseemly acts, rebellious and disloyal speech against the crown prince designate Ashurbanipal, or his brothers by the mother of the crown prince designate Ashurbanipal, and conceal it and do not report it to our lord, the crown prince designate Ashurbanipal, if, as long as we, our sons and our grandsons live, the crown prince designate Ashurbanipal will not be our king and lord, if we place another king, another prince over ourselves, our sons, our grandsons—may all the gods mentioned (here) call us, our offspring, and our descendants, to account."

58. (513) If you sin against this treaty which [your] lord Esarhaddon, king of Assyria, has established with you on behalf of the crown prince designate Ashurbanipal, his brothers by the mother of the crown prince designate Ashurbanipal, and the rest of the sons begotten by Esarhaddon, king of Assyria, may Ashur, father of the gods, strike you down with his fierce weapons.

59. (519) May Palil, lord of first rank, let eagles and vultures eat your flesh.

60. (521) May Ea, king of the *apsu*, lord of the springs, give you deadly water to drink, and fill you with dropsy.

61. (523) May the great gods of heaven and earth make water and oil an abhorrence to you.

62. (524) May Girra, who provides food for young and old, burn your offspring and descendants.

63. (526) (Ditto, ditto). May all the gods who are named in this treaty tablet reduce your soil in size to be as narrow as a brick, turn your soil into iron, so that no one may cut a *furrow* in it.

64. (530) Just as rain does not fall from a copper sky, so may there come neither rain nor dew upon your fields and meadows, but let it rain burning coals in your land instead of dew.

65. (534) Just as lead does not resist fire, so may you not resist your enemies, but take your sons and daughters by the hand (and flee).

66. (537) Just as a mule has no offspring, may your name, offspring and descendants disappear from the land.

67. (540) Just as the "horn" of [the *plow*] is within it (the soil) and does not cut a *furrow* in the *soil*, [...] does not return to its [...], so may your offspring, and the offspring of your sons and daughters disappear from the face of the earth (variant?: from the land).

68. (545) May Shamash plow up your cities and districts with an iron plow.

69. (547) Just as this ewe is cut open and the flesh of its young placed in its mouth, so may he (Shamash?) make you eat in your hunger the flesh of your brothers, your sons, and your daughters.

70. (551) Just as (these) yearlings and spring lambs, male and female, are cut open and their entrails are rolled around their feet, so may the entrails of your sons and daughters be rolled around your feet.

71. (555) Just as a snake and a mongoose do not enter the same hole and do not live there, but plot of cutting each other's throat, so may you and your women not enter the same house, (not lie down in the same bed) but plot of cutting each other's throat.

72. (560) Just as bread and wine enter the intestines, so may they (the gods) let this oath enter your intestines and the intestines of your sons and daughters.

73. (563) Just as you can blow water out of a *tube*, so may they blow away you, your women, your sons, your daughters, may they make your rivers, your springs, and their wells flow backward.

74. (567) May they let go gold ... from your land (uncertain).

75. (568) Just as honey is sweet, so may the blood of your women, your sons and daughters taste sweet in your mouths.

76. (570) Just as the ... is ... alive, so may, while you are alive, your flesh, the flesh of your women, your sons and daughters ... be ...

77. (573) May they break your bow and make you crouch at the feet of your enemies, may they make the bow refuse to bend in your hands, may they turn backward your chariots.

78. (576) Just as a stag is chased and killed, so may your avengers chase and kill you, your brothers, your sons.

79. (579) Just as a butterfly does not fit into (lit.: own) and does not return to its cocoon, so may you not return to your women in your houses.

80. (582) Just as a bird is caught by means of a decoy, so may they deliver you, your brothers, your sons, into the hand of your avengers.

81. (585) May they blacken your flesh/skin, the flesh/skin of your women, your brothers, your sons and daughters [with . . .], pitch and naphtha.

82. (588) Ditto. Just as a *ḫarušḫu*-beast is caught in a snare, so may you, your brothers, your sons and daughters be caught by the hand of your enemy.

83. (591) May your flesh, the flesh of your women, your brothers, your sons and daughters be used up like the flesh of a chameleon.

84. (594) Just as a honeycomb is pierced through and through with holes, so may holes be pierced through and through in your flesh, the flesh of your women, your brothers, your sons and daughters while you are alive.

85. (599) May they (the gods) let lice, caterpillars, and other field pests eat up your land and your district as if locusts.

86. (601) May they *squash* you as a fly in the hand of your enemies, may your enemies mash you.

87. (603) Just as this bedbug stinks, so may your breath stink before god, king, and men.

88. (606) May they strangle you, your women, your sons and daughters, with a cord.

89. (608) Just as one burns a wax figurine in fire, dissolves a clay one in water, so may they burn your figure in fire, submerge it in water.

90. (612) Just as this chariot is spattered with blood up to its running board, so may they spatter your chariots in the midst of your enemy with your own blood.

91. (616) May they spin you like a spindle whorl, may they use you like women in the sight of your enemy.

92. (618) May they cause you, your brothers, your sons and daughters to go backward like a crab.

93. (621) May they surround you like an evil fire.

94. (622) Just as (this) oil enters your flesh, so may they make this oath enter your flesh, the flesh of your brothers, your sons and daughters.

95. (626) Just as one cuts off the hands and feet and blinds the eyes of those who blaspheme against the god or the lord, so may they bring about your end, may they make you sway like a marsh reed, may they tear you *out* like blood from the bandage of the enemy.

96. (632) If you abandon Esarhaddon, king of Assyria, or the crown prince designate Ashurbanipal, and disperse right and left, may swords consume the one who goes to the right, may swords consume the one too who goes to the left.

96A. May they [*slaughter*] you, your women, your brothers, your sons and daughters like kids.

97. (637) Just as the squeak produced by this door pivot, so may you, your women, your sons and daughters never rest nor sleep, not even your bones should stay together.

98. (641) Just as the inside of (this) hole is empty, so may they make your insides be empty.

99. (643) When your enemy pierces you, may there be no wax, oil, *zinzaru'* or cedar balsam available to put on your wounds.

100. (646) Just as (this) gall is bitter, so may you, your women, your sons and daughters be bitter to each other.

101. (649) May Shamash clamp his bronze trap over you, throw you into a trap from which there is no escape, and not save you (from it).

102. (652) Just as this waterskin is slit and its water *runs out,* so may your waterskins be *slit* in a region of thirst and famine, and you die of lack of water.

103. (656) Just as (this) *shoe* is slit, [. . . so may your shoe be slit] in a terrain of thorns [. . .].

104. (662) May Enlil, lord of the throne, [. . .]

105. (663) May Nabu, who holds the tablets of fate of the gods, erase your name, and make your descendants disappear from the land.

106. (665) May the door [. . .] in your face, may your doors [. . .]

Date (669) (Dated) the 16th day of the month Ajaru, in the eponymy of Nabu-bel-usur, governor of Khorsabad. Treaty established (by Esarhaddon) concerning Ashurbanipal, crown prince designate of Assyria, and Shamashshumukin, crown prince designate of Babylonia.

VII

Egyptian Historical Texts

TRANSLATOR: JOHN A. WILSON

ANET, 233–34 ## The Expulsion of the Hyksos

It is an irony of history that out best contemporaneous source on the expulsion of the Hyksos from Egypt comes from the biographical record of a relatively modest citizen of Upper Egypt, the captain of a Nile vessel. In relating his participation in the campaigns of Ah-mose I (about 1570–1545 B.C.) and of Thutmose I (about 1525–1495 B.C.), Ah-mose, son of the woman Eben, tells of the successive attacks on the Hyksos in Egypt and then of the follow-up campaigns into Asia.

The commander of a crew, Ah-mose, son of Eben, the triumphant, says:

I speak to you, all mankind, that I may let you know the favors which have come to me. I have been awarded gold seven times in the presence of the entire land, and male and female slaves in like manner, and I have been vested with very many fields.[1] The reputation of a valiant man is from what he has done, not being destroyed in this land forever.

He speaks thus:

Fig. 42   I had my upbringing in the town of el-Kab, my father being a soldier of the King of Upper and Lower Egypt: Seqnen-Re, the triumphant,[2] his name being Bebe, (5) the son of (the woman) Ro-onet. Then I served as soldier in his place in the ship, "The Wild Bull," in the time of the Lord of the Two Lands: Neb-pehti-Re, the trium-

---

[1] In his tomb, Ah-mose gives a list of 9 male and 10 female slaves which were his booty. His grants of land from the king came to something like 70 acres.

[2] One of the pharaohs named Seqnen-Re in the 17th dynasty.

phant,[3] when I was (still) a boy, before I had taken a wife, (but) while I was (still) sleeping in a *net hammock.*[4]

But after I had set up a household, then I was taken on the ship, "Northern," because I was valiant. Thus I used to accompany the Sovereign—life, prosperity, health!—on foot, following his excursions in his chariot.[5] When the town of Avaris was besieged, then I showed valor of foot in the presence of his majesty. Thereupon I was appointed to the ship, "Appearing in Memphis." Then there was fighting on the water in *the canal PaDjedku* of Avaris. Thereupon I made a capture, (10) and I carried away a hand.[6] It was reported to the king's herald. Then the Gold of Valor was given to me. Thereupon there was fighting again in this place. Then I made a capture again there and brought away a hand. Then the Gold of Valor was given to me over again.

Then there was fighting in the Egypt which is south of this town.[7] Thereupon I carried off a man (as) living prisoner. I went down into the water—now he was taken captive on the side of the town[8]—and crossed over the water carrying him. Report was made to the king's herald. Thereupon I was awarded gold another time.

Then Avaris was despoiled. Then I carried of spoil from there: one man, three women, a total of four persons. Then his majesty gave them to me to be slaves.[9]

Then (15) Sharuhen was besieged for three years.[10] Then his majesty despoiled it. Thereupon I carried off spoil from there: two women and a hand. Then the Gold of Valor was given to me, *and* my spoil was given to me to be slaves. $\qquad$ Josh. 19:6

Now after his majesty had killed the Asiatics, then he sailed southward to Khenti-hen-nefer, to destroy the Nubian nomads. . . .

After this (Thut-mose I) went forth to Retenu,[11] to assuage his heart throughout the foreign countries. His majesty reached Naharin,[12] (37)

---

[3] Ah-mose I.

[4] Perhaps: "I was (still) sleeping with the phallic sheath attached"?

[5] Note the first use of the horse and chariot by the Egyptians. The Hyksos had introduced this war force into Egypt.

[6] It was an Egyptian army custom to cut off the hand of a dead enemy as a proof of killing.

[7] South of Avaris. This looks like a temporary retirement by the Egyptians.

[8] Beside the town, but across a body of water from the Egyptian army.

[9] In Ah-mose's "list of the male and female slaves of the spoil," most of the 19 names are good Egyptian. However, there appear a Pa-'Aam, "The Asiatic," a T'amutj, which is a feminine name similar to Amos, and an Ishtar-ummi, "Ishtar is My Mother."

[10] It lay in the extreme southwestern corner of the land of Canaan, in the territory of the tribe of Simeon. Perhaps it was modern Tell el-Fâr'ah.

[11] Syria-Palestine in general.

[12] "The Two Rivers," the area of the Euphrates bend.

and his majesty—life, prosperity, health!—found that enemy[13] while he was marshaling the battle array. Then his majesty made a great slaughter among them. There was no number to the living prisoners whom his majesty carried off by his victory. Now I was in the van of our army,[14] and his majesty saw how valiant I was. I carried off a chariot, its horse, and him who was in it as a living prisoner. They were presented to his majesty. Then I was awarded gold another time. . . .[15]

The Asiatic Campaign of Thut-mose III

ANET, 234–38

The Battle of Megiddo

Thut-mose III (about 1490–1436 B.C.) was the conquering pharaoh who set the Egyptian Empire on a foundation firm for almost a century. For twenty years he led campaigns into Asia almost every year. Some of these campaigns involved serious fighting, others were parades of strength. We have detailed information on his first campaign (perhaps 1468 B.C.), which attacked the focus of Asiatic resistance in the Canaanite city of Megiddo.

The "Annals" of Thut-mose III's military campaigns are carved on the walls of the Temple of Karnak, in recognition of the fact that the god Amon-Re had given victory.

Fig. 106

The Horus: Mighty Bull, Appearing in Thebes; . . . (Thut-mose III).

His majesty commanded that [the victories which his father Amon had given to him] should be established [upon] a monument in the temple which his majesty had made for [his father Amon, in order to set down] (5) each individual campaign, together with the booty which [his majesty] carried [off from it, *and the dues of*] every [*foreign country*] which his father Re had given to him.

Year 22, 4th month of the second season, day 25.[16] [*His majesty passed the fortrees of*] Sile,[17] on the first campaign of victory [*which*

---

[13] "That fallen one," a frequent designation of a major enemy.

[14] It has been pointed out that only in the stretch of patriotic enthusiasm of the first century of the 18th dynasty did the Egyptians speak of "our army," instead of ascribing the troops to the pharaoh.

[15] In the quarries of Maâsara is a record of the reopening of the quarries for stone to be used in certain temples. Part of the inscription runs: "The stone was dragged by the cattle which his [*victories*] throughout the lands of the Fenkhu had carried off." The accompanying scene shows Asiatics driving the cattle. Djahi and Fenkhu apply to the Phoenician coast running down into Palestine and including the hinterland— further north than southern Palestine.

[16] Tentatively, April 16, 1468 B.C., for the battle of Megiddo. The precise date will depend upon what the ancient Egyptians meant by a "new moon."

[17] Or Tjaru, the Egyptian frontier post, at or near modern Kantarah.

his majesty made to extend] the frontiers of Egypt, in valor, [in victory, in power, and in justification]. Now this was a [long] time in years ... (10) plunder, while every man *was* [*tributary*] before ... But it happened in later times that the garrison which was there was in the town of Sharuhen, while from Iursa to the outer ends of the earth[18] had become rebellious against his majesty.

Josh. 19:6

Year 23, 1st month of the third season, day 4, the day of the feast of the king's coronation—as far as the town of "That-Which-the-Ruler-Seized," [*of which the Syrian name is*] Gaza.[19]

[Year 23,] (15) 1st month of the third season, day 5—departure from this place, in valor, [in victory,] in power, and in justification, in order to overthrow that wretched enemy,[20] and to extend the frontiers of Egypt, according to the command of his father Amon-Re, the [*valiant*] and victorious, that he should capture.

Fig. 99

Year 23, 1st month of the third season, day 16[21]—as far as the town of Yehem. [His majesty] ordered a conference with his victorious army, speaking as follows: "That [wretched] enemy (20) of Kadesh has come and has entered into Megiddo. He is [there] at this moment. He has gathered to him the princes of [every] foreign country [which had been] loyal to Egypt, as well as (those) as far as Naharin and M[*itanni*], them of Hurru, them of Kode, their horses, their armies, [and their people], *for* he says—so it is reported—'I shall wait [here] (25) in Megiddo [to fight against his majesty].' Will ye tell me [what is in your hearts]?"[22]

They said in the presence of his majesty: "What is it like to go [on] this [road] which becomes (so) narrow? It is [reported] that the foe is there, waiting on [the outside, while they are] becoming (more) numerous. Will not horse (have to) go after [horse, and the army] (30) and the people similarly? Will the vanguard of us be fighting while the [rear guard] is waiting here in Aruna, unable to fight?[23] *Now* two (other) roads are here. One of the roads—behold, it is [*to the east of*] us, so that *it* comes out at Taanach. The order—behold, it

Judg. 5:19

---

[18] From southern Palestine to northern Syria.

[19] On Borchardt's reckoning, the Egyptians reached Gaza on April 25, 1468, having traveled at the respectable rate of 150 miles in 9 or 10 days. As this date was the anniversary of Thut-mose III's coronation, the year number changed from 22 to 23.

[20] The Prince of Kadesh was the leader of the coalition against Egypt.

[21] May 7, 1468 (Borchardt). After leaving the Egyptian-held city of Gaza, the army's rate was notably slower through territory which was actually or potentially rebellious. Perhaps 80 miles were covered in 11 or 12 days. Yehem (possibly Jahmai or similar) is tentatively located by Nelson at Yemma on the south side of the Carmel ridge.

[22] It is probable from the nature of this coalition and from Thut-mose's subsequent campaigns that this Kadesh was the city on the Orontes.

[23] If they went straight ahead on the narrow track debouching just south of Megiddo, they had to go in single file and would be particularly vulnerable.

is to the (35) north side of Djefti,[24] and we will come out to the north of Megiddo. Let our victorious lord proceed on the one of [them] which is [satisfactory to] his heart, (but) do not make us go on that difficult road!"

Then messages [were brought in *about that wretched enemy, and discussion was continued*] of [that] problem on which they had previously spoken. That which was said in the majesty of the Court—life, prosperity, health![25]—"I [swear], (40) as Re loves me, as my father Amon favors me, as my [nostrils] are rejuvenated with life and satisfaction, my majesty shall proceed upon this Aruna road! Let him of you who wishes go upon these roads of which you speak, and let him of you who wishes come in the following of my majesty! '*Behold*,' they will say, these (45) enemies whom Re abominates, 'has his majesty set out on another road because he has become afraid of us?'—so they will speak."

They said in the presence of his majesty: "May thy father Amon, Lord of the Thrones of the Two Lands, Presiding over Karnak, act [*according to thy desire*]! Behold, we are following thy majesty everywhere that [thy majesty] goes, for a servant will be after [his] lord."

[*Then* his majesty *laid a charge*] (50) upon the entire army: "[*Ye*] shall [*hold fast to the stride of your victorious lord on*] that road which becomes (so) na[rrow. Behold, his majesty has taken] an oath, saying: 'I will not let [my victorious army] go forth ahead of my majesty in [this place!'" *Now his majesty had laid it in his heart*] that he himself should go forth at the head of his army. [Every man] was made aware (55) of his order of march, horse following horse, while [his majesty] was at the head of his army.

Year 23, 1st month of the third season, day 19[26]—the awakening in [life] in the tent of life, prosperity, and health, at the town of Aruna. Proceeding northward by my majesty, carrying my father Amon-Re, Lord of the Thrones of the Two Lands, [that he might open the ways] before me,[27] while Har-akhti established [*the heart of my victorious army*] (60) and my father Amon strengthened the arm [of my majesty]. . . .

Then [his] majesty issued forth[28] [at the head of] his [army], which was [prepared] in many ranks. [*He had not met*] a single [*enemy.* Their] southern wing was in Taanach, [while their] nothern wing was

Num. 10:33

Deut. 1:33

---

[24] Two safer mountain tracks were offered as alternatives, one debouching at Taanach, 4 or 5 miles southeast of Megiddo, and one debouching at an unknown point north(west) of Megiddo.

[25] That is, the voice from the throne. The Court moved with the pharaoh.

[26] Three days after arrival in Yehem.

[27] The standard of Amon led the way.

[28] From the pass on to the Megiddo plain.

on the south side [of *the Qina Valley.*[29] Then] (65) his majesty *rallied them saying*: ". . . ! They are fallen! While that [wretched] enemy . . . [*May*] ye [*give praise*] to (70) [*him; may ye extol the might of*] his majesty, because his arm is greater than (that of) [*any king. It has indeed protected the rear of*] his majesty's army in Aruna!"

Now while the rear of his majesty's victorious army was (still) at [the town] of Aruna, the vanguard had come out into the [Qi]na Valley, and they filled the mouth of this valley.

Then they said to his majesty—life, prosperity, health!—(75) "Behold, his majesty has come forth with his victorious army, and they have filled the valley. Let our victorious lord listen to us this time, and let our lord guard for us the rear of his army and his people. When the rear of the army comes forth for us into the open, then we shall fight against these foreigners, then we shall not trouble our hearts [about] the rear of (80) our army."

A halt was made by his majesty outside, [*seated*] there and guarding the rear of his victorious army. Now the [*leaders*] had just finished coming forth on this road when the shadow turned.[30] His majesty reached the south of Megiddo on the bank of the Qina brook, when the seventh hour was in (its) course in the day.

Then a camp was pitched there for his majesty, and a charge was laid upon the entire army, [saying]: "Prepare ye! Make your weapons ready, since one[31] will engage in combat with that wretched enemy in the morning, because one is . . . !"

Resting in the enclosure of life, prosperity, and health.[32] Providing for the officials. *Issuing rations* to the retinue. Posting the sentries of the army. Saying to them: "Be steadfast, be steadfast! Be vigilant, be vigilant!" Awakening in life in the tent of life, prosperity, and health. They came to tell his majesty: "The desert is well, and the garrisons of the south and north also!"

Year 23, 1st month of the third season, day 21, the day of the feast of the *true* new moon.[33] Appearance of the king at dawn. Now a charge was laid upon the entire army to *pass by* . . . (85) His majesty set forth in a chariot of fine gold, adorned with his accoutrements of combat, like Horus, the Mighty of Arm, a lord of action like Montu, the Theban, while his father Amon made strong his arms.

[29] The Qina is still represented by a brook flowing south of Megiddo. When he said: "They are fallen!" he was anticipating the fall of the Asiatics, because they had failed to guard the pass.

[30] It was noon, and the shadow clock should be turned around. The Egyptian van thus reached the Megiddo plain seven hours before the rear of the army emerged and Thut-mose could go into camp.

[31] Pharaoh.

[32] The royal enclosure was doubtless an elaborate pavillon.

[33] Borchardt's date for the battle is May 12, 1468.

The southern wing of his majesty's army was at a hill south of [the] Qina [*brook*], and the northern wing was to the northwest of Megiddo, while his majesty was in their center, Amon being the protection of his person (in) the melee and the strength of [*Seth pervading*] his members.

Thereupon his majesty prevailed over them at the head of his army. Then they saw his majesty prevailing over them, and they fled headlong [to] Megiddo with faces of fear. They abandoned their horses and their chariots of gold and silver, so that someone might draw them (up) into this town by *hoisting* on their garments. Now the people had shut this town against them, (but) they [let down] garments to *hoist* them up into this town. Now, if only his majesty's army had not given up their hearts to capturing the possessions of the enemy, they would [have captured] Megiddo at this time, while the wretched enemy of Kadesh and the wretched enemy of this town were being dragged (up) *hastily* to get them into their town, for the fear of his majesty entered [their bodies], their arms were weak, [*for*] his serpent-diadem had overpowered them.

Then their horses and their chariots of gold and silver were captured as an easy [prey. *Ranks*] of them were lying stretched out on their backs, like fish in the *bight of a net,* while his majesty's victorious army counted up their possessions. Now there was captured [that] wretched [enemy's] tent, which was worked [with *silver*], . . .

Then the entire army rejoiced and gave praise to Amon [because of the victory] which he had given to his son on [this day. They *lauded*] his majesty and extolled his victories. Then they presented the plunder which they had taken: hands,[34] living prisoners, horses, and chariots of gold and silver and of *painted work.* (90) . . .

[Then his majesty commanded] his army with the words: "Capture ye [effectively, my] victorious [army]! Behold, [*all foreign countries*] have been put [*in this town by* the command] of Re on this day, inasmuch as every prince of every [northern] country is shut up within it, for the capturing of Megiddo is the capturing of a thousand towns! Capture ye firmly, firmly! . . ."

[*Orders were issued to* the com]manders of the troops to pro[*vide for their divisions and to inform*] each [man] *of* his place. They measured [this] city, which was corralled with a moat and enclosed with fresh timbers of all their pleasant trees, while his majesty himself was in a fortress east of this town, [being] watchful . . . . . . [enclosed] with a girdle wall, . . . *by* its girdle wall. Its name was called "Men-kheper-Re-is-the-Corraller-of-the-Asiatics." People were appointed as sentries at the enclosure of his majesty, and they were told: "Be steadfast, be steadfast! Be vigilant, [be vigilant]!" . . . his majesty. . . .

---

[34] Cut off from the fallen foe as tokens of battle accomplishment.

[Not one] of them [was permitted to go] outside from behind this wall, except to come out *at a knock* on the door of their fortress.[35]

Now everything which his majesty did to this town and to that wretched enemy and his wretched army is set down by the individual day, by the individual expedition, and by the individual [troop] commanders. . . . They [are] set down on a roll of leather in the temple of Amon today.

Now the princes of this foreign country came on their bellies to kiss the ground to the glory of his majesty and to beg breath for their nostrils, because his arm was (so) great, because the prowess of Amon was (so) great [over (95) every] foreign [country] . . . [all] the princes whom the prowess of his majesty carried off, bearing their tribute of silver, gold, lapis lazuli, and turquoise, and carrying grain, wine, and large and small cattle for the army of his majesty, with one gang of them bearing tribute southward. Then his majesty appointed princes anew for [*every town*]. . . .

[List of the booty which his majesty's army carried off from the town of] Megiddo: 340 living prisoners and 83 hands; 2,041 horses, 191 foals, 6 stallions, and . . . colts; 1 chariot worked with gold, with a *body* of gold, belonging to that enemy, [*1*] fine chariot worked with gold belonging to the Prince of [*Megiddo*] . . . , and 892 chariots of his wretched army—total: 924; 1 fine bronze coat of mail belonging to that enemy, [*1*] fine bronze coat of mail belonging to the Prince of Meg[iddo, and] 200 [*leather*] coats of mail belonging to his wretched army; 502 bows; and 7 poles of *meru*-wood, worked with silver, of the tent of that enemy.

Fig. 93

Now the army [of his majesty] carried off [*cattle*] . . . : 387 . . . , 1,929 cows, 2,000 goats, and 20,500 sheep.

List of what was carried off afterward by the king from the household goods of that enemy, who [was in] Yanoam, Nuges, and Herenkeru,[36] together with the property of those towns which had made themselves subject to him . . . : . . . ; 38 [*maryanu*] belonging to them,[37] 84 children of that enemy and of the princes who were with him, 5 *maryanu* belonging to them, 1,796 male and female slaves, as well as their children, and 103 pardoned persons, who had come out from that enemy because of hunger—total: 2,503—apart from bowls of costly stone and gold, various vessels, (100) . . . , a large *akunu*-jar in Syrian work, jars, bowls, *plates,* various drinking vessels, large

---

[35] The besieged Asiatics were permitted to appear only if Egyptians called them out?

[36] "Upper Retenu" properly stands for the mountain territory of north Palestine and southern Syria, and Yanoam seems to have been in the Lake Huleh area. The three towns would then be somewhere in that area.

[37] The *maryanu* were the warrior or officer class in Asia at this time.

kettles, [x +] 17 knives—making 1,784 *deben*;[38] gold in discs, found in the process of being worked, as well as abundant silver in discs— 966 *deben* and 1 *kidet*;[39] a silver statue *in the form of* . . . , [*a statue*] . . . ,

Fig. 4 with head of gold; 3 walking sticks with human heads; 6 carrying-chairs of that enemy, of ivory, ebony, and *carob*-wood, worked with gold, and the 6 footstools belonging to them; 6 large tables of ivory and *carob*-wood; 1 bed belonging to that enemy, of *carob*-wood, worked with gold and with every (kind of) costly stone, in the manner of a *kerker*,[40] completely worked in gold; a statue of that enemy which was there, of ebony worked with gold, its head of lapis [lazuli] . . . ; bronze vessels, and much clothing of that enemy.

Now the fields were made into arable plots and assigned to inspectors of the palace—life, prosperity, health!—in order to reap their harvest. List of the harvest which his majesty carried off from the Megiddo acres: 207,300 [+ x] sacks of wheat,[41] apart from what was cut as forage by his majesty's army, . . .

A Campaign of Seti I in Northern Palestine

Internally and externally the Amarna Revolution had dealt a serious blow to Egyptian empire. Domestic reorganization was the first need. Then, when Seti I (about 1318–1301 B.C.) became pharaoh, he returned to campaigning in Asia. This stela from Palestinian soil gives a brief statement of his energy in meeting an attempted coalition of Asiatic princes.

Year 1, 3rd month of the third season, day 10.[42] Live the Horus: Mighty Bull, Appearing in Thebes, Making the Two Lands to Live; the Two Goddesses: Repeating Births, Mighty of Arm, Repelling the Nine Bows; the Horus of Gold: Repeating Appearances, Mighty of Bows in All Lands; the King of Upper and Lower Egypt, Lord of the Two Lands: Men-maat-Re [Ir]-en-Re; the Son of Re, Lord of Diadems: Seti Mer-ne-Ptah, beloved of Re-Har-akhti, the great god. The good god, potent with his arm, heroic and valiant like Montu, rich in captives, (5) knowing (how to) place his hand, alert wherever he is; speaking with his mouth, acting with his hands, valiant leader of his army, valiant warrior in the very heart of the fray, a Bastet[43] terrible

---

[38] About 435 lb. troy of metal value (probably reckoned in silver) in the listed pieces.

[39] About 235 lb. troy. Uncertain whether of silver only, or of the combined value of gold and silver.

[40] An unknown object of wood.

[41] Something like 450,000 bushels.

[42] Around 1318 B.C., this date fell late in May.

[43] Bastet, an Egyptian cat-goddess, merged with Sekhmet, the lioness goddess of war.

in combat, penetrating into a mass of Asiatics and making them prostrate, crushing the princes of Retenu, reaching the (very) ends of (10) him who transgresses against *his* way. He causes to *retreat* the princes of Syria,[44] *all* the boastfulness *of whose* mouth was *(so) great.* Every foreign country of the ends of the earth, their princes say: "Where shall we go?" They spend the night *giving testimony* in his name, *saying: "Behold it, behold it!" in* their hearts. It is the strength of his father Amon that decreed to him valor and victory.

On this day[45] one came to speak to his majesty, as follows: (15) "The wretched foe who is in the town of Hamath[46] is gathering to himself many people, while he is seizing the town of Beth-Shan. *Then there will be* an alliance with them of Pahel. He does not permit the Prince of Rehob to go outside."[47]

Thereupon his majesty sent the first army of Amon, (named) "Mighty of Bows," to the town of Hamath, the first army of the (20) Re, (named) "Plentiful of Valor," to the town of Beth-Shan, and the first army of Seth, (named) "Strong of Bows," to the town of Yanoam.[48] When the space of a day had passed, they were overthrown to the glory of his majesty, the King of Upper and Lower Egypt: Menmaat-Re; the Son of Re: Seti Mer-ne-Ptah, given life.

The Report of a Frontier Official

ANET, 259

In a group of letters which served as models for schoolboys, one communication presents the form in which an official on the eastern frontier of Egypt might report the passage of Asiatic tribes into the better pasturage of the Delta.

---

[44] *Kharu*, Syria-Palestine in general.

[45] The date at the beginning of the inscription.

[46] Not necessarily the Prince of Hamath. This may have been a prince from the north; note that Seti sends one army division north to Yanoam.

[47] Ancient Beth-Shan is modern Tell el-Ḥuṣn, just northwest of modern Beisan. Hamath is almost certainly Tell el-Ḥammeh, about 10 mi. south of Beisan. Pahel or Pella is Khirbet Faḥil, about 7 mi. southeast of Beisan and across the Jordan. Rehob is probably Tell eṣ-Ṣârem, about 3 mi. south of Beisan. These cities all seem to have lain within a small range. It would seem that Hamath and Pahel were acting against Beth-Shan and Rehob.

[48] Seti I's dispositions were rapid and effective. One problem here is the reason for sending a unit against Yanoam, which was apparently considerably north of the center of disaffection. Yanoam may be modern Tell en-Nâʿameh, north of Lake Huleh and thus nearly 50 mi. north of Beisan. Perhaps the real opposition to Egypt lay to the north, in the territory dominated by the Hittites. By throwing a road-block against reinforcements from the north, Seti I would be able to deal with a localized rebellion around Beth-Shan, without outside interference.

(51) The Scribe Inena communicating to his lord, the Scribe of the Treasury Qa-g[abu], . . . :—In life, prosperity, health! This is a letter [to] let [my lord] know: An[other communication to] my lord, to wit:

[I] have carried out every commission laid upon me, in good shape and strong as metal. I have not been lax.

Gen. 46:28; 47:1

Another communication to my [lord], to [wit: We] have finished letting the Bedouin tribes of Edom pass the Fortress [of] Mer-ne-Ptah Hotep-hir-Maat—life, prosperity, health!—which is (in) Tjeku,[49]

Exod. 1:11

(56) to the pools[50] of Per-Atum[51] [of] Mer-[ne]-Ptah Hotep-hir-Maat, which are (in) Tjeku, to keep them alive and to keep their cattle alive, through the great *ka* of Pharaoh—life, prosperity, health!— the good sun of every land, in the year 8, 5 [intercalary] days, [the Birth of] Seth.[52] I have had them brought in a copy of the *report* to the [place where] my lord is, *as well as* the other names of days when the Fortress of Mer-ne-Ptah Hotep-hir-Maat—life, prosperity, health!—which is (in) [Tj]ek[u], may be passed. . . .

ANET, 260

A Syrian Interregnum

For an unknown number of years between the Nineteenth and Twentieth Dynasties Egypt was in a chaotic state and for a part of the time was under the rule of a Syrian. All that we know of this episode comes from the following text.

The Great Papyrus Harris comes from Thebes and dates to the end of the reign of Ramses III (about 1164 B.C.), forming a kind of last will and testament for him. The troubles which he here describes lay between the reign of the last king of the Nineteenth Dynasty (about 1205 B.C.) and the beginning of the reign of Ramses III's father, Set-nakht (about 1197 B.C.).

SAID King User-maat-Re Meri-Amon[53]—life, prosperity, health!— the great god,[54] to the officials and leaders of the land, the infantry, the chariotry, the Sherden,[55] the many bowmen, and all the souls of Egypt:

[49] The location is the eastern end of the Wadi Tumilat, the "land of Goshen." The Fortress of Mer-ne-Ptah will have been a frontier fortress. Tjeku—or probably Teku— could only with difficulty be Succoth and seems to be a broad designation for the region.

[50] The Semitic word *birkeh* is used.

[51] Per-Atum, "the House of Atum," is probably biblical Pithom.

[52] "The Birth of Seth" was the 3rd intercalary day at the end of the year. Around 1215 B.C. this would be after the middle of June.

[53] Ramses III (about 1195–1164 B.C.).

[54] The epithet normally means that the king is already dead.

[55] Egyptian captive or mercenary troops, from the Mediterranean area.

Hear ye, that I may make you aware of my benefactions which I accomplished while I was king of the people. The land of Egypt had been cast aside, with every man being his (*own standard of*) right. They had no chief spokesman for many years previously up to other times. The land of Egypt was officials and mayors,[56] one slaying his fellow, both exalted and lowly. Other *times* came afterwards in the empty years,[57] and . . . ,[58] a Syrian (5) with them, made himself prince. He set the entire land as tributary before him. One joined his companion that their property might be plundered. They treated the gods like the people, and no offerings were presented in the temples.

But when the gods reversed themselves to show mercy and to set the land right as was its normal state, they established their son, who had come forth from their body, to be Ruler—life, prosperity, health!—of every land, upon their great throne: User-kha-Re Setep-en-Re Meri-Amon—life, prosperity, health!—the Son of Re: Set-nakht Merer-Re Meri-Amon—life, prosperity, health! He was Khepri-Seth when he was enraged. He brought to order the entire land, which had been rebellious. He slew the disaffected of heart who had been in Egypt. He cleansed the great throne of Egypt.

The War against the Peoples of the Sea

ANET, 262–63

In the latter half of the second millennium B.C. there were extensive movements in the eastern Mediterranean area. Masses of homeless peoples moved slowly across the sea and its coastlands, displacing or merging with the older populations. These migrations ended the Minoan civilization in Crete, contributed to the historical populations of Greece and Italy, wiped out the Hittite Empire, thrust the Philistines into Canaan, and washed up on the shores of Egypt. In Ramses III's eighth year (about 1188 B.C.) the pharaoh met and checked their attempt to push into the rich lands of the Nile. The victory was only a check, because the Egyptian Empire in Asia ended shortly after. The following accounts of this war come from Ramses III's temple of Medinet Habu at Thebes.

Fig. 7

Fig. 92

(1) Year 8 under the majesty of (Ramses III) . . .

(16) . . . The foreign countries made a *conspiracy* in their islands. All at once the lands were removed and scattered in the fray. No land could stand before their arms, from Hatti, Kode, Carchemish, Arzawa,

---

[56] That is, broken down under local rule only, without king or other central government.

[57] Either years void of orderly rule, or years of emptiness, i.e., of economic distress.

[58] The rule of an otherwise unknown Syrian ("Horite") is certain.

Fig. 95

and Alashiya on,[59] being cut off *at [one time]*. A camp [was set up] in one place in Amor.[60] They desolated its people, and its land was like that which has never come into being. They were coming forward toward Egypt, while the flame was prepared before them. Their confederation was the Philistines, Tjeker, Shekelesh, Denye(n), and Weshesh,[61] lands united. They laid their hands upon the lands as far as the circuit of the earth, their hearts confident and trusting: "Our plans will succeed!"

Now the heart of this god, the Lord of the Gods, was prepared and ready to ensnare them like birds. . . . I organized my frontier in Djahi,[62] prepared before them:—princes, commanders of garrisons, (20) and *maryanu.* I have the river-mouths[63] prepared like a strong wall, with warships, galleys and coasters, *(fully) equipped,* for they were manned completely from bow to stern with valiant warriors carrying their weapons. The troops consisted of every picked man of Egypt. They were like lions roaring upon the mountain tops. The chariotry consisted of runners, of *picked men,* of every good and capable chariot-warrior. The horses were quivering in every part of their bodies, prepared to crush the foreign countries under their hoofs. I was the valiant Montu,[64] standing fast at their head, so that they might gaze upon the capturing of my hands. . . .

Those who reached my frontier, their seed is not, their heart and their soul are finished forever and ever. Those who came forward together on the sea, the full flame was in front of them *at* the river-mouths, while a stockade of lances surrounded them on the shore.[65] They were dragged in, enclosed, and prostrated on the beach, killed,

---

[59] Hatti was the Hittite Empire, Kode the coast of Cilicia and northern Syria, Carchemish the city on the Euphrates, Arzawa somewhere in or near Cilicia, and Alashiya probably Cyprus.

[60] Perhaps in the north Syrian plain or in Coele-Syria.

[61] Except for the Philistines (Peleset), these names are rendered close to the Egyptian writings. For the Tjeker, cf., the Wen-Amon story. The Shekelesh might be the Siculi, the Denyen (cuneiform Danuna) might be the Danaoi. The Weshesh cannot easily be related to any later people.

[62] The Phoenician coast, running down into Palestine. From what little we know of Ramses III's sway, his defensive frontier was not north of Palestine. It is possible that the land battle against the Peoples of the Sea was in Asia, whereas the sea battle was on the coast of Egypt.

[63] Normally used for the mouths of the branches of the Nile in the Delta. Hence probably the line of defense in Egypt. Just possibly, the word might have been extended to harborages on the Asiatic coast.

[64] The god of war.

[65] One body had to be met on land (in Djahi?), whereas another body had to be met on sea (in the Delta?). The scenes show the boats of the Peoples of the Sea and also a movement by land in oxcarts, with women, children, and goods.

and made into heaps from tail to head. Their ships and their goods were as if fallen into the water.

I have made the lands turn back from (even) mentioning Egypt; for when they pronounce my name in their land, then (25) they are burned up. Since I sat upon the throne of Har-akhti and the Great-of-Magic[66] was fixed upon my head like Re, I have not let foreign countries behold the frontier of Egypt, to boast thereof to the Nine Bows.[67] I have taken away their land, their frontiers being added to mine. Their princes and their tribespeople are mine with praise, for I am on the ways of the plans of the All-Lord, my august, divine father, the Lord of the Gods.

The Megiddo Ivories

ANET, 263

A large collection of "Phoenician ivories" was found by excavation in a palace at Megiddo in Palestine. The carved designs were cosmopolitanly derived *Figs. 29–31, 90* from various culture areas of the ancient Near East. The excavator tentatively dates the manufacture of the pieces between 1350 and 1150 B.C. Among the ivories are five bearing Egyptian hieroglyphs. A model pen case of an Egyp- Ezra 2:65; tian envoy to foreign countries bears the name of Ramses III (about 1195– Neh. 7:67 1164 B.C.), setting the *terminus ad quem* for the collection.

Three plaques, which may have been used for inlay in furniture, bear the name of the Singer of Ptah, South-of-His-Wall, Lord of the Life of the Two Lands, and Great Prince of Ashkelon, Kerker.

The Campaign of Sheshonk I

ANET, 263–64

Sheshonk I (about 945–924 B.C.) is the Shishak of the Old Testament. It is I Kings 14:25–26; disappointing to find that the Egyptian texts do not enlarge our understand- II Chron. 12:2–9 ing of his campaign in Palestine in a sense which constitutes a real addition to the biblical account. To be sure, he has left us a listing of the Palestinian *Fig. 94* and Syrian towns which he claimed to have conquered, and this list may be reconstructed into a kind of itinerary. There is, however, no narrative ac- count of the campaign by the pharaoh. The references in his inscriptions to "tribute of the land of Syria" or to his victories over the "Asiatics of distant foreign countries" are vague and generalized. How unhistorical his large claims were is clear from a statement to the pharaoh by the god Amon: "I have subjugated [for] thee the Asiatics of the armies of Mitanni." Mitanni as a nation had ceased to exist at least four centuries earlier.

In addition to the list of towns, we do possess two documents attesting the name of Sheshonk on Asiatic soil. At Megiddo in Palestine was found a

---

[66] The uraeus-serpent, symbol of kingship.

[67] Traditional enemies of Egypt.

fragment of a monumental stela bearing the name of Sheshonk I and permitting the conclusion that the pharaoh had set up a triumphal monument there. At Byblos in Phoenicia another fragment, this time the chair of a seated statue, bears his name, although this monument may well be a princely gift, rather than a symbol of conquest.

Finally, the Walters Art Gallery in Baltimore has a basalt statuette of an Egyptian, the "Envoy of the Canaan and of Palestine, Pa-di-Eset, the son of Apy," which may date to the Twenty-second Dynasty. This piece does not involve conquest, but rather diplomatic relations.[68]

ANET³, 553–54

Asiatics in Egyptian Household Service

In the Thirteenth Dynasty (mid-eighteenth century B.C.) there is evidence for the presence of numerous Asiatics serving in Egyptian households. Whether they should specifically be called "slaves" is not certain, even if probable. Since there is no contemporaneous evidence for military capture of Asiatics, the Joseph story (Gen. 37:28, 36) may supply the solution, in a trade in Asiatics carried on by Asiatics themselves.

The present text deals with more than eighty servants of a single Theban household, of whom more than forty are stated to be Asiatic. There are many more women than men. Among the males are "house-men," cooks, a brewer, and a tutor(?). The majority of the women worked in the weaving rooms. The adults are usually listed with an Asiatic name, followed by an Egyptian name. Again the analogy of Joseph's two names seems apt. One Asiatic has only an Egyptian name, followed by the entry: "It is his name." The children usually have only an Egyptian name. Were they born in bondage?

(viii 1) The king's servant, Renes-seneb's son, Ankhu—he is called Hedjri—house-man.

The maidservant, Iy's daughter, Sat-Gemeni—it is her name—hairdresser.

Her daughter, Renes-seneb—it is her name—child.

The king's servant, Iusni's son, Ashau—it is his name—fieldhand.

(5) (The king's servant), Iy's son, Ibu—it is his name—fieldhand.

The Asiatic, Seneb-Res-seneb—it is his name—cook.

The Asiatic woman, Rehui—she is called Kai-pu-nebi—*warper* of cloth.

Her son and Nefu's son, Res-seneb—he is called Renefres—child.

[The Asia]tic, [A]pra-Reshpu—[he is called . . .]—brewer.

(10) The Asiatic woman, Haiimmi—she is called . . .—weaver of linen.

The Asiatic woman, Menahem—she [is called . . .]—weaver of linen.

---

[68] G. Steindorff points out that the father's name may be Canaanite in origin.

The Asiatic, Su . . .—he is called Ankhu-seneb—cook.

The Asiatic woman, Sekratu[69]—she is called Wer-dit-ni-Nub—
weaver of linen.

(The Asiatic woman), Immi-Sukru—(she is called) Seneb-[Sen]-
Usert—[weaver of] linen.

(15) (The Asiatic woman), Aduttu—(she is called) Nub . . .—
[weaver of li]nen.

(The Asiatic woman), [Se]kratu—(she is called) Sen[eb . . .]—
weaver of cloth.

(ix 17) The Asiatic woman, Akhati-mer—she is called Henuti-pu-
Wadjet—*warper* of linen.

The Asiatic, Tuti-uit—he is called Ankh-em-hesut—house-man.

The Asiatic, Qui . . .—he is called Res-seneb—house-man.

(20) The king's servant, Ii . . .—it is his name—house-man.

The Asiatic woman, Shepra[70]—she is called Seneb-henutes—weaver
of linen.

The Asiatic woman, Sukra-*iputy*—she is called Merit-Nub—*warper*
of cloth.

The Asiatic woman, Asher—[she is] called Wer-Intef . . .—weaver
. . .

Her daughter, Senebtisy—it [is her name]—child.

(25) The Asiatic woman, An[ath . . .]—she [is called] Nub-em-mer-
Kis—weaver of linen.

The Asiatic woman, Shamashtu—she is called Seneb-henut . . .—
warper of linen.

The Asiatic Isibtu—he is called Amen-em . . .—*tutor.*

The maidservant, Wewi's daughter, Irit—it is her name—. . .

The Asiatic [woman, . . .]i-huti—she is called Men-hesut—. . .

(30) Her daughter, *Dedet-Mut* . . .—[it is her name]—child.

Her son, Ankhu-seneb—. . .—child.

The Asiatic [woman], Akh . . .—. . .—. . . linen.

(x 33) The Asiatic [woman], Aduna—she is called Seneb-he[nut
. . .]—. . .

Her son Ankhu—he is called Hedjru—child.

(35) The Asiatic woman, Baaltuya—she is called
Wah-Res-seneb—*work-staff.*

Her daughter Senebtisy—it is her name—child.

The Asiatic woman, Aqaba[71]—she is called Res-seneb-wah—*warper*
of linen.

[The maidservant], Senaa-ib's daughter, Ren-seneb—it is her
name—gardener.

---

[69] A name related to Issachar.

[70] Related to the name Sapphira.

[71] A name related to Jacob.

Her [daughter], Henuti-pu—it is her name—child. . . .

(xi 58) Her son, Ankhu—he is called Pa-Amu—*child*.

The Asiatic woman, Anath . . .—she is called Iun-er-in—*warper* of linen.

(60) The maidservant, Iiti—she is called Bebi-sherit's daughter, Iit—weaver . . .

The Asiatic woman, Ro-inet—she is called Seneb-h[enut]es—weaver of linen.

The Asiatic woman, Hiabi-ilu—she is called Neh-ni-em-khasut—workhouse (worker).

Her son, Abi . . . m—he is called Seneb-nebef.

(xii 64) [The Asiatic woman, . . .]i-Baal—she is called Netjeri-em-sai—*warper* of linen.

. . . hau—it is her name—*warper* of cloth.

Her son, Res-seneb—it is his name.

The Asiatic woman, Sakar—she is called Nub-erdis—. . .

The king's servant, Res-seneb—it is his name—house-man.

The Asiatic woman, Tjenatisi—she is called Peti-menti—workhouse (worker). . . .

ANET³, 554–55 # The War against the Hyksos

It is a fortunate chance that provides a new discovery which continues a known inscription. Ka-mose's attack on the Hyksos was first known through a schoolboy's tablet and then brought into monumental compass in the fragments of a stela. It now appears that that stela was the first of a pair erected at Karnak. In 1954, among the foundation slabs used under statues at Karnak, Labib Habachi discovered an essentially complete stela, which gives the continuation and conclusion of the Ka-mose story.

The stela is of the conventional shape, with a rounded top and the winged sun disk above. However, the first line simply continues a context from the lost final lines of the stela previously known. In a corner of the base is carved the figure of a man, with the label, "the Chief Treasurer Neshi" (also mentioned in 1. 37 of the text).

(1)[72] "a miserable answer out of your town. (Yet) you have been forced away in the company of your army. Your speech is mean when you make me a (mere) 'prince,' whereas you are a 'ruler,' as if to beg for yourself the execution-block to which you will fall. Your back has been seen, O wretch! My army is after you. The women of Avaris will

---

[72] The text opens in the middle of a sentence, continuing the other stela. Apparently Ka-mose wrote the Hyksos ruler Apophis and received an abusive reply. Supply some such prior words as: "[You sent me]."

not conceive; their hearts will not *open* within their bodies when my army's battle-cry is heard."

I moored at Per-djed*qen*, my heart glad, for I had made Apophis see a miserable time, the Prince of Retenu,[73] weak of arms, who planned many things in his heart, (but) they have not come to pass for him. I reached *the depot* (5) *of going south*. I crossed over to them to address them. I formed the fleet, *arrayed* one after another. I put the prow (of one) at the rudder (of another), with my bodyguard, flying upon the river as if a falcon. My own ship of gold was at the head thereof; (it) was like a *divine* falcon in front of them. I set the valiant *mek*-ship *probing* toward the desert-edge, the *djat*-ship following it, as if (it) were *a kite ravaging the djat*-lands of Avaris. I saw his women upon his roof peering from their *loopholes* toward the shore, without their bodies *stirring* when they heard me. They peered out with their noses on their walls like the young of *inhet*-animals from inside their holes, while (I was) saying: "*This is the attack!* (10) Here am I. I shall succeed. What is left over is in my hand. My lot is fortunate. As the valiant Amon endures, I will not leave you, I will not let you set foot in the fields unless I am upon you! So your wish has failed, miserable Asiatic! See, I shall drink of the wine of your vineyard, which the Asiatics of my own capturing will press out for me. I shall destroy your dwelling-place and cut down your trees, after I have *confined* your women to the holds of ships. l shall take over the chariotry." I have not left a plank *under* the hundreds of ships of new cedar, filled with gold, lapis lazuli, silver, turquoise, and countless battle-axes of metal, apart from moringa-oil, incense, fat, honey, *itren*-wood, *sesedjem*-wood, wooden *planks*, (15) all their valuable timber, and all the good produce of Retenu.[74] I *seized* them all. I did not leave a thing of Avaris, because it is *empty*, with the Asiatic vanished.

So your wishes have failed, miserable Asiatic, who had been saying: "I am a lord without peer. As far as Her-mopolis *and to* the House of Hat-Hor[75] *are bringing tribute to* Avaris in the two rivers."[76] I shall leave it in desolation, without people therein, after I have destroyed their towns. I shall burn up their places, made into red mounds forever, because of the damage which they did in this (part of) Egypt, they who gave themselves over to serving the Asiatics, after they had abandoned Egypt, their mistress.

[73] Syria-Palestine generally, but here used derivatively for the Hyksos ruler in Egypt.

[74] The "hundreds" of ships and the range of merchandise testify to the commercial activities of the Hyksos.

[75] Perhaps Pathyris, modern Gebelein in Upper Egypt.

[76] Two branches of the Nile in the Delta?

I captured a message of his *above* the oasis, going south to Cush, upon a letter of papyrus. I found on it, in written words from the ruler of Avaris:—

(20) "Aa-user-Re, the Son of Re: Apophis, sending greetings to my son, the ruler of Cush. Why do you arise as a ruler without letting me know? Do you see what Egypt has done to me: the ruler who is in it, Ka-mose the Strong, given life, attacking me on my own soil, (although) I had not assailed him—just like everything that he has done to you? He picks out these two lands to persecute them, my land and yours. He has destroyed them. Come north. *Do not falter.* See, he is here in my hand, and there is no one who is waiting for you in this (part of) Egypt. See, I will not give him leave until you have arrived. Then we shall divide the towns of this Egypt, and *our* [*two lands*] will be happy in joy."

Wadj-kheper-Re the Strong, given life, who controls situations— (25) foreign lands have been given to me, *the Two Lands* are under me, and the rivers as well. No way can be found *for trespass against me*, and I have not been neglectful of my army. *The face of the northerner was not averted;* he became afraid of me while I was sailing south, before we had fought, before I had reached him. He saw my fiery blaze, and he sent (a despatch) as far as Cush to seek protection for himself. I captured it on the way and did not let it arrive. Then I had it taken back again to him, left on the east side near Atfih.[77] My strength entered into his heart, and his body was ravaged when his messenger told him what I had done to the Nome of Cynopolis,[78] which had been his property. I despatched a strong brigade, which went overland to lay waste the Oasis of Bahariyah, while I was in Sako,[79] in order to permit no rebel to be (30) to the rear of me.

I sailed south in strength of heart, joyful, destroying every rebel who was on the way. Oh what a happy journey south for the Ruler— life, prosperity, health!—having his army before him! There was no loss of them; no man missed his companion. Their hearts did not weep, as I bestirred myself to the District of Thebes at the season of Inundation. Every face was bright; the land was in affluence; the river-bank ran wild; Thebes was in festival. Women and men came to see me. Every woman embraced her companion. There was no face with tears. *I burned incense to Amon* at the inner sanctuary and at the place where it is said: "Receive good things," just as he gives the

---

[77] Aphroditopolis on the east bank was a northern point of Upper Egypt, about 55 miles south of Cairo. It must have been within Ka-mose's control.

[78] The seventeenth Upper Egyptian nome, near modern Maghagha, about 110 miles south of Cairo.

[79] Modern el-Qais of the Cynopolite Nome, about 125 miles south of Cairo. Bahariyah lies about 100 miles west of this.

sword to the Son of Amon—life, prosperity, health!—the enduring king, Wadj-kheper-Re, the Son of Re: Ka-mose the Strong, given life, (35) who has subdued the south and overthrown the north, who has taken over the land in strength, given life, stability and satisfaction, while his heart is glad with his *ka*, like Re forever and ever.

[His] majesty issued a command to the Hereditary Prince and Count, the Privy Councillor of the Palace, the Headman of the Entire Land, the Sealbearer of the King of Lower Egypt, the *Helmsman* of the Two Lands, the Leader, the Overseer of Courtiers, and [*Chief*] Treasurer, *the strong of arm,* Neshi: "Have everything which my majesty has done by strength put upon a stela which occupies its place in Karnak in the Theban Nome forever and ever." Then he said to his majesty: "I will act [*in conformance with*] *that which* [*my*] *lord* [*has commanded me*]." Favors of the king's presence *were decreed.*

Assyrian and Babylonian Historical Texts

TRANSLATOR: A. LEO OPPENHEIM

The Dedication of the Shamash Temple
ANET³, 556–57 **by Yahdun-Lim**

On nine bricks found by A. Parrot in 1953 in Mari, we have the longest brick inscription ever to come out of Mesopotamian soil, 147 to 157 lines in five columns. It contains the dedication of the temple of Shamash by Yahdun-Lim, the father of Zimri-Lim, after his campaign to the Mediterranean Sea and the defeat of an alliance of nomadic enemies.

(i) (Dedicated) to Shamash, the king of the heaven and the nether world, who pronounces orders and decisions for god and man, whose office is (the dispensation of) justice and to whom it has been given (to protect) what is right, the shepherd of all the black-headed, the famous god, judge of everything endowed with life, agreeable to supplication, ready to listen to vows, to accept prayers, who gives to those who worship him a long-lasting life of happiness, the overlord of Mari, (by) Yah-dun-Lim, the son of Yag(g)id-Lim, king of (the city of) Mari and of the Hana country, who digs canals, builds city walls, erects stelae mentioning (his) name, provides his people with superabundance, furnishes his country with everything (needed), the *mighty* king, the famous hero, on the occasion when Shamash was agreeable to his supplication and listened to his prayer.

Indeed, Shamash did *promptly* come to the aid of Yahdun-Lim and while no other king residing in Mari had ever—since, in ancient days, the god built the city of Mari—reached the (Mediterranean) Sea, (ii) nor reached and felled timber in the great mountains, the Cedar Mountain and the Boxwood Mountain, he, Yahdun-Lim, son of Ya(g)gid-Lim, the powerful king, the wild bull among the kings, did march to the shore of the sea, an unrivaled feat, and offered sacrifices to the Ocean as (befitting) his high royal rank while his troops washed themselves in the Ocean. He (also) entered the great mountains, the Cedar Mountain and the Boxwood Mountain, and felled such trees as boxwood, cedar, cypress, and *elammakku*-trees. He made (this) razzia, established (thus) his fame and proclaimed his power. He subjected that (entire) region on the shore of the Ocean, united it under (his) command, made it furnish him troops. (iii) He imposed a permanent tribute upon it and they are still bringing him their tribute.

In that same year the following kings rebelled against him: La'um, king of Samanum and the country of the Ubrabians, Bahlu-kulim, king of Tuttul and of the country Amnanum, Ajalum, the king of Abattum and the country of the Rabbeans; an army of Sumu-epuh from the country of Jamhad came to their help, in the town of Samanum, they all gathered against him, the center of *nomads,* (but) he (Yahdun-Lim) defeated these three kings of the *nomads* in a big battle. He routed their army and the army who had come to their help, made a massacre (among them). (Then) he erected piles of their corpses. He razed the walls of their (cities), turning them into mounds of rubble. The city of Haman (belonging to) the center of the Haneans, which all the sheikhs of Hana had built, he razed and (iv) made into mounds of rubble. He also defeated its king, Kasuri-hala, annexed their (the Haneans') country.

Then he built up the embankment of the Euphrates (in Mari) and erected (there) the temple of his lord Shamash for his (own) well-being; he made for him (Shamash) a temple of perfect construction in every aspect of craftsmanship, befitting his godhead, and installed him in this magnificent abode. He named this temple: Egirzalanki (which means): "The-temple-which-is-the-pride-of-Heaven-and-Nether-World."

May Shamash who resides in this temple grant for ever to Yahdun-Lim, who built his temple, his beloved king, a mighty weapon (able) to defeat the enemies, a long and happy rule and everlasting years of abundance and happiness.

Whoever desecrates this temple, *assigns* it to evil and untoward purposes, does not reinforce its foundation, does not replace what has fallen down or (v) stops the food offerings (destined) for it, erases my name (in this inscription)—or gives orders for erasing it—, inscribes his own name not previously inscribed—or gives orders for writing it—, or prompts somebody else (to do these things) on account of the curses (inscribed here), be this man a king, or a general, or a mayor, or whoever else, Enlil who pronounces decisions for (all) the gods, should make the kingdom of this man smaller than that of all the other kings; Sin, the elder brother among the gods, his brothers, should curse him with the "Great Curse"; Nergal, the armed god, should break his weapon and not accept him (in the nether world when he appears there) slain (in battle). Ea, the master (lit.: king) of fates, should make his fate a bad one; the great lady, Aja the Bride, should forever represent his case in a bad light before Shamash; Bunene, the great plenipotentiary of Shamash, should end his life, eliminate every offspring of his, so that neither descendant nor progeny of his should ever live under the sun (text: Sun god).

ANET³, 557–58 ## The Story of Idrimi, King of Alalakh

Found in 1939 at Atchana in Syria, the statue showing King Idrimi of Alalakh seated on his throne was not published until 1949 because of war conditions. An inscription of 101 lines indiscriminately covers the front of the figure, with a postscript of three lines incised on one side of the beard and whiskers.

I am Idrimi, the son of Ilimilimma, the servant of Adad, of Hepat and of Ishtar, the Lady of Alalakh, my lady.

An evil deed happened in Halab, the seat of my family, and we fled to the people of Emar, brothers of my mother, and we lived (then) in Emar. My brothers, who were older than I, stayed with me but none of them had the plans I had. I (said to) myself: "Whoever owns the seat of his family is a ... (while) who does not is but a slave in the eyes of the people of Emar!" (So) I took with me my horse, my chariot, and my groom, went away and crossed over the desert country and even entered into the region of the Sutian warriors. I stayed with them (once) overnight in my ... chariot, but the next day I moved on and went to the land of Canaan. I stayed in Ammia in the land of Caanan; in Ammia lived (also) natives of Halab, of the country Mukishkhi, of the country Ni' and also warriors from the country Amaʾe. They discovered that I was the son of their overlord and gathered around me. There I grew up and stayed for a long time. For seven years I lived among the Hapiru-people. (Then) I released birds (to observe their flight) and looked into (the entrails of) lambs (and found) that after seven years Adad had become favorable to me. So I built boats, made ... soldiers board them, approached the country Mukishkhi via the sea and reached shore below Mt. Casius. I went ashore and when my country heard of me they brought me cattle and sheep. And in one day, and as one man, the countries Ni', Amaʾe, Mukishkhi and my city Alalakh turned to me. My brothers heard (about this) and they came into my presence. As soon as they had become reconciled with me, I established my brothers as such.

However, for seven years, Barattarna, the mighty king, the king of the Hurrian warriors, treated me as an enemy. In the seventh year,

I sent Anuanda (as messenger) to King Barattarna, the king of the ⟨Hurrian⟩ warriors, and told (him) about the services of my forefathers when my forefathers had been in their (the kings') service and (when) what we had said was pleasing to the kings of the Hurrian warriors, and (that) they had made an alliance based on a solemn oath among themselves. The mighty king *heard* of our former services and of the oath they had sworn to each other—they had *read* the wording of the oath to him, word by word as well as (the list of) our services. He accepted my messenger (lit.: my greeting). I increased the *gifts indicating* my loyalty, which were *heavy*, and returned to him (his) lost household. I swore him a mighty *oath* as to my status as a loyal vassal.

And (so) I became king in charge of Alalakh. Kings from right and left came up to me and just as they used to *bring presents* upon *presents* for my forefather in . . . , I had them *bring* (them to me) in. . . . And I . . . ed them.

I took . . . soldiers and went up against the country of the Hittites and I destroyed seven of their fortified *places*; these are the . . . fortified *places*: Pashshakhe, Damarut-re'i, Hulahhan, Zise, Ie, Uluzina and Zaruna. The country of the Hittites did not mobilize (its troops), did not march against me, I could do what I wanted. I took prisoners from them, plundered their riches, possessions, and property, and distributed it to my soidiers, my auxiliary troops, my brothers, and friends. I myself took a share like theirs. Then I returned to the country of Mu-kishkhi and entered (in triumph) into my city Alalakh.

I had a house built by means of the prisoners, the provisions, riches, possessions, and property which I had brought down from the country of the Hittites; I made my throne like the throne of kings, my brothers like brothers of kings, my children like their children, and my guardsmen like their guardsmen. I made the Sutians within my country settle in secure settlements and those who did not want to live in settlements I made do so. And I placed my country on a firm footing and made my towns as they were before like. . . . As to the cultic *regulations* which the gods of Alalakh had established, and the sacrifices and offerings which our forefathers had performed for them, I have constantly performed them exactly as they had performed them and now I have entrusted (the responsibility for) them to my son Adad-nirari.

May the god of heaven extirpate every offspring of whosoever steals this statue of mine, and curse him, extirpate his sons and offspring also of his . . . servants, may the gods of heaven and nether world *destroy* his kingship and his country. May Adad, the lord of heaven and nether world and (all) the great gods make the son and progeny of whosoever changes or erases it(s inscription), disappear from his country.

Sharruwa, is the scribe, . . .

May the gods of heaven and nether world keep the scribe Sharruwa who has written (the text of) this statue in good health and protect him; they should be his . . . , Shamash the lord of those above the earth and below, the lord of the spirits of the dead should be his caretaker.

(Postscript on the right cheek of the statue): I was king for 30 years. I wrote my achievements on my statue. Let people [read it] and ble[ss me].

Ashurnasirpal II (883–859): Expedition to the Lebanon

ANET, 275–76

From the annals inscribed on the large pavement slabs of the temple of Ninurta in Calah, the new royal residence built by Ashurnasirpal II.

Fig. 118

(iii 84–90)

At that time I seized the entire extent of the Lebanon mountain and reached the Great Sea of the Amurru country. I cleaned my weapons in the deep sea and performed sheep-offerings to (all) the gods. The tribute of the seacoast—from the inhabitants of Tyre, Sidon, Byblos, Mahallata, Maiza, Kaiza, Amurru, and (of) Arvad which is (an island) in the sea, (consisting of): gold, silver, tin, copper, copper containers, linen garments with multicolored trimmings, large and small monkeys, ebony, boxwood, ivory from walrus tusk—(thus ivory) a product of the sea,—(this) their tribute I received and they embraced my feet.

I ascended the mountains of the Amanus (*Ḫama-ni*) and cut down (there) logs of cedars, stone-pines, cypresses (and) pines, and performed sheep-offerings to my gods. I (had) made a sculptured stela (commemorating) my heroic achievements and erected (it) there. The cedar beams from the Amanus mountain I *destined/sent* for/to the temple Esarra for (the construction of) a *iasmaku*-sanctuary as a building for festivals serving the temples of Sin and Shamash, the light(giving) gods.

The Banquet of Ashurnasirpal II

ANET³, 558–60

On a sandstone block placed near the doorway to the throne-room of the palace of Ashurnasirpal in Calah was found in 1951 a figural representation with an inscription (total: 154 lines) in an unusual arrangement. The upper part of the stone shows the king in a square recess, flanked by inscribed columns, under an awkwardly arranged row of divine symbols. The text, apart from its stereotyped titulary and historical summary, is mainly concerned with the building of the new capital Calah, the royal garden and the festival in celebration of the opening of the royal palace.

(i)

(This is) the palace of Ashurnasirpal, the high priest of Ashur, chosen by Enlil and Ninurta, the favorite of Anu and of Dagan (who is) destruction (personified) among all the great gods—the legitimate king, the king of the world, the king of Assyria, son of Tukulti-Ninurta, great king, legitimate king, king of the world, king of Assyria (who was) the son of Adad-nirari, likewise great king, legitimate king, king of the world and king of Assyria—the heroic warrior who always acts upon trust-inspiring signs given by his lord Ashur and (therefore) has no rival among the rulers of the four quarters (of the world); the shepherd of all mortals, not afraid of battle (but) an onrushing flood which brooks no resistance; the king who subdues the unsubmissive (and) rules over all mankind; the king who always acts upon trust-inspiring signs given by his lords, the great gods, and therefore has personally conquered all countries; who has acquired dominion over the mountain regions and received their tribute; he takes hostages, triumphs over all the countries from beyond the Tigris to the Lebanon and the Great Sea, he has brought into submission the entire country of Laqe and the region of Suhu as far as the town of Rapiqu; personally he conquered (the region) from the source of the Subnat River to Urartu.

I returned to the territory of my own country, (the regions) from the pass (which leads to) the country Kirrure as far as Gilzani, from beyond the Lower Zab River to the town of Til-bari which is upstream of the land of Zamua—from Til-sha-abtani to Til-sha-sabtani—(also) Hirimu and Harrutu (in) the fortified border region of Babylonia (Karduniash). I listed as inhabitants of my own country (the people living) from the pass of Mt. Babite to the land of Hashmar.

Ashur, the Great Lord, has chosen me and made a pronouncement concerning my world rule with his own holy mouth (as follows): Ashurnasirpal is the king whose fame is power!

I took over again the city of Calah in that wisdom of mine, the knowledge which Ea, the king of the subterranean waters, has bestowed upon me, I removed the old hill of rubble; I dug down to the water level; I heaped up a (new) terrace (measuring) from the water level to the upper edge 120 layers of bricks; upon that I erected as my royal seat and for my personal enjoyment 7 (text: 8) beautiful halls (roofed with) boxwood, *Magan-ash,* cedar, cypress, terebinth, *tarpi'u* and *mehru* (beams); I sheathed doors made of cedar, cypress, juniper, boxwood and *Magan-ash* with bands of bronze; I hung them in their doorways; I surrounded them (the doors) with decorative bronze bolts; to proclaim my heroic deeds I painted on their (the palaces') walls with vivid blue paint how I have marched across the mountain ranges, the foreign countries and the seas, my conquests in all countries; I had lapis lazuli colored glazed bricks made and set (them in the wall) above their gates. I brought in people from the countries over which I rule, those who were conquered by me personally, (that is) from the country Suhi (those of) the town Great [. . .], from the entire land of Zamua, the countries Bit-Zamani and [Kir]rure, the town of Sirqu which is across the Euphrates, and many inhabitants of Laqe, of Syria and (who are subjects) of Lubarna, the ruler of Hattina; I settled them therein (the city of Calah).

I dug a canal from the Upper Zab River; I cut (for this purpose) straight through the mountain(s); I called it Patti-hegalli ("Channel-of-Abundance"); I provided the lowlands along the Tigris with irrigation; I planted orchards at its (the city's) outskirts, with all sorts of fruit trees.

I pressed the grapes and offered (them) as first fruits in a libation to my lord Ashur and to all the sanctuaries of my country. I (then) dedicated that city to my lord Ashur.

[I collected and planted in my garden] from the countries through which I marched and the mountains which I crossed, the trees (and plants raised from) seeds from wherever I discovered (them, such as): cedars, cypress, *šimmešallu*-perfume trees, *burāšu*-junipers, myrrh-producing trees, *daprānu*-junipers, nut-bearing trees, date palms, ebony, *Magan-ash,* olive trees, *tamarind,* oaks, *tarpi'u*-terebinth trees, *luddu*-nut-bearing trees, pistachio and *cornel*-trees, *mehru*-trees, ŠE.MUR-trees, *tijatu*-trees, Kanish oaks, willows, *sadānu*-trees, pomegranates, plum trees, fir trees, *ingirašu*-trees, *kameššeru*-pear trees, *supur-gillu*-bearing trees, fig trees, grape vines, *angašu*-pear trees, aromatic *sumlalu*-trees, *titip*-trees, *hip/būtu*-trees, *zanzaliqqu*-trees, "swamp-apple" trees, *hambuqūqu*-trees, *nuhurtu*-trees, *urzīnu*-trees, resinous *kanaktu*-trees [. . .]. In the gardens in [Calah] they vied with each other in fragrance; the paths i[n the gardens were well *kept*], the irrigation weirs [distributed the water *evenly*]; its pomegranates glow in the pleasure garden like the stars in the sky, they are interwoven like grapes on the vine; . . . in the pleasure garden [. . .] in the garden of happiness flourished like ce[dar trees] (break).

(ii)

I erected in Calah, the center of my overlordship, temples such as those of Enlil and Ninurta which did not exist there before; I rebuilt in it the (following) temples of the great gods: the temples of Ea-sharru (and) Damkina, of Adad (and) Shala, of Gula, Sin, Nabu, Belet-nathi, Sibittu (and of) Ishtar-kidmuri. In them I established the (sacred) pedestals of the(se), my divine lords. I decorated them splendidly; I roofed them with cedar beams, made large cedar doors, sheathed them with bands of bronze, placed them in their doorways. I placed figural representations made of shining bronze in their doorways. I made (the images of) their great godheads sumptuous with red gold and shining stones. I presented them with golden jewelry and many other precious objects which I had won as booty.

I lined the inner shrine of my lord Ninurta with gold and lapis lazuli, I placed right and left of it IM objects made of bronze, I placed at his pedestal fierce *ušumgallu*-dragons of gold. I performed his festival in the months Shabatu and Ululu. I arranged for them (the materials needed for) scatter and incense offerings so that his festival in Shabatu should be one of great display. I fashioned a statue of myself as king in the likeness of my own features out of red gold and polished stones and placed it before my lord Ninurta.

I organized the abandoned towns which during the rule of my fathers had become hills of rubble, and had many people settle therein; I rebuilt the old palaces across my entire country in due splendor; I stored in them barley and straw.

Ninurta and Palil, who love me as (their) high priest, handed over to me all the wild animals and ordered me to hunt (them). I killed 450 big lions; I killed 390 wild bulls from my open chariots in direct assault as befits a ruler; I cut off the heads of 200 ostriches as if they were caged birds; I caught 30 elephants in pitfalls. I caught alive 50 wild bulls, 140 ostriches (and) 20 big lions with my own [. . .] and *stave.*

(iii)

I received five live elephants as tribute from the governor of Suhu (the Middle Euphrates region) and the governor of Lubda (S.E. Assyria toward Babylonia); they used to travel with me on my campaigns.

I organized herds of wild bulls, lions, ostriches and male and female monkeys and had them breed like flocks (of domestic animals).

I added land to the land of Assyria, *many* people to its people.

When Ashurnasirpal, king of Assyria, inaugurated the palace in Calah, a palace of joy and (erected with) great ingenuity, he invited into it Ashur, the great lord and the gods of his entire country, (he prepared a banquet[1] of) 1,000 fattened head of cattle, 1,000 calves,

---

[1] The Gargantuan bill of fare given here provides us, in spite of all its lexical difficulties, with the basic features of a banquet menu. The list is structured as follows: (1) meat dishes (sheep, cattle, with some game; fowl consisting mostly of small birds with aquatic birds in the second place) and equal amounts of fish and jerboa with assorted eggs in large number; (2) bread; (3) beer and wine in equal amounts; (4) side dishes consisting

10,000 stable sheep, 15,000 lambs—for my lady Ishtar (alone) 200 head of cattle (and) 1,000 *siḫḫu*-sheep—1,000 spring lambs, 500 stags, 500 gazelles, 1,000 *ducks,* 500 *geese,* 500 *kurkû*-geese, 1,000 *mesuku*-birds, 1,000 *qāribu*-birds, 10,000 doves, 10,000 *sukanūnu*-doves, 10,000 other (assorted) small birds, 10,000 (assorted) fish, 10,000 jerboa, 10,000 (assorted) eggs; 10,000 loaves of bread, 10,000 (jars of) beer, 10,000 skins with wine, 10,000 pointed bottom vessels with *šu'u*-seeds in sesame oil, 10,000 small pots with *ṣarhu*-condiment, 1,000 wooden crates with vegetables, 300 (containers with) oil, 300 (containers with) salted *seeds,* 300 (containers with) mixed *raqqūte*-plants, 100 with *kudimmu*-spice, 100 (containers with) . . . , 100 (containers with) parched barley, 100 (containers with) green *abaḫšinnu*-stalks, 100 (containers with) fine mixed beer, 100 pomegranates, 100 bunches of grapes, 100 mixed *zamru*-fruits, 100 pistachio cones, 100 with the fruits of the *šūši*-tree, 100 with garlic, 100 with onions, 100 with *kuniphu* (seeds), 100 with the . . . of turnips, 100 with *hinhinnu*-spice, 100 with *budû*-spice, 100 with honey, 100 with rendered butter, 100 with roasted . . . barley, 100 with roasted *šu'u*-seeds, 100 with *karkartu*-plants, 100 with fruits of the *ti'atu*-tree, 100 with *kasû*-plants, 100 with milk, 100 with cheese, 100 jars with "mixture," 100 with pickled *arsuppu*-grain, ten homer of shelled *luddu*-nuts, ten homer of shelled pistachio nuts, ten homer of fruits of the *šūšu*-tree, ten homer of fruits of the *ḫabba-qūqu*-tree ten homer of dates, ten homer of the fruits of the *titip*-tree, ten homer of *cumin,* ten homer of *saḫḫunu,* ten homer of *uriānu,* ten homer of *andaḫšu*-bulbs, ten homer of *šišanibbe*-plants, (iv) ten homer of the fruits of the *simbūru*-tree, ten homer of thyme, ten homer of perfumed oil, ten homer of sweet smelling matters, ten homer of . . . , ten homer of the fruits of the *naṣubu*-tree, ten homer of *zimzimmu*-onions, ten homer of olives.

When I inaugurated the palace at Calah I treated for ten days with food and drink 47,074 persons, men and women, who were bid to come from across my entire country, (also) 5,000 important persons, delegates from the country Suhu, from Hindana, Hattina, Hatti, Tyre, Sidon, Gurguma, Malida, Hubushka, Gilzana, Kuma (and) Musasir, (also) 16,000 inhabitants of Calah from all ways of life, 1,500 officials of all my palaces, altogether 69,574 invited guests from all the (mentioned) countries including the people of Calah; I (furthermore) provided them with the means to clean and anoint themselves. I did them due honors and sent them back, healthy and happy, to their own countries.

---

mainly of pickled and spiced fruit, and seeds of a wide variety, also onion; (5) dessert (sweet fruits, nuts, honey, cheese) and savories, most of which cannot be identified yet. At the end, the list mentions perfumed oil and sweet smelling substances.

Shalmaneser III (858–824): The Fight against the Aramean Coalition

ANET, 277–81

First Year according to the so-called Monolith Inscriptions.

(i.49–ii 13)

At that time, I paid homage to the greatness of (all) the great gods (and) extolled for posterity the heroic achievements of Ashur and Shamash by fashioning a (sculptured) stela with myself as king (depicted on it). I wrote thereupon my heroic behavior, my deeds in combat and erected it beside the source of the Saluara river which is at the foot of the mountains of the Amanus. From the mountain Amanus I departed, crossed the Orontes river (*A-ra-an-tu*) and approached Alimush, the fortress town of Sapalulme from Hattina. To save his life, Sapalulme from Hattina [called for] Ahuni, man of Adini, Sangara from Carchemish, Haianu from Sam'al, Kate from Que, Pihirim from Hilukka, Bur-Anate from Iasbuq, Ada[. . .] . . . Assyria. . . .

(ii)

[Their/his army] I scattered, I stormed and conquered the town . . . I carried away as booty . . . , his horses, broken to the yoke. I slew with the sword. . . . During this battle I personally captured Bur-Anate from [Iasbuk]. I con[quered] the great cities (*maḫâzu*) of Hattina. . . . I overthrew the . . . of the Upper [Sea] of Amurru and of the Western Sea (so that they became) like ruin-hills (left by) the flood. I received tribute from the kings of the seashore. I marched straightaway, unopposed . . . throughout the wide seashore, I fashioned a stela with an image of myself as overlord in order to make my name/fame lasting forever and e[rected it] near the sea. I ascended the mountains of the Amanus, I cut there cedar and pine timber. I went to the mountain region Atalur, where the statue of the god Hirbe is set up and erected (there) a(nother) statue (of mine) beside his statue. I de[parted] from the sea; I, conquered the towns Taia, Hazazu, Nulia (and) Butamu which (belong) to the country Hattina. I killed 2,900 of [their] battle-experienced soldiers; 14,600 I brought away as prisoners of war. I received the tribute of Arame, man of Gusi, (to wit): silver, gold, large [and small] cattle, wine, a couch of *whitish* gold.

Sixth Year according to the Monolith-Inscription.

(ii 78–102)

In the year of (the eponym) Daian-Ashur, in the month Aiaru, the 14th day, I departed from Nineveh. I crossed the Tigris and approached the towns of Giammu on the river Balih. They became afraid of the terror emanating from my position as overlord, as well as of the splendor of my fierce weapons, and killed their master Giammu with their own weapons. I entered the towns Sahlala and Til-sha-Turahi and brought my gods/images into his palaces. I performed the *tašiltu*-festival in his (own) palaces. I opened (his) treasury, inspected what he had hidden; I carried away as booty his possessions, bringing (them) to my town Ashur. From Sahlala I departed and approached Kar-Shalmaneser. I crossed the Euphrates another time at its flood on rafts (made buoyant by means) of (inflated) goatskins. In Ina-Ashur-utir-asbat, which the people of Hattina call Pitru, on the other side of the Euphrates, on the river Sagur, I received tribute from the kings of the other side of the Euphrates—that is, of Sanagara from Car-chemish, Kundashpi from Commagene, of Arame, man of Gusi, of Lalli from Melitene (*Melid*), of Haiani, son of Gabari, of Kalparuda from Hattina, (and) of Kalparuda of Gurgum—(consisting of): silver, gold, tin, copper (or bronze), copper containers. I departed from the banks of the Euphrates and approached Aleppo (*Ḫal-man*). They (i.e., the inhabitants of A.) were afraid to fight and seized my feet (in submission). I received silver and gold as their tribute and offered sacrifices before the Adad of Aleppo. I departed from Aleppo and approached the two towns of Irhuleni from Hamath (*Amat*). I captured the towns Adennu, Barga, (and) Argana his royal residence. I removed from them his booty (as well as) his personal (lit.: of his palaces) possessions. I set his palaces afire. I departed from Argana and approached Karkara, I destroyed, tore down and burned down Karkara, his (text: my) royal residence. He brought along to help him 1,200 chariots, 1,200 cavalrymen, 20,000 foot sol-

II Sam. 8:3   diers of Adad-'idri (i.e., Hadadezer) of Damascus (*Imērišu*), 700 chariots, 700 cavalrymen, 10,000 foot soldiers of Irhuleni from Hamath,

I Kings 16:29   2,000 chariots, 10,000 foot soldiers of Ahab, the Israelite (*A-ḫa-ab-bu* ^mat^*Sir-'i-la-a-a*), 500 soldiers from Que, 1,000 soldiers from Musri, 10 chariots, 10,000 soldiers from Irqanata, 200 soldiers of Matinu-ba'lu from Arvad, 200 soldiers from Usanata, 30 chariots, 1[0?],000 soldiers of Adunu-ba'lu from Shian, 1,000 camel-(rider)s of Gindibu', from Arabia, [...],000 soldiers of Ba'sa, son of Ruhubi, from Ammon—(all together) these were twelve kings. They rose against me [for a] decisive battle. I fought with them with (the support of) the mighty forces of Ashur, which Ashur, my lord, has given to me, and the strong weapons which Nergal, my leader, has presented to me, (and) I did inflict a defeat upon them between the towns Karkara and Gilzau. I slew 14,000 of their soldiers with the sword, descending upon them like Adad when he makes a rainstorm pour down. I spread their corpses (everywhere), filling the entire plain with their widely scattered (fleeing) soldiers. During the battle I made their blood flow down the *ḫur-pa-lu* of the district. The plain was too small to let (all) their (text: his) souls descend[2] (into the nether world), the vast field gave out (when it came) to bury them. With their (text: sing.) corpses I spanned the Orontes before there was a bridge. Even during the battle I took from them their chariots, their horses broken to the yoke.

Eighteenth Year according to the fragment of an annalistic text.

In the eighteenth year of my rule I crossed the Euphrates for the sixteenth time. Hazael of Damascus (*Imērišu*) put his trust upon his numerous army and called up his troops in great number, making the mountain Senir (Sa-ni-ru), a mountain, facing the Lebanon, to his fortress. I fought with him and inflicted a defeat upon him, killing with the sword 16,000 of his experienced soldiers. I took away from him 1,121 chariots, 470 riding horses as well as his camp. He disappeared to save his life (but) I followed him and besieged him in Damascus (*Di-maš-qi*), his royal residence. (There) I cut down his gardens (outside of the city, and departed). I marched as far as the mountains of Hauran (*šadê^emat Ha-ú-ra-ni*), destroying, tearing down and burning innumerable towns, carrying booty away from them which was beyond counting. I (also) marched as far as the mountains of Ba'li-ra'si which is a promontory (lit.: at the side of the sea) and erected there a stela with my image as king. At that time I received the tribute of the inhabitants of Tyre, Sidon, and of Jehu, son of Omri (*Ia-ú-a mâr Hu-um-ri-i*).

Inscription from a marble bead.

Booty (*kišitti^ti*) of the temple of Sheru from the town of Mallaha, the royal residence of Hazael of Damascus (*Imērišu*) which Shalmaneser, son of Ashurnasirpal, has brought into the walls of Libbiali.[3]

II Kings 8:7–15; Amos 1:4

Epigraphs

From the rich iconographic documentation left by Shalmaneser III, five representations fall into the orbit of this book. They are provided with epigraphs which are given below in translation.

(a) From the Bronze Gates of Balawat

(Band III—Phoenicia, Tyre, Sidon, Gaza)
I received the tribute (brought) on ships from the inhabitants of Tyre and Sidon.

Fig. 98

---

[2] This expression seems to indicate that the "souls" of the numerous dying soldiers were conceived as slipping down to the nether world through holes or cavities in the ground and that the massed corpses actually did cover the battlefield so completely as to make this descent difficult.

[3] The name *Libbi-âli* denotes the central section of the town Ashur.

(Band XIII—Syria)
I conquered Ashtamaku, the royal residence of Irhuleni of Hatti, together with 86 (other towns).

(b) From the Black Obelisk.

II

I Kings 19:16–17   The tribute of Jehu (*Ia-ú-a*), son of Omri (*Ḫuum-ri*); I received from
Fig. 100   him silver, gold, a golden *saplu*-bowl, a golden vase with pointed
bottom, golden tumblers, golden buckets, tin, a staff for a king, (and)
wooden *puruḫu*.

Adad-Nirari III (810–783): Expedition to

ANET, 281   # Palestine

Stone slab. From a broken stone slab found at Calah.

(1–14)

Property of Adad-nirari, great king, legitimate king, king of the
world, king of Assyria—a king whom Ashur, the king of the Igigi
(i.e., the dei superi) had chosen (already) when he was a youngster,
entrusting him with the position of a prince without rival, (a king)
whose shepherding they made as agreeable to the people of Assyria
as (is the smell of) the Plant of Life, (a king) whose throne they established firmly; the holy high priest (and) tireless caretaker of the
temple é. s á r. r a, who keeps up the rites of the sanctuary, who acts
(only) upon the trust-inspiring oracles (given) by Ashur, his lord;
who has made submit to his feet the princes within the four rims
of the earth; conquering from the Siluna mountain of the Rising
Sun, the countries Saban, Ellipi, Harhar, Araziash, Mesu, the (country of the) Medians, Gizilbunda in its (full) extent, the countries
Munna, Persia (*Parsua*), Allabria, Apdadana, Na'iri with all its regions, Andiu which lies far away in the *pitḫu* of the mountains with
all its regions, as far as the Great Sea of the Rising Sun (and) from
the banks of the Euphrates, the country of the Hittites, Amurru-
country in its full extent, Tyre, Sidon, Israel (*mat Ḫu-um-ri*), Edom,
Palestine (*Pa-la-as-tu*), as far as the shore of the Great Sea of the
Setting Sun, I made them submit all to my feet, imposing upon
them tribute.

Year 5: The king of Akkad (stayed) in his country. He organized
his chariots and many horses.

Year 6, month Kislimu: The king of Akkad moved his army into
Hatti land. He dispatched his army from Hatti land, they raided the
desert, took much booty from the land of the Arabs, (also) their

herds and divine images in great number. In the month Addaru, the king returned to his country.

Year 7, month Kislimu: The king of Akkad moved his army into Hatti land, laid siege to the city of Judah (*Ia-a-ḫu-du*) and the king took the city on the second day of the month Addaru. He appointed in it a (new) king of his liking, took heavy booty from it and brought it into Babylon.

Year 8, month Tebetu: The king of Akkad (went) into Hatti land as far as Carchemish [. . .] from [. . .] and in the month Shabatu he returned to his country.

The Assyrian King List

ANET³, 564–66

(i)

Tudiya, Adamu, Yangi, Kitlamu, Harharu, Mandaru, Imsu, Harsu, Didanu, Hanu, Zuabu, Nuabu, Abazu, Belu, Azarah, Ushpiya, Apiashal—
Total: 17 kings living in tents.

Aminu (was) the son of Ilu-kabkabi, Ilu-kabkabi the son of Yazkur-ilu, Yazkur-ilu the son of Yakmeni, Yakmeni the son of Yakmesi, Yakmesi the son of Ilu-Mer, Ilu-Mer the son of Hayani, Hayani the son of Samanu, Samanu the son of Hale, Hale the son of Apiashal, (and) Apiashal the son of Ushpiya—
Total: 10 kings who are ancestors.

Sulilu son of Amini, Kikkiya, Akiya, Puzur-Ashur, (I), Shallim-ahhe, Ilu-shuma—
Total: 6 kings [*mentioned* on] brick (inscriptions); their (*lists* of) *eponyms* are *missing*.

Erishu (I) son of Ilu-shuma whose [. . .]; he ruled as king for 40 years.

Ikunu son of Erishu; he ruled as king for [x years].

Sharru-kin (I) son of Ikunu; he ruled as king for [x years].

Puzur-Ashur (II) son of Sharru-kin; he ruled as king for [x] years.

Naram-Sin son of Puzur-Ashur; he ruled as king for [x] years.

Erishu (II) son of Naram-Sin; he ruled as king for [x] years.

Shamshi-Adad (I), the son of Ilu-kabkabi, went away to Babylonia in the time of Naram-Sin; in the eponymy of Ibni-Adad, Shamshi-Adad came back from Babylonia; he seized Ekallate; he stayed in Ekallate for three years; in the eponymy of Atamar-Ishtar, Shamshi-Adad came up from Ekallate and removed Erishu, son of Naram-Sin, from the throne,

(ii)

seized the throne, (and) ruled as king for 33 years.

Ishme-Dagan (I) son of Shamshi-Adad; he ruled as king for 40 (var.: 50) years.

Ashur-dugul, the son of a nobody, without right to the throne; he ruled as king for six years.

During the lifetime of that same Ashur-dugul, son of a nobody, (the following) six kings, (likewise) sons of nobodies, ruled as kings in periods of less than one *year*: Ashur-apla-idi, Nasir-Sin, Sin-namir, Ibqi-Ishtar, Adad-salulu (and) Adasi.

Bel-bani son of Adasi; he ruled as king for ten years.

Libaya son of Bel-bani; he ruled as king for 17 years.

Sharma-^{d}IM (I) son of Libaya; he ruled for 12 years.

Ib-tar-Sin son of Sharma-^{d}IM; he ruled for 12 years.

Bazaya son of *Ib*-tar-Sin; he ruled for 28 years.

Lullaya son of a nobody; he ruled as king for six years.

Kidin-Ninua son of Bazaya; he ruled as king for 14 years.

Sharma-^{d}IM (II) son of Kidin-Ninua; he ruled as king for three years.

Erishu (III) son of Kidin-Ninua; he ruled as king for 13 years.

Shamshi-Adad (II) son of Erishu; he ruled as king for six years.

Ishme-Dagan (II) son of Shamshi-Adad; he ruled as king for 16 years.

Shamshi-Adad (III), son of Ishme-Dagan, brother of Sharma-^{d}IM (II), son of Kidin-Ninua; he ruled as king for 16 (var.: 15) years.

Ashur-nirari (I) son of Ishme-Dagan; he ruled as king for 26 years.

Puzur-Ashur (III) son of Ashur-nirari; he ruled as king for [x] (variants: 14 and 24) years.

Enlil-nasir (I) son of Puzur-Ashur; he ruled as king for 13 years.

Nur-ili son of Enlil-nasir; he ruled as king for 12 years.

Ashur-shaduni son of [Nur-ili]; he ruled as king for one full month.

Ashur-rabi (I), the son of Enlil-nasir, removed [Ashur-shaduni,] seized the throne (and) [ruled as king for x years].

Ashur-nadin-ahhe (I) son of Ashur-rabi; [he ruled as king for x years].

(iii)
His brother Enlil-nasir (II) remo[ved him] from the throne (and) ruled as king for six years.

Ashur-nirari (II) son of Enlil-nasir (I or II); he ruled as king for seven years.

Ashur-bel-nisheshu son of Ashur-nirari (II); he ruled as king for nine years.

Ashur-rim-nisheshu son of Ashur-bel-nisheshu; he ruled as king for eight years.

Ashur-nadin-ahhe (II) son of Ashur-rim-nisheshu; he ruled as king for 10 years.

Eriba-Adad (I) son of Ashur-bel-nisheshu; he ruled as king for 27 years.

Ashur-uballit (I) son of Eriba-Adad; he ruled as king for 36 years.

Enlil-nirari son of Ashur-uballit; ditto ten years.

Arik-den-ili son of Enlil-nirari; ditto 12 years.

Adad-nirari (I) brother of Arik-den-ili; he ruled as king for 32 years.

Shulmanu-ashared (I) son of Adad-nirari; ditto 30 years.

Tukulti-Ninurta (I) son of Shulmanu-ashared; ditto 37 years.

While Tukulti-Ninurta was . . . , his son Ashur-nadin-apli seized his throne (and) ruled for three (var.: four) years.

Ashur-nirari (III) son of Ashur-nasir-apli; he ruled as king for six years.

Enlil-kudur-usur son of Tukulti-Ninurta; he ruled as king for five years.

Ninurta-apli-Ekur, the son of Ili-ihadda, a descendant of Eriba-Adad, went to Babylonia; he came back from Babylonia, seized the throne (and) ruled as king for three (var.: 13) years.

Ashur-dan (I) son of Ninurta-apil-Ekur; ditto 46 (var.: 36) years.

Ninurta-Tukulti-Ashur son of Ashur-dan ruled as king for less than a *year*.

His brother Mutakkil-Nusku fought with him and defeated him; he sent him away to Babylonia. Mutakkil-Nusku held the throne for less than a *year*; he (then) disappeared forever.

Ashur-resh-ishi (I) son of Mutakkil-Nusku; he ruled as king for 18 years.

Tukulti-apil-Esharra (I) son of Ashur-resh-ishi; he ruled as king for 39 years.

Ashared-apil-Ekur son of Tukulti-apil-Esharra; he ruled as king for two years.

Ashur-bel-kala son of Tukulti-apil-Esharra; he ruled as king for 18 years.

Eriba-Adad (II) son of Ashur-bel-kala; ditto two years.

(iv)
Shamshi-Adad (IV), the son of Tukulti-apil-Esharra, came from Babylonia; he removed Eriba-Adad, the son of Ashur-bel-kala, from the throne; he seized the throne (and) ruled as king for four years.

[Ashur-nasir-apli (I) son of] Shamshi-Adad (IV); ditto for 19 years.

Shulmanu-ashared (II), son of Ashur-nasir-apli; he ruled as king for 12 years.

Ashur-nirari (IV) son of Shulmanu-ashared (II); ditto six years.

Ashur-rabi (II) son of Ashur-nasir-apli; ditto 41 years.

Ashur-resh-ishi (II) son of Ashur-rabi; he ruled as king for five years.

Tukulti-apil-Esharra (II) son of Ashur-resh-ishi; he ruled as king for 32 years.

Ashur-dan (II) son of Tukulti-apil-Esharra; he ruled as king for 23 years.

Adad-nirari (II) son of Asbur-dan; he ruled as king for 21 years.

Tukulti-Ninurta (II) son of Adad-nirari; ditto seven years.

Ashur-nasir-apli (II) son of Tukulti-Ninurta; he ruled as king for 25 years.

Shulmanu-ashared (III) son of Ashur-nasir-apli; he ruled as king for 35 years.

Shamshi-Adad (V) son of Shulmanu-ashared; he ruled as king for 13 years.

Adad-nirari (III) son of Shamshi-Adad; he ruled as king for 28 years.

Shulmanu-ashared (IV) son of Adad-nirari; he ruled as king for ten years.

Ashur-dan (III) brother of Shulmanu-ashared; he ruled as king for 18 years.

Ashur-nirari (V) son of Adad-nirari (III); he ruled as king for 10 years.

(The earlier copy ends here with the subscript:)
Copy from Ashur; written by (lit.: hand of) Kandalanu, the scribe of the temple inside of Arbela, Month Lulubu, the 20th day;

eponym: Adad-bel-ukin, governor of the inner city of Ashur, in his second eponymy.

(The later copy continues:)

Tukulti-apil-Esharra (III) son of Ashur-nirari (V); he ruled as king for 18 years.

Shulmanu-ashared (V) son of Tukulti-apil-Esharra; he ruled as king for 5 years.

Written and checked against its original. A tablet of the *mašmāšu*-priest, Bel-shum-iddin, a native of Ashur. May Shamash take away him who takes (this tablet) away.

Tiglath-pileser III (744–727): Campaigns against Syria and Palestine

ANET, 282–84

Fig. 119   From a building inscription on clay preserved in various copies.

(56–63)

I installed Idi-bi'li as a Warden of Marches on the border of Musur. In all the countries which . . . [I received] the tribute of Kushtashpi of Commagene (*Kummuḫu*), Urik of Que, Sibitti-be'l of Byblos, . . . Enil of Hamath, Panammu of Sam'al, Tarhulara of Gumgum, Su-lumal of Militene, . . . Uassurme of Tabal, Ushhitti of Tuna, Urballa of Tuhana, Tuhamme of Ishtunda, . . . [Ma]tan-be'l of Arvad, Sanipu of Bit-Ammon, Salamanu of Moab, . . . Mitinti of Ashkelon, Jeho-ahaz (*Ia-ú-ḫa-zi*) of Judah (*Ia-ú-da-a-a*), Kaush-malaku of Edom (*Ú-du-mu-a-a*), Muzr[i . . .], Hanno (*Ḫa-a-nu-ú-nu*) of Gaza (*Ḫa-za-at-a-a*) (consisting of) gold, silver, tin, iron, antimony,[4] linen garments with multicolored trimmings, garments of their native (industries) (being made of) dark purple wool . . . all kinds of costly objects be they products of the sea or of the continent, the (choice) products of their regions, the treasures of (their) kings, horses, mules (trained for) the yoke. . . .

Year unknown.

(150–57)

I received tribute from Kushtashpi of Commagene (*Kummuḫu*),

II Kings 15:17   Rezon (*Ra-ḫi-a-nu*) of Damascus (*Ša-imērišu*), Menahem of Samaria

---

[4] The term *abaru* (Sumerogram: A.BAR) denotes a rarely used metal, probably magnesite. For unknown reasons, it has mostly been used for small objects and tools (spoon, axe, etc.) prescribed for ritual purposes.

(*Me-ni-ḫi-im-me* ᵃˡ*Sa-me-ri-na-a-a*), Hiram (*ḫi-ru-um-mu*) of Tyre,
Sibitti-bi'li of Byblos, Urikki of Que, Pisiris of Carchemish, I'nil of
Hamath, Panammu of Sam'al, Tarḫulara of Gurgum, Sulumal of Militene, Dadilu of Kaska, Uassurme of Tabal, Ushhitti of Tuna, Urballa
of Tuhana, Tuhamme of Ishtunda, Urimme of Hubishna (and) Zabibe,
the queen of Arabia,⁵ (to wit) gold, silver, tin, iron, elephant-hides,
ivory, linen garments with multicolored trimmings, blue-dyed wool,
purple-dyed⁶ wool, ebony-wood boxwood-wood, whatever was precious (enough for a) royal treasure; also lambs whose stretched hides
were dyed purple, (and) wild birds whose spread-out wings were
dyed blue,⁷ (furthermore) horses, mules, large and small cattle, (male)
camels, female camels with their foals.

Year unknown. From a fragmentary annalistic text.

... the town Hatarikka as far as the mountain Saua, [... the towns:]
Byb[los], ... Simirra, Arqa, Zimarra, ... Uznu, [Siannu], Ri'-raba,
Ri'-sisu, ... the towns ... of the Upper Sea, I brought under my rule.
Six officers of mine I installed as governors over them. [... the town
R]ashpuna which is (situated) at the coast of the Upper Sea, [the
towns ...]nite, Gal'za, Abilakka which are adjacent to Israel (*Bît Ḫu-
um-ri-a*) [and the] wide (land of) [...]li, in its entire extent, I united
with Assyria, Officers of mine I installed as governors upon them.

As to Hanno of Gaza (*Ḫa-a-nu-ú-nu* ᵃˡ*Ḫa-az-za-at-a-a*) who had
fled before my army and run away to Egypt, [I conquered] the town of
Gaza, ... his personal property, his images ... [and I placed (?)] (the
images of) my [... gods] and my royal image in his own palace ...
and declared (them) to be (thenceforward) the gods of their country.
I imposed upon th[em tribute]. [As for Menahem I ov]erwhelmed
him [like a snowstorm] and he ... fled like a bird, alone, [and bowed
to my feet(?)]. I returned him to his place [and imposed tribute upon
him, to wit:] gold, silver, linen garments with multicolored trimmings, ... great ... [I re]ceived from him. Israel (lit.: "Omri-Land"
Bît Ḫumria) ... all its inhabitants (and) their possessions I led to
Assyria. They overthrew their king Pekah (*Pa-qa-ḫa*) and I placed
Hoshea (*A-ú-si-'*) as king over them. I received from them 10 talents   II Kings 15:30
of gold, 1,000(?) talents of silver as their [tri]bute and brought them
to Assyria.

⁵ The female rulers of Arab tribes attested in cuneiform documents from Tiglath-
pileser III to Ashurbanipal, and perhaps Nabonidus.
⁶ The terms used in this context are *takiltu* and *argamannu*; the first denoting a
darker, the second a reddish shade of blue purple.
⁷ This unique reference seems to mention stuffed and decorated animals.

ANET, 284–87

Sargon II (721–705): The Fall of Samaria

(A) Inscriptions of a General Nature

"Pavé des Portes," No. IV, lines 31–44.

Fig. 120

II Kings 18:9–10

(Property of Sargon, etc., king of Assyria, etc.) conqueror of Samaria (*Sa-mir-i-na*) and of the entire (country of) Israel (*Bît-Ḫu-um-ri-a*) who despoiled Ashdod (and) Shinuhti, who caught the Greeks who (live on islands) in the sea, like fish, who exterminated Kasku, all Tabali and Cilicia (*Ḫilakku*), who chased away Midas (*Mi-ta-a*) king of Musku, who defeated Musur (*Mu-ṣu-ri*) in Rapihu, who declared Hanno, king of Gaza, as booty, who subdued the seven kings of the country Ia', a district on Cyprus (*Ia-ad-na-na*), (who) dwell (on an island) in the sea, at (a distance of) a seven-day journey.

(B) From Annalistic Reports

So-called Annals and their parallels taken from the Display Inscriptions. The Annals are quoted here according to A. G. Lie, *The Inscriptions of Sargon II, King of Assyria*, Part 1. The Annals (Paris, 1929).

First Year.

(10–17)

At the begi[nning of my royal rule, I . . . the town of the Sama]rians [I besieged, conquered] (2 lines destroyed) [for the god . . . who le]t me achieve (this) my triumph. . . . I led away as prisoners [27,290 inhabitants of it (and) [equipped] from among [them (soldiers to man)] 50 chariots for my royal corps. . . . [The town I] re[built] better than (it was) before and [settled] therein people from countries which [I] myself [had con]quered. I placed an officer of mine as governor over them and imposed upon them tribute as (is customary) for Assyrian citizens.

According to the Display Inscriptions.

(23–26)

I besieged and conquered Samaria (*Sa-me-ri-na*), led away as booty 27,290 inhabitants of it. I formed from among them a contingent of 50 chariots and made remaining (inhabitants) assume their (social) positions. I installed over them an officer of mine and imposed upon them the tribute of the former king. Hanno, king of Gaza and also II Kings 17:4ff. Sib'e, the *turtan* of Egypt (*Mu-ṣu-ri*), set out from Rapihu against me to deliver a decisive battle. I defeated them; Sib'e ran away, afraid when he (only) heard the noise of my (approaching) army, and has not been seen again. Hanno, I captured personally. I received the tribute from Pir'u of Musuru, from Samsi, queen of Arabia (and) It'amar the Sabaean, gold in dust-form, horses (and) camels.

According to the Annals of the Room XIV.

(11–15)
Iamani from Ashdod, afraid of my armed force (lit.: weapons), left his wife and children and fled to the frontier of M[usru] which belongs to Meluhha (i.e., Ethiopia) and hid (lit.: stayed) there like a thief. I installed an officer of mine as governor over his entire large country and its prosperous inhabitants, (thus) aggrandizing (again) the territory belonging to Ashur, the king of the gods. The terror(-inspiring) glamor of Ashur, my lord, overpowered (however) the king of Meluhha and he threw him (i.e., Iamani) in fetters on hands and feet, and sent him to me, to Assyria. I conquered and sacked the towns Shinuhtu (and) Samaria, and all Israel (lit.: "Omri-Land" *Bît Ḫu-um-ri-ia*). I caught, like a fish, the Greek (Ionians) who live (on islands) amidst the Western Sea.

According to the Display Inscription.

(33–37)
Ia'ubidi from Hamath, a commoner[8] without claim to the throne, a cursed Hittite, schemed to become king of Hamath, induced the cities Arvad, Simirra, Damascus (*Di-maš-qa*[ki]) and Samaria to desert me, made them collaborate and fitted out an army. I called up the masses of the soldiers of Ashur and besieged him and his warriors in Qarqar, his favorite city. I conquered (it) and burnt (it). Himself I flayed; the rebels I killed in their cities and established (again) peace and harmony. A contingent of 200 chariots and 600 men on horseback I formed from among the inhabitants of Hamath and added them to my royal corps.

Seventh Year.

(120–25)
Upon a trust(-inspiring oracle given by) my lord Ashur, I crushed the tribes of Tamud, Ibadidi, Marsimanu, and Haiapa, the Arabs who live, far away, in the desert (and) who know neither overseers nor official(s) and who had not (yet) brought their tribute to any king. I deported their survivors and settled (them) in Samaria.

From Pir'u, the king of Musru, Samsi, the queen of Arabia, It'amra, the Sabaean,—the(se) are the kings of the seashore and from the

---

[8] With *hubšu* denoting in Akkadian texts a special social class.

desert—I received as their presents, gold in the form of dust, precious stones, ivory, ebony-seeds,[9] all kinds of aromatic substances, horses (and) camels.

Eleventh Year according to the Display Inscription.

(90–112)

Azuri, king of Ashdod, had schemed not to deliver tribute any more and sent messages (full) of hostilities against Assyria, to the kings (living) in his neighborhood. On account of the(se) act(s) which he committed, I abolished his rule over the people of his country and made Ahimiti, his younger brother, king over them. But the(se) Hittites, always planning evil deeds, hated his reign and elevared to rule over them a Greek (*Ia-ma-ni*) who, without any claim to the throne, had no respect for authority—just as they themselves. In a sudden rage, I did not (wait to) assemble the full might of my army (or to) prepare the camp(ing equipment), but started out towards Ashdod (only) with those of my warriors who, even in friendly areas, never leave my side. But this Greek heard about the advance of my expedition, from afar, and he fled into the territory of Musru—which belongs (now) to Ethiopia—and his (hiding) place could not be detected. I besieged (and) conquered the cities Ashdod, Gath, Asdu-dimmu; I declared his images, his wife, his children, all the possessions and treasures of his palace as well as the inhabitants of his country as booty. l reorganized (the administration of) these cities (and) settled therein people from the [regions] of the East which I had conquered personally. I installed an officer of mine over them and declared them Assyrian citizens and they pulled (as such) the straps (of my yoke). The king of Ethiopia who [lives] in [a distant country], in an inapproachable region, the road [to which is . . .], whose fathers never—from remote days until now—had sent messengers to inquire after the health of my royal forefathers, he did hear, even (that) far away, of the might of Ashur, Nebo (and) Marduk. The awe-inspiring glamor of my kingship blinded him and terror overcame him. He threw him (i.e., the Greek) in fetters, shackles and iron bands, and they brought him to Assyria, a long journey.

Isa. 20:1

(C) From Broken Prisms

According to the broken Prism A.

[Aziru, king] of Ashdod (lacuna) on account of [this crime . . .] *from* . . . Animiti . . . his younger brother over [them . . .] I made (him)

---

[9] These are part of the Mesopotamian pharmacopoeia.

ruler . . . tribute . . . like (those of) the [former] kings, I imposed upon him. [But these] accursed [Hittites] conceived [the idea] of not delivering the tribute and [started] a rebellion against their ruler; they expelled him . . . (*Ia-ma-ni*) a Greek, comm[oner without claim to the throne] to be king over them, they made sit down [on the very throne] of his (former) master and [they . . .] their city of (or: for) the at[tack] (lacuna of 3 lines) . . . its neighborhood, a moat [they prepared] of a depth of 20 + x cubits . . . it (even) reached the underground water, in order to . . . Then [to] the rulers of Palestine (*Pi-liš-te*), Judah (*Ia-ú-di*), Ed[om], Moab (and) those who live (on islands) and bring tribute [and] *tâmartu* -gifts to my lord Ashur—[he spread] countless evil lies to alienate (them) from me, and (also) sent bribes to Pir'u, king of Musru—a potentate, incapable to save them—and asked him to be an ally. But I, Sargon, the rightful ruler, devoted to the pronouncements (uttered by) Nebo and Marduk, (carefully) observing the orders of Ashur, led my army over the Tigris and the Euphrates, at the peak of the(ir) flood, the spring flood, as (if it be) dry ground. This Greek, however, their king who had put his trust in his own power and (therefore) did not bow to my (divinely ordained) rulership, heard about the approach of my expedition (while I was still) far away, and the splendor of my lord Ashur overwhelmed him and . . . he fled. . . .

Nimrud Inscription.

(8)
(Property of Sargon, etc.) the subduer of the country Judah (*Ia-ú-du*) which is far away, the uprooter of Hamath, the ruler of which— Iau'bidi—he captured personally.[10]

Sennacherib (704–681): The Siege of Jerusalem

From the Prism of Sennacherib.   ANET, 287–88

(ii 37–iii 49)
In my third campaign I marched against Hatti. Luli, king of Sidon, whom the terror-inspiring glamor of my lordship had overwhelmed, fled far overseas and perished. The awe-inspiring splendor of the "Weapon" of Ashur, my lord, overwhelmed his strong cities (such as) Great Sidon, Little Sidon, Bit-Zitti, Zaribtu, Mahalliba, Ushu (i.e., the mainland settlement of Tyre), Akzib (and) Akko, (all) his fortress cities, walled (and well) provided with feed and water for his garrisons,

---

[10] After his victory over Iau-bi'di at Qarqar, Sargon erected various stelae commemorating this event.

and they bowed in submission to my feet. I installed Ethba'al (*Tuba'lu*) upon the throne to be their king and imposed upon him tribute (due) to me (as his) overlord (to be paid) annually without interruption.

As to all the kings of Amurru—Menahem (*Mi-in-ḫi-im-mu*) from Samsimuruna, Tuba'lu from Sidon, Abdili'ti from Arvad, Uru-milki from Byblos, Mitinti from Ashdod, Buduili from Beth-Ammon, Kammusun-adbi from Moab (and) Aiarammu from Edom, they

Fig. 102

brought sumptuous gifts (*igisû*) and—fourfold—their heavy *tâmartu* -presents to me and kissed my feet. Sidqia, however, king of Ashkelon, who did not bow to my yoke, I deported and sent to Assyria, his family-gods, himself, his wife, his children, his brothers, all the male descendants of his family. I set Sharruludari, son of Rukibtu, their former king, over the inhabitants of Ashkelon and imposed upon him the payment of tribute (and of) *katrû* -presents (due) to me (as) overlord—and he (now) pulls the straps (of my yoke)!

In the continuation of my campaign I besieged Beth-Dagon, Joppa, Banai-Barqa, Azuru, cities belonging to Sidqia who did not bow to my feet quickly (enough); I conquered (them) and carried their spoils away. The officials, the patricians and the (common) people of Ekron[11]—who had thrown Padi, their king, into fetters (because he was) loyal to (his) solemn oath (sworn) by the god Ashur, and had handed him over to Hezekiah, the Jew (*Ha-za-qi-(i)a-ú* ^amel^*Ia-ú-da-ai*)—(and) he (Hezekiah) held him in prison, unlawfully,

II Kings 18:21, 24

as if he (Padi) be an enemy—had become afraid and had called (for help) upon the kings of Egypt (*Muṣ(u)ri*) (and) the bowmen, the chariot(-corps) and the cavalry of the king of Ethiopia (*Meluḫḫa*), an army beyond counting—and they (actually) had come to their assistance. In the plain of Eltekeh (*Al-ta-qu-ú*), their battle lines were drawn up against me and they sharpened their weapons. Upon a trust(-inspiring) oracle (given) by Ashur, my lord, I fought with them and inflicted a defeat upon them. In the mêlée of the battle, I personally captured alive the Egyptian charioteers with the(ir) princes and (also) the charioteers of the king of Ethiopia. I besieged Eltekeh (and) Timnah (*Ta-am-na-a*), conquered (them) and carried their spoils away. I assaulted Ekron and killed the officials and patricians who had committed the crime and hung their bodies on poles surrounding the city. The (common) citizens who were guilty of minor crimes, I considered prisoners of war. The rest of them, those who were not accused of crimes and misbehavior, I released. I made Padi, their king, come from Jerusalem (*Ur-sa-li-im-mu*) and set him as their lord on the throne, imposing upon him the tribute (due) to me (as) overlord.

As to Hezekiah, the Jew, he did not submit to my yoke, I laid siege to 46 of his strong cities, walled forts and to the countless small

---

[11] Note the social stratification indicated in this passage.

villages in their vicinity, and conquered (them) by means of well-stamped (earth-)ramps, and battering-rams brought (thus) near (to the walls) (combined with) the attack by foot soldiers, (using) mines, breeches as well as sapper work. I drove out (of them) 200,150 people, young and old, male and female, horses, mules, donkeys, camels, big and small cattle beyond counting, and considered (them) booty. Himself I made a prisoner in Jerusalem, his royal residence, like a bird in a cage. I surrounded him with earthwork in order to molest those who were leaving his city's gate. His towns which I had plundered, I took away from his country and gave them (over) to Mitinti, king of Ashdod, Padi, king of Ekron, and Sillibel, king of Gaza. Thus I reduced his country, but I still increased the tribute and the *katrû*-presents (due) to me (as his) overlord which I imposed (later) upon him beyond the former tribute, to be delivered annually. Hezekiah himself, whom the terror-inspiring splendor of my lordship had overwhelmed and whose irregular and elite troops which he had brought into Jerusalem, his royal residence, in order to strengthen (it), had deserted him, did send me, later, to Nineveh, my lordly city, together with 30 talents of gold, 800 talents of silver, precious stones, antimony,[12] large cuts of red stone, couches (inlaid) with ivory, *nîmedu*-chairs (inlaid) with ivory, elephant-hides, ebony-wood, box-wood (and) all kinds of valuable treasures, his (own) daughters, concubines, male and female musicians. In order to deliver the tribute and to do obeisance as a slave he sent his (personal) messenger.

II Kings 18:15

Epigraph from a relief showing the conquest of Lachish.   *Fig. 121*

Sennacherib, king of the world, king of Assyria, sat upon a *nîmedu*-throne and passed in review the booty (taken) from Lachish (*La-ki-su*).

II Kings 18:14
II Kings 19:8

Esarhaddon (680–669): The Syro-Palestinian Campaign

ANET, 291

From the Prism B.

(v 54–vi 1)

I called up the kings of the country Hatti and (of the region) on the other side of the river (Euphrates) (to wit): Ba'lu, king of Tyre,

---

[12] This refers probably to stibnite, which might have been used as an eye paint (beside the cheaper and efficient substitute, burnt shells of almond and soot). Stibium is easily reduced and the metal is sporadically attested to in Mesopotamia since the Neo-Sumerian period.

II Chron. 33:11 Manasseh (*Me-na-si-i*), king of Judah (*Ia-ú-di*), Qaushgabri, king of Edom, Musuri, king of Moab, Sil-Bel, king of Gaza, Metinti, king of Ashkelon, Ikausu, king of Ekron, Milkiashapa, king of Byblos, Matanba'al, king of Arvad, Abiba'al, king of Samsimuruna, Puduil, king of Beth-Ammon, Ahimilki, king of Ashdod—12 kings from the seacoast;

Ekishtura, king of Edi'il (Idalion), Pilagura (Pythagoras), king of Kitrusi (Chytros), Kisu, king of Sillu'ua (Soli), Ituandar, king of Pappa (Paphos), Erisu, king of Silli, Damasu, king of Kuri (Curium), Atmesu, king of Tamesi, Damusi, king of Qarti-hadasti (Carthage), Unasagusu, king of Lidir (Ledra), Bususu, king of Nuria,—10 kings from Cyprus (*Iadnana*) amidst the sea, together 22 kings of Hatti, the seashore and the islands; all these I sent out and made them transport under terrible difficulties, to Nineveh, the town (where I exercise) my rulership, as building material for my palace: big logs, long beams (and) thin boards from cedar and pine trees, products of the Sirara and Lebanon (*Lab-na-na*) mountains, which had grown for a long time into tall and strong timber, (also) from their quarries (lit.: place of creation) in the mountains, statues of protective deities (lit.: of Lamassû and Shêdu) made of a š n a n -stone, statues of (female) *abzaztu*, thresholds, slabs of limestone, of a š n a n -stone, of large- and small-grained breccia, of *alallu*-stone, (and) of g i . r i n . h i . l i . b a -stone.

ANET, 301 ## Receipt of Tribute from Palestine

The BrM text K 1295 is a receipt of tribute brought from Palestine.

Two minas of gold from the inhabitants of Bit-Ammon (*mat Bit-Am-man-na-a-a*); one mina of gold from the inhabitants of Moab (*mat Mu-'-ba-a-a*); ten minas of silver from the inhabitants of Judah (*mat Ia-ú-da-a-a*); [. . . mi]nas of silver from the inhabitants of [Edom] (*mat [U-du-ma]-a-a*). . . .

(reverse)

. . . the Inhabitants of Byblos, the district officers of the king, my lord, have brought.

ANET, 304–5 ## The Fall of Nineveh

C. J. Gadd, *The Newly Discovered Babylonian Chronicle*, No. 21,901, in the British Museum (London, 1923), with transliteration and translation. Excerpt given is for the fourteenth year of Nabopolassar.

(reverse)

[Fourteenth year:] The king of Akkad cal[led up] his army and [Cyaxar]es, the king of the Mandahordes (*Umman-manda*) marched

towards the king of Akkad, [in] . . . they met each other. The king of
Akkad . . . and [Cyaxar]es . . . [the . . .]s he ferried across and they
marched (upstream) on the embankment of the Tigris and . . .
[pitched camp] against Nineveh. . . . From the month Simanu till the
month Abu, three ba[ttles were fought, then] they made a great attack
against the city. In the month Abu, [the . . . th day, the city was seized
and a great defeat] he inflicted [upon the] entire [population]. On
that day, Sinsharishkun, king of Assy[ria fled to] . . . , many prisoners
of the city, beyond counting, they carried away. The city [they turned]
into ruin-hills and hea[ps (of debris). The king] and the army of Assyria escaped (however) before the king (of Akkad) and [the army] of
the king of Akkad. . . . In the month Ululu, the 20th day, Cyaxares and
his army returned to his country. Afterwards, the king of A[kkad] . . .
marched as far as Nisibis. Booty and *ga-lu-tu* of . . . and (of) the country Rusapu they brought to the king of Akkad, to Nineveh. [In the
month] . . . Ashuruballit . . . sat down in Harran upon the throne to
become king of Assyria. Till the month . . . [the king of Akkad stayed]
in Nineveh. . . . From the 20th day of the month [Tashritu] the king
[of Akkad] . . . in the same month of Tashritu in the town . . .

The Fall of Jerusalem

(reverse 11–13)
Text from the seventh year of Nebuchadnezzar II. D. J. Wiseman, *Chronicles
of Chaldaean Kings (626–556 B.C.) in the British Museum* (London, 1956).
Tablet B.M. 21946 on plates V and XIVff., also pp. 66ff.

Seventh year: In the month Kislimu, the king of Akkad called up his
army, marched against Syria (lit.: Hattu-land), encamped against the   *Fig. 58*
city of Judah (URU Ia-a-hu-du) and seized the town on the second day
of the month Adar. He captured the king. He appointed there a king of
his own choice. He took much booty from it and sent (it) to Babylon.

The Conquest of Jerusalem

ANET³, 563–64

From the tablet which deals with the period from the last (21st) year of Nabopolassar to the eleventh year of his son and successor Nebuchadnezzar II,
the section reporting on the events before and after the conquest of Jerusalem has been translated here. The preceding years saw the conquest of Hatti
land by Nabopolassar and his son's annual campaigns through the West
(conquest of Askelon, first year), the subsequent campaign against Elam
(Year 9), a short rebellion (Year 10), and more campaigns in Hatti land.

Year 4: The king of Akkad sent out his army and marched into Hatti
land. [They marched] unopposed through Hatti land. In the month

of Kislimu he took the lead of his army and marched toward Egypt. The king of Egypt heard (of it) and sent out his army; they clashed in an open battle and inflicted heavy losses on each other. The king of Akkad and his army turned back and [returned] to Babylon.

Year 5: The king of Akkad (stayed) in his country. He organized his chariots and many horses.

Year 6, month Kislimu: The king of Akkad moved his army into Hatti land. He dispatched his army from Hatti land, they raided the desert, took much booty from the land of the Arabs, (also) their herds and divine images in great number. In the month Addaru, the king returned to his country.

Year 7, month Kislimu: The king of Akkad moved his army into Hatti land, laid siege to the city of Judah (*Ia-a-ḫu-du*) and the king took the city on the second day of the month Addaru. He appointed in it a (new) king of his liking, took heavy booty from it and brought it into Babylon.

Year 8, month Tebetu: The king of Akkad (went) into Hatti land as far as Carchemish [. . .] from [. . .] and in the month Shabatu he returned to his country.

ANET, 308

Nebuchadnezzar II (605–562)

(1) From administrative documents found in Babylon, some information concerning the fate of Jehoiachin, king of Judah, can now be gathered. These cuneiform tablets list deliveries of oil for the subsistence of individuals who are either prisoners of war or otherwise dependent upon the royal household. They are identified by name, profession, and/or nationality. The two tablets, so far published, also mention, beside Judeans, inhabitants of Ashkelon, Tyre, Byblos, Arvad, and, further, Egyptians, Medeans, Persians, Lydians, and Greeks.

II Kings 25:27–30

Jer. 52:31–34

    (text Babylon 28122, obverse 29–33)
. . . t[o?] *Ia-'-ú-kin,* king . . .
to the *qîpūtu-house* of . . .
. . . for Shalamiamu, the . . .
. . . for 126 men from Tyre . . .
. . . for Zabiria, the Ly[dian] . . .
    (text Babylon 28178, obverse ii 38–40)
10 (*sila* of oil) to . . . [*Ia*]-'-*kin,* king of *Ia*[. . .]
2½ *sila* (oil) to [. . . so]ns of the king of Judah (*Ia-a-ḫu-du*)
4 *sila* to 8 men from Judah (*amelIa-a-ḫu-da-a-a*) . . .
    (text Babylon 28186, reverse ii 13–18)
1½ *sila* (oil) for 3 carpenters from Arvad, ½ *sila* each
11½ *sila* for 8 ditto from Byblos, 1 sila each . . .
3½ *sila* for 7 ditto, Greeks, ½ sila each

½ *sila* to *Nabû-êṭir* the carpenter

10 (*sila*) to *Ia-ku-ú-ki-nu,* the son of the king of *Ia-ka-du* (i.e.,
	Judah)

2½ *sila* for the 5 sons of the king of Judah (*Ia-ku-du*) through
	Qana'a [. . .]

(2) From a fragmentary historical text (BrM 78–10–15, 22, 37, and 38).

(13–22)

. . . [in] the 37th year, Nebuchadnezzar, king of Bab[ylon] mar[ched
against] Egypt (*Mi-ṣir*) to deliver a battle. [*Ama*]*sis* (text: [. . .]-*a(?)-
su*), of Egypt, [called up his a]rm[y] . . . [. . .]*ku* from the town *Putu-
Iaman* . . . distant regions which (are situated on islands) amidst the
sea . . . many . . . which/who (are) in Egypt . . . [car]rying weapons,
horses and [chariot]s . . . he called up to assist him and . . . did [. . .]
in front of him . . . he put his trust . . . (only the first signs at the beginning and the end of the following 7 or 8 lines are legible).

The Mother of Nabonidus

ANET³, 560–62
Fig. 265

On two stelae found in Harran, one in 1906 and one as recently as 1956, we
have what appears, stylistically, as a tomb inscription of the mother of Nabonidus. The fact that two such objects are found in proximity seems, however, to suggest that they represent some atypical form of memorial tablets,
since these stelae were placed, together with two likewise identical stelae of
Nabonidus himself (see the following text, "Nabonidus and His God"), in an
architecturally oriented arrangement in or near the temple in Harran, the
reconstruction of which is clearly the main concern of both texts.

(i)

I am Adad-guppi', the mother of Nabonidus, king of Babylon, a devotee of Sin, Ningal, Nusku, and Sadarnunna, my gods, with whom
(lit.: with whose godhead) I always, even since my childhood, took
refuge, I who—(even) in the 16th year of Nabopolassar, king of Babylon, when Sin, the king of all gods, became angry with his city
(i.e., Harran) and his temple, and went up to heaven and the city and
the people in it became desolate—visited the sacred places of Sin,
Ningal, Nusku, and Sadarnunna in (the city and) remained devoted
to them (lit.: to their godhead); I who have laid hold of the hem of
the garment of Sin, the king of all gods, and have taken refuge with
his great godhead every day and night; I who have been piously devoted all my lifetime to Sin, Shamash, Ishtar and Adad, who are in
the heaven and in the nether world. For whatever precious possessions they have given me, I *thanked* them with gifts day and night for
months and years.

I laid hold of the hem of the garment of Sin, the king of all gods, my eyes were directed toward him day and night; I bowed down before him(!) in prayers and prostrations, saying: "If you would return to your city, all the black-headed people would worship your great godhead!" In order to appease (the anger of) my personal god and goddess, I did not permit apparel made of fine wool, gold and silver jewelry, any new garment, perfumes, and scented oil to touch my body, I was clad in a torn garment and when I left (my house) it was in silence, I constantly pronounced benedictions for them, the praise of my personal god and goddess was in my thoughts and I performed the services for them. I did not spare whatever precious possession I had but brought it to them (as votive offering).

From the 20th year of Ashurbanipal, king of Assyria, when I was born, until the 42nd year of Ashurbanipal, the 3rd year of his son Ashur-etil-ili, the 21st year of Nabopolassar, the 43rd year of Nebuchadnezzar, the 2nd year of Awel-Merodach, the 4th year of Neriglissar, during (all) these 95 years in which I visited the temple of the great godhead of Sin, the king of all the gods in heaven and in the nether world, he looked with favor upon my pious good works and listened to my prayers, accepted my vows.

(Eventually) his wrathful heart quieted down and he became reconciled with the temple Ehulhul, the temple of Sin in Harran, the divine residence in which his heart rejoices, and he had a change of heart. Sin, the king of all the gods, looked with favor upon me and called Nabonidus, my only son, whom I bore, to kingship and entrusted him with the kingship of Sumer and Akkad, (also of) all the countries from the border of Egypt, on the Upper Sea, to the Lower Sea. Then I lifted my hands to Sin, the king of all the gods, [I asked] reverently and in a pious mood: (ii) "Since you have called to kingship [Nabonidus, my son, whom I bore, the beloved of his mother,] and have elevated his status, let all the other gods—upon your great divine command—help him (and) make him defeat his enemies, do (also) bring to completion the (re)building of the temple Ehulhul and the performance of its ritual!" In a dream Sin, the king of all the gods, put his hands on me saying: "The gods will return on account of you! I will entrust your son, Nabonidus, with the divine residence of Harran; he will (re)build the temple Ehulhul and complete this task. He will restore and make Harran more (beautiful) than it was before! He will lead Sin, Ningal, Nusku, and Sadarnunna in solemn procession into the temple Ehulhul!"

I heeded the words which Sin, the king of all the gods, had spoken to me and I saw (them come true). Nabonidus, the only son whom I bore, performed indeed all the forgotten rites of Sin, Ningal, Nusku, and Sadarnunna, he completed the rebuilding of the temple Ehulhul, led Sin, Ningal, Nusku, and Sadarnunna in procession from Babylon

(Shuanna), his royal city, installed (them again) in gladness and happiness into Harran, the seat which pleases them.

Out of his love for me who worships him and have laid hold to the hem of his garment, Sin, the king of all gods, did what he had not done before, had not granted to anybody else, he gave me (a woman) an exalted position and a famous name in the country. He added (to my life) many days (and) years of happiness and kept me alive from the time of Ashurbanipal, king of Assyria, to the 9th year of Nabonidus, king of Babylon, the son whom I bore, (i.e.) one hundred and four happy years (spent) in that piety which Sin, the king of all gods, has planted in my heart. My eyesight was good (to the end of my life), my hearing excellent, my hands and feet were sound, my words well chosen, food and drink agreed with me, my health was fine and my mind happy. I saw my great-great-grandchildren, up to the fourth generation, in good health and (thus) had my fill of old age.

Let me entrust to you, Sin, my lord, my son Nabonidus, king of Babylon (NUN^ki) (since) you have looked upon me with favor and have given me (such) a long life; he should not sin against you as long as he lives. Assign to him the favorable *šēdu* and *lamassu* protective spirits whom you have assigned to me and who have made me reach ripe old age. Do not forgive him (easily) his trespassing and sins against your great godhead, may he (always) be in awe of your great godhead.

I have obeyed with all my heart and have done my duty (as a subject) during the 21 years in which Nabopo-lassar, the king of Babylon, the 43 years in which Nebuchadnezzar, the son of Nabopolassar, and the four years in which Neriglissar, the king of Babylon, exercised their kingship, (altogether) 68 years; I have made Nabonidus, the son whom I bore, serve Nebuchadnezzar, son of Nabopolassar, and Neriglissar, king of Babylon, and he performed his duty for them day and night by doing always what was their pleasure. He also made me a good name before them and they gave me an elevated position as if I were their real daughter. (break) And (for this reason) I have been making funerary offerings for them, performing and instituting for them permanent incense offerings, abundant (and) of sweet smell.

(Postscript:) She died a natural death in the 9th year of Nabonidus, king of Babylon. Nabonidus, king of Babylon, the son whom she bore, laid her body to rest [wrapped in] fine [wool garments and] shining white linen. He deposited her body in a hidden tomb with splendid [ornaments] of gold [set with] beautiful stones, [. . .] stones, expensive stone beads, [containers with] scented oil, and [. . .]. He slaughtered fat rams and assembled into his presence [the inhabitants] of Babylon and Borsippa together with [people] from far off provinces, he [summoned even kings, princes] and governors from the [borders] of Egypt on the Upper Sea, to the Lower Sea, for the mourning and [. . .] and they made a great lament, scattered [dust] on their heads. For seven days and seven nights they walked about, heads hung low, [dust strewn], stripped of their attire. On the seventh day [. . .] all the people of the country shaved and cleaned themselves, [*threw away*] their (mourning) attire [. . .] [I had] chests with (new) attire [brought] for them *to* their living quarters, [treated them] with food [and drink], provided them richly with fine oil, poured scented oil over their heads, made them glad (again) and looking presentable. I provided them well for their [long] journey and they returned to their homes.

[Whoever] you are, king, prince [or . . .] [take refuge] with the great godhead of Sin, the king [of all gods], the lord of the gods of heaven and nether world, worship Shamash, Adad and Ishtar, the lords [of heaven] and the nether world who [. . .], [the gods] who reside in Esagila and E[zida] and pray to them lest they [. . .]; the command of Sin and of Ishtar which can save [you . . .]. Keep [yourself] and your offspring safe forever and ever.

ANET³, 562–63 ## Nabonidus and His God

In 1956 D. S. Rice discovered in the ruins of the Great Mosque in Harran two stelae of Nabonidus used there secondarily as paving stones. Both are in typical stela form ending in a semicircle which contains in bas-relief the figure of the king in adoration before the symbols of the Sun, Ishtar, and the Moon. The lower part of each monolith contains the inscription in three columns of about 50 lines.

(i)

(This is) the great miracle of Sin that none of the (other) gods and goddesses knew (how to achieve), that has not happened to the country from the days of old, that the people of the country have ⟨not⟩ observed nor written down on clay tablets to be preserved for eternity, that (you), Sin, the lord of all the gods and goddesses residing in heaven, have come down from heaven to (me) Nabonidus, king of Babylon! For me, Nabonidus, the lonely one who has nobody, in whose (text: my) heart was no thought of kingship, the gods and goddesses prayed (to Sin) and Sin called me to kingship. At midnight he (Sin) made me have a dream and said (in the dream) as follows: "Rebuild speedily Ehulhul, the temple of Sin in Harran, and I will hand over to you all the countries."

But the citizens of Babylon, Borsippa, Nippur, Ur, Uruk (and) Larsa, the administrators (and) the inhabitants of the urban centers of Babylonia acted evil, careless and even sinned against his great divine power, having not (yet) experienced the awfulness of the wrath of the Divine Crescent, the king of all gods; they disregarded his (text: their) rites and there was much irreligious and disloyal talk. They devoured one another like dogs, caused disease and hunger to appear among them. He (Sin) decimated the inhabitants of the country, but he made me leave my city Babylon on the road to Tema, Dadanu, Padakku, Hibra, Jadihu, even as far as Jatribu. For ten years I was moving around among these (cities) and did not enter my own city Babylon.

Upon the order of Sin, the king of all gods, the lord of lords, which the gods and goddesses living in heaven (then) executed, upon the order of the Divine Crescent, Sin, they appointed Shamash, Ishtar, Adad, and Nergal to watch over my well-being. (Thereupon) in one and the same year (twice), to wit in the month of Nisannu as well as Tashritu, the people of Babylonia and Upper Syria could collect the products of the (open) country and the sea, and throughout all these years, without exception, Adad, the dike warden of heaven and nether world provided them upon the command of Sin with rain even in the height of the summer, in the following months: Simanu, Du'uzi, Abu, (and) Ululu, and so they could *bring* me (in order to support me) their abundance without hardship. Upon the command of Sin «and» Ishtar, the Lady-of-Battle, without whom neither hostilities nor reconciliation can occur in the country and no battle can be fought, extended her protection (lit.: hand) over them, and the king of Egypt, the Medes and the land of the Arabs, all the hostile kings, were sending me messages of reconciliation and friendship. As to the land of the Arabs which [is the eternal enemy] of Babylonia [and which] was (always) *ready* to rob and carry off its possession, (ii) Nergal broke their weapons upon the order of Sin, and they all bowed down at my feet. Shamash, the lord of oracular decisions, without whom no prediction can be uttered (lit.: no mouth can be opened or shut), made, in execution of a command of his own father, the Divine Crescent, the words and the hearts of the people of Babylonia and Upper Syria, who are in my charge, turn (again) to me so that they began to serve me and to execute my command throughout all the distant mountain regions and inaccessible paths I was moving about.

Then the (predicted) term of ten years arrived, it happened on the very day which the king of the gods, the Divine Crescent, had (in the dream) predicted, i.e., the 17th day of Tashritu, of which it is said (in the hemerologies): a day on which Sin is gracious.

O Sin, lord of the gods, whose name on the first day (of his appearance) is "Weapon-of-Anu," (you) who are able to illuminate (lit.: touch with light all) the heaven and to crush the nether world, who hold in your (text: the) hands the power of the Anu-office, who wield all the power of the Enlil-office, who have taken over the power of the Ea-office, holding thus in your (text: his) own hand all the heavenly powers; Enlil among the gods, king of kings, lord of lords, whose command they do not contradict, you who do not have to repeat your (text: his) order, of whose great awe the heaven and the nether world are full, with whose sheen heaven and nether world are covered—who can do anything without you? You place religious awe of your great godhead in the heart of any country in which you desire to dwell and its foundation remains steadfast forever; you remove awe toward you from any country which you choose to destroy and you overthrow it forever. ⟨You⟩ are the one whose utterance all the gods and goddesses living in heaven observe; they execute the command of the Divine Crescent, their own father, who wields the powers of heaven and nether world, without whose exalted command, which is given in heaven every day, no country can rest in security and no light can be in the world; the gods shake like reeds and the Anunnaki quiver; those who [bow down] before his divine command which cannot be changed . . . [. . .].

(iii)

[Before that moment] my visits to the diviner (or) the dream expert [for the interpretation of signs] did not cease, (but) whenever I lay down to sleep, (my) dreams at night were confused, until the word [came true, the time] was full, the right moment had arrived which [Sin had *foretold*]. [Then I dispatched a messenger] from Tema [and he went to] Babylon, my lordly city. When they saw [him . . .] they took gifts and presents be[fore him], the kings of the nearby regions came up (to Babylon) to kiss his (text: my) feet and those far off heard (about it) and were filled with awe of his (Sin's) great divine power. The gods and goddesses who had fled and withdrawn returned to give blessings. Then, my good fortune was found (again) in the victims used for the decisions of the diviner.

I arranged for my followers in the distant mountain regions (to live) in great plenty and abundance and I myself took the road home undisturbed.

(Thereupon) I carefully executed the command of his (Sin's) great godhead, I was not careless nor negligent but set in motion people from Babylon and Upper Syria, from the border of Egypt on the Upper Sea to the Lower Sea, all those whom Sin, the king of the gods, had entrusted to me, (thus) I built anew the Ehulhul, the temple of Sin, and completed this work. I (then) led in procession Sin, Ningal, Nusku, and Sadarnunna, from Shuanna (in Babylon), my royal city, and brought (them) in joy and happiness (into the temple), installing them on a permanent dais. I made abundant offerings before them and lavished gifts (on them).

I filled Ehulhul with happiness and made its personnel rejoice.

(Thus) I fulfilled the command of Sin, the king of the gods, the lord of lords who dwells in heaven, whose name surpasses that of (all) the (other) gods in heaven, (i.e.) of Shamash, who is *installed* by him, Nusku, Ishtar, Adad, (and) Nergal who have (only) executed the command of the Divine Crescent, who surpasses them (all).

Whenever I armed myself with weapons and set my mind to do battle, it was (solely) to execute the command of the Divine Crescent (hence) whoever you be whom Sin will (later on) name to kingship and whom he will call "My son," [do visit] the sacred places of Sin, who dwells in heaven [whose command cannot be changed] and whose order needs no [repetition] and [he will assist *you*] with his weapon in [battle . . .].

The Fall of Babylon

ANET, 306–7

Eleventh year: The king (stayed) in Tema;[13] the crown prince, the officials and his army (were) in Akkad. The king did not come to Babylon for the (ceremonies of the) month Nisanu, Nebo did not come to Babylon, Bel did not go out (from Esagila in procession), the festival of the New Year was omitted, (but) the offerings for the gods of Babylon and Borsippa were given according to the complete (ritual).

(iii reverse)

. . . Tigris . . . [In the month of] Addaru the (image of the) Ishtar of Uruk . . . the . . . [the . . .]s of the Sea Country . . . [arm]y [made an] at[tack]. . . .

[Seventeenth year:] . . . Nebo [went] from Borsippa for the procession of [Bel . . .] [the king] entered the temple É . t ù r . k a l a m . ma, in the t[emple] . . . (partly unintelligible).[14] [Be]l went out (in procession), they performed the festival of the New Year according to the complete (ritual). In the month of . . . [Lugal-Marada and the other gods] of the town Marad, Zababa and the (other) gods of Kish, the goddess Ninlil [and the other gods of] Hursagkalama entered Babylon. Till the end of the month Ululu (all) the gods of Akkad . . . those from above the IM and (those from) below the IM, entered Babylon. The gods from Borsippa, Kutha, . . . and Sippar (however) did not enter. In the month of Tashritu, when Cyrus attacked the army of Akkad in Opis on the Tigris, the inhabitants of Akkad revolted, but he (*Nabonidus*) massacred the confused inhabitants. The 14th day, Sippar was seized without battle. Nabonidus fled. The 16th day, Gobryas (*Ugbaru*), the governor of Gutium and the army of Cyrus entered Babylon without battle. Afterwards Nabonidus was arrested in Babylon when he returned (there). Till the end of the month, the shield(-carrying) Gutians were staying within Esagila (but) nobody carried arms in Esagila and its (pertinent) buildings, the correct time

---

[13] Nabonidus' prolonged and apparently unmotivated stay in Tema has given rise to an extended literature.

[14] This incident seems to have occurred during the New Year's Festival.

(for a ceremony) was not missed. In the month of Arahshamnu, the 3rd day, Cyrus entered Babylon, green twigs were spread in front of him—the state of "Peace" (*šulmu*) was imposed upon the city. Cyrus sent greetings to all Babylon. Gobryas, his governor, installed (sub-) governors in Babylon. From the month of Kislimu to the month of Addaru, the gods of Akkad which Nabonidus had made come down to Babylon . . . returned to their sacred cities. In the month of Arahshamnu, on the night of the 11th day, Gobryas died. In the month of [Arahshamnu, the . . . th day, the wi]fe of the king died. From the 27th day of Arahshamnu till the 3rd day of Nisanu a(n official) "weeping" was performed in Akkad, all the people (went around) with their hair disheveled. When, the 4th day, Cambyses, son of Cyrus, went to the temple é. níg.pa .k a l a m . m a . s u m . m a, the é. p a priest of Nebo who . . . the bull . . . they came (and) made the "weaving" by means of the *handles* and when [he le]d the image of Ne[bo . . . sp]ears and leather quivers, from. . . . Nebo returned to Esagila, sheep-offerings in front of Bel and the god *Mâ[r]-b[îti]*.

(iv reverse)

(After lacuna, only the ends of 9 lines are preserved.)

ANET, 315–16

Cyrus (557–529)

Fig. 195 Inscription on a clay barrel.

(one line destroyed)

. . . [r]ims (of the world) . . . a weakling has been installed as the *enû*[15] of his country; [the correct images of the gods he removed from their thrones, imi]tations he ordered to place upon them. A replica of the temple Esagila he has . . . for Ur and the other sacred cities inappropriate rituals . . . daily he did blabber [incorrect prayers]. He (furthermore) interrupted in a fiendish way the regular offerings, he did . . . he established within the sacred cities. The worship of Marduk, the king of the gods, he [chang]ed into abomination, daily he used to do evil against his (i.e., Marduk's) city. . . . He [tormented] its [inhabitant]s with corvée-work (lit.: a yoke) without relief, he ruined them all.

Upon their complaints the lord of the gods became terribly angry and [he departed from] their region, (also) the (other) gods living among them left their mansions, wroth that he had brought (them) into Babylon (Š u . a n . n aᵏⁱ). (But) Marduk [who does care for] . . .

---

[15] The old Sumerian title appears here in a context which seems to indicate that the primitive concept concerning the intimate connection between the physical vitality of the ruler and the prosperity of the country, was still valid in the political speculations of the Babylonian clergy.

on account of (the fact that) the sanctuaries of all their settlements were in ruins and the inhabitants of Sumer and Akkad had become like (living) dead, turned back (his countenance) [his] an[ger] [abated] and he had mercy (upon them). He scanned and looked (through) all the countries, searching for a righteous ruler willing to lead him (i.e., Marduk) (in the annual procession). (Then) he pronounced the name of Cyrus (*Ku-ra-aš*), king of Anshan, declared him (lit.: pronounced [his] name) to be(come) the ruler of all the world. He made the Guti country and all the Manda-hordes bow in submission to his (i.e., Cyrus') feet. And he (Cyrus) did always endeavour to treat according to justice the black-headed whom he (Marduk) has made him conquer. Marduk, the great lord, a protector of his people/worshipers, beheld with pleasure his (i.e., Cyrus') good deeds and his upright mind (lit.: heart) (and therefore) ordered him to march against his city Babylon (K á . d i n g i r . r a). He made him set out on the road to Babylon (DIN.TIR^{ki}) going at his side like a real friend. His widespread troops—their number, like that of the water of a river, could not be established—strolled along, their weapons packcd away. Without any battle, he made him enter his town Babylon (Š u . a n . n a), sparing Babylon (K á . d i n g i r . r a^{ki}) any calamity. He delivered into his (i.e., Cyrus') hands Nabonidus, the king who did not worship him (i.e., Marduk). All the inhabitants of Babylon (DIN.TIR^{ki}) as well as of the entire country of Sumer and Akkad, princes and governors (included), bowed to him (Cyrus) and kissed his feet, jubilant that he (had received) the kingship, and with shining faces. Happily they greeted him as a master through whose help they had come (again) to life from death (and) had all been spared damage and disaster, and they worshiped his (very) name.

I am Cyrus, king of the world, great king, legitimate king, king of Babylon, king of Sumer and Akkad, king of the four rims (of the earth), son of Cambyses (*Ka-am-bu-zi-ia*), great king, king of Anshan, grandson of Cyrus, great king, king of Anshan, descendant of Teispes (*Ši-iš-pi-iš*), great king, king of Anshan, of a family (which) always (exercised) kingship; whose rule Bel and Nebo love, whom they want as king to please their hearts.

When I entered Babylon (DIN.TIR^{ki}) as a friend and (when) I established the seat of the government in the palace of the ruler under jubilation and rejoicing, Marduk, the great lord, [induced] the magnanimous inhabitants of Babylon (DIN.TIR^{ki}) [to love me], and I was daily endeavouring to worship him. My numerous troops walked around in Babylon (DIN.TIR^{ki}) in peace, I did not allow anybody to terrorize (any place) of the [country of Sumer] and Akkad. I strove for peace in Babylon (K á . d i n g i r . r a^{ki}) and in all his (other) sacred cities. As to the inhabitants of Babylon (DIN.TIR^{ki}), [who] against the will of the gods [had/were . . . , I abolished] the corvée (lit.: yoke) which was against their (social) standing. I brought relief to their dilapidated housing, putting (thus) an end to their (main) complaints. Marduk, the great lord, was well pleased with my deeds and sent friendly blessings to myself, Cyrus, the king who worships him, to Cambyses, my son, the offspring of [my] loins, as well as to all my troops, and we all [praised] his great [godhead] joyously, standing before him in peace.

All the kings of the entire world from the Upper to the Lower Sea, those who are seated in throne rooms, (those who) live in other [types of buildings as well as] all the kings of the West land living in tents,[16] brought their heavy tributes and kissed my feet in Babylon (Š u . a n . n a). (As to the region) from . . . as far as Ashur and Susa, Agade, Eshnunna, the towns Zamban, Me-Turnu, Der as well as the region of the Gutians, I returned to (these) sacred cities on the other side of the Tigris, the sanctuaries of which have been ruins for a long time, the images which (used) to 'live therein and established for them permanent sanctuaries. I (also) gathered all their (former) inhabitants and returned (to them) their habitations. Furthermore, I resettled upon the command of Marduk, the great lord, all the gods of Sumer and Akkad whom Nabonidus has brought into Babylon (Š u . a n . n a^{ki}) to the anger of the lord of the gods, unharmed, in their (former) chapels, the places which make them happy.

May all the gods whom I have resettled in their sacred cities ask daily Bel and Nebo for a long life for me and may they recommend me (to him); to Marduk, my lord, they may say this: "Cyrus, the king who worships you, and Cambyses, his son, . . ." . . . all of them I settled in a peaceful place . . . ducks and doves, . . . I endeavoured to fortify/repair their dwelling places. . . .

(six lines destroyed)

The Uruk King List from Kandalanu to

ANET³, 566 ## Seleucus II

[x] years [. . .]
  Other *name*: [. . .]
21 years: K[anda]lan
1 year: Sin-shum-lishir
  and Sin-shar-ishkun
21 years: Nabopolassar
43 [ye]ars: Nebuchadnezzar (II)
2 [ye]ars: Amel-Marduk

---

[16] This phrase refers either to the way of life of a nomadic or a primitive society in contradistinction to that of an urban.

[x] + 2 years, 8 months: Neriglissar
[. . .] 3 months: Labashi-Marduk
[x] + 15 years: Nabonidus
[9 years: Cy]rus
[8 years: Cambys]es
[36 years: Dari]us

(break)
    (rev.)
[whose] second name (is) Nidin-ᵈB[el]
5 [y]ears: Darius (III)
7 years: Alexander
6 years: Philip
6 years: Antigonus
31 years: Seleucus (I)
22 years: Antiochus (I)
15 years: Antiochus (II)
20 [years]: Seleucus (II)

(break)

A Seleucid King List

ANET³, 566–67

[. . .] Alexander (the Great) [. . .]
Philip, the brother of Alexander [did . . .].
For [x] years there was no king in the country.
    Antigonus, the commander of the army was [. . .].
Alexander, the son of Alexander (was reckoned as king) for
    six years.
Year 7 is the first year (of Seleucus). Seleucus (I, Nicator) became
    king; he ruled for 25 years.
Year 31, month Elulu: king Seleucus (I) was killed in the West.
Year 32: Antiochus (I, Soter), son of Seleucus (I) became king. He
    ruled for 20 years.
Year 51, month Ajaru, 16th (day): Antiochus (I), the great king,
    died.
Year 52: Antiochus (II, Theos), son of Antiochus (I), became king.
    He ruled for 15 *years.*
Year 66, month Abu: The following (rumor) was he[ard] in
    Babylon: Antiochus (II), the great king [has died].
    (rev.)
[Year] 67: Seleucus (II, Gallinicus) [. . .]
[. . .]
[Year] 87: Seleucus (III, Soter) [. . .]
[Year] 90: King Antiochus (III, the Great) asc[ended] the throne.
He ruled for 35 [years].

[From] the Year 102 to the Year 119, Antiochus [. . .] [. . .] and
Antiochus, ⟨his⟩ sons ruled as kings.

Year 125, month Simanu: the following (rumor) was heard in
Babylon: Antiochus (III), the king, was killed in Elam.

In the same year, his son Seleucus (IV, Philipator) ascended the
throne. He ruled for 12 years.

Year 137, month Elulu, 10th day: Seleucus (IV), the king, died. . . .
In the same month, his son Antiochus (IV, Epiphames)
ascended the throne. He ruled for 11 years.

In the same year, month Arahsamnu, Antiochus (IV)
and his son Antiochus were kings.

[Year 1]42, month Abu: Antiochus, the king was put to death upon
the command of his father, King Antiochus (IV).

[Year 14]3: Antiochus became king.

[Year 148], month Kislimu: It was heard that K[ing] Antiochus
(V, Eupator) [died . . .]

[. . .]

[. . .]

on left edge: Demetrius son of Demetrius [. . .] Arsaces, king [. . .].

Palestinian Inscriptions

TRANSLATOR: W. F. ALBRIGHT

The Gezer Calendar

ANET, 320

This little inscription was discovered at Gezer in 1908 by R.A.S. Macalister; it is on a school exercise tablet of soft limestone. For a number of years its date was uncertain, but recent discoveries establish its relative archaism and point to the second half of the tenth century or the very beginning of the ninth as its probable time. The writer would date it in or about the third quarter of the tenth century—about 925 B.C. in round numbers. The language is good biblical Hebrew, in a very early spelling; it is written in verse and seems to have been a kind of mnemonic ditty for children.

Fig. 65

His two months are (olive) harvest,   (tricolon, 2:2:2)
    His two months are planting (grain),
        His two months are late planting;
His month is hoeing up of flax,   (tricolon, 3:3:3)
    His month is harvest of barley,
        His month is harvest and *feasting*;
His two months are vine-tending,   (bicolon, 2:2)
    His month is summer fruit.

The Moabite Stone

ANET, 320–21

This important inscription was discovered intact in 1868; it was subsequently broken by the Arabs and in 1873 it was taken to the Louvre.

Fig. 74

    The date of the Mesha Stone is roughly fixed by the reference to Mesha, king of Moab, in II Kings 3:4, after 849 B.C. However, since the contents of the stela point to a date toward the end of the king's reign, it seems probable that it should be placed between 840 and 820, perhaps about 830 B.C. in round numbers.

reading class

Evidence Moabites attacked Israel

I (am) Mesha, son of Chemosh-[. . .], king of Moab, the Dibonite—my father (had) reigned over Moab thirty years, and I reigned after my father,—(who) made this high place for Chemosh in Qarhoh [. . .] because he saved me from all the kings and caused me to triumph over all my adversaries. As for Omri, (5) king of Israel, he humbled Moab many years (lit., days), for Chemosh was angry at his land. And his son followed him and he also said, "I will humble Moab." In my time he spoke (thus), but I have triumphed over him and over his house, while Israel hath perished for ever! (Now) Omri had occupied the land of Medeba, and (Israel) had dwelt there in his time and half the time of his son (Ahab), forty years; but Chemosh dwelt there in my time.

And I built Baal-meon, making a reservoir in it, and I built (10) Qaryaten. Now the men of Gad had always dwelt in the land of Ataroth, and the king of Israel had built Ataroth for them; but I fought against the town and took it and slew all the people of the town as satiation (intoxication) for Chemosh and Moab. And I brought back from there Arel (or Oriel), its chieftain, dragging him before Chemosh in Kerioth, and I settled there men of Sharon and men of Maharith. And Chemosh said to me, "Go, take Nebo from Israel!" (15) So I went by night and fought against it from the break of dawn until noon, taking it and slaying all, seven thousand men, boys, women, girls and maid-servants, for I had devoted them to destruction for (the god) Ashtar-Chemosh. And I took from there the [. . .] of Yahweh, dragging them before Chemosh. And the king of Israel had built Jahaz, and he dwelt there while he was fighting against me, but Chemosh drove him out before me. And (20) I took from Moab two hundred men, all first class (warriors), and set them against Jahaz and took it in order to attach it to (the district of) Dibon.

It was I (who) built Qarhoh, the wall of *the forests* and the wall of the citadel; I also built its gates and I built its towers and I built the king's house, and I made both of its reservoirs for water inside the town. And there was no cistern inside the town at Qarhoh, so I said to all the people, "Let each of you make (25) a cistern for himself in his house!" And I cut *beams* for Qarhoh with Israelite captives. I built Aroer, and I made the highway in the Arnon (valley); I built Beth-bamoth, for it had been destroyed; I built Bezer—for it lay in ruins—with fifty men of Dibon, for all Dibon is (my) loyal dependency.

And I reigned [*in peace*] *over* the hundred towns which I had added to the land. And I built (30) [. . .] Medeba and Beth-diblathen and Beth-baal-meon, and I set there the [. . .] of the land. And as for Hauronen, there dwelt in it [. . . . And] Chemosh said to me, "Go down, fight against Hauronen. And I went down [and I fought against the town and I took it], and Chemosh dwelt there in my time. . . .

The Ostraca of Samaria

ANET, 321

This name is applied to a homogeneous group of 63 dockets on Israelite pot-sherds which were found by G. A. Reisner in 1910, while excavating a floor-level from the first phase of the second period of palace construction at Samaria. Owing to a mistake in stratigraphy, which was subsequently corrected by J. W. Crowfoot and his associates, this level was first attributed to Ahab; it is now reasonably certain that it should be assigned to the reign of Jeroboam II (about 786–746 B.C.). The four regnal years mentioned on the Ostraca extend from the ninth to the seventeenth (about 778–770 B.C.). These documents, though jejune in themselves, are of great significance for the script, spelling, personal names, topography, religion, administrative system, and clan distribution of the period.

Samaria Ostracon, No. 1

In the tenth year. To Shamaryau (Shemariah) from Beer-yam, a jar of old wine. Pega (son of) Elisha, 2; Uzza (son of) . . . , 1; Eliba, 1; Baala (son of) Elisha, 1; Jedaiah, 1.

Samaria Ostracon, No. 2

In the tenth year. To Gaddiyau from Azzo. Abibaal, 2; Ahaz, 2; Sheba, 1; Merib-baal, 1.

Samaria Ostracon, No. 18

In the tenth year. From Hazeroth to Gaddiyau. A jar of fine oil.

Samaria Ostracon, No. 30

In the fifteenth year. From Shemida to Hillez (son of) Gaddiyau. Gera (son of) Hanniab.

Samaria Ostracon, No. 55

In the tenth year. (From the) vineyard of Yehau-eli. A jar of fine oil.

An Order for Barley from Samaria

In 1932 several ostraca were found at Samaria, and were published the following year by E. L. Sukenik. One of them is outstanding because of its length and relative completeness. The script belongs to the eighth century, probably to its third quarter; it is characterized by extraordinarily long shafts of such letters as *l, m, n*, like other Israelite documents of this general period. The text is difficult, and the rendering below is tentative.

Baruch (*son of*) *Shallum* [. . .]
    O Baruch . . . pay attention and [give (?) to . . . (son of)] Yimnah (Imnah) barley (to the amount of) two (or three?) *measures.*

ANET, 321

The Siloam Inscription

Fig. 73   Accidentally discovered in 1880 in the rock wall of the lower entrance to the tunnel of Hezekiah south of the temple area in Jerusalem, the inscription is now in the Museum of the Ancient Orient at Istanbul. Its six lines occupy the lower half of a prepared surface, the upper part of which was found bare of inscription. It is, accordingly, almost certain that the first half of the original document is missing. Its contents and script point to the reign of Hezekiah (about 715–687 B.C.), a dating confirmed by II Kings 20:20 and especially II Chron. 32:30.

[. . . when] (the tunnel) was driven through. And this was the way in which it was cut through:—While [. . .] (were) still [. . .] axe(s), each man toward his fellow, and while there were still three cubits to be cut through, [there was heard] the voice of a man calling to his fellow, for there was *an overlap* in the rock on the right [and on the left]. And when the tunnel was driven through, the quarrymen hewed (the rock), each man toward his fellow, axe against axe; and the water flowed from the spring toward the reservoir for 1,200 cubits, and the height of the rock above the head(s) of the quarrymen was 100 cubits.

ANET³, 568

A Letter from the Time of Josiah (Mesad Hashavyahu Ostracon)

Fig. 236   In 1960 J. Naveh excavated a fortress on the Mediterranean seven km. northwest of Jamnia and three km. south of the mouth of the Wadi Rubin (Nahal Soreq). The name then given the site turned out to be based on an erroneous reading of the ostracon in question. The life of the fortress could be dated within narrow limits by the typical late pre-exilic and early Ionian (Southwest-Anatolian Greek) pottery found on the site, as well as by historical considerations, which suggest a date about 630 B.C. This would be just after the death of the Assyrian king Ashurbanipal and before the occupation of the Philistine Plain by Psammetichus of Egypt. The script of the ostracon is unfortunately quite slovenly, and it might be dated almost anywhere in the seventh century. The language is also uneven, and there are orthographic inconsistencies, but it is, in general, a fluent late pre-exilic Hebrew.

Let my lord commander hear the case of his servant! As for thy servant, thy servant was harvesting at Hazarsusim (?). And thy servant was (still) harvesting as they finished the storage of grain, as usual before the Sabbath. While thy servant was finishing the storage of grain with his harvesters, Hoshaiah son of Shobai came and took thy servant's mantle. (It was) while I was finishing with my harvesters (that) this one for no reason took thy servant's mantle. And all my companions will testify on my behalf—those who were harvesting with me in the heat (?) [. . .] all my companions will testify on my behalf! If I am innocent of gui[lt, let him return] my mantle, and if not, it is (still) the commander's right to take [my case under advisement (?) and to send word] to him [(asking) that he return the] mantle of thy servant. And let not [the plea of his servant] be displeasing to him! . . . .

Three Ostraca from Arad

ANET³, 568–69

During the excavation of the citadel mound of biblical Arad, in the extreme south of the hill country of Judah, south of Hebron and northeast of Beersheba, since 1962 hundreds of Hebrew and Aramaic ostraca have been found. The most important single find (1964) consisted of a group of seventeen ostraca, mostly in a good state of preservation, and probably all dating from shortly before the conquest of Judah by the Chaldaeans and their allies in the late winter of 598/97. This date has subsequently been confirmed by the discovery of an ostracon mentioning steps which were to be taken against an expected Edomite raid. The value of the new material for political, administrative and especially religious history is considerable; it is exceeded only by the excavation of a local, but Yahwist sanctuary of the ninth–sixth centuries B.C.

A

To my lord Eliashib: May Yahweh grant thy welfare! And (as) of now, give Shemariah half an aroura (of ground) and to Kerosi give a quarter aroura and to the sanctuary (give) what thou didst recommend to me. As for Shallum, he shall stay at the temple of Yahweh.

Fig. 235

B

To Eliashib—and (as) of now: Give the *Kittiyîm* three baths of wine and write the exact date. And from what is left of the old wheat grind up one (*kor*) of wheat to make bread for them. Serve the wine in punch bowls.

C

To Nahum, and (as) of now: Go to the house of Eliashib, son of Oshiyahu, and get from him one (bath) of oil, and send it to m[e] in haste, sealing it with thy seal.

On the 24th of the month Nahum delivered the oil into the hand of the *Kittî*.

ANET, 321–22 # The Lachish Ostraca

These ostraca were discovered in the ruins of the latest Israelite occupation at Tell ed-Duweir in southern Palestine, which unquestionably represents biblical Lachish. The first 18 were found by the late J. L. Starkey in 1935; three more (making 21 in all) were added during a supplementary campaign in 1938. Most of the ostraca were letters, while others were lists of names, etc., but only a third of the documents are preserved well enough to be reasonably intelligible throughout. Nearly all of the ostraca come from the latest occupation level of the Israelite gate-tower, and they are generally placed immediately before the beginning of the Chaldean siege of Lachish, perhaps in the autumn of 589 (or 588) B.C. Since they form the only known corpus of documents in classical Hebrew prose, they have unusual philological significance, quite aside from the light which they shed on the time of Jeremiah.

Lachish Ostracon II

II Sam. 9:8

To my lord Yaosh: May Yahweh cause my lord to hear tidings of peace this very day, this very day! Who is thy servant (but) a dog that my lord hath remembered his servant? May Yahweh afflict those who re[port] an (evil) rumor about which thou art not informed!

Lachish Ostracon III

Thy servant Hoshaiah hath sent to inform my lord Yaosh: May Yahweh cause my lord to hear tidings of peace! And now thou hast sent a letter, but my lord did not enlighten thy servant concerning the letter which thou didst send to thy servant yesterday evening, though the heart of thy servant hath been sick since thou didst write to thy servant. And as for what my lord said, "Dost thou not understand?— call a scribe!", as Yahweh liveth no one hath ever undertaken to call a scribe for me; and as for any scribe who might have come to me, truly I did not call him nor would I give anything at all for him!

And it hath been reported to thy servant, saying, "The commander of the host, Coniah son of Elnathan, hath come down in order to go into Egypt; and unto Hodaviah son of Ahijah and his men hath he sent to obtain . . . from him."

And as for the letter of Tobiah, servant of the king, which came to Shallum son of Jaddua through the prophet, saying, "Beware!", thy servant hath sent it to my lord.

Fig. 80 ## *Lachish Ostracon IV*

May Yahweh cause my lord to hear this very day tidings of good! And now according to everything that my lord hath written, so hath thy servant done; I have written on the door according to all that my lord hath written to me. And with respect to what my lord hath written about the matter of *Beth-haraphid,* there is no one there.

And as for Semachiah, Shemaiah hath taken him and hath brought him up to the city. And as for thy servant, I am not sending *anyone* thither [today(?), but I will send] tomorrow morning.

And let (my lord) know that we are watching for the signals of Lachish, according to all the indications which my lord hath given, for we cannot see Azekah.

Lachish Ostracon V

May Yahweh cause my lord to hear [tidings of peace] and good [this very day, this very day!] Who is thy servant (but) a dog that thou hast sent to thy servant the [letters . . . Now] thy servant hath returned the letters to my lord. May Yahweh cause thee to see [. . .]. How can thy servant benefit or injure the king?

Lachish Ostracon VI

To my lord Yaosh: May Yahweh cause my lord to see this season in good health! Who is thy servant (but) a dog that my lord hath sent the [let]ter of the king and the letters of the prince[s, say]ing, "Pray, read them!" And behold the words of the pr[inces] are not good, (but) to weaken our hands [and to sla]cken the hands of the *m[en] who are informed about them* [. . . And now] my lord, wilt thou not write to them, saying, "Why do ye thus [*even*] in Jerusalem? Behold unto the king and unto [*his house*] are ye doing this thing!" [And,] as Yahweh thy God liveth, truly since thy servant read the letters there hath been no [*peace*] for [thy ser]vant. . . .

Jer. 38:4

Lachish Ostracon VIII

May Yahweh cause my lord to hear tidings of good this very day! [. . .]. *The Lord hath humbled me* before thee. *Nedabiah* hath fled to the mountains [. . .]. Truly I lie not—let my lord *send* thither!

Lachish Ostracon IX

May Yahweh cause my lord to hear [tidings] of peace! [. . .] let him send [. . .] *fifteen* [. . .]. Return word to thy servant through *Shele-miah* (telling us) what we shall do tomorrow!

Canaanite and Aramaic Inscriptions

Building Inscriptions

TRANSLATOR: FRANZ ROSENTHAL

ANET, 499 ## Yehimilk of Byblos

This inscription records the dedication of a new building, possibly a temple, and is now quite generally dated in the tenth century. It was found in Byblos in 1929.

A house built by Yehimilk, king of Byblos, who also has restored all the ruins of the houses here.

May Ba'lshamem and the Lord of Byblos[1] and the Assembly of the Holy Gods of Byblos prolong the days and years of Yehimilk in Byblos, for (he is) a righteous king and an upright king before the Holy Gods of Byblos!

ANET, 499–500 ## Azitawadda of Adana

This unusually long inscription comes from a locality called Karatepe situated about thirty-eight miles southwest of Mar'ash beside the River Jeyhan. Three versions of the Phoenician text, together with some Hittite versions, were discovered in 1946–47. They contain an autobiographical account which king Azitawadda composed on the occasion of the dedication of a citadel and city founded by him. The exact date of the inscriptions is still uncertain and depends on a further study of the archaeological and historical

---

[1] A correction to "Lady of Byblos," a frequently mentioned deity, has been suggested.

evidence. The text seems to antedate events described in the inscription of Kilamuwa (see no. 3), but at present a much later, eighth-century date cannot be ruled out.

One version of the inscription is written in four columns on four sides of a statue. Another version starts on a gate lion and is continued on two orthostats. The third version consists of three columns distributed over four orthostats and continued on the bases of the fourth and adjacent orthostats to a gate lion.

I am Azitawadda, the blessed of Baʻl,[2] the servant of Baʻl, whom Awrikku[3] made powerful, king of the Danunites.

Baʻl made me a father and a mother to the Danunites. I have restored the Danunites. I have expanded the country of the Plain of Adana from the rising of the sun to its setting. In my days, the Danunites had everything good and plenty to eat and well-being. I have filled the storehouses of Paʻr. I have added horse to horse, shield to shield, and army to army, by virtue of Baʻl and the Gods (El). I shattered the wicked. I have removed all the evil that was in the country. I have set up my lordly houses in good shape and I have acted kindly toward the roots of my sovereignty.[4]

I have been sitting upon the throne of my father. I have made peace with every king. Yea, every king considered me his father because of my righteousness and my wisdom and the kindness of my heart.

I have built strongholds in all the outposts at the borders in places where there were evil men, gangleaders, none of whom had been subservient to the House of Mupsh. I, Azitawadda, placed them underneath my feet. I have built strongholds in those places, so that the Danunites might dwell in peace of mind.

I have subdued powerful countries in the west which the kings who were before me had not been able to subdue. I, Azitawadda, subdued them. I have brought them (their inhabitants) down and established them at the eastern end of my borders, and I have established Danunites there (in the west). In my days, there was, within all the borders of the Plain of Adana, from the rising of the sun to its setting, even in places which had formerly been feared, where a man was afraid to walk on the road but where in my days a woman was able *to stroll, peaceful activity*,[5] by virtue of Baʻl and the Gods (El). And in all my days, the Danunites and the entire Plain of Adana had plenty to eat and well-being and a good situation and peace of mind.

[2] Or perhaps: "chief official (*habarakku*) of Baʻl."

[3] Awrikku most probably was the father of Azitawadda.

[4] The "roots" may be the residential and capital cities of the realm, or the royal offspring.

[5] Literally: "*work* (Akk. *dullu*) *with spindles*."

I have built this city. I have given it the name of Azitawaddiya, for Ba'l and Reshef-*Şprm* commissioned me to build it. I have built it, by virtue of Ba'l and by virtue of Reshef-*Şprm,* with plenty to eat and well-being and in a good situation and in peace of mind to be a protection for the Plain of Adana and the House of Mupsh, for in my days, the country of the Plain of Adana had plenty to eat and well-being, and the Danunites *never* had *any night* in my days.

Having built this city and having given it the name of Azitawaddiya, I have established Ba'l-*Krntryš* in it. A sacrific(ial order) was established for all the molten images: for the yearly sacrifice an ox, at the [time of pl]owing a sheep, and at the time of harvesting a sheep.

May Ba'l-*Krntryš* bless Azitawadda with life, peace, and mighty power over every king, so that Ba'l-*Krntryš* and all the gods of the city may give Azitawadda length of days, a great number of years, good authority, and mighty power over every king! And may this city possess plenty to eat and wine (to drink), and may this people that dwells in it possess oxen and small cattle and plenty to eat and wine (to drink)! May they have many children, may they be strong numerically, may they serve Azitawadda and the House of Mupsh in large numbers, by virtue of Ba'l and the Gods (*El*)!

If there be a king among kings and a prince among princes or a man who is (just) called a man who shall wipe out the name of Azitawadda from this gate and put down his own name, even if he has good intentions toward this city but removes this gate which was made by Azitawadda and makes for the (new) gate a (new) *frame* and puts his name upon it, whether he removes this gate with good intentions or out of hatred and evil, let Ba'lshamem and El-the-Creator-of-the-Earth and the Eternal-Sun and the whole Group of the Children of the Gods (*El*) wipe out that ruler and that king and that man who is (just) called a man! However, the name of Azitawadda shall endure forever like the name of sun and moon!

Kilamuwa of *Y'dy*-Sam'al

ANET, 500–501

This autobiographical account, composed in connection with the dedication of a palace, was discovered in 1902 in modern Zinjirli in northwest Syria. It dates from the second half of the ninth century B.C. The text consists of two parts. In the first part, king Kilamuwa boasts of his success in foreign policy, and in the second part, he praises his domestic accomplishments. He states that he improved the position of the *mškbm,* possibly an oppressed sedentary element of the population, on whose undisturbed relations with another group, the *b'rrm,* possibly referring to "wild" Bedouins, peace in his realm depended.

Y'dy, whose vocalization is uncertain, might be the capital city of the realm, to be vocalized Yu'addiya or the like (cf., Azitawadda-Azitawaddiya), which later on came to be known as Sam'al. The latter, however, might have been the name of a larger region or country.

I am Kilamuwa, the son of Hayya. Gabbar became king over *Y'dy* but he was ineffective. There was *Bmh* but he was ineffective. There was my father Hayya but he was ineffective. There was my brother Sha'il but he was ineffective. But I, Kilamuwa, the son of *Tm*,[6] what I achieved, the former (kings) did not achieve.

My father's house was in the midst of mighty kings. Everybody stretched forth his hand to eat it. But I was in the hands of the kings like a fire that eats the beard, like a fire that eats the hand. The king of the Danunites (tried to) overpower me, but I hired against him the king of Assyria, (who) gave a maid for a lamb, a man for a garment.[7]

I, Kilamuwa, the son of Hayya, sat upon the throne of my father. Before the former kings, the *mškbm* went (cowed) like dogs. I, however, to some I was a father. To some I was a mother. To some I was a brother. Him who had never seen the face of a sheep, I made the possessor of a flock. Him who had never seen the face of an ox, I made the possessor of a herd of cattle and a possessor of silver and a possessor of gold. He who had not (even) seen linen since his youth, in my days he was covered with byssus. I took the *mškbm* by the hand. They were disposed (toward me) as an orphan is to his mother.

If one of my children who shall sit in my place should damage this inscription, may the *mškbm* not respect the *b'rrm*, and may the *b'rrm* not respect the *mškbm*!

He who smashes this inscription, may his head be smashed by Ba'l-Samad who belongs to Gabbar, and may his head be smashed by Ba'l-Hamman who belongs to *Bmh*, and by Rakabel, the Lord of the dynasty!

Barrakab of *Y'dy*-Sam'al

ANET, 501

This inscription of a remote successor of the afore-mentioned Kilamuwa was found in Zinjirli in 1891. It was set up about 730 B.C.

Fig. 127

I am Barrakab, the son of Panamu, king of Sam'al, servant of Tiglath-pileser, the lord of the (four) quarters of the earth.

---

[6] Many suggestions have been made to explain these two letters but the one considering them the name of Kilamuwa's mother—to be corrected to Tammat—remains the most plausible one for the time being.

[7] Kilamuwa apparently used a proverb in which a buyer boasts of a good bargain. He not only hired the mighty king of Assyria, but was able to do so cheaply.

Because of the righteousness of my father and my own righteousness, I was seated by my Lord Rakabel and my Lord Tiglath-pileser upon the throne of my father. The house of my father has profited more than anybody else, and I have been running at the wheel of my Lord, the king of Assyria, in the midst of mighty kings, possessors of silver and possessors of gold. I took over the house of my father and made it more prosperous than the house of one of the mighty kings. My brethren, the kings, *are envious* because of all the prosperity of my house.

My fathers, the kings of Sam'al, had no good house. They had the house of Kilamu, which was their winter house and also their summer house. But I have built this house.

Cultic Inscriptions

ANET, 501   ### Ben-Hadad of Damascus

Fig. 139   The stela with this inscription was discovered, apparently in 1939, in an ancient cemetery about four miles north of Aleppo, probably not *in situ*. It may, however, have originally been set up somewhere in the neighborhood of Aleppo. It dates from about 860 B.C.

A stela set up by Barhadad, the son of T[abrimmon, the son of Hezion], king of Aram, for his Lord Melqart, which he vowed to him and he (then) heard his voice.

ANET, 501   ### Kilamuwa of *Y'dy*-Sam'al

A gold sheath found in Zinjirli.

A *smr* (*sheath, scepter?*) fashioned by Kilamuwa, the son of Hayya, for Rakabel. May Rakabel give him a long life!

ANET, 501–2   ### Zakir of Hamat and Lu'ath

This historical inscription, dating from the early years of the eighth century B.C., was composed in connection with the dedication of a statue of Ilu-Wer, an avatar of Hadad. It was found in 1904 in a place about twenty-five miles southeast of Aleppo, which in modern times is called Afis and which appears to have been mentioned in this inscription as Apish.

A stela set up by Zakir, king of Hamat and Lu'ath, for Ilu-Wer, [*his god*].

I am Zakir, king of Hamat and Lu'ath. A humble man I am. Be'elshamayn [*helped me*] and stood by me. Be'elshamayn made me king over Hatarikka (Hadrach).

Barhadad, the son of Hazael, king of Aram, united [seven of] a group of ten kings against me: Barhadad and his army; Bargush and his army; the king of Cilicia and his army; the king of 'Umq and his army; the king of Gurgum and his army; the king of Sam'al and his army; the king of Milidh and his army. [All these kings whom Barhadad united against me] were seven kings and their armies. All these kings laid siege to Hatarikka. They made a wall higher than the wall of Hatarikka. They made a moat deeper than its moat. But I lifted up my hand to Be'elshamayn, and Be'el-shamayn heard me. Be'elshamayn [spoke] to me through seers and through diviners. Be'elshamayn [said to me]: Do not fear, for I made you king, and I shall stand by you and deliver you from all [these kings who] set up a siege against you. [Be'elshamayn] said to me: [*I shall destroy*] all these kings who set up [a siege against you and *made this moat*] and this *wall* which. . . .

[. . .] *charioteer* and *horseman* [. . .] its king in its midst [. . .]. I [*enlarged*] Hatarikka and added [to it] the entire district of [. . .] and *I made him ki*[*ng* . . .] all these strongholds everywhere within the bor[ders].

I built houses for the gods everywhere in my country. I built [. . .] and Apish [. . .] and the house of [. . .].

I set up this stela before Ilu-Wer, and I wrote upon it my achievements [. . .]. Whoever shall remove (this record of) the achievements of Zakir, king of Hamat and Lu'ath, from this stela and whoever shall remove this stela from before Ilu-Wer and banish it from its [place] or whoever shall stretch forth his hand [to . . .], [may] Be'elshamayn and I[lu-Wer and . . .] and Shamash and Sahr [and . . .] and the Gods of Heaven [and the Gods] of Earth and Be'el-'[. . . deprive him of h]ead and [. . . and] his root and [. . . , *and may*] the name of Zakir and the name of [*his house endure forever*]!

Yehawmilk of Byblos

ANET, 502

This ex-voto has been known since 1869, but a fragment completing most of its lower right-hand corner was found only sixty years later. It appears to date from the fifth or fourth century. The identity of the second of the three main objects which Yehawmilk here dedicates to his goddess has not yet been fully cleared up. Instead of an *engraved object*, it might have been a *door*.

Fig. 130

I am Yehawmilk, king of Byblos, the son of *Yehar-ba'l*, the grandson of Urimilk, king of Byblos, whom the mistress, the Lady of Byblos, made king over Byblos.

I have been calling my mistress, the Lady of Byblos, [and she heard my voice]. Therefore, I have made for my mistress, the Lady of Byblos, this altar of bronze which is in this [*courtyard*], and this *engraved object* of gold which is in front of this *inscription* of mine, with the *bird* (?) of gold that is set in a (*semiprecious*) stone, which is upon this *engraved object* of gold, and this portico with its columns and the [*capitals*] which are upon them, and its roof: I, Yehawmilk, king of Byblos, have made (these things) for my mistress, the Lady of Byblos, as I called my mistress, the Lady of Byblos, and she heard my voice and treated me kindly.

May the Lady of Byblos bless and preserve Yehawmilk, king of Byblos, and prolong his days and years in Byblos, for he is a righteous king. And may [the mistress,] the Lady of Byblos, give [him] favor in the eyes of the gods and in the eyes of the people of this country and (that he be) pleased with the people of this country.

[Whoever you are,] ruler and (ordinary) man, who might [*continue*] to do work on this altar and this *engraved work* of gold and this portico, my name, Yehawmilk, king of Byblos, [you should put with] yours upon that work, and if you do not put my name with yours, or if you [*remove*] this [*work and transfer this work from its foundation*] *upon this* place *and* [. . . , may] the mistress, the Lady of Byblos, [*destroy*] that man and his seed before all the Gods of Byblos.

ANET, 502–3 ## The Marseilles Tariff

The two blocks of stone containing this inscription were found in Marseilles in 1845. The stone used for them is known to occur in the region of Carthage. Thus, it is possible that the document originally belonged to a temple in Carthage. However, the possibility that a similar kind of stone might also have been quarried in the neighborhood of Marseilles apparently has not yet been sufficiently explored. The date of the inscription is uncertain; it may date from the third century or the early part of the second century B.C. The text is carefully engraved. It is provided with a title, and each paragraph begins with a new line.

Temple of Ba'l-[*Zaphon*]

Tariff of payments set up [by the men in charge of] the payments in the time of [the lords Hilles]ba'l, the suffete, the son of Bodtanit, the son of Bod[eshmun, and Hillesba'l,] the suffete, the son of Bodeshmun, the son of Hillesba'l, and their colleagues.

For an ox, as a whole offering or a *substitute offering* or a complete whole offering, the priests shall have ten—10—silver (pieces) for each. In the case of a whole offering, they shall have, over and above this payment, meat [weighing *three hundred*—300]. In the case of a *substitute offering,* they shall have *neck* and *shoulder joints (chuck),* while the person offering the sacrifice shall have the skin, *ribs,* feet, and the rest of the meat.

For a calf whose horns are *still lacking somewhat and* . . . , or for a stag, as a whole offering or a *substitute offering* or a complete whole offering, the priests shall have five—5—silver [pieces for each. In the case of a whole offering, they shall have, over and] above this payment, meat weighing one hundred and fifty—150. In the case of a *substitute offering,* they shall have *neck* and *shoulder joints,* while [the person offering the sacrifice] shall have the skin, *ribs,* feet, [and the rest of the meat].

For a ram or a goat, as a whole offering or a *substitute offering* or a complete whole offering, the priests shall have one—1—shekel of silver and 2 *zr*[8] for each. In the case of a *substitute offering,* they shall have, [over and above this payment, *neck*] and *shoulder joints,* while the person offering the sacrifice shall have the skin, *ribs,* feet, and the rest of the meat.

For a lamb or for a kid or for a *young* stag, as a whole offering or a *substitute offering* or a complete whole offering, the priests shall have three quarters of silver and [2] *zr* [for each. In the case of a *substitute offering,* they shall have, over and] above this payment, *neck* and *shoulder joints,* while the person offering [the sacrifice] shall have the skin, *ribs,* feet, and the rest of the meat.

For an *'gnn* bird or a *ṣṣ*(bird), as a complete whole offering or a *šṣf offering* or a *ḥzt offering,* the priests shall have three quarters of silver and 2 *zr* for each. [The person offering the sacrifice] shall have the meat.

[For] any (other) bird or a holy *oblation* or a hunt offering or an oil offering, the priests shall have 10 *'a* of silver for each [. . .].

For any *substitute offering* which they shall have to carry to the God, the priests shall have *neck* and *shoulder joints,* and for a *substitute offering* [. . .].

Upon a *cake*[9] and upon milk and upon fat and upon any sacrifice which someone is to offer as a meal-offering, [the priests shall have . . .].

For any sacrifice which shall be offered by persons poor[10] in cattle or poor in fowl, the priests shall have nothing [whatever].

---

[8] *zr* is the name of a small coin or, possibly, the abbreviation for such a coin, as *'a* below is an abbreviation of the name of another unit smaller than *zr.*

[9] *bll* may mean "fodder" as in Hebrew. It is certainly possible that fodder was offered for the animals of the temple.

[10] Or rather: "without."

Any *citizen* and any scion (*of a noble clan*) and any participant in a banquet for the God and anybody who shall offer a sacrifice [...], those men shall make payment per sacrifice as specified in a written document [which was set up under ...].

Any payment which is not specified in this tablet shall be made according to the written document which [was also set up ... under Hillesbaʻl, the son of Bodtan]it and Hillesbaʻl, the son of Bodeshmun, and their colleagues.

Any priest who shall accept a payment contrary to what is specified in this tablet shall be fined [...].

Any person offering a sacrifice who shall not give the [*money for*] the payment [which is specified in this tablet ...].

ANET, 503   The Carthage Tariff

A number of fragments very similar in contents to the preceding Marseilles Tariff have also been found in Carthage itself over a number of years beginning with 1858. Three of those fragments, though not parts of the same monument, were recognized by J.-B. Chabot as belonging to identical texts, and Chabot's reconstruction has been followed in this translation. The date of the Carthage Tariff is about the same as that of the Marseilles Tariff.

Tariff of payments set up by [the men in charge of the payments ...].

[For an ox, as whole offerings or *substitute offerings*], the priests [shall have] the skins, and the person offering the sacrifice the *fat parts* [...].

For a stag, [as whole offerings or *substitute offerings*], the priests [shall have] the skins, and the person offering the sacrifice the *fat parts* [...].

For a ram or a goat, as whole offerings or as *substitute offerings,* the priests shall have the skins of the goats, and the person offering the sacrifice shall have the *ribs* [...].

For a lamb or for a kid or for a *young* stag, as whole offerings or *substitute offerings,* the priests shall have the skins [...].

For any sacrifice which shall be offered by persons poor in cattle, the priest shall have nothing whatever.

For an 'gnn bird or for a ṣṣ(bird), 2 *zr* of silver for each.

[For any *substitute offering* wh]ich he shall have to carry to the God, the priest shall have *necks* and *shoulder joints* [...].

[Upon any] holy [*oblation*] and upon a hunt offering and upon an oil offering [...].

Upon a *cake* (*fodder*) and upon milk (fat) and upon a sacrifice as a meal-offering and upon [...].

Any payment which is not specified in this tablet shall be made [according to the written document ...].

Any priest who shall take [...].

Any person offering a sacrifice who [...].

Any person who shall trade [..., and who] shall shatter this tablet [...].

Pds, the son of Eshmunhilles [...].

Other Inscriptions
The King of Kedar

One of four silver bowls with brief Aramaic inscriptions found, it seems, around 1950 at Tell el-Maskhuta about twelve miles west of Ismailia in Egypt and dating from the fifth century B.C.

Offered to Han-Ilat by Qaynu, the son of Gashm, king of Kedar.

Punic Ex-voto Inscriptions

The first two of these stelas were discovered at Salammbo between 1945 and 1950 and published by J.-G. Février in *CIS*, 1, Nos. 5684 and 5685, Pls. XCVIII and XCIX. They appear to belong among the oldest Punic inscriptions known so far, possibly dating from about as early as 600 B.C. The other two stelas, dating from a considerably later period, were found at El-Hofra in Constantine in 1950 and published by A. Berthier and R. Charlier, *Le Sanctuaire punique d'El-Hofra* (Paris, 1955), Nos. 28 and 55, pp. 29–31, 49–51, Pls. II A and VII A. All of them belong to a type of monument that over the last century and a half has become known in hundreds of specimens, most of them inscribed with basically identical inscriptions. A few of the texts contain the word *mlk* which has been recognized as a cultic term denoting some kind of sacrifice. *Mlk* appears at times modified by such words as *'mr*, "lamb," *'dm*, "man" (?), or *b'l* ("Ba'al," or "citizen," or, rather unlikely, "instead of an infant"). Occasionally, one also finds other cultic expressions added, such as *bshrm btm*, of which the first, crucial element is most obscure and has again been thought to refer to human (infant) sacrifices. Whatever their precise significance, the relevance of these monuments and the inscriptions they bear to Canaanite cult practices characterized by the OT terms *molech* (*moloch*) and *topheth* seems quite well established and has been discussed extensively,

a. A stela of *mlkt b'l* made by Bodisi, the son of Melqartgadd, for the Lord Ba'al Hammon.

b. A stela of *mlk bʻl* given by Magon, the son of Hanno, to Baʻal Hammon.

c. For the Lord, for Baʻal Hammon, *mlk ʼdm bshrm, completely,* vowed by *ʼAfishshihar,* because He heard his voice and blessed him.

d. For the Lord, for Baʻal Hammon, *mlk ʼmr (mol-chomor),* a vow vowed by *Akborat,* the daughter of [...].

ANET³, 658

The Amulet from Arslan Tash

The limestone plaque containing this inscription was purchased in 1933 at Arslan Tash, the ancient Hadattu. At the time, two such plaques were obtained but only one has been published so far. The language of the inscription is an undetermined Canaanite dialect; the writing is of an Aramaic type. It would seem to date from the seventh century B.C. According to the interpretation presented below, we have here the text of an incantation named after a certain *Ssm,* possibly a mythological being of Anatolian (or Egyptian?) provenance but not a full-fledged god such as is pictured on the reverse of the plaque. The incantation is directed against the winged sphinx and the she-wolf devouring a human being, both pictured on the obverse and collectively called the "stranglers," that is, female demons supposed to cause the death of infants and children. It may have been intended to facilitate childbirth and to make sure that the newborn infant would not fall prey to the "stranglers." However, the reading of the crucial passage at the end which is often translated: "May her womb be opened and may she give birth! ... When the sun rises, travail and give birth!" is based upon the doubtful reconstruction of missing words and upon an uncertain and, it seems, unwarranted emendation of what is actually written.

An incantation for *the female flying demon.* The "bond" of *Ssm,* the son of *Pdrsh* (?).

Take *these* and say to the strangling females: The house I enter you shall not enter, and the courtyard I tread you shall not tread. An eternal bond has been established for us. *Ashshur* has established (it) for us, and all the divine beings and *the majority of the group* of all the holy ones, through the bond of heaven and earth *for ever,* through the bond of Baʻl, *the lord of* the earth, through the bond *of the wife of* Hawron, *whose utterance is pure,* and *her* seven co-wives and the eight wives of Baʻl. ...

(On the sphinx:) To *the female demon that flies* in the dark chamber (say): Pass by, time and again, Lili(t)!

(On the she-wolf:) *To the robbing, slaying female* (say): Go away!

(On and around the deity:) *Sz zt,* may his [*mouth*] *not* (?) *open* ... Let the sun rise, *eternally, eternally!*

The Uruk Incantation

ANET³, 658–59

A tablet inscribed with cuneiform characters originating from Uruk (Erech) was acquired by the Louvre in 1913. Already its first editor, F. Thureau-Dangin, tentatively determined its language as Aramaic. The date of the tablet is uncertain. It may possibly come from the third century B.C.

I have taken a (magic) bond from the wooden roof, in silence, from the threshold of the gate. I have put it underneath my tongue. I have entered a house full of words, a tongue-tied table, a mixing bowl (full) of poison. When they saw me, the house full of words fell silent, the tongue-tied table was upset, the mixing bowl (full) of poison was poured out.

I have been successful, and I am successful . . . [. . .], before adults and children, women and men, . . . and those assembled and sitting at the gate, before so-and-so, from *everything*.

Remove, drive out pains! Defective one, be wh[ole]! Lame one, run! Find companions, excessive one! *Finally*, (you all) rise!

Speak, dumb one! Rise, silent one!

Who is angry, who is enraged, who is clothed in the garment of anger, (has) fire in his mouth, (has) *mixtures (of spittle)* underneath his tongue? So-and-so, the son of so-and-so, is angry and enraged, is clothed in the garment of anger, (has) fire in his mo[uth], (has) *mixtures (of spittle)* underneath his tongue. I am wise . . . [. . .].

I have taken a (magic) knot from [*the threshold?*], soundless(ly), from the room [*(below) the roof*]. I have entered into the presence of so-and-so . . . [. . .]. I have made him take off the garment of anger. I have clothed him in the garment of . . . I have taken the fire from his mouth, the *mixtures (of spittle)* from underneath [his tongue]. My good things from his mouth [*come forth*], my evil things from *his posterior* [. . .], before adults and children, women and men, [. . . and those assembled] and sitting at the gate, and before s[o-and-so . . .].

[*Remove, drive out pains*!] Defective one, [be whole]! Lame one, run! Find companions, excessive one! *Finally*, (you all) rise!

Speak, dumb one! Rise, silent one!

The Treaty between *KTK* and Arpad

ANET³, 659–61

The inscriptions containing this treaty originate from a locality called Sujin near Sfire, or, as seems more likely, from the village of Sfire itself, about sixteen miles southeast of Aleppo. The block of basalt on which the portion of the treaty designated Sfire I is inscribed was broken horizontally into two parts, with the loss of a few lines in between. In addition to the text inscribed upon the front and the back of the block (designated I A and I B, although it is by no means clear which is the recto and which is the verso), one side of it is also inscribed (Sfire I C). Another version is preserved in a very fragmentary fashion (Sfire II). It is similarly inscribed upon a stela reconstituted from a number of preserved fragments. Another portion of the treaty (Sfire III) has been recovered from nine fragments of a stela. In this case, only one inscribed side, apparently the verso, is preserved.

The treaty dates from about 750 B.C. The identity of *Ktk* has not yet been established. *Ktk* has been vocalized Katikka (Alt), and it has been identified with Kas/shku or Urartu (Dupont-Sommer), Hatarikka-Hadrach (Landsberger), Assyria (Dossin), and a locality named Kis(s)ik (Noth).

(Sfire I A)

A treaty of Barga'yah, king of *Ktk*, with Matti'el, the son of 'Attarsamak, king of [Arpad; a t]reaty of the sons of Barga'yah with the sons of Matti'el; a treaty of the sons of the sons [and the offspring] of Barga'yah with the offspring of Matti'el, the son of 'Attarsamak, king of Arpad; a treaty of *Ktk* with [a treaty of] Arpad; a treaty of the inhabitants of *Ktk* with a treaty of the inhabitants of Arpad; a treaty of . . . [. . .] and with all Aram and with Musr and with his (*Matti'el's*) sons who will come up after him, and [. . .] all upper and lower Aram, and with anybody entering and l[eaving] the royal house, [all those who have h]ere set up this treaty.

This treaty concluded by Barga'[yah *is set up* before . . .] and *Mullesh* (?), before Marduk and Zerpanit, before Nabu and T[ashmet, before Irra and Nus]k, before Nergal and Las, before Shamash and *Nur,* before S[in and Nikkal, be]fore Nikkar and *Kd'h,* before all the Gods of *Rḥbh* and *'dm,* [before . . . Hadad of A]leppo, before Sibitti, before El and 'Elyon, before Heaven [and Earth, before A]byss and Sources, and before Day and Night. Witnesses all [you] G[ods be for it]! Open your eyes to behold the treaty of Barga'yah [*with Matti'el, king of Arpad*]!

If Matti'el, the son of 'Attarsamak, kin[g of Arpad,] is false to [*the Gods of this treaty,* and i]f the offspring of Matti'el is false [to . . . (large break) . . . . Seven rams shall tup] a ewe, and she shall not become pregnant. Seven [wetn]urses shall anoint [*their breasts* and] suckle a boy, and he shall not be sated. Seven mares shall suckle a colt, and it shall not be s[ated. Seven] cows shall suckle a calf, and it shall not be sated. Seven ewes shall suckle a lamb, and [it shall not be s]ated. His seven *daughters* shall go *in search of* food, and they shall not *arouse concern.*

If Matti'el is false [to Barga'yah and to] his son and to his offspring, his kingdom shall be a kingdom of sand, (nay) a kingdom (like) a dream that *fades* like fire. [May Ha]dad [*pour out*] everything evil on earth and in heaven, and every trouble. And may he pour out hai[*lstones*] upon Arpad. Seven years shall the locust eat. Seven years shall the worm eat. Seven [years shall] *blight* come upon the face of *its* land, and no grass shall sprout, so that nothing green can be seen and its vegetation does not [appear]. The sound of the cithara shall not be heard in Arpad and among its people, *only* . . . and *only* [mournful sou]nds and lamentation. The Gods shall send every kind of devouring pest against Arpad and against its people. The mo[uth] of snakes [*shall devour*], the mouth of scorpions, the mouth of *bears,* the mouth of panthers, and moths and lice. [There shall be no] *foliage. Defoliated*, it will be laid waste. Its vegetation will not ripen. Arpad shall be a (desolated) mound for [. . . and] gazelles, foxes, hares, wild-cats, owls, [. . .], and *magpies.* [*This tow*]*n,* and *Mdr', Mrbh, Mzh, Mblh, Shrn, Tw'm, Byt'l, Bynn,* [. . . , ']*rnh,* Ḥ*zz,* and *'dm* shall not *be mentioned (ever after).*

As this wax is consumed by fire, thus Arpad [and its dependencies] shall be consumed *ext*[*ensively*]. Hadad shall sow in them salt and water cress. And *it shall* not *be mentioned (ever after).*

This *bandit* and [. . .] *is* Matti'el. *It is he himself.*

As this wax is consumed by fire, thus M[atti'el] shall be consumed [by fi]re.

As this bow and these arrows are broken, thus *Inurta* (*Ninurta*) and Hadad shall break [the bow of Matti'el] and the bow of his nobles.

As a man of wax *is blinded,* thus Matti'el shall *be blinded.*

[As] this calf is cut up, thus Matti'el and his nobles shall be cut up.

As [. . .], thus the wives of Matti'el and the wives of his offspring and the wives of his nobles shall *work as slaves.*

As [. . .] and have her face boxed, thus . . . [. . .].

(The text of the upper part of Sfire I B is quite similar to that in I A. The lower portion spells out, as does Sfire III, details of the obligations incumbent upon the parties to the treaty. Only three or four paragraphs seem reasonably clear so far.)

(Sfire I C)

[If . . .] *they thus* say and *write* whatever [I, Matti'el,] have written as a reminder for my son [and the son of] my son who will come up [after m]e, [*they*] will be made prosperous [before] the Sun, [and no]thing evi[l will be done to] my ro[yal hou]se, [and] the house of M[atti'el . . .].

May [he who observes the words of this stela] be guarded by the Gods as to his day and as to his house. But whoever does not observe the words of the inscription on this stela but says: I shall *efface* some of its words, or I shall upset the good things and put down evil ones, on the day he will do so, that man and his house and all that is *in it* shall be upset by the Gods, and *he* (*his house*) be turned upside down, and that (man) shall not *acquire* a name!

(Sfire II C)

(While most of the preserved text of Sfire II A and B permits a coherent translation only where the missing links can be supplied on the basis of Sfire I and III, the concluding portion is quite clear.)

[... and he who inten]ds to *efface* these inscriptions from the bethels where they are set up and says: I shall destroy the inscriptions, and *tomorrow* I shall destroy *Ktk* and its king, but (who) himself is afraid to *efface* the inscriptions from the bethels and (therefore) says to someone who does not know: I shall hire (you), and commands (him) to *eff*[*ace* these inscri]ptions from the bethels ... [...].

[*But if they observe this treaty* ...], the God]s of the trea]ty in this inscription [*shall guard*] Matti'el, his son, the son of his son, his offspring, all the kings of Arpad, all his nobles, and their people, as to their houses and their days.

(Sfire III)

[...] or to your son or to your offspring or to one of the kings of Arpad and s[pea]ks [ag]ainst me or against my son or against the son of my son or against my offspring in the manner of any one man who blows hot and speaks evil words, you must not accept from him the words (he says) to my detriment [and to the detriment of my son]. You must turn them over into my hands. Your son must turn (them) over to my son. Your offspring must turn (them) over to my offspring. The offspring of [anyone of the k]ings of Arpad must turn (them) over to me. Whatever is good in my eyes, I shall do to them. If you do not do so, you will have been false to all the Gods of the treaty in [this] inscription.

If one of my officials or one of my brothers or one of my eunuchs or one of the people under my control flees from me and becomes a fugitive and goes to Aleppo, you must not pro[vide f]ood for them, and you must not say to them: Stay peacefully in your place, and you must not cause them to be disdainful of me. You must placate them and return them to me. If not, they shall [remain] in your land to be quiet there until I come and placate them. If you cause them to be disdainful of me and provide food for them and say to them: Stay where you are and pay no attention to him, you will have betrayed this treaty.

When I send my messenger to anyone of the kings around me or to anyone who is a friend of mine, to (exchange) greetings or for any of my business, or he sends his messenger to me, the road shall be open to me. You must not (try to) exercise control over me in this respect and you must not contest i[t](s use) with me. If you do not do so, you will have betrayed this treaty.

If it happens that one of my brothers or one of the house of my father or one of my sons or one of my *officers* or one of my officials or one of the people under my control or one of my enemies seeks my head to kill me and to kill my son and my offspring, if it is me they kill, you must come and avenge my blood from the hand of my enemies. Your son must come to avenge the blood of my son from his enemies. The son of your son must come to avenge the bl[ood of the s]on of my son. Your offspring must come to avenge the blood of my offspring. If it is a city, you must slay it with the sword. If it is one of my brothers or one of my slaves or [one] of my officials or one of the people under my control, you must slay him and his offspring, his *supporters,* and his friends with the sword. If you do not do so, you will have been false to all the Gods of the treaty in this inscription.

If the idea to kill me comes to your mind and you bring it upon your lips, and the idea to kill the son of my son comes to the mind of the son of your son and he brings it upon his lips, or if the idea to kill my offspring comes to the mind of your offspring and they bring it upon their lips, and if (such an) idea comes to the mind of the kings of Arpad, whenever someone dies (as a result), you will have been false to all the Gods of the treaty in this inscription.

If [my] son who will sit upon my throne quarrels with one of his brothers or *conceives a hatred of him,* you must not let loose your tongue among them, saying to them: Kill your brother, or imprison him and [do not] set him free! For if you make peace among them, he will not be killed and he will not be imprisoned. So, if you do not make peace among them, you will have betrayed this treaty.

When a fugitive of mine flees to one of the kin[gs around] me and a fugitive of theirs flees and comes to me, if mine is returned, I shall return [theirs and] you must not (try to) hinder me. If you do not do so, you will have betrayed this treaty.

You must not let loose your tongue in my house and among my sons and among [my] bro[thers and among] my offspring and among my people, saying to them: Kill your lord, and be in his place, for he is not better than you! Someone will avenge [my blood. If you] commit treachery against me or against my sons and against my offspring, you will have been false to all the Gods of the treaty in this inscription.

[*Tl'y*]*m*, its villages, its inhabitants, and its territory belong to my father and to [his house for]ever. When the Gods drove out the house [of my father, it] came to belong to someone else. But now, the Gods have brought about the return of the hou[se of my father . . .] my father and *Tl'ym* has returned to [. . .] and to his son and to the son of his son and to his offspring forever. [If . . .] my son, and my offspring quarrels [with your offspring concern]ing *Tl'ym*, its villages, and its inhabitants, whoever *brings up* [. . . k]ings of Arpad [. . .], you will have betrayed this treaty.

If [. . .] and they bribe whatever king who [. . . all tha]t is beautiful and all that is go[od . . .].

ANET³, 661 ## Ahiram of Byblos

This inscription, found in 1923, is the oldest of the documents translated here and is now quite generally dated in the early tenth century B.C. Its technical execution leaves much to be desired, and it should be noted that sepulchral inscriptions occasionally are less carefully executed than other types of monumental inscriptions.

A sarcophagus made by [It]tobaʻl, the son of Ahiram, king of Byblos, for Ahiram, his father, as his eternal ⟨dwelling-⟩place.

If there be a king among kings and a governor among governors and an army commander up in Byblos who shall uncover this sarcophagus, let his judicial staff be broken, let his royal throne be upset! May peace flee from Byblos, and he himself be wiped out!
Written by (before ?) . . .

ANET³, 661 ## Agbar, Priest of the Moon-god in Nerab

Found in 1891 at Nayrab in the immediate neighborhood of Aleppo, the monument probably dates from the seventh century.

Belonging to Agbar, priest of Sahr, in
Nerab. This is his picture.
Because of my righteousness before him, he gave me a good name and prolonged my days. On the day I died, my mouth was not closed to words, and with my eyes, what do I see? Children of the fourth generation, who wept for me, being distraught.

They did not place with me a vessel of silver and bronze. With my garments they placed me (here), lest in the future my *couch* be removed.

Whoever you are who shall do wrong and remove me, may Sahr, Nikkal, and Nusk cause him to die a miserable death, and may his posterity perish!

ANET³, 662 ## Tabnit of Sidon

This inscription, which was excavated in 1887, dates, as is now generally held on historical and archaeological grounds, from Achaemenid times, apparently the early fifth century.

I, Tabnit, priest of Astarte, king of Sidon, the son of Eshmunʻazar, priest of Astarte, king of Sidon, am lying in this sarcophagus.

Whoever you are who might find this sarcophagus, don't, don't open it and don't disturb me, for no silver has been *given* me, no gold and no *jewelry* whatever has been *given* me! Only I (myself) am lying in this sarcophagus.

Don't, don't open it, and don't disturb me, for such a thing would be an abomination to Astarte! But if you do open it and if you do disturb me, may ⟨you⟩ not have any seed among the living under the sun or resting-place together with the shades!

Eshmun'azar of Sidon

ANET³, 662

Eshmun'azar's great sarcophagus was found near Sidon in 1855. It is dated about fourteen years later than the preceding inscription.

In the month of Bul, in the year fourteen—14—of the reign of Eshmun'azar, king of Sidon, the son of king. Tabnit, king of Sidon, king Eshmun'azar, king of Sidon, spoke as follows:

I have been snatched away before my time, the son of a *number* of *restricted* days, an orphan, the son of a widow. I am lying in this casket and this grave, in a place which I (myself) built.

Whoever you are, ruler and (ordinary) man, may he not open this resting-place and may he not search in it for anything, for nothing whatever has been placed into it! May he not take the casket in which I am resting, and may he not carry me away from this resting-place to another resting-place! Even if people goad you, do not listen to their talk, for any ruler and any man who shall open this resting-place or who shall take up the casket in which I am resting or who shall carry me away from this resting-place—may they not have a resting-place with the shades, may they not be buried in a grave, and may they not have son and seed to take their place! And may the Holy Gods abandon them to a mighty ruler who (might) rule them, in order to cut down that ruler or man who shall open this resting-place or who shall take up this casket, as well as the seed of that ruler or those men! May they have no root down below and no fruit up on top, and *may they be cursed* among the living under the sun, for I *am to be pitied*, I was snatched away before my time, the son of a *number* of *restricted* days, an orphan, the son of a widow, I am.

For I, Eshmun'azar, king of Sidon, the son of king Tabnit, king of Sidon, the grandson of king Eshmun'azar, king of Sidon, and my mother, Amo'ashtart, priestess of Astarte, our mistress the queen, the daughter of king Eshmun'azar, king of Sidon, (we are) the ones who built the houses of the gods, the house of [*Astarte*] in Sidon-by-the-Sea, and we (also) established Astarte in Shamem-Addirim. We are the ones who built a house for Eshmun, the Holy Prince, (at) the *Ydll* Spring in the mountain, and we established him in Shamem-Addirim. We are the ones who built houses for the gods of Sidon in Sidon-by-the-Sea, a house for the Lord of Sidon and a house for

'Ashtart-Shem-Ba'l. Furthermore, the Lord of Kings gave us Dor and Joppa, the mighty lands of Dagon, which are in the Plain of Sharon, in accordance with the important deeds which I did. And we added them to the borders of the country, so that they would belong to Sidon forever.

Whoever you are, ruler and (ordinary) man, may he not open it and may he not uncover me and may he not carry me away from this resting-place and may he not take up the casket in which I am resting, lest these Holy Gods abandon them and cut down that ruler and those men and their seed forever!

South-Arabian Inscriptions

TRANSLATOR: A. JAMME

The historical period of South Arabia begins, according to common opinion, with the eighth century B.C., and is definitively closed by the Moslem occupation in the first half of the seventh century A.D. Its inscriptions are chiefly in the dialects spoken in the four great kingdoms of Saba', Maʿîn, Qatabân, and Ḥaḍramawt.

Sabaean Inscriptions   ANET³, 663–65

1. Mâreb, capital of Saba', is famed for the dam west of the city, and the great temple 'Awwâm southeast of it. The following text mentions the building of the enclosure wall of this sanctuary, and was carved on the outside of the wall itself.

Yadaʿʾil Ḏariḥ, son of Sumhuʿalay, *mukarrib* of Saba', walled 'Awwâm, the temple of 'Ilumquh, when he sacrificed to 'Aṭtar and [when] he established the whole community [united] by a god and a patron and by a pact and a [secret] trea[ty. By 'Aṭtar and by Hawbas and by] 'Ilumquh.

2. On the top of Jebel el-Falag (near Mâreb), is a beautiful votive stela, on the lower part of which a boustrophedon inscription commemorates the reason for its erection by a man who was granted transport for an important building.

←   Bi'aṭtar, he of [the family of] Ḥa(lil), son of 'Ilqawwâm,   (1)
→   he of [the clan of] Barahum, erected [and] built the stela of 'Aṭ-
←   tar and Samî' and of Ḏât-Ḥimyâm and of Wadd-
→   um, when he was appointed for transport for the building of
      the entrance court

←   of Sumhuʿalay and [for] the building [which] he planned
and   (5)

→   made strong.

3. Another stela found in Maʿrib (north-northwest of Mâreb) bears a boustrophedon text commemorating both the erection of this monument and
the hunt which took place on that occasion.

←   sym-   Yataʿamar Bayyin, son of Sumhu-   (1)
→   bols   ʿalay, *mukarrib* of Sabaʾ, erected
←   the stela of the two gates of Nûmum, when he hunted
→   the hunting by ʿṭtr and by pits.

4. The funeral stela was in common use among the South-Arabian peoples.
On this stela, found at Mâreb in 1947, the "identity card" of the person is engraved on the top above the depression in which a human head is shown in
relief.

Ḥay(û)m [of the Family of] Gaʾirân

5. A large number of Sabaean texts are dedicatory inscriptions. The present
text from Mâreb tells of the offering of a bronze statue; it probably mentions
the judicial clearing of a man who was falsely considered as a member of a
conspiracy, although he had resisted the propaganda made by ʾAwsum. This
text also mentions the punishment of a girl ordered by the divinity.

(1) [....]rwadd and [.] (2) [....]m, dedi(ca)[ted to ʾIlumquh
Ṭah]wân, master of ʾAww[âm] (3), this [sta]tue in bronze in praise
because vouchsafed (4) [and assist]ed ʾIlumquh Ṭahwân His servant
Yaṣ[baḥ and] (5) his [brother *or* son] from the interdict he incurred
when [tried to incite] (6) him [to revolt] ʾAwsum, the Ḫawlânî,
against (thei)[r] lord (7) the king; and because ʾIlumqu[h] vouchsafed and assisted (8) His servant Yaṣbaḥ in showering down upon
him the favor he (9) [be]sought Him in order to punish and give
away the (10) girl, who was called ʾAbwafay in Kab(g)ân (11) in the
city of Šibâmum. And that ʾIlumquh may continue to gr[ant] (12)
His servant Yaṣbaḥ the favors he may beseech (13) [Him]; and that
He may vouchsafe him the esteem and the grace of h[is] lord (14)
[Našaʾkar]ib Yuʾ[m]in Yuharḥib, king of Sabaʾ and (15) [Raydân, son
of ʾIlšar]aḥ Yaḥḍub and Yaʾzil Bayyin, King[s (16) of Sabaʾ and Ray-
dân; and that] He [may] protect their persons; and that He may preserve (17) [them from the hostility and the wicked]ness of enemy. By
ʾIlumquh.

6. The public confession was known among the South-Arabian peoples. The
present text in relief on a bronze tablet from Medînet Haram mentions five
transgressions, all of which concern ritual sexual purity.

(1) Ḥarim, son of Ṯawbân, avowed and did (2) penance to Ḏû-Samâwî because he drew near a (3) woman during a period illicit to him [or her] and fondled a woman during her menses (4); and that he came together with a woman in childbed; and that he went without any purification and wore his clothes (6) without purification ; and that he touched women (7) during their menses and did not wash himself; and that he (8) moistened his clothes with ejections. And he humbled himself (9) and abased himself and repented. And that he may be rewarded.

7. In spite of particular favors received from the divinity, the offering of a statue was sometimes ordered by the god himself through his oracle.

(1) Karib'aṭat, (son of Ha)yṯân, high (2) official of Wahab'aṭat, of [the tribe of] Gadanum (3), dedi(cated) to 'Ilumquh Ṯahwân, master of (4) 'Awwâm, this statue in praise because preser[ved] (5) him 'Ilumquh in life and [because] he arose from (6) the illness he suffered in the year of Naša'karib, son of (7) Sumkarib, as He bade him (8) [by] His ora[cle]; and that 'Ilumquh may continue to shower down upon (9) His servant Karib'aṭat all the favors [which] he may (10) beseech from Him; and that He may assist [and] protect him from (11) all illness and [from] the hostility and the wickedness of enemy. By 'Aṭṭar (12) and 'Ilumquh and by Ḏât-Ḥimyâm and by Rub' [of] Hirr[ân].

Minaean Inscriptions

ANET³, 665–67

8. A few Minaean fragmentary inscriptions discovered in El-'Ela have been interpreted as containing South Arabian parallels to the Hebrew Levite; this opinion does not seem to be right.

(1) [... and his] son 'A[w]s ... (2) [... and all what he pos]sess to Wadd as pledge ... (3) ... disturbs Waddum ... (4) ... reduced him into his subjection; and when ... (5) ... 'A]ws to Wadd against whoever would remove it ... (6) ... in the temple of ... (7) ... Yaḏkur'il, he of [the clan of] 'Aḥram ...

9. In a depression called el-Miḥyar approximately twenty minutes from the ancient capital Ma'în, J. Halévy found a stela, the four sides of which are covered with inscriptions, and only copied a part of them.

(Glaser 1278:) (1) Ḥayû, son of 'Aways, he of [the family of] Ḥazmân, (2) he of the clan of Niswar, appointed (?) and secluded (?) (3) his wife Masqî, free woman of (4) Liḥyân.

(Glaser 1256:) (1) 'Ilwahab, son of Ḥayû, he of [the family of] Namḫân, (2) he of the clan of Gabaʾân, appointed (?) (3) and secluded (?) 'Abbaʿ from (4) Gaza.

(Glaser 1252:) (1) Wahabʾil, son of Yaḥamʾil, he of [the family of] (2) Radaʿ, he of the clan of Gabaʾân, appointed (?) (3) and secluded (?) 'Absamî from (4) Sidon.

10. The following text, engraved above the door of the temple located at el-Miḥyar, mentions the restoration of this sanctuary by a Minaean king. Two symbols are on the sides of the text, a door on the left, and on the right, a hand on a square.

(1) Ḥalkarib Ṣaduq, son of 'Abyadaʿ, king of Maʿîn, built and renewed Riṣâfum, the temple of 'Attar, He of [the temple of] Qabḍum, and entrusted the temple (2) Riṣâfum to the care of 'Attar Šarqân and all the divinities of [the] tribes [united] by a god and a patron and a pact and a secret treaty against anyone who would change it and against anyone who would (3) let it come to an end and against anyone who would strip [it] and against anyone who would commit foul acts in the temple Riṣâfum, in war and peace, in both periods of earth and heaven.

11. A large inscription engraved on the wall near the western door of the ancient Minaean capital mentions the building of towers and communication trenches and also the farming of a large estate granted by the king and the high council of Maʿîn.

(1) 'Almân, son of 'Ammkarib, he of [the family of] Ḥadʾar, father of Yaʾwisʾil and Yadkurʾil and Saʿadʾil and Wahabʾil and Yasmiʿʾil, [people of the clan of] Gabaʾân, favourites of 'Abyadaʿ Yataʿ, king of Maʿîn, consecrated and built and dedicated to 'Attar, He of Qabḍum, and to Waddum and Nakraḥum, all the upper building and the pier support of six communication trenches and of six towers in the wall of the city

(2) Qarnawu, on the conduit of the quarter Ramśawu from the tower [which] the judges built, to the crossroads of the city; [those trenches and those towers] which he ['Almân] built and raised—which he covered with a roof—in wood and hewn stones, and the sloping banks of their escarpments from the building of the counter escarpment to the top, with the taxes [which] 'Attar, He of Qabḍ, imposed on him and with the first fruits he has taken for the divinities and with what he added from his own, when

(3) he offered [perfum]es to Wadd and sacrificed to 'Attar, He of Qabḍ, and to Wadd victims in [the temple] courts //15// ; and when 'Abyadaʿ Yataʿ, king of Maʿîn, and the council of Maʿîn, [deliberating]

in the high council, invested 'Almân with the administration and the organization of what has been commanded for his god and his patron and his king and his tribe in war and peace; and [when] they farmed out to him the land [which contributed to] the building

(4) by means of the income from the spinning mill of the king, forty-seven cubits //47// [in height] and in breadth seventeen cubits //17// and by means of [the] contribution [granted] by the law of Ma'în through public allocation of cereal: forty-seven ẓbr //47//; and with regard to its boundaries and its directions: from the weir [which] the clan of Ḥanḏar repaired and in the direction—upstream—of the water conduit of the clan of Hawar

(5) and the irrigation canal [which] the clan of Ganad repaired, and in the direction—on the west—of the land of Ṭanuf, and in the direction—Yaṭil—of the two water conduits of the clan of 'Amam and of the water conduit of the clan of "Ašar, in conformity with the document of his archives. By 'Aṭṭar Šarqân and by 'Aṭṭar, He of Qabḍ, and Wadd and Nakrahum and by 'Aṭṭar, He of [the temple of] Yu-hariq, and by all the divinities of Ma'în and Yaṭil, and by 'Abyada' Yaṭa', king

(6) of Ma'în, and by their tribe of Ma'în and Yaṭil. And 'Almân and his sons entrusted their offering and their farming and their usufruct to 'Aṭṭar Šarqân and 'Aṭṭar, He of Qabḍ, and to Wadd and Nakrahum and all the divinities of Ma'în and Yaṭil and Ḥirrân, the torrent of Wadd against anyone who would change them and their documents during the days of earth.

12. The present inscription, found in Ḥaribat Ma'în in 1944, mentions several offerings of buildings, possessions and animals, brought to different divinities by a family of priests of high rank, who were in the service of the lunar god Waddum and whose chief was Ḥalyafa' Fayš.

(1) Ḥalyafa' Fayš, priest of Waddum, (so)n of 'Abkarib, father of Na(ba)ṭkarib Riyyâm and 'Ilṣaduq, the two priests of Waddum, and their sons Ḥalyafa' Riyyâm and Sa'ad'il and 'A(b)karib and 'Ammsamî', [people of the] clan of Yada', consecrated and dedicated to 'Aṭṭar,

(2) He of [the temple of] Qabḍum, and to Waddum and Nakrah<>um, all the building of the tower Yahir and of its passage Rata', in wood and in hewn stones, from the foundation to the top, from the jamb of the door to the tower [which] he dedicated [in] Ḏû-Ḥaḍr ; when he sacrificed to 'Aṭṭar, He of Qabḍ,

(3) four offerings,—each including forty-four [units]—; and when he sacrificed to the divinities black cattle and sucklings in the name of all Ma'în: freemen and workers and hirelings (and) overseers of employees ; and when he sacrificed to 'Aṭṭar, He of Qabḍ, and to

(4) Waddum victims on the [temple] courts; and when he built [and] dedicated to ʿAṭṭar, He of [the temple of] Yuhariq and to Nakraḥ(um) three cubits of the wall of Yaṭil, in hewn stones, from the foundation to the top; and when he consecrated (and) dedicated to (his) god ʿAṭṭar, (He) of Qabḍ, (what) he possessed.

ANET³, 667–69

Qatabanian Inscriptions

13. A Qatabanian *mukarrib* tells us his titles, some connected with the lunar god and his sanctuaries, others relating to landed properties; and he finally mentions the dedication of some property to the moon divinity ʾAnbay; from Wâdî Beihân.

(a 1) Šahar Hilâl . . . , son of Yadaʿʿab, *mukarrib* (a 2) of Qatabân, first born of ʾAnbay and Ḥawkum, He of ʾAmar and Šamar, (b 1) procurator of the clerk of the priest of ʿAmmum (b 2) Ṭantum, priest and administrator of ʿAmm Rayʿân, (b 3) master of the possessions [which] he measured in Ḍabaḥtum (b 4) and including (the) stone-cased wells in the estate (b 5) [which the tribe] Hawrân possessed, dedicated to ʾAnbay, (b 6) master of the feast, his possession against (b 7) calamity (?).

14. The present text mentions the opening of a road in the mountains, commanded by the principal Qatabanian god ʿAmm and executed by ʾAwsʿamm, the same man who opened the road at the Meblaqah pass, according to the order of the *mukarrib* of Qatabân. On the left and the right of the lines 4–7, a bucranium and above it, a monogram.

(1) Yadaʿʿab Ḍubayyin, (2) son of Šahar, *mukarrib* of Qatabân and all the (3) children of ʿAmm and ʾAwsân and Kaḥid and (4) Dahasum and Tabnaw and Yarfaʾ, the southerners (5) and the northerners, pierced and bored and put through the mountain road (6) and the pass of Ẓarrum on the command of ʿAmm, He of [the temple of] Šaqr. By ʿAmm and by (7) ʾAnbay and by ʿAmm, He of [the temple of] Raymatum, and by ʿAmm, He of Šaqr, and by (8) Ḥawkum and by Ḍât-Ṣantum and by Ḍât- Ẓahrân and by Ḍât-Raḥbân. (9) ʾAwsʿamm, son of Yaṣurrʿamm, of [the family of] Madahum, directed and controlled all (10) the work and the boring and the paving of the pass Ẓarrum by the order of his lord (11) Yadaʿʿab.

15. This inscription engraved on Jebel Šeqîr (northeast of Hajar Ḥenû az-Zurîr) mentions a work which probably was the opening of a road, by an ordinary man who entrusted it to the care of several divinities not only for himself, but also for his children and his colonists.

(1) Nabaṭʿamm, son of Yaqahmalik, he of [the tribe of] Ḍaraʾân, performed and pierced a boring on the top of the fortified hill (2) Ḍû-Mawẓadum, for his ground Ḍû-Daraʿat and Ḍû-ʾAṭirat; and he entrusted it to the care of ʿAṭtar and ʿAmm, He of Šaqr, and (3) of Ḥawkum and Ḍât-Raḥbân for him and his children and his colonists. By ʿAṭtar and by ʿAmm and by (4) ʿAmm, He of Šaqr, and by ʾAnbay and by Ḥawkum and by Ḍât-Raḥbân and by Šahar Hilâl and his son (5) Nabaṭʿamm, both kings of Qatabân.

16. A concession is granted by a Qatabanian king to several people regarding their contribution to a temple; from Hajar Koḥlân (ancient Timnaʿ).

(1) Šahar Hilâl Yuhanʿim, son of Yadaʿʿab, king of Qatabân, granted and decreed on account of Ḥaṭabum, the temple of ʿAmm, He of Dawanum, and on account of Riṣâfum, the temple (2) of ʾAnbay Šaymân and by obedience to Šams and Rubʿ Šahar for his people ʿAmmyadaʿ and Hufnum, both sons of Haybar, and for Hawfʾil, son of Haybar (3) ʾAbân, and for Raʾabʿamm, son of Ḥayû, and for ʿAlayum and Yašriḥʿamm, both sons of Rabaḥ and to their brothers the administrators of ʿAmm, He of Labaḫ, and to their female relationship (4) and to their children: from [the] owed part and [the definitive] arrangement [as regards the preceding part] and [the] seizure and [the] income, [they may use them] to pay their due in voluntary offering and gift and promise to ʿAmm and ʾAṭirat (5), so that will be informed the administrators of ʿAmm, He of Labaḫ, and their female relationship and their sons and their daughters according to this stipulation and this concession (6). And Šahar granted to his people the administrators of ʿAmm, He of Labaḫ, and to their female relationship and to their sons by privileging them according to this stipulation and this concession and (7) his [inscribed] lines. And Šahar ordered his people the administrators of ʿAmm, He of Labaḫ, to write and engrave these [inscribed] lines on the valley of Labaḫ and in the apartment reserved to them in (8) the temple of ʿAmm, He of Labaḫ, in Ḍû-Gaylum and at the entrance Ḍû-Šadaw in Timnaʿ, in the month of Ḍû-Timnaʿ, during the second eponym of Šaharum, he of [the tribe of] Yagur. (9) And may the administrators of ʿAmm, He of Labaḫ, submit and do justice to this stipulation and this concession and to the concessions which wrote for them (10) Šahar Yagul. And Šahar signed it with his own hand.

17. Inscription found during the excavation at Ḥeid bin ʿAqîl, the cemetery of Timnaʿ, mentioning a statue as votive offering.

(1) ʾAbṣaduq ʿArim [woman of the family of]. Wahabʾil, he of [the clan of] Hirrân, (2) and he of [the clan of] Ḍaraʾân, dedicated to

'Anbay Šaymân (3) her votive offering in Riṣâfum. She entrusted [to 'Anbay's care] her female statue (4) against anyone who would change [it] from its place.

18–19. Bases of proscynemata mentioning the "identity card" of the persons who were in some way represented on the upper plate, but now actually missing.

> (30-47-28 = *RÉS* 4569) Yaṭi'um [of the family of] Faqaḍ.
> (30-47-30 = *RÉS* 4571) Na'ammum [of the family of] Waqaš.

ANET³, 669–70

Hadrami Inscriptions

20. An inscription in relief on a bronze plate commemorates its offering to the principal Ḥaḍrami lunar god and also the consecration to several divinities of two very precious things of the dedicator, the light of his eye and the thought of his heart; from Šabwa.

(1) Ṣaduqḍakar Barrân, prefect of the property of the king of Ḥaḍramawt, son of (2) 'Ilšaraḫ, dedicated to Sîn, He of [the temple of] 'Ilum, an offering in bronze of which the (3) weight is true, reddish-brown bronze—and he offered it—, which he promised to Sîn (4) as He bade him by His oracle. And Ṣaduqḍakar consecrated in submission (5) to Sîn, He of 'Ilum, and to 'Aṭṭar, his father, and to the goddesses of His temple 'Ilum, (6) and to the gods and goddesses of the city Šabwa, his person and his understanding and his (7) children and his possessions and the light of his eye and the thought of his heart as homage (8) and submission which may be agreeable."
    On the reverse of the plate, the monogram "Sa'adšamsum (?)."

21. A Ḥaḍrami king commemorates the rebuilding of the temple and the fortress of his capital which he has transformed; on the occasion he gave a hunting party which was particularly successful; engraved on the cliff called 'Uqla about 15 km. west of Šabwa.

(1) Yada"il Bayyin, king of Ḥaḍramawt, son of Rabbšams, of the freemen of Yuhab'ir, he who transformed and altered the city Šabwat (2) and rebuilt in stone the temple, roofed [and] paved the fortress, when they [the temple and the fortress] collapsed and [when] they [Yada"il and his party] killed thirty-five bovines and eighty-two young camels and twenty-five gazelles and eight cheetahs at the fortress 'Anwadum.

22. An inscription, engraved on the same cliff as the preceding, enumerates the people who accompanied their Ḥaḍrami king on a sojourn in the fortress where coronation honors were distributed.

(1) Naṣrum, son of Nahadum, and Raqšum, (2) son of 'Aḏmar, and Wa'ilum, son (3) of Yu'allid, and Wa'ilum, son of Baqilum (4), and 'Abkarib, he of [the family of] Waddum, accompanied (5) their lord 'Il'aḏḏ Yaluṭ, king of Ḥaḏramawt (6), son of 'Ammḏaḥar, when he proceeded to the fortress (7) 'Anwadum in order to sojourn and give titles.

23. A fragmentary inscribed clay stamp unearthed at Beitîn, biblical Bethel, in 1957, by James L. Kelso; 7 × 8 cm. and 1.5 cm. thick; almost identical with, but different from, the one seen by Th. Bent at al-Mašhad (about 62 km. in a straight line southeast of Šibâm, in Ḥaḏramawt) and whose paper squeeze, A 727, belongs to the Glaser collection. The inscription, identical in the two stamps, although slightly different from a palaeographic viewpoint, is the seal of a Ḥaḏrami *fdn* "delegate" living at Bethel and whose function was to authenticate with his seal, shipments of goods sent back to Ḥaḏramawt.

1 [. . . Ḥa-]
2 miyân, the de-
3 legate.

24. A Qatabanian rock inscription discovered by Major M. D. Van Lessen in the Soames Hill near the Yemeni border in the vicinity of Mukérâs, with the name of a previously unknown name of a god, whose *scriptio plena*, *'lyn*, may be graphically compared with the divine epitheton in the Old Testament, 'ĕlyôn ('*lywn*; e.g., Dt 32:8).

1 Ḥazîyân 'Ayizân
2 Laḥay has written to the honor of 'Aliyân,
3 He of one hundred years.

XII

Egyptian Execration Texts

TRANSLATOR: JOHN A. WILSON

ANET, 328–29 ## The Execration of Asiatic Princes

Fig. 153
Jer. 19:10–11 In the Middle Kingdom period the Egyptians practiced the magical cursing of their actual or potential enemies. In the Berlin Museum are fragments of pottery bowls which had been inscribed with the names of such foes and then smashed. In the Cario and Brussels Museums inscribed figurines carry the same kind of curse. As they smashed such pottery, so they thought to break the power of their enemies. The exorcised elements were Nubians, Asiatics, Libyans, hostile Egyptians, and evil forces. The translations below, from the Berlin material, gives some Asiatics, some Egyptians, and the forces.

Asiatics

(e 1) The Ruler of Iy-ʿanaq,[1] *Erum,* and all the *retainers*[2] who are with him; the Ruler of Iy-ʿanaq, Abi-*yamimu,* and all the retainers who are with him; the Ruler of Iy-ʿanaq, ʿAkirum, and all the *retainers* who are with him;

Num. 24:17 (4) the Ruler of Shutu,[3] Ayyabum,[4] and all the *retainers* who are with him; the Ruler of Shutu, Kushar and all the *retainers* who are with him; the Ruler of Shutu, Zabulanu,[5] and all the *retainers* who are with him; . . .

Deut. 2:10 [1] Many of the geographic names are unknown, and identifications for most of the others must be tentative. The present name has been related to the ʿAnaqim "giants" who were in the land of Canaan at the time of the Conquest.

[2] Taken as the Egyptian word for "trusted men." Perhaps the same word as the *hanik* of Gen. 14:14.

[3] Probably Moab.

[4] Job; cuneiform Ayyab.

[5] Similarly cuneiform, for Zebulon.

(23) the Ruler of Asqanu,[6] *Khalu-kim*, and all the *retainers* who are with him; . . .

(27) the Ruler of Jerusalem, Yaqar-ʿAmmu, and all the *retainers* who are with him; the Ruler of Jerusalem, *Setj*-ʿAnu, and all the *retainers* who are with him; . . .[7]

(31) all the rulers of *Iysipi* and all the *retainers* who are with them;

(f 1) all the Asiatics—of Byblos, of Ullaza, of Iy-ʿanaq of Shutu, of *Iymuʿaru*, of *Qehermu*, of *Rehob*,[8] of Yarimuta, of *Inhia*, of *Aqhi*, of ʿArqata,[9] of Yarimuta, of *Isinu*,[10] of Asqanu, of *Demitiu*, of *Mut-ilu*, of Jerusalem of ʿAkhmut, of *Iahenu*, and of *Iysipi*;

(g 1) their strong men, their swift runners, their allies, their associates, and the Mentu[11] in Asia;

(h 1) who may rebel, who may plot, who may fight who may talk of fighting, or who may talk of rebelling—in this entire land.

Egyptians

(m 1) All men, all people, all folk, all males, all *eunuchs,* all women, and all officials,

(n 1) who may rebel, who may plot, who may fight, who may talk of fighting, or who may talk of rebelling, and every rebel who talks of rebelling—in this entire land.

Josh. 1:18

(o 1) Ameni shall die, the tutor of Sit-Bastet, the *chancellor* of Sit-Hat-Hor, (daughter of) Nefru.[12]

Sen-Usert the younger, called Ketu, shall die, the tutor of Sit-Ipi, (daughter of) Sit-Hat-Hor, and tutor of Sit-Ipi, (daughter of) Sit-Ameni, the *chancellor* of Ii-menet, (daughter of) Sit-Hat-Hor . . .

(8) Ameni, born to Hetep and son of Sen-Usert, shall die.

Baneful Forces

(p 1) Every evil word, every evil speech, every evil slander, every evil thought, every evil plot, every evil fight, every evil quarrel, every evil plan, every evil thing, all evil dreams, and all evil slumber.

---

[6] Ashkelon; cuneiform Ashqaluna.

[7] The figurines in Brussels and Cairo have further identifiable names.

[8] Probably any one of several Rehobs.

[9] Or ʿIraqtum, another name for the same, in Phoenicia.

[10] This has been compared to (Beth)-Shan.

[11] The "Mentu is Setet" is an old designation of Egypt's immediate neighbors to the northeast.

[12] There are two significant factors about these specifically named Egyptians. First, the names are names characteristic of the Twelfeth Dynasty royal family. Second, several of them are functionaries of women who seem to be princesses or queens. One thinks of the harem conspiracy as the setting for such curses.

Egyptian Hymns

TRANSLATOR: JOHN A. WILSON

ANET, 369–71

The Hymn to the Aton

The Pharaoh Amen-hotep IV broke with the established religion of Egypt and instituted the worship of the Aton, the sun disc, as the source of life. The "Amarna Revolution" attempted a distinct break with Egypt's traditional and static ways of life in religion, politics, art, and literature. Pharaoh changed his name to Akh-en-Aton (perhaps "He Who Is Serviceable to the Aton") and moved his capital from Thebes to Tell el-Amarna. Pharaoh's own attitude to the god is expressed in the famous hymn which follows. Beyond doubt, the hymn shows the universality and beneficence of the creating and re-creating sun disc. A similarity of spirit and wording to the 104th Psalm has often been noted, and a direct relation between the two has been argued.[1] Because Akh-en-Aton was devoted to this god alone, the Amarna religion has been called monotheistic. This is a debatable question, and a reserved attitude would note that only Akh-en-Aton and his family worshiped the Aton, Akh-en-Aton's courtiers worshiped Akh-en-Aton himself, and the great majority of Egyptians was ignorant of or hostile to the new faith.

Figs. 108, 110

Praise of Re Har-akhti, Rejoicing on the Horizon, in His Name as Shu Who Is in the Aton-disc,[2] living forever and ever; the living great Aton who is in jubilee, lord of all that the Aton encircles, lord of heaven, lord of earth, lord of the House of Aton in Akhet-Aton;[3] (and praise of) the King of Upper and Lower Egypt, who lives on truth, the Lord of the Two Lands: Nefer-kheperu-Re Wa-en-Re; the Son of

---

[1] As in J. H. Breasted, *The Dawn of Conscience* (New York, 1933), 281–86.

[2] The Aton had a dogmatic name written within a royal cartouche and including the three old solar deities, Re, Har-of-the-Horizon, and Shu.

[3] Akhet-Aton was the name of the capital at Tell el-Amarna.

Re, who lives on truth, the Lord of Diadems: Akh-en-Aton, long in his lifetime; (and praise of) the Chief Wife of the King, his beloved, the Lady of the Two Lands: Nefer-neferu-Aton Nefert-iti, living, healthy, and youthful forever and ever; (by) the Fan-Bearer on the Right Hand of the King . . . Eye. He says:

Thou appearest beautifully on the horizon of heaven,
Thou living Aton, the beginning of life!
When thou art risen on the eastern horizon,
Thou hast filled every land with thy beauty.
Thou art gracious, great, glistening, and high over every land;
Thy rays encompass the lands to the limit of all that thou hast
    made:
As thou art Re, thou reachest to the end of them;[4]
(Thou) subduest them (for) thy beloved son.[5]
Though thou art far away, thy rays are on earth;
Though thou art in *their* faces, *no one knows thy* going.

When thou settest in the western horizon,
The land is in darkness, in the manner of death.
They sleep in a room, with heads wrapped up,
Nor sees one eye the other.
All their goods which are under their heads might be stolen,
(But) they would nor perceive (it).
Every lion is come forth from his den;
All creeping things, they sting.
Darkness *is a shroud,* and the earth is in stillness,
For he who made them rests in his horizon.   Ps. 104:20–21

At daybreak, when thou arisest on the horizon,
When thou shinest as the Aton by day,
Thou drivest away the darkness and givest thy rays.
The Two Lands are in festivity *every day,*
Awake and standing upon (their) feet,
For thou hast raised them up.
Washing their bodies, taking (their) clothing,   (5)
Their arms are (raised) in praise at thy appearance.
All the world, they do their work.   Ps. 104:22–23

All beasts are content with their pasturage;
Trees and plants are flourishing.
The birds which fly from their nests,
Their wings are (stretched out) in praise to thy *ka.*
All beasts spring upon (their) feet.

---

[4] Pun: *Ra* "Re," and *er-ra* "to the end."
[5] Akh-en-Aton.

Whatever flies and alights,

Ps. 104:11–14   They live when thou hast risen (for) them.

The ships are sailing north and south as well,
For every way is open at thy appearance.
The fish in the river dart before thy face;

Ps. 104:25–26   Thy rays are in the midst of the great green sea.

Creator of seed in women,
Thou who makest fluid into man,
Who maintainest the son in the womb of his mother,
Who soothest him with that which stills his weeping,
Thou nurse (even) in the womb,
Who givest breath to sustain all that he has made!
When he descends from the womb to *breathe*
On the day when he is born,
Thou openest his mouth completely,
Thou suppliest his necessities.
☞ When the chick in the egg speaks within the shell,
Thou, givest him breath within it to maintain him.
When thou hast made him his fulfillment within the egg, to break it,
He comes forth from the egg to speak at his completed (time);
He walks upon his legs when he comes forth from it.

Ps. 40:5   How manifold it is, what thou hast made!

They are hidden from the face (of man).
O sole god, like whom there is no other!
Thou didst create the world according to thy desire,

Ps. 104:24   Whilst thou wert alone:

All men, cattle, and wild beasts,
Whatever is on earth, going upon (its) feet,
And what is on high, flying with its wings.

The countries of Syria and Nubia, the *land* of Egypt,
Thou settest every man in his place,
Thou suppliest their necessities:

Ps. 90:10   Everyone has his food, and his time of life is reckoned.

Ps. 104:27   Their tongues are separate in speech,

And their natures as well;
Their skins are distinguished,
As thou distinguishest the foreign peoples.
Thou makest a Nile in the underworld,
Thou bringest it forth as thou desirest
To maintain the people (of Egypt)[6]

---

[6] The Egyptians believed that their Nile came from the waters under the earth, called by them Nun.

According as thou madest them for thyself,
The lord of all of them, wearying (himself) with them,
The lord of every land, rising for them,
The Aton of the day, great of majesty.

All distant foreign countries, thou makest their life (also),
For thou hast set a Nile in heaven,
That it may descend for them and make waves upon
    the mountains,   (10)   Ps. 104:6, 10
Like the great green sea,
To water their fields in their towns.[7]
How effective they are, thy plans, O lord of eternity!
The Nile in heaven, it is for the foreign peoples
And for the beasts of every desert that go upon (their) feet;
(While the true) Nile comes from the underworld for Egypt.

Thy rays suckle every meadow.
When thou risest, they live, they grow for thee.
Thou makest the seasons in order to rear all that thou hast made,   Ps. 104:19
The winter to cool them,
And the heat that *they* may taste thee.
Thou hast made the distant sky in order to rise therein,
In order to see all that thou dost make.
Whilst thou wert alone,
Rising in thy form as the living Aton,
Appearing, shining, *withdrawing or approaching,*
Thou madest millions of forms of thyself alone.
Cities, towns, fields, road, and river—
Every eye beholds thee over against them,
For thou art the Aton of the day over *the earth. . . .*

Thou art in my heart,
And there is no other that knows thee
Save thy son Nefer-kheperu-Re Wa-en-Re,[8]
For thou hast made him well-versed in thy plans and in thy
    strength.[9]

The world came into being by thy hand,
According as thou hast made them.
When thou hast risen they live,   Ps. 104:30
When thou settest they die.   Ps. 104:29

---

[7] The rain of foreign countries is like the Nile of rainless Egypt.

[8] Even though the hymn was recited by the official Eye, he states that Akh-en-Aton alone knows the Aton.

[9] Pharaoh was the official intermediary between the Egyptians and their gods. The Amarna religion did not change this dogma.

Thou art lifetime thy own self,
For one lives (only) through thee.
Eyes are (fixed) on beauty until thou settest.
All work is laid aside when thou settest in the west.
(But) when (thou) risest (again),
[*Everything is*] made to flourish for the king, . . .
Since thou didst found the earth
And raise them up for thy son,
Who came forth from thy body:
the King of Upper and Lower Egypt, . . . Akh-en-Aton, . . . and the
    Chief Wife of the King . . . Nefert-iti, living and youthful
    forever and ever.

Nefertiti

Hymn of Victory of Mer-ne-Ptah ("The Israel Stela")

ANET, 376, 378

The date of this commemorative hymn (or series of hymns) relates it to Mer-ne-Ptah's victory over the Libyans in the spring of his fifth year (about 1230 B.C.). However, the text is not historical in the same sense as two other records of that victory, but is rather a poetic eulogy of a universally victorious pharaoh. Thus it was not out of place to introduce his real or figurative triumph over Asiatic peoples in the last poem of the hymn. In that context we meet the only instance of the name "Israel" in ancient Egyptian writing.

. . . .
The princes are prostrate, saying: "Mercy!"[10]   *coalition of Canaanites*
    Not one raises his head among the Nine Bows.
Desolation is for Tehenu; Hatti is pacified;
    Plundered is the Canaan with every evil;
Carried off is Ashkelon; seized, upon is Gezer;
    Yanoam is made as that which does not exist;[11]

Fig. 96
Jer. 49:10
Lam. 1:1

Israel is laid waste, his seed is not;[12]

[10] Or "Peace!" The Canaanite word *shalam* is used here.

[11] Hatti was the land of the Hittites. Yanoam was an important town of northern Palestine.

[12] Much has been made of the fact that the word "Israel" is the only one of the names in this context which is written with the determinative of people rather than land. Thus we should seem to have the Children of Israel in or near Palestine, but not yet as a settled people. This would have important bearing on the date of the Conquest. This is a valid argument. Determinatives should have meaning, and a contrast between determinatives in the same context should be significant. This stela does give the country determinatives to settled peoples like the Rebu, Temeh, Hatti, Ashkelon, etc., and the determinative of people to unlocated groups like the Madjoi, Nau, and

Hurra is become a widow for Egypt![13]
All lands together, they are pacified;
Everyone who was restless, he has been bound by the King of Upper and Lower Egypt: Ba-en-Re Meri-Amon; the Son of Re: Mer-ne-Ptah Hotep-hir-Maat, given life like Re every day.

Tekten. The argument is good, but not conclusive, because of the notorious carelessness of Late-Egyptian scribes and several blunders of writing in this stela.

The statement that the "seed," i.e., offspring, of Israel had been wiped out is a conventional boast of power at this period.

[13] The land of the biblical Horites, or Greater Palestine.

1. Ö 1st historical mention of Israel

2. Ö It is a propaganda text
   b/c canaanites were revolting
   against Egypt.
   " claiming victory when they
       were losing"

archaeology : seca drop of Egyptian
              Culture

Israel is a proper name, note: → Semi-nomadic tribes moving into Canaan
Egyptians wrote in hieroglyphics
letter aloph - bull w/ horns
   X k A ∀ ⊥

* Issue in hieroglyphics -
   as a reader, you do not know
   what the name refers to w/o a clue.
→ After each inscription you see a picture
   to say what it is.

Mesopotamian Hymns

Sumerian Hymns
TRANSLATOR: S. N. KRAMER

ANET³, 576–77   ## Hymn to Ninurta as God of Vegetation

This is a rather rare type of lyrical hymn addressed to Ninurta as the deity in charge of fertility and vegetation.[1] The poem begins with a four-line strophe typical of Sumerian hymnal compositions, in which the first two lines and second two lines are identical except that the epithet of the first half of the strophe is replaced by the proper name to which it belongs. Then follows at least three strophes of three lines each characterized by a simple, though not ineffective repetition pattern.

> (obv.)
> Life-giving semen, life-giving seed,   (1)
> King whose name was pronounced by Enlil,
> Life-giving semen, life-giving seed,
> Ninurta whose name was pronounced by Enlil.
>
> My king, I will pronounce your name again and again,
> Ninurta, I your man, your man,
> I will pronounce your name again and again.

[1] Ninurta was conceived and worshipped in a rather contradictory twofold aspect. As the deity in charge of the South Wind, he is the god of battle who destroys the rebellious land, and in accordance with some as yet unknown Sumerian myth, avenges his father Enlil. On the other hand Ninurta is "the farmer of Enlil," and as such is of course the god of fertility, prosperity, and long life. It is this latter aspect of Ninurta that the poet of this hymn exalts in lyric song.

My king, the ewe has given birth to the lamb,
The ewe has given birth to the lamb, the ewe has given birth to the
    good sheep,
I will pronounce your name again and again.   (10)

My king, the mother-goat [has given birth] to the kid,
[The mother-goat] has given birth [to the kid, the mother-goat] has
    given birth [to the goat]
[I will pronounce your name again and again]
              (remainder of obv. destroyed)
    (rev.)
. . . .   (1)
The king . . . .
As long as he was king . . . .
In the river [there flowed fresh water].
In the field grew the rich grain.
The sea was filled with carp and . . . -fish.
In the canebrake grew "old" reeds and young reeds,
The forests were filled with deer and wild goats,
In the steppe grew the *mashgur*-tree,
The watered gardens were filled with honey (and) wine,   (10)
In the palace "grew" long life.

It is a *balbale*-song.

Hymn to Ninurta as a God of Wrath   ANET³, 577

This composition exalts Ninurta as a god of wrath who roams about in the night, and is dedicated to battle, like the pest-god Irra; he is a monstrous dragon and venomous snake who crushes the evil and rebellious lands; he is a judge whose verdict is awesome; he brings about the destruction of the enemy and of the contentious and disobedient. Structurally, the entire poem consists of two-line strophes, with each line divided into two hemistichs; the two lines are identical except that the first begins with "My king," and the second with "Lord Ninurta."

[My king . . .
    Who like Irra roams about in the night,]
[Lord Ninurta] . . .
    Who like Irra roams about in the night.
[My king] who like Irra has perfected heroship,
    Dragon with the "hands" of a lion, the *claws* of an eagle,
Lord Ninurta who like Irra has perfected heroship,
    Dragon with the "hands" of a lion, the *claws* of an eagle,

My king who vanquishes the houses of the rebellious lands, great
    lord of Enlil,
    You, with power you are endowed.
Lord Ninurta who vanquishes the houses of the rebellious lands,
    great lord of Enlil,
    You, with power you are endowed.

My king, when your heart was seized (by anger),
    You spat venom like a snake,
Lord Ninurta, when your heart was seized (by anger),
    You spat venom like a snake,

My king, toothed (*pickaxe*) that uproots the evil land,
    Arrow that breaks up the rebellious land,
Lord Ninurta, toothed (*pickaxe*) that uproots the evil land,   (10)
    Arrow that breaks up the rebellious land,

My king, your verdict is a great verdict, ineffable,
    Your word no *god* can gaze upon,
Lord Ninurta, your verdict is a great verdict, ineffable,
    Your word, no *god* can gaze upon.

My king, when you approached the enemy, you scattered him like
    rushes,
    You meted out to him . . . ,
Lord Ninurta, when you approached the enemy, you scattered him
    like rushes,
    You meted out to him . . . ,

[My king], of the house of the foe you are its adversary,
    Of his city, you are its enemy,
Lord Ninurta, of the house of the foe, you are its adversary,
    Of his city, you are its enemy.

[My king], of the house of the contentious (and) disobedient, you
    are its adversary,
    Of their city, you are its enemy.
Lord Ninurta, of the house of the contentious (and) disobedient,
    you are its adversary,
    Of their city, you are its enemy.

Hymnal Prayer of Enheduanna:
ANET³, 579–82 # The Adoration of Inanna of Ur

This remarkable composition, whose text is virtually complete, consists of
two unequal parts. The first, and the longer by far (lines 1–142), is a hymnal
prayer to Inanna, purportedly uttered by Enheduanna, the daughter of

Sargon the Great, founder of the Dynasty of Akkad, who appointed her as *en,* or high-priestess of Nanna (also known as Sin) the tutelary deity of Ur. The second, and very brief, section (lines 143–50) contains the author's pronouncement that Enheduanna's prayer had been accepted by the goddess, who was now made welcome in Ur by Nanna and his wife Ningal. The document is of significance for the religious and political history of Sumer, though unfortunately not a little of its content is ambiguous and obscure.

Enheduanna begins her orison to Inanna as the deity in charge of all the *me,* the divine norms, duties, and powers, assigned to all cosmic and cultural entities at the time of creation, in order to keep them operating harmoniously and perpetually (lines 1–8). She then proceeds to depict the more cruel, destructive, and vindictive aspects of the goddess: she is a venomous, thundering, flood-and-fire raining deity whose rites are unfathomable (lines 9–16); she is an awesome storm deity before whom all mankind trembles and quakes (lines 17–28); she is an irate, relentless, and intractable goddess of war before whom even the great gods flee in terror (lines 26–42); she is the cruel conqueror of Mt. Ebih and its rebellious people (lines 43–50); as the goddess of love, as well as war, she deprives the unsubmissive city of all procreation and vegetation (lines 51–57).

Following a brief chant of adoration of Inanna as a great, wise, merciful and life-giving goddess (lines 58–65), comes a long passage in which Enheduanna pictures the misery and suffering that have overtaken her (lines 66–108); it is this passage that is interspersed with what seem to be several references to political events. This is followed in turn by a brief prayer of the high-priestess to Inanna as her dear and powerful queen to keep her out of her bitter straits (109–21). Enheduanna then proceeds to invoke Inanna with a resounding magnificat that recounts her immense powers, and closes with a plea to the goddess to turn a friendly heart to her adoring, devout, and pious votary (lines 122–42). The composition concludes with Inanna's, acceptance of Enheduanna's supplication (lines 143–50), and a summary three-line invocation of the goddess by the author-poet (lines 151–53).

Queen of all the *me,* radiant light,   (1)
Life-giving woman, beloved of An (and) Urash,
Hierodule of An, much bejewelled,
Who loves the life-giving tiara, fit for *en*-ship,
Who grasps in (her) hand, the seven *me,*
My queen, you who are the guardian of all the great *me,*
You have lifted the *me,* have tied the *me* to your hands,
Have gathered the *me,* pressed the *me* to your breast.

You have filled the land with venom, like a dragon.
Vegetation ceases, when you thunder like Ishkur,   (10)
You who bring down the Flood from the mountain,
Supreme one, who are the Inanna of heaven (and) earth,

Who rain flaming fire over the land,
Who have been given the *me* by An, queen who rides the beasts,
Who at the holy command of An, utters the (divine) words,
Who can fathom your great rites!

Destroyer of the foreign lands, you have given wings to the storm,
Beloved of Enlil you made it (the storm) blow over the land,
You carried out the instructions of An.
My queen, the foreign lands cower at your cry,   (20)
In dread (and) fear of the South Wind, mankind
Brought you their anguished clamor,
Took before you their anguished *outcry*
Opened before you wailing and weeping,
Brought before you the "great" lamentations in the city streets.

In the van of battle, everything was struck down before you,
My queen, you are all devouring in your power,
You kept on attacking like an attacking storm,
Kept on blowing (louder) than the howling storm,
Kept on thundering (louder) than Ishkur,   (30)
Kept on moaning (louder) than the evil winds,
Your feet grew not weary,
You caused wailing to be uttered on the "lyre of lament."

My queen, the Anunna, the great gods,
Fled before you like fluttering bats,
Could not stand before your awesome face,
Could not approach your awesome forehead.
Who can soothe your angry heart!
Your baleful heart is beyond soothing!
Queen, happy of "liver," joyful of heart,   (40)
(But) whose anger cannot be soothed, daughter of Sin,
Queen, paramount in the land, who has (ever) paid you (enough)
    homage!

The mountain who kept from paying homage to you—vegetation
    became "tabu" for it,
You burnt down its great gates,
Its rivers ran with blood because of you, its people had nothing to
    drink,
Its troops were led off willingly (into captivity) before you,
Its forces disbanded themselves willingly before you,
Its strong men paraded willingly before you,
The amusement places of its cities were filled with turbulence,
Its adult males were driven off as captives before you.   (50)

Against the city that said not "yours is the land,"
That said not "It belongs to the father who begot you,"

You promised your holy word, turned away from it,
Kept your distance from its womb,
Its woman spoke not of love with her husband,
In the deep night she whispered not (tenderly) with him,
Revealed not to him the "holiness" of her heart.

Rampant wild cow, elder daughter of Sin,
Queen, greater than An, who has (ever) paid you (enough) homage!
You who in accordance with the life giving *me*, great queen of
    queens,   (60)
Have become greater than your mother who gave birth to you, (as
    soon as) you came forth from the holy womb,
Knowing, wise, queen of all the lands,
Who multiplies (all) living creatures (and) peoples—
    I have uttered your holy song.
Life-giving goddess, fit for the *me*, whose acclamation is exalted,
Merciful, life-giving woman, radiant of heart, I have uttered it
    before you in accordance with the *me*.

I have entered before you in my holy *gipar*,
I the *en*, Enheduanna,
Carrying the *masab*-basket, I uttered a joyous chant,
(But now) I no longer dwell in the goodly place you established.
Came the day, the sun scorched me   (70)
Came the shade (of night), the South Wind overwhelmed me,
My honey-sweet voice has become *strident*,
Whatever gave me pleasure has turned into dust.

Oh Sin, king of heaven, my (bitter) fate,
To An declare, An will deliver me,
Pray declare it to An, he will deliver me.

The kingship of heaven has been seized by the woman (Inanna),
At whose feet lies the flood-land.
That woman (Inanna) so exalted, who has made me tremble
    together the city (Ur),
Stay *her*, let her heart be soothed by me.   (80)
I, Enheduanna will offer supplications to her,
My tears, like sweet drinks.
Will I proffer to the holy Inanna, I will greet her in peace,
Let not Ashimbabbar (Sin) be troubled.

She (Inanna) has changed altogether the rites of holy An,
Has seized the Eanna from An,
Feared not the great An,
That house (the Eanna) whose charm was irresistible, whose allure
    was unending,

That house she has turned over to destruction,
Her . . . that she brought there has . . .   (90)
My wild cow (Inanna) assaults there its men, makes them captive.

I, what am I among the living creatures!
May An give over (to punishment) the rebellious lands that hate
      your (Inanna's) Nanna,
May An split its cities asunder,
May Enlil curse it,
May not its tear-destined child be soothed by her mother,

Oh queen who established lamentations,
Your "boat of lamentations," has *landed* in an inimical land,
There will I die, while singing the holy song.
As for me, my Nanna watched not over me,   (100)
I have been attacked most cruelly.
Ashimbabbar has not spoken my verdict.
But what matter, whether he spoke it or not!
I, accustomed to triumph, have been driven forth from (my) house,
Was forced to flee the cote like a swallow, my life is devoured,
Was made to walk among the mountain thorns,
The life-giving tiara of *en*-ship was taken from me,
Eunuchs were assigned to me—"These are becoming to you," it was
      told me.

Dearest queen, beloved of An,
Let your holy heart, the noble, return to me,   (110)
Beloved wife of Ushumgalanna (Dumuzi),
Great queen of the horizon and the zenith,
The Anunna have prostrated themselves before you.
Although at birth you were the younger *sister,*
How much greater you have become than the Anunna, the great
      gods!
The Anunna kiss the ground before you.

It is not my verdict that has been completed, it is a strange verdict
     that has been *turned* into my verdict,
The fruitful bed has been abolished,
(So that) I have not interpreted to man the commands of Ningal.
For me, the radiant *en* of Nanna,   (120)
May your heart be soothed, you who are the queen beloved of An.
"You are known, you are known"—it is not of Nanna that I have
     recited it, it is of you that I have recited it.
"You are known by your heaven-like height,
You are known by your earth-like breadth,
You are known by your destruction of rebel-lands,
You are known by your massacring (their people),

You are known by your devouring (their) dead like a dog,
You are known by your fierce countenance.
You are known by the raising of your fierce countenance,
You are known by your flashing eyes. (130)
You are known by your *contentiousness* (and) disobedience,
You are known by your many triumphs"—
It is not of Nanna that I have recited it, it is of you that I have
    recited it.
My queen, I have extolled you, who alone are exalted,
Queen beloved of An, I have *erected* your daises,
Have heaped up the coals, have conducted the rites,
Have set up the nuptial chamber for you, may your heart be
    soothed for me,
Enough, more than enough innovations, great queen, have I made
    for you.
What I have recited to you in the deep night,
The *gala*-singer will repeat for you in midday. (140)
It is because of your captive spouse, your captive son,
That your wrath is so great, your heart so unappeased.
The foremost queen, the prop of the *assembly*,
Accepted her prayer.
The heart of Inanna was restored,
The day was favorable for her, she was clothed with beauty, was
    filled with joyous allure,
How she carried (her) beauty—like the rising moonlight!
Nanna who came forth in wonder true, (and) her mother Ningal,
    proffered prayers to her,
Greeted her at the doorsill (of the temple). (150)
To the hierodule whose command is noble,
The destroyer of foreign lands, presented by An with the *me*,
My queen garbed in allure, O Inanna, praise!

The King of the Road: A Self-Laudatory Shulgi Hymn

ANET³, 584–86

This rather unusual hymn, that is partly narrative in character, is of considerable significance not only for the nature and role of the institution of kingship in Sumer, but also for such little known aspects of its cultural life as communications and athletic prowess. It begins with a hyperbolic itemizing of Shulgi's virtues and endowments, including those granted him as a favorite of the great gods, that is typical of Sumerian royal hymnography, except that, rather surprisingly they include love of the road and a passion for speed (lines 1–19). Moreover, following another brief, typical eulogistic passage (lines 20–26), Shulgi elaborates on his great interest in travel, claiming that he saw to it that the roads of the land were always in good repair, and that he constructed on them resthouses for the weary traveller (lines 27–35). He then asserts that, eager to establish his name and fame as a champion runner, he made a journey from Nippur to Ur, a distance of fifteen "double hours"—roughly about 100 miles—as if it were only a distance of one "double hour" (lines 36–45). Arriving at Ur amidst the plaudits of the multitudes, he offered immense sacrifices in the Ekishnugal, the far-famed temple of Sin, to the accompaniment of music and song (lines 46–54). After resting, bathing, and eating in his palace, he returned to Nippur in spite of a raging hailstorm, and thus could celebrate the *ešeš*-feasts in both Ur and Nippur on one and the same day (lines 55–78). There in Nippur, moreover he banqueted with the sun-god Utu, and his (Shulgi's) divine spouse, the fertility goddess Inanna (lines 79–85). There, too, An invested him with the royal insignia, so that he became a mighty king whose power and glory were exalted in the four corners of the universe (lines 86–101).

I, the king, a hero from the (mother's) womb am I,	(1)
I, Shulgi, a mighty man from (the day) I was born am I,	
A fierce-eyed lion, born of the *ushumgal* am I,	
King of the four corners (of the universe) am I,	
Herdsman, shepherd of the blackheads am I,	
The trustworthy, the god of all the lands am I,	
The son born of Ninsun am I,	
Called to the heart of holy An am I,	
He who was blessed by Enlil am I,	
Shulgi, the beloved of Ninlil am I,	(10)
Faithfully nurtured by Nintu am I,	
Endowed with wisdom by Enki am I,	
The mighty king of Nanna am I,	
The open-jawed lion of Utu am I,	
Shulgi chosen for the vulva of Inanna am I,	
A princely donkey all set for the road am I,	
A horse that swings (his) tail on the highway am I,	
A noble donkey of Sumugan eager for the course am I,	
The wise scribe of Nidaba am I.	
Like my heroship, like my might,	(20)
I am accomplished in wisdom (as well),	
I *vie* with its (wisdom's) true word,	
I love justice,	
I do not love evil,	
I hate the evil word,	
I, Shulgi, a mighty king, supreme, am I.	
Because I am a powerful man rejoicing in his "loins,"	

I *enlarged* the footpaths, straightened the highways of the land,
I made secure travel, built there "big houses,"
Planted gardens alongside of them, established
    resting-places,   (30)
Settled there friendly folk,
(So that) who comes from below, who come from above,
Might refresh themselves in its cool (shade),
The wayfarer who travels the highway at night,
Might find refuge there like in a well-built city.

That my name be established unto distant days that it leave not the
    mouth (of men),
That my praise be spread wide in the land,
That I be *eulogized* in all the lands,
I, the runner, rose in my strength, *all set* for the course,
(And) from Nippur to Ur,   (40)
I resolved to traverse as if it were (but a distance) of one *danna*.

Like a lion that wearies not of its virility, I arose,
Put a *girdle* about my loins,
I swing (my) arms like a dove feverishly fleeing a snake,
I spread wide the knees like the Indugud-bird that has lifted (its)
    eye toward the mountain.
(The inhabitants of) the cities that I had established in the land,
    swarmed all about me,
My blackheaded people, as numerous as ewes, marvelled at me,
Like a mountain-kid hurrying to its shelter,
(As) Utu who sheds (his) broad light on (man's) habitations,
I entered the Ekishnugal,   (50)
Filled with abundance the great stall, the house of Sin,
Slaughtered there oxen, multiplied (the slaughtering of) sheep,
Made resound there the drum and the timbrel,
Took charge there of the *tigi*-music, the sweet.

I, Shulgi, the all bountiful, brought there bread-offerings,
Have inspired dread from (my) royal seat like a lion,
In the lofty palace of Ninegal,
I *rested* (my) knees, bathed in fresh water,
Bent (my) knees, ate bread,
Like an owl (and) a falcon I arose,   (60)
Returned to Nippur in my . . .

On that day, the storm howled, the tempest swirled,
Northwind (and) Southwind roared eagerly,
Lightning devoured in heaven alongside the seven winds,
The deafening storm made the earth tremble,

Ishkur thundered throughout the heavenly expanse,
The winds on high embraced the waters below,
Its (the storm's) little stones, its big stones,
Lashed at my back.

(But) I, the king was unafraid, uncowed, (70)
Like a young lion (prepared to) *spring* I shook myself *loose,*
Like a donkey of the steppe, I *covered up* my . . . ,
My heart full of happiness *took delight* in the course,
Coursing like a noble donkey travelling all alone,
Like Utu eager (to come) home,
I traversed the journey of 15 *danna* (in distance),
My *sagursag* gazed at me (in wonder),
As in one (and the same) day I celebrated the *ešeš*-feasts in (both)
    Ur (and) Nippur.

With valiant Utu my brother and friend,
I drank strong drink in the palace founded by An, (80)
My minstrels sang for me the seven *tigi*-songs.
By the side of my spouse, the maid Inanna, the queen, the "vulva"
    of heaven (and) earth,
I sat at its (the palace's) banquet.
She spoke not my *judgment* as a (final) judgment,
Wheresoever I lift my eyes, thither I go,
Wheresoever my heart moves me, thither I proceed.

An set the holy crown upon my head,
Made me take the scepter in the "lapis-lazuli" Ekur,
On the radiant dais, he raised heaven high the firmly founded
    throne,
He exalted there the power of (my) kingship. (90)
I bent low all the lands, made secure the people,
The four-corners of the universe, the people in *unison*, call my
    name,
Chant holy songs,
Pronounce my exaltation (saying):

"He that is nurtured by the exalted power of kingship,
Presented by Sin, out of the Ekishnugal,
With heroship, might, and a good life,
Endowed with lofty power by Nunamnir,
Shulgi, the destroyer of all the foreign lands, who makes all the
    people secure,
Who in accordance with the *me* of the universe, (100)
Shulgi, cherished by the trusted son of An (Sin)!"
Oh, Nidaba, praise!

An Akkadian Hymn

Translator: Ferris J. Stephens

Hymn to Ishtar

ANET, 383

After extolling the charms and virtues of the goddess, the hymn concludes by enumerating the blessings which she has bestowed upon the king, Ammiditana. While these are represented as accomplished facts, the statements should be taken as indications of the hope of the king for their eventual realization. The text publication does not indicate the provenience of the tablet. It was written in the latter part of the First Dynasty of Babylon, approximately 1600 B.C. Text: *RA*, xxii, 170–71; translation: *RA*, xxii, 174–77; metrical transcription: *ZA*, xxxviii, 19–22.

Praise the goddess, the most awesome of the goddesses.
Let one revere the mistress of the peoples, the greatest of the Igigi.[2]
Praise Ishtar, the most awesome of the goddesses.
Let one revere the queen of women, the greatest of the Igigi.

She is clothed with pleasure and love.   Song of Sol. 4:1–3
She is laden with vitality, charm, and voluptuousness.
Ishtar is clothed with pleasure and love.
She is laden with vitality, charm, and voluptuousness.

In lips she is sweet; life is in her mouth.
At her appearance rejoicing becomes full.   (10)
She is glorious; veils are thrown over her head.
Her figure is beautiful; her eyes are brilliant.

The goddess—with her there is counsel.
The fate of everything she holds in her hand.
At her glance there is created joy,
Power, magnificence, the protecting deity and guardian spirit.

She dwells in, she pays heed to compassion and friendliness.
Besides, agreeableness she truly possesses.
Be it slave, unattached girl, or mother, she preserves (her).
One calls on her; among women one names her name.   (20)

Who—to her greatness who can be equal?
Strong, exalted, splendid are her decrees.
Ishtar—to her greatness who can be equal?
Strong, exalted, splendid are her decrees.

---

[2] A collective name for the great gods of heaven.

She is sought after among the gods; extraordinary is her station.
Respected is her word; it is *supreme* over them.
Ishtar among the gods, extraordinary is her station.
Respected is her word; it is *supreme* over them.

She is their queen; they continually cause her commands to be
    executed.
All of them bow down before her.   (30)
They receive her light before her.
Women and men indeed revere her.

In their assembly her word is powerful; it is dominating.
Before Anum their king she fully supports them.
She rests in intelligence, cleverness, (and) wisdom.
They take counsel together, she and her lord.

Indeed they occupy the throne room together.
In the divine chamber, the dwelling of joy,
Before them the gods take their places.
To their utterances their attention is turned.

The king their favorite, beloved of their hearts,
Magnificently offers to them his pure sacrifices.
Ammiditana, as the pure offering of his hands,
Brings before them fat oxen and gazelles.

From Anum, her consort, she has been pleased to ask for him
An enduring, a long life.
Many years of living, to Ammiditana
She has granted, Ishtar has decided to give.

By her orders she has subjected to him
The four world regions at his feet;
And the total of all peoples
She has decided to attach them to his yoke.

Didactic and Wisdom Literature

Egyptian Instructions
TRANSLATOR: JOHN A. WILSON

The Instruction of the Vizier Ptah-hotep   ANET, 412–14

The Egyptians delighted in compilations of wise sayings, which were direc-
tive for a successful life. To them, this was "wisdom." One of the earliest of
these compilations purports to come from Ptah-hotep, the vizier of King
Izezi of the Fifth Dynasty (about 2450 B.C.). The old councilor is supposed to
be instructing his son and designated successor on the actions and attitudes
which make a successful official of the state. Excerpts from the document
follow.

. . . . Then he said to his son:

Let not thy heart be puffed-up because of thy knowledge; be not
confident because thou art a wise man. Take counsel with the ignorant as well as the wise. The (full) limits of skill cannot be attained,
and there is no skilled man equipped to his (full) advantage.[1] Good
speech is more hidden than the emerald, but it may be found with   Prov. 2:4
maidservants at the grindstones. . . .

IF THOU ART A LEADER (85) commanding the affairs of the multitude, seek out for thyself every beneficial deed, until it may be that
thy (own) affairs are without wrong. Justice is great, and its appropri-
ateness is lasting; it has not been disturbed since the time of him who
made it, (whereas) there is punishment for him who passes over its
laws. It is the (right) path before him who knows nothing. Wrongdoing

---

[1] *Ma'at* "justice" or "truth," was an inheritable value.

has never brought its undertaking into port. (It may be that) it is fraud that gains riches, (95) (but) the strength of justice is that it lasts, and a man may say: "It is the property of my father." . . .

Prov. 23:1–3   IF THOU ART ONE OF THOSE SITTING (120) at the table of one greater than thyself, take what he may give, when it is set before thy nose. Thou shouldst gaze at what is before thee. Do not pierce him with many stares, (for such) an aggression against him is an abomination to the *ka*.[2] Let thy face be cast down until he addresses thee, and thou shouldst speak (only) when he addresses thee. (130) Laugh after he laughs, and it will be very pleasing to his heart and what thou mayest do will be pleasing to the heart. No one can know what is in the heart.

As for the great man when he is at meals, his purposes conform to the dictates of his *ka*. He will give to the one whom he favors. (140) The great man gives to *the man whom he can reach,* (but) it is the *ka* that lengthens out his arms. The eating of bread is under the planning of god[3]—it is (only) a fool who would *complain of* it.

Prov. 25:13   IF THOU ART A MAN OF INTIMACY, whom one great man sends to another, be thoroughly reliable when he sends thee. Carry out the errand for him as he has spoken. (150) Do not be reserved about what is said to thee, and beware of (any) act of forgetfulness. Grasp hold of truth, and do not exceed it. (*Mere*) *gratification is by no means to be repeated.* Struggle against making words worse, (thus) *making one great man hostile to another through vulgar speech.* (160) A great man, a little man—it is the *ka's* abomination.[4] . . .

(175) IF THOU ART A POOR FELLOW, FOLLOWING A MAN OF DISTINCTION, one of good standing with the god, know thou not his former insignificance. Thou shouldst not be puffed-up against him because of what thou didst know of him formerly. Show regard for him in conformance with what has accrued to him—property does not come of itself. It is their law for him who wishes them. *As for him who oversteps, he is feared.* It is god who makes (a man's) quality, (185) and he defends him (even) while he is asleep. . . .

If thou art one to whom petition is made, (265) be calm as thou listenest to the petitioner's speech. Do not rebuff him before he has swept out his body or before he has said that for which he came. A petitioner likes attention to his words better than the fulfilling of that for which he came. He is rejoicing thereat more than any (other)

---

[2] The *ka* was the protecting and guiding vital force of a man, and thus his social mentor.

[3] "God" in these wisdom texts sometimes means the king, sometimes the supreme or creator god, and sometimes the force which demands proper behavior—a force not clearly defined, but perhaps the local god.

[4] Do not draw invidious distinctions?

petitioner, (even) before that which has been heard has come to pass. As for him who plays the rebuffer of a petitioner, men say: "Now why is he doing it?" (275) It is not (*necessary*) that everything about which he has petitioned *should* come to pass, (but) a good hearing is a soothing of the heart.

IF THOU DESIREST to make friendship last in a home to which thou hast access as master, as a brother, or as a friend, into any place where thou mightest enter, beware of approaching the women. It does not go well with the place where that is done. *The face has no alertness by splitting it.*[5] A thousand men *may be distracted from* their (own) advantage. (285) One is made a fool by limbs of fayence, as she stands (there), become (all) carnelian. A mere trifle, the likeness of a dream—and one attains death through knowing her. . . . Do not do it—it is really an abomination—(295) and thou shalt be free from sickness of heart every day. As for him who escapes from gluttony for it, all affairs will prosper with him. . . .

Prov. 6:29
Prov. 6:24
Prov. 7:5

Prov. 7:27

DO NOT BE COVETOUS AT A DIVISION. Do not be greedy, unless (it be) for thy (own) portion. Do not be covetous against thy (own) kindred. Greater is the respect for the mild than (for) the strong. (320) He is a mean person who *exposes* his kinsfolk; he is empty of *the fruits of conversation.*[6] It is (only) a little of that for which one is covetous that turns a calm man into a contentious man.

Prov. 15:27

IF THOU ART A MAN OF STANDING, THOU SHOULDST FOUND THY HOUSEHOLD and love thy wife at home as is fitting. Fill her belly; clothe her back. Ointment is the prescription for her body. Make her heart glad as long as thou livest. (330) She is a profitable field for her lord.[7] Thou shouldst not contend with her at law, and keep her far from gaining control. . . . Her eye is her stormwind. Let her heart be soothed through what may accrue to thee; it means keeping her long in thy house. . . .

Prov. 31:10–12, 31

Prov. 12:4

IF THOU ART (NOW) IMPORTANT AFTER THY (FORMER) UNIMPORTANCE, so that thou mayest do things after a neediness (430) formerly in the town which thou knowest, in contrast to what was thy lot before, do not be miserly with thy wealth, which has accrued to thee as the gift of god. Thou art not behind[8] some other equal of thine to whom the same has happened. . . .

Eccles. 6:2

IF A SON ACCEPTS WHAT HIS FATHER SAYS, (565) no project of his miscarries. He whom thou instructest as thy obedient son, who will stand well in the heart of the official, his speech is guided with

---

[5] Perhaps: He who has a wandering eye for the women cannot be keen.

[6] A mean person is he who goes out (from?) under his kinsfolk.

[7] The desire for children—particularly male children—was perennial in the orient.

[8] Not behind or ahead of, but the same as?

respect to what has been said to him, one regarded as obedient. . . .
(But) the *induction*[9] of him who does not hearken miscarries. The
wise man rises early in the morning to establish himself, (but) the
fool rises early in the morning (only) to *agitate* himself. . . .

ANET, 421–24 ## The Instruction of Amen-em-Opet

A general parallelism of thought or structure between Egyptian and Hebrew
literature is common. It is, however, more difficult to establish a case of direct literary relation. For this reason, special attention is directed to the Instruction of Amen-em-Opet, son of Ka-nakht, and its very close relation to
the Book of Proverbs, particularly Prov. 22:17–24:22. Amen-em-Opet dif-
fers from earlier Egyptian books of wisdom in its humbler, more resigned,
and less materialistic outlook.[10]

The hieratic text is found in British Museum Papyrus 10474 and (a portion only) on a writing tablet in Turin. The papyrus is said to have come
from Thebes. The date of the papyrus manuscript is debated. It is certainly
subsequent to the Egyptian Empire. A date anywhere between the 10th and
6th centuries B.C. is possible, with some weight of evidence for the 7th–6th
centuries. Some introductory lines have been omitted here.

HE SAYS: FIRST CHAPTER:
Give thy ears, hear what is said,
Give thy heart to understand them. (10)

Prov. 22:17–18a   To put them in thy heart is worth while,
(But) it is damaging to him who neglects them.
Let them rest in the casket of thy belly,
That they may be a *key* in thy heart.
At a time when there is a whirlwind of words, (15)

Prov. 22:18–19   They shall be a mooring-stake *for* thy tongue.
If thou spendest thy time while this is in thy heart,
Thou wilt find it a success;
Thou wilt find my words a treasury of life, (iv 1)
And thy body will prosper upon earth.

SECOND CHAPTER:

Prov. 22:22   Guard thyself against robbing the oppressed
And against overbearing the disabled. (5)
Stretch not forth thy hand against the approach of an old man,
Nor *steal away* the speech of the *aged*.
Let not thyself be sent on a dangerous errand,

---

[9] Induction into the official service?

[10] The shifting of the course of the Nile brought new lands into being. Apparently
these were crown domains.

Nor love him who carries it out.
Do not cry out against him whom thou hast attacked,   (10)
Nor return him answer on thy own behalf.
He who does evil, the (very) river-bank abandons him,
And his *floodwaters* carry him off.
The north wind comes down that it may end his hour;
It is joined to the tempest;   (15)
The thunder is loud, and the crocodiles are wicked.
Thou heated man,[11] how art thou (now)?
He is crying out, and his voice (reaches) to heaven.
O moon,[12] establish his crime (against him)!
So steer that we may bring the wicked man across,   (v 1)
For we shall not act like him—
Lift him up, give him thy hand;
Leave him (in) the arms of the god;
Fill his belly with bread of thine,   (5)   Prov. 25:21–22
So that he may be sated and may *be ashamed.*
Another good deed in the heart of the god
Is to pause before speaking. . . .

FOURTH CHAPTER:
As for the heated man of a temple,   (vi 1)   Ps. 1; Jer. 17:5–8
He is like a tree growing in the open.
In the completion of a moment (comes) its loss of foliage,
And its end is reached in the shipyards;
(Or) it is floated far from its place,   (5)
And the flame is its burial shroud.
(But) the truly silent man holds himself apart.
He is like a tree growing in a *garden.*
It flourishes and doubles its yield;
It (stands) before its lord.   (10)
Its fruit is sweet; its shade is pleasant;
And its end is reached in the garden. . . .

SIXTH CHAPTER:
Do not carry off the landmark at the boundaries of the arable land,
Nor disturb the position of the measuring-cord;
Be not greedy after a cubit of land,
Nor encroach upon the boundaries of a widow. . . .   (vii 15)   Prov. 22:28; 23:10
Guard against encroaching upon the boundaries of the fields,
Lest a terror carry thee off.   (viii 10)
One satisfies god with the will of the Lord,

---

[11] The "hot" man is the passionate or impulsive man, in contrast to the "silent" or humbly pious man.

[12] Thoth was the barrister of the gods.

Prov. 23:11	Who determines the boundaries of the arable land. . . .	
	Plow in the fields, that thou mayest find thy needs,	(17)
	That thou mayest receive bread of thy own threshing floor.	
	Better is a measure that the god gives thee	
	Than five thousand (taken) illegally.	
	They do not spend a day (in) the granary or barn;	(ix 1)
	They make no provisions for the beer-jar.	
	The completion of a moment is their lifetime in the storehouse;	
	At daybreak they are sunk (from sight).	
	Better is poverty in the hand of the god	(5)
	Than riches in a storehouse;	
Prov. 15:16–17	Better is bread, when the heart is happy,	
	Than riches with sorrow.	

SEVENTH CHAPTER:

	Cast not thy heart in pursuit of riches,	(10)
	(For) there is no ignoring Fate and Fortune.[13]	
	Place not thy heart upon externals,	
	(For) every man belongs to his (appointed) hour.	
	Do not strain to seek an excess,	
	When thy needs are safe for thee.	(15)
	If riches are brought to thee by robbery,	
	They will not spend the night with thee;	
	At daybreak they are not in thy house:	
	Their places may be seen, but they are not.	
	The ground has opened its mouth . . . that it might swallow them up,	
	And might sink them into the underworld.	(x 1)
	(Or) they have made themselves a great breach of their (own) size	
	And are sunken down in the storehouse.	
	(Or) they have made themselves wings like geese	
Prov. 23:4–5	And are flown away to the heavens.	(5)
	Rejoice not thyself (over) riches (gained) by robbery,	
	Nor mourn because of poverty.	
	If an archer *in the van* advances (too far),	
	Then his *squad* abandons him.	
	The ship of the covetous is left (in) the mud,	(10)
	While the boat of the silent man (has) a fair breeze.	
	Thou shouldst make prayer to the Aton when he rises,	
	Saying: "Give me prosperity and health."	
	He will give thee thy needs for this life,	
	And thou wilt be safe from terror. . . .	

---

[13] The god *Shay* and the goddess *Renenut* were two deified concepts, whose governing role was particularly strong at this time.

NINTH CHAPTER:

Do not associate to thyself the heated man,   Prov. 22:24
Nor visit him for conversation.
Preserve thy tongue from answering thy superior,   (xi 15)
And guard thyself against reviling him.
Do not make him cast his speech to lasso thee,
Nor make (too) free with thy answer.
Thou shouldst discuss an answer (*only*) *with* a man of thy (own)
     size,
And guard thyself against plunging headlong into it.
Swifter is speech when the heart is hurt   (xii 1)
Than wind *of the head-waters.* . . .
Do not leap to hold to such a one,   Prov. 22:25
Lest a terror carry thee off.

TENTH CHAPTER: (xiii 10)

Do not greet thy heated (opponent) in thy violence,
Nor hurt thy own heart (thereby).
Do not say to him: "Hail to thee!" falsely,
When a terror is in thy belly.
Do not talk with a man falsely—   (15)   Prov. 12:22
The abomination of the god.
Do not cut off thy heart from thy tongue,
That all thy affairs may be successful.
Be sincere in the presence of the common people,
For one is safe in the hand of the god.   (xiv 1)
God hates him who falsifies words;
His great abomination is the contentious of belly.

ELEVENTH CHAPTER:

Be not greedy for the property of a poor man,   (5)
Nor hunger for his bread.
As for the property of a poor man, it (is) a blocking to the throat,
It makes a *vomiting* to the gullet.
If he has *obtained* it by false oaths,
His heart is perverted by his belly. . . .   (xiv 10)   Prov. 23:6–7
The mouthful of bread (too) great thou swallowest and
     vomitest up,   (xiv 17)
And art emptied of thy good. . . .   Prov. 23:8

THIRTEENTH CHAPTER:

Do not confuse a man with a pen upon papyrus—   (xv 20)
The abomination of the god.
Do not bear witness with false words,   (xvi 1)   Prov. 14:15
Nor *support* another person (*thus*) with thy tongue.
Do not take an accounting of him who has nothing,

Nor falsify thy pen.

Prov. 22:26–27   If thou findest a large debt against a poor man,   (5)

Make it into three parts,

Forgive two, and let one stand.

Thou wilt find it like the ways of life;

Thou wilt lie down and sleep (soundly); in the morning

Thou wilt find it (again) like good news.   (10)

Better is praise as one who loves men

Prov. 16:8   Than riches in a storehouse;

Better is bread, when the heart is happy,

Than riches with sorrow. . . .

SIXTEENTH CHAPTER:

Do not *lean on* the scales nor falsify the weights,

Prov. 20:23   Nor damage the fractions of the measure.

Do not wish for a (common) country measure,   (xvii 20)

And neglect those of the treasury.

The ape[14] sits beside the balance,

And his heart is the plummet.   (xviii 1)

Which god is as great as Thoth,

He that discovered these things, to make them?

Make not for thyself weights which are deficient;

Prov. 16:11   They *abound in grief* through the will of god. . . .

EIGHTEENTH CHAPTER: (xix 10)

Do not spend the night fearful of the morrow.

Prov. 27:1   At daybreak what is the morrow like?

Man knows not what the morrow is like.

God is (always) in his success,

Whereas man is in his failure;   (15)

Prov. 19:21   One thing are the words which men say,

Another is that which the god does.

Prov. 20:9   Say not: "I have no wrongdoing,"

Nor (yet) strain to seek quarreling.

As for wrongdoing, it belongs to the god;   (20)

It is sealed with his finger.

There is no success in the hand of the god,

But there is no failure before him.

If he[15] pushes himself to seek success,   (xx 1)

In the completion of a moment he damages it.

Be steadfast in thy heart, make firm thy breast.

Steer not with thy tongue (alone).

If the tongue of a man (be) the rudder of a boat,   (5)

The All-Lord is its pilot. . . .

[14] The animal sacred to Thoth, god of just measure.
[15] A man.

TWENTIETH CHAPTER:
Do not confuse a man in the law court,
Nor *divert* the righteous man.
Give not thy attention (only) to him clothed in white,   (xxi 1)
Nor give consideration to him that is unkempt.
Do not accept the bribe of a powerful man,
Nor oppress for him the disabled.
As for justice, the great reward of god,   (5)
He gives it to whom he will. . . .
Do not falsify the *income* on the records,
Nor damage the plans of god.
Do not discover for thy own self the will of god,   (15)
Without (reference to) Fate and Fortune. . . .

TWENTY-FIRST CHAPTER:
Do not say: "I have found a strong superior,   (xxii 1)   Prov. 20:22
For a man in thy city has injured me."
Do not say: "I have found a *patron*,
For one who hates me has injured me."
For surely thou knowest not the plans of god,   (5)
Lest thou *be ashamed* on the morrow.
Sit thou down at the hands of the god,   Prov. 20:22; 27:1
And thy silence will cast them down. . . .
Empty not thy belly to everybody,
Nor damage (thus) the regard for thee.
Spread not thy words to the common people,   Prov. 20:19; 23:9
Nor associate to thyself one (too) outgoing of heart.
Better is a man whose talk (remains) in his belly   (15)   Prov. 12:23
Than he who speaks it out injuriously.
One does not run to reach success,
One does not *throw* to his (own) damage. . . .

TWENTY-THIRD CHAPTER:
Do not eat bread before a noble,
Nor lay on thy mouth at first.
If thou art satisfied with false chewings,   (xxiii 15)
They are a pastime for thy spittle.
Look at the cup which is before thee,   Prov. 23:1–3
And let it serve thy needs.
As a noble is great in his office,
He is as a well abounds (in) the drawing (of water). . . .

TWENTY-FIFTH CHAPTER:
Do not laugh at a blind man nor tease a dwarf   Prov. 17:5
Nor injure the affairs of the lame.   (xxiv 10)
Do not tease a man who is in the hand of the god,[16]

---

[16] The insane.

Nor be fierce of face against him if he errs.

Ps. 103:14   For man is clay and straw,
And the god is his builder.
He is tearing down and building up every day.   (15)
He makes a thousand poor men as he wishes,
(Or) he makes a thousand men *as overseers,*
When he is in his hour of life.
How joyful is he who reaches the West,
When he is safe in the hand of the god.[17] . . .

TWENTY-EIGHTH CHAPTER:
Do not *recognize* a widow if thou catchest her in the fields,[18]
Nor fail to be *indulgent* to her reply.   (xxvi 10)
Do not neglect a stranger (with) thy oil-jar,
That it be doubled before thy brethren.

Prov. 22:22–23   God desires respect for the poor
More than the honoring of the exalted. . . .

THIRTIETH CHAPTER:
See thou these thirty chapters:
They entertain; they instruct;
They are the foremost of all books;
They make the ignorant to know.   (xxvii 10)
If they are read out before the ignorant,
Then he will be cleansed by them.
Fill thyself with them; put them in thy heart,
And be a man who can interpret them,
Who will interpret them as a teacher.   (15)

Prov. 22:29   As for the scribe who is experienced in his office,
He will find himself worthy (to be) a courtier. (colophon:)
          It has come to its end
In the writing of Senu, son of the God's Father Pa-miu.[19]   (xxviii 1)

Sumerian Didactic and Wisdom Literature

ANET³, 589–91   # Man and His God

TRANSLATOR: S. N. KRAMER

A Sumerian Variation of the "Job" Motif

This "lamentation to a man's god," as the ancient author himself describes it,
is an edifying poetic essay composed, no doubt, for the purpose of prescribing

---

[17] Death releases a man from the helplessness of this world.
[18] Literally: "Do not find a widow." The reference is to the poor gleaning in the fields.
[19] Senu was the scribe who made this copy.

the proper attitude and conduct for a victim of cruel and seemingly undeserved misfortune. The Sumerians, like all peoples throughout the ages, were troubled by the problem of human suffering, particularly relative to its rather enigmatic causes and potential remedies. Their teachers and sages believed and taught the doctrine that man's misfortunes were the result of his sins and misdeeds. They were convinced, moreover, that no man is without guilt; as our Sumerian poet-theologian puts it: "Never was a sinless child born to its mother." In spite of surface appearances to the contrary, therefore, there are no cases of unjust and undeserved human suffering; it is always man who is to blame, not the gods. But the truth of such theological premises and conclusions is by no means readily apparent, and in moments of adversity, more than one sufferer must have been tempted to challenge the fairness and justice of the gods, and to blaspheme against them. It may well be that it was in an effort to forestall such resentment against the gods and to ward off potential disillusionment with the divine order, that one of the sages of the Sumerian academy, the *edubba,* composed this instructive essay.

The main thesis of our poet is that in cases of suffering and adversity, no matter how seemingly unjustified, the victim has but one valid and effective recourse, and that is to continually glorify his god and keep wailing and lamenting before him until he turns a favourable ear to his prayers. The god concerned is the sufferer's "personal" god, that is the deity who, in accordance with the accepted Sumerian credo, acted as the man's representative and intercessor in the assembly of the gods. To prove his point our author does not resort to philosophical speculation and theological argumentation. Instead, with characteristic Sumerian pragmatism, he cites a case: Here is a man, unnamed to be sure, who had been wealthy, wise, and righteous, or at least seemingly so, and blest with both friends and kin. One day sickness and suffering overwhelmed him. Did he defy the divine order and blaspheme? Not at all! He came humbly before his god with tears and lamentation, and poured out his heart in prayer and supplication. As a result his god was highly pleased and moved to compassion; he gave heed to his prayer, delivered him from his misfortunes, and turned his suffering to joy.

Structurally speaking, our poetic tract may be tentatively divided into five sections. First comes a brief introductory exhortation that man should praise and exalt his god and soothe him with lamentations (lines 1–9). The poet then introduces the unnamed individual who, upon being smitten with sickness and misfortune, addresses his god with tears and prayers (lines 10–20 plus). There follows the sufferer's petition which constitutes the major part of the poem (lines 26 minus–116). It begins with a description of the ill treatment accorded him by his fellow men—friend and foe alike (lines 26–55); continues with a lament against his bitter fate, including a rhetorical request to his kin and to the professional singers to do likewise (lines 56–95); and concludes with a confession of guilt and a direct plea for relief and deliverance (lines 96–116). Finally comes the "happy ending," in which the poet informs us that the man's prayer did not go unheeded, and that his god accepted the entreaties and delivered him from his afflictions (lines 117–29). All this leads, of course, to a further glorification of his god (lines 130–end).

Let a man utter constantly the exaltedness of his god,
Let the young man praise artlessly the words of his god,
Let the inhabitant of the straightforward land *moan*,
In the house [of] s[ong] let him *interpret* . . . to his woman-friend
    and man-friend,
Soothe [*his* he]art,
Bring forth . . . , utter . . . ,
Measure out . . . ,
Let his lament soothe the heart of his god,
(For) a man without a god would not obtain food.

The young man—he uses not his strength for evil *in* the place of
    deceit, (10)
(*Yet*) . . . , sickness, bitter suffering . . . d him,
. . . , fate, . . . brought . . . close to him,
Bitter . . . *confused its* . . . , covered his . . . ,
. . . placed an evil hand on him, he was treated as . . . .
. . . of his god,
. . . in his . . . , . . . he *weeps*,
. . . he directed a . . . ,
Speaks [tearfully] to him of his suffering . . . ,
. . . *in* his . . . wrath,
. . . s . . . . (20)
    (approximately 5 lines destroyed)
"I am a young man, a discerning one, (yet) who *respects* me *prospers*
    not,
My righteous word has been turned into a lie,
The man of deceit has covered me (with) the South-wind, I (am
    forced to) serve him,
Who *respects* me not has shamed me before you.

You have doled out to me suffering ever anew, (30)
I entered the house, heavy is the spirit,
I, the young man, went out to the street, oppressed is the heart,
With me, the *valiant*, my righteous shepherd has become angry, has
    looked upon me inimically,
My herdsman has sought out evil forces against me who am not
    (his) enemy,
My companion says not a true word to me,
My friend gives the lie to my righteous word.
The man of deceit has *conspired* against me,

(And) you, my god, do not thwart him,
You carry off my understanding,
The wicked has *conspired* against me   (40)
Angered you, stormed about, planned evil.
I, the wise, why am I bound to the ignorant youths?
I, the discerning, why am I counted among the ignorant?
Food is all about, (yet) my food is hunger,
On the day shares were allotted to all, my allotted share was
    suffering.

The *brother* . . . quarrelled, planned [evi]l,
[He . . . s] my . . . ,
. . . ,
Raises up . . . ,
Carries off . . . ,   (50)
Writes on clay . . . the wise . . . ,
Seeks out the . . . *of* the journey,
Cuts down like a tree the . . . of the road,
. . . [. . . s] the supervisor,
. . . [. . . s] the steward.

My god, [I would stand] befo[re yo]u,
Would speak to you, . . . , my word is a groan,
I would tell you about it, would bemoan the bitterness of my path,
[Would bewail] the confusion of . . . .
Let the wise . . . *in* my plans, lament will not cease,   (60)
I . . . to my friend,
I . . . to my companion.

Lo, let not my mother who bore me cease my lament before you,
Let not my sister [utter] the happy song and chant,
Let her utter tearfully my misfortunes before you,
Let my wife voice *mournfully* my suffering,
Let the expert singer bemoan my bitter fate.

My god, the day shines bright over the land, for me the day is
    black,
The bright day, the good day has . . . like the . . . ,
Tears, lament, anguish, and depression are lodged within me,   (70)
Suffering overwhelms me like one who does (nothing but) weep,
(The demon of) fate in its hand . . . s me, carries off my breath of
    life,
The malignant sickness-demon bath[es] in my body,
The bitterness of my path, the e[vil] of [*my* . . .],
. . . s the *kindly* . . . ,
. . . s the *unsettled* . . . .

I who am not the . . . of the . . . ,
I who am not the . . . of the . . . ,
[L]ike . . . I . . . before you,
                    (lines 80–94 largely destroyed)
. . . *I* weep *not*.

My god, you who are my father who begot me, [*lift up*] my face,
Like an innocent cow, in *pity* . . . the groan,
How long will you neglect me, leave me unprotected?
Like an ox, . . . ,
(How long) will you leave me unguided?   (100)
They say—the sages—a word righteous (and) straightforward:
'Never has a sinless child been born to its mother,
. . . a sinless *workman* has not existed from of old.'
My god, the . . . of destruction which I have . . . d against you,
The . . . of . . . which I have prepared before you,
Let them not . . . the man, the *wise*; utter, (my god), *words of grace*
     upon *him*,
(*When*) the day is not (yet) *bright*, in my . . . , in my . . . , make me
     walk before you,
My impure (*and*) my lack-lustre . . . —*touch* their . . . ,
Utter words of grace upon *him* whom you . . . d *on* the day *of* wrath,
Whom you . . . d *on* the day . . . —pronounce joy *upon* him.   (110)
My god, now that you have *shown* me my sins . . . ,
In the gate of . . . , I would speak . . . ,
I, the young man, would *confess* my sins before you.
May you *rain* upon the assembly . . . like a cloud,
May you . . . *in* your *chamber* my groaning *mother* . . . ,
Me, the *valiant*, may you . . . *in wis*[*dom* my] groaning. . . . "

. . . .

The man—his bitter weeping was heard by his god,
When the lamentation and wailing that filled him had soothed the
     heart of his god for the young man,
The righteous words, the artless words uttered by him, his god
     accepted,   (120)
The words which the young *man* prayerfully confessed,
Pleased the . . . , the *flesh* of his god, (and) his god withdrew his
     hand from the evil word,
. . . which oppresses the heart, . . . he embraces,
The encompassing sickness-demon, which had spread wide its
     wings, he *swept away*,
The . . . , which had smitten him like a . . . , he dissipated,
The (demon of) fate, who had been placed (there) in *accordance*
     with his *sentence*, he turned *aside*,
He turned the you[ng *m*]an's suffering into joy,

Set by him the . . . *good* . . . spirit (as a) watch (and) guardian,
Gave him . . . the tutelary genii of friendly mien.

[The man uttered] constantly the exaltedness of his god,   (130)
Brought forth . . . , made known . . . ,

(lines 132–37 destroyed)

" . . . may he return for me,
. . . may he release,
. . . may he set straight for me."   (140)

The antiphon of the lamentation to a man's (personal) god.

Proverbs from Mesopotamia

TRANSLATOR: ROBERT H. PFEIFFER

A. K 4347

ANET, 425

(20) Deal not badly with a matter, then [no sor]row [will fa]ll into your heart. (21) Do [no] evil, then you will [not] clutch a lasting [sorr]ow. (27) Without copulation she conceived, without eating she became plump![20] (28) Copulation causes the breast to give suck.[21] (29) When I labor they take away (my reward): when I increase my efforts, who will give me anything? (34) The strong man is fed through the price of his hire, the weak man through the price (or: the wages) of his child. (37) He is fortunate in everything, since he wears a (fine) garment. (38) Do you strike the face of a walking ox with a strap? (39) My knees keep walking, my feet are tireless, yet a man devoid of understanding pursues me with sorrow. (40) Am I (not) a thoroughbred steed? Yet I am harnessed with a mule and must draw a wagon loaded with reeds. (44) I dwell in a house of asphalt and bricks, yet some clay . . . pours over me.[22] (50) The life of the day before yesterday is that of any day. (53) You are placed into a river and your water becomes at once stinking; you are placed in an orchard and your date-fruit becomes bitter.[23] (55) If the shoot is not right it will not produce the stalk, nor create seed. (56) Will ripe grain grow? How do we know? Will dried grain grow? How do we know? (57) Very soon he will be dead; (so he says), "Let me eat up (all I have)!" Soon he will be well; (so he says), "Let me economize!"

Eccles. 9:11

Eccles. 1:9–10

Isa. 22:13

---

[20] To indicate something impossible; cf. Amos 6:12a. The Sumerian original reads: "Without his cohabiting with you, can you be pregnant? Without his feeding you, can you be fat?"

[21] I.e., cause and effect.

[22] The Sumerian seems to mean: "In the house the asphalt was removed from the brick; . . . last year the roof drain was dripping on me."

[23] Said of a man afflicted with persistent bad luck, or of one bringing misfortune to others through the evil eye.

(60) From before the gate of the city whose armament is not power-ful the enemy cannot be repulsed. (64) You go and take the field of the enemy; the enemy comes and takes your field.

The following Sumerian proverbs appear on tablets dating to the Early Old Babylonian period which have been found at Nippur and Ur. The transla-tions here provided are by Edmund I., Gordon, Research Associate, Babylo-nian Section, University Museum, University of Pennsylvania.

(1) A perverse child—his mother should never have given birth to him; his (personal) god should never have fashioned him! (2) The fox had a stick with him: "Whom shall I hit?" He carried a legal doc-ument with him: "What can I challenge?" (3) Upon my escaping from the wild-ox, the wild-cow confronted me! (4) As long as he is alive, he is his friend; on the day of (his) death, he is his greatest ad-versary! (5) He could not bring about an agreement; the women were all talking to one another! (6) Into an open mouth, a fly will enter! (7) Like a barren cow, you are looking for a calf of yours which does not exist! (8) The horse, after he had thrown off his rider, said: "If my burden is always to be this, I shall become weak!" (9) The dog understands "Take it!" He does not understand "Put it down!"

Akkadian Didactic and Wisdom Literature
Observations on Life: A Pessimistic Dialogue
ANET, 437–38 ## between Master and Servant
TRANSLATOR: ROBERT H. PFEIFFER

(I) ["Servant,] obey me." Yes, my lord, yes. ["Bring me at once the] chariot, hitch it up. I will ride to the palace." [Ride, my lord, ride! All your wishes] will be realized for you. The king] will be gracious to you. (5) ["No, servant,] I shall not ride [to] the palace." [Do not ride], my lord, do not ride. [To a place . . .] he will send you. [*In a land which*] you know [not] he will let you be captured. [Day and] night he will let you see trouble.

(II) (10) "Servant, obey me." Yes, my lord, yes. ["Bring me at] once water for my hands, and give it to me: I wish to dine." [Dine,] my lord, dine. To dine regularly is the opening of the heart (i.e., brings joy). [To a dinner] eaten in happiness and with washed hands (the sun-god) Shamash comes. "No, [servant,] I shall not dine." (15) Do not dine, my lord, do not dine. To be hungry and eat, to be thirsty and drink, comes upon (every) man.

(III) "Servant, obey me." Yes, my lord, yes. "Bring me at once the chariot, hitch it up. I will ride to the wilderness." Ride, my lord, ride.

The fugitive's stomach is full. (20) The hunting dog will break a bone; the fugitive *ḫaḫur* bird will build its nest; the wild ass running to and fro will. . . . "No, servant, to the wilderness I will not ride." Do not ride, my lord, do not ride. (25) The fugitive's mind is variable. The hunting dog's teeth will break; the house of the fugitive *ḫaḫur* bird is in [*a hole*] of the wall; and the abode of the wild ass running to and fro is the desert.

(IV) "Servant, [obey me." Yes, my lord, yes.] (20–31) (fragments). . . . the silence of the evil one make complete. ["My enemy] I shall capture and *quickly* shackle. I shall lie in wait for my adversary." (35) Lie (in wait), my lord, lie (in wait). . . . A house you will not build. He who proceeds [rashly] destroys his father's house.

(V) . . . "I will not build a house." You will not build it.

(VI) ["Servant, obey me." Yes, my lord, yes.] "At the [word of my adversary I shall remain silent."] (40) Remain silent, my lord, remain [silent. Silence is better than speech.] "No, servant, at the [word of my adversary I shall not remain silent."] Do not remain silent, my lord, [do not remain silent.] If you do not speak with your mouth. . . . Your adversary will be angry with you. . . .

(VII) (45) "Servant, obey me." Yes, my lord, yes. "I intend to start a rebellion." Do (it), my lord, [do (it)]. If you do not start a rebellion what becomes of your clay?[24] Who will give you (something) to fill your stomach? "No, servant, I shall not do something violent." (50) [Do (it) not, my lord, do (it) not.] The man doing something violent is killed or [*ill-treated*], or he is maimed, or captured and cast into prison.

Prov. 24:21–22

(VIII) "Servant, obey me." Yes, my lord, yes. (55) "A woman will I love." Yes, love, my lord, love. The man who loves a woman forgets pain and trouble. "No, servant, a woman I shall not love." [Do not love,] my lord, do not [love]. Woman is a well, (60) woman is an iron dagger—a sharp one!—which cuts a man's neck.

(IX) "Servant, obey me." Yes, my lord, yes. "Bring me at once water for my hands, and give it to me: I will offer a sacrifice to my god." Offer, my lord, offer. A man offering sacrifice to his god is happy, loan upon loan he makes. "No, servant, a sacrifice to my god will I not offer." Do not offer (it), my lord, do not offer (it). You may teach a god to trot after you like a dog when he requires of you, (saying), "(Celebrate) my ritual" or "do not inquire (by requesting an oracle)" or anything else.

(X) ["Servant,] obey me." Yes, my lord, yes. (70) "I shall give food to our country." Give it, my lord, give it! [The man who] gives food [to his country]—his barley (remains) his own but his receipts from interest (payments) become immense. ["No, servant,] food to my

---

[24] "Your clay" means of course "your body" (cf., Gen., 2:7).

country I shall not give." [Do not give, my lord,] do not give. Giving is like *lov*[*ing*]. . . . giving birth to a son. (75) . . . they will curse you. [They will eat] your barley and destroy you.

(XI) "Servant, obey me." Yes, my lord, yes. "I will do something helpful for my country." Do (it), my lord, do (it). The man who does something helpful for his country,—his helpful deed is placed in the bowl of Marduk.[25] (80) "No, servant, I will not do something helpful for my country." Do it not, my lord, do it not. Climb the mounds of ancient ruins and walk about: look at the skulls of late and early (men); who (among them) is an evildoer, who a public benefactor?

(XII) "Servant, obey me." Yes, my lord, yes. "Now, what is good? (85) To break my neck, your neck, throw (both) into the river—(that) is good." Who is tall enough to ascend to heaven? Who is broad enough to embrace the earth? "No, servant, I shall kill you and send you ahead of me." (Then) would my lord (wish to) live even three days after me? (Colophon) Written according to the original and collated.

ANET³, 592–93

An Akkadian Fable

TRANSLATOR: ROBERT D. BIGGS

Dispute between the Tamarisk and the Date Palm

I

The tamarisk [opened] his mouth [saying],   (3)
"My flesh compared with [your] flesh [is . . .]
My precious, fine *climbing-belt* you [. . .]
[You] are like a slave girl who be[*trays*] her mistress."

The [date palm] answered proudly   (7)
" . . . your *pods* with a rod [. . .]
When we call on a god [*your*] flesh [*is only good*] against sin.
The tamarisk does not know the best of the . . . or the best of [. . .]."

Ditto (Tamarisk speaks). "I am better than you, a master of every
    craft. The *far*[*mer* . . .]   (11)
All he has, the farmer has cut from the crooks of me, [. . .]
He makes his spade from my trunk and with the spade made
    from me
He opens the irrigation canal so the field gets water. I have [. . .]
And for the moisture of the soil, the grain . . . [. . .]   (15)
I thresh, and grain, on which people thrive, I thresh."

Ditto (Date palm speaks). "I am better than you, a master of every
    craft. The farmer [. . .]   (17)
All he has: reins, whips, rope for the team and the see[der-plow]
Harness, . . . , rope for the . . . , net *for* the wagon, [. . .]

---

[25] The tablets listing men's deeds were stored in Marduk's bowl.

... the farmer's equipment, all there is of it, ... [...]."   (20)

Ditto (Tamarisk speaks). "Think of the equipment made from me
     in the king's palace. What [...]   (21)

[In] the king's house. The king eats from a dish made from me,
     from a *cup* [made from me the queen drinks],

With a spoon made from me the warriors eat, from a trough made
     from me [...]

(And) the baker scoops out the flour. I am a weaver [beating up]
     the thread (and thus)

I clothe the people [...]   (25)

The ... of the god. I am the chief exorcist and (ritually) renew the
     temple. [I am] indeed a fine thing

[And] can have no equal."
          (rev.)

Ditto (Date palm speaks). "At the place of the offering to the god
     Sin ... Sin the noble [...]   (1)

The king cannot make a libation anywhere where I am not present,
     in ... [...]

Rites are performed with me, my leaves heaped up on the ground,
     ... [...]

Then the palm is also a brewer; ... [...]."

Ditto (Tamarisk speaks). "Come, let us go, you and I, to the city
     of Kish. [...]   (5)

There are signs of me where the scholar works. The [...] are not
     full [of ... *and*]

Not full of incense. The *qadishtu*-woman sprinkles water and [...]

Takes [the ...] and they worship and hold a festival. Then [...]

Is for the hand of the butcher and his leaves ... [...]."

Ditto (Date palm speaks). "Come, let us go, you and I, to the
     city of [...]   (10)

Wherever there are sins, there is work for you, O Tamarisk. The
     carpenter with [...]

And he respects me and daily praises [me]."

(Tamarisk speaks). "Who ... [...]   (13)

I bear. The *shepherd boy* [*uses*] great staves [of me]

Splits the ... , like a reed worker who [...]

I shall rejoice in the greatness of my strength [...]

I have made you into something effective, very strong [...]."

(Date palm speaks). "I am better than you. Six times I excel,
     seven times I [...]   (18)

I am one who alternates with the goddess of grain. For three
     months [...]

The orphan girl, the widow, the poor man, [...]

Eat without stint my sweet dates [...] broken
                    (rest of text damaged or destroyed)

II

In long-ago days, *in far-off years*
The Fates dug the rivers;
The gods of the lands, Anu, Enlil, and Ea convened an assembly.
Enlil and the (other) gods took counsel,
Among them was seated Shamash,   (5)
Among them was seated the great lady among the gods.
Once there was no kingship in the lands
And the rule was given to the gods.
                    (two lines unintelligible)
The king planted
A palm in his palace.
With it he planted a . . . tamarisk.
In the shade of the tamarisk a dinner
Was given and in the shade of the palm   (15)
. . .
The opening of . . . the way of the king.
Each other's worth [they insulted];
The tamarisk and the date palm [had a dispute].
The tamarisk (spoke) thus, "*I* . . . greatly.   (20)
If the date palm is so wonderful . . . . "
"You, tamarisk, are a useless tree.
What are your branches? Only wood without any fruit at all!
My fruit is . . .
. . .
The gardener speaks well of me,
Of use to both slave and official.
My fruit makes the infant grow;
Grown men (also) eat my fruit"
" . . . the equal of the king . . .   (30)
The equipment in the king's palace—
What made from me is to be found in the king's palace?
The king eats from a *table* made of me,
The queen drinks from a *cup* made of me.
I am a weaver and beat up the threads. [. . .]
I am the chief exorcist and purify [the house]."
                    (rest of text fragmentary or destroyed)

ANET³, 595–96 ## Counsels of Wisdom

TRANSLATOR: ROBERT D. BIGGS

                    (beginning of text badly damaged)
Do not talk [with a tale]bearer,   (21)
Do not consult [with a . . .] . . . who is an idler;

Because of your good qualities, you will be made into an *example*
  for them.
Then you will reduce your own work, forsake your path,
And will let your wise, modest opinion be perverted.
Let your mouth be restrained and your speech guarded;
(That) is a man's pride—let what you say be very precious.
Let insolence and blasphemy be an abomination for you;
Speak nothing profane nor any unjust report.
A talebearer is looked down upon.   (30)
Do not set out to stand around in the assembly.
Do not loiter where there is a dispute,
For in the dispute they will have you as an *observer*.
Then you will be made a witness for them, and
They will involve you in a lawsuit to affirm something that does
  not concern you.
In case of a dispute, get away from it, disregard it.
If a dispute involving you should flare up, calm it down.
A dispute is a *covered* pit,
A . . . wall which can *cover over* its foes;
It brings to mind what one has forgotten and makes an accusation
  against a man.   (40)
Do not return evil to your adversary;
Requite with kindness the one who does evil to you,
Maintain justice for your enemy,
Be friendly to your enemy.
     (a number of lines damaged)
Give food to eat, beer to drink,   (61)
Grant what is requested, provide for and treat with honor.
At this one's god takes pleasure.
It is pleasing to Shamash, who will repay him with favor.
Do good things, be kind all your days.

Do not honor a slave girl in your house;
She should not rule [your] bedroom like a wife.
. . . , do not give yourself over [to] slave girls.
If she goes up your . . . , you will not go down.
Let this be said [among] your people: (70)
"The household which a slave girl rules, she disrupts."
Do not marry a prostitute, whose husbands are legion,
An *ishtarītu*-woman who is dedicated to a god,
A *kulmashītu*-woman whose . . . is much.
When you have trouble, she will not support you,
When you have a dispute she will be a mocker.
There is no reverence or submissiveness in her.
Even if she is powerful in the household, get rid of her,

For she pricks up her ears for the footsteps of another man.
Variant: Whatever household she enters (as wife) will be scattered
    and the one who marries her will not be stable.   (80)

My son, if it be the wish of a ruler that you belong to him,
If you are entrusted with his closely guarded seal
Open his treasure house (and) enter it,
For no one but you may do it.
Uncounted wealth you will find inside,
But do not covet any of that,
Nor set your mind on a secret crime,
For afterwards the matter will be investigated
And the secret crime which you committed will be exposed.
The ruler will hear of it (and) will [. . .],   (90)
His happy face will [. . .],
           (a number of lines damaged)
Do not speak ill, speak (only) good.   (127)
Do not say evil things, speak well of people.
He who speaks ill and says evil—
People will waylay him because of his debt to Shamash.   (130)
Do not talk too freely, watch what you say.
Do not express your innermost thoughts even when you are alone.
What you say in haste you may *regret* later.
Exert yourself to restrain your speech.

Worship your god every day.
Sacrifice and (pious) utterance are the proper accompaniment of
    incense.
Have a freewill offering for your god,
For this is proper toward a god.
Prayer, supplication, and prostration
Offer him daily, then your prayer *will be granted,*   (140)
And you will be in harmony with your god.
Since you are learned, read in the tablet:
"Reverence begets favor,
Sacrifice improves life
And prayer dispels guilt.
He who worships the gods is not slighted by [. . .],
He who worships the Anunnaki will thus prolong [his days]."
With a friend or comrade do not speak [*evil things*].
Do not say unworthy things, [speak] what is good.
If you have promised something, give [. . .],   (150)
If you have created trust, you should [. . .],
[And fulfill] the wish of a comrade.
[If] you have created trust in friends [. . .]
[Since] you are learned, [read in the tablet]:
           (rest of text fragmentary)

Ludlul Bēl Nēmeqi, "I Will Praise the Lord of Wisdom"

Translator: Robert D. Biggs

Tablet I

I will praise the lord of wisdom, the [*deliberative*] god,   (1)
Who lays hold of the night, but frees the day,
Marduk, the lord of wisdom, the [*deliberative*] god,
Who lays hold of the night, but frees the day,
Whose fury surrounds him like a storm wind,
But whose breeze is as pleasant as a morning zephyr,
Whose anger is irresistible, whose rage is a devastating flood,
But whose heart is merciful, whose mind forgiving,
The . . . of whose hands the heavens cannot hold back,
But whose gentle hand sustains the dying,   (10)
Marduk, the . . . of whose hands the heavens cannot hold back,
But whose gentle hand sustains the dying,
                    (long break)
The lord [. . .] the *confusion*   (41)
And the warrior *Enlil* [. . .] his . . .
My god has forsaken me and *disappeared*,
My goddess has cut me off and stayed removed from me.
The benevolent spirit who was (always) beside [me] has departed,
My protective spirit has flown away and seeks someone else.
My dignity has been taken away, my manly good looks jeopardized,
My pride has been cut off, my protection has skipped off.
Terrifying omens have been brought upon me,
I was put out of my house and wandered about outside.   (50)
The omens concerning me are confused, daily there *is*
      inflammation.
I cannot stop going to the diviner and dream interpreter.
What is said in the street portends ill for me.
When I lie down at night my dream is terrifying.
The king, the very flesh of the gods, the sun of his peoples,
His heart is enraged (with me) and cannot be appeased.
Even though I stand *praying* they . . . against me.
They gather together telling things that ought not be said.
Thus the first, "I have made him want to end his life."
The second says, "I made him vacate his post."   (60)
Likewise the third, "I shall take over his position."
"I will take over his house," says the fourth.
The fifth . . . .
The sixth and seventh will pursue his . . . .
The group of seven has assembled their forces,
Merciless as a storm demon, they are like . . . .

They are one in flesh, united in purpose.
Their hearts rage against me and they are ablaze like fire.
They agree on slander and lies about me.
They have sought to muzzle my respectful mouth. (70)
I, whose lips always prattled, have become like a mute.
My hearty shout is [reduced] to silence,
My proud head is bowed to the ground,
Fear has weakened my brave heart.
Even a youngster has turned back my broad chest.
My arms, (though once) strong, are . . .
I, who used to walk like a proud man, have learned to slip by
    unnoticed.
Though I was a respectable man, I have become a slave.
To my *many relations* I have become like a recluse.
If I walk the street, fingers are pointed at me; (80)
If I enter the palace, eyes blink.
My own town looks on me as an enemy;
Even my land is savage and hostile.
My friend has become a stranger,
My companion has become an evil person and a demon.
In his rage my comrade denounces me,
Constantly my associate *furbishes* his weapons.
My close friend has brought my life into danger;
My slave has publicly cursed me in the assembly.
. . . the crowd has defamed me. (90)
When someone who knows me sees me, he *passes by on the other
    side.*
My family treats me as if I were not related to them,
The grave is ready for anyone who speaks well of me,
But he who speaks ill of me is promoted.
The one who slanders me has the god's help;
The . . . who says "god have mercy" when death is imminent
Without delay becomes well through his protective god.
I have no one to go at my side, nor have I found anyone
    understanding.
They divided all my possessions among foreign riffraff.
They stopped up the source of my canal with silt. (100)
They have stopped the joyous harvest song in my fields,
And silenced my city like an enemy city.
They have let another take over my duties,
They appointed someone else to be present at the rites (where I
    should be).
By day there is sighing, by night lamentation,
The month is wailing, the year is gloom.
I moan like a dove all day long.

[Instead of singing a] song I *groan loudly.*
My eyes are . . . [through] constant weeping,
My lower eyelids are swollen [from *ceaseless*] tears.   (110)
[. . .] before me the fears of my heart
[. . .] panic and fear.
                    (The rest of the tablet is badly damaged.)

Tablet II

I survived to the next year; the appointed time passed.   (1)
I turn around, but it is bad, very bad;
My *ill luck* increases and I cannot find what is right.
I called to my god, but he did not show his face,
I prayed to my goddess, but she did not raise her head.
Even the diviner with his divination could not make a prediction,
And the interpreter of dreams with his libation could not elucidate
     my case.
I sought the favor of the *zaqīqu*-spirit, but he would not
     enlighten me;
The exorcist with his ritual could not appease the divine wrath
     against me.
What strange conditions everywhere!   (10)
When I look behind (me), there is persecution, trouble.
Like one who has not made libations to his god,
Nor invoked his goddess when he ate,
Does not *make* prostrations nor recognize (the necessity of)
     bowing down,
In whose mouth supplication and prayer are lacking,
Who has even *neglected* holy days, and ignored festivals,
Who was negligent and did not observe the gods' rites,
Did not teach his people reverence and worship,
But has eaten his food without invoking his god,
And abandoned his goddess by not bringing a flour offering,   (20)
Like one who has gone crazy and forgotten his lord,
Has frivolously sworn a solemn oath by his god, (like such a one)
     do I *appear.*
For myself, I gave attention to supplication and prayer:
My prayer was discretion, sacrifice my rule.
The day for worshipping the god was a joy to my heart;
The day of the goddess's procession was profit and gain to me.
The king's blessing—that was my joy,
And the accompanying music became a delight for me.
I had my land keep the god's rites,
And brought my people to value the goddess's name.   (30)
I made the praise for the king like a god's,
And taught the people respect for the palace.

I wish I knew that these things would be pleasing to one's god!
What is good for oneself may be offense to one's god,
What in one's own heart seems despicable may be proper to one's
    god.
Who can know the will of the gods in heaven?
Who can understand the plans of the underworld gods?
Where have humans learned the way of a god?
He who was alive yesterday is dead today.
One moment he is worried, the next he is boisterous.   (40)
One moment he is singing a joyful song,
A moment later he wails like a professional mourner.
Their condition changes (as quickly as) opening and shutting (the
    eyes).
When starving they become like corpses,
When full they oppose their god.
In good times they speak of scaling heaven,
When they are troubled they talk of going down to hell.
I am *perplexed* at these things; I have not been able to understand
    their significance.
As for me, exhausted, a windstorm is driving me on!
Debilitating Disease is let loose upon me: (50)
An Evil Wind has blown [from the] horizon,
Headache has sprung up from the surface of the underworld,
An Evil Cough has left its *Apsu*,
The Irresistible Demon has left *Ekur,*
[The Lamashtu-demon came] down from the Mountain,
Cramp set out [with . . .] the flood,
Weakness breaks through the ground along with the plants.
[They all joined in] and came on me together.
[They *struck*] my head, they enveloped my skull;
[My] face is gloomy, my eyes flow.   (60)
They have wrenched my neck muscles and made (my) neck limp.
They struck [my chest,] beat my breast.
They affected my flesh and made me shake,
[In] my epigastrium they kindled a fire.
They churned up my bowels, . . . [they] . . . my . . .
Causing the discharge of phlegm, they tired out my [lungs].
They tired out my limbs and made my *fat* quake.
My upright stance they knocked down like a wall,
My robust figure they laid down like a rush,
I am thrown down like a . . . and cast on my face.   (70)
The *alû*-demon has clothed himself in my body as with a
    garment;
Sleep covers me like a net.
My eyes stare straight ahead, but cannot see,

My ears are open, but cannot hear.
Feebleness has overcome my whole body,
An attack of illness has fallen upon my flesh.
Stiffness has taken over my arms,
Weakness has come upon my knees,
My feet forget their motion.
[A stroke] has got me; I choke like someone prostrate.   (80)
Death has [*approached*] and has covered my face.
If someone is concerned about me, I am not even able to answer
    the one who inquires.
[My . . .] weep, but I cannot control myself.
A snare is laid on my mouth,
And a bolt keeps my lips barred.
My "gate" is barred, my "drinking place" blocked,
My hunger is . . . , my windpipe constricted.
I eat grain as though it were a vile thing,
Beer, the sustenance of mankind, is distasteful to me.
My malady is indeed protracted.   (90)
Through not eating, my looks have become strange,
My flesh is flaccid, and my blood has ebbed away.
My bones look separated, and are covered (only) with my skin.
My flesh is inflamed, and the . . . -disease has afflicted me.
I have taken to a bed of *bondage*; going out is a pain;
My house has become my prison.
My arms are powerless—my own flesh is a manacle,
My feet are fallen flat—my own person is a fetter.
My afflictions are grievous, my wound is severe.
A whip full of needles has struck me,   (100)
The goad that pricked me was covered with barbs.
All day long the tormentor torments [me],
And at night he does not let me breathe easily for a minute.
Through twisting my joints are parted,
My limbs are splayed and knocked apart.
I spent the night in my dung like an ox,
And wallowed in my excrement like a sheep.
My symptoms are beyond the exorcist,
And my omens have confused the diviner.
The exorcist could not diagnose the nature of my sickness,   (110)
Nor could the diviner set a time limit on my illness.
My god has not come to the rescue nor taken me by the hand;
My goddess has not shown pity on me nor gone by my side.
My grave was waiting, and my funerary paraphernalia ready,
Before I was even dead lamentation for me was finished.
All my country said, "How he is crushed!"
The face of him who gloats lit up when he heard,

The news reached her who gloats, and her heart rejoiced.
I know the day for my whole family,
When, among my friends, their Sun-god will have mercy.   (120)

Tablet III

His hand was heavy upon me, I could not bear it.   (1)
My dread of him was alarming, it [. . . me]
His fierce wind [*brought on*] a destructive flood.
His stride was . . . , it . . . [. . .]
. . . the severe illness does not [leave] my person,
I forget *wakefulness,* it makes [my mind] stray.
Both day and night I groan,
Whether awake or dreaming I am equally miserable.
A remarkable young man of outstanding physique,
Splendid in body, clothed in new garments—   (10)
Since in waking moments . . .
Clad in splendor, robed in dread,
          (The rest of the first dream is mainly destroyed.)
A second time [I had a dream,]   (21)
And in the dream I had at night
A remarkable priest [was . . .]
Holding in his hand a piece of purifying tamarisk wood.
"Laluralimma, resident of Nippur,
Has sent me to purify you."
The water he was carrying he poured over me,
Recited the life-restoring incantation, and massaged [my body].
A third time I had a dream,
And in the dream I had at night   (30)
A remarkable young woman of shining countenance,   (30a)
. . . , equal to a god.   (31)
A queen of the peoples . . . [. . .]
She entered and [sat down . . .]
She spoke my deliverance [. . .]
"Fear not," she said, "I [will . . . you]."
. . . *had* a dream [. . .]
She said, "Be delivered from your very wretched state,
Whoever has had a vision during the night."
In the dream Urnindinlugga, [. . .]
A bearded young man wearing a head covering,   (40)
An exorcist, carrying a (cuneiform) tablet,
"Marduk has sent me.
To Shubshi-meshre-Shakkan I have brought prosperity,
From Marduk's pure hands I have brought prosperity."
He (Marduk) had entrusted me into the hands of my ministrant.
[*In*] waking hours he sent a message

And showed his favorable sign to my people.
In the . . . sickness [. . .]
My illness was quickly over and [my . . .] broken.
After the mind of my Lord had quietened   (50)
And the heart of merciful Marduk rejoiced,
[After he had] received my prayers [. . .]
To whom turning is pleasant. [. . .]
                    (several lines badly damaged)

    Si 55
[He brought] near his spell which binds. [. . .]   (4)
[He drove] away the Evil Wind to the horizon,
To the surface of the underworld he took [the Headache,]
[He sent] down the Evil Cough to its *Apsû,*
The Irresistible Demon he returned [to] *Ekur,*
He overthrew the Lamashtu-demon, sending her off to the
      Mountain,
He sent the chills to the flowing water and the sea.
He tore up the root of Weakness as if it were a plant.   (10)
Troubled Sleep, the (continual) sleepiness
He took far away like smoke with which the heavens get filled.
Woe and Alas, . . . he raised like a mist and [put] in the
      underworld.
The persistent complaint in the head which . . . ,
He dispelled like dew of the night, and removed it from me.
My clouded eyes, which were cloaked in a deathly shroud—
He drove (the shroud) a thousand leagues away and brightened
      [my] vision.
My ears which were clogged and blocked like a deaf man's—
He removed their obstructions and opened my hearing.
My nose, whose [breathing] was choked by the onset of fever— (20)
He soothed its affliction and now I breathe [freely].
My impetuous lips which had . . . [. . .]—
He removed their terror and loosed their shackles.
My mouth, which had been closed so that talking was diffi[cult]—
He wiped like copper and [removed] its dirt.
My teeth, which were clenched and held tightly together—
He opened their lock and . . . their roots.
My tongue, which was tied and [could] not converse—
[He] wiped away its . . . and my speech *became clear.*
My throat, which was tight and choking as though with lumps
      of earth,   (30)
He restored, and *it sang* songs which were like a flute.
My gullet, which was swollen so that it could not take [in food]—
Its swelling diminished, and he opened its blockage.

(The remaining three lines of this text are damaged. The remainder of Tablet III is preserved only for certain lines quoted in the ancient commentary, here given by letters rather than numbers.)

The large intestine, which was always empty through lack of food,
    and was twined like a reed basket— (a)
It receives food and takes drink. (b)
My neck, which was limp and bent at the base— (c)
He gave rigidity and made it upright like a *fir tree.* (d)
He made my physique like that of one perfect in strength. (e)
He *trimmed* my fingernails *as if expelling a tabooed woman.* (f)
He drove out their fatigue and made their . . . good. (g)
My knees, which were fettered and [bound like]
    the *būṣu*-bird's, (h)
The frame of my body he . . . [. . .] (i)
He wiped away the . . . and cleansed its filth. (j)
My gloomy appearance was made light. (k)
Beside the river, where people's lawsuits are decided, (l)
Half my body was stricken, but I was freed from the fetters. (m)
. . . (n)
I proceeded along the Kunush-kadru Street—free (from my
    afflictions). (o)
He who has done wrong in respect to Esagil, let him learn
    from me! (p)
It was Marduk who put a muzzle on the mouth of the lion who
    was eating me. (q)
It was Marduk who took away the sling of the one who was
    pursuing me and turned back his sling-stone. (r)
    (The rest of the text is badly damaged or destroyed.)

Tablet IV

The Lord . . . me, (1)
The Lord took hold of me,
The Lord set me on my feet,
The Lord restored me to health,
He rescued me [from the pit],
He summoned me [from] destruction,
[. . .] he pulled me from the *Ḫubur* river,
[. . .] he took my hand.
[The one who] (once) struck me down,
Marduk, (now) raised me up. (10)
He struck the hand of the one who struck me;
It was Marduk who made him drop his weapon.
    (a number of lines damaged and missing)
The feast of the Babylonians . . . [. . .] (27)

The grave I had made [. . .] at the banquet.
The Babylonians saw how [Marduk] restores to health,
And all mouths proclaim [his] greatness: (30)
Who would have thought that he would see his Sun?
Who would have thought that he would walk along his street?
Who but Marduk could have restored the dying to life?
Apart from Sarpanitum which goddess could have granted life?
Marduk can even restore to life someone already in the grave,
Sarpanitum knows how to save from destruction.
Wherever the earth is laid, and the heavens are extended,
Wherever the sun god shines, and the fire god blazes,
Wherever water flows and winds blow,
Creatures whose clay Aruru took in her fingers,   (40)
Those endowed with life, who walk about,
Humanity, all of it, gives praise to Marduk!
[. . .] . . . , who give utterance,
[. . .] may he rule all the peoples,
[. . .] shepherd of all inhabited places.
[. . .] the beneficial waters from the deep,
[. . .] the gods [. . .]
[. . .] the extent of heaven and [earth].
                    (some lines damaged or destroyed)
[. . .] which with my prayers [. . .]   (76)
[With] prostration and supplication [*I entered*] into the temple
      Esagil.
[I who went] down to the grave have returned to the "Gate of the
      [Sun Rise]."
[In the] "Gate of Prosperity" prosperity was [given to me],
[In the] "Gate of the . . . Guardian Spirit" a guardian spirit came
      [up to me],   (80)
[In the] "Gate of Well-being" I found well-being,
In the "Gate of Life" I was granted life,
In the "Gate of the Sun Rise" I was reckoned among the living,
In the "Gate of Splendid Wonderment" the omens concerning me
      were very plain,
In the "Gate of Release of Guilt" I was released from my bond,
In the "Gate of Worship" my mouth made inquiry,
In the "Gate of Resolving of Sighs" my sighs were resolved,
In the "Gate of Pure Water" I was sprinkled with water of
      purification,
In the "Gate of Well-being" I communed with Marduk,
In the "Gate of Exuberance" I kissed the foot of the goddess
      Sarpanitum.   (90)
I persisted in supplication and prayer before them,
Sweet incense I placed before them,

I presented an offering, a gift, accumulated donations,
I slaughtered fat oxen, and butchered *fattened sheep,*
I repeatedly libated honey-sweetened beer and pure wine.
The protecting genius and guardian spirit, divine attendants of the
    brickwork of Esagil,
[*With*] libation I made their hearts glow,
[With] the many [meals] I made them joyful.
[The threshold, the bolt] socket, the bolt, the doors,
[I *offered*] oil, butter, and choicest grain. (100)
[. . .] . . . the rites of the temple.

ANET³, 601–4

The Babylonian Theodicy

TRANSLATOR: ROBERT D. BIGGS

The Theodicy is an acrostic poem of twenty-seven stanzas of eleven lines each, not all of which are preserved, and takes the form of a dialogue. The acrostic reads: *a-na-ku sa-ag-gi-il-ki-*[*i-na-am-u*]*b-bi-ib ma-âš-ma-šu ka-ri-bu ša i-li ú šar-ri,* "I Saggil-kīnam-ubbib, the exorcist, am an adorant of the god and the king."

    Sufferer I
O sage [. . .] come, [let] me tell you. (1)
[. . . let] me inform you.
[. . .] . . . [. . .] . . . you,
I [. . .], who suffered greatly, will not cease to reverence you.
Where is the wise man of your caliber?
Where is the scholar who can rival you?
Where is the counsellor to whom I can relate my trouble?
I am finished. Anguish has come upon me.
When I was still a child, fate took my father;
My mother who bore me went to the Land of No Return. (10)
My father and mother left me without anyone to be my guardian.
    Friend II
Respected friend, what you say is sad.
Dear friend, you have let your *mind* dwell on evil.
You have made your good sense like that of an incompetent
    person;
You have changed your beaming face to scowls.
Our fathers do indeed give up and go the way of death.
It is an old saying that they cross the river Hubur.
When you look upon all of mankind
. . . it is not . . . that has made the impoverished first-born rich.
Who prefers as a favorite the rich man? (20)
He who looks to his god has a protective spirit;
The humble man who fears his goddess accumulates wealth.

Sufferer III

My friend, your mind is a spring whose depth has not been found,
The high swell of the sea, which does not subside.
I will ask you a question; listen to what I say.
Pay attention for a moment; hear my words.
My body is . . . hunger is my fear;
My success has vanished, my *stability* has gone.
My strength is weakened, my prosperity has ended,
Moaning and trouble have darkened my features.   (30)
The grain of my fields is far from satisfying [me],
Beer, the people's sustenance, is far from *being enough for me.*
Can a life of happiness be assured? I wish I knew how!

Friend IV

What I say is restrained, . . . [. . .]
But you [. . .] your reason contrarily.
You make [your . . .] diffuse and irrational,
You [turn] your select . . . blind.
As to your persistent unending desire for . . . [. . .]
[The former] security . . . [is . . .] by prayers.
The appeased goddess returns with [. . .]   (40)
[. . .] without setting things aright, takes pity on [. . .]
Ever seek the [correct standards] of justice.
Your . . . , the mighty one, will show kindness,
[. . .] will grant mercy.

Sufferer V

I have bowed to you, my [comrade], I have taken your . . .
[. . .] . . . the utterance of [your . . .].
[. . .] . . . come, let me [say something to you].
The onager, the wild ass, who filled itself with . . .
Did it pay attention to *the giver of assured* divine oracles?
The savage lion who devoured the choicest meat,   (50)
Did it bring its flour offering to appease the goddess's anger?
. . . the prominent person who has multiplied his wealth,
Did he weigh out precious gold for the goddess Mami?
[Have I] withheld offerings? I have prayed to my god,
I have pronounced the blessing over the goddess's regular sacrifices,

. . .

Friend VI

O date palm, tree that gives wealth, my precious brother,
Endowed with all wisdom, jewel of [. . .]
You are as stable as the earth, but the plan of the gods is remote.
Look at the superb wild ass on the [plain;]
The arrow will turn to the gorer who trampled down the fields. (60)
Come, consider the lion that you mentioned, the enemy of cattle,
For the deed which the lion did the pit awaits him.

The opulent prominent person who heaps up goods
Will be burned to death by the king before his time.
Would you wish to go the way these have gone?
Rather seek the lasting reward of (your) god!

    Sufferer VII

Your mind is the north wind, a pleasant breeze for the people.
Dearest friend, your advice is good.
Just one word would I put before you.
Those who do not seek the god go the way of prosperity,   (70)
While those who pray to the goddess become destitute and
    impoverished.
In my youth I tried to find the will of my god;
With prostration and prayer I sought my goddess.
But I was pulling a yoke in a useless corvée.
My god decreed poverty instead of wealth (for me).
A cripple does better than I, a dullard keeps ahead of me.
The rogue has been promoted, but I have been brought low.

    Friend VIII

My just, knowledgeable friend, your thoughts are perverse.
You have now forsaken justice and *blaspheme* against your god's
    plans.
In your mind you think of disregarding the divine
    ordinances.   (80)
[. . .] the sound rules of (your) goddess.
The clever plans of the god [are . . .] like the center of heaven,
The decrees of the goddess are not . . .
. . . humanity has learned well.
Their ideas [. . .] to mankind;
To grasp the way of a goddess [. . .]
Their reason is close at hand [. . .]
. . . [. . .]

    (stanzas IX–XII lacking or badly damaged)

Sufferer XIII

I will abandon my home [. . .]   (133)
I will desire no property [. . .]
I will disregard my god's regulations and trample on his rites.
I will slaughter a calf and will . . . the food,
I will take the road and go to distant places,
I will dig a well and let loose a flood,
I will roam over the remote open country like a robber.
I will go from house to house to ward off my hunger;   (140)
I will search in hunger and roam the streets.
Like a beggar I will [. . .] inwards [. . .]
Happiness is far away . . . [. . .]

    (stanza XIV badly damaged)

Sufferer XV

The daughter speaks [unjust things] to her mother.   (159)

The fowler who casts [his net] is fallen.   (160)

All in all, which person [has] success?

The many wild creatures which . . . [. . .]

Which among them has [. . .]?

Should I seek a son and daughter [. . .]?

May I not lose what I find . . . [. . .]

　　　Friend XVI

Humble and submissive one . . . [. . .]

Your will ever submits [. . .] precious.

　　　　　(rest of stanza damaged or missing)

　　　Sufferer XVII

The crown prince is clothed in [*rags*]   (181)

The son of the destitute and naked is clad in [fine garments]

The one who keeps watch over the malt (as it dries) [accumulates]
　　　gold.

The one who measures out the red gold must bear the [. . .]

The one who (normally) eats only vegetables [eats] the dinner of a
　　　noble.

The son of the important and the rich has only a carob to eat.

The rich man is fallen. [His *wealth*] is far away.

　　　　　(stanzas XVIII and XIX badly damaged)

　　　Friend XX

You have let your cunning mind go astray.   (212)

[. . .] you have scorned wisdom,

[. . .] you despise what is proper, you profane the ordinances.

[. . .] . . . the carrying-hod is far away from him.

[. . .] is made into a person of influence,

[. . .] is called a savant;

He is looked after and gets what he wants.

Follow in the way of the god, *observe his rites*,

[. . .] is considered righteousness.   (220)

　　　　　(stanza XXI badly damaged)

　　　Friend XXII

As for the rogue whose favor you want,   (235)

His . . . soon vanishes.

The rogue who has acquired wealth [in a manner] which is against
　　　the will of the gods

Is persecuted by a murderer's weapon.

Unless you seek the will of the god, what success can you have?

He that bears his god's yoke never lacks food, even though it be
　　　sparse.   (240)

Seek the favorable breath of the god,

What you have lost in a year you will make up in a moment.

Sufferer XXIII

I have looked around in the world, but things are turned around.
The god does not impede the way of even a demon.
A father tows a boat along the canal,
While his son lies in bed.
The eldest son makes his way like a lion,
The second son is happy to be a mule driver.
The heir goes about along the streets like a *peddler*,
The younger son (has enough) that he can give food to the
    destitute.   (250)
What has it profited me that I have bowed down to my god?
I must bow even to a person who is lower than I,
The rich and opulent treat me, as a youngest brother, with
    contempt.

Friend XXIV

O wise one, O savant, who masters knowledge,
Your heart has become hardened and you accuse the god wrongly.
The mind of the god, like the center of the heavens, is remote;
Knowledge of it is very difficult; people cannot know it.
Among all the creatures whom Aruru formed
Why should the oldest offspring be so . . . ?
In the case of a cow, the first calf is a runt,   (260)
The later offspring is twice as big.
A first child is born a weakling,
But the second is called a mighty warrior.
Though it is possible to find out what the will of the god is, people
    do not know how to do it.

Sufferer XXV

Pay attention, my friend, understand my clever ideas,
Heed my carefully chosen words.
People extol the word of a strong man who has learned to kill
But bring down the powerless who has done no wrong.
They confirm (the position of) the wicked for whom what should
    be an abomination is considered right
Yet drive off the honest man who heeds the will of his god.   (270)
They fill the [storehouse] of the oppressor with gold,
But empty the larder of the beggar of its provisions.
They support the powerful, whose . . . is guilt,
But destroy the weak and trample the powerless.
And as for me, an insignificant person, a prominent person
    persecutes me.

Friend XXVI

Narru, king of the gods, who created mankind,
And majestic Zulummar, who pinched off the clay for them,
And goddess Mami, the queen who fashioned them,

Gave twisted speech to the human race.
With lies, and not truth, they endowed them forever.　　　(280)
Solemnly they speak favorably of a rich man,
"He is a king," they say, "riches should be his,"
But they treat a poor man like a thief,
They have only bad to say of him and plot his murder,
Making him suffer every evil like a criminal, because he has no . . .
Terrifyingly they bring him to his end, and extinguish him like
　　　glowing coals.
　　　Sufferer XXVII
You are kind, my friend; behold my trouble,
Help me; look on my distress; know it.
I, though humble, wise, and a suppliant,
Have not seen help or aid even for a moment.　　　(290)
I have gone about the square of my city unobtrusively,
My voice was not raised, my speech was kept low.
I did not raise my head, but looked at the ground,
I did not worship even as a slave in the company of my associates.
May the god who has abandoned me give help,
May the goddess who has [forsaken me] show mercy,
The shepherd, the sun of the people, pastures (his flock) as a god
　　　should.

Aramaic Proverbs and Precepts

Translator: H. L. Ginsberg

The Words of Ahiqar

ANET, 427–30

The text is preserved as the more recent writing on eleven sheets of palimpsest papyrus of the late fifth century B.C. recovered by German excavators from the debris of Elephantine, Upper Egypt, in the years 1906–7. The first four papyri, with a total of five columns, contain the story of Ahiqar, which is in the first person; the remaining seven, with a total of nine columns, contain Ahiqar's sayings. The composition of the work may antedate the preserved copy by as much as a century.

Prior to the recovery of the old Aramaic text, several post-Christian recensions of the book of Ahiqar were known, the Syriac one being the oldest. The man Ahiqar is mentioned in the book of Tobit (1:22; 14:10; etc.).

. . .

(vi 79–94) [Wh]at is stronger than a braying ass?
The l[o]ad. The son who is trained and taught and on [whose] feet the fetter is put [*shall prosper*]. Withhold not thy son from the rod,

else thou wilt not be able to save [him from *wickedness*]. If I smite thee, my son, thou wilt not die, but if I leave thee to thine own heart [thou wilt not live]. A blow for a bondman, *a reb[uke]* for a bond-woman, and for all thy slaves dis[cipline. One who] buys a run[away] slave [or] a thievish handmaid *squanders his fortune and disgraces]* the name of his father and his offspring with the reputation of his wantonness.—The scorpion [finds] bread but is not p[leased, and *something b]ad* and is more pleased than if one fe[eds it . . .] The lion will *lie in wait* for the stag in the concealment of the . . . and he [. . .] and will shed its blood and eat its flesh. Even so is the meeting of [*me*]*n.*— . . . a lion. . . . An ass which leaves [*its load*] and *does not carry it* shall take a *load* from its companion and take the b[urde]n which is not its [own with its own] and shall be made to bear a camel's load.—The ass *bend[s down]* to the she-ass [from lo]ve of her, and the birds [. . .]. Two things [which] are meet, and the third pleasing to Shamash: one who dr[inks] wine and gives it to drink, one who guards wisdom, and one who hears a word and does not tell.—Behold that is dear [to] Shamash. But he who drinks wine and does not [give it to drink], and one whose wisdom goes astray, [and . . .] is seen.— [. . . Wisdom . . .].

(vii 95–110) To gods also she is dear. F[or all time] the kingdom is [hers]. In he[av]en is she established, for the lord of holy ones has exalted [her.—My s]on, ch[at]ter not overmuch so that thou speak out [every w]ord [that] comes to thy mind; for men's (eyes) and ears are everywhere (trained) u[pon] thy mouth. Beware lest it be [thy] *undoing.* More than all watchfulness watch thy mouth, and [over] what [*thou*] h[*earest*] harden thy heart. For a word is a bird: once re-leased no man *can re[capture it].* First co[un]t *the secrets of* thy mouth; then bring out thy [words] by *number.* For the *instruction* of a mouth is stronger than the *instruction* of war. Treat not lightly the word of a king: let it be healing for thy [flesh]. Soft is the utterance of a king; (yet) it is sharper and stronger than a [two]-edged knife. Look before thee: a hard look [on the f]ace of a k[ing] (means) "Delay not!" His wrath is swift as lightning: do thou take heed unto thyself that he disp[lay i]t not against thine ut[tera]nces and thou perish [be]fore thy time. [The wr]ath of a king, if thou be commanded, is a burning fire. Obey [it] at once. Let it not be kindled against thee and cover (read: *burn*) thy hands. [Cov]er up the word of a king with the veil of the heart.—Why should wood strive with fire, flesh with a knife, a man with [*a king*]? I have tasted even the bitter medlar, and [*I have eaten*] endives; but there is naught which is more [bi]tter than poverty. Soft is the tongue of *a k[ing]*, but it breaks a dragon's ribs; like a plague, which is not seen.—Let not thy heart rejoice over the multitude of children [nor grieve] over their fewness. A king is like *the Merciful*; his voice also is loud: who is there that can stand before

Prov. 4:23

Prov. 4:22; 16:24

Eccles. 8:2–3

Eccles. 6:10

Prov. 25:15

him, except one with whom is God? Beautiful is a king to behold, and noble is his majesty to them that walk the earth as [free]men. A good vessel cove[rs] a word in its heart, and a broken one lets it out. The lion approached to [greet the ass]: "Peace be unto thee." The ass answered and said to the lion: . . .

(viii 111–25) I have lifted sand, and I have carried salt; but there is naught which is heavier than [rage].

Prov. 27:3; Job. 6:2–3

I have lifted bruised straw, and I have taken up bran; but there is naught which is lighter than a sojourner.[26] War troubles calm waters between good friends. If a man be small and grow great, his words soar above him. For the opening of his mouth is an utte[ra]nce of gods, and if he be beloved of gods they will put something good in his mouth to say. Many are [the st]ar[s of heaven wh]ose names no man knows. By the same token, no man knows mankind.

Prov. 16:1

Isa. 40:26; Ps. 147:4

There is [n]o lion in the sea, therefore they call a flood a lb'. The leopard met the goat when she was cold. The leopard answered and said to the goat, "Come, I will cover thee with my hide." The goat [answered] and said to the leopard, "What need have I for it, my lord? Take not my skin from me." For he does not greet the gazelle[27] except to suck its blood.—The bear went to the lam[bs. "Give me one of you and I] will be content." The lam[bs] answered and said to him, "Take whichever thou wilt of us. We are [thy] la[mbs]." Truly, 'tis not in the power of m[e]n to li[ft u]p their feet or to put them down with[out the gods]. Truly, 'tis not in thy power to li[ft u]p thy foot [o]r to put it down.—If a good thing come forth from the mouths of m[en, it is well for them], and if an evil thing come [forth] from their mouths, the gods will do evil unto them.—If God's eyes are on men, a man may chop wood in the dark without seeing, like a thief, who demolishes a house and . . . (ix 123–41) [Bend not] thy [b]ow and shoot not thine arrow at a righteous man, lest God come to his help and turn it back upon thee. [If] thou [be hungry], my son, take every trouble and do every labor, then wilt thou eat and be satisfied and give to thy children. [If thou be]nd thy bow and shoot thine arrow at a righteous man, from thee is the arrow but from God the guidance. [If] thou [be needy], my son, borrow corn and wheat that thou mayest eat and be sated and give to thy children with thee. Take not a heavy loan, from an evil man. More[over, if] thou take a loan, give no rest to thyself until [thou repay the l]oan. [A loa]n is sweet as [. . .], but its repayment is grief. My [son, hearken not] with thine ears to [a lying man]. For a man's charm is his truthfulness; his repulsiveness, the lies of his lips. [At fi]rst a throne [is set up] for the liar, but in the e[nd they fi]nd out his lies and spit in his face. A liar's neck is cut

[26] I.e., there is nothing less respected.

[27] The goat seems to have become a gazelle through inadvertence.

[i.e., he speaks very softly?] like a . . . virgin that [is hidden] from sight, like a man who causes misfortune which does not proceed from God.—[Despise not] that which is in thy lot, nor covet a wealth which is denied thee. [Multiply not] riches and make not great thy heart. [Whosoever] *takes no pride* in the names of his father and mother, may the s[un] not shine [upon him]; for he is a wicked man. [From myself] has my misfortune proceeded: with whom shall I be justified?—The son of my body has spied out my house: [wh]at can I say to strangers? [*My son* has] been a false witness against me: who, then, has justified me?—From my house has gone forth wrath: with whom shall I strive? Reveal not thy [*secrets*] before thy [fri]ends, lest thy name become despised of them. (x 142–58) With him who is more exalted than thou, *quarrel not.* With him who is . . . and stronger than thou, [*contend not; for he will take*] of thy portion and [*add it to*] his. Behold even so is a small man (who strives) with [a great one]. Remove not wisdom from thee [. . .]. Gaze not overmuch [les]t thy vi[sion] be dimmed. Be not (too) sweet, lest they [swallow] thee: be not (too) bitter [*lest they spit thee out*]. If thou wouldst be [exalted], my son, [humble thyself before God], who humbles an [exalted] man and [exalts a lowly man]. What me[n's] l[i]ps curse, God does n[ot] curse. (Lines 152–55 badly damaged and omitted here.) God shall twist the twister's mouth and tear out [his] tongue. Let not good [ey]es be darkened, nor [good] ears [be stopped, and let a good mouth love] the truth and speak it. (xi 159–72) A man of [beco]ming conduct whose heart is good is like a mighty c[it]y which is si[*tuated*] upon a m[*ountain*]. There is [*none that can bring him down. Except*] a man *dwell* with God, how can he be guarded by his own refuge? . . . , but he with whom God is, who ca[n cas]t him down? (Line 162 difficult and omitted here.) A man [knows not] what is in his fellow's heart. So when a good man [se]es a wi[cked] man [let him beware of him]. Let him [not] join with him on a journey or be a *neighbor* to him—a good man [wi]th a ba[d] m[an]. The [bram]ble sent to [the] pomegranate tree [saying], "The bramble to the pomegranate: Wherefore the mul(titude) of (thy) thorns [to him that to]uches thy [fru]it?" . . . The [pomegranate tree] answered and said to the bramble, "Thou art al[l] thorns to him that touches thee." All that come in contact with a righteous man are on his side. [*A city*] of wicked men shall on a gusty day be pulled apart, and in . . . its gates be brought low; for the spoil [of the righteous are they].—Mine eyes which I lifted up unto thee and my heart which I gave thee in wisdom [hast thou scorned, and thou ha]st brought my name into disg[race]. If the wicked man seize the corner of thy garment, leave it in his hand. Then approach Shamash: he will [t]ake his and give it to thee.

Prov. 20:20

Prov. 25:9–10

(xii 173–90) (Ends of all lines and beginnings of some missing. Only the point of line 188 is entirely clear: "Hunger makes bitterness sweet, and thirst [sourness]." In column xiii 191–207, only of a few sayings is enough preserved for making out the point.)

Prov. 27:7

… If thy master entrust to thee water to keep [*and thou do it faithfully, he may*] leave gold with thee. … [A man] one [day said] to the wild ass, "[Let me ride] upon thee, and I will maintain thee [… ." Said the wild ass, "Keep] thy maintenance and thy fodder, and let me not see thy riding."—Let not the rich man say, "In my riches I am glorious."

Jer. 9:23

(Column xiv 208–23 has only shreds preserved; the point of the first one can be guessed: "[*Do not sh*]ow an Arab the sea nor a Sidonian the *de*[*sert*]; for their work is *different*.")

XVI

Oracles and Prophecies

ANET, 444–46 ## The Egyptian Prophecy of Nefer-rohu

TRANSLATOR: JOHN A. WILSON

The Middle Kingdom delivered Egypt from the civil war and anarchy which had followed the Old Kingdom. These troubles and their ultimate resolution produced a sense of messianic salvation, a feeling which the early pharaohs of the Middle Kingdom probably fostered in their own interests. The following text was apparently composed at that time of happy deliverance, although the earliest extant copies happen to date from the Eighteenth Dynasty, about five centuries later. The text purports to relate how King Snefru of the Fourth Dynasty sought entertainment and how a prophet foretold the downfall of the Old Kingdom and the reestablishment of order by Amenem-het I, the first king of the Twelfth Dynasty.

NOW IT HAPPENED THAT the majesty of the King of Upper and Lower Egypt: Snefru, the triumphant, was the beneficent king in this entire land. On one of these days it happened that the official council of the Residence City entered into the Great House—life, [prosperity], health!—to offer greeting. Then they went out, that they might offer greetings (elsewhere), according to their daily procedure. Then his majesty—life, prosperity, health!—said to the seal-bearer who was at his side: "Go and bring me (back) the official council of the Residence City, which has gone forth hence to offer greetings on this [day]." (Thereupon they) were ushered in to him (5) immediately. Then they were on their bellies in the presence of his majesty a second time.

Then his majesty—life, prosperity, health!—said to them: "(My) people, behold, I have caused you to be called to have you seek out for me a son of yours who is wise, or a brother of yours who is competent, or a friend of yours who has performed a good deed, one who may say to me a few fine words or choice speeches, at the hearing of which my [majesty] may be entertained."

Then they put (themselves) upon their bellies in the presence of his majesty—life, prosperity, health!—once more. THEN THEY SAID BEFORE his majesty—life, prosperity, health!: "A great lector-priest of Bastet,[1] O sovereign, our lord, (10) whose name is Nefer-rohu—he is a commoner valiant [with] his arm, a scribe competent with his fingers; he is a man of rank, who has more property than any peer of his. Would that he [*might be permitted*] to see his majesty!" Then his majesty—life, prosperity, health!—said: "Go and [bring] him to me!"

Then he was ushered in to him immediately. Then he was on his belly in the presence of his majesty—life, prosperity, health! Then his majesty—life, prosperity, health!—said: "Come, pray, Nefer-rohu, my friend, that thou mayest say to me a few fine words or choice speeches, at the hearing of which my majesty may be entertained!" Then the lector-priest Nefer-rohu said: "Of what has (already) happened or of what is going to happen, O Sovereign—life, prosperity, health!—[my] lord?" (15) Then his majesty—life, prosperity, health!—said: "Rather of what is going to happen. *If it has* taken place *by* today, *pass it* [*by*]."[2] Then he stretched forth his hand for the box of writing equipment; then he drew forth a scroll of papyrus and a palette; thereupon he put (it) into writing.[3]

What the lector-[priest] Nefer-rohu said, that wise man of the east, he who belonged to Bastet at her appearances, that child of the Heliopolitan nome,[4] AS HE BROODED over what (was to) happen in the land, as he called to mind the state of the east, when the Asiatics would move about with their strong arms, would disturb the hearts [of] those who are at the harvest, and would take away the spans of cattle at the plowing. (20) He said:

Reconstruct, O my heart, (*how*) thou bewailest this land in which thou didst begin! To be silent is *repression.* Behold, there is something about which men speak as *terrifying,* for, behold, the great man is a thing passed away (in the land) where thou didst begin. BE NOT LAX; BEHOLD, IT is before thy face! Mayest thou rise up against what is before thee, for, behold, although great men are concerned with the land, what has been done is as what is not done. *Re must begin the*

---

[1] The lector-priest (literally, "he who carries the ritual") was initiated into the sacred writings and thus was priest, seer, and magician. Bastet was the cat-goddess of Bubastis in the eastern half of the Delta.

[2] This must be the general sense, although the wording is obscure. An Egyptian interest in the future, rather than the past, was not normal, but a prophecy which promised that the future would restore the past would be acceptable.

[3] The pharaoh himself wrote down the prophecy. The Egyptian texts treat Snefru as a friendly and approachable ruler.

[4] Although now serving in Bubastis, he was born in the Heliopolitan nome.

Isa. 24:3

foundation (*of the earth over again*). The land is completely perished, (so that) no remainder exists, (so that) not (even) the black of the nail survives from what was fated.[5]

Amos 8:9

THIS LAND IS (SO) DAMAGED (that) there is no one who is concerned with it, no one who speaks, no eye that weeps. How is this land? The sun disc is covered over. (25) It will not shine (so that) people may see. No one can live when clouds cover over (the sun). Then everybody is deaf for lack of it.

I shall speak of what is before my face; I cannot foretell what has not (yet) come.

Isa. 19:5
Ezek. 30:12

THE RIVERS of Egypt are empty, (so that) the water is crossed on foot. Men seek for water for the ships to sail on it. Its course is [become] a sandbank. The sandbank *is against* the flood; the place of water *is against* the [flood]—(*both*) the place of water *and* the sandbank.[6] The south wind will oppose the north wind; the skies are no (longer) in a single wind.[7] A foreign bird will be born in the marshes of the Northland. It has made a nest beside (30) men, and people have let it approach through want of it.[8] DAMAGED INDEED ARE

Isa. 19:8

THOSE good things, those fish-ponds, (where there were) those who clean fish, overflowing with fish and fowl. Everything good is disappeared, and the land is prostrate because of woes from that *food,*[9] the Asiatics who are throughout the land.

Isa. 19:18

Foes have arisen in the east, and Asiatics have come down into Egypt. . . . No protector will listen. . . . Men will enter into the *fortresses.* Sleep will *be banished* from my eyes, (35) as I spend the night

Zeph. 2:15

wakeful. THE WILD BEASTS OF THE DESERT WILL drink at the rivers of Egypt and be at their ease on their banks for lack of *some one to scare them away.*

This land is helter-skelter, and no one knows the result which will come about, which is hidden from speech, sight, or hearing. The face is deaf, for silence *confronts.* I show thee the land topsy-turvy. That which never happened has happened. Men will take up weapons of warfare, (so that) the land lives in (40) confusion. MEN WILL MAKE ARROWS of metal,[10] beg for the bread of blood, and laugh with the laughter of sickness.[11] There is no one who weeps because of death;

[5] Not so much of the "Black Land" of Egypt survives as might be under a fingernail.

[6] Perhaps mistranslated, but attempting to hold the idea that neither the banks nor the bed of the stream would receive the life-giving inundation.

[7] The pleasant north wind is the normal wind of Egypt.

[8] A strange passage, which either emphasizes the unnaturalness of nature in the distressed times or else is an oblique reference to Asiatics infiltrating into the Delta.

[9] The Asiatics are a bitter diet for the Egyptians?

[10] Note that metal arrow-points were first used in Egypt in the Eleventh Dynasty (about 2100 B.C.).

[11] Hysteria.

there is no one who spends the night fasting because of death; (but) a man's heart pursues himself (alone). (Dishevelled) mourning is no (longer) carried out to-day, (for) the heart is completely *separated from* it. A man sits *in his corner,* (*turning*) his back while one man kills another. I show thee the son as a foe, the brother as an enemy, and a man (45) killing his (own) father. **Isa. 19:2**

EVERY MOUTH IS FULL OF "LOVE ME!", AND everything GOOD has disappeared. The land is perished, (*as though*) laws *were* destined *for it:* the damaging of what had been done, the emptiness of what had been found,[12] and the doing of what had not been done. Men take a man's property away from him, and it is given to him who is from outside. I show thee the possessor in need and the outsider satisfied. He who never filled for himself (*now*) *empties.*[13] Men will [*treat*] (fellow) citizens as hateful, in order to silence the mouth that speaks. If a statement is answered, an arm goes out with a stick, and men speak with: "Kill him!" THE UTTERANCE OF SPEECH IN THE HEART is like a fire. (50) Men cannot suffer what issues from *a man's* mouth.

The land is diminished, (but) its administrators are many; bare, (but) its taxes are great; little in grain, (but) the measure is large, and it is measured to over-flowing.[14]

Re separates himself (from) mankind. If he shines forth, it is (but) an hour. No one knows when midday falls, for his shadow cannot be distinguished.[15] There is no one bright of face when seeing [him]; the eyes are not moist with water, when he is in the sky like the moon. His prescribed time does not fail. His rays are indeed in (men's) faces in his former way.

I SHOW THEE THE LAND TOPSY-TURVY. The weak of arm is (now) **Isa. 24:1**
the possessor of an arm. Men (55) salute (respectfully) him who (formerly) saluted. I show thee the undermost on top, turned about *in proportion to* the turning about *of my belly.* Men live in the necropolis. The poor man will make wealth. . . . It is the paupers who eat the offering-bread, while the servants *jubilate.* The Heliopolitan nome, the birthplace of every god, will no (*longer*) *be on earth.*

(THEN) IT IS THAT a king WILL COME, BELONGING TO THE SOUTH, Ameni, the triumphant, his name. He is the son of a woman of the land of Nubia; he is one born in Upper Egypt.[16] He will take the

---

[12] A pious obligation resting upon the Egyptians was to restore the inscriptions of the ancestors which were "found empty," i.e., damaged or containing lacunae. Under the present unsettled conditions what was found empty was left empty.

[13] Perhaps: he who never had to insist on full measure for himself now scrapes the bottom.

[14] A land smaller and poorer has more bureaucrats and higher and more exacting taxes.

[15] The sun's shadow on the shadow-clock determined the hour of noon.

[16] Ameni was an abbreviated name for Amen-em-het (I).

[White] Crown; he will wear the Red Crown; (60) he will unite the Two Mighty Ones;[17] he will satisfy the Two Lords[18] with what they desire. The encircler-of-the-fields (will be) in his grasp, the oar . . . [19]

REJOICE, ye people of his time! The son of a man will make his name forever and ever. They who incline toward evil and who plot rebellion have subdued their speech for fear of him. The Asiatics will fall to his sword, and the Libyans will fall to his flame. The rebels belong to his wrath, and the treacherous of heart to (65) the awe of him. The uraeus-serpent which is on his brow stills for him the treacherous of heart.

THERE WILL BE BUILT the Wall of the Ruler—life, prosperity, health![20]—and the Asiatics will not be permitted to come down into Egypt that they might beg for water in the customary manner, in order to let their beasts drink. And justice will come into its place, while wrongdoing is *driven* out.[21] Rejoice, he who may behold (this) (70) and who may be in the service of the king!

The learned man will pour out water for me,[22] when he sees what I have spoken come to pass.

IT HAS COME (TO ITS END) in [success], by the *Scribe* . . .

Akkadian Oracles and Prophecies
Divine Revelations in Letters from Mari
and Ashur

ANET³, 623–26, 629–32

TRANSLATOR: WILLIAM L. MORAN

With the exception of (j), all the letters are from the Mari archives.

The letters are grouped according to the recipients of the revelations: private persons (a–d), ecstatics (e–g), those designated by the term *āpilum* (variant, *aplûm;* fem. *āpiltum;* h–i), a prophetess (j).

a

The writer is known both as the governor of Nahur (cf., Nahor, Gen. 11:26) on the upper Habur, and as an official at the court of Mari. It is in the latter

---

[17] The two tutelary goddesses of Upper and Lower Egypt, who united as the Double Crown.

[18] Horus and Seth.

[19] As one act of the coronation ceremonies, the pharaoh, grasping an oar and some other object, dedicated a field by running around it four times.

[20] A series of fortresses along the eastern frontier, as in *Si-nuhe.*

[21] The coronation of each pharaoh reinstituted the old order of *ma'at* "justice," and expelled "deceit."

[22] As a libation at the tomb.

capacity that he seems to have sent this letter to the king Zimri-Lim, who must therefore have been absent from Mari. Hence our tablet, unless it was never sent, must be a copy.

Speak to my lord: Thus Itur-Asdu your servant. (5) The day I dispatched this tablet of mine to my lord, Malik-Dagan, a man from Shakka, ca⟨m⟩e and spoke to me as follows: "In a dream of mine I was set on going in the company of a(nother) man (10) from the fortress of Sagaratum, in the Upper District, to Mari. *On my way* I entered Terqa, and right after entering I entered the temple of Dagan and (15) prostrated myself. As I was prostrate, Dagan opened his mouth and spoke to me as follows: "Did the kings of the Yaminites and their forces make peace with the forces of Zimri-Lim (20) who moved up here?" I said, "They did not make peace." Just before I went out he spoke to me as follows: "Why are the messengers (25) of Zimri-Lim not in constant attendance upon me, and why does he not lay his full report before me? Had this been done, I would long ago have delivered (30) the kings of the Yaminites into the power of Zimri-Lim. Now go, I send you. Thus shall you speak to Zimri-Lim, saying: (35) 'Se[nd] me your messengers and lay your full report before me, and then I will have the kings of the Yaminites [*coo*]*ked* on a fisherman's *spit,* and I will lay them before you.'"

(40) This is what this man saw in his dream and then recounted to me. I now hereby write to my lord; my lord should deal with this dream. (45) Furthermore, if my lord so desires, my lord shall lay his full report before Dagan and the messengers of my lord shall be constantly on their way to Dagan. (50) The man who told me this dream was to offer a *pagrum*-sacrifice to Dagan, and so I did not send him on. Moreover, since this man was trustworthy, I did not take any of his hair or the fringe of his ga⟨r⟩ment.

b

The writer was the governor of Terqa; he writes to Zimri-Lim.

Speak to my lord: Thus Kibri-Dagan your servant. (5) Dagan and Ikrub-El are safe and sound; the ci[ty of Terqa and] the district are safe and sound. (A badly preserved line and a break of about six lines.) (rev.) He saw the following (dream): "You (pl.) shall not (re-)build this *deserted* house. If this house is (re)built, I will make it collapse into the river." (5′) The day he saw this dream, he said nothing to anyone. The next day he again saw the following dream: "It was a god. 'You (pl.) shall not (re)build this house. (10′) If you (re)-build it, I will make it collapse into the river.'" I now hereby (15′) dispatch to my lord the fringe of his garment and a lock from his head. From that day [this] servant has been ill.

c

The same correspondents and introduction as in b.

Furthermore, a man repeated the dre[am . . .] . . . [saying]: [x] thousand men . . . (10′) in the forti[fied] cities of [Ma]ri, Terqa, and [Sa]garatum (three badly preserved lines). (16′) [This man repea]ted this dream of his, and then [sh]ifted the responsibility onto me, saying, "Write to the ki[ng]." For this reason I wrote to my lord.

d

The same correspondents as in b and c; introduction omits reference to the gods and city.

(5) The day I sent this tablet of mine to my lord, a man's wife came to me before the darkness of the mountain (sundown) and (10) spoke to me on the news about Babylon as follows: "Dagan sent me. Write to your lord. He is not to worry, nor is he *ev*[*er*] to worry. (15) [Ha]mmurabi [the king o]f Babylon . . ." (rest of tablet almost entirely illegible).

e

The same correspondents as in b–d; the usual introduction.

Moreover, the day I sent this tablet of mine to my lord, [an ec]static of Dagan (10) came and addressed me as follows: "The god sent [me]. Hurry, write to the ki[ng] that they are to offer the mortuary-sacrifices for the sha[de] of Yahdun-Li[m]." This is what this ecstatic (20) said to me, and I have therefore written to my lord. Let my lord do what pleases him.

f

The same correspondents as in b–e; the usual introduction.

I have not been remiss in harvesting the barley of the district and storing it in the granaries. (10) [Moreover], with regard to the [construc]tion of the new gate, [. . .] the ecstatic came here earlier, [*the wor*]*k* (15) [*was started*] and [*we set abo*]*ut* [*the construction of*] that [ga]te. [*Now the day*] I sent this tablet of mine to my lord, (20) this [ec]static returned here and addressed [a wor]d to me, giving me [an ulti]matum: "[*I*]*f* you (pl.) do not build that gate, (25) [*a la*]*mentation* will be held! You are not numerous enough!" [Th]is is what this ecstatic [sa]id to me. Besides, I am [worr]ied for the har[vest]; (30) I cannot turn my [ne]ck. [*Heaven forbid that*] my lord should say . . .

g

The same correspondents as in b–f; lines 7–12 are concerned with the flocks of the Yaminites along the Euphrates.

(13) [The day I sent th]is tablet of mine [to] my lord, [. . . the *ecstatic* o]f Dagan ad[dressed me] as follows: "Dagan se[nt me] concerning the performance of the sacrifice [*for the dead*]. (20) Write to your lord that in the coming month, on the fourteenth day, the sacrifice *for the dead* is to be performed. Under no circumstances are they to omit this sacrifice." This is what this man said to me. (25) I now hereby write to my lord. May my lord do what in accordance with his deliberation pleases him.

h

Solecisms, barbarisms, and orthographic errors mark the letter as the work of a provincial scribe.

(Beginning broken.) [With regar]d to the *zukrum* and the cattle about which Abi-[. . .] said to me in the presence of Zu-Hadnim, "Hand over the *zuk*[*rum* and the cattle]," my lord told me (5) to hand over the *zukrum* in the presence of the kin[gs and . . .], saying, "In the future he is not to break the agreement with me." I provided witnesses against him. My lord should know this.

At (the inspection of) the omens Adad the lord of Kallassu [spoke] as follows: "Am I not (10) Adad the lord of Kallassu who reared him between my thighs and restored him to the throne of his father's house? After restoring him to the throne of his father's house, I again gave him a dwelling-place. Now, since I (15) restored him to the throne of his father's house, I should receive from him an hereditary property. If he does not give (it), I am the lord of throne, territory, and city, and what I gave I will take away. If on the other hand (20) he grants my request, I will give him throne upon throne, house upon house, territory upon territory, city upon city; even the land from east to west will I give him." This is what the *āpilu's* said. Furthermore, (25) they are constantly appear⟨ing⟩ at (the inspection of) the omens, (and) now to boot the *āpilum* of Adad the lord of Kallassu is guarding the *threshing-floor* of Alahtum as the hereditary property. My lord should know this.

(30) Previously, when I was living in Mari, I reported to my lord every word the *āpilum* and the *āpiltum* told me. Now I am living [in] a different country, (but) am I not to write to my lord what I hear and they tell me? (35) If in the future something amiss should happen, would my lord not say, "Why did you not write to me the word the *āpilum* told you and that he was guarding your *threshing-floor*." I have now (40) written to my lord. My lord should know this.

[More]over, the *āpilum* of Adad the lord of Halab (Aleppo) came [to Abu]-Halum and said, "[Wr]ite to your lord (break)." (Edge of tablet) "[. . . from the east] to the west [*it is I*] who will give him." [This] is what Adad the lord of Halab said in the presence of Abu-Halum. My lord should know this.

i

The writer was a high official at Mari; he writes to Zimri-Lim.

Speak to my lord: Thus Mukannishum your servant. (5) I offered a sacrifice to Dagan for the life of my lord, and then the *aplûm* of Dagan of Tut[tul] arose and spoke as follows: "O Babylon! How must you be constantly treated? (10) I am going to gather you into a net . . . I will d[eli]ver into the power of Zimri-Li[m] the houses of the seven confederates and all their poss⟨ess⟩ions." Moreover, the *aplûm* of D[agan] . . . he s[poke] as follows (rest destroyed).

j

The writer, who is well known from other reports to Esarhaddon, the one addressed in this letter, served as a kind of ambassador at large.

[To the king] my [lord] your servant [Mar-Ishtar]. [Greetings] to the king my lord. [May Nabu and Bel] bless [the king] my lord. [A long life], health and happiness may [the great gods] (5) grant the king my lord. [Damqi], the son of the bishop of Ak[kad], [. . .] of the land of Ashur and Babylon [. . .] exercised hegemony over the universe. He [and his queen] have . . . [. . .]; (10) the substitution for the king my lord, [the queen-mother] (and) the . . . of Shamash-shum-ukin [he . . .]. For their redemption he went to (his) fate. We built the mausoleum, he (and) his queen (15) were outfitted in their finery, solemnly laid in state, buried, (and) mourned. The burning (of magical figurines) has been performed; all (evil) portents have been rendered ineffective; many rituals against (evil) portents, (the ceremonies) "House of (ritual) bathing," "House of dipping in water," (as well as other) incantation-rituals (and) lamentations for the pacification of the gods, (20) have been carried out punctiliously, in the traditional formulae of the scribal guild. For the information of the king my lord.

I have heard that (even) before these ceremonies (of enthronement), the prophetess prophesied, (and) to Damqi, the bishop's son, she said: (25) "You shall bear my kingship." (reverse) Moreover, the prophetess said to him in an assembly of the people: "I have indicated the . . . of my lord, I have turned you over (to the assembly)."

The apotropaic (5) rituals which were performed went perfectly. The king my lord should be exceedingly gratified. (Of course) the

Akkadians were frightened, (but) we reassured them (and) they calmed down. I heard (too) that the bishops and the high (temple-) officials of Akkad were frightened. (10) (Thus) have Bel and Nabu (and) all the great gods prolonged the life of the king my lord. However, during the *eternity* of the eclipse and the conjunction of the gods he (the king) must not in fact go to the (palace?) *limits*.

If it is acceptable to the king my lord, (15) a commoner should be appointed to the bishopric as previously. He should offer the daily sacrifices before the high-altar; on the days of the monthly-feasts and (the feast) of the "Greeting of the temple" he should pour out the incense on the censor-stands [before] the Lady of Akkad, (and then) should (the moon) bring about an eclipse (and with it) affe[ct] Akkad, (20) [...] he should serve as the king's substitute. (21–25 fragmentary) Whoever is acceptable to the king my lord, the king my lord should appoint in his (Damqi's) place.

k

The writer of the letter was the daughter of Yarim-Lim of Aleppo, who helped Zimri-Lim regain the throne of Mari. She sends this and letters l–o and t to her husband. That the words of the unnamed man and woman, who are so prominent in this letter, were considered revelations in some sense is clear from their being designated "word, utterance" (with oracular significance, Akk. *igerrûm*, lines 6, 10) and, implicitly, "signs, portents" (line 4). However, why they were so esteemed remains obscure.

Speak to my lord: Thus Shibtu your maid-servant. For a report on the campaign my lord is waging, I inquired (5) of a man and a woman ... for the signs, and the (oracular) word was very favorable to my lord. Similarly, I inquired of the man and woman with regard to Ishme-Dagan, (10) and the (oracular) word concerning him was not favorable. As to the report on him, he has been placed under the foot of my lord. Thus they (spoke): "My lord raised the *ḫumāšum* to Ishme-Dagan, (15) saying, 'I shall beat you (in a contest) with the *ḫumāšum*. Just wrestle and I shall beat you in wrestling.'" Thus I (spoke): "Is my lord approaching battle?" Thus they (spoke): (20) "No battle will be fought. Right after arriving his (Ishme-Dagan's) auxiliary troops will be scattered, (25) and they will cut off the he[ad of Ishme]-Dagan and then put it under the foot of my lord. Thus (my lord will say): 'The army of Ishme-Dagan is large, and if I [arriv]e, (30) will his auxiliary forces be sca[tt]ered from him? They have hemmed in my own auxiliary forces.' It is Dagan, Adad, Itur-Mer, and Belet-ekallim—and Adad is indeed the lord of decision—who are march[ing] at the side of my lord. (35) Heaven forbid that my lord should s[ay] this, 'With arms I [*must defeat* t]hem.'"

(I am not making them sp[eak]. They speak on their own, and on their own they ag[ree]). (40) Thus they (spoke): "The auxiliary forces of Ishme-[Dagan] are (made up of) captives. With acts of treason *and treachery* they are constantly . . . They do not accept [. . .] [Be]fore my lord his army will be scattered."

l

An otherwise unknown cult-player seems to have been granted a revelation by the goddess Annunitum regarding an enemy (Hammurabi of Babylon?) of the king. It was not only very favorable, but it agreed with the report that the queen had received when on the same question she had made inquiries on her own, in all probability from the haruspex. This remarkable coincidence is urged as confirmation of the trustworthiness of the oracle.

Sp[e]ak to my lord: Thus Sh[i]btu your maid-servant. The palace is safe and sound. (5) I[li-kha]snaya, the c[ul]t-p[la]ye[r] of . . . , in [. . . *enter*]ed [*the temple of Annunitum*] and [*concerning the man of . . . the goddess* (10) has s]ent him here [*to my lord*]. [*Thus she* spo]ke, [*saying:* "I . . ."] (Break) (rev.) . . . I inquired, and this man is determining many things for this land. He will not succeed. (5') My lord will see what the goddess will do to this man. You will conquer him and over him you will stand. His days are short. He will not survive. My lord should know this. (10') Before the report of Ili-khasnaya which Annunitum sent here, on the fifth [d]ay (of the month) I myself had made inquiry, and the [re]port which Annunitum sent here to you (15) and that which I asked for agree perfectly.

m

This is a public prophecy, and with the new evidence of *ARM,* x [Archives Royales de Mari series, vol. X] the rule seems to be that in such cases the legal symbols of the lock of hair and the fringe of the tunic were required; see lines 23ff., and letters m, p, w. This and the following letter especially make it clear that extraordinary psychic states were characteristic of prophecies delivered in the temples; the evidence suggests trance of the lucid type in which the medium does not lose all consciousness of self and surroundings.

Speak to my lord: Thus Shibtu your maid-servant. The palace is safe and sound. (5) In the temple of Annunitum, on the third day (of the month), Shelebum went into a trance. Thus (spoke) Annunitum: "O Zimri-Lim, with a revolt (10) they would put you to the test. Guard yourself. At your side put servants, your controllers whom you love. (16) Station them so they can guard you. Do not go about by yourself. (20) And as for the men who would put you [to the test], I shall deliver [th]ese m[en] into your hand." Now I have hereby dispatched to my lord the ha[ir and fringe] (25) of the cu[lt-player].

n

Speak to my lord: Thus Shibtu your maid-servant. (5) In the temple of Annunitum in the city, Akhatum, the servant of Dagan-malik, went into a trance and spoke as follows, saying: "O Zimri-Lim, even though you for your part have spurned me, (10) I for my part shall embrace you. I shall deliver your enemies into your hand, (15) and the men of Sharrakiya I shall seize and gather them to the destruction of Belet-ekallim." On the following day (20) Akhum the priest brought me this report (together with) the hair and fringe, and I have written to my lord, sealed the hair (25) and fringe, and sent (them) to my lord.

o

[Speak to my lord: Th]us Shibtu your maid-servant. The temples, the gods, the palace, and the workshops are safe and sound. (5) More-over, Kakkalidi had the following vision in the temple of Itur-Mer: Two huge transports were blocking the river, and the king with the soldiers (10) was already on board in the center. Those on the right and the left were [sh]outing. Thus they (spoke): "Kingship, [sce]pter and throne, (15) the upper and lower *region* have been given to Zimri-Lim." And the soldiers to a man were answering: "To Zimri-Lim alone have they been given." These transports to the gate of the palace . . . (break).

p

The writer of the letter is known as a woman of some means and high position at the court of Mari. A disturbing dream of years back has returned, and this is made all the more ominous by a recent warning of an ecstatic which indicates the king is in danger.

Speak to my lord: Thus Addu-duri your maid-servant. Since the peace of your father's house I have never had this dream. These were my signs before. In my dream I entered the temple of Belet-ekallim and Belet-ekallim (10) was not in residence nor the statues before her present. And I saw this and went on weeping. This dream of mine was in the evening-watch. Again (I dreamt) and Dada, the priest (15) of Ishtar-pishra, was on duty in the gate of Belet-ekallim, and an eery voice was crying this over and over, saying: "Come back, O Dagan! (20) Come back, O Dagan!" This it was crying over and over. Moreover, the ecstatic arose in the temple of Annunitum and thus (spoke), saying: "O Zimri-Lim, do not go on an expedition. (25) Stay in Mari, and then I alone will take responsibility." My lord must not be negligent in guarding himself. (30) I m[y-self] hereby seal my hair and fringe and send (them) to my lord.

q

Speak to my lord: Thus Addu-duri. Iddin-ili, the priest (5) of Itur-Mer, saw a dream. Thus he (spoke): "In my dream Belet-biri stepped up to me and (10) spoke as follows. Thus she (spoke): '... is [*his*] ki[*ng-sh*]*ip* and the rule is his permanent possession. (15) Why does he keep going up again and again to the family-house? Let him guard himself.'" Now my lord must not be negligent in guarding himself.

r

The writer seems to have lived with the king's daughter in the palace of the ruler of Ilanṣura, a vassalage of Mari.

[Speak] to my lord [the Star]: Thus Shibat[um your maid-servant].... (rev.)... (5′) In the dream (it went) thus: A man of [...] stepped up and thus he (spoke): "Let the girl, the daughter of ... pahim ... , Tagidnate, be sum[moned]." This he said to me. Now, (10′) let my lord have the har[us]pex look into the matter, and if this [dr]eam was s[e]en, my lord, have confidence in this girl and let her be summoned. And may the *health* of my lord ...

s

Speak to my lord: Thus ... nana, your maid-servant. When I lived in Ganibatum, (5) I sent Kukkimkhiya to Rubben, and on her way they made off with her. But Dagan, your lord, protected me and no one touched me. Dagan said this to me. Thus he (spoke): (10) "Did you head up (or) down?" Thus I (spoke): "Down, and I came here and did not find my girl. When (15) my lord went to Andariq, the very image of my girl appeared here with Sammetar, and I went to him and he gave [me] his consent. (20) Again he broke faith with me and did not give me my girl." Dagan said this to me. Thus he (spoke): "Until the time Zimri-Lim frees your girl, no one (25) will release ⟨her⟩ to you." Now, in accordance with the wrath of Dagan, my lord must not detain my girl.

t

Speak to Addu-duri, my mistress: Thus Timlu yo[ur] maid-servant. Let it be a sign that at the time of ... (5) Yar'ib-Abba expelled me from Kasapa and I cam[e and] said [this] to you. Thus I (spoke): "I had a [dre]am about yo[u, and] (10) in my dr[eam] Annum ..."

u

Speak to my lord: Thus Shibtu your maid-servant. The palace is safe and sound. (5) Qishti-Diritim, the prophet of Diritum, on the second day (of the month) [came] to the gate of the palace [and] sent [t]his message to me. [Thus he (spoke)]: "Before the throne of *Ma*[*ri*]

(10) no one . . . To Zimri-Lim *ala'ītum* has been gi[ven]. The lance of the . . ." This is the message [he sent me]. (15) More[over, . . .] (break) (rev.) . . . (8') [*He spoke*] a word to E[a]. What Asumum [*said to Ea*] I did not hear. He ar[*ose and thus*] he spoke, saying: "[*Before*] we pronounce [the oath], let them take the di[rt] and door-frame of the gate [of Mari] . . . , and then [*let us pronounce*] the oath." (15') They took the dirt and the door-frame of the ga[te] of Mari and they dissolved (them) in water. Then the gods and goddesses drank. Thus (spoke) Ea: "Swear to the gods that [you will not] harm the brickwork or the *commissioner* [⟨of Mari⟩]." The gods and goddesses [swore]: "We will not harm the brickwork or the *commissioner* of Mari."

v

[Sp]eak [to] my lord: [Th]us Addu-duri your [maid]-servant. (5) [A pro]phet, Işi-akhu by name, [a]rose in the temple of [Kh]ishametum, and (spoke) thus: "Only your [*fo*]*llowers* will eat your [*ram* and (10) dri]nk your [*cu*]p. . . . Your [ad]versaries will be . . . [I al]one have trampled them down." (break)

w

Inibshina was a daughter of Zimri-Lim and dedicated to the god Adad as an *ugbabtu*-priestess. The prophetess probably delivered her oracle publicly, though no temple is mentioned. In view of letter n, the god inspiring her was probably Annunitum.

Speak to the Star: Thus Inibshina. Innibana the prophetess (5) arose and spoke as follows, saying: "O Zimri-Lim, the city Sharrakiya (10) [*I shall give to*] its enemies and those [en]circling it. . . . (16) I hereby give you my hair and fringe. Let them declare (me) free (of legal claims)." I now hereby send (20) the hair and the fringe to the Star. Let the Star [have] an omen taken so that he may act in accordance with his omens. Let the Star guard himself.

x

Speak to the Star: Thus Inibshina. Earlier Shelebum the cult-player (5) gave [m]e an oracle and I wrote to you. Now the *qamatum* of Dagan of Terqa came here and spoke as follows. (10) Thus she (spoke): "The peace-moves of the man of Eshnunna are sheer deception. 'Under the straw the water courses,' but (15) I am going to gather him into a net which holds fast. I shall put an end to his city, and his property, which from ancient times has [n]ot been destroyed, I shall destroy." (20) This she said to me. Now guard yourself. Without an omen do not enter the city. (25) Here is what I hear: "He keeps moving about by himself." You are not to keep moving about by yourself!

ANET³, 605

Oracles concerning Esarhaddon

TRANSLATOR: ROBERT D. BIGGS

(i 5) [Esarhad]don, king of the lands, fear not! *That* wind which blows against you—I need only say a word and I can bring it to an end. Your enemies, (10) like a (young) boar in the month of Simanu, will flee even at your approach. I am the great Belet—I am the goddess Ishtar of Arbela, she who (15) has destroyed your enemies at your mere approach. What order have I given you which you did not rely upon? I am Ishtar of Arbela! (20) I shall lie in wait for your enemies, I shall give them to you. I, Ishtar of Arbela, will go before you and behind you. (25) Fear not! You who are paralyzed (saying), "Only in crying Woe can I either get up or sit down."

(This oracle is) from the woman Ishtar-la-tashiat (30) of Arbela.

O king of Assyria, fear not! The enemy of the king of Assyria I will deliver to slaughter. (i 34–40 and ii 1–8 are too fragmentary for translation.)

(This oracle is) from the woman Sin-qisha-amur of Arbela.

(11) I rejoice over Esarhaddon, my king; Arbela rejoices! (This oracle is) from the woman Rimute-allate of the town Darahuya (15) which is in the mountains.

(16) Fear not, Esarhaddon! I, the god Bel, am speaking to you. (20) I watch over your inner heart as would your mother who brought you forth. Sixty great gods are standing together with me and protect you. The god Sin is at your right, the god Shamash at your left. (25) The sixty great gods are standing around you, ranged for battle. Do not trust human beings! Lift your eyes to me, look at me! (30) I am Ishtar of Arbela; I have turned Ashur's favor to you. When you were small, I *chose* you. Fear not! Praise me! Where is there any enemy who *overcame* you while I remained quiet? Those who are (now) behind will (soon) be the leaders. I am the god Nabu, god of the stylus. Praise me!

(40) (This oracle is) from the woman Baia of Arbela.

(A number of lines are destroyed or damaged.)

(iii 15) I am Ishtar of Arbela, O Esarhaddon, king of Assyria. In the cities Ashur, Nineveh, Calah, Arbela I shall grant you many days, endless years. I am the great midwife (who helped at your birth), (25) the one who gave you suck, who has established your rule under the *wide* heavens for many days, endless years; from a golden chamber in the heavens I will watch. I will light a lamp of *elmeshu*-stone for Esarhaddon, king of Assyria. (35) I will watch him like my very own crown. Fear not, O king! Because I have spoken to you (in an oracle), (40) I will not abandon you. (iv 1) Because I have encouraged you, I shall not let you come to shame. I will help you cross the river safely. (5) O Esarhaddon, legitimate heir, son of the goddess

Ninlil! I am . . . for you. With my own hands, your foes (10) I shall annihilate. (lines 11 and 12 obscure) O Esarhaddon, in the city Ashur I shall grant you long days, endless years. O Esarhaddon, in Arbela I am your good shield. O Esarhaddon, legitimate heir, son of the goddess Ninlil, I am thinking of [you]. I love [you] very much. (lines 26–39 obscure)

(v 1–3 obscure) I will *cut to pieces* before him those who speak . . . *blasphemies.* (lines 8 and 9 obscure)

(10) (This oracle is) from the woman Ishtar-bel-dayani, the . . . of the king.

(12) I, the Lady of Arbela, (say) to the king's mother: "Because you have complained against me saying 'He who is at the right and he who is at the left you hold on your lap, but where is my own offspring? You make him run about (unprotected) in the open country!'" Now, O king, fear not! Yours is the kingship! Yours is the might! (24–25) (This oracle is) from the woman Belit-abisha of Arbela.

(26) Greeting to Esarhaddon, king of Assyria! Ishtar of Arbela has gone out to the open country. Greeting to her son (i.e., the king)! You will send into the city . . . (lines 31–35 and vi 1–4 destroyed or badly damaged)

(vi 4) [. . . with which Ishtar] of Arbela fills his *arms.* Why did you not act on the earlier oracle which I gave to you? Now you should act on this later one. Praise me! When the day *declines,* let them hold torches *facing (me).* Praise me! (20) I will make the *riffraff* go out of my palace. You shall eat the best food and drink the best water. You shall live well in your palace. Your son and your grandson will exercise rule on the lap of the god Ninurta.

(30) (This oracle is) from the man La-dagal-ili of Arbela.

A Letter to Ashurbanipal

ANET³, 605–6

TRANSLATOR: ROBERT D. BIGGS

The text is a letter of Marduk-shum-usur to Ashurbanipal (668–633 B.C.).

(7) In a dream the god Ashur spoke to the grandfather of the king my lord (i.e., Sennacherib), the sage, [saying], "O king, lord of kings, offspring of the sage and of Adapa. . . . You surpass in knowledge even the *Apsû* and all the wise men." (10) When the father of the king my lord (i.e., Esarhaddon) went to Egypt, he saw in the region of Harran the temple made of cedar. The god Sin, leaning on a staff, had two crowns on his head. The god Nusku was standing in front of him. The father of the king my lord entered and he (i.e., Nusku) placed [a crown] on his head, saying, "You will go and will make conquests in several countries." (15) He left and in fact conquered Egypt. Other

lands, not yet submissive to Ashur and Sin, the king, lord of kings, will conquer. (rest too damaged for translation)

ANET³, 606

An Oracular Dream concerning Ashurbanipal

TRANSLATOR: ROBERT D. BIGGS

(v 46) The goddess Ishtar heard my anxious sighs and said "Fear not!" and gave me confidence, (saying) "Since you have lifted your hands in prayer and your eyes have filled with tears, I have had mercy." During the night in which I appeared before her, (50) a *šabrû*-priest lay down and had a dream. He awoke with a start and then Ishtar caused him to see a nocturnal vision. He reported to me as follows: "The goddess Ishtar who dwells in Arbela came in. Right and left quivers were suspended from her. She was holding a bow in her hand, (55) and a sharp sword was drawn to do battle. You were standing in front of her and she spoke to you like a real mother. Ishtar called to you, she who is most exalted among the gods, giving you the following instructions: 'Wait with the attack; (for) wherever you intend to go, I am also ready to go.' You said to her, 'Wherever you go, I will go with you, O goddess of goddesses!' She repeated her command to you as follows: 'You shall stay here where you should be. (65) Eat, drink wine, make merry, praise my divinity, while I go and accomplish that work to help you attain your heart's desire. Your face will not be pale, nor your feet shaky, and you need not wipe off your (cold) sweat in the height of battle.' She wrapped you in her lovely babysling, protecting your entire body. Her face shone like fire. Then [she went out in a frightening way] to defeat your enemies, (75) against Teumman, king of Elam, with whom she was angry."

ANET³, 606–7

Prophecies

TRANSLATOR: ROBERT D. BIGGS

(ii)

[That ruler's days will be sh]ort. That land
    [will have another ruler].   (1)

[A ruler will arise], he [will rule] for eighteen years.
The country will live safely, the interior of the country will be
    happy, the people will [have abun]dance.
The gods will make beneficial decisions for the country, favorable
    winds [will blow].
The date palm and the furrow will bring in good yield.
Shakkan and Nisaba will . . . in the land.
There will be (favorable) rain and high water, the people of the land
    will observe a festival.

That ruler will be killed in an uprising.

A ruler will arise, he will rule for thirteen years. (8)

There will be an attack of Elam against Akkad, and

The booty of Akkad will be carried off.

The temples of the great gods will be destroyed, the defeat of
    Akkad will be decreed (by the gods).

There will be confusion, disturbance, and unhappy events in the
    land, and

The reign will diminish (in power); another man, whose name is
    not mentioned (as a successor) will arise, and

Will seize the throne as king and will put to death his officials.

He will fill with the *corpses* of half the army the lowlands of Tupliash,

Plain and level ground, and

The people of the land will experience a severe famine.

A ruler will arise, his days will be few, and he will not
    rule the land. (19)

A ruler [will arise], he will rule for three years. (20)

The canals [*of that land*] will fill up with silt.
           (rest of column damaged or destroyed)
    (iii)

[A ruler will arise, he will rule for . . . years].
           (several lines destroyed)

That king [will rule] all the regions. (2)

His people will [have] abundance and . . .

The regular offerings for the Igigi-gods which had ceased he will
    re-establish, the gods [will . . .]

Favorable winds will blow, [there will be] abundance, and . . . in
    [the land.] (5)

Cattle [will lie down] safely in the open.

The vegetation of winter [will last] through the summer, the
    vegetation of sum[mer will last through the winter].

The offspring of the domestic animals [will thrive].

A ruler will arise, he will rule for eight years.
           (rest of obverse destroyed)
    (iv)

A ruler will arise, he [will rule] for three years. (2)

The remainder of the people [will return to their homes].

Abandoned cities will be reinhabited. [. . .]

There will be rebellions, and then [. . .]

For Akkad [there will be] enmity, [. . .]

The rites of Ekur and of Nippur will [*be transferred*] to [another]
    country.

The . . . of *Enlil* will [*return*] to Nippur.

That ruler [will defeat] the land of Amurru.

A ruler will arise, he will [rule] for eight years. (10)
The temples of the gods [will be restored], at the *advice* [of the king]
The rites of the great gods [will be restored].
[There will be] (favorable) rain and high water in the land.
The people who have experienced evil [will experience good].
The rich will become poor, the poor will become rich. [. . .]
The one who was *rich* will stretch out his hand to the poor.
. . . , the mother will speak what is right to her daughter.
[The *elders*] will *sit* and will give advice to the land.
[Locusts will ar]ise and devour the land, the king will [bring] hard times upon his land.

(rest of text too damaged for translation)

Love Poetry

Egyptian Love Songs

ANET, 467–69

TRANSLATOR: JOHN A. WILSON

The later Egyptian Empire (1300–1100 B.C.) has provided us with several collections of love songs. They were apparently intended to be sung to the accompaniment of some musical instrument. They express an enjoyment of nature and the out-of-doors. As in the Song of Songs, the lovers are called "my brother" and "my sister."

a

The voice of the swallow speaks and says:
"The land has brightened—What is thy road?"[1]
Thou shalt not, O bird, *disturb* me!
I have found my brother in his bed,
And my heart is still more glad,
(*When he*) said to me:
"I shall not go afar off.
My hand is in thy hand,
I shall stroll about,
And I shall be with thee in every pleasant place."
He makes me the foremost of maidens.
He injures not my heart.
THE END.

Song of Sol.
2:12–13

b

SEVENTH STANZA.[2]
Seven (days) to yesterday I have not seen the sister,
    And a sickness has invaded me.

Song of Sol. 2:5; 5:8

---

[1] Where are you walking in the early morning?
[2] Here the word "seven" is employed in place of a pun.

My body has become heavy,
    Forgetful of my own self.[3]
If the chief of physicians come to me,
    My heart is not content (with) their remedies;
The lector priests,[4] no way (out) is in them:—
    My sickness will not be probed.
To say to me: "Here she is!" is what will revive me;
    Her name is what will lift me up;
The going in and out of her messengers
    Is what will revive my heart.
More beneficial to me is the sister than any remedies;
    She is more to me than the collected writings.
My health is her coming in from outside:
    When (I) see her, then (I) am well.
If she opens her eye, my body is young (again);
    If she speaks, then I am strong (again);
When I embrace her, she drives evil away from me—
    But she has gone forth from me for seven days!

c

Would that thou wouldst come (to the sister speedily),
    Like a horse of the king,

Song of Sol. 1:9

Picked from a thousand of all steeds,
    The foremost of the stables!
It is distinguished in its food,
    And its master knows its paces.
If it hears the sound of the whip,
    It knows no delay,
And there is no foremost of the chasseurs[5]
    Who can stay before it (to hold it).
How well the sister's heart knows
    That he is not far from the sister!
    THE END.

Sumerian Love Poetry

TRANSLATOR: S. N. KRAMER

ANET[3], 638

Dumuzi and Inanna: Love in the Gipar

This narrative poem is divided into two stanzas by the rubric s a – g í d – d a – à m (line 25). The first six lines are quite obscure; the remainder of the first

---

[3] Often in the sense of losing consciousness.

[4] Who read magic spells for the cure of disease.

[5] *Teher*, a foreign word (perhaps Hittite) for a chariot-warrior.

stanza is taken up with a detailed account of Inanna's bedecking the various parts of her body with precious stones, jewels, and ornaments, which she selects from what seems to be a treasure-heap brought to her by a "date-gathering" devotee. The second stanza tells of the meeting between the be-jeweled Inanna and Dumuzi in the Eanna of Erech, a meeting which so fills Inanna with desire and passion that she sends a special messenger to her father (no doubt the god Sin) with the request that he (that is, perhaps, her father) make her house "long" so that she and her lover can take their plea-sure in it.

. . . ,

Holy Inanna . . . .
He who gathers the dates, . . . the date palm,
Who gathers the dates, . . . the date palm for Inanna,
He brought her water, he brought her water, for the seed, the black,
He brought Inanna a *heap* (of precious stones) *by* the water for the
    seed, the white.
He brought her, he brought her, he brought her a heap of (precious)
    stones to pick from,
He brought the maid Inanna, he brought her a heap of (precious)
    stones to pick from,
Of the heap—he gathers the lapis lazuli (stones) onto its "breast,"
Of the heap, for Inanna he gathers the lapis lazuli (stones) onto its
    "breast."   (10)
She picks the buttocks-stones, puts them on her buttocks,
Inanna picks the head-stones, puts them on her head,
She picks the *duru*-lapis lazuli stones, puts them on her nape,
She picks *ribbons* of gold, puts them in her hair of the head,
She picks the narrow gold earrings, puts them on her ears,
She picks the bronze eardrops, puts them on her ear-lobes,
She picks "that which drips honey," puts it on her face,
She picks "that which *covers* the princely house," puts it on her nose,
She picks "the house which . . . ," puts it on her . . . ,
She picks cypress (and) boxwood, the lovely wood, puts them on
    her navel,   (20)
She picks a sweet "honey well," puts it about her loins,
She picks bright alabaster, puts it on her anus,
She picks black . . . willow, puts it on her vulva,
She picks ornate sandals, puts them on her feet.

   It is a *sagidda*.

For whom the heap of lapis lazuli stones had been gathered—the *en*
    met her,
Inanna for whom the heap of lapis lazuli stones had been
    gathered—Dumuzi met her,
In the "*navel* of heaven," the house of Enlil, the *en* met her,

In the Eanna, Enlil's herdsman Dumuzi met her,
Who was standing at the lapis lazuli door of the *gipar*—the *en*
    met her, (30)
Who was standing by the *narrow* door of the storehouse of
    Eanna—Dumuzi met her.
When to the "breast" of the heap she returned them,
When Inanna, to the "breast" of the heap, she returned them,
The woman . . . her *ilulamma*-song.
The maid, singing, sent a messenger to her father,
Inanna, dancing, sent a messenger to her father:
"My *house,* my *house,* let him make it 'long' for me,
I the queen—my *house,* my *house* let him make it 'long' for me,
My *gipar-house* let him make it 'long' for me,
The people will set up my fruitful bed, (40)
They will cover it with plants (the color of) *duru*-lapis lazuli,
I will bring there my sweetheart,
I will bring there Amaushumgalanna,
He will put his hand by my hand,
He will put his heart by my heart,
His putting of hand to hand—its *sleep* is so refreshing,
His pressing of heart to heart—its pleasure is so sweet."

ANET³, 639–40

Dumuzi and Inanna: The Ecstasy of Love

The formal structure of this tender and ardent love song is rather unusual. It consists of two soliloquies by the goddess separated from each other by a brief tête-à-tête between the goddess and her lover Dumuzi; the first soliloquy and its ensuing tête-à-tête make up the first stanza, designated by the scribe as a *sagidda,* while the second soliloquy takes up the entire second stanza, designated by the scribe as a *sagarra.* In Inanna's first soliloquy (obv. lines 1–8), the goddess relates that one night, while she was innocently singing and dancing about, presumably in heaven, Dumuzi met her, held her hand, and embraced her. There follows a brief dialogue between them consisting of Inanna's plea (obv. lines 9–12) to Dumuzi to let go of her since on coming home she will have to deceive her mother and she does not know how, and Dumuzi's suggestion (obv. lines 13–22) to tell her mother that she whiled away the hours with a girl friend in the public square, an excuse that will enable them to spend the night making love by the moonlight. The extant part of Inanna's second soliloquy which is rather elliptical and allusive, begins with an exulting pronouncement of her arrival at the "gate" of her mother Ningal accompanied by Dumuzi who "will say the word" to her, that is, no doubt, ask for her daughter's hand (rev. lines 4–13); it concludes with an ecstatic eulogy of her husband-to-be and the fertility insured by their sacred marriage (rev. lines 14–21).

(obverse)
Last night, as I, the queen, was shining bright,
Last night, as I, the queen of heaven, was shining bright,
As I was shining bright, as I was dancing about,
As I was uttering a song at the brightening of the *oncoming* night,
He met me, he met me,
The Lord Kuli-Anna met me,
The lord put his hand into my hand,
Ushumgalanna embraced me.

"*Come now,* wild bull, set me free, I must go home,
Kuli-Enlil, set me free, I must go home,   (10)
What shall I say to deceive my mother!
What shall I say to deceive my mother Ningal!"

"Let me inform you, let me inform you.
Inanna, most deceitful of women, let me inform you:
'My girl friend took me with her to the public square,
She *entertained me* there with *music* and dancing,
Her chant, the sweet, she sang for me.
In sweet rejoicing I whiled away the time there'—
Thus deceitfully stand up to your mother,
While we by the moonlight indulge (our) passion,   (20)
I will [prepare] for you a bed pure, sweet, (and) noble,
Will while away the sweet *time* with you in joyful fulfillment."

    It is a *sagidda.*

    (remainder of the obverse and first three lines of reverse destroyed)

    (reverse)
I have come to our mother's gate,
I, in joy I walk,
I have come to Ningal's gate,
I, in joy I walk.
To my mother he will say the word,
He will sprinkle cypress oil on the ground,
To my mother Ningal he will say the word,   (10)
He will sprinkle cypress oil on the ground,
He whose dwelling is fragrant,
Whose word brings deep joy.

My lord is seemly *for* the holy lap,
Amaushumgalanna, the son-in-law of Sin,
The lord Dumuzi is seemly *for* the holy lap,
Amaushumgalanna, the son-in-law of Sin.
My lord, sweet is your increase,

Tasty your plants (and) herbs in the plain,
Amaushumgalanna, sweet is your increase, (20)
Tasty your plants (and) herbs in the plain.

It is a *sagarra*. A *tigi*-song of Inanna.

Inanna and the King: Blessing on the Wedding Night

ANET³, 640–41

This poem is an epithalamion in the Emesal dialect which is in some respects a companion piece to the last stanza of the Inanna hymn that celebrates the *hieros-gamos* between King Iddin-Dagan and the goddess. The poet begins with an address, probably to the goddess Inanna, informing her that Gibil had purified for her "the great shrine" in her Eanna temple, and that the king had erected an altar and carried out the lustration rites for her (col. i 1–12); this is followed by a prayer that in the evening when "the day had gone to sleep," and it was time for the goddess "to caress the lord" in the favored sleeping place, she should give the king life and the staff and crook (col. i lines 13–17). The poet then sings of the preparation of the "sleeping place" of kingship and queenship which "rejoices the heart" and "sweetens the lap" (col. i lines 18–31). After a break we find Inanna speaking to the king(?) "words of life, words of long days" (col. ii lines 1–3). Following which Ninshubur takes him by his right forearm(?), leads him to Inanna's lap, and asks her to bless him with everything essential for the well-being of the king and his people: a good reign, a firmly founded throne, a well-governing scepter, a staff and crook for the control of Sumer and Akkad and the lands beyond (col. ii lines 4–18); she should grant him, too, that "he (the king) like a farmer set the fields in order, like a faithful shepherd multiply the sheepfolds" (col. ii lines 19–20); and that under his reign, the land should have all it need: plants and grains, overflow by the rivers, late grain in the fields, fish and birds in the marshes, fresh and mature reeds in the canebrake, *mashgur*-trees in the plains, deer and wild-goats in the forest, honey and wine in the well-watered gardens, vegetables in the trenches (between the furrows), long life in the palace, high water brought by the Tigris and Euphrates to make verdant their banks and watered acres, grain heaps and mounds piled high by the goddess Nidaba (col. ii line 18–col. iii line 4). Following a further request by Ninshubur that the king be allowed to spend a long time in Inanna's lap (col. iii lines 5–6), the king proceeds with "lifted head" to the lap of Inanna and is embraced by her (col. iii lines 7–12).

(col. i)
"
. . . ,
Of the house of Eridu—its guidance,
Of the house of Sin—its radiance,
Of the Eanna—its *habitation*;

The house—it has been presented (to you).
(In) my enduring house which floats like a cloud,
(Whose) name in truth, is a goodly vision,
(Where) a fruitful bed, lapis-bedecked,
Gibil had purified for you in the great shrine,
He who is well-suited for 'queenship,' (10)
The lord has *erected* his *altar*,
In his *reed-filled* house which he has purified for you, he performs
    your rites.

The sun has gone to sleep, the day has *passed*,
As in bed you gaze (lovingly) upon him,
As you caress the lord,
Give life unto the lord,
Give the staff and crook unto the lord."
She craves it, she craves it, she craves the bed,
She craves the bed of the rejoicing heart, she craves the bed,
She craves the bed of the sweet lap, she craves the bed, (20)
She craves the bed of kingship, she craves the bed,
She craves the bed of queenship, she craves the bed.
By his sweet, by his sweet, by his sweet bed,
By his sweet bed of the rejoicing heart, by his sweet bed,
By his sweet bed of the sweet lap, by his sweet bed,
By his sweet bed of kingship, by his sweet bed,
By his sweet bed of queenship, by his sweet bed,
He covers [the bed] . . . for her, covers the bed for her,
He covers [the bed] . . . for her, covers the bed for her. (30–31)
    (col. ii)
[To] the k[ing] . . . ,
The *beloved* speaks on his sweet bed,
Speaks to him words of life, words of "long days."

Ninshubur, the trustworthy vizier of the Eanna,
Took him by his right *forearm*,
Brought him blissfully to the lap of Inanna:
"May the lord whom you have called to (your) heart,
The king, your beloved husband, enjoy long days at your holy lap,
    the sweet,
Give him a reign favorable (and) glorious,
Give him the throne of kingship on its enduring foundation, (10)
Give him the people-directing scepter, the staff (and) the crook,
Give him an enduring crown, a diadem which *ennobles* the head,
From (where) the sun rises, to (where) the sun sets,
From south to north,
From the Upper Sea to the Lower Sea,
From (where grows) the *halub*-tree to (where grows) the cedar,

Over all Sumer and Akkad give him the staff (and) the crook,
May he exercise the shepherdship of the blackheads (wherever)
    they dwell,
May he make productive the fields like the farmer,
May he multiply the sheepfolds like a trustworthy shepherd.   (20)

Under his reign may there be plants, may there be grain,
At the river, may there be overflow,
In the field may there be late-grain,
In the marshland may the fish (and) birds make much *chatter*,
In the canebrake may the 'old' reeds, the young reeds grow high,
In the steppe may the *mashgur*-trees grow high.
In the forests may the deer and the wild goats multiply,
May the watered garden produce honey (and) wine,
In the trenches may the lettuce and cress grow high,
In the palace may there be long life,   (30)
    (col. iii)
Into the Tigris and Euphrates may flood water be brought,
On their banks may the grass grow high, may the meadows be
    covered,
May the holy queen of vegetation pile high the grain heaps and
    mounds,
Oh my queen, queen of the universe, the queen who encompasses
    the universe,
May he enjoy long days [at your holy] lap."

The king goes with lifted head [to the holy lap],
He goes with lifted head to [the holy] lap [of Inanna],
The king going with [lifted head],
Going to my queen with lifted head,   (10)
From . . . ,
Embraces the hierodule . . . .

"The Honey-man": Love-song to a King

ANET³, 645

This song, too, was no doubt chanted by a *lukur*-priestess in connection with the *hieros-gamos,* although the name of the participating king is not mentioned in the text. Instead, he is described in sensuous, concrete, fertility imagery: he is lettuce planted by the water, a well-stocked garden, luxuriant, grain in the furrow, a fruit-bearing apple tree, and above all, a "honey-man" who sweetens her body, or rather that of the goddess Inanna whom she represents. Structurally, the poem may be divided into three parts: (1) an initial four-line strophe characterized by "vegetation" symbolism and an identical refrain for three of its lines; (2) a four-line "honey-man" strophe with an identical refrain for three of its lines; (3) a summary two-line strophe ending in the refrain characteristic of the first strophe.

He has *sprouted,* he has *burgeoned,* he is lettuce *planted by* the
    water,
My well-stocked garden of the . . . plain, my favored of the *womb,*
My grain luxuriant in its furrow—he is lettuce *planted by* the
    water,
My apple tree which bears fruit up to (its) top—he is lettuce *planted*
    by the water.

The "honey-man," the "honey-man" sweetens me ever,
My lord, the "honey-man" of the gods, my favored of the *womb,*
Whose hand is honey, whose foot is honey, sweetens me ever.
Whose limbs are honey sweet, sweetens me ever.

My sweetener of the . . . *navel,* [my favored of the *womb*],
My . . . of the fair thighs, he is lettuce [*planted by* the water].   (10)

It is a *balbale* of Inanna.

"Set Me Free, My Sister": The Sated Lover   ANET³, 645

As far as can be determined at present, the extant part of this poem consists
of several speeches. Lines 21–22 end an address to Inanna by some female
deity informing her of some of the virtues and prerogatives presented to her.
This is followed by a soliloquy on the part of Inanna reminiscent of "Inanna
and Dumuzi: The Ecstasy of Love" in which she chants of meeting her beloved, further designated here as "brother," and "my brother of fairest face,"
and uniting with him in love so much so that he became "sated" (lines 23–34).
The remainder of the poem (lines 35–38) consists of the lover's plea to Inanna,
to "set him free," so that he can return with her to the palace where she will
be treated as a "young daughter" by the father.

". . . , sweet allure,
My holy Inanna, I presented to you."

"As . . . the beloved of my eye,
My beloved met me,
Took his pleasure of me, rejoiced *together* with me.
The brother brought me to his house
Made me lie on its . . . honey bed,
My precious sweet, having lain by my heart,
In unison, the 'tongue-making' in unison,
My brother of fairest face, made 50 times.   (30)
I . . . for him like a *weakling,*
I set it up for him in the . . . together with . . . from the earth,
My brother who . . . in his anger,
My precious sweet is sated with me."

"Set me free, my sister, set me free,
Come, my beloved sister, I would go to the palace,
You will be a little daughter before my father,
I will set free for you . . ."

It is a *balbale* of Inanna.

Other Literary Texts

An Egyptian Poem
In Praise of the City Ramses

ANET, 470–71

Translator: John A. Wilson

The pharaohs of the Nineteenth Dynasty established their residence city, the biblical Ramses or Raamses, in the northeastern Delta. The glories of this new capital were celebrated in poetical compositions like the following.

The Scribe Pai-Bes communicating to his lord, the Scribe Amen-em-Opet: In life, prosperity, health! It is a letter to let [my] lord know. Another communication to my lord, to wit:

I have reached Per-Ramses, and have found (ii 1) it in [very, very] good condition, a beautiful district, without its like, after the pattern of Thebes. It was [Re] himself [who founded it.]

The Residence is pleasant in life; its field is full of everything good; it is (full) of supplies and food every day, its *ponds* with fish, and its lakes with birds. Its meadows are verdant with grass; its banks bear dates; its melons are abundant on the sands. . . . Its granaries are (so) full of barley and emmer (that) they come near to the sky. Onions and leeks (5) are *for food,* and lettuce of the *garden,* pomegranates, apples, and olives, figs of the orchard, sweet wine of *Ka*-of-Egypt,[1] surpassing honey, red *wedj*-fish of the canal of the Residence City, *which* live on lotus-flowers, *bedin*-fish of the *Hari*-waters, . . .

Num. 11:5

The Shi-Hor[2] has salt, and *the Her canal* has natron. Its ships go out and come (back) to mooring, (so that) supplies (10) and food are

Josh. 13:3

---

[1] A well-known vineyard of the Delta.

[2] The biblical "the Shihor (which is before Egypt)," or "the Waters of Horus." Presumably the Tanite branch of the Nile, with its salt-flats.

in it every day. One rejoices to dwell within it, and there is none who says: "Would that!" to it.[3] The small in it are like the great.

Come, let us celebrate for it its feasts of the sky, as well as its feasts at the beginning of the seasons.[4]

The reed-thicket[5] comes to it with papyrus; the Shi-Hor with rushes. ... (iii 1) ... The young men of "Great of Victories" are dressed up every day, with sweet oil upon their heads and newly dressed hair. They stand beside their doors, their hands bowed down with flowers, with greenery of the House of Hat-Hor and flax of *the Her canal,* on the day when User-maat-Re Setep-en-Re—life, prosperity, health!—Montu-in-the-Two-Lands enters in, on the morning of the Feast of Khoiakh. (5) Every man is like his fellow in uttering their petitions.

The ale of "Great of Victories" is sweet; ... beer of Kode[6] from the harbor, and wine of the vineyards. The ointment of the *Segbeyen* waters is sweet, and the garlands of the *garden.* The singers of "Great of Victories" are sweet, being instructed in Memphis.

(So) dwell content of heart and free, without stirring from it, O User-maat-Re Setep-en-Re—life, prosperity, health!—Montu-in-the-Two-Lands, Ramses Meri-Amon—life, prosperity, health!—thou god!   THE END.

Sumerian Literature

TRANSLATOR: S. N. KRAMER

ANET³, 646–51

The Curse of Agade
The Ekur Avenged

This rather unusual "historiographic" document, first composed (probably) about 2000 B.C. by a Sumerian theologian-poet with a reflective and inventive turn of mind, is of significance for the history of religious thought. Its central theme concerns national catastrophe as a direct consequence of divine wrath kindled by a defiant act on the part of man. In the case of Sumer, the disastrous catastrophe came in the guise of a humiliating and destructive invasion by the barbarous, ruthless Gutians from the Zagros ranges, that

---

[3] No one feels a lack in the city Ramses.

[4] The "feasts of the sky" were those astronomically set, such as those of the phases of the moon. The seasonal feasts included the Coronation Feast, the Rising of the Dog-Star, the Feast of Opet, etc.

[5] The word used appears also in Hebrew in "the Sea of Reeds" (conventionally translated "Red Sea").

[6] Kode or Qedi was the north Phoenician coast, carrying into Cilicia.

brought confusion and anarchy in the land for about a century or so. This cruel event preyed on the hearts and minds of the more thoughtful and literate of the Sumerians, and pressed for an explanation within the framework of the Sumerian world view. It is this need for a satisfying rationale which seems to have led to the composition of the document by a deeply religious poet imbued with the conviction that it was the desecration of Sumer's holiest shrine by a bitter and defiant king which led to the calamity that overwhelmed the king's capital city and the land as a whole.

The culprit chiefly responsible for this catastrophe, according to our author, was Naram-Sin, the fourth king of the Dynasty of Akkad, that ruled from its capital, the still unlocated city of Agade. The founder of the dynasty was Sargon the Great, Naram-Sin's grandfather. According to our author, Sargon's rise to power was due to Enlil, the leading deity of the Sumerian pantheon, who turned over both the temporal and religious control of Sumer, after Kish and Erech, its two great political centers, had been destroyed by the angered god (lines 1–6). But it was primarily the goddess Inanna who devoted all her efforts to make Agade a prosperous and affluent city whose sway over Sumer, and indeed over virtually the entire ancient world, was supreme and unchallenged, and especially so when Naram-Sin began his reign (lines 7–53).

But then, our author continues, Inanna, acting, it seems, in accordance with "the word of the Ekur," that is presumably, the word of Enlil, abandoned her shrine Eulmash in Agade and turned inimical to the city (lines 54–65). At the same time some of the other gods—Ninurta, Utu, and Enki—deprived the city of the powers and endowments they had conferred upon it, and Agade became weak and impoverished (lines 66–84). At first Naram-Sin, according to our author, accepted this cruel fate in humility and self-abasement, especially after he had a highly mysterious vision concerned with the Ekur (lines 85–90). But when after seven years of this contrite behavior he sought an oracle from the Ekur in Nippur and was not granted his request, his humility turned to defiance (lines 91–98). He mobilized his troops and proceeded to devastate the Ekur, desecrate its holy places, and despoil it of its possessions (lines 97–144).

But no sooner had he done so, our document continues, than the angered Enlil began to avenge the destruction of his beloved Ekur. He brought down from their mountain lairs, the Gutians, an uncivilized, uncontrollable, multitudinous horde who spread over the land like swarming locusts, and brought about the suspension of all avenues of communication by land or sea (lines 145–69). Cities became desolate; fields and gardens were abandoned; famine raged, and death stalked the inhabitants of Sumer (lines 170–91). The land was filled with wailing, lamenting, hair-tearing, and bodily laceration, but Enlil turned a deaf ear to the people's suffering; he went into his cella, and laid himself down to sleep (lines 192–208). It was then that some of the great gods of Sumer decided to mollify Enlil, and thus presumably save Sumer from total destruction, by pronouncing a terrible oath against Agade, dooming her to a fate worse than that inflicted by her on Nippur: she would become a city deprived of all human friendship and filled with wailing and lamentation; all its holy places would be destroyed, and starvation and desolation would be rampant; she would become a place unfit for human habitation (lines 209–69). And, concludes our author, that is just what happened: Agade was destroyed, and became a desolate uninhabitable ruin.

After the frowning forehead of Enlil
Had killed (the people of) Kish like the "Bull of Heaven,"
After he had ground the house of Erech into dust, like a giant bull,
After in due time, to Sargon the king of Agade,
From below to above, Enlil
Had given him lordship and kingship,
Then did holy Inanna, the shrine of Agade,
Erect as her noble chamber,
In Ulmash did she set up a throne.

Like a "little fellow" building (his) house anew,   (10)
Like a young son, erecting the (wife's) chamber—
That everything be collected (safely) in the storehouses,
That their city be a firmly established dwelling place,
That its people eat "dependable" food,
That its people drink "dependable" water,
That the bathed "heads" make the courtyards joyous,
That the people beautify the places of festivity,
That the men of the city "eat" in harmony,
That the outsiders scurry about like "unknown" birds,
That Marhashi be turned to *clay,*   (20)
That in future *days* the giant elephant, (and) the *ahzaza,* the beasts
    of distant lands,
Roam about all together in the midst of (its) boulevards,
(Also) the "princely" dogs, the Elamite dogs, the "asses" of the
    mountain, *long-haired alum*-sheep,
Inanna allowed herself no sleep.

In those days the dwelling of Agade were filled with gold,
Its bright-shining houses were filled with silver,
Into its granaries were brought copper, lead, (and) slabs of lapis
    lazuli,
Its silos *bulged* at the sides,
Its old women were endowed with counsel,
Its old men were endowed with eloquence,   (30)
Its young men with endowed with the "strength of weapons,"
Its little children were endowed with joyous hearts,
The nurse-raised children of the governors,

Played on the *algarsur*-instruments,
Inside, the city (was full of) *tigi*-music,
Outside it (was full of) reed-pipe (and) *zamzam*-music,
Its quay where the boats docked were all abustle,
All lands lived in security,
Their people witnessed (nothing but) happiness,
Their king Naram-Sin, the shepherd,   (40)
Stepped forth like the sun on the holy dais of Agade,
Its walls reached skyward like a mountain,

The gates—like the Tigris emptying its water into the sea,
Holy Inanna opened its gates.
The Sumerians eagerly sailed (their) goods-(laden) boats to it
     (Agade),
The Martu, (the people of) the lord that knows not grain,
Brought her perfect oxen, perfect sheep,
The Meluhhaites, the people of the black land,
Brought up to her the (exotic) wares of the foreign lands,
The Elamites (and) Subaraeans carried for her (all sorts of) goods,
     like sack-carrying donkeys,   (50)
Ensi's *sanga*'s,
The comptroller of the Guedinna
Conduct their monthly and New Year gift (to Agade).

(But then) in the palace of Agade—what prostration!
Holy Inanna accepted not its gifts,
Like a princely son who . . . , she *shared* not its wealth,
The "word of the Ekur" was upon it like a (deathly) silence,
Agade was all atremble,
The Ulmash was in terror,
She who had lived there, left the city,   (60)
Like a maiden forsaking her chamber,
Holy Inanna forsook the shrine Agade,
Like a warrior hastening to (his) weapon,
She went forth against the city in battle (and) combat,
She attacked as if it were a foe.

In days not five, in days not ten,
The *fillet* of lordship, the tiara of kingship,

Mansium, the throne given over to kingship,
Ninurta brought into his Eshumesha.
Utu carried off the "eloquence" of the city,   (70)
Enki *poured out* its wisdom.
Its awesomeness that had reached towards heaven,
An brought up to the midst of heaven,
Its boats that had been carefully *caulked*,

Enki [brought down] into the Abzu,
Its weapons were . . .
The shrine Agade . . .
The city . . . ,
Like a huge elephant . . . ,
Like a huge bull . . . ,
Like a fierce *ushumgal*-dragon . . . ,   (80)
Its battles were [decreed] a bitter fate,
The kingship of Agade was prostrated,
Its future is extremely unhappy,
At the "month house" the treasures lay scattered about.

(Then) Naram-Sin in a vision . . . ,
He kept it to himself, put it not in speech, spoke with nobody
    about it,
Because of the Ekur, he dressed in sackcloth,
Covered his chariot with a boat-covering mat,
Loaded not his boat with . . . ,
Gave away everything desirable for Kingship.   (90)

Seven years Naram-Sin remained firm,
Who had ever seen that a king should "put hand on head for seven
    years!"
(But then) seeking an oracle at the house,
In the "built" house there was no oracle,
Seeking an oracle a second time at the house,
In the "built" house there was no oracle.
(Whereupon) changing his line of *action*,
He defied the word of Enlil,
Crushed those who had submitted to him (Enlil),
Mobilized his troops,   (100)
Like a mighty man *accustomed* to high-handed (action),
He put a restraining hand on the Ekur.
Like a runner *contemptuous* of (his body's) strength,
He treated the *giguna* like thirty shekels.
Like a bandit who plunders a city,
He erected large ladders against the house.
To destroy the Ekur like a huge boat,
To turn it into dust like a mountain mined for silver,
To cut it to pieces like a mountain of lapis lazuli,
To prostrate it like a city, ravaged by Ishkur,   (110)
Against the house that was not a mountain where cedar was
    felled,
He forged great axes,
Sharpened double-edged "axes of destruction,"
Fixed copper *spikes* at the bottom of it,

Levelled it down to the "foundation" of the land,
Fixed axes at the top of it,
The house lay stretched "neck to ground," like a man who had been
    killed (in battle).
He tore up its *mes*-trees,
The raining dust rose sky high.   (120)
He struck down its doorposts, cut off the vitality of the land,
At the "Gate of no Grain Cutting," he cut grain,
Grain was cut off from the "hand" of the land.
Its "Gate of Peace" he broke down with the pickaxe,
Peace was estranged from the lands,
(And) from the "noble" fields (and) acres of the wide . . .

The Ekur—he *forged* its bronze *spikes* in (heaps of) firewood,
The people (now) saw its cella, the house that knew not light,
The Akkadian saw the holy vessels of the gods.
Its great *laḫama* of the *dubla,* who stood at the house,   (130)
(Although) they were not among those who ate that which is tabu,
Naram-Sin cast into the fire.
Cedar, cypress, *zabalum*-tree, and boxtree,
Its *giguna*-trees, he *pulverized,*
Its gold he brought into . . . -bags,
Its silver he brought into . . . leather sacks,
Its copper he piled up on the quay like huge (heaps of) grain (ready
    to be) carried away,
Its silver was worked over by the silversmith,
Its precious stone was worked over by the jeweller,
Its copper was hammered by the smith.   (140)
(Although all these) were not the possessions of an attacking city,
He docked large boats at the quay by the house,
Docked large boats at the quay by the house of Enlil,
Carried off the possessions from the city,
(But with) the carrying off the possessions of the city,
Counsel departed from the city,
As the boats *took off* from the quay, the good sense of Agade turned
    to folly,
The . . . storm that . . . ,
The rampant Flood who knows no rival,
Enlil, because his beloved Ekur had been attacked, what
    destruction he wrought!   (150)
He lifted his eyes to the . . . -mountain,
Mustered the "wide" mountain as one.
The unsubmissive people, the land (whose people) is without
    number,
Gutium, the land that brooks no control,

Whose understanding is human, (but) whose form (and) *stuttering*
    words are that of a dog,
Enlil brought down from the mountain.
In vast numbers, like locusts, they covered the earth,
Their "arm" stretched out for him in the steppe like an *animal-trap*,
Nothing escaped their "arm,"
No one *eluded* their "arm."   (160)
The herald took not to the road,
The (sea)-rider sailed not his boat along the river.
The . . . -goats of Enlil that broke out of their sheepfold—their
    shepherd made them follow him,
The cows that broke out of their stalls, their cowherd made them
    follow him.
On the *trees* of the *(river)-banks* watches were set up,
Brigands dwelt on the road.
In the gates of the land the doors stood (deep) in dust,
All the lands raised a bitter cry on their city walls
Furrows embedded the cities although (their) inside was not a
    steppe, (their) outside was not wide (open land).

After the cities had been built, after they had been
    struck down,   (170)
The large fields (and) acres produced no grain,
The flooded acres produced no fish,
The watered gardens produced no honey (and) wine,
The heavy *clouds* brought not rain, there grew no *mashgur*-tree.
Then did half a *sila* of oil equal one shekel,
Half a *sila* of grain—one shekel,
Half a *mina* of wool—one shekel,
One *ban* of fish—one shekel.
The *commodities* of their cities were bought up like good
    "words,"
Who slept on the roof died on the roof,   (180)
Who slept inside the house was not brought to burial,
The people droop helplessly because of their hunger.

By the *kiur,* the "great place" of Enlil,
The cedar-cutter held back (his) speech in (deathly) *silence,*
In its *midst* men by *two's* were devoured,
In its . . . men by *three's* were devoured,
Heads were *crushed,* heads were . . . ,
Mouths were *crushed,* "heads" were turned to seeds,
The faithful *"slaves"* were changed into treacherous *"slaves,"*
The valiant lay on top of the valiant,   (190)
The blood of the treacherous flowed over the blood of the
    faithful.

Then did Enlil, out of his immense shrine,
Make a small reed-shrine,
From sunrise to sunset its treasures decreased,
The old women who were cut off from the day,
The old men who were cut off from the day,
The chief *gala*'s who were cut off from the year,
For seven days, seven nights,
Like "the seven lyres standing at the horizon," followed him (Enlil)
    about,
Like Ishkur played for him the *shem, mezi,* and *lilis.*   (200)

The old women ceased not (crying) "Oh, my city,"
The old men ceased not (crying) "Oh, its men,"
The *gala*'s ceased not (crying) "Oh, the Ekur,"
Its maidens ceased not tearing (their) hair
Its youths ceased not (their) maceration,
Their tears, the tears of the mothers and fathers of Enlil,
They bring again and again in the awe-filled *duku* of holy Enlil.
Because of all this, Enlil entered (his) holy cella, lay down on (his)
    katabba.
Then did Sin, Enki, Inanna, Ninurta, Ishkur, (and) Utu, the great
    gods,
They who soothe (and) *comfort* the heart of Enlil, utter a prayer
    to him: (210)
"Oh, valiant Enlil, the city that has destroyed your city may it
    become like your city,
(The city) that has demolished your *giguna,* may it become like
    Nippur,
Of that city, may *skulls* fill its wells,
May no sympathizing friends be found there,
May brother not recognize his brother,
May its maiden flagellate herself in her chamber,
May its father utter bitter cries in the house of his dead wife,
May he moan like a dove in its hole,
May he thrash about like a swallow in its cranny,
May he scurry about like a dove in terror."   (220)

A second time did Sin, Enki, Inanna, Ninurta, Ishkur, Utu, Nusku,
    (and) Nidaba, the great gods,
Direct their face to the city,
Curse Agade with a baleful curse:
"City, you who dared assault the Ekur—it is Enlil (whom you
    assaulted),
Agade, you who dared assault the Ekur—it is Enlil (whom you
    assaulted),
At your holy wall, lofty as it is, may wailing resound,

May your *giguna* be heaped up like dust,
May your *laḥama* that stand in the *dubla,*
Lie prostrate like huge (fighting) men drunk with wine,
May your clay return to its Abzu,   (230)
May it be clay cursed by Enki,
May your grain return to its furrows,
May it be grain cursed by Ashnan,
May your trees return to their forests,
May they become trees cursed by Ninildu,
May the oxen-slaughterer, slaughter (his) wife (instead),
May your sheep-butcher, butcher his child (instead),
May your poor hurl his *precious* children into the water,
May the prostitute stretch herself out in the gate of her brother,
May your hierodule mother, your courtesan mothers give back
     (their) children,   (240)
May your gold be sold as silver,
May your silver be sold as *zaḥa*-metal,
May your copper be sold as lead.

Agade, may your strong man be deprived of his strength,
May he not be able to lift a leather bag . . . ,
May your *wrestler* rejoice not in his strength, may he lie in
     'darkness,'
May famine kill (the people of) that city,
May the princely children who ate (only) the very best bread, lie
     about in the grass,
May your man who used to carry off the first *fruits,* eat the *scraps*
     of his tables,
The leather thongs of the door of his father's house,   (250)
May he munch these leather thongs with his teeth;
May your palace built in joy, fall to ruins in anguish,
May the evil ones, the ghosts of 'silent places' howl (there)
     evermore;
Over your *usga*-place established for lustrations,
May the 'fox of the ruined mounds,' glide (his) tail;
In your great gates (firmly) established in the land,
May the '*ukuku*-birds of anguished heart' set up (his) nest,
In your city where you (no longer) sleep to (the sound of)
     tigi-music,
Where you (no longer) go to bed with a joyful heart,
May the oxen of Nanna, that (used to) fill the stalls,   (260)
Moan evermore like ghosts who roam the 'silent places';
May your canalboat towpaths grow (nothing but) tall grass,
May your wagon-roads grow (nothing but) the 'wailing-plant';

Moreover, on your canalboat towpaths, the places where the
    channel is narrow,
May no one walk among the wild goats, 'darting snakes of the
    mountain,'
May your steppe where grew the succulent plants,
Grow (nothing but) the 'reed of tears,'
Agade (instead of) your sweet-flowing water, may salt water flow
    (there),
May he who said 'I would sleep in that city,' not find a good
    dwelling there,
May he who said 'I would sleep in Agade,' not find a good sleeping
    place there."   (270)

(And) lo, with Utu's bringing forth the day, so it came to pass!
Its canalboat towpaths grew (nothing but) tall grass,
Its wagon-roads grew (nothing but) the "wailing-plant."
Moreover, on its canalboat towpaths, the places where the channel
    is narrow,
No one walks among the wild goats and darting snakes of the
    mountain,
Its steppe where grew the succulent plants,
Grew (nothing but) the "reed of tears."
Agade, (instead of) its sweet-flowing water, salt water flowed
    (there),
He who said, "I would dwell in that city," found not a good dwelling
    place there.
He who said, "I would sleep in Agade," found not a good sleeping
    place there,   (280)
Agade is destroyed! Praise Inanna.

Ua-aua

ANET³, 651–52

A Sumerian Lullaby

This composition, the only one of its kind thus far known from the Ancient
Near East, probably consists entirely of a chant purported to be uttered by the
wife of Shulgi, the preeminent and long-lived ruler of the Third Dynasty of
Ur, who seemed to have been anxious and troubled by the ill-health of one of
her sons. Being a mother's lullaby, one might have expected her to address her
words directly to the child. This is true, however, only of the greater part of
the poem (cf., lines 6–11, 19–23, 39–63, 92–100). In the other preserved passages she seems to soliloquize about her son in the third person (cf., lines 1–5,
24–38, 64–91), and in one passage she addresses Sleep personified (lines
12–18): In detail the contents of the composition may be sketched as follows:

The poem begins with a rather wistful and wishful soliloquy in which the mother seems to reassure herself that as she envisions it in the very chant she is uttering, her son will grow big and sturdy (lines 1–5). She then seems to try to buoy up her son's spirit with the promise of care and oncoming sleep (lines 6–11). Having mentioned sleep, she addresses it directly and urges it to close her son's wakeful eyes as well as his babbling tongue (lines 12–18). She now turns again to her ailing son, and promises to provide him with the sweet little cheeses that will serve to heal him, who is none other than the son of Shulgi (lines 19–23). He will also eat her well-watered lettuce, she continues (lines 24–26). She now sees herself—again while uttering her chant—providing him with loving wife and beloved child nursed and tended by a joyous nursemaid (lines 27–38).

Now anxiety about the illness of her son begins to dominate her mood, and in her next soliloquy addressed directly to her son whom she seems to see in her troubled fancy as dead and mourned by professional mourners and crawling insects (lines 39–50). Following a fragmentary passage in which sleep is mentioned once again (lines 51–56), we find the mother blessing her son with a wife and son, abundance of grain, a good angel, a happy and joyous reign (lines 57–63). Following another fragmentary and obscure passage which ends in two lines concerned with a palm-tree (lines 64–91), the mother turns once again to her son and future king, and admonishes him to stand by Ur and Erech, to seize and pinion the enemy, a dog who, unless cowed, will tear him to pieces (lines 92–100).

ua! *aua*!
In my song of joy—he will grow stout,
In my song of joy—he will grow big,
Like the *irina*-tree he will grow stout of root,
Like the *šakir*-plant he will grow broad of crown.

Lord, from . . . you know . . . ,
Among those burgeoning apple trees by the river arrayed,
Who . . . will spread his hand on you,
Who lies there will lift his hand on you,
My son, sleep is about to overtake you,   (10)
Sleep is about to settle on you.

Come Sleep, come Sleep,
Come to my son,
Hurry Sleep to my son,
Put to sleep his restless eyes,
Put your hand on his (kohl)-painted eyes,
And (as for) his babbling tongue,
Let not the babbling hold back (his) sleep.

He will fill your lap with *emmer*.
I—I will make sweet for you the little cheeses,   (20)

Those little cheeses that are the healer of man,
The healer of man, the son of the Lord,
The son of the Lord Shulgi.

My garden is lettuce well-watered,
It is *gakkul*-lettuce . . . ,
The Lord will eat that lettuce.
In my song of joy—I will give him a wife,
[I will] give him [a wife], I will give him a [son],
The nursemaid, joyous of heart, will converse with him,
The nursemaid, joyous of heart, will suckle him;   (30)
I—I will [take] a wife for my son,
She will [bear] him a son so sweet,
The wife will lie on his burning lap,
The son will lie in his outstretched arms,
The wife will be happy with him,
The son will be happy with him,
The young wife will rejoice in his lap,
The son will grow big on his sweet knee.
You are in pain,
I am troubled,   (40)
I am struck dumb, I gaze at the stars,
The new moon *shines* down on my face,
Your bones will be arrayed on the wall,
The "man of the wall" will shed tears for you,
The *keeners* will pluck the harps for you,
The gekko will gash the cheek for you,
The fly will pluck the beard for you,
The lizard will *bite* his tongue for you,
Who "makes sprout" woe, will make it sprout all about you,
Who spreads woe, will spread it all about you.   (50)
                    (lines 51–56 fragmentary)
May the wife be your support,
May the son be your lot,
May the winnowed barley be your bride,
May Ashnan, the *kusu*-goddess be your ally,   (60)
May you have an eloquent guardian-angel,
May you *achieve* a reign of happy days,
May your feasts make bright the fore [head].
                    (lines 64–91 fragmentary)
And you, lie you in sleep!
Array the branches (of) your palm-tree,
It will fill you with joy like . . .
Stand at the side of Ur *as* a *ḫuldubba-demon*
Stand at the side of Erech as . . . -demon,

Seize the mouth of the dog as a . . . -demon,
Pinion his "arms" as with a net of reeds,
Make the dog cower before you,
Lest he will rip your back like a sack.

(remainder of the text very fragmentary)

Letters

Akkadian Letters
The Mari Letters

ANET, 482–83

TRANSLATOR: W. F. ALBRIGHT

In 1935–38 André Parrot excavated the palace of king Zimri-Lim (about 1730–1700 B.C.) at Tell el-Hariri, ancient Mari on the Middle Euphrates. Among nearly 20,000 cuneiform tablets found in this palace were some 5,000 letters, mostly written by native Amorites (Northwestern Semites) in a Babylonian full of West-Semitic words and grammatical usages. Personal names, language and customs reflect the culture of the Patriarchal Age in Genesis.

a

Published and translated by G. Dossin in *Revue d'assyriologie et d'archéologie orientale,* XXXV (1938), pp. 178f.

To my lord say: Thus Bannum, thy servant. Yesterday, (5) I departed from Mari, and spent the night at Zuruban. All the Benjaminites raised fire-signals.[1] (10) From Samanum to Ilum-Muluk, from Ilum-Muluk to Mishlan, all the cities of the Benjaminites (15) of the Terqa district raised fire signals in response, and so far I have not ascertained the meaning of those signals. Now, I shall (20) determine the meaning, and I shall write to my lord whether it is thus or not. Let the guard of the city of Mari be strengthened, (25) and let my lord not go outside the gate.

Jer. 6:1

---

[1] With their aid the ancients were able to communicate with great rapidity over considerable distances.

b

Published by C. F. Jean in *Archives royales de Mari,* 11, No. 22. For his preliminary translation see *Revue d'assyriologie et d'archéologie orientale,* XXIX, pp. 64f.; the following is fully revised.

To my lord say: Thus Ibal-pi-Il, thy servant. (5) Hammurabi spoke to me as follows: "A heavily armed force had gone out to raid the enemy column, but there was no suitable base to be found, so that force has returned empty-handed and the column of the enemy is proceeding in good order without panic. Now let a light armed force go to raid the enemy column and capture informers."

Thus Hammurabi spoke to me. I am sending Sakirum with three hundred troops to Shabazum, (20) and the troops which I have sent are one hundred fifty [Hanu], fifty Suhu, and one hundred troops from the bank of the Euphrates River; and there are three hundred troops of Babylon. In the van of the troops of my lord there goes Ilu-nasir, the seer,[2] the subject of my lord, (25) and one Babylonian seer goes with the troops of Babylon. These six hundred troops are based in Shabazum, and the seer assembles the omens. When the appearance of their (30) omens is favorable, one hundred fifty go out and one hundred fifty come in. May my lord know this. The troops of my lord are well.

Num. 22–24

c

Published by C. F. Jean in *Archives royales de Mari,* 11, No. 37, and translated in *Revue des études sémitiques,* 1944, pp. 10f.; the following is fully revised.

To my lord say: Thus Ibal-Il, thy servant. The tablet of Ibal-Adad from Aslakka (5) reached me and I went to Aslakka to "kill an ass"[3] between the Hanu and Idamaras. A "puppy and lettuce" they brought, but I obeyed my lord and (10) I did not give the "puppy and lettuce." I caused the foal of an ass to be slaughtered. I established peace between the Hanu and Idamaras. (15) In Hurra, in all of Idamaras, the Hanu are victorious, as a victor who has no enemy.[4] May my lord be pleased. This tablet of mine (20) I will have delivered to my lord in Rataspatum. I will reach my lord by the third day after this tablet of mine. (25) The camp and the Banu-Sim'al are well.

Zech. 9:9

---

[2] Cuneiform *barum.* In later times Balaam was just such a *baru.*

[3] This expression is always in Amorite, transcribed in cuneiform *hayaram qatalum* (Heb., *qatol 'air*); it means simply "make a treaty," which was solemnized by the sacrifice of a young ass, much as the later Saracens of St. Nilus' time sacrificed a camel.

[4] The cuneiform text must be read *Jabi'um gerem ul išu,* obviously referring to the bloodless victory of the Hanu (the most important tribe of Mari) over their former foes in the southeastern marches.

d

Published by C. F. Jean in *Archives royales de Mari,* 11, No. 131, and translated in *Revue des études sémitiques,* 1944, pp. 26f.; the following is fully revised.

To my lord say: Thus Mashum, thy servant. (5) Sintiri wrote to me for help, and I reached him with troops at Shubat-Shamash. The next day word of the enemy (10) came as follows: "Yapah-Adad has made ready the settlement Zallul on this side on the bank of the Euphrates River, and with two thousand troops of the Hapiru of the land (15), is dwelling in that city." This word came to me, and from Shubat-Shamash, with troops of my command and with troops of the command of (20) Sintiri, I hurried, and made ready the town of Himush over against the town of Zallul. Between the two (25) cities (there is a distance of) thirty "fields." When I had made ready the city of Hi-   Jer. 6:1
mush over against him, and he saw that the land was hastening to (my) aid, (30) he raised a fire signal, and all the cities of the land of Ursum on the other side acknowledged it. The *security* forces which are stationed within the brick-*enclosure* are numerous, and, lest they (35) wipe out the troops, I did not draw near the city. This tablet of mine I send to my lord from the bank of the Euphrates River. The troops and *cattle* are well.

The Amarna Letters

ANET, 483–90

TRANSLATOR: W. F. ALBRIGHT

In 1887 an Egyptian peasant woman discovered a collection of cuneiform tablets at Tell el-Amarna in Middle Egypt, the site of Akh-en-Aton's capital in the early fourteenth century B.C. These tablets were sold to European museums and private dealers; some of them escaped attention for nearly thirty years. Subsequently excavation disclosed enough additional tablets to bring the total collection up to about 377 numbers. Almost all of them are letters belonging to the royal archives of Amen-hotep III and his son Akh-   *Fig. 107*
en-Aton. Nearly 300 letters were written by Canaanite (or rarely Egyptian) scribes in Palestine, Phoenicia, and southern Syria, about half of them in Palestine proper. These letters are written in a conventional vulgar Akkadian, full of canaanitisms in grammar and vocabulary. Occasionally we find a letter written mostly in Canaanite with scattered Akkadian formulas and ideograms. They date from the last years of Amen-hotep III and the reign of his successor; a very few may date from the ephemeral reign of Akh-en-Aton's son-in-law and successor, Smenkhkere.

    The translations offered below represent the combined work of W. F. Albright and George E. Mendenhall, with a few corrections by W. L. Moran, S.J.

EA, No. 234[5]

To the king, my lord, the Sun-god from heaven: Thus Zatatna, prince of Accho, thy servant, the servant of the king, and (5) the dirt (under) his two feet, the ground which he treads. At the two feet of the king, my lord, the Sun-god from heaven, seven times, seven times I fall, both prone and supine. (10) Let the king, my lord, hear the word of his servant! [Zir]damyashda has withdrawn from Biryawaza. [He was] with Shuta, the s[ervant] of the (15) king in the city of [. . . .] He did not say anything to him. The army of the king, my lord, has departed. He was with it in Megiddo. (20) I said nothing to him, but he deserted to me, and now Shuta has written to me: "Give (25) Zirdamyashda to Biryawaza!" But I did not consent to give him up. Behold, Accho is (as Egyptian) as Magdal (30) in Egypt, but the king, my lord, has not heard that [Shut]a has turned against me. Now let the king, my lord, send (35) his commissioner and fetch him.

Exod. 14:2

EA, No. 244[6]

To the king, my lord, and my Sun-god, say: Thus Biridiya, the faithful servant of the (5) king. At the two feet of the king, my lord, and my Sun-god, seven and seven times I fall. Let the king know that (10) ever since the archers returned (to Egypt?), Lab'ayu has carried on hostilities against me, and we are not able to pluck the wool, and we are not able to go outside the gate in the presence of Lab'ayu, since he learned that thou hast not given (20) archers; and now his face is set to take Megiddo, (25) but let the king protect his city, lest Lab'ayu seize it. (30) Verily, the city is destroyed by death from pestilence and *disease*. Let the king give (35) one hundred garrison troops to guard the city lest Lab'ayu seize it. Verily, there is no other purpose in (41) Lab'ayu. He seeks to destroy Megiddo.

EA, No. 245[7]

Further, I said to my brethren, "If the gods of the king, our lord, grant (5) that we capture Lab'ayu, then we will bring him alive to the

[5] This letter comes from the time of Akh-en-Aton. Shuta (pronounce *Suta*) was an Egyptian officer, probably the great-grandfather of Ramses II; Biryawaza (whose name was formerly read erroneously *Namyawaza*) was prince of Damascus under Egyption suzerainty. All personal names (except Shuta) are Indo-Aryan.

[6] Biridiya was prince of Megiddo at the end of the reign of Amen-hotep III and the beginning of the reign of Akh-en-Aton; his name is Indo-Aryan like most other princely names of northern Palestine at that time. Lab'ayu (whose name meant approximately "lion-like" in Canaanite) was prince of Shechem in the central hill-country and was constantly raiding the territory and caravans of his neighbors on all sides.

[7] This is the latter part (all that is preserved) of a continued letter from Biridiya of Megiddo. Zurata, whom Biridiya accuses of treachery, was prince of Acre (biblical Accho).

king, our lord"; but my mare was felled by an arrow, and I alighted
(10) afterwards and rode with Yashdata, but before my arrival, they
had slain him. (15) Verily, Yashdata is thy servant, and he entered the
battle with me. And verily, [. . .] (20) the life of the king, m[y lord]
[and] [. . .] all in [. . .] of the king, [my] lord, [. . .], and Zurata
(25) removed Lab'ayu from Megiddo, saying to me: "I will send him
by ship (30) to the king," and Zurata took him and sent him home
from Hannathon, for Zurata had received his ransom money (35) in
his hand.

Further, what have I done to the king, my lord, that he should despise me and honor (40) my younger brothers? Zurata has sent
Lab'ayu, and Zurata has sent Ba'lu-mihir to their homes, and let the
king, my lord, be informed!

RA, xix, p. 97[8]

To the king, my lord, and my Sun-god say: Thus Biridiya, the true
servant of the king. (5) At the feet of the king, my lord, and my Sun-
god, seven times and seven times I fall. Let the king be informed
concerning his servant and concerning his city. (10) Behold, I am
working in the town of Shunama, and I bring men of the corvée, Gen. 49:15
(15) but behold, the governors who are with me do not as I (do): they
do not (20) work in the town of Shunama, and they do not bring
men for the corvée, but I alone (25) bring men for the corvée from
the town of Yapu. They come from Shu[nama], and likewise from
the town of Nuribda. (30) So let the king be informed concerning
his city!

EA, No. 250[9]

˹To˺ the king, my lord, say: Thus Ba'lu-UR.SAG, thy servant. At the
feet of the king, my lord, seven times, seven times, I fall. Let the king,
my lord, know that (5) the two sons of a rebel against the king my
lord, the two sons of Lab'ayu, have determined to destroy the land of
the king, my lord, after their father's death. And let the king, my lord,
know that (10) many days the two sons of Lab'ayu have *accused* me
(saying): "Why hast thou given the town of Giti-padalla into the hand
of the king, thy lord—the city which Lab'ayu, our father, captured?"

---

[8] This letter from the prince of Megiddo is very instructive because of the light it
throws on forced labor for the king in the Plain of Esdraelon, several of whose towns
and villages are mentioned. The word for "corvée" is the Hebrew *mas*, which is employed a little later of the tribe of Issachar in this very region.

[9] The prince from whom this letter comes was in control of a district in the northern coastal plain of Palestine, south of Carmel. Here Lab'ayu's sons are described as
continuing their father's activities. Biryawaza, whose help is wanted to subdue the re-
calcitrants, was prince of Damascus. Milkilu was prince of Gezer, whose territory ad-
joined the territory of Ba'lu-UR.SAG ("Baal is a warrior") on the south.

(15) So thus the two sons of Lab'ayu spoke to me: "Declare war against the people of the land of Qena, because they slew our father; and if you do not declare war, then we are hostile to you."

But I answered them: (20) "May the god of the king, my lord, preserve me from making war against the people of the land of Qena, the servants of the king, my lord!" Now may it be agreeable to the king, my lord, to send one of his officers to Biryawaza (25) and let him say to him: "Wilt thou march against the two sons of Lab'ayu, or art thou a rebel against the king?" And after him, let the king, my lord, send to me [. . .] the deed (30) ⌈of the king,⌉ thy ⌈lord⌉, against the two sons of Lab'ayu [. . .] Milkilu *has gone in to them* [? . . .] (35) . . . ⌈land of the king, my lord, with them after Milkilu and Lab'ayu died.⌉ (40) And thus the two sons of Lab'ayu spoke: "Be hostile to the king, thy lord, like our father, when he attacked Shunama and Burquna and Harabu, and (45) destroyed them/smote them. And he took Giti-rimuni, and he betrayed the helpers of the king, thy lord."

But I answered them: "The god of the king, my lord, preserve me from making (50) war against the king, my lord. The king, my lord, I serve, and my brothers who hearken to me." But the courier of Milkilu does not move from the two sons of Lab'ayu (55) a (*single*) day. Behold, Milkilu seeks to destroy the land of the king, my lord. But there is no other intention with me—I serve the king, my lord, and the word which the king, my lord, speaks do I hear.

EA, No. 252[10]

To the king, my lord, say: Thus Lab'ayu, thy servant. At the feet of my lord I fall. (5) As for what thou hast written, "Are the people strong who have captured the town? How can the men be arrested?" (I reply) "By fighting was the town captured, (10) in spite of the fact that I had taken an oath of conciliation and that, when I took the oath, an (Egyptian) officer took the oath with me! The city as well as my god are captured. I am slandered/blamed (15) before the king, my lord."

Further, when (even) ants are smitten, they do not accept it (passively), but they bite the hand of the man who smites them. (20) How could I hesitate this day when two of my towns are taken?

Further, even if thou shouldst say: "(25) Fall beneath them, and let them smite thee," I should still repel my foe, the men who seized the town and (30) my god, the despoilers of my father, (yea) I would repel them.

---

[10] This letter is written in almost pure Canaanite and was not understood until very recently. Lab'ayu virtuously protests that he was only repelling aggressors who had attacked his native town (not Shechem, which was his capital) in spite of a previous treaty sworn in the presence of an Egyptian official.

EA, No. 254[11]

To the king, my lord and my Sun-god: Thus Lab'ayu, thy servant, and the dirt on which thou dost tread. At the feet of the king, my lord, (5) and my Sun-god, seven times and seven times I fall.

I have heard the words which the king wrote to me, and who am I that the king should lose his land (10) because of me? Behold, I am a faithful servant of the king, and I have not rebelled and I have not sinned, and I do not withhold my tribute, and I do not refuse (15) the requests of my commissioner. Now they wickedly slander me, but let the king, my lord, not impute rebellion to me!

Further, (20) my crime is namely that I entered Gezer and said publicly: (25) "Shall the king take my property, and not likewise the property of Milkilu?" I know the deeds which Milkilu has done against me.

(30) Further, the king wrote concerning my son. I did not know that my son associates with the 'Apiru (36), and I have verily delivered him into the hand of Addaya.

Further, if the king should write for my wife, (40) how could I withhold her? If the king should write to me, "Plunge a bronze dagger into thy heart and (45) die!", how could I refuse to carry out the command of the king?

EA, No. 256[12]

To Yanhamu, my lord say: Thus Mut-ba'lu, thy servant. At the two feet of my lord I fall. How is it said (5) before thee, "Mut-ba'lu has fled, Ayab has hidden himself?" How can the prince of Pella flee from the face of the commissioner (10) of the king, his lord? As the king my lord lives, as the king my lord lives, Ayab is not in Pella. Behold, he has not been (here) for two months(?). (15) Indeed, ask Ben-ilima, ask Taduwa, ask Yashuya. Again, *at the instance of* (20) the house of Shulum-Marduk, the city of Ashtartu came to (my) help, when all the cities of the land of Garu were hostile, (namely) Udumu, Aduru, (25) Araru, Meshqu, Magdalu, Eni-anabu and Zarqu, and when Hayanu and Yabilima were captured.

---

[11] In this letter Lab'ayu protests his innocence of all charges against him and assures the king (Amen-hotep III) that he is more loyal than the neighbors who complain against him.

[12] Mut-ba'lu (literally "Man of Baal") was prince of Pella in the northern Jordan Valley, opposite Beth-Shan; Ayab (Ayyab, Hebrew Job) was prince of Ashtartu (biblical Ashtaroth) in Bashan. The land of Garu lay in southern Golan between Pella and Ashtartu. Yanhamu, to whom the letter is addressed, was a high Egyptian official of Canaanite (possibly of Hebrew) origin, who seems to have been the Egyptian governor of Palestine at the beginning of the reign of Akh-en-Aton.

Further, behold—after (30) thy writing a tablet to me, I wrote to him. Before thou dost arrive with thy caravan, behold, he will have reached Pella, and he will hear (thy) words.

EA, No. 270[13]

To the king, my lord, my pantheon, my Sun-god, say: Thus Milkilu, thy servant, (5) the dirt (under) thy feet. At the feet of the king, my lord, my pantheon, my Sun-god, seven times, seven times I fall. Let the king, my lord, know (10) the deed which Yanhamu did to me after I left the presence of the king, my lord. Now he seeks (15) two thousand (shekels) of silver from my hand, saying to me: "Give me thy wife and (20) thy children, or I will smite!" Let the king know this deed, and let my lord send to me (26) chariots, and let him take me to himself lest I perish!

EA, No. 271[14]

To the king, my lord, my pantheon, my Sun-god, say: Thus Milkilu, thy servant, (5) the dirt (under) thy feet. At the feet of the king, my lord, my pantheon, my Sun-god, seven times, seven times, I fall. Let the king know (10) that powerful is the hostility against me and against Shuwardata. Let the king, my lord, protect his land (15) from the hand of the 'Apiru. If not, (then) let the king, my lord, send chariots (20) to fetch us, lest our servants smite us.

Further, let the king, my lord, ask (25) Yanhamu, his servant, concerning that which is done in his land.

RA, xxxi, pp. 125–36[15]

To Milkilu, prince of Gezer. Thus the king. Now I have sent thee this tablet to say to thee: Behold, (5) I am sending to thee Hanya, the commissioner of the archers, together with goods, in order to procure fine concubines (i.e.) *weaving women:* silver, gold, (linen) garments, (10) *turquoise,* all (sorts of) precious stones, chairs of *ebony,* as well as every good thing, totalling 160 deben. Total: 40 concubines: the price of each concubine is 40 (shekels) of silver. (15) So

[13] Milkilu (Heb., Malchiel) was prince of Gezer. For Yanhamu see the previous letter.

[14] For Milkilu see the previous letter. Shuwardata (with an Indo-Aryan name) was prince of the Hebron region in the southern hill-country, and frequently appears in association with Milkilu. The 'Apiru (formerly called Habiru) were a strong semi-nomadic people, or rather class of population in Syria and Palestine. While there is much reason to identify them with the Hebrews of the Patriarchal Age, the combination still remains uncertain and cannot be made the basis for any historical inferences.

[15] This letter from pharaoh to Milkilu of Gezer throws an interesting light on the role of the Canaanite princes in organizing royal commerce an Asia; Egyptian products and manufactured articles are to be exchanged for the best quality of slave-girls.

send very fine concubines in whom there is no blemish. (19) And let the king, thy lord, say to thee, "This is good. To thee life has been *decreed*." And mayest thou know that (25) the king is well, like the Sun-god. His troops, his chariots, his horses are very well. Behold, the god Amon has placed the upper land, (30) the lower land, the rising of the sun, and the setting of the sun under the two feet of the king.

EA, No. 280[16]

To the king, my lord, my pantheon, my Sun-god, say: Thus Shuwardata, (5) thy servant, the dirt (under) thy feet! At the feet of the king, my lord, my pantheon, my Sun-god, seven times, seven times, I fall! (9) The king, my lord, sent me to make war against Keilah. I have made war (and) I was successful; my town has been restored (15) to me. Why did 'Abdu-Heba write to the people of Keilah (saying): "Take (my) silver and (20) follow me!" And let the king, my lord, know that 'Abdu-Heba had taken the town from my hand.

Further, (25) let the king, my lord, investigate; if I have taken a man or a single ox or an ass from him, then he is in the right! (30)

Further, Lab'ayu is dead, who seized our towns; but behold, 'Abdu-Heba is another Lab'ayu, and (35) he (also) seizes our towns! So let the king take thought for his servant because of this deed! And I will not do anything until the king sends back a message to his servant.

RA, XIX, p. 106[17]

To the king, my lord, my Sun-god, my pantheon say: Thus Shuwardata, thy servant, servant of the king (5) and the dirt (under) his two feet, the ground (on) which thou dost tread! At the feet of the king, my lord, the Sun-god from heaven, seven times, seven times I fall, both (10) prone and supine.

Let the king, my lord, learn that the chief of the 'Apiru has risen (in arms) against the lands which the god of the king, my lord, gave me; (16) but I have smitten him. Also let the king, my lord, know that

---

[16] Shuwardata, prince of the Hebron district, here protests to pharaoh (Akh-en-Aton) that 'Abdu-Heba, prince of Jerusalem, is just as aggressive as the unlamented Lab'ayu (see the previous letters).

[17] This letter, from the beginning of Akh-en-Aton's reign, is an extraordinarily illuminating illustration of the situation in Palestine at that time. Just who this redoubtable 'Apiru chieftain was we do not learn, since the proud feudal princes disdained even to mention names of the semi-nomadic 'Apiru. However, he was sufficiently dangerous to unite the arch-foes, 'Abdu-Heba and Shuwardata, and to induce them to offer fifty chariots (a very considerable offer for Palestinian chieftains) to the princes of Accho and Achshaph in the Plain of Acre, far to the north. One suspects that Milkilu of Gezer and Lab'ayu of Shechem, who are not mentioned at all, were—either or both—involved with the 'Apiru.

all my brethren have abandoned me, and (20) it is I and 'Abdu-Heba (who) fight against the chief of the 'Apiru. And Zurata, prince of Accho, and Indaruta, prince of Achshaph, it was they (who) hastened (25) with fifty chariots—for I had been robbed (by the 'Apiru)—to my help; but behold, they are fighting against me, so let it be agreeable to the king, my lord, and (30) let him send Yanhamu, and let us make war in earnest, and let the lands of the king, my lord, be restored to their (former) limits!

EA, No. 286[18]

To the king, my lord, say: Thus 'Abdu-Heba, thy servant. At the two feet of my lord, the king, seven times and seven times I fall. (5) What have I done to the king, my lord? They blame me before the king, my lord (saying): "'Abdu-Heba has rebelled against the king, his lord." Behold, as for me, (it was) not my father (10) and not my mother (who) set me in this place; the arm of the mighty king brought me into the house of my father! Why should I commit (15) transgression against the king, my lord? As long as the king, my lord, lives, I will say to the commissioner of the king, my lord, "Why do ye favor the 'Apiru and oppose the governors?"—And thus (21) I am blamed in the presence of the king, my lord. Because it is said, "Lost are the lands of the king, my lord," thus am I blamed to the king, my lord! (25) But let the king, my lord, know that (when) the king had established a garrison, Yanhamu took ⌐it all⌐ away, [and . . .] ⌐the troops⌐ (30) [of archers(?) . . .] the land of Egypt [. . .] O king, my lord, there are no garrison troops (here)! [So] let the king take care of his land! (35) Let the king take care of his land! [The land]s of the king have all rebelled; Ilimilku is causing the loss of all the king's land. So let the king take care of his land! I keep saying, "Let me enter (40) into the presence of the king, my lord, and let me see the two eyes of the king, my lord." But the hostility against me is strong, so I cannot enter into the presence of the king, my lord. So may it please the king (45) to send me garrison troops in order that I may enter and see the two eyes of the king, my lord. As truly as the king, my lord, lives, when the commis[sioners] go forth I will say, "Lost are the lands of the king! (50) Do you not hearken unto me? All the governors are lost; the king, my lord, does not have a (single) governor (left)!" Let the king

---

[18] This letter is characteristic of the continuous requests of 'Abdu-Heba, prince of Jerusalem, for Egyptian assistance in his chronic struggle with the 'Apiru. However, it seems certain from other letters that he was inclined to lump his enemies among the "governors" (i.e., the native princes) with the 'Apiru. It is uncertain whether the Ilimilku (Elimelech) of lines 35ff. was an 'Apiru chieftain, was one of the sons of Lab'ayu, or was even Milkilu of Gezer (whose name might have been transposed accidentally by the scribe).

turn his attention to the archers, and let the king, my lord, send out (55) troops of archers, (for) the king has no lands (left)! The 'Apiru plunder all the lands of the king. If there are archers (here) in this year, the lands of the king, my lord, will remain (intact); but if there are no archers (here) (60) the lands of the king, my lord, will be lost!

To the scribe of the king, my lord: Thus 'Abdu-Heba, thy servant. Present eloquent words to the king, my lord.—All the lands of the king, my lord, are lost!

EA, No. 287[19]

[To the kin]g, my lord, [say:] [Thus] 'Abdu-Heba, thy servant. [At the feet] of my lord seven t[imes and seven times I fall.] [Let my king] [know (?) this] matter! [Milkili and Tagu (?)] (5) have caused [their troops (?)] to enter [the town of Rubutu (?)] [Behold] the deed which [Milkilu (?)] has done; [bows] (and) copper arrows [. . . he has given (?) . . .] word [. . . (10) . . .] into the town of [Rubutu (?)] they brought in. Let my king know that all the lands are at peace (but that) there is war against me. So let my king take care of his land!

Behold the land of Gezer, the land of Ashkelon, (15) and ⌈Lachish,⌉ they have given them grain, oil, and all their requirements; and let the king (thus) take care of his archers! Let him send archers against the men who transgress against the king, my lord. (20) If there are archers (here) in this year, then the lands and the governor⟨s⟩ will (still) belong to the king, my lord; [but] if there are no archers, the lands and the governors will (no longer) belong to the king! (25) Behold this land of Jerusalem: (It was) not my father (and) not my mother (who) gave (it) to me, (but) the arm of the mighty king (which) gave (it) to me.

Behold, this deed is the deed of Milkilu (30) and the deed of the sons of Lab'ayu who have given the land of the king to the 'Apiru. Behold, O king, my lord, I am right!

With reference to the Nubians, let my king ask the commissioners whether my house is (not) very strong! (35) Yet they attempted a

---

[19] In this letter the prince of Jerusalem complains about a number of events which recur in other letters. In the first place he excoriates Milkilu of Gezer and Tagu of the northern Coastal Plain of Palestine for their aggression against Rubutu, which lay somewhere in the region southwest of Megiddo and Taanach. In the second place he urges the king to instruct his officers to supply the Egyptian archers from the towns of the Philistine Plain and Sharon (in order to avert heavy drain on the scanty supplies of Jerusalem). He goes on to complain that the Nubian (biblical Cushite) slave-troops (or mercenaries) of Egypt, stationed as garrison in Jerusalem, had burglarized the residence of 'Abdu-Heba himself, nearly killing the prince in his own house. He finally complains that his last caravan containing tribute and captives for the king was attacked and robbed near Ajalon, presumably by the men of Milkilu of Gezer and the sons of Lab'ayu.

very great crime; they took their implements and breached . . . of the roof. [If] they send into the land [of Jerusalem] ⌜troops⌝, let them come up with [an (Egyptian) officer (40) for] (regular) service. Let [my king] take heed for them—for [all] the lands are impoverished by them—[and] let my king requisition for them much grain, much oil, (and) much clothing, (45) until Pawure, the royal commissioner, comes up to the land of Jerusalem.

Addaya has left, together with the garrison (and) the (Egyptian) officer which my king had given (me). Let the king know! Addaya spoke to me, (saying,) (50) [Loo]k, let me go, (but) do not thou leave it (the city)! So send me a garrison this [year], and send me a commissioner likewise, O my king. I have sent [gifts (?)] to the king, my lord: [. . .] captives, five thousand [silver (shekels)] (55) and eight porters for the caravans of the king, *my lord*; (but) they were captured in the plain of Ajalon. Let the king, my lord, know that I cannot send a caravan to the king, my lord. For thy information!

II Kings 21:4, 7   (60) Behold, the king has set his name in the land of Jerusalem for ever; so he cannot abandon the lands of Jerusalem!

To the scribe of the king, my lord, (65) say: Thus ʿAbdu-Heba, thy servant. At thy two feet I fall—thy servant am I! Present eloquent words to the king, my lord. I am (only) a petty officer of the king; (70) I am more insignificant (?) than thou!

But the men of the land of Nubia have committed an evil deed against ⟨me⟩; I was almost killed by the men of the land of Nubia (75) in my own house. Let the king [call] them to (account). Seven

Gen. 4:24   times and seven times let the [king,] my lord, [avenge (?)] me!

EA, No. 288[20]

To the king, my lord, my Sun-god, say: Thus ʿAbdu-Heba, thy servant. At the two feet of the king, my lord, seven times and seven times I fall. (5) Behold the king my lord, has set his name at the rising of the sun, and at the setting of the sun! (It is) vile what they have done against me. Behold, I am not a governor (10) (nor even a) petty officer of the king, my lord; behold, I am a shepherd of the king, and a bearer of the royal tribute am I. It was not my father (and) not my mother, (but) the arm of the mighty king (15) (which) placed me in the house of my father. [. . .] came to me [. . .] I delivered ten slaves [into his] hand. Shuta, the royal commissioner, came (20) to me. Twenty-one maidens (and) eighty captives I delivered into the hand of Shuta as a gift for the king, my lord. Let my king take thought for

---

[20] This letter continues the complaints of the previous letter, and incidentally paints a vivid picture of the anarchic condition of the country early in the reign of Akh-en-Aton. The references to "the very gate of Sile (Zilu)" mean that the outrages against the *pax Aegyptiaca* extend to the frontiers of Egypt itself, near modern Qantarah.

his land! The land of the king is lost; in its entirety (25) it is taken
from me; there is war against me, as far as the lands of Seir (and) as
far as Gath-carmel! All the governors are at peace, but there is war
against me. I have become like an 'Apiru (30) and do not see the two
eyes of the king, my lord, for there is war against me. I have become
like a ship in the midst of the sea! The arm of the mighty king (35)
conquers the land of Naharaim and the land of Cush, but now the
'Apiru capture the cities of the king. There is not a single governor
(remaining) (40) to the king, my lord—all have perished! Behold,
Turbazu has been slain in the (very) gate of Sile, (yet) the king holds
his peace. Behold Zimreda, the townsmen of Lachish have smitten
him, slaves who had become 'Apiru. (45) Yaptih-Hadad has been
slain [in] the (very) gate of Sile, (yet) the king holds his peace.
[Wherefore] does not [the king] call them to account? [So] let the
king take care of his land; [and l]et the king decide, and let the king
send (50) archers to his land! [But] if there are no archers (here) this
year, all the lands of the king, my lord, will be lost. They shall not say
to the king, my lord, (55) that the land of the king, my lord, has been
lost, and (that) all of the governors have perished! If there are no archers (here) this year, let the king send a commissioner, and let him
take me (60) to himself (!) together with ⟨my⟩ brothers, and we shall
die near the king, our lord!

[To] the scribe of the king, my lord: [Thus] 'Abdu-Heba, ⟨thy⟩
servant. At [thy (?)] two feet I fall. Present eloquent words (65) [. . .]
to the king, [my lord! Thy] servant [and] thy son am I.

EA, No. 289[21]

To the king, my lord, [say]: Thus 'Abdu-Heba, thy servant. At the two
feet of my lord, the king, seven times and seven times I [fall.] (5) Behold, Milkilu does not break (his alliance) with the sons of Lab'ayu
and with the sons of Arzayu in order to covet the land of the king for
themselves. As for a governor who does (such a) deed (as) this, (10)
why does not my king call him to account? Behold Milkilu and Tagu!
The deed which they have done is this, that they(!) have taken it, the
town of Rubutu. And now as for Jerusalem—(15) Behold this land
belongs to the king, or why like the town of Gaza is it loyal to the
king? Behold the land of the town of Gath-carmel, it belongs to Tagu,
and the men of Gath (20) have a garrison in Beth-Shan. Or shall we
do like Lab'ayu, who gave the land of Shechem to the 'Apiru? (25)
Milkilu has written to Tagu and the sons of ⟨Lab'ayu⟩, (saying) "Ye
are (members of) my house. Yield all of their demands to the men of
Keilah, and let us break our alliance ⟨with⟩ Jerusalem!" (30) The garrison which thou didst send through Haya, son of Miyare, Addaya

---

[21] Addaya was the Egyptian resident governor of Palestine, with his seat at Gaza.

has taken (and) has put into his residence in Gaza, [and] twenty men to Egypt (35) he has sent. Let my king know (that) there is no royal garrison with me. So now, as my king lives, truly the commissioner, Puwure, has taken leave of me (40) and is in Gaza; and let my king look out for him! And let the king send fifty men as a garrison to guard the land! The entire land of the king has revolted. (45) Send me Yanhamu and let him take care of the land of the king!

To the scribe of the king, [my lord]: Thus 'Abdu-Heba, [thy] servant. Present eloquent words (50) to the king. I am much more insignificant than thou; I am thy servant.

EA, No. 290[22]

[To] the king, my lord, say: Thus ['Abdu]-Heba, thy servant. At the two feet of the [king,] my lord, seven times and seven times I fall. (5) Behold the deed which Milkilu and Shuwardata did to the land of the king, my lord! They rushed troops of Gezer, troops of Gath (10) and troops of Keilah; they took the land of Rubutu; the land of the king went over to the 'Apiru people. But now even (15) a town of the land of Jerusalem, Bit-*Lahmi* by name, a town belonging to the king, has gone over to the side of the people of Keilah. Let my king hearken to 'Abdu-Heba, thy servant, (20) and let him send archers to recover the royal land for the king! But if there are no archers, the land of the king will pass over to the 'Apiru people. (25) This was done at the command of Milkilu [and at] the command of Shuwardata (?) . . . So let my king (30) take care of [his] land!

EA, No. 292[23]

To the king, my lord, my pantheon, my Sun-god say: Thus Ba'lu-shipti, thy servant, the dirt (under) thy two feet. (5) At the feet of the king, my lord, my pantheon, my Sun-god, seven times, seven times I fall. I have looked this way, and I have looked that way, (10) but it was not bright. I looked toward the king, my lord, and it was bright. A brick may move from beneath its companions, (15) but I will not move from beneath the two feet of the king, my lord. I have heard the words, which the king, my lord, wrote to his servant: (20) "Guard thy

[22] In lines 15ff. there is an almost certain reference to the town of Bethlehem, which thus appears for the first time in history. Keilah may have been the home of Shuwardata, prince of the Hebron district.

[23] Ba'lu-shipti was prince of Gezer in the period following the death of Milkilu, and this letter comes from the middle of the reign of Akh-en-Aton. Maya was a high Egyptian official at the court of the latter, then acting as commander of the Egyptian forces in Palestine. Peya bears an Egyptian name, in spite of the Canaanite name of his mother(?), and he was probably a minor Egyptian officer.

commissioner, and guard the cities of the king, thy lord." Behold, I guard, and behold, I hearken day (25) and night to the words of the king, my lord. But let the king, my lord, *learn* concerning his servant, (that) there is hostility against me from the mountains, so I have built (30) a house—Manhatu is its name—in order to make ready before the archers of the king, my lord; but Maya took it from my hands, and installed (35) his commissioner within it. So command Reanap, my commissioner, to restore the city to my hands, that I may make ready for (40) the archers of the king, my lord.

Further, behold the deed of Peya, the son of Gulate, against Gezer, the maidservant of the king, my lord, how many days he plundered it, so that it has become an empty cauldron because of him. From the mountains (50) people are ransomed for thirty (shekels) of silver, but from Peya for one hundred (shekels) of silver; so know these words of thy servant!   Exod. 21:32

EA, No. 297[24]

To the king, my lord, my pantheon, my Sun-god, say: Thus Yapahu, thy servant, the dirt (under) thy two feet. (5) At the feet of the king, my lord, my pantheon, my Sun-god, seven times, seven times, I fall. Everything which the king, my lord, said to me (10) I have heard most attentively.

Further: I have become like an empty bronze cauldron (because of) the debt (15) at the hands of the Sutu, but now I have heard the sweet breath of the king, and it goes out (20) to me, and my heart is very serene.

EA, No. 298

To the king, my lord, my pantheon, my Sun-god, the Sun-god of heaven. Thus Yapahu, the prince of (5) Gezer, the dirt (under) thy two feet, the groom of thy horse. At the two feet of the king, my lord (10) the Sun-god of heaven, seven times and seven times I fall, both prone and supine; and everything (15) which the king, my lord, commands me I hear very attentively. A servant of the king am I, and the dirt of thy two feet. (20) Let the king my lord know that my youngest brother is estranged from me, and has entered (25) Muhhazu, and has given his two hands to the chief of the 'Apiru. And now the [land of . . .]anna is hostile to me. (30) Have concern for thy land! Let my lord write to his commissioner concerning this deed.

---

[24] Yapakhu was prince of Gezer after the death of Milkilu. By *Sutu* is meant the nomadic tribesmen of Semitic origin who were in Egyptian service, as we know from other documents.

EA, No. 320[25]

To the king, my lord, my pantheon, my Sun-god, the Sun-god of heaven: Thus (5) Widia, the prince of Ashkelon, thy servant, the dirt (under) thy feet, the groom of thy horse. (10) At the feet of the king, my lord, seven times and seven times verily I fall, both prone and (15) supine.

Now I am guarding the place of the king which is with me, and whatever the king, my lord, has sent to me (20) I have heard very attentively. Who is the dog that does not hearken to the words of the king, his lord, (25) the son of the Sun-god?

Letter from Tell el-Hesi[26]

[To] the (Egyptian) officer say: [Thus P]a'pu. At thy feet I fall. Thou shouldst know that (5) Shipti-ba'lu and Zimreda have plotted publicly and Shipti-ba'lu said to Zimreda: ["The pr]ince of Yaramu wrote to me: 'Give me ⌜six⌝ bows, and three daggers, and three swords. (15) Verily I am going out against the land of the king, and thou art my ally!'" And yet he returns (the charge of) (20) lèse-majesté (saying): "The one who plots against the king is Pa'pu! And send him to (confront) me!" And [now] I have sent Rabi-ilu (25) to bring him (to thee) [because of] this matter.

Shechem Letter

To Birashshena say: Thus Baniti-[. . .]. From three years ago until now (5) thou hast caused me to be paid. Is there no grain nor oil nor wine which thou canst send? What is my offense that thou hast not paid me? (10) The children who are with me continue to learn. I am their father and their mother every day alike [. . . (15) . . . .] Now [behold] whatever [there is] beneath the feet [of my lord] let him [send] to me (20) and let him infor[m me].

Taanach, No. 1[27]

To Rewashsha say: Thus Guli-Adad. Live well! (5) May the gods take note of thy welfare, the welfare of thy house, of thy children! Thou

---

[25] Note the Indo-Aryan name of the prince of Ashkelon, whose servile words illustrate the impotence to which he was condemned by his nearness to the Egyptian residence, at Gaza, as well as by the smallness of his territory.

[26] This letter vividly characterizes the atmosphere of mutual suspicion and treachery which prevailed in Palestine in the early part of Akh-en-Aton's reign. Zimreda was prince of Lachish (Tell ed-Duweir) and Shipti-Ba'lu was to succeed him in that capacity. As shown by his name, Pa'pu was an Egyptian official, perhaps the local commissioner at Lachish.

[27] This letter and the other letters found by Ernst Sellin at Taanach, five miles southeast of Megiddo in northern Palestine, unquestionably belong to the fifteenth century B.C., and they may be dated roughly about three generations before the bulk

hast written to me concerning silver (10) and behold I will give fifty (shekels) of silver, truly I will do (so)!

Further, and if (20) there is a wizard of Asherah, let him *tell our fortunes* and let me hear *quickly,* and the omen and the interpretation send to me. (25)

I Kings 18:19ff.

As for thy daughter who is in the town of Rubutu, let me know concerning her welfare; and if she grows up thou shalt give her to become *a singer,* (30) or to a husband.

The Substitute King

ANET³, 626

TRANSLATOR: WILLIAM L. MORAN

The same correspondents and introduction as in the letter j of chapter XVI.

(5) The [substitute] king, who on the evening of the fourteenth took his se[at] (upon the throne), then spent the night of the fifteenth in the palace [of *Ashur*], (and) whom (the moon) affected with the eclipse, entered (10) Akkad safe and sound on the evening of the twentieth, (and) took his seat (on the throne). In the light of day I had (him) recite the traditional formulae of the scribal guild; he took upon himself all the signs of heaven and earth, (and) assumed the hegemony over all the universe. For the informa[tion] of the king my lord.

(15) This eclipse, which (the moon) brought about in (the month of) Tebet, concerned the land of Amurru. The king of the land of Amurru will die, his land will diminish, (or) in another interpretation, will disappear. Surely the scholars can tell the king my lord (20) something about the land of Amurru: the land of Amurru means the land of the Hittites and the land of the Sutaeans, (or) in another interpretation, the land of Chaldaea. Someone or other of the kings of the land of the Hittites, or of the land of Chaldaea, (reverse) or of the land of the Arabs, must bear (the consequences of) this sign. For the king my lord (there is to be) contentment: the king my lord will achieve his desire. The rites and prayers (5) of the king my lord are acceptable to the gods. Either the king of Cush, or the king of [Tyre], or Mugallu must meet the appointed death; (10) or, the king my lord will cap[ture him], the king my lord will diminish his land, the women of his harem will enter the service of the king [my lor]d. The king my lord should be gratified.

---

of the Amarna Tablets. Rewashsha was the prince of Taanach; his Egyptian name illustrates the extent of Egyptian penetration about a century after the initial conquest. The word here rendered "wizard" is Akkadian *ummanu,* which passed into Hebrew as *omman* and into later Phoenician as *ammun,* always with the general sense of "learned, skilled man, expert." The diviners of Asherah appear in the time of Elijah as "prophets of Asherah": they also figure in the Baal Epic of Ugarit.

However, the king my lord, should be careful, and (his) vigilance great. The apotropaic rituals, the lamentations for the pacification (of the gods), the spell against malaria (and other forms of) (15) pestilence should be carried out for the k[ing my lor]d and the sons of the king, my lords. (Several lines fragmentary or destroyed.)

ANET³, 626–27

A Happy Reign

TRANSLATOR: WILLIAM L. MORAN

To the king [my lord] your servant Adad-shum[usur]. Greetings to the ki[ng my lord]. May Nabu and Marduk bless the king [my lord] (5) most richly. Ash[ur the king of the go]ds has pronounced the name of the [king] my lord for the kingship over the land of Ashur. In their reliable oracle Shamash and Adad have established for the king my lord, for his kingship over the lands, a happy reign: days (10) of justice, years of equity, heavy rains, waters in full flood, a thriving commerce. The gods are reconciled, divine worship is widespread, the temples are enriched. (This) the great gods of heaven and earth have brought about (15) in the time of the king my lord.

Old men dance,
    young men sing,
Women and maidens
    are gl[ad (and) ma]ke merry.

Wives they take,
    deck with *ear-[ri]ngs,*
Beget sons and daughters—   (20)
    the offspring are instructed.
Whom his crime had condemned to death,
    the king my lord has let live;
[who] was held prisoner many [ye]ars,
    is set free;
[wh]o were sick many days,
    have recovered.
The hungry have been sated;   (reverse)
    the lice-infested have been anointed;
    the naked have been clad in garments.

ANET³, 627

A Royal Decree of Equity

TRANSLATOR: WILLIAM L. MORAN

The writer was the son and successor of Hammurabi of Babylon.

Speak to Etel-pi-Marduk: Thus Samsu-iluna. The king my father i[s ill]. (5) In order to [. . .] the land, I have taken [my seat] on the throne of [my father's] house. Moreover, in order to bol[ster up] the ten[ant(s)], [I ha]ve remitted (10) the arrears of the [. . .], the tenant-farmers (and) [*the shepherds*]; [the deb]t-tablets of the soldier, the fisherman, and the *muškēnu* (15) I have broken, (and) I have established equity in the land. In the land of [. . .] no one *is to make demands* on the house of a soldier, a fisherman, or a *muškēnu*. (20) As soon as you re[ad] my tablet, you and the elders of the land under your command are to come up here and have an audience with me.

A Letter to a God

ANET³, 627

Translator: William L. Moran

Speak to Ida (the river-god) my lord: Thus Zimri-Lim your servant. I herewith send a gold cup to my lord. At an earlier date I wrote my report to my lord; my lord reveal[ed] a sign. May my lord (10) make the sign which he revealed come true for me. Moreover, may my lord not neglect to protect my li[fe], may my lord not turn [his f]ace elsewhere, (15) besides me may my lord have need of no one el[se].

Punishment by Fire

ANET³, 627–28

Translator: William L. Moran

The writer was the king of Carchemish.

Speak to Zimri-Lim: Thus Yatar-Ami your son. Now as to these two men from here (5) whom I sent off with Napsuna-Addu, in this report on the city of Irrid which was picked up, they mentioned these men, saying, "They talked (10) with Mebisa, the servant of Bunuma-Addu; they know about the affair." So I have now had them conducted to Ida, (15) but their accuser is being guarded here in prison. A trustworthy servant of yours, in the company of Napsuna-Addu, should lead these men (20) to Ida. If these men are saved, I will burn their accuser in fire; if the men (25) die, here I will give their houses (and) their people to their accuser. May my father report on them to me.

Treaties and Coalitions

ANET³, 628

Translator: William L. Moran

The writer is the king of Assyria who ousted the dynasty of Yahdun-Lim from Mari; he here writes to a vassal in Shemshara (ancient Shusharra) in the Zagros Mountains to the east, where this tablet was found.

a

Speak to Kuwari: Thus Shamshi-Adad. Surely you have heard about the hostility of Yashub-Addu (5) the Ahzaean. Prior to this he had followed the man of the Shimurraeans, deserted the man of the Shimurraeans and followed the man of the Tirukkaeans. He deserted the man of the Tirukkaeans and (10) followed the Ya'ilanum (tribe). He deserted the Ya'ilanum (tribe) and followed me. Even me he deserted and has been following the man of Kakmu. Moreover, to all (15) these kings he has sworn an oath. It is scarcely three years since he became an ally and an enemy of these kings.

When he became an ally, (20) he swore an oath to me in the temple of Adad of Arrapha. Again, on the bank of the (Lower) Zab, in A'innum, he swore an oath to me; moreover, I swore an oath to him. Twice he swore an oath to me. (25) From the time he took the hem of my garment, I never collected any silver, oxen, sheep, or grain from his land; (30) I did not seize a single town in his land. (Nevertheless), having now become my enemy, he has been following the man of Kakmu. He becomes the ally of a king and (35) and swears an oath, (then) he becomes the ally of a(nother) king and swears an oath, while becoming an enemy of the first king with whom he was allied. His alliance with, and then hostility to, the king he is allied with [*take place*] within *two* months. With me [he was allied] for [x] months, and again he is hosti[le]. (45) I have now arri[ved] (and been here) these [x] months, but he has given me no help. When he moves up (for battle), you will he[ar] all that I am doing in his land.

b

The letter is addressed to Zimri-Lim; this excerpt, the only part published, tells much about political power before Hammurabi imposed the *pax babyloniaca*.

(22) Moreover, with regard to what my lord wrote here to the kings, saying, "Come to the sacrifice in honor of Ishtar," I gathered the kings to Sharmaneh and conveyed this message to them: "There is no king who is strong just by himself. Ten (to) fifteen kings are following (25) Hammurabi the man of Babylon; so, too, Rim-Sin the man of Larsa; so, too, Ibal-pi-el the man of Eshnunna; so, too, Amut-pi-el the man of Qatanum; (and) twenty kings are following Yarim-Lim the man of Yamhad."

ANET³, 628–29

"The God of My Father"

TRANSLATOR: WILLIAM L. MORAN

The correspondents are the king of Qatna in Syria and Ishme-Dagan, the older brother of Yasma'-Addu of Mari and the successor of Shamshi-Adad on the Assyrian throne. The presence of this letter in the Mari archives is perhaps to be explained by the intervention of Yasma'-Addu, who, aware of the letter's tone and anxious to avoid any form of retaliation by his brother, stopped it on its way through Mari. Possibly, however, Ishme-Dagan sent it back to Mari for the consideration of his brother, who was the son-in-law of the king of Qatna.

Speak to Ishme-Dagan: Thus Ishhi-Addu your brother. (5) Right now, just to relieve my feelings, I must speak about this matter which should not be spoken about. You are a great king; you made a request to me for two horses, and I had them conducted to you. But you sent me (10) twenty minas of tin! Without any formal agreement with me you have not gone wanting (what you requested), (and yet) you sent me this bit of tin! Had (15) you simply not sent me (anything), by the name of the god of my father my feelings would not have been hurt. The price of these horses over here by us in Qatna was (20) six hundred shekels of silver, yet you sent me twenty minas of tin! What will the one who hears of this say? Will he not *vilify* us? (25) This house is your house. What is missing in your house (that) a brother does not grant a request to a brother? Had you (30) not sent me the tin, my feelings would not have been hurt at all. You are not a great king! Why have you acted so? (35) This house is your house.

A Loan between Gentlemen   ANET³, 629

TRANSLATOR: WILLIAM L. MORAN

Speak to Muarihu the commissioner: Greetings to you. As to your writing here and saying: "He has acquired your servants from the hands of Hehea the Egyptian for 400 shekels of silver, but there are 140 shekels of my own money (10) which are outstanding. Moreover, he has *now* entered the temple and indeed said under oath (that) in fact he had not handed over your servants. I (still) have (15) their ransom money."—I shall give (you) the money you personally disemburse, and he has returned my servants to me, so give (20) your 80 shekels and do not put interest (on a loan) between us. We are each of us gentlemen.

A Boy to His Mother   ANET³, 629

TRANSLATOR: WILLIAM L. MORAN

The writer's father, Shamash-hazir, was a high official in the administration of Larsa under Hammurabi. The script is very clumsy, the language shows a boy's mistakes and (probably) colloquial speech, and the complaint belongs to the "letter home" through the ages.

Speak to Zinu: Thus Iddin-Sin. May Shamash, Marduk and Ilabrat for my sake forever (5) keep you well. Gentlemen's clothes improve year by year. (10) You are the one making my clothes cheaper year by year. By cheapening and scrimping my clothes (15) you have become rich. While wool was being consumed in our house like bread, you were the one making my clothes cheaper. The son of Adad-iddinam, (20) whose father is (only) an underling of my father, *has [recei]ved two* new garments, (but) you keep getting upset over just one garment for me. Whereas you (25) gave birth to me, his mother [acquir]ed him by adoption, (30) but whereas his mother loves him, you do not love me.

Aramaic Letters

TRANSLATOR: H. L. GINSBERG

ANET, 491–92

Letters of the Jews in Elephantine

"The Passover Papyrus"

A very defective strip of papyrus with writing on both sides. Text: Sachau, 6; Ungnad, 6; Cowley, 21. Date: 419 B.C.

[To] my [brethren Yedo]niah[28] and his colleagues the [J]ewish gar[rison], your brother Hanan[iah].[29] The welfare of my brothers may God [seek at all times]. Now, this year, the fifth year of King Darius, word was sent from the king to Arsa[mes[30] saying, *"Authorize a festival of unleavened bread for the* Jew]ish [garrison]." So do you count fou[rteen days of the month of Nisan and] obs[erve *the passover*],[31] and from the 15th to the 21st day of [Nisan observe the festival of unleavened bread]. Be (ritually) clean and take heed. [Do n]o work [on the 15th or the 21st day, no]r drink [beer,[32] nor eat] anything [in] which the[re is] leaven [from the 14th at] sundown until the 21st of Nis[an. For seven days it shall not be seen among you. Do not br]ing it into your dwellings but seal (it) up between these date[s. *By order of King Darius.* To] my brethren Yedoniah and the Jewish garrison, your brother Hanani[ah].

[28] A priest and head of the Jewish community (military colony) of Elephantine.

[29] Apparently a secretary for Jewish affairs to Arsames.

[30] Satrap of Egypt from 455/4 to at least 407.

[31] The word *psh'* in two ostraca from Elephantine may mean "passover (offering)."

[32] This restoration is only correct if Hananiah's tradition, like rabbinic law, included under "leaven" fermented corn but not fermented fruit (wine). The Samaritans take a more rigorous view.

Contributions to the Cult of Yaho

A very broad sheet of papyrus with 7 columns of Aramaic; traces of palimpsest. Text: Sachau, 17–19; Ungnad, 19; Cowley, 22. Date: 419 or 400 B.C.[33] See the special study of U. Cassuto in *Kedem*, 1, pp. 47–52.

On the 3rd of Phamenoth,[34] year 5. This is (*sic!*) the names of the Jewish garrison which (*sic!*) gave money to the God Yaho, [2 shekels] each.

(Lines 2–119, 126–135 name 123 contributors of both sexes.)

(120-125) Cash on hand with Yedoniah the son of Gemariah on the said day of the month of Phamenoth: 31 *karash*, 8 shekels. Comprising: for Yaho 12 *k.*, 6 sh.;[35] for Ishumbethel[36] 7 *k.*; for Anathbethel[37] 12 *k.*

Settlement of Claim by Oath

Text: Sayce-Cowley, F; Cowley, 14. Date: 440 B.C.

The Jewess Mibtahiah (*Mbṭhyh*) had apparently married the Egyptian Pi' and then the marriage had been dissolved. The marriage had meant Mibtahiah's exit from the Jewish community and adoption into the Egyptian. Even its liquidation necessitated her swearing by an Egyptian deity. The witnesses to this document are neither Jewish nor Egyptian.

On the 14th of Ab, being the 19th day of Pahons, in the year 25 of King Artaxerxes, Pi' the son of Pahi (*Pḥy*), builder, of the fortress of Syene, said to Mibtahiah, daughter of Mahseiah the son of Yedoniah, an Aramean of Syene of the detachment of Varizata (as follows): In accordance with the action which we took at Syene, *let us make a division* of the silver, grain, raiment, bronze, iron, and all goods and possessions and marriage contract. Then an oath was imposed upon you, and you swore to me concerning them by the goddess Sati. I was satisfied with the oath which you took to me concerning your goods, and I renounce all claim on you from this day for ever.

---

[33] Depending on whether the fifth year is that of Darius II or of the native Egyptian king Amyrtaeus.

[34] A month in the Egyptian calendar.

[35] Since 1 *karash* = 20 (light) shekels, this is the correct total for 123 contributions of 2 shekels each. The monies for the other two deities were doubtless contributed by non-Jews, Yedoniah acting as treasurer or banker for all the Arameans of Elephantine.

[36] Male divinity.

[37] Probably female divinity.

Petition for Authorization to Rebuild the Temple of Yaho

A well-preserved papyrus with writing on both sides, apparently a copy of one sent to Jerusalem. Text: Sachau, 1–2; Ungnad, 1; Cowley 30. Date: 407 B.C. (Another, defective copy, with some variants: Sachau, 3; Ungnad, 2; Cowley 31.)

To our lord Bagoas, governor of Judah, your servants Yedoniah and his colleagues, the priests who are in the fortress of Elephantine. May the God of Heaven seek after the welfare of our lord exceedingly at all times and give you favor before King Darius and the nobles a thousand times more than now. May you be happy and healthy at all times. Now, your servant Yedoniah and his colleagues depose as follows: In the month of Tammuz in the 14th year of King Darius,[38] when Arsames (5) departed and went to the king, the priests of the god Khnub, who is in the fortress of Elephantine, conspired with Vidaranag, who was commander-in-chief here, to wipe out the temple of the god Yaho from the fortress of Elephantine. So that wretch Vidaranag sent to his son Nefayan, who was in command of the garrison of the fortress of Syene, this order, "The temple of the god Yaho in the fortress of Yeb is to be destroyed." Nefayan thereupon led the Egyptians with the other troops. Coming with their weapons to the fortress of Elephantine, they entered that temple and razed it to the ground. The stone pillars that were there they smashed. Five (10) "great" gateways built with hewn blocks of stone which were in that temple they demolished, but their doors *are standing,* and the hinges of those doors are of bronze; and *their* roof of cedar-wood, all of it, with the . . . and whatever else was there, everything they burnt with fire. As for the basins of gold and silver and other articles that were in that temple, they carried all of them off and made them their own.—Now, our forefathers built this temple in the fortress of Elephantine back in the days of the kingdom of Egypt, and when Cambyses came to Egypt he found it built. They knocked down all the temples of the gods of Egypt, but no one did any damage to this temple. (15) But when this happened, we and our wives and our children wore sackcloth, and fasted, and prayed to Yaho the Lord of Heaven, who has let us see our desire upon that Vidaranag. The dogs took the fetter out of his feet,[39] and any property he had gained was lost; and any men who have sought to do evil to this temple have all been killed and we have seen our desire upon them.—We have also sent a letter before now, when this evil was done to us, ⟨to⟩ our lord and to

---

[38] 410 B.C.

[39] Perhaps a mistake for "his feet out of the fetter."

the high priest Johanan and his colleagues the priests in Jerusalem and to Ostanes the brother of Anani and the nobles of the Jews. Never a letter have they sent to us. Also, from the month of Tammuz, year 14 of King Darius, (20) to this day, we have been wearing sackcloth and fasting, making our wives as widows, not anointing ourselves with oil or drinking wine. Also, from then to now, in the year 17 of King Darius,[40] no meal-offering, in[cen]se, nor burnt offering have been offered in this temple. Now your servants Yedoniah, and his colleagues, and the Jews, the citizens of Elephantine, all say thus: If it please our lord, take thought of this temple to rebuild it, since they do not let us rebuild it. Look to your well-wishers and friends here in Egypt. Let a letter be sent from you to them concerning the temple of the god Yaho (25) to build it in the fortress of Elephantine as it was built before; and the meal-offering, incense, and burnt offering will be offered in your name, and we shall pray for you at all times, we, and our wives, and our children, and the Jews who are here, all of them, if you do thus, so that that temple is rebuilt. And you shall have a merit before Yaho the God of Heaven more than a man who offers to him burnt offering and sacrifices worth a thousand talents of silver and (because of) gold. Because of this we have written to inform you. We have also set the whole matter forth in a letter in our name to Delaiah and Shelemiah, the sons of Sanballat the governor of Samaria. (30) Also, Arsames knew nothing of all that was done to us. On the 20th of Marheshwan, year 17 of King Darius.

Neh. 12:22–23
I Chron. 3:24

Neh. 2:19

Advice of the Governors of Judah and Samaria to the Jews of Elephantine

Text: Sachau, 4; Ungnad, 3; Cowley, 32.

Memorandum of what Bagoas and Delaiah said to me: Let this be an instruction to you in Egypt to say before Arsames about the house of offering of the God of Heaven which had been in existence in the fortress of Elephantine (5) since ancient times, before Cambyses, and was destroyed by that wretch Vidaranag in the year 14 of King Darius: to rebuild it on its site as it was before, and the meal-offering and incense[41] to be made on (10) that altar as it used to be.

---

[40] 407 B.C.

[41] The Mazdean Arsames was likely to react more favorably if no mention was made of burnt offering, since it involved the profaning of fire by contact with dead bodies.

Petition by Elephantine Jews, Perhaps to Arsames

Text: Sachau, 4; Ungnad, 4; Cowley, 33.

Your servants Yedoniah the son of Ge[mariah] by name 1, Ma'uzi the son of Nathan by name [1], Shemaiah the son of Haggai by name 1, Hosea the son of Yatom by name 1, (5) Hosea the son of Nathun by name 1, 5 men in all, Syenians who [ho]ld proper[ty] in the fortress of Elephantine, say as follows: If your lordship is [favo]rable, and the temple of ou[r] God Yaho [is rebuilt] in the fortress of Elephantine as it was for[merly buil]t, (10) and n[o] *sheep,* ox, or goat are offered there as burnt offering, but (only) incense, meal-offering, [and drink-offering], and (if) your lordship giv[es] orders [to that effect, then] we shall pay into your lordship's house the s[um of ... and] a thous[and] *ardabs* of barley.

Assignment to a New Lessor of Land Abandoned in the Egyptian Rebellion of 410 B.C.

ANET³, 633

This is one of a collection of documents and fragments of documents, written on leather and enclosed in a leather bag, which were acquired by the late Ludwig Borchardt in Egypt.

The sender of the letter, Arsames, was the Persian satrap of Egypt (and of Babylonia and Transeuphrates as well?) in the last two decades of the fifth century B.C. It may have been written less than a year after the rebellion to which it refers, and it probably originated in Babylon, which is named in some of the other letters. Arsames is known to have been absent from Egypt during, and for a couple of years after, the rebellion.

(outside)
(1) From Arsames to the officer Nakht-Hor the Comptroller and his colleagues the accountants in Egypt.

(inside)
(1) From Arsames to Nakht-Hor the Comptroller and his colleagues.

Now, Petosiri (as he is called), a *forester,* a servant of mine, has written to me as follows: "In the matter of [my father] Pamun (as he [was called). When] (2) the rebellion occurred in Egypt, in the course of it my father the said Pamun (as he was called) perished and the farm occupied by him, measuring a seed requirement of 30 ardabs, was abandoned; for our staff pe[rished] to a man. [Therefore, let them assign] (3) the farm of my father Pamun to me. Take thought on my behalf: let them assign it to me to occupy."

Arsames, therefore, commands thus: If the facts accord with the above statement of Petosiri in his letter to [me concerning] his father the said [Pamun] (4) (as he was called)—if he did perish together with [his] st[aff] when the rebellion occurred in Egypt, [and] the farm of his father [the said] Pamun, measuring a seed requirement of 30 ardabs, was abandoned—and if it has (5) not been (re)joined [to my estate] and assigned by me to another servant of mine, then I hereby assign the farm of the said Pamun to Petosiri. You for your part advise him (thus): Let him occupy it and let him pay (6) the land-tax to my estate just as it was formerly paid by his father Pamun.

(7) Artohi is cognizant of this order; Rasht is the clerk.

Illustration Credits

Albright, W. F.: 33. Aharoni, Y.: 199, 231, 232. Aharoni, Y., and Arad Expedition: 234, 235, 301, 302. Allegro, J. M.: 173. American Schools of Oriental Research: 83. Amiran, R., and Arad Expedition: 293. Archives Photographiques, Paris: 67, 68, 74, 96, 132, 134. Bar-Adon, P., and Department of Antiquities and Museums, Israel: 266, 267, 270. Birnbaum, S. A.: 81. Bothmer, B. V.: 191. British Museum: 5, 16, 17, 28, 58, 69, 72, 97, 98, 100, 102, 114, 115, 118, 119, 122, 124, 142, 144, 146, 151, 155, 156, 157, 158, 161, 163, 164, 165, 167, 168, 239, 287. British School of Archaeology in Iraq: 221, 228, 247, 249. Brooklyn Museum: 70, 82, 160. Bulloz, J. E., Paris: 40. Cairo Museum: 4, 42, 84, 105, 106, 111, 129. Cameron, G. G.: 62. Cross, F. M., Jr.: 233. Dajani, A. K., and Department of Antiquities of Jordan: 282. Department of Antiquities, Israel: 27, 211, 212, 213, 214, 248. De Vaux, R.: 294. Dothan, M.: 201, 269 Dunand, M.: 103. École Biblique: 217. Éditions "TEL," Paris: 86, 147. Felbermeyer, J.: 112. Foto Marburg: 6, 43, 93, 107, 108, 109, 110, 125, 127, 193. Franken, H. J.: 240. Gaddis, A.: 88, 94. Garber, P. L.: 182. Giraudon, Paris: 59, 117. Hebrew Union College: 295. Hessische Treuhandver-waltung des früheren preussischen Kunstgutes, Wiesbaden: 8, 87, 89, 91. Hirmir Fotoarchiv Munchen: 223, 230, 284. Holladay, J. S.: 204. Horn, S. H.: 73. Iraq Museum: 36, 169, 209, 271, 286. Kenyon, K.: 49, 172, 205, 207, 208. Mazar, B.: 38. Metropolitan Museum of Art, New York: 12, 19, 21, 26, 32, 41, 45, 46, 113, 159, Musées Royaux d'Art et d'Histoire, Brussels: 153. Museo di Antichità, Turin: 14, 120. Museum of the Ancient Orient, Istanbul: title page. Museum of Fine Arts, Boston: 104. Oriental Institute, Chicago: 3, 7, 10, 29, 30, 31, 48, 55, 92, 95, 123, 148, 149, 170, 175, 181, 185, 186, 196, 197, 203, 241, 275, 276, 277. Palestine Archaeological Museum, Jerusalem: 9, 11, 22, 37, 39, 47, 49, 53, 80, 90, 135, 152, 166, 177, 178, 187. Palestine Institute, Pacific School of Religion: 23, 76, 176. Parrot, A.: 206, 220, 226, 227, 242, 274, 279. Perrot, J.: 250, 251, 252. Photo Rostemy, Teheran: 195. Porada, E.: 57. Pritchard, J. B.: 24, 78, 79, 116, 126, 128, 130, 136, 137, 139, 140, 143, 179, 180, 202, 210, 215, 216, 218, 219, 224, 225, 237, 238, 268, 288, 289, 305, 306. Reed, W. L.: 280, 281. Schaeffer, C.F.A.: 63, 133, 244, 245, 246, 257. School of Oriental and African Studies: 265. Staatliche Museen, Berlin: 121, 189. Trans World Airlines: 192. University Museum, University of Pennsylvania: 1, 13, 15, 34, 35, 44, 60, 61, 66, 71, 85, 99, 131, 150, 154, 188, 194. Virginia Museum of Fine Arts: 198. Winchester College: 258. Wright, G. E.: 253, 296, 297. Yadin, Y.: 174, 259, 260, 261, 262, 263, 264, 272, 273, 283, 285, 292, 298, 300. Yale University News Bureau: 56.

Illustrations from Books

2: C. R. Lepsius, *Denkmäler aus Ägypten und Äthiopien*, Berlin, 1848–1859, vol. 2, pl. 133.—18: N. de G. Davies, *The Tomb of Rekh-mi-Ré' at Thebes*, New York, 1943, pl. 58.—20: A. Moortgat, *Vorderasiatische Rollsiegel*, Berlin, 1940, no. 526.—25, 138: *Syria*, XVIII, pl. 24, pl. 17.— 50, 51: *Journal of the Palestine Oriental Society*, vol. 14, 1934, pl. 1, p. 180, fig. 2,—52: H, Junker, *Gîza*, vol. 2, Vienna and Leipzig, 1934, pl. 7b.—54, 101: A. H. Layard, *A Second Series of the Monuments of Nineveh*, London, 1853, pls. 35, 21.—64: H. Grimme, *Althebräische Inschriften vom Sinai*, Darmstadt, 1923, pl. 9, below.—65: D. Diringer, *Le iscrizioni antico-ebraiche palestinesi*, Florence, 1934, pl. 1.—75: A. Reifenberg, *Ancient Hebrew Seals*, London, 1950, p. 27.—77: W. F. Albright, *The Excavation of Tell Beit Mirsim*, vol. 1, *AASOR*, 12, New Haven, 1932, p. 78, fig. 13.—141: F. H. Weissbach, *Babylonische Miscellen, WVDOG*, 4, Leipzig, 1903, p. 16, fig. 1.—145: A. H. Layard, *The Monuments of Nineveh*, London, 1849, pl. 65.— 162: A. J. Gayet, *Le temple de Louxor, Mémoires, Mission archéologique française au Caire*, vol. 15, Paris, 1894, pl. 63 (71).—171: H. Frankfort, *Cylinder Seals*, London, 1939, pl. 22k.—183: The Megiddo Expedition, *Megiddo II*, Text, Chicago, 1948, fig. 107.—184: *Bulletin of the American Schools of Oriental Research*, no. 52, 1933, fig. 1.—190: V. Place, *Ninive ft l'Assyrie*, vol. 3, plates, Paris, 1867, pl. 18bis.—200, 290, 291, 299: Y. Yadin et al., *Hazor III–IV*, Jerusalem, 1961, pls. 339:1, 1, 2, 121:2.—222, 229, 278: E. Akurgal, *Orient und Okzident*, Baden-Baden, 1966, pls. 34a, 32, 33.—236: *Israel Exploration Journal*, vol. 10, 1960, pl. 17.—243: *Ugaritica III*, pl. III.—254, 255, 256: *Syria*, vol. 43, 1966, pls. 2, 3 left, 1 left.—303: Y. Yadin et al., *Hazor II*, Jerusalem, 1960, pl. 4:2.—304: J. B. Pritchard, *Gibeon, Where the Sun Stood Still*, Princeton, 1962, fig, 5.—307: *Syria*, vol. 32, 1955, pl. 15:2.

Index to Biblical References

Index

Plates

1. Statuettes of Sumerians which stood before the god of the Nintu Temple V at Khafajah early in the third millennium.

Show Semi-nomads from Canaan

Carrying gifts for the King

2. Ibsha, "the ruler of a foreign country," leads a caravan of "thirty-seven" Asiatics bringing eye-paint to Egypt; a tomb painting dating from about 1890 B.C. The bellows on each of the donkeys suggests traveling metalworkers (cf. Gen. 4:19-22).

Pictorial analogy of Joseph's many-colored coat.

3. Head of a Mede, with hair and beard elaborately curled, carved on a decorated stairway at Persepolis; from the time of Darius and Xerxes.

4. Bound Syrian captive on the head of a ceremonial walking stick of Tut-ankh-Amen found his tomb at Thebes.

5. Syrian tribute bearers, bringing ointment horn, quiver, vessels, rhyton, and child; on a fragment of plaster from the wall of a fifteenth-century tomb at Thebes.

6. A beardless Hittite prisoner with a rope around his neck; on the wall of the great temple at Abu Simbel.

7. Prisoners of Ramses III from his campaign in Amor—Lybian, Syrian, Hittite, one of the Sea Peoples (perhaps a Philistine), Syrian; on wall of temple at Medinet Habu.

8. Kneeling Syrians and Negroes decorate the platform (footstool) of Amen-hotep III enthroned.

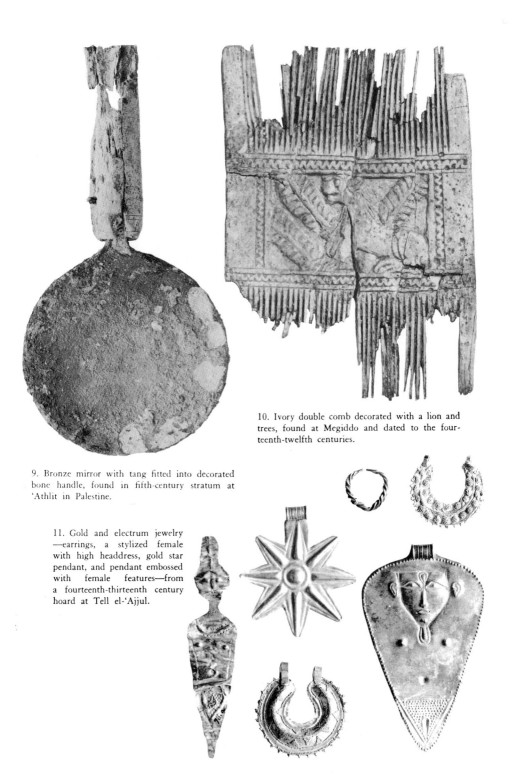

10. Ivory double comb decorated with a lion and trees, found at Megiddo and dated to the fourteenth-twelfth centuries.

9. Bronze mirror with tang fitted into decorated bone handle, found in fifth-century stratum at 'Athlit in Palestine.

11. Gold and electrum jewelry —earrings, a stylized female with high headdress, gold star pendant, and pendant embossed with female features—from a fourteenth-thirteenth century hoard at Tell el-'Ajjul.

12. An Egyptian barber dresses the hair of one of the recruits of Amen-hotep II; fifteenth century.

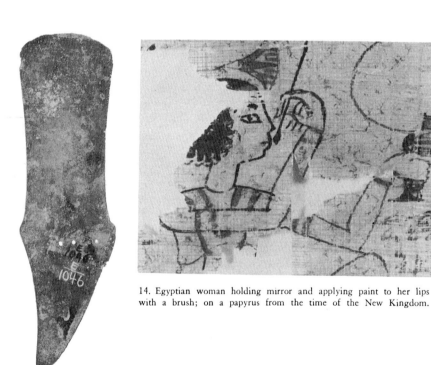

14. Egyptian woman holding mirror and applying paint to her lips with a brush; on a papyrus from the time of the New Kingdom.

13. Egyptian razor blade of bronze with holes for attaching to handle; possibly Eighteenth Dynasty.

15. Dairy scene on frieze from Tell el-Obeid: milking of cow, doorposts of the sacred precincts, and preparation of milk products; limestone figures set against a black shale background held within copper borders; middle of third millennium.

16. Wooden model of a man plowing with a two-handled wooden plow drawn by two yoked oxen; late third millennium.

17. Seed plow with drill on a basalt stela of Esarhaddon.

18. Traditional brickmaking in Egypt: workmen with hoes knead clay moistened with water, as laborers carry material to two brickmakers; from fifteenth-century tomb painting of Rekh-mı-Re at Thebes.

20. Mesopotamian god and worshiper drinking (beer?) through tubes.

21. Wooden model of a boat equipped with rudder, mast, sail, and cabin, in which sits Meket-Re with his son and a singer; Eleventh Dynasty.

19. Gathering grapes from an arbor, treading, and storage of wine in jars with stoppers; fifteenth century.

22. Clay figure bending over a trough kneading dough; from a cemetery of 900-600 B.C. at ez-Zib.

23. Limestone weight inscribed with *pym* from Tell en-Nasbeh (cf. I Samuel 13:21).

24. Clay weight with inscription found at Gibeon.

25. Weight in form of human head found at Ras Shamra; fourteenth-thirteenth century.

26. Model of potter's shop, in which one figure turns clay on a wheel as another tends a kiln; twenty-first century, from Sakkarah.

27. Profiles of characteristic pottery types from the principal archaeological periods in Palestine.

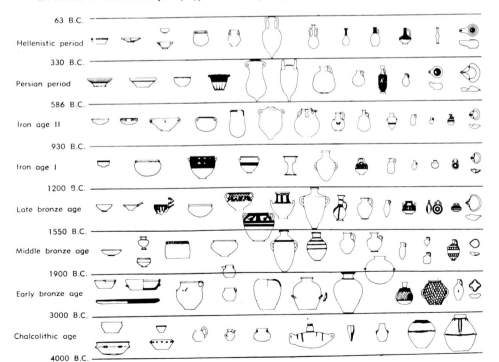

28. Woman's head framed by recessed window (cf. I Kings 6:4), carved from ivory for an inset in woodwork (cf. II Kings 9:30); from Nimrud, possibly first half of eighth century.

29. Box from one piece of ivory with sphinxes and lions carved in high relief; from Megiddo, 1350-1150 B.C.

30, 31. Ivory carving of nude woman; and ivory figurine with eyes of glass, of a woman holding staff, probably used as an inset for furniture (cf. Amos 6:4); from Megiddo, 1350-1150 B.C.

32. Painting of spinning and weaving scene on wall of Middle Kingdom tomb.

33. A dye plant consisting of two cylindrical stone vats and two rectangular basins, from eighth-century level at Tell Beit Mirsim.

34, 35. Gold helmet of Mes-kalam-dug (not the king), hammered out of one piece of metal, and gold dagger and sheath; twenty-fifth century tomb at Ur.

36. Coat of mail made of bronze plates laced together with thongs, from a level dated to the middle of the second millennium at Nuzi.

37. A pottery mold for casting implements with two axes or chisels in place; from Shechem, Middle Bronze Age.

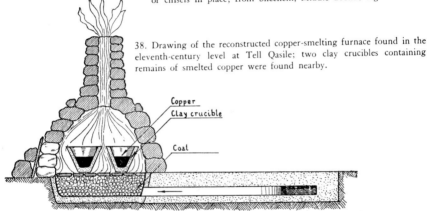

38. Drawing of the reconstructed copper-smelting furnace found in the eleventh-century level at Tell Qasile; two clay crucibles containing remains of smelted copper were found nearby.

Copper
Clay crucible

Coal

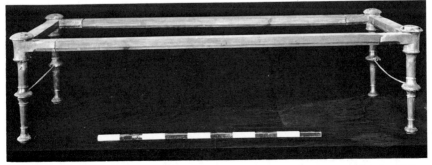

39. A bed of the Persian period reconstructed from bronze fittings and iron tie-rods found at Tell el-Far‘ah (south).

40. Ashurnasirpal hunting lions, on a ninth-century bas-relief found at Nimrud.

41. Tut-ankh-Amon, standing in his chariot with drawn bow, charges a herd of gazelles and ostriches fleeing before the king's hounds; painting on the lid of a box found in the king's tomb at Thebes.

42. Wooden model of Egyptian soldiers arranged in four columns, armed with lances and shields; from Siut, Middle Kingdom.

43. Assyrian soldiers leading away prisoners of war and transporting women in a cart; from seventh-century palace of Ashurbanipal at Nineveh.

44. Reconstructed lyre with sound-box ending in a gold bull's head; found in a twenty-fifth century tomb at Ur.

45. Egyptian musicians: harpist, lutist, dancer, player of double pipe, lyrist; fifteenth-century tomb painting at Thebes.

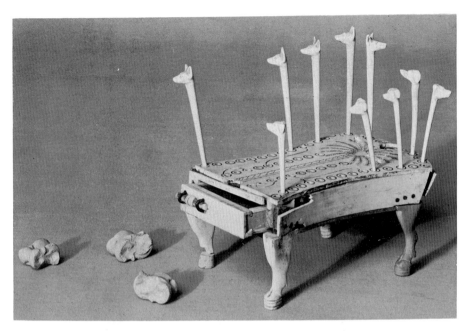

46. Game board of ivory and ebony veneer, ivory pins, and knucklebones, for playing "hounds and jackals"; from a Theban tomb.

47. Game board with ten playing pieces and an ivory teetotum pierced on four sides with varying number of holes; from Middle Bronze stratum at Tell Beit Mirsim.

48. An ivory game board with fifty-eight holes, from Megiddo, 1350-1150 B.C.

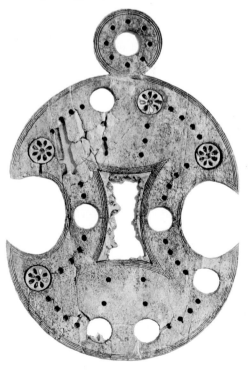

49. Plastered skull found in a Neolithic stratum at Jericho.

50. Fourth-century Jewish coin with bearded figure seated on a winged wheel.

51. Fourth-century coin from Beth-zur, inscribed with "Hezekiah" and "Judaea."

52. Seated scribes, equipped with sharpened rush pens and palettes; Fourth Dynasty.

53. Ink-wells of terra-cotta and bronze found in the remains of scriptorium at Qumran.

54. Scribes list the booty and the slain of a town captured by Sennacherib.

55. Restored writing equipment of an Egyptian scribe: rush pen, palette, and water jar.

56. Legal document in cuneiform from Cappadocia with its envelope.

57. Cylinder seals, varying in size and shape, carved with scenes which were impressed on wet clay for purposes of identification.

58. Cuneiform tablet with account of the conquest of Jerusalem by Nebuchadnezzar in 598 B.C.

59. The stela of Hammurabi inscribed with laws; from Susa.

60. Historical records of Esarhaddon on an octagonal prism.

61. Ancient clay map of the town of Nippur, showing locations of temple, walls, gates, and canals; found at Nippur.

62. Relief and inscription of Darius at Behistun; the inscription provided a key for reading Akkadian cuneiform.

63. Clay tablet containing the Ugaritic alphabet of thirty characters in order.

64. Alphabetic inscription in Sinaitic script containing the phrase "for Ba'alat"; fifteenth century.

66. Clay cylinder inscribed with a text of Nebuchadnezzar.

67. Ceremonial adzehead inscribed in the cuneiform alphabet of Ras Shamra; possibly fourteenth century.

65. Limestone tablet inscribed with a school text of an agricultural calendar; from Gezer, about tenth century.

68. Portion of the text of the legend of Aqhat on clay tablet from Ras Shamra.

69. Fragment of clay tablet from Nineveh inscribed with the Babylonian account of the flood.

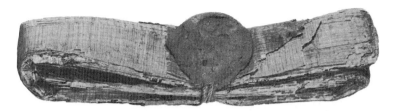

70. Sheet of papyrus rolled, tied, and sealed with an impression on mud, containing, a marriage contract in Aramaic.

71. Section of the Theban recension of the "Book of the Dead," written on papyrus and illustrated with a vignette.

72. The Rosetta stone, inscribed in hieroglyphic, demotic, and Greek.

73. The Siloam inscription cut into the rock wall of the tunnel of Hezekiah south of the temple area in Jerusalem.

74. Inscription ot Mesha, king of Moab, on a black basalt stela; carved about 840-820 B.C.

75. "Belonging to Shema, servant of Jeroboam"; eighth century, from Megiddo. 76. "Belonging to Jaazaniah, servant of the king" (cf. II Kings 25:23); from Tell en-Nasbeh, about 600 B.C. 77. Impression on a jar handle: "Belonging to Eliakim, steward of Joiachin"; from Tell Beit Mirsim, sixth century.

78. Jar handle stamped with a "royal stamp," inscribed "For the king, *mmšt*; from Gibeon. 79. Jar handle stamped with later "royal stamp," "For the king, Ziph"; from Gibeon.

80. Reverse of Ostracon IV from Tell ed-Duweir with mention of Lachish; early sixth century.

81. Table of Semitic alphabets; outlined letters indicate carving; solid letters, writing with ink.

82. Portion of an Aramaic papyrus, dated 404 B.C., describing the gift of a house by Anani bar Azariah to his daughter.

83. Column of Isaiah manuscript from Dead Sea cave; contains Isaiah 33:1-24.

85. Registers of the Ur-Nammu stela from Ur, showing the building of a ziggurat; from about 2060-1955 B.C.

86. Naram-Sin of Agade stands victorious over the Lullubians; twenty-third century, from Susa.

87. The fortress of 'the town of the Canaan" under attack by Seti I; on wall at Karnak.

88. A portion of the list of the Asiatic conquests of Thut-mose III; from Karnak. Each name-ring is surmounted by the figure of a bound Asiatic.

89. Chiefs of Lebanon felling cedars and assuring an Egyptian officer of Seti I of their submission; at Karnak.

90. The Prince of Megiddo celebrates a victory with feasting and music and the procession of prisoners; he sits upon a cherub throne; from Megiddo, 1350-1150 B.C.

91. The fortress of Ashkelon being conquered by the forces of Ramses II; men on the tower raise their hands in a gesture of submission; at Karnak.

92. Ship of Ramses III engaged in battle with the Philistines and other Sea Peoples who wear feather crowns.

93. Counting and recording the hands of Hittites killed in battle with Ramses II (cf. I Samuel 18:25 ff.).

94. Part of the scene and list of conquests in Palestine by Sheshonk I (cf. I Kings 14:25-26; II Chron. 12:2-4).

95. Ramses III attacks a walled fortress in Amor manned by Syrian lancers, on a relief at Medinet Habu.

96. Detail of the name "Israel" from the stela of Mer-ne-Ptah, found at Thebes.

97. The "war panel" from a standard found at Ur, depicting the triumph of the king over his enemies; twenty-fifth century.

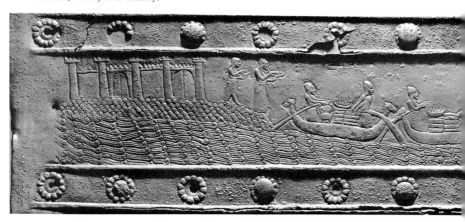

98. Bronze bands from Balawat: tribute taken from Tyre by Shalmaneser III (above); sacrifice prepared at the source of the Tigris (below).

99. Ramses II before Amon-Re, on a thirteenth-century stela found at Beth-shan.

100A. Scenes from the Black
Obelisk of Shalmaneser III
from Nimrud; in second reg-
ister from top, "Jehu, son of
Omri" presents his tribute to
the king.

100B. Opposite side of the "Black Obelisk" depicting camels, an elephant, monkeys, and other tribute for Shalmaneser III.

101. Attack upon Lachish by siege-engines pushed up an incline and accompanied by archers who shoot from behind shields; archers, spearmen, and sling-throwers support the siege-engines; three nude figures impaled; relief of Sennacherib found at Nineveh.

102, *opposite*. Sennacherib seated on his throne receiving the booty taken from Lachish; inhabitants of the town kneel before him; from Nineveh.

103. Reliefs of Ramses II and Shalmaneser III (?) carved on the cliff at Nahr el-Kelb, near Beirut.

104. Thut-mose IV as a sphinx treading upon his foes; throne fragment from Thebes.

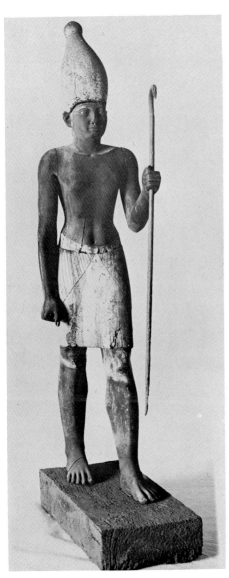

106. Thut-mose III, upper part of basalt statue from Karnak.

105. Wooden figure of Sen-Usert I wearing the white crown of Upper Egypt.

107. Amen-hotep III wearing blue crown with uraeus.

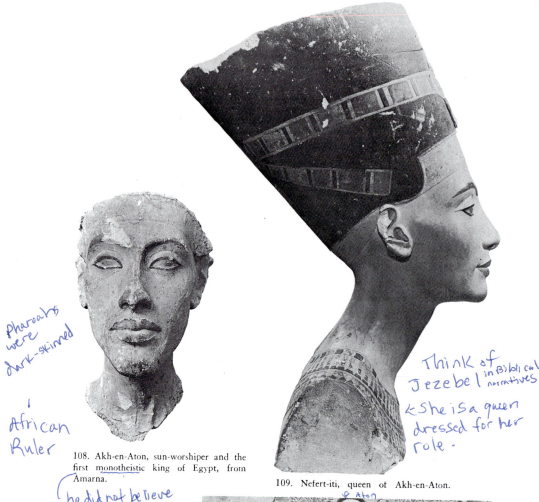

108. Akh-en-Aton, sun-worshiper and the first monotheistic king of Egypt, from Amarna.

109. Nefert-iti, queen of Akh-en-Aton.

110. Family scene of Akh-en-Aton, Nefert-iti, and their daughters, under the sun-disc with radiating arms; from Amarna.

111. Gold mask of King Tut-ankh-Amon, son-in-law of Akh-en-Aton, found in his tomb at Thebes.

112. Ramses II wearing the blue crown and broad collar; probably from Karnak.

113. King Mer-ne-Ptah, from Thebes.

note muscular features

114. Seti II sitting on throne holding a small shrine.

115. Enannatum, king of Lagash, about
2500 B.C.

116. Lamgi-Mari, king of Mari, dedication
to Ishtar; middle of third millennium.

117. Gudea, e n s i of Lagash, dedication to Nin-
gizzida; from Tello, beginning of twenty-first
century.

119. King Tiglath-pileser III of Assyria (744-727 B.C.); from Nimrud.

118. Ashurnasirpal II; from Nimrud.

120. Sargon II of Assyria, from Khorsabad.

121. King Esarhaddon holding two royal captives on leash; from Zinjirli.

122. King Ashurbanipal banqueting in a garden with his queen, attended by servants and musicians, while an enemy's head hangs on a tree nearby.

123. King Darius seated on his throne, Crown Prince Xerxes behind him, with attendants; Persepolis.

124. Ashurbanipal carrying a basket for rebuilding of the temple of Esagila in Babylon.

125. King Merodach-baladan of Babylon (II Kings 20:12) making a grant to an official.

126. Ahiram, king of Byblos, seated on a cherub throne, before an offering table.

127. King Barrakab of Sam'al seated on his throne, with his scribe.

128. Nude female figurines, cultic objects of fertility worship, from 2000-600 B.C.

129. Nude goddess standing on a lion, flanked by a worshiper and the god Seth.

130. King Yehawmilk presents a libation to his goddess, the "Lady of Byblos."

131. The goddess with two horns, and a worshiper holding a lotus, on a
thirteenth-century stela from Beth-shan.

132. Silver goddess with gold collar and skirt from Ras Shamra; 2000-1800 B.C.

133. Copper goddess from Ras Shamra; 1900-1600 B.C.

134. Bronze god overlaid with gold and silver; from Minet el-Beida, 1500-1300 B.C.

135. Nude goddess with a *was* scepter on a fourteenth-century gold pendant from Beth-shan.

137. God with headdress, from Ras Shamra, 2000-1800 B.C.

136. The "Baal of Lightning," 1900-1750 B.C., from Ras Shamra.

138. Presentation of offering to god "El," on a thirteenth-century stela from Ras Shamra.

140. Storm-god astride a bull, with lightning bolts in his hands; from Arslan Tash, eighth century.

139. The god Melqart on a dedicatory stela "which he vowed to him" (see Chapter IX), erected by Barhadad (Ben-Hadad), king of Aram about 860 B.C.

141. The god Marduk on a piece of lapis lazuli; from Babylon, middle of ninth century.

142. Boundary-stone of Nebuchadnezzar I, with symbols
of various gods and goddesses; twelfth century.

143. Upper part of a statue of a goddess with
flowing vase; from Mari, 2000-1500 B.C.

144. Shamash enthroned within his shrine, to whom Nabuaplaiddin is presented; from Abu Habbah, middle of ninth century.

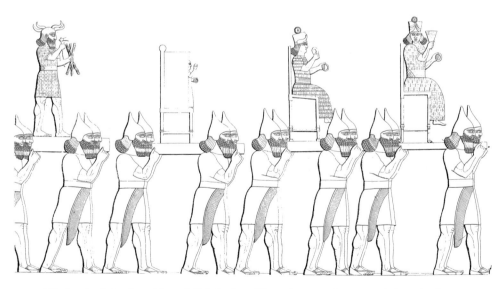

145. Squads of Assyrian soldiers of Tiglath-pileser III carrying away the statues of the gods of a captured town; from Nimrud.

146, *opposite*. Isis protecting Osiris with her wings (cf. Ps. 17:8); from Karnak, sixth century.

147. Bronze model of the ritual of the dawn, with representations of cultic objects; from Susa, twelfth century.

148. Horned incense altar from Megiddo; tenth-ninth century.

149. Bronze openwork stand from Megiddo; 1050-1000 B.C. (?).

150. Cylindrical cult object from Beth-shan, decorated with birds and serpents; eleventh century.

151, 152. Clay models of the liver. One inscribed with omens and magical formulae for use of diviners (cf. Ezek. 21:26), from about 1830-1530 B.C.; other uninscribed, from Megiddo, 1350-1150 B.C.

153. Clay figurine of a bound prisoner with a curse upon the enemies of Egypt written over the body; the figurine was broken in order to make the inscribed curse take effect (cf. Jer. 19:10-11); from Sakkarah, eighteenth century.

155. Shalmaneser III sacrificing to his gods, before his own royal image cut in the rock at Lake Van.

156. Ashurbanipal pouring a libation over dead lions before an offering table and incense stand, to the accompaniment of music; from Nineveh.

157. Ceremony of "opening the mouth" for giving the deceased a new body in the hereafter; New Kingdom.

158. Egyptian sky-goddess Nut, arched as the heavens, supported by the air-god Shu; at his feet, the earth-god Geb; a vignette in the "Book of the Dead" from Deir el-Bahri, tenth century.

160. The god Osiris.

161. Gods of Egypt lead a soul in the land of the dead and weigh his heart.

159. The king as Amon.

162. The god Khnum fashions the prince Amen-hotep III and his *ka* on a potter's wheel, as the goddess Hathor extends the *ankh* sign, the emblem of life; at Luxor.

163. Winged lion of Ashurnasirpal.

164. Goat upright beside a tree from "Great Death Pit" at Ur twenty-fifth century.

165. Winged creature, from Carchemish.

166. Ivory sphinx in lotus thicket, inset for panel (cf. Ps. 45:8); from Samaria, ninth century.

167. Sun-god with Ea to his right; to the left, a "Flora" and Ninurta.

168. The sun-god before the enthroned Ea, god of wisdom; from Ur.

CYLINDER SEALS OF THE AKKADIAN ERA (2360-2180 B.C.)

169. Sun-god, holding a plow, travels in his boat.

170. Seven-headed fiery dragon attacked by two gods; from Tell Asmar.

171. Fighting gods and the building of a temple tower.

172. Massive tower of Neolithic Jericho, nine meters in diameter, a part of the city defenses; in its center is a stone staircase with twenty steps leading downward to a horizontal passage.

173. The east city-gate at Shechem.

174. Hazor: "House of Makhbiram" of eighth century (upper); pillared building of time of Ahab (center); Solomonic gate and casemate wall (below and left).

175. Ancient Megiddo.

176. City wall and gate at Tell en-Nasbeh; with stone benches at the gate.

177. Foundation of city wall, near a gate of ninth-century Samaria.   178. Hellenistic tower at Samaria.

179. Rock-cut pool and spiral stairway with 79 steps leading to water 25 meters below the surface; excavated at el-Jib, ancient Gibeon (cf. II Samuel 2:13).

180, *opposite*. Tunnel cut in the rock at Gibeon, leading down 93 steps from inside the city wall to the spring at the base of the hill.

181. Model of the Solomonic stables at Megiddo; tenth century; cf. I Kings 9:15, 19, etc.

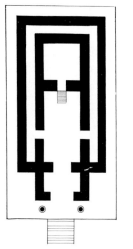

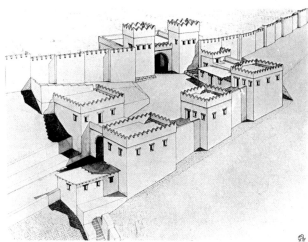

182. Suggested floor plan of the temple of Solomon in Jerusalem.

183. Plan of tenth-century gateway at Megiddo; cf. Ezek. 40:5-16.

184. An eleventh-century fortress at Gibeah of Saul, preserved at only one corner.

185. Plan of the chapel and palace at Tell Tainat in Syria; eighth century; similar in plan to Jerusalem temple.

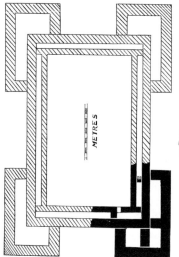

186. Shrine with a large altar; at Megiddo, about 3000 B.C.

187. Temple with mud-brick platform, altar, and benches for offerings, from the Late
Bronze period at Lachish.

188. The temple tower, or ziggurat, at Ur; cf. the "tower" of Babel in Gen. 11:1-9.

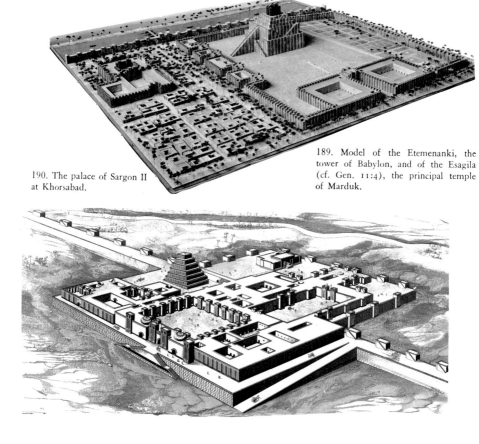

190. The palace of Sargon II at Khorsabad.

189. Model of the Etemenanki, the tower of Babylon, and of the Esagila (cf. Gen. 11:4), the principal temple of Marduk.

191. Tomb for King Djoser of the Third Dynasty, in the form of a step pyramid, at Sakkarah.

192. A sphinx with the head of King Khaf-Re guards the necropolis of Giza with its three great pyramids.

193. The Ishtar gate of Nebuchadnezzar II at Babylon.

194. Bound enemy carved on a door socket from Hierakonpolis.

195. The tomb of Cyrus at Pasargadae in Iran, erected about 529 B.C.

196. Tombs of Darius I, Artaxerxes I, and Darius II, cut in the rock at Naqsh-i-Rustam in Iran.

197. The apadana, or audience hall, of Darius and Xerxes at Persepolis.

198. Bronze statuette of a kneeling Asiatic captive.
199. Dignitary seated on a throne, painted on shard from Ramat Raḥel.

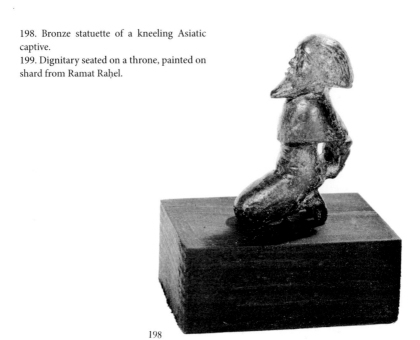

198

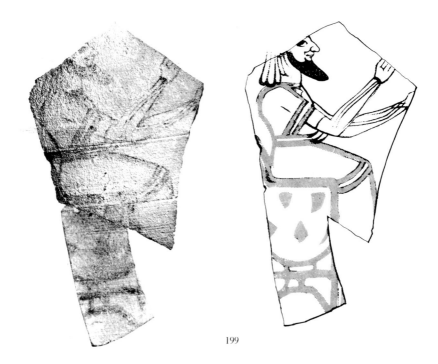

199

200. Bronze plaque of a Canaanite, from Hazor.
201. Gold earring in form of a goat's head, from Ashdod.
202. Two electrum toggle pins decorated with herringbone design.
203. A peasant riding upon a humped bull.

201

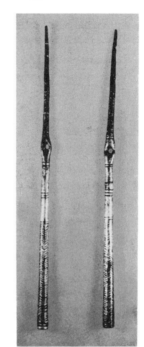

202

200

203

204. Stone weights inscribed with their values.
205. Furniture found in a tomb of the Middle Bronze Age at Jericho.

204

205

206. Carpenter at work with an adze.
207a–c. Wooden stool with string seat, from a
tomb at Jericho.

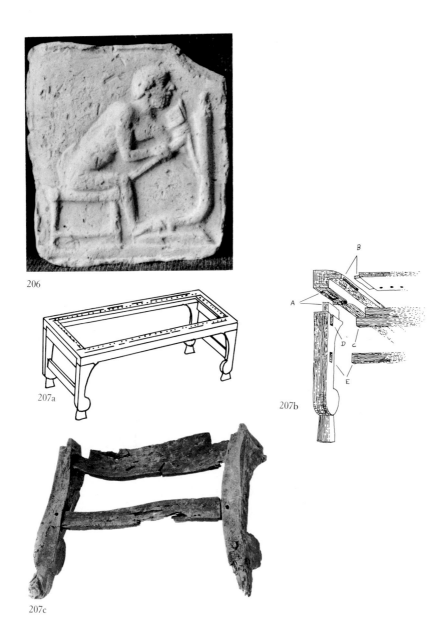

206

207a

207b

207c

208. Wooden bowl from a funerary offering at Jericho.
209. Woman's head carved from ivory; from Nimrud.
210. Ivory head of the Phoenician period; from Sarepta.
211. Saw (and detail) found at Kfar Monash.

208

209

210

211

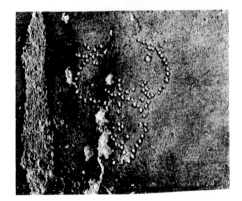

212. Axeheads from Kfar Monash.
213. Tools of the Early Bronze Age, found at Kfar Monash.
214. Spearheads from Kfar Monash.
215. Laver, bowl, strainer, and juglet, from a tomb at Tell es-Saʻidiyeh.
216. Sword with hornlike projections and tang fitted into bronze handle from Tell es-Saʻidiyeh.

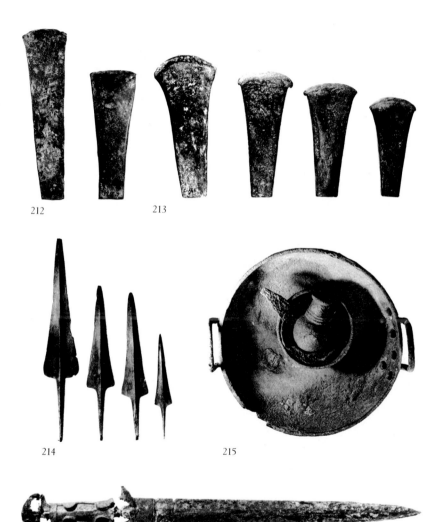

212   213

214   215

216

217

218

217. Closed pottery kiln of the Early Bronze Age, at Tell el-Far'ah (North).
218. Firing chamber of pottery kiln at Sarepta.

219. Clay stopper and a wine jar, from Gibeon.
220. Helmeted warrior carved on shell, from Mari.
221. Sections of scale armor found at Nimrud.

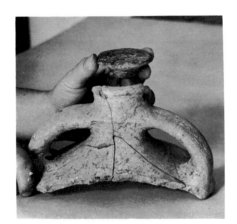

219

220

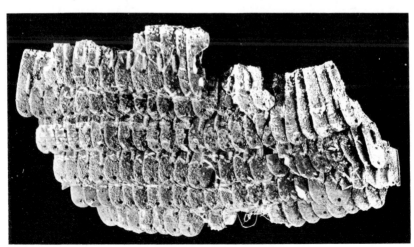

221

222

222. Warrior carrying a calf on his shoulder, from Karatepe.
223. Hunter with a bow and arrows, from Karatepe.
224. Bird incised within a six-pointed star, from Gibeon.
225. Fowl incised on the handle of a cooking pot, from Gibeon.

224

223

225

226. Musician with a horizontal harp of seven strings.
227. Musician seated on a folding stool and playing a harp.
228. Pyxis carved with musicians playing lyre, drum, and double flute.

226

227

228a

228b

228c

228d

229. Musicians in bas-relief, from Karatepe.
230. Mother nursing a child beside a palm tree.

229

230

231. Window balustrade, found at Ramat
Raḥel.
232. Carved proto-Aeolian capital, from
Ramat Raḥel.
233. Three javelin heads inscribed with
alphabetic characters.

231

232

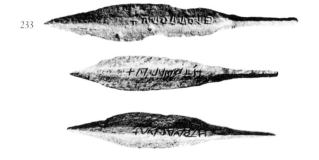

233

234. Bowl from Tell Arad incised with "Arad."
235. Letter to Eliashib that mentions "the house of Yahweh."
236. Hebrew letter of the seventh century, from "Meṣad Hashavyahu."

234

235

236

237. Judaean royal stamp–seal impressions on jar handles.

238. Jar handles from el-Jib inscribed with "Gibeon."

239. Hebrew inscription on the lintel of a tomb at Silwan.

240a–b. Inscribed clay tablet, from Deir'Alla.

241. Oxcarts carrying the Sea Peoples, on bas-relief at Medinet Habu.

239

240a

240b

241

242. King Itur-Shamagan of Mari.
243. Seal impression of Tudhaliyas, King of the Hittites.

242

243

244. A portrait head of an important woman of Ugarit.

245. A king of Ugarit triumphs over his enemy.

246. A royal person of Ugarit embraces his consort.

244

245

246

247

247. Statue of Shalmaneser III inscribed with a cuneiform text.
248. A dignitary served and entertained by attendants.
249. Shalmaneser III greets his royal visitor under a canopy.

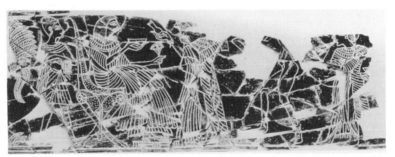

248

249

250. Clay figurine of a seated woman, from
Munḥata.
251. Ivory statuette of a woman, from Bir
Safadi.
252. Statuette of a male figure, from Bir
Safadi.

250

251

252

253. Bronze figurine of a god, from Shechem.
254. Bronze statuette of the seated "El," from Ras Shamra.
255. Two identical statuettes of a god with upraised hand.

254

253

255

256. Bronze figure of a bull, from Ras Shamra.
257. A goddess nursing two children, from
Ras Shamra.
258. Bas-relief of Qudshu-Astarte-Anath.

256

257

258

259. Seated deity with rounded cap, from Hazor.
260. Bull figurine, found in Canaanite temple at Hazor.
261. Seated god with high conical headdress.

260

259

261

262. Bronze cult standard decorated with religious symbols.
263. Statue of a deity standing on a bull, from Hazor.

262

263

264. Statuette of an enthroned figure, from Hazor.

265. Upper part of Nabonidus stela, found at Harran.

266. Bronze crown from Naḥal Mishmar.
267. Wand decorated with heads of ibexes, from Naḥal Mishmar.
268. Bronze tripod with bowl for burning incense, from Tell es-Saʻidiyeh.
269. Late Philistine pottery cult stand, from Ashdod.

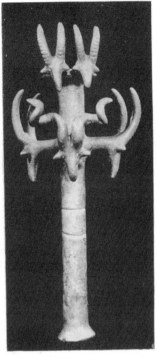

267

266

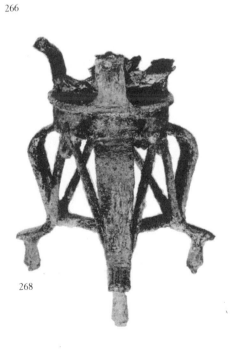

268

269

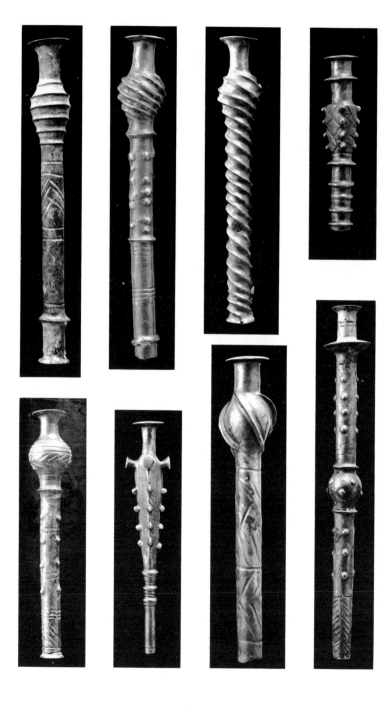

271. Model house built upon two goats.
272. Clay mask of human face.
273. Inscribed liver model, from Hazor.

271

272

273

274. Slaughter of a ram by two men.
275. Upper half of a votive plaque, from the
Inanna temple at Nippur.

274

275

276. Banquet scene on a votive plaque from Nippur.
277. Hero between two lions, carved on plaque from Nippur.

276

277

278. Banquet scene, from Karatepe.

279. Worshipper carrying a sacrificial kid, from Mari.
280. Detail of coffin lid molded with human face.
281. Clay coffin from Dhiban.

279

280

281

282. Clay coffin from Amman.

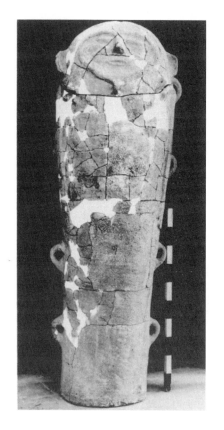

283. Four-winged figure carved on bone handle, from Hazor.
284. Composite creature supporting a winged sun-disk, from Karatepe
285. Lion orthostat from Hazor.

283

284

285

286. A Pazuzu plaque from Nimrud.

287. A god sits beside a sacred tree, a woman and snake beyond.

288. Banquet scene on a seal from Tell es-Saʿidiyeh.

289. Dancing animals and dignitary, on a seal from Tell es-Saʿidiyeh.

287

288

289

291. Air view of Area A at Hazor at the end of
the 1958 season.

292. Water system in Area L at Hazor.
293. Early Bronze Age city wall with tower, at Arad.

292

293

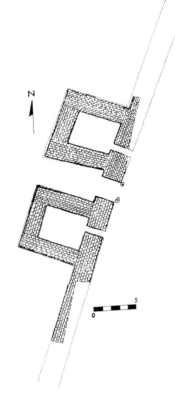

294. Early Bronze Age city gate at Tell el-Far'ah (North).
295. Tenth-century city gate at Gezer.

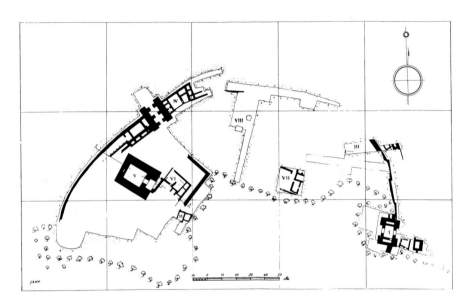

296

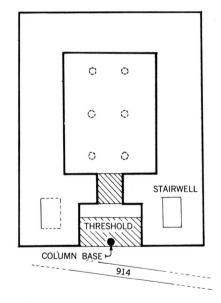

297

298. Cultic objects in situ within the Hazor
temple.
299. The "Holy of Holies" of a Canaanite
temple at Hazor.

298

299

300. Canaanite shrine with stelae and offering table at Hazor.

301. "Holy of Holies" of the temple at Tell Arad.
302. Altar in the sanctuary room of the Arad temple.

301

302

303. Large building with two rows of pillars at Hazor.
304. Section of tunnel to the spring at Gibeon.

303

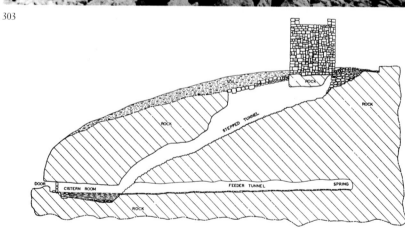

304

305. Stairway from the top to the base of Tell es-Saʻidiyeh.

306. Section of pool-and-stairway at Gibeon.

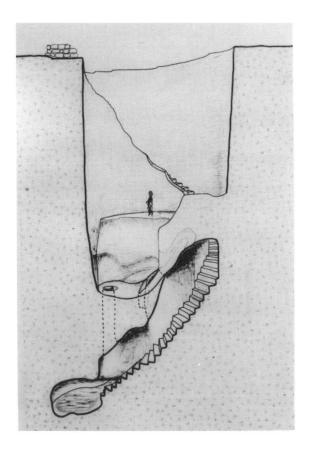

307. Model house of nine rooms, from Mari,
Damascus.